*The*

# POWER

*of*

# SOUND

# The
# POWER
## *of*
# SOUND

## *Edmund Gurney*

WITH AN INTRODUCTORY ESSAY BY

## *Edward T. Cone*

BASIC   BOOKS,   INC.,   PUBLISHERS

*New York*                    *London*

First published in 1880

© 1966 by Basic Books, Inc.
Library of Congress Catalog Card Number: 66-28360
Printed in the United States of America

# THE POWER OF *The Power of Sound*

EDWARD T. CONE

*The Power of Sound* was published in 1880. Although it is a treatise on musical aesthetics, you will search your *Grove* in vain for an entry on its author. The fourteenth edition of the *Encyclopaedia Britannica* will summarize his life and work for you in a few lines, but you will have to read them carefully to find any mention of his interest in music. Even the eleventh edition, which awards him a respectable column, relegates his accomplishments in music to a few sentences. What chiefly interests the *Britannica* is his role as a founder of the Society for Psychical Research and his work in what we should today call parapsychology.

A more comprehensive view can be obtained from the *Dictionary of National Biography* (Oxford, 1917). From its four-column account emerges the picture of a man of energetic and omnivorous intellect, of talent in both speculative and experimental science, who pathetically tried—but in vain—to pursue just those careers for which he apparently had insufficient gifts. Music was one of these.

Edmund Gurney was born in 1847 in Hersham, Surrey. From boyhood his ambition was to become a violinist; nevertheless, his education was standard for the Anglican clergyman's son that he was: Blackheath, then Trinity College, Cambridge. He showed ability as a classical scholar and was awarded a fellowship at Trinity in 1872; but throughout this period of his life his primary interest continued to be music. It was not necessary for him to earn a living, so he soon gave up any idea he may have had of an academic career. Instead, he devoted himself to the study of violin, piano, and composition—until he faced the first and probably the greatest of his disappointments: the painful realization that, whether from lack of basic ability or from inadequate training, he would never become a professional musician.

With characteristic resolution, he now turned his attention to philosophy and science. The results of his researches in aesthetics, psychology, physiology, and physics, applied to his vivid musical experiences, produced *The Power of Sound*. But during this period he seemed to feel a new vocation, for from 1877 to 1881 he studied medicine at University

College, London. Once again he was forced to admit that he had missed his calling; for, although he took another bachelor's degree, he never qualified as a physician. He turned instead to yet another profession; he began reading law at Lincoln's Inn. This course of action, too, proved abortive.

It was in psychical research that Gurney finally found the career he had been looking for. The independent income that had supported him through the years of his over-extended schooling now enabled him to engage in a remarkable series of researches in telepathy, hypnotism, and spiritualism. Approaching these subjects from a scientific point of view, he tried to formulate theories that could be experimentally tested and to frame rationally acceptable explanations for so-called supernatural phenomena. The results are to be found chiefly in a collection entitled *Phantasms of the Living* and in articles written for the *Proceedings of the Society for Psychical Research.*

Gurney published a final collection of essays, *Tertium Quid,* in 1887. His premature death the following year was caused by an apparently accidental overdose of a medicinal drug.

At first glance there seems to be little connection between Gurney's later researches and those that produced *The Power of Sound.* Yet a similar intent underlies both undertakings: the desire to approach as systematically as possible a peculiarly recalcitrant subject—one that had previously been relegated for the most part to the realm of the subjective and emotional. As Gurney says in the preface to the present work, "little attempt [heretofore] has been made to apply scientific treatment to the musical phenomena themselves." To be sure, "the views to which I have tried to supply a scientific basis are the very ones I find more or less explicitly held by scores of reasonable people . . . none the less must I hold it important to get at the scientific basis for them, if possible" (pp. xviii–xix).

This basis Gurney attempts to establish by a twofold effort, arguing from acoustics, physiology, and psychology on the one hand and from the theory of evolution on the other. From the former he attempts to derive a systematic division of the senses into aesthetic and non-aesthetic and an explanation of the delight of the aesthetic senses in the perception of form. From the latter he argues that the "impressiveness" of music (its powerful effect on the listener) derives from its associations with the most primitive emotions and activities of the human race.

Although this is the portion of the book in which, we may infer from the preface, Gurney probably took most pride, it seems the least satisfactory today. The advances of our own century in the physiology of the ear and psychology of hearing naturally date much of what Gurney has to say; yet it must be admitted that they have not been so startling as to invalidate all his conclusions. Indeed, if one turns from *The Power of Sound* to an up-to-date textbook in the field, one is surprised at how little seems to have been definitively established since Gurney wrote. In the field of evolution, however, Gurney, although apparently a convinced Darwinian, had some strange ideas. One of his favorite characters, for example, is a "creature who got the rudiment of an eye by habitually lying in the sun" (p. 544; see Appendix A *passim*). And I can explain his condescension toward Haydn and Mozart only as the result of his attempt to apply evolutionary principles to the history of music.

On the other hand, the author's attempt at the scientific fertilization of aesthetics results in some amazingly perceptive remarks, often casual asides, that anticipate the thought of a much later day. The recent photographer who tried to show the abstract beauty of such objects as cancerous stomachs might have been inspired by Gurney's appreciation of a frog's gall bladder—"I have seldom seen a more beautiful tint of blue" (p. 294). His observation of our "instinct of having around us a certain amount of space in which we are alone," such that "any sudden violation to this instinct is very unnerving" (p. 37), has been confirmed by recent experiments. And his objection to analogies among the arts because of the danger that "lies in the loose application of terms which are common to more than one of them" (p. 288) has a Wittgensteinian ring.

Turning to his treatment of literature and fine arts, we find the analysis of English metrics in Chapter XIX to be close to some that are in high favor today. His discussions of painting and sculpture are generally disappointing, being heavily influenced by Victorian views on art; nevertheless, he analyzes, with specific reference to Rembrandt, the relation of abstract to representational values in a passage of exemplary criticism. (See pp. 395–396.)

These points alone, however, would not justify a book of five hundred pages, especially one written in a ponderous and turgid style that seems almost incapable of producing a simple sentence. There are other shortcomings as well. Gurney has many deaf spots—the music of Donizetti and Verdi, for example. His tastes are admittedly conservative—nay, reactionary. His knowledge of music before 1700 is deficient, even for a man of his day. He can speak with awe of "the overpowering effect of Schubert's *Ave Maria*, played by wind-instruments and accompanied by strings" (p. 408). (Of course the nineteenth century did not share our puristic attitude toward such arrangements. Elsewhere Gurney discusses very wisely the educational role of piano transcriptions in the learning of orchestral and choral music. See pp. 297–298.) He finds Cellier superior to Offenbach. But, as Gurney himself puts it with uncharacteristic succinctness, ''differences of musical taste are as striking as they are ultimate'' (p. 535). We must not allow such lapses (as we consider them) to deflect our attention from the main course of the author's argument. It is here, and not in details of musical judgment, that his strength is to be found.

F. L. Lucas, in his essay on tragedy, says that ''we should go back to Aristotle not so much for the right answers as for the right questions.''[1] Gurney, like Aristotle, asks the right questions. Why do we enjoy music? Why do we enjoy some compositions more than others? What does it mean to say that some compositions are better than others? What, if anything, can music express? Is there a correlation between such expression and musical excellence? What is musical form? What is its relation to expression and to excellence? What relations between music and words make a text-setting seem appropriate or inappropriate? Is valid musical criticism possible? In what way, if at all, is music affected by other forms of artistic and intellectual activity, and by social and political conditions?

It should be clear from the above that Gurney's book is no typical guide to the understanding or ''appreciation'' of music, even though he is ''not writing for musicians, but for those who care for music'' (p. xvi). Take the subject of form, for example. You will find here only passing reference to sonata and rondo and fugue. You will find an inadequate and highly questionable discussion of musical phrase- and sentence-structure. What Gurney is interested in is a much more fundamental issue. What is the nature of musical form? Is it controlled primarily by succession—moment-to-moment progression? Or by agglutination—the addition of part to part? Or by accretion—organic growth? Or if by all three, in what relationship? His discussion is illuminating, not because it begins where most books on form and analysis leave off, but because it leaves off before they begin. Indeed, most such books show no recognition that there is a problem here. One must therefore give Gurney great credit for its mere formulation, regardless of whether one accepts or rejects his solution.

This solution, nonetheless, is worth close study. As it happens, the problem of form is one of several connected topics that occupy the author's attention, explicitly or implicitly, throughout the book. They

[1] F. L. Lucas: *Tragedy, Serious Drama in Relation to Aristotle's Poetics,* revised    edition (London: The Hogarth Press, 1957), p. 12.

are central to his musical aesthetic—for that matter, to any proper musical aesthetic. They are therefore as relevant to our contemporary musical thought as to that of Gurney's day. Whether or not one admits the cogency of his arguments—often difficult to determine, owing to his verbosity—one must find his conclusions especially interesting in the light of certain opinions now in vogue on composition, analysis, and criticism.

Let us return, then, to the question of musical form. What is its nature? Is it determined primarily by the moment-to-moment succession of one tone or chord or motif to the next? Or does it consist rather of relationships among parts—the contrasts and similarities heard as each one is added to the preceding? Or is it to be thought of as the organic growth of a generating idea—or conversely as a central organism whose over-all structure influences or even controls every detail? Of these three possibilities, the second will be recognized as the one governing most academic treatises on form, or rather on "forms." The third is in the ascendancy today, especially as the result of the work of Heinrich Schenker and his school. It may come as a surprise, then, to find Gurney insisting firmly on the primacy of the first. The basic requirement of musical form is indicated by "the test that each bit shall necessitate, as it were, and so enter into organic union with the *one next to it.*" In other words, "the cardinal idea of organic form in any musical sentence or paragraph is not to be connected with this length or that length, but with *cogency of sequence* at each point" (p. 204).

What then of larger forms—of sonata form, rondo, and the like? Gurney admits that in successful examples "a close artistic coherence may pervade and bind together the several successive segments of form." Nevertheless, this "laxer order of a longer movement" is by no means "parallel in kind to the order which dominates the note-units of the segments themselves" (pp. 96–97). The author is only voicing here a discomfort many of us feel but are usually unwilling to mention. Hearing the successive themes of a rondo, or noting the contrast between a scherzo and its trio, we wonder whether these various parts are bound together by strict necessity. The interrelations we find among them often testify more to our own ingenuity than to the cogency of the thematic connections. Gurney is clear on this point: "The central principle of form, entire mutual interdependence of elements, admits of gradual relaxation as the size of the elements increases; up to the point where it becomes absurd to attempt to apply it, as when we take as elements the separate movements of a sonata" (p. 213).

Does he then rule out the possibility of an organic view of form?

Not entirely, for at least in some cases ''the whole may be, or may become through familiarity, so truly organic as to make each part seem an unalterable phase of the continuous motion: but for all that it is in our enjoyment of the parts, one after another, that that quality of close and vital organism takes effect.'' We can never apprehend the whole of a composition simultaneously, except by an artificial abstraction: ''We never get our impressions of a long musical movement, as we commonly do those of a great architectural structure, through views which sweep over and embrace the whole rather than dwell on the parts.'' To do that would involve a contradiction in terms: ''to enjoy something the essence of which is a *succession* of impressions by a *simultaneous* review of all the impressions'' (pp. 214–215).

Above all, we should never be tempted to find in adherence to an abstract formal design an explanation of musical excellence: ''The abstract type has no beauty or meaning for us, no ideal place in our imagination; it is nothing in favour of any piece that the mechanical part of it, its skeleton, so to speak, places it under one head or another'' (p. 100). Gurney had in mind the academic classification of musical ''forms,'' but his warning is equally apposite today. Students of Schenker, for example, often assume that the presence of an *Urlinie* in the background of a piece ensures its quality; actually it guarantees only that the piece will make a modicum of tonal sense of a certain type.

Gurney's approach is indeed one-sided; but it is useful today because it reminds us that the musical surface is after all there to be enjoyed for its own sake. Indeed, only if the surface is enjoyable (Gurney is not afraid to use the word ''beautiful'') can the underlying framework have any value. As he puts it, ''Pleasure in the whole has no meaning except as expressing the sum of our enjoyments from moment to moment; a sum which will be increased in proportion as the organic principle pervades the whole'' (p. 214).

This must sound like a heretical reversal of values to theorists trained in modern analytical methods—as well as to those composers who consider the surface of a composition important only insofar as it shows its relationships to an underlying framework. But—to return to a previous instance—an *Urlinie* cannot save a piece whose themes are trivial or dull. A canon, too, is only as interesting as its material; the close relationship among its polyphonic parts is wasted unless the parts themselves deserve it. Similarly, anyone can reverse the direction of a melody, but why do so unless both the original and the retrograde make musical sense? These are simple and superficial examples, but they clarify Gurney's principle that the composer's first responsibility is to the musical surface itself—"the successive notes and smallest fragments, as they turn up moment after moment" (p. 214).

Today we hear compositions—by reputable composers—apparently determined by the demands of structural abstractions, or of special compositional methods, or even of improvised performance. The composer of such a work has deliberately relinquished control of the surface. What he seems to be asking us to enjoy (if that is the right word) is not the composition itself, but the idea behind it. In fact, one often wonders whether the composer even considers it necessary for the piece to be heard; an analysis, or an account of the way it was composed, or a description of how it should be performed, would seem to do as well. And although these examples are extreme, they only exaggerate tendencies clearly discernible in the music of many others writing today. Gurney flatly rejects the concept embodied in this approach to composition. In a passage outstanding for its bluntness—even to the use of a simple sentence!—he declares: "In Music the notion of a larger and *more* essential design, in reference to which shorter individual strains are *details* in the sense of being *less* essential, has no application. The scheme has no value apart from the bits" (p. 216).

This brings us to a second point: What are these "bits"? For Gurney, music is first and always melody. The "bits" are bits of melody (note the word "strains" in the first sentence of the quotation). Musical form is melodic form: tone succeeding tone to produce a phrase, phrase following phrase in a period, and so on to what Gurney calls a musical paragraph, which itself may be only a "bit" of the whole composition. Gurney's concern for the detail, for the individual part, is by no means either a Wagnerian or an Impressionist desire to locate ultimate value in the single motif; it is simply his assertion of the primacy of the tune. But the tune is not a mere succession of pitches. Melody, as here defined, includes rhythm and is usually supported by harmony. It is thus the chief vehicle of what Gurney calls "Ideal Motion"—or, as we should be more likely to call it today, musical progression.

Gurney is especially insistent about the integral role of the rhythmic element in creating melodic form. By an ingenious series of familiar tunes rhythmically deformed, he tries to demonstrate the inseparability of pitch-succession and temporal relationship (see pp. 151–155). The fact that his examples are so loaded as to be unfair suggests that the principle may not be of universal applicability; yet there is a moral to be drawn and seriously pondered. To what extent are either isorhythmic or isomelic forms, without further musical support, generally perceptible? Liszt, Wagner, and Strauss have so long accustomed us to motivic

transformation that we take it for granted as a universally applicable
procedure; our docility in this respect has probably prepared us for the
unconditional acceptance of the serial principle. As a consequence, many
musicians now seem to hold, a priori, that any sequence of the elements
of the chromatic scale maintains its identity regardless of rhythm, register, or tone-color, whether undergoing inversion, retrogression, both, or
neither. As a matter of abstract mathematical definition such a position
is as valid as any other; but surely a musician should submit each
specific case to the judgment of his ear. What does it mean to say that
a musical relationship exists where we cannot hear one? Gurney's position, as applied to contemporary music, would no doubt be impossibly
limiting, but it is crucial to realize that limits may exist. And there was,
after all, in the music Gurney knew best, some justification for his
statement, splendidly dogmatic in its confident italics, that ''in *all* impressive form the rhythm is not something superposed, or more or less
consciously suggested or referred to, but is essentially *there*'' (p. 158).

Harmony, too, is subsumed under Ideal Motion. It ''supports and
defines the form, and intensifies the sense of its coherence and the satisfaction in following it'' (p. 246). Its main function, then, is to clarify
and enrich melody. A series of chords, rhythmically embodied, can even
create a sort of ''chord-melody''; but what is important in every case
is the progression and what we should today call its harmonic rhythm.
Gurney realizes at the same time that with harmony a static principle
enters music, one that must be carefully controlled if it is not to become
dominant. He senses in Wagner an over-reliance on chordal sound for
its own sake, and he is fearful of Wagner's influence in this respect.
Fortunately for him, Impressionism is still a few years off; and he is
happily unaware that less than a hundred years later the monotonous
reiterations of a single chord can be exhibited as a musical composition.
One hopes that this last example is a rare aberration; yet a great deal
of contemporary music seems to renounce progression on principle. What
is left is a series of sounds, or motifs, or gestures, each experienced for
its own sake. Gurney warns against the danger of ''simple incoherence,
of a loss of the feeling for true unity of sequence and development.''
Although over-elaborate constructions ''may, on the one hand, degenerate into complicated patterns and ingenious mazes, still more easily,
on the other, may they dissolve into a formless chaos of flying fragments.'' We can all suggest recent examples of each extreme, even
though we may not all agree with the suggested remedy: ''Musical
composition can be rendered vital by new and beautiful themes, and by
nothing else; failing that, it would lose the popular element which is

the mainstay of its existence, and would become the ingenious amusement of a clique'' (p. 228).

The fact that the foregoing treatment of the nature of form and of music as movement has to a certain extent been able to reverse Gurney's own order of discussion shows how closely related the two concepts are. Either can be derived from the other, as Gurney implies in his own explanation of Ideal Motion. ''It is the *oneness of form and motion* which constitutes the great peculiarity of melody. . . . Melodic form and the motion in question are aspects of the same phenomenon. . . . I can think of no better term to express this unique musical process than *Ideal Motion*'' (pp. 164–165).

The gravest shortcoming of this approach to musical analysis is that it is unable to distinguish various levels of musical activity. Gurney refuses to hear any tones of a melody as ornamental details, or even as less important than others—just as he fails to realize that a long movement can elaborate a simple underlying structure. His great virtue is that he conceives form as the concrete reality of a composition. It is even misleading on this view to speak of the form *of* a piece of music: the form *is* the music.

One other problem constantly stressed during the discussion of Ideal Motion concerns the recognition of musical excellence. It is not enough to know what music is; we must be able to tell good from bad, or even good from less good. It should be clear that the locus of what Gurney calls the ''impressiveness'' of a work must be its melodic form, but on what grounds is one melodic form to be judged superior to another? The answer is unconditional: ultimate judgment is intuitive. The appreciation of melodic form must ''involve a special exercise, belonging to what I shall have to designate again and again as the *musical faculty*. . . . Whatever explanations of musical effect turn out to be possible, the exercise of the musical faculty will present an ultimate and inexplicable element.'' Thus a melodic form that ''seems right seems so in a way peculiar to itself, and the sense of the rightness appears strictly intuitive'' (p. 86).

This conclusion is stated very early in the argument, but the author devotes much space later on to its justification, especially in Chapter IX, ''The Relations of Reason and Order to Beauty.'' Here he argues that all attempted explanations of artistic beauty are bound to fall short. At most they define necessary, but never sufficient conditions. For example, ''unity under variety is a characteristic, or rather is the definition, of all form, not specially of beautiful form'' (p. 189). No matter what feature may be adduced as a criterion of musical beauty or ''impressiveness,'' one can always find (or compose) examples that, while exhibiting the feature in question, are clearly neither beautiful nor impressive.

The musical faculty that operates in the evaluation of melodies is naturally the arbiter in all other aspects of musical structure. In particular, ''as a melody is judged, so its adequate or inadequate harmonisation is judged.'' There are rules of harmony, to be sure—and they afford an unusually clear example of the criteria that define necessary but insufficient conditions. ''We cannot say such and such is the right harmony *because* it obeys the rules, seeing that what in that place would sound wrong may also obey them'' (pp. 248–249).

On this point Gurney's studies in psychology and physics can give him no help. Explanations appealing to psychological principle are illusory or circular. ''It *sounds* more rational to say 'the mind is so ordered as to enjoy order' than to say 'the mind is so ordered as to enjoy disorder.' And yet the latter statement would serve quite as often as the former, if we could at all rest in either as an adequate explanation'' (p. 186). What most attempts at formulation come out with, when correctly analyzed, is a tautology: ''The mind perceives and feels a particular thing, beauty of this or that kind, as it has been by nature constituted to perceive and feel it'' (p. 185). Helmholtz's appeal to the physics of tone is equally bootless. What Gurney says of it could apply just as well to more recent efforts to erect musical aesthetics on a physical basis: ''The *rationale* of relationship of notes in pitch is known. . . . But this goes no further in accounting for the beauty of free form than the possession of convenient stones and plenty of cement would go in explaining Giotto's tower. The relation of note to note is parallel to the fact that one stone rests naturally on or is firmly bound to another; such facts of course make the form possible, but they do not account for it'' (p. 197). If Gurney is right, present-day hopes of developing a scientific method of musical pedagogy, composition, and criticism are misguided. So, too—some of us would be happy to believe—are attempts to produce acceptable music in any desired style by means of an appropriately programmed computer.

There is one other direction where, as Gurney takes special pains to warn us, it is useless to wander in search of an explanation of musical impressiveness: toward the misty realm of emotional expression. Unlike other writers too well known to require citation, he denies neither the possibility nor the relevance of expression. But expressiveness is not to be identified, or even correlated, with impressiveness. After listing some of the specific emotions typically associated with musical effects, Gurney points out that ''the very act of cataloguing a few of these definite emotional characters makes one feel how transient and uncertain they often are; how little they sum up the substance of the thing which is actually delighting us" (p. 336, marginal summary). Indeed, much music of undeniable beauty can be enjoyed without reference to its emotional expressiveness, which may be minimal. And if expression is to provide a basis for judgment, how does one choose among several tunes, all equally expressive of the same mood? These and related considerations force the author to the conclusion that "a tune is no more constituted beautiful by an expression, e.g., of mournfulness or of capriciousness than a face is" (p. 318).

At the same time, there is another and quite different kind of emotion associated with the enjoyment of music. Indeed, the source of the impressiveness of all music is to be found in "its perpetual production in us of an emotional excitement of a very intense kind, which yet cannot be defined under any known head of emotion. So far as it can be described, it seems like a fusion of strong emotions transfigured into a wholly new experience" (p. 120). Whatever we may think of Gurney's explanation of this phenomenon, based as it is on Darwin's theories about the origin of music, most of us will recognize the accuracy of his description. Is there not, then, some justification for the widespread opinion that there is a connection between music and what may be called—without specific emotional connotation—the "inner life"? Gurney believes that there is. His discussion of it, though brief, foreshadows much that has been written in our own day. Since musical form seems to move with a life and an emotional power of its own, it is not surprising that the listener, in following it, seems to recognize phases of his own inner experience—passages "of change and crisis and contrast, of expectation, memory, and comparison." For this reason, "we may feel, at the end of a musical movement, that we have been living an engrossing piece of life." The intensity of the musical emotion is such that it "condenses a very large amount of inner life . . . into a very brief space of actual time." The reality of these sensations is probably what accounts for our usually fruitless attempts to connect a given composition with specific emotions or other manifestations of the inner life. Whatever the validity of such connections may be, for the most part they "lie in a region where thought and language struggle in vain to penetrate" (pp. 347–348).

It will probably come as a disappointment to many that Gurney, after promising a scientific treatment of musical phenomena, should, at a crucial point in his argument, take refuge in intuition, in "the musical faculty," and in a unique musical emotion. The frustrated reader may even unkindly suggest that the investigation of psychic phenomena is indeed the proper field for one who finds such phantasms inhabiting the musical world. Now, it is true, as I have suggested earlier, that Gurney's approaches to music on the one hand and to the supernatural on the other arise from the same mental outlook, but it is one of skepticism rather than of credulity. One might well characterize Gurney as a skeptical empiricist: his skepticism distrusts abstractions and insists on the limitations of scientific knowledge even while relying on scientific method: his empiricism accepts the concrete facts of human experience as fundamental. The solutions he offers to the problems he raises are often unsatisfactory, but he performs valuable service by simply raising them, by trying to solve them, and by letting us see how he goes about the job. His point of view, a healthy corrective for some of those popular today, is what is important. It is one that values the music above its analysis and that respects the hearer's delight as the final test of its quality—indeed, as the purpose of its existence.

*Princeton, N.J.*
*July 1966*

# PREFACE

————◆◆————

A CONSIDERABLE part of the substance of this book has already
appeared in the shape of articles in the *Fortnightly Review*, the
*Nineteenth Century*, *Fraser's* and *Macmillan's Magazines*, and
*Mind*. This disconnected mode of publication was specially
unfavourable to a subject where the prevailing doubt and dis-
agreement as to the very first principles precludes taking anything
for granted. In their present more coherent form, I trust that
my main positions may at any rate have gained in clearness.
One word may be said as to arrangement. My primary concern
being with the æsthetics of Hearing, and in particular with Music,
the various analogies and contrasts which other regions of experience present have been introduced in connection with the different
divisions of the main subject; which has led to a somewhat
sporadic notice of other arts. To those who believe in transcendental links, making all the arts One, this treatment may
appear unsatisfactory; but it certainly conduces to the distinctness of my humbler line of argument.

My chief object, after certain preliminary explanations, has
been to examine, in such a way as a person without special technical knowledge may follow, the general elements of musical
structure, and the nature, sources, and varieties, of musical effect;
and by the light of that enquiry to mark out clearly the position
of Music, in relation to the faculties and feelings of the individual,
to the other arts, and to society at large. Since the publication
of Helmholtz's *Tonempfindungen*, an epoch-making book in the
branch of physics which deals with musical sound, the study of

that subject has been widely popularised. But while the indispensable *material* of musical phenomena has thus met with exceptionally complete treatment, and has been in its salient points exceptionally well understood in this country, little attempt has been made to apply scientific treatment to the musical phenomena themselves. Many special fields of enquiry—history, biography, criticism, the various technical aspects of the art—have found able and zealous workers : but very few English writers have attempted any separate treatment of the more general facts and problems which underlie the whole subject and are appreciable apart from technical detail. It is the more unfortunate that I find myself distinctly at variance with the greater part of these previous attempts, as well as with Helmholtz himself in respect of several questions lying on the borderland of the physical and the æsthetic enquiry.[1] This isolation has been to me a source of most serious misgiving, and has considerably delayed the completion of my task. I will not forestall what has to follow by mentioning particular points ; but will only say that, after repeated reconsideration, the various analyses and expositions which I have met with still seem to me greatly to fail, not only in recognition of the difficulties which the phenomena of Music present, but (what is more important) in recognition of the phenomena themselves ; these last being actual more or less ascertainable facts, and mainly implicit of course in the musical experiences of those who, wisely enough, take their enjoyment without troubling their heads about the how and the why. These are the facts which I have given my utmost endeavours to realise as they are, apart

---

[1] I have not read any of the German systems of æsthetics, general or musical. Among many which are confessedly in the clouds, which replace scientific enquiry by barren systematisation or abstract metaphysics, and either ring the changes on arbitrary hierarchies of the arts and the emotions, or inform us, *e.g.*, that 'when Music shall have thrown off the tyranny of rhythm, then and only then will she attain self-consciousness' (and these are invariably the ones from which I find extracts quoted), there must doubtless be others of a more instructive kind ; but I have not happened to hear of any in which the fundamental facts and problems of Music, as they appear to me, are connectedly considered. Dr. Pole's *Philosophy of Music* came out too late for me to consult it, and I do not know how far his ground coincides with mine. My debt to Mr. Darwin on one very fundamental topic will appear abundantly in the sequel.

from theories, and it is only through its harmony with them that I have felt any confidence in working out the more theoretic part of my exposition. On this more tangible ground, the sense of speculative isolation is at any rate relieved by abundance of unspeculative sympathy; and even as regards conclusions and applications, the views to which I have tried to supply a scientific basis are the very ones I find more or less explicitly held by scores of reasonable people, who have observed for themselves and are keenly interested in the position and prospects of the musical art. But though many may be led to them by individual instinct and experience, none the less must I hold it important to get at the scientific basis for them, if possible; less for the satisfaction of holding connected and logical views than to obtain definite ground for opposing dangerous tendencies; for refuting fallacies which are the more insidious and elusive in proportion as the æsthetic impressions themselves have an appearance of vagueness; and for insisting with authority on the truest and noblest functions of the people's art.

It is in this last point, in the convergence of my arguments to conclusions concerning the popular bearings and possibilities of Music, that my chief encouragement has lain throughout. It is to my growing conviction on that subject that I chiefly aim at winning others; the conviction that this art, if its conditions were better understood, might do far more for numbers in all classes who at present feel themselves at sea in it, and get comparatively little out of it; but more particularly that it has a unique message for the uncultivated and ignorant, for the publicans and sinners; and not in the millennium, but now; not after but before they cease to be uncultivated and ignorant. I may add, that if such phrases have here an *ad captandum* and exaggerated air, and suggest irrelevant rhetoric about the general soundness and impressibility for good of the popular heart, my support of them in the sequel, with restricted reference to this most isolated region of experience, will probably prove only too persistently plain and rigorous.

And this brings me to a few words of explanation and

apology as to the general method of treatment.    The words
*theoretic* and *speculative* which I have used above need not
alarm any reader with a vision of remote hypotheses and recondite arguments.    Even the parts of the investigation where
I have been most driven to the use of abstract words deal, for
the most part, with quite concrete matters: for instance, the
long account of Melody and Harmony is an analysis as to the
rightness or wrongness of which any intelligent person who has
felt an interest in listening to Music, and who will follow my
method of interrogating his experience, will be competent to form
a very fair opinion.    Still less need the most ardent believer in
the spiritual character of the art fear to find the domain of genius
measured by mechanical rules, or the feelings whose indescribable and mysterious nature no one, I think, can have realised
more deeply than myself, docketed off under cut-and-dry psychological formulæ.    So far am I from the thought or desire of

> Untwisting all the chains that tie
> The hidden soul of Harmony,

that one of the first results of my analysis is to define the
boundary of the vast region that lies beyond it; and one of the
most direct conclusions from my general explanations is the hopelessness of penetrating Music in detail, and of obtaining, whether
in objective facts of structure or in fancied analogies and interpretations, any standpoint external to the actual inward impression, from which to judge it.    At the same time I have not been
able to avoid a considerable amount of definition and distinction,
nor can I hope to be of service to any reader who is not willing to accompany me for a certain distance over dull ground.
The region is naturally a foggy one; and in it any *bonâ fide*
enquirer, who aspires to be in some degree a guide, has to reckon
with very singular conditions in the feelings and ideas prevailing
around him.    For while Music, on the clear side of its direct
utterances, its actual pleasure-giving qualities, is a subject which
a vast number of people care about deeply and appreciate truly,
not one in a hundred of these has ever had a moment's independ-

ent curiosity to look beyond this direct delight, and to distinguish
even the most general characteristics of the things which impress
him or of his own impressions. The consequence is that among
the deluge of musical talk and writing which the days bring
forth there is hardly a view or a phrase too shallow or fantastic
to obtain unquestioning assent. Many genuine lovers of Music, I
am sure, are vaguely stimulated with a sense of the dignity of the
art, when they hear that Beethoven was a prophet who 'disentangled the confused web of human existence,' or that Schumann
'stated the riddle' (of the painful earth) 'and left the solution to the
hearer;' or when they read in a popular text-book that a composer
has to 'dive into the psychological mysteries of the human heart,'
being instinctively aware how indispensable this practice is, in
order 'to appreciate the different degrees of feeling produced by
various phases of mental disposition;' and that he is thus led to
the profound psychological discovery that as a single feeling, like
melancholy, cannot always remain at the same strength, he must
not make his themes all alike. But none the less must talk like
this (and more, compared to which this is sober reason), on the
part of accredited musicians, react damagingly on the art; and
its prevalence might excuse even pedantic efforts after precision.

Controversy, again, which I would gladly have avoided, has
been unavoidable where what appear to me fallacies are in
possession of the field. My best apology on this head will
perhaps be that my argument, so far as it is true, cuts the
ground from under the sort of musical controversy which is most
rampant and useless—the endless disputation and dogmatism
about the comparative merits of composers and compositions—
by showing how little tangible basis such disputation has; how
utterly unconvincing it is doomed to be; and how the application
of the only possible test distinctly points to the wisdom, in this
region, of exceptionally wide tolerance.

In conclusion, I must repeat that I am not writing for
musicians, but for those who care for Music. I should be sorry
indeed that the excellent musicians, both practical and literary,

who from time to time have expressed to me their agreement with many of the views here set forth, should not know what valuable help I have found in their sympathy. But members of a skilled minority, who have spent years of labour on a subject, or who have been used to regard it as intimately bound up with refined culture, may very naturally look with suspicion on an attempt to strip it to some extent of its esoteric character and its intellectual pretensions. While, then, I shall be doubly grateful for any favours I meet with in this quarter, I do not feel that I am depending on a verdict of experts. Though there are many points on which musicians must be the judges, or rather the most accredited witnesses, these are not the points which I am chiefly interested in discussing : and failure for me would be failure to be understood by educated persons outside the technical circle. It is true that I have been unable to adopt 'popular treatment' even in what is to some extent an advocacy of the popular cause. But as regards musicianship, such amount of it as is implied in remembering any simple melody is all I ask to begin with : while, in return, I hope to prove to any one who possesses this faculty, that he knows much more about Music than he perhaps imagines. A slight amount of technical information will present itself as we go along; and if a very elementary point is sometimes emphasised, it is because I often find people who have been enjoying Music all their lives, to whom it is still a piece of information, *e.g.*, that the *quality* of a musical note is something different from its *pitch.* Lastly, as to examples. A writer on this art of sound is keenly sensible of his disadvantage in this respect, as compared with those who deal with visible things ; for he can but set on the page the symbols, and not the faintest shadow of the reality, of his illustrations, while they can put before even an untutored eye the very traits they are describing. Still no reader I am likely to find will have any difficulty in getting the quotations played to him, even if he cannot himself make them out : and examples are of such immense help that I would gladly have much increased their number. I have continually had the mortification of feeling that I was obliged to sacrifice to reasons of space what would have been to me the easiest and to others the most interesting part of my work. Such as they are, the examples have been chosen with a special view to simplicity, and will be found to embody in the most direct way possible the points they are meant to illustrate.

E. G.

# CONTENTS.

*The*
# POWER
*of*
# SOUND

# THE
# POWER OF SOUND.

---◦◦◦✕◦◦---

## CHAPTER I.

### THE ORGANS AND IMPRESSIONS OF THE HIGHER SENSES.

IT is now generally admitted that our organs of special sense, the channels by which we keep up our constant and various intercourse with what we call the external world, have been formed in past ages by gradual processes in correspondence with stimuli which that external world supplied; and that as the physical organs themselves are the highly modified descendants of undifferentiated and comparatively simple tissues, so the sensibilities connected with them must have been represented, in the embryonic stage of evolution, by something analogous to those modes of feeling which we find in ourselves to be the simplest, the least differentiated, and the most crudely suggestive of actual bodily affection. These are connected with the general continuous covering of our bodies, as distinguished from our special sense-organs; and are comprised, broadly speaking, under the heads of touch, and of heat and cold. The very fact that more than one of these modes of feeling can be mentioned shows, of course, that as regards the sensibilities themselves, differentiation is not wholly absent; heat and cold are felt as something quite different from touch, and if they are not connected with some special nervous apparatus, they must at any rate be connected with some special mode of nervous action; but they resemble touch in that they belong to no special localised organ, being felt in the same way over almost the whole of the outer (and in some degree over the inner) surfaces of the body. With these may be included certain other modes of sensation which, though more restricted in locality, are still hardly conceived of as falling within the domain of a special sense-organ; those, namely (apart from taste), which have to do with food and drink.

§ 1. The modes of sensation, as distinguished by presence or absence of a special sense-organ;

If now we compare these simpler sensations with those belonging to the more differentiated organs, in respect of one special aspect which is common to both kinds, the aspect of agreeableness and disagreeableness, we immediately encounter a striking contrast. We are accustomed

contrasted in respect of varieties of taste;

to use the two correlative words, Pleasure and Pain, in respect of all our sensations; but it is only in respect of the less differentiated class that we find anything like universal agreement as to what is pleasurable and what is painful. A blow or a burn are objected to by all alike; the feelings of hunger and its satisfaction (as apart from the differentiated sense of taste) are universal experiences: whereas in respect of the differentiated class, be it smell, taste, sight, or sound, the varieties of opinion are infinite; the greater differentiation of the organs seeming to carry with it an ever-increasing possibility of such varieties in the experiences of individuals. And not only are the tastes of individuals extremely various —savages delighting in food, in odours, in gaudy colours, and harsh sounds, which are revolting and distressing to more civilised senses—but there are possibilities of great variation in the same individual at different times. Habit may act both by deadening and by cultivating the sensibilities; association may modify and even reverse previous preferences and antipathies.

and of Pleasure and Pain.

Further, if we arrange our modes of sensation in a series, putting sight and hearing first, and descending through smell and taste to the modes which are unconnected with any differentiated organ, we find special peculiarities in respect both of Pleasure and Pain. The *pleasure* which is obtainable by this latter class seems to depend almost wholly on some pre-existing distress or craving, or, at the very least, desire. It is delightful to eat and drink when one is hungry and thirsty, and to plunge into cold water when the skin is hot or irritated: but to eat when one is not hungry can only give pleasure by the effect on the specialised sense of taste; and similarly, when the body is in a normal state, unnoticed from the very fact that it is neither pleasurable nor painful, contact with warm or cold bodies yields the very slightest satisfaction; and in the case of merely tactile impressions the possibilities seem smaller still. Relief and contrast then seem necessary factors; the previous state must have presented a decided divergence from the line of neutrality or indifference, if the change is to give a distinctly positive result; for in this less specialised region, divergences from a purely neutral state in the direction of pleasure are so slight that they seem scarcely worthy of the same name as we apply to our more vivid experiences. *Pain*, on the other hand, applies with such force and reality to this very same region, and especially to the modes of impression whose area is largest,[1] that its use in connection with the higher senses seems by comparison quite metaphorical. Doubtless the sensations of the

---

[1] I am speaking only of the sensations due to stimuli from foreign sources; there are, of course, other sensations due simply to changes in our own frames. These, when *passive*, as in the case of thirst or toothache, seem to be entirely of the painful kind, and to have no pleasurable counterparts: that is to say, unless we have been previously suffering, no involuntary change in our organism, which is not connected with some external stimulus, seems capable of giving us pleasure. The *active* pleasure of muscular movement, on the other hand, is as marked as is the pain of muscular fatigue.

higher senses may often be to sensitive persons a source of acute distress : but whatever may be thought at a moment when the choice is not absolutely presented, I do not believe that even the shrillest shriek of a railway whistle, or the most glaring and discordant colour, could be so much an object of dread to any one as a sharp cut or blow. In this respect unpleasant smells and tastes seem to occupy an intermediate position ; a nauseous taste being less disagreeable than a blow, but more so than a jarring sound. To revert now to what was said in the last paragraph as to agreement and variety of taste, we find that there is indeed a consensus as to what is pleasurable and painful in connection with the most fundamental bodily needs ; but that if we confine our attention to such modes of contact with the external world as are, so to speak, quasi-accidental and adventitious, which are over and above the satisfaction of these primary cravings, Pain, where it appears, has practically no correlative, being the sole and certain result of any wide divergence from the neutral state, and that here, in its literal sense, it constitutes the great thing about which people are all agreed ; while those regions of higher sense where Pain becomes less distinct and positive, and where the effects of distressing experiences are comparatively transient, are just those where Pleasure, in a distinct and positive form, appears on the scene, and also where varieties and modifications of likes and dislikes become prominent facts ; and in these more differentiated regions we begin to be able to mark off certain feelings and sets of feelings by the word *æsthetic*, and to reason or dogmatise about higher and lower and more or less cultivated tastes. We shall have much to do later with the ideas and distinctions represented by these words : at present I am only concerned with the point that the region of sensation which has æsthetic possibilities is also the region of variety of taste ; broadly illustrated by the fact that in this same region we do not find as the correlative of Pleasure anything to which the word Pain, with its implication of what all alike agree in shunning and dreading, can be literally applied.[1]

---

[1] These general principles may seem to admit of exceptions. For instance, the sensibility to pain from external contact varies enormously in degree : sensitive and delicate persons may shudder at the mere sound of the slaps on the back which their coarser or more robust fellows regard as an agreeable and friendly mode of salutation. Such an exception, however, is but apparent : for the difference here is clearly only in the degree of the external stimulus ; the amount of what is necessary to produce pain may vary, but the stimulus may always reach a point at which the stoutest will object to it. There are, however, exceptions of a more real kind. The sense of touch admits of great specialisation under certain circumstances, and the absence of one or more of the normal senses may probably contribute much to this result. Thus, a boy called 'Blind Peter' found it the height of luxury to stroke velvet, and probably experienced in so doing a delight the nature of which others can hardly conceive ; so that here the sense of touch was really elevated to the æsthetic class. Many of the lower animals differ from man in having more localised *organs* of touch ; but whether this involves superior specialisation and variety in their tactile sensations we cannot tell.

Of the physiological concomitants of agreeable and disagreeable sensation very little can be said with certainty; but the accepted doctrine is
worth noticing here, if only to show what a short way it takes us. The
doctrine is that, as sensation depends on nervous stimulation, agreeable
sensation depends on a certain limit of amount in the stimulation, on its
reaching a point short of that degree of violence which would fatigue and
wear the organ. Now if this is merely taken to mean that, if we are to
receive sensuous pleasure through an organ, this organ must be in a
tolerably fresh and responsive state, it is doubtless true: but the form
in which the right conditions are usually described, as combining *the
maximum of stimulation with the minimum of fatigue*, has an air of
scientific precision which is rather delusive. At first sight, indeed, the idea
seems attractively simple through our familiarity with the agreeable sense
of *muscular* activity, rising in intensity up to a certain point, and capable
both of keeping short of, and of reaching, the painful pitch which we call
fatigue. But when the nervous changes are represented in consciousness
not by *fatigue*, but by a *special mode of discomfort*, as in the case of a
nasty taste or a grating sound, though it may still be a most reasonable
assumption that some sort of nervous wear and tear is going on, yet a
phrase which seems to assume a scale of degrees of stimulation, or, more
accurately, of ratios of stimulation to wear and tear, answering to degrees
of agreeableness or disagreeableness, seems quite out of place. Of many
tastes and odours, the faintest possible suggestion is disagreeable; and a
harsh sound can in no way be made to appear like the excess of a sweet
one. Again, the organ of smell, if continuously stimulated, will quickly
cease to appreciate either an agreeable or a disagreeable odour; that is, it
reaches the same state of indifference and insensibility through a stage
in the one case of entirely agreeable, in the other of entirely disagree-
ble sensation. The natural inference is surely that the corresponding
physiological processes must differ in *kind* rather than in *degree*; for that
the degrees of stimulation in the two cases must be tolerably equal, seems
indicated by the fact that the times during which the agreeable and disagreeable sensations are respectively appreciated, previous to the deadening of the sensibility, will not differ much in length. The very fact that
we can roughly compare and equate an agreeable and a disagreeable taste
or odour, in respect of intensity or pungency, points to the same conclusion. Once more, the over-stimulation which *deadens* must apparently
be something different from the over-stimulation which *excites and
annoys* a sense-organ. For example, a sensation of fragrance (provided it
be not over-strong) remains enjoyable, but gradually decreases in vividness up to the point when we become insensible to it; while a continuous
musical tone, however sweet, will force itself more and more on our
attention, and end by thoroughly annoying us; so that under continuous

stimulation of a kind accounted agreeable, the sense of smell passes to a
deadened state without any stage of discomfort, while the sense of tone
passes to a state of increased wakefulness with continually growing discomfort; and if our sliding scale of wear and tear is to run parallel with both
these subjective phenomena, its character as the physiological basis of
either does not seem to have much explanatory force. The fact is that the
actual molecular processes which accompany sensation are unknown
to us: we know neither the chemical changes nor the transformations
of energy which are involved in the course of nervous wear and repair.
And even if this knowledge were revealed to us, if we could actually
apply our mechanical conceptions of wear and repair to these inmost processes, if we could calculate a scale showing how the wear of a nerve
might be variously well or ill adjusted to its opportunities of repair (somewhat as we might calculate degrees of reason or unreason in various
modes of adjusting a man's food and sleep to the work required of him),
we should have no right to assume that the relation of such a scale of
measurements to the variations of our sensations would be at all perceptible to us; for we have no proof that the physiological conditions of
those variations are completely and exhaustively summed up under the
heads of amount of action and repair.[1]

The essential indefiniteness of the formula, in spite of its air of precision, may be seen in another way. For what, according to it, should we
consider the *best* condition? Would it not be the condition when the ratio
of stimulation to wear and tear is largest, that is, when the repair is going
on as fast as the wear? But this would seem very contrary to our experience

*and essentially
indefinite.*

---

[1] The application of the above-mentioned
principle, even in some of the simpler cases
where it might be expected to succeed,
presents great difficulties. For example, the
eye dwells on a moderately illuminated white
surface without fatigue or discomfort, but
with very little positive gratification; but if
the blue which is present as a constituent in
that white light be separately presented, by
elimination of the other constituents, the
gratification is instantly increased. The
experiment may be fairly made by looking
at a piece of fairly bright white sky, first
with the naked eye, and then through a
beautifully tinted blue glass. Clearly the
increase of pleasure is not due to an increase
of stimulus on the retina, for the physical
stimulus is *diminished* by the whole amount
of light eliminated; as little can it be due
to a prevention or cessation of the conditions
of fatigue, for the white was not at all
fatiguing. The only possible application of
the physiological theory would seem to be
that the nervous action was in some way
freer and easier in the less complicated action belonging to the perception of a single
tint, than in the response to the larger
number of different stimuli which make up
for us white light. But in the face of the
facts that the comparative lack of freedom
and ease, thus assumed in the case of the
more neutral sensation, is not *felt* as any
mode of discomfort, and is compatible with
some amount of gratification, and that the
same assumed lack has absolutely no effect
in reducing the *general* quality of the light,
*brightness* (for the white was perceived as
brighter than the blue), it would seem that
the *particular* quality of *blueness* must have
the physiological correlative of its superior
enjoyableness entirely in the *mode*, not the
*degree*, of nervous action, in a set of events
comprising essential elements beyond any
which our mechanical notions of wear and
tear could possibly reach.

of those higher pleasures for which our senses are the channels: for we often receive our greatest æsthetic delights at the expense of great subsequent dulness and exhaustion of the head, which shows that nervous wear has far outrun repair at the time of enjoyment. And experience seems to point to a similar fact, though less marked in proportion as the periods of enjoyment and subsequent fatigue are usually far shorter, in the case of purely sensuous pleasures. But if we once admit this third element of *time* for nervous repair, all certainty as to our original ratio vanishes. It is intelligible to speak of the maximum of stimulation compatible with an amount of wear which shall be reparable at the moment; but to speak of the maximum of stimulation compatible with an amount of wear reparable at some future moment, is to make the ratio between stimulation and wear utterly indefinite, unless that moment is fixed and named; and there is nothing in the formula or in the facts to suggest an idea of a general rule as to the fixation of such a moment, much less the rule itself. Moreover, even if it seemed conceivable that such a ratio could be adjusted, the attempt to connect it with the phenomena of pleasure would land us, on the subjective side, in all the complications of measurement by intensity and measurement by duration.

§ 3. The origin of Pleasure and Pain is inscrutable; and their early development lies outside the theory of natural selection.

Still more obscure than the physiological basis of agreeable and disagreeable sensation is its history. The origin of Pleasure and Pain (to adopt the more convenient phrase, in which Pain must be understood in its larger and looser sense) is exactly as inscrutable as the origin of sensation itself. Like sensation in general, Pleasure and Pain must be regarded as psychical concomitants of certain nervous processes, starting in an embryonic form probably with the very dawn of consciousness, and equally with consciousness beyond the reach of explanation and derivation. It is necessary to notice this, inasmuch as it is not uncommon to encounter more or less definite views which refer Pleasure and Pain, or at all events their early development, to the theory of natural selection. The prominent facts of pleasure felt in certain common actions which are obviously advantageous to the existence of living individuals and their species, and of pain felt in deprivations or occurrences which as obviously tend to destroy or shorten such existences, with the concomitant impulses *towards* the advantageous and *from* the disadvantageous things, are enough to account for a vague idea that natural selection must have had a direct part in fostering the pleasurable and painful sensibilities, as in fostering so many other conditions favourable to survival. To pursue this subject here would, however, carry us too far.[1]

Passing then from this somewhat dubious ground to the specialised senses, those of smell, taste, seeing, and hearing, as now indisputably known to us, we at once recognise very great differences in the way in which their

---

[1] An enquiry into the relations of pleasure and pain to advantage and advantageous impulses will be found in the first Appendix.

several functions are exercised; and with these differences are connected varying degrees of intensity in the pleasures they afford. Thus according to a generally recognised law, the more intense pleasures of sense would be naturally those connected with organs whose activity is intermittent, so that the nerve-organs concerned have long periods of repose. And if sensations be looked at in isolation this appears to be the case: a strawberry probably gives keener pleasure than any single ungradated tint of colour, isolated from all associations with nature and from all mental elements of comparison and contrast; or than any single sound on a musical instrument. Judged, then, on this ground, the organs of sight and hearing, with their constant and to a great extent unselecting activity, would apparently labour under a great disadvantage: their being always ready for their work would seem to mean that the work is not to be rewarded: and if, notwithstanding this, sight and hearing are universally acknowledged to be the highest of our senses, to be the æsthetic senses *par excellence,* we must seek a further reason. Various facts have been adduced which hardly seem to touch the root of the acknowledged superiority; as, for instance, that the pleasures of sight and hearing are unconnected with any directly life-serving function, and that in the outlet to nervous force which they give without being clogged by prosaic utilitarian aims, they partake of the nature of play. But though this is true, one fails to see *à priori* why connection with the preservation of life should derogate from the character of a pleasure: even if we allow that it is a higher thing to enjoy life than to live, such a principle could not of itself elevate experiences which, without being proved superior in enjoyableness, are only proved inferior in usefulness. Again, it has been said with truth that the two higher senses are those whose pleasures can be shared by numbers of people simultaneously, so that they are ennobled above other pleasures by their social character. But even if all mankind could be fed at once and gratis on heavenly manna, it would hardly alter the accepted view as to the comparative inferiority of the pleasure of eating.

§ 4. The differentiated senses: various characteristics of the pleasures they afford.

The real distinction is a much more fundamental one, and introduces us to two words with which we shall have much to do—Form and Colour. The great fact which places sight and hearing in a totally distinct and unique position as regards pleasure, is the power which we possess of *grouping* the separate impressions received by the eye and the ear, and *combining* a number of them in distinct wholes; in other words, our power, in connection with these senses, of perceiving *Form*: *Colour,* on the other hand, is undistinctive, having analogues in connection with all the senses. The special characteristics on which the power of perceiving Form rest, and its peculiarities in the respective domains of sight and hearing, will be examined directly: for the moment, the mention of the bare word and fact was desirable for the better understanding of what will more conveniently precede, the facts and contrasts presented by the correla-

§ 5. The great distinction, as regards pleasure, of the two higher senses is the perception of Form.

tive, Colour.   Both the words present difficulties as regards our purposes;
Colour being employed strictly of one set of impressions only, those of
sight, and so confined within limits which we shall have largely to extend;
while Form is commonly used with very wide latitude, and very vague
apprehension of what it can and cannot mean in its various applications;
whence the importance of getting its most fundamental meaning, as the
correlative of Colour, clear from the very outset.

Colour, on the other hand, has its analogues in all the senses.

        Colour, then, apart from Form, represents, in the sense of sight, that mode
of consciousness which is common to *all* the senses : it represents sensuous
impression, simply as such, without any supervention of a grouping and
coordinating faculty.   A colour unbounded by a line (as the blue of the
sky when we gaze straight up into it and see nothing else), an isolated
musical sound, the scent of a rose, the taste of a peach, are all truly
parallel things.   They are all perfectly simple and self-complete experiences: none of them has any reference to other experiences of a kindred
sort, preceding or following them.   Preceding circumstances may of course
affect our powers of receiving the normal sensation from these sources, by
affecting the respective organs: if we have already eaten peaches *ad nauseam*, our present peach may disgust instead of delight us; if we have
dazzled our eyes by looking at the sun, we shall see instead of the pure blue
sky the sun's image printed thereon.   Equally, what we are now experiencing may affect our next experience: if we look from the bright sky to the
foliage near us, it may look blanched and withered; if we sip a delicate
wine while the taste of the peach is still in our mouths, its flavour may
be lost to us.   But the necessity that our organs should be in a special and
unfatigued state, if they are to convey to us what we hold to be the
normal impression from the object, in no way affects the fact that the
impression, when we really get it, is of a perfectly simple and independent
kind.   It may indeed have associations linked with it, and in this way be
connected with our supersensuous nature; but it has no inherent relationship, and makes up no connected whole, with the impressions of the same
sense which are contiguous to it in time; it carries its whole character and
essence with it in the moment of its presentation.

        There is, unfortunately, no generic word to express these simple and
unanalysable sensuous experiences, derived through the channels of our
various specialised sense-organs.   Smell and taste are most intimately
allied, the impressions of the one sense being sometimes even mistaken
for those of the other; and words like *aroma* and *bouquet* seem to contain a reference to both senses, or to the region where one shades into the
other.   Similarly, colour and musical tone possess affinities of a dimmer
kind; affinities which, as we shall see hereafter, have been a most fruitful
source of misapprehension, but which are at any rate distinct enough to
constitute these sensations a separate sub-group.   As regards the relation

of the isolated and purely sensuous impressions to the forms and combinations into which the mental faculties organise them, and in the contrast between sensuous and formal elements as connected with contrasts in character, value, and duration of effect, the tone-sense and the light-sense are often very comparable; and as we shall have to trace out this resemblance in various directions, no apology seems necessary for sometimes combining the two modes of impression under the term *colour*. A single term is absolutely needed; and it would be no more reasonable to refuse the word *colour* to the *timbre* or quality of musical tones than to refuse such terms as *harmony* and *discord* to the phenomena of visual colour.

Our sensuous experiences of colour and tone are of course so completely bound up with those combinations and forms in connection with which we have received them, that it needs a considerable effort to disentangle the purely sensuous element, and it is probably quite impossible to judge of it entirely on its own merits. Even when we lie on our back and see nothing but blue sky, the sense of space and freedom, involving complex mental elements, comes in as a factor of our pleasure : the same colour would not move us as it does if it were a yard from our eyes. But so far as we can succeed in isolating the purely sensuous element of our visual and auditory experiences, and comparing them with their analogues of taste and smell, the view which was stated above, that amount of pleasure depends on intermittences of nervous activity in the organ, seems just. As regards colour and its analogues, it is in the appreciation of harmonies, gradations, and contrasts, that is, in the *perception of relations*, that one sense proves its superiority to another; and this depends ultimately on the very points of structure and action to which we shall trace, in a moment, the general superiority of the two higher senses. But apart from such relations, it is hard to see in what sense the ear and eye, in enjoying a tone or colour merely as such, reach a higher level than does the nose in enjoying a sweet scent; and indeed, if the further element of association be allowed to count, the sense of smell might put in a good claim for the highest place of all. Looked at merely on this common ground of purely sensuous impression, colours and tones present a perfect parallel with the experiences of the lower senses, not only in nature, but in many of the phenomena found in connection with them. The piercing shouts and laughter of children in the streets, the harsh and noisy music of savages, an undiscriminating love of gaudy tints, a preference for coarse and highly flavoured food, and so on, are all signs of uncultivated and unrefined organs, which are susceptible, if taken in time, of considerable modification and education. This uncritical love of violent stimulation is common to all the senses, and is often found in connection with all of them in the same individual. In the same way delicacy of organisation implies, for the most part, a preference for delicate flavours throughout the whole gamut

§ 6. Grades of rank are hard to establish among the pure and simple sense-impressions.

of sensation ; nose and palate, ear and eye, each claiming consideration
and resenting violence.

§ 7. Ultimate grounds of the superiority of the eye and ear; the power of discrimination.

But there is a fundamental peculiarity of the eye and ear which utterly
differentiates them from the other sense-organs, and which sets them, as
regards the scope of their activities and the enjoyment attainable through
them, in a position totally apart. This peculiarity is extreme delicacy
and complexity—the possession by both organs of a multitude of terminal
elements capable of separate individual action, and, by the eye, of apparatus for innumerable distinct movements—combined with extremely rapid
power of recuperation ; a combination which renders them most rapidly
sensitive to an immense number of differences in the impressions they
receive. It is owing to this that the experiences are possible, which constitute these two senses beyond all comparison our most important channels
of communication with the world of people and things, and place the
impressions received through them in a wholly unique relation to our intellectual and emotional activity. True, it is not hard to find other grounds
of superiority. Thus, the eye and ear are able to act at a great distance
from their object ; and again, their readiness to act at any moment,
and comparative unsusceptibility to fatigue, must be reckoned an advantage, provided that their enjoyments are provided for (as it will be further
shown that they are) by some other means than the mere recuperation
of nervous energy and of the power of responding to stimulus, which the
lower senses attain by long intervals of repose. There is another very principal characteristic of these senses in relation to impressive general conceptions, as of size, force, and pace, which we shall study more conveniently
later. But these further points we shall find to be also connected ultimately with the enormous power which the eye and ear possess of rapidly
discriminating impressions ; so that this power may be stated generally to
be at the root of their superiority.

Double nature of discrimina-tion.

Discrimination of sense-impressions is of two sorts—discrimination of
the sensations in respect of their individual *character*, including both
quality and intensity, and discrimination of their relative *positions* in
space or time.[1] Discrimination of the first sort may be wide or narrow ;
discrimination of the second sort may be rapid and complete, or slow and
slight. The enormous superiority of the eye and ear, as channels of perception and intercourse, consists rather in the pre-eminent degree in which
they combine the second sort of discrimination with the first than in a
monopoly of either. The senses of taste and smell are open to a very
great variety of impressions, distinguished as different in individual

---

[1] Impressions of hearing may present a
unique sort of difference, describable indeed
as a difference of individual quality, but really
connected with a perfectly unique analogue
of space and time in which relative *positions*
of elements are held and distinguished,
namely, *pitch* ; but into the detailed discussion of this it would be premature to enter.

character. But in connection with them there is no discrimination in space, and only the barest rudiment of discrimination in time, appearing just in the moment of transition from one to another : if we recall the order in which we have experienced many various tastes, as at a dinner of many courses, it is by deliberate and separate efforts of memory, where moreover some reference to the name or look of each dish will probably have to precede recollection of its taste ; not by summoning up a connected passage of sensation where each item falls instinctively into its place. Here the ear, with its enormously greater speed of operation, is pre-eminent. It might take a minute to realise in succession a dozen or even half a dozen distinct tastes, each requiring as it does some time for its appreciation, and then again an interval being necessary before we are in a state to appreciate the next ; while we can easily count a dozen aloud in a second, where each word entails several distinct auditory impressions ; and a whole string of nonsense-syllables can be recalled in a flash. Again, in connection with muscular and tactile impressions, we have some power of discrimination in space, and, owing to the rapidity with which they are realised, a very considerable amount of instinctive appreciation of their order in time ; but then in their case the varieties of individual impression are comparatively insignificant in number and interest.

In connection with discrimination of the individual and qualitative characteristics of impressions, one special point as to these favoured organs is worth noticing ; namely, that the complexity of arrangement which constitutes the physiological basis of the phenomena is not of a precisely similar sort in the two cases ; and this can be understood without any minute acquaintance with anatomical details. The eye and ear agree, indeed, in the delicacy and intricacy of their terminal nervous apparatus, which is immensely greater than anything found in connection with the lower senses. But as regards the actual differentiation of structure in the organ itself, the actual assignment of different parts of it to different sorts of affection, the ear stands completely apart, containing an enormously large number of structurally distinct elements,[1] each responsive to a special mode, or at most to a very narrow range, of physical stimulus. In the eye, on the other hand, it is held that the kinds of elements differentiated in actual *structure* for the reception of colour-impressions, are only three ; and the differentiation is rather in the numerous modes of nervous *process*, to which variously combined affections of these few elements are able to give rise. As regards sensation, however, this difference has no value ;

*The kinds of complexity of arrangement in the eye and ear respectively.*

[1] These elements are not distinct in the sense of being anatomically disconnected from one another ; they form part of what is known as the basilar membrane, which is a long narrow membrane tightly stretched in the direction of its breadth, but compara- tively loosely in the direction of its length. Its transverse fibres may thus, as Helmholtz has shown, be regarded as forming a system of stretched strings, each capable of vibrating independently in response to a special exciting tone.

the variety of impression provided for by the variety of degree in which each kind of element takes its part, in a combined response to the variously constituted rays of light, is of such a sort that we get a multiplicity of colour-impressions not less simple, distinct, and rapidly changeable, than if we had a separate sort of retinal element for every shade of colour.

§ 8. Great difference between the senses of sight and hearing, in the ordinary use made of their wide discriminative powers.

The eye and the ear agree then in this superiority. But examining a little further into the respective modes in which their discriminating powers are commonly utilised, we at once encounter a striking difference; the first, and perhaps the most fundamental, of the many differences between these two privileged senses which we shall come across in the course of our inquiry. In the case of sight we *habitually* make use of the eye's power of discriminating a multitude of individual impressions, to combine these into groups or objects. Into the physiological details of the process we need not enter: roughly speaking, the muscular mechanism of the eye enables us to distinguish the numerous instantaneous movements by which impressions are brought from the various less sensitive points to the most sensitive point of the retina; whence we obtain our conceptions, not only of the outsideness to one another of the various parts of objects, but of their relative positions. Turning now to the ear, we find no such habitual grouping of impressions. Incomparably the most important use that the ear makes of its discriminative power is connected with speech :[1] and in this it is occupied merely with symbols, the attention being directed not to sense-impressions, but to the ideas symbolised. Quite different sounds in another language might convey precisely the same ideas; and the sounds, merely as such (altering perhaps even in repetitions of a single familiar phrase by a single voice), present no certain group having the character of an object.

§ 9. Reasons why series of ordinary auditory impressions make up, as a rule, no objective groups or forms.

This is not sufficiently accounted for by a mere reference to the commonly recognised distinctions between time and space. For though in the case of the ear we have not, as in the case of the eye, the means of discriminating impressions in space, still, if we can discriminate their relative positions in time, there seems no *à priori* reason why a series of them should not form for us groups with a certain character of objectivity and permanence. And indeed this *may* occur up to a certain limited point. Any known word or phrase partakes of the character; and the rapidity with which the ear grasps the elements presented to it, and learns to associate each separate impression with its predecessors and successors, enables even a set of nonsense-syllables to obtain, by repetition, an objectivity at least to this extent, that if a change be made in the order, it is instantly recognised and, it may be, resented, as baulk-

---

[1] In some animals the sense of smell seems to reach a perfection and scope which adapts its impressions for symbols; it is conjectured that ants have a language of smell, and even that articulata possess senses of which we have no knowledge.

ing an expectation ; an experience quite beyond the scope of the slow-acting and rest-needing senses of smell and taste. Still this objectivity is not even remotely comparable to that which we associate with sight : and for this there seem to be two main reasons. First, the sense of permanence in visible objects depends greatly on the passivity and indestructibility of *matter*. Sound is the result of *motion*, usually of visible motion, and even when the same series of sounds is repeated and is familiar to us, we still are conscious of its dependence on movements in its source, movements which it lay within the option of ourselves or of another to make or not to make. When the source is impersonal, sounds are rarely sufficiently rapid or various to make up any recognisable group, besides being hardly ever repeated in regular order ; and, moreover, here also we feel that the exciting causes are transient and accidental, and may be at any moment destroyed by human or natural agencies. Secondly, the things we see gain a quite unique-character of objectivity and permanence from the associations of the senses of touch and muscular movement. It is probably impossible to overestimate the effect of these factors in the formation of our conception of objects. We can of course touch the things which yield to us sounds, smells, and tastes : but the objects of sight we can not only touch, but can trace out, part by part, in space, by a series of muscular and tactual sensations which run exactly parallel at every step with the accompanying visual sensations. We thus acquire an instinctive assurance that it is possible to obtain exact confirmation of what we see, by another line of different but exactly corresponding experience, of experience too which naturally gives the most vivid sense of external contact and resistance ; and this mutual reaction of the two lines of feeling seems at every moment to witness to the validity of each.

So far we have been considering the general everyday activity of the eye and ear ; not their enjoyments. As regards enjoyment, the fact that the. eye is normally and habitually perceiving forms is no special advantage to it. It is for the most part busy either with symbols, as in reading, or with objects the interest of which (if there be any) is mainly owing to the mental activity they evoke, not to special delight in the contours of the objects themselves. People may vary in the comparative amounts of interest they gain by sight and by sound, by reading and looking about them and by intercourse with their kind : as regards the respective use of the two senses in the ordinary course of life, it would perhaps be hard, on the average, to assign a superiority to one over the other. But then, among a number of uninteresting forms, the eye does at times encounter something wholly distinct, something which has not as yet been mentioned, something which, if it could not be paralleled by the ear, would at once turn the balance ; namely, Beauty. Has, then, the perception of beautiful forms an analogue in the domain of sound ? We have seen that the

§ 10. There is one region of experience where auditory impressions are combined into real groups ; and so attain *beauty*.

sets of impressions which the ear receives in the ordinary course of things cannot be said to make up groups or forms at all, much less beautiful ones : is there any exceptional region where this rule does not apply ? Fortunately there is : there does exist one special region of auditory phenomena, where organised groups and forms do exist, and not only exist but attain to perfect and unsurpassable beauty. What that region is need hardly be said ; how it comes to exist, and to contain within it such marvellous possibilities, we shall inquire in subsequent chapters : at present it is enough to notice the unique place which it occupies in the domain of auditory impressions, and the æsthetic rank which the sense of hearing derives through it. Indeed the very word Beauty, which we have just used, is a standing testimony to the fact that, in respect of enjoyment, the eye and ear hold a position of as striking and unique superiority to the other sense-organs as we have seen that they do in respect of varied activity : the world of Beauty is preeminently the world of Form.

§ 11. Recapitulation as regards Form. The perception of form, to recapitulate, takes place through the supervention of a combining and coordinating faculty on sets of elementary sense-impressions. To any one who is familiar with it, this point seems so obvious and fundamental that it is hard for him to realise how commonly it is ignored, at any rate in the case of sound. Even people with sufficient education to know what nerves are, will be found to explain Music as an agreeable stimulation of the nerves of hearing ; and concurrently with such a view there naturally goes a failure to perceive what we have noticed above, that on the purely sensuous side the superior senses may fall far short of the inferior, and that too at the very moment when they are engaged in the delighted contemplation of beauty. Compare a melody or a face with the scent of roses. The perception of a melody, like that of a face, consists in the combination of a number of sense-impressions ; and what truly corresponds to the perception of the scent, as a simple and ultimate phenomenon due to nerve-stimulation, is not the *combination* of units, but each *separate* unit, whether of sound or colour. And these units, though corresponding with the sensation of sweet smell in respect of their simple and ultimate character, are probably extremely inferior to it in respect of enjoyableness. For just as the perception of a face, drawn in pencil, is made up of neutral units of impression, of simple black and white, so each note of a tune, whistled with the truest musical enjoyment, may be and commonly is, as regards sound, a very poor affair indeed ; so that the reference, the only possible one in the case of a sweet scent to simple physical stimulation of the nerves, is not only wrong, but especially delusive. The supervention of the higher faculties we found to be possible in the two cases of sight and hearing, through the enormous variety of the possible impressions and the rapidity with which they are grasped ; this variety and rapidity, again, being connected with the extraordinarily complex nature of the organs concerned. In the case of the eye we found the super-vention to take place *habitually*, and to lead to our ordinary perception of external objects; in respect of which we have assumed, as a fact generally recognised, that some possess beauty and some do not, but have at present sought no explanation of this difference. In the case of the ear, on the other hand, we have seen that the combination of sense-impressions into coherent groups of any complexity takes place *exceptionally*, but with a resulting beauty often comparable in degree to the very best attained by visual forms; of which beauty, again, we have deferred all account and explanation.

I cannot quit the special subject of this chapter without pointing out that the subtler physical peculiarities, connected with qualitative discrimination of impressions by the two higher senses, present to the evolutionist certain very noticeable problems; more especially noticeable in the case of the ear, both in themselves, and because we shall find that (over and above that rapid discrimination *in time* which has been mentioned) certain *qualitative* differences, those of *pitch*, have an essential relation to the higher sort of auditory forms; whereas qualitative differences of retinal impressions, being simply *colour*-differences, have no such relation to visual forms. The case of the eye, however, had better be considered first, as it is by comparison and contrast with this that the still more remarkable facts as to the ear will be best realised.

§ 12. Difficulties in accounting for the extreme delicacy and complexity of the higher sense-organs.

If we consider that sense-organs have had two principles of development—gradual adaptation through subjection and response to particular stimuli, and the stamping of favourable variations by natural selection—it naturally occurs to ask at what stages and in what proportions the two influences have respectively acted. But there are some preliminary questions. It may seem that often the power of delicate discrimination of sense-impressions is a faculty acquired by the *individual*, and cannot be directly referred to inherited or transmissible modifications of structure. This view seems specially applicable to the senses whose organs have not, like the ear, a multiplicity of elements, each structurally differentiated from all the others; since, in their case, we can account for a new sensation, or an increased power of discrimination, by a new and more refined mode of nervous action,[1] developed through exercise into a greater

The case of the eye: how far is the delicate discrimination of colour a faculty acquired by individuals?

---

[1] It is not necessary to go into the disputed point as to whether stimulation of one and the same nerve-fibre is susceptible of qualitative as well as quantitative differences; that is to say, whether, in the case of any particular sense, differences of sensation are based on different *modes* of nervous discharge possible to one and the same fibre, and caused by the different effects of different stimuli on its terminal structure. If the individual fibres are *not* so susceptible of various *modes*, but only of various *degrees*, of affection, and if the sensations received through them are *numerous* in kind, while

nicety of response to stimuli, and comparable to some of the acquired and individual aptitudes and feats of skill which are so familiar to us ; and we are not encumbered by having to account for structures whose complete differentiation would involve periods far beyond the individual life. The senses of taste and smell are of this kind, admitting as they do of an enormous amount of cultivation and of the most various degrees of discriminative power. This is well exemplified in the case of taste by men's relative faculty for judging of wines and vintages ; while those who have had experience of chemical work will bear witness to the same power of improvement and varieties of cleverness in respect of the sense of smell. Now it cannot be denied that the colour-sense seems to a certain extent to come under this class. While perceptible shades of colour seem almost infinite, the actually differentiated sorts of retinal elements, as has been mentioned, are only three ; and the various ways in which the component parts of the retinal response are combined, under the various physical stimuli, might seem referable to those modes of nervous action in which it might not seem unreasonable to imagine a considerable amount of individual acquirement : while the wide agreement in the mode of action, the less degree of individual and quasi-accidental variations, such as corresponded in our instances of taste and smell to very marked variety and uncertainty of discriminative power, might be attributed to the altogether exceptional constancy and universality of the physical stimuli. But this view will hardly stand examination. For though the presence of colour-stimuli of some sort is no doubt a constant and universal fact, the conditions seem quite sufficiently variable (*e.g.* in the environment of a town-child and of a country-child) to produce, were they truly effective, far greater variations than we find to exist.

and how far is it a recent phe-nomenon,

There are not lacking, however, other grounds of doubt as to the degree of parallelism and connection between increasing discrimination of colour and structural changes in the sensory apparatus. For as regards optical facts, it is specially easy to imagine that they may have been there without being noticed ; and that modes of effort, interest, and atten-

they, as distinguished by their terminal structures, are *few* in kind, all we have to do is to refer the differences in the 'mode of nervous action' to the higher centre, to what goes on at the cerebral point where the variously proportioned stimulations reach their junction and terminus. Thus, we do not imagine we have a separate gustatory fibre for every imaginable taste. We may then leave *sub judice* the question whether the same fibres, by different modes of action, or several distinct sets of fibres, by different combinations of degrees of action (as in the colour sense), give rise to the different tastes : but what is clear is that there must be *somewhere* a particular affection of nervous substance for each particular simple sensation, whether originating in the actual passing of the telegraphic messages, or only on their arrival. Whatever view be adopted on the disputed point, the ear seems to stand quite alone in the immense number of its actually differentiated terminal structures : and this distinction is too striking not to connect itself with the all-important sensory distinction that the ear alone has, in pitch, a true *scale* of sensations, presenting not only *differences* but *distances*.

tion are at the root of the changes, which on that view, it might be alleged, would easily be rapid. On the very natural and common view which connects discrimination of tints with enjoyment of them, it may seem specially easy to refer the later elaboration of the faculty to psychical concomitants of concentration and attention, and to modes of relation to the environment which are not only far withdrawn from the struggle for existence, but may be represented as matters of comparatively recent occurrence. It has been urged with considerable force that a very large part of the power of delicately discriminating tints (a power which must be carefully distinguished from length, keenness, and quickness of vision) has been developed within a time which in the history of evolution is a mere nothing : and a very extreme hypothesis of marked deficiency of colour-sense in the most gifted people of antiquity attracted lately a good deal of attention.

If this were so, we should certainly find the readiest explanation of the fact in connecting it with the action of higher nervous centres than that of vision. Experience shows us how much the power of perceiving depends on interest in the thing seen, which may have the most various sources ; and how great are the differences which exist in individuals all possessing what passes for normally good sight, and in the same individual at different times. And this alone would be enough to suggest that the physiological part of the phenomenon must be to a great extent behind and beyond definable points of structure and action, in nervous tracts where we cannot trace or even guess at the course of variations. The line where the differentiating facts begin is quite impossible to draw. It is matter of common recognition how possible it is for stimuli of various sorts to take actual effect on the physical organism without being at all noticed ; how sometimes gradually, sometimes suddenly, by a seeming accident we wake up to them, or how by an act of will we can make ourselves notice them ; how sometimes we become alive once for all to a difference we had never detected, and how one order of impression may be found pleasurable and interesting by one person, and attended to accordingly with gradually increasing powers of discrimination, and another by another ; whence we may perceive the evident impossibility, in many cases, of knowing how far perception and discrimination, when they come, are due to the formation of a power of physical response previously absent in the organ immediately concerned, and how far the facts must be referred to the exercise of attention and the deliberate dwelling on differences. It is enough to realise that this latter element cannot but play an important part ; and that the sorts of physiological events which accompany the adjustment of the attention, and which result in the improvement of the faculty, must have to do with much more unstable nervous structures and functions than the definitely hereditary ones associated with a particular

*[marginal note: and connected with the action of higher nervous centres ?]*

organ of sense. These remarks apply of course chiefly to the superior orders of sensation, and pre-eminently to vision, which affords such wide and perpetual scope to the advanced mental activities involved in rapid distinction and comparison; while the lower senses, with their slow one-by-one impressions and long periods of rest, offer less chance for such subtleties.

§ 13. Reasons for not regarding the faculty as of recent origin.

At the same time, there are very weighty reasons for hesitating to assign to the more delicate discrimination of colour at all a recent origin. As regards the points last noticed, we shall find it hard indeed, when we look round us, to accept an hypothesis of immense increase in the individual *attention* to colour; to believe that an observant *interest*, absent in the Greeks, is active now in the great mass of mankind. And the interest, it must be noticed, would have to be special and original in each case; since we lack evidence that that sort of improvement which we observe in a sensory faculty in connection with interest and attention is transmissible to descendants. Still more untenable of course would be the hypothesis that a large proportion of the actual *structure* of the optical apparatus has been a matter of recent development. Again, notions of artistic discrimination are in this connection decidedly dangerous; since they easily lead to confounding the *pleasure* derived from the shades and gradations of beautiful colour with the actual *power* to discriminate. But coarseness in the one sense does not at all imply coarseness in the other. A savage's eye may be in a sense as discriminative and as attentive as our own, though he may prefer the most barbarous and crude effects of colour. And when we consider the excellence of sight which is a common characteristic of savages, and also the exceptional advantages which that characteristic undoubtedly entails in the vicissitudes of primitive life, it seems not unnatural to imagine two separate stages in the later history of the faculty; one in which the sense had attained, through constant and attentive use, a very high level of discriminative power, a level which natural selection would tend to preserve if not to heighten; and another in which the faculty remains, or has been revived, to a great extent in direct connection with pleasure, as a part of the higher nervous sensibility, and with such amount of hereditary character as that may involve. Between the two stages, when the power is neither a prime necessity in the struggle for existence nor a special source of artistic enjoyment, it is easy to conceive that it might considerably decline; though again it would be rash to affirm this decline, in respect, for example, of the less civilised members of civilised communities, unless experiments were made which obviated the risk of confusing want of taste with want of discriminative power.

If we agree, then, that the development of the colour-sense must be referred back at any rate beyond the historic human times, when the accidents of individual habit and the varieties of taste would greatly obscure the problem, our two principles—of natural selection and of gradual adaptation to an increasing variety of stimulus through exercise of function—stand clear. Now of these two principles we should at first be inclined to regard the influence of the *latter* as having been here, not only exceptionally powerful and precise (owing to the peculiarly precise and close relation between a sense-organ and the external condition of its action), but exceptionally independent of the aid of natural selection. Recalling Mr. Spencer's argument, that ' as fast as essential faculties multiply, and as fast as the number of organs that co-operate in any given function increases, indirect equilibration by natural selection becomes less and less capable of producing specific adaptations, and remains fully capable only of maintaining the general fitness of constitutions to conditions ; ' and again, ' as fast as the number of bodily and mental faculties increases, and as fast as the maintenance of life comes to depend less on the amount of any one, and more on the combined action of all, so fast does the production of specialities of character by natural selection alone become difficult ; ' we may certainly find grounds for including discrimination of colour among the faculties to which that argument applies. For it must be noticed that advanced power of discriminating colours is of far less service for the mere *recognition* of objects than for their *distinction* among a number of others ; and this distinction would apparently only be of advantage to creatures whose mental and locomotive powers were decidedly advanced, and who thus belonged to the later stage of evolution described in the passages just quoted. The difference from, *e.g.*, the sense of taste may be thus represented. An enormous number of tastes are recognised by us as entirely and individually distinct ; and whatever might be the limits of this faculty in lower organisms, it is at any rate plain that the sense of taste could only be advantageous at all so far as it truly recognised individual impressions. But in colour the innumerable varieties are for the most part varieties of *shade* of a few orders of colour, blue, green, brown, and so on, as to which moreover the same object, in different lights and weathers, may vary between extremely wide limits : and to recognise a number of such tints as individually distinct, without seeing them in actual juxtaposition, is to a great extent even now beyond the power of any but cultivated sensibilities. On this ground alone, then, it would be difficult to credit primitive organisms with any appreciable share of such a faculty ; while as regards advantage, the extent to which it would have helped them in the important acts of recognising living-creatures or specimens of vegetable growth, is as nothing compared with what would be naturally effected by simple sensibility to degrees of light and dark and the power to perceive shapes and movements. As soon, however, as we come to the *distinction* of one object among a number of

Natural selection can apparently have had little to do with the final development of the colour-sense.

Difference from taste as regards discrimination.

others, we have a condition where shades of colour are of the utmost importance, and to which taste hardly presents the slightest parallel. Now this, as I have said, seems to belong naturally to a stage of advanced locomotive and co-ordinative power, when attention could be concentrated with advantage on a multitude of definite points, when food would be hunted for in various localities, and danger detected at considerable distances. And the extent and complication of the various actions involved in the useful exercise of this discriminative faculty might certainly seem to warrant us in assigning the later stages at all events of its development to the time when, according to Mr. Spencer's view, natural selection had ceased to be concentrated on the enhancement of particular modifications.[1]

§ 14. Difficulties in the principle of direct adaptation;

But now comes the curious point. The seemingly natural reference of the more delicate perception of colour to gradual adaptations, caused by the perpetual presence of coloured objects in the environment, will be found to present some very unexpected grave difficulties of its own.[2] The

---

[1] I cannot entirely harmonise Mr. Spencer's statements on this point. After explaining the differentiation of the higher sensory organs from the general integument, he says it is an open question whether these differentiations are due wholly to indirect equilibration (that is practically natural selection), or partly also to direct equilibration, that is, to differentiation of structure through the actual exercise of a function; in the case of the sense-organs through response to external stimuli. He grants that possibly light might 'aid in setting up certain of the modifications by which the nervous parts of visual organs are formed : ' but adds that 'it seems clear that the *complexities* of the sensory organs are not thus explicable;' that 'they must have arisen by the natural selection of favourable variations.' Surely those parts of the organs for the explanation of which we can only look to favourable variation and selection (since they could not have been developed through the exercise of function in response to stimuli), are the less complex and more mechanical parts which Mr. Spencer has been describing, such as the anterior chamber of the eye, and the auditory sac formed by infolding of the external integument; but as regards the far greater 'complexities' more immediately connected with sensation (as of the retinal elements), in spite of the difficulties to be immediately suggested as to modification through exercise in response to stimuli, Mr. Spencer's own remarks, quoted above in the text, seem sufficiently to mark natural selection as merely or chiefly a *conservative* factor.

[2] The points respecting environment which follow by no means exhaust the problem as to the share which direct stimulation and exercise of function, apart from natural selection, may have had in the development of the senses. There exists a more fundamental difficulty, at any rate as regards actual formation of new structural elements; which will at once appear if we compare the case of sense-organs with some other imaginable case of structural growth. For instance, there seems little *à priori* difficulty in conceiving a large development and differentiation of the muscular system, including the appearance of actually new elements, through the exercise of elements already present; muscular effort being applicable in all sorts of directions, for all sorts of known and desired results, and not depending on the presence of any special order of stimulus. In such a case, the fact and its cause, the relation between function and structure, and the parallel development of the two, would be entirely comprehensible. If, on the other hand, a new *sensibility* appeared, *e.g.* to some new colour, due to rays beyond those of the spectrum as at present known to us, we might, indeed, infer the existence of some new sort of retinal element, by such means as have already led us to infer the existence of the present three sorts; but how could we conceive that it had been developed through exercise of the elements

very fact that admiration of colour is supposed to have played an important part in the processes of sexual selection, the admiration being clearly of something recognised as *exceptional*, suggests the question how the requisite sensitiveness could have been developed. The point is the better worth noticing, as the colours themselves have received much more attention than the means of perceiving and enjoying them : while the rarity of certain colours in the environment, however much a reason for enjoying them when the perception has once become possible, certainly makes that perception the harder to account for in creatures who were entirely dependent in such matters on what nature presented to them.

On the theory, then, that the perpetual response to the stimuli of light especially as to red and orange. received from various objects may have gradually differentiated the means of distinguishing colours, how are we to account for the differentiation of the means to perceive such an exceptional colour as bright red ? It is impossible to imagine that the coloured environment of any creature (unless perchance a secreter of coral) can at any time have contained more than an infinitesimal fraction of this element ; and even the white of which it is a factor is comparatively rare in objects. The preponderance of browns, greens, and blues, whether on land or water, seems as if it must always have been overpowering ; and the fact that the general environment would be less noticed than exceptional features in it is irrelevant ; as what we are considering is a purely physical effect, the natural condition for which is

already present, which depend for exercise on one particular sort of stimulus, and would obviously be quite incapable of active efforts towards an unknown result ? How, in this case, could we conceive development of the new element by exercise, till it was itself *there*, at any rate in a rudimentary form, to be exercised ? which rudimentary form would imply an origin not by direct stimulus but by accidental variation. And in application to the past history of our organs, a similar hypothesis of accidental variation clearly carries with it the necessity of imagining some indirect means for preserving the variation ; that is, brings us round to the natural selection whose aid we were trying to dispense with.

This difficulty as to the *origin* of new structural elements does not apply to our conceptions of their *subsequent development* by exercise ; but all speculation on the subject must be very uncertain, owing to the limited range of possible experiment. For in the case of sense-organs, with their nervous apparatus, structure really means to a great extent molecular and chemical constitution, and so far its modifications entirely transcend our powers

of direct observation. We are reduced, therefore, for our views of development, to inferences from subjective facts, and as animals cannot describe their sensations, we are almost confined to our own species. Nor, even if careful records of sensation had been made for many generations, showing the modifications producible in the experience of an individual, the degree in which modifications can be transmitted, should we feel any confidence in using the results as evidence of pre-historic facts, except so far as they were of a distinctly positive kind. In spite, however, of all obscurities, there seems no choice between largely admitting the method of direct modification through subjection and response to stimuli, and invoking the whole machinery of natural selection for a multitude of small changes of little or no advantage in the struggle for existence ; and belonging, moreover, to a stage of development when the relations between organism and environment must have become so complex as to make the invocation of that principle for improvements in any *single* sense-organ decidedly unsafe.

that the physical stimulus shall be sufficiently frequent and continuous, not that it shall attract special attention. And the difficulty is even greater than it at first sight appears : for not only is red perceived, but it is one of three colours for which one of the three sorts of retinal elements connected with colour sensations has a maximum of excitability. It is comparatively easy to imagine a new mode of stimulation, a new nervous action set up by the application of a new stimulus to given nerve-endings, as when we experience a new taste for the first time : but here in the retina we have a distinct structure gratuitously differentiated, so to speak, for a certain stimulus of which the experience must have been of the most minute and intermittent kind. That the stimulus of red is relatively violent when it does occur seems shown by the manner in which it fatigues the eye ; but this clearly goes a very little way towards relieving the difficulty.[1]

§ 15. The case of the ear ;  In the case of the ear, where we have nothing analogous to the muscular action by which the eye perceives shapes and movements, the only perceptive and discriminative power which it would be advantageous to possess would be concerned with the character of sounds, as signs of this or that object ; and even at a very early stage the advantage in being

---

[1] I cannot think that this point has been sufficiently recognised. Mr. Grant Allen, in his *Physiological Æsthetics*, draws attention to what he calls the adaptation of eyes to colours, noticing that the converse adaptation had been more dwelt on by Mr. Darwin and others. But he appears to me to mix up the advantages of this adaptation with its *origin*, without perceiving that the facts of the former are precisely those which make the latter obscure. Thus, given animals who can appreciate red and orange, and who feed on red and orange fruits and berries, it is clearly advantageous to them to be attracted by the vividness with which a few specks of red stand out among acres of green ; and the simplest contrivance for effecting this end, according to Mr. Allen, would be to give the greatest possible rest to such retinal elements as respond to red and orange rays : but this rarely broken rest would scarcely be the simplest contrivance for establishing the assumed power of response. Again, he says, as though intending it for an explanatory account of the method of adaptation, that by a natural consensus, '*pari passu* with the development of brilliant colour in the vegetable world, must have come the development of a taste for brightness in the animal world.' Now if the requisite physiological elements are *there already*, such a consensus is intelligible : thus, a taste for new gustatory or olfactory sensations might readily follow on the appearance of new sorts of food. But what we want to understand is the actual differentiation of a special physiological element for red colour ; the differentiation is at any rate something different from gratification of the taste which it makes possible. We have found this differentiation hard enough to account for even on the widest supposition of red and orange already there in the environment. So far as we accept Mr. Allen's view, that 'the very existence of reds, yellows, and purples in the outer world is indirectly almost entirely owing to their special effect upon animal organism,' we are cutting away our only possible condition for making out the eye's adaptation to red to be historically at all parallel with its adaptation to blue and green ; namely, that the environment shall do at any rate all it can, by having some of its reds, the more marked and brilliant the better, there and ready to act as the blues and greens are. The last quoted statement is opposed to the authority of Mr. Darwin, who is careful to point out that brilliantly coloured substances must have continually originated chemically in the tissues of animals and plants, without any relation to perception or advantage. Similar considerations must doubtless apply to the natural conditions of fragrance in the external world.

made aware of the proximity of prey or of friends or enemies might be considerable. Natural selection may thus be credited with a most important part in the development of such early perceptions: while the generally neutral character of sounds, and the want of precision and regularity in their physical conditions, would lead us to expect the differentiation through the direct influence of environment to be very insignificant. The number of distinct sounds in nature, even including the noises made by friends and enemies, would be necessarily limited, and the general run of them, footsteps, rustlings, cracklings, and so on, are absolutely colourless. And in this general lack of variety, advantage would lie less in the power of marking differences than in susceptibility to very slight impressions, analogous to long and keen sight, and like that a very common characteristic of savages.

So far the case of the ear seems pretty plain, as this very monotony and neutrality of character precludes any difficulties connected with fine shades of discrimination, individual peculiarities of predilection and attention, and extraordinarily rapid development. But this immunity only extends to what we know as *noises*, not to what we know as *tones*. This is an all-important distinction, which will occupy us fully in the next chapter: for the present purpose I need not do more than appeal to the reader's general appreciation of the difference between the two things; merely adding that while the perception of noises requires comparatively simple structural elements, tones are discriminated by means of a separate and most elaborate part of the auditory apparatus. And when we consider this more elaborate part, standing as it does completely alone in amount of structural differentiation of elements, and try to apply the general theory of development through direct adaptation to surrounding conditions, we have the sort of difficulty just suggested by the perception of red colour multiplied a thousand-fold. We shall see further on what a small part definite musical tone plays in the natural environment: yet a very large part of the auditory apparatus, as we know it in man, seems set apart for the most minute discrimination of the pitch and quality of tones and for nothing else. It is true that this part of the apparatus comes into play in the perception of the pitch and quality of sounds in speech: but in the first place the tone-element there, as we shall find, is extremely unremarkable and caused by little infinitesimal and irregular fragments of the sort of vibration for which the various parts of the auditory organ are respectively differentiated, so that to imagine the differentiation to have taken place through them seems like imagining a person to learn swimming by flapping one hand in a basin of water; and in the second place the range of pitch within which musical tone is perceived extends on both sides immensely beyond the furthest limits of speech. And if we look lower in the scale of creation, the faculty of

*simple, when we regard it as merely an organ for noises; exceptionally difficult, when we regard it as an organ for discrimination of tones.*

discriminating tones, though there doubtless immensely inferior to our own, seems scarcely less strikingly out of proportion to the apparent means for forming it. Artificial tones are of course as unknown in the animal world as artificial colours : and in comparing what nature has done for animals in respect of the two modes of sensation, we have to set off such sounds as animals have the power of making for themselves, inconsiderable in variety and of most intermittent occurrence, against the perpetual and lavish display of visual colour in the external world. And the very fact which we shall notice later, that the power of making such sounds seems in many cases to have been developed greatly for the sake of the pleasure it gave, seems to involve the idea that the auditory changes necessary for responsive vibration and consequent enjoyment kept ahead of, or at any rate parallel with, the increasing variety of stimulus ; or at the very least must have followed with miraculous speed.

On the whole, then, the relation between the development of the tone-sense and the conditions of physical environment seems to constitute a most obscure problem. In the case of the eye and colour, whatever minor difficulties may be found, we at any rate are certain of the physical conditions of light and colour, as prime constituents of the environment, long before there was any germ of living organism to be environed : while tones to the very last remain exceptional phenomena ; comprise elements at both ends of the scale which are exceptions even among the exceptions; and moreover are still heard by many persons, and must have been heard by the immense majority of our progenitors, under the constant disadvantage of great unsteadiness and poverty of *timbre*, entailing on the physiological side a very feeble and imperfect exercise of function by the organ, and a correspondingly small chance of development.

# CHAPTER II.

## UNFORMED SOUND.

IN our sketch of the senses we passed on rapidly to a point whence we could obtain at once a clear view of the ground which really gives to sight and hearing their unique position in the hierarchy; and also could glance at the fundamental peculiarity presented by the sense of hearing, in the very occasional character of that highest activity which gives it its place in relation to Beauty, and makes it equally with sight the key to an otherwise unimaginable world. Having done this, we may now conveniently retrace our steps to the region of simple and unformed sense-impressions; and as this same sense of hearing is to be henceforth the main subject of our enquiry, we may proceed to examine some of the characteristics of sound, regarded for the present simply as such, apart from any grouping and co-ordination of elements. A few of these peculiarities, as has been already seen, are common also to the sense of sight; while others mark off hearing from all the other senses. §1. Peculiarities in the impressions of sight and sound.

To begin with, then, the feelings of sound are extremely unlocal, presenting strong contrast to those of taste and smell. Sight agrees with hearing in this respect, as, though the eye is the great organ for appreciation of external locality, the impressions it receives are not noticed as belonging locally to it and to no other part of the body. When the eye is fatigued, however, it may experience pain or discomfort of a quite local kind, connected, not with the actual seeing elements of the retina, but with the associated apparatus. The ear is not liable to this experience, and impressions of sound may therefore be said to be the most unlocal of all; the discomfort caused by a sudden loud noise, or, in some cases, by extreme shrillness, being not so much connected with the actual sound as with a less differentiated sense of shock or jar. Unlocal sensations.

Again, the means of access, the media through which the impressions of light and sound are received, ether in the one case, air in the other, constitute a fundamental difference in the sort of material, so to speak, which the external world presents to the two higher senses. The existence of these media is of course connected with the power of the eye and the ear to act at a distance from the exciting cause, which affects them by vibrations set up in the medium, not by direct contact: Impression by vibrations.

such a power, however, is not confined to these senses, for the organ of
smell, though needing direct contact of exciting particles, may encounter
these particles at a considerable distance from their main source, whence
they are enabled to spread by reason of their extraordinary minuteness. A

more noticeable point lies in the omnipresence of the ethereal and aerial
media; since only by this omnipresence could the organism be connected
with every object and movement in its vicinity. We saw in the last
chapter that the priority attaching to sight and hearing in virtue of this
connection entailed no superiority of sensuous *pleasure*: it may now be
added that the more universal phenomena of sight and sound are in some
ways more beyond the choice and control of individuals than any others.
Ordinary light means something very different in London and in Athens,
and languages, like voices, may be harsh as well as sweet. And on an
average of cases, the ear and eye certainly do not get more than a very
insignificant fraction of the amount of agreeable sensation of which they are
capable: the ratio of opportunity to capacity would probably prove, if a
census could be taken, to be very much smaller in their case than in that
of taste. Moreover, their constant liability to impressions, owing to the

universal presence of their media, places these higher senses at a disadvantage in a more positive way; for they are perpetually liable to be
taken unawares, and to be condemned to what they dislike without the
chance of escape. The ear is in this respect especially helpless, since it
cannot by its own action shut out what displeases it; while, unfortunately,
the excessive and wearing sounds of city-life are, of all outrages to the
senses, those of which one can least foresee the cessation. Nor can we
foresee the slightest chance of improvement in this respect through
change in the organism. The jar on the nerves produced by disagreeable
sound represents too infinitesimal a piece of unfitness for conditions to
stand any chance of being weeded out: we may even regard the general
nervous susceptibility implied in such experiences as a natural concomitant
of the superior physical and mental organisation which tends to supremacy
and survival. Nor can more be hoped from gradual adaptation; since it
is exactly the sudden and intermittent character of the annoyance which
both gives it its character and prevents our getting indifferent to it. I
fear we must take our unfitness to our conditions in this respect as a set-
off against the development of our ears to a point so remote from
utility and so conducive to enjoyment as that implied in the main subject
of this book.

We pass now to a distinction which is altogether peculiar to sound,
and is of the greatest importance. We have seen already that the impressions of all the sense-organs, of the eye and ear as well as of the nose
and palate, as long as they are regarded merely as isolated impressions,
and not as combined by a superior faculty into complex groups or wholes,

have a common character of ultimate and irreducible simplicity; and
further, that in the cases of light and tone this common character might
be fairly represented by the term *colour*. Now every impression which
the ear receives from moment to moment, just like every separate impression of light on the retina, has a particular quality which makes it
a distinct and recognisable phenomenon; as we know white or blue or
yellow when we see them, so we know the sound of a fiddle or of
thunder or of running water when we hear them. But when we think of
various sounds, when we recall what the sense-impressions really are in
the several cases, they seem to separate themselves into two classes which,
though they may merge into one another, are in nature quite distinct,
the class of *tones* and the class of *noises*; these may be provisionally dis- Tones and
tinguished as the class where that quality of sound exists which is noises.
generally described as *musical*, and the class where that quality is absent.
And it is only to the former class that such a term as *colour* seems at all
applicable; the colour-quality of a voice or an instrument is at once
understood as signifying its tone or *timbre*; but to speak of the sound of
a cough or a cart-wheel as having colour-quality would be thought absurd.
Not but that it may be important for us to distinguish the sound of
wheels on a road from any other sounds which may be audible at the
same time; we constantly avoid being run over by our power so to distinguish. But the characteristics of non-musical sounds never strike us as
shades of some common character in reference to which they can be compared. A cough is one thing, the sound of a waterfall is another, the
grating of a saw is another. The first may be neutral, the second pleasant,
the third unpleasant; they may present varying degrees of suddenness
or of loudness, and in these respects we can certainly compare them; but
in their lack of any essential common nature, they are disparate things;
and the only generic word for them is just *noises*, which is here really a
negative and quasi-technical term, implying absence of musical tone.

The *physical* difference (I may be allowed to remind my readers) between Their physical
musical tones and non-musical noises, is the difference between regular and physiologi-
and irregular stimulus. In the case of tones, the aerial vibrations are cal difference;
regular, precisely similar condensations and rarefactions of the air
succeeding each other in unvarying order, so many to the second; and the
auditory apparatus is so constituted that a parallel regularity of nervous
stimulation is set up in it. Noises, on the other hand, are due to an
irregular disturbance of the air; the state of which in their case, as compared with the state which produces musical tones, finds a rough
parallel in the surface of a pond blown by gusts of wind and churned by
oars and paddle-wheels, as compared with the same surface on a still day
with regular waves circling out from some point where a stone has been
dropped.

and one important consequence of it in respect to sensation.

The exceptional occurrence of true musical tones in our experience of sounds suggests one consequence which we shall find to be of great importance; namely, that when they do occur, they reap the benefit of rare and intermittent stimulation, which was noticed in the last chapter as characteristic of the keener bodily pleasures. The full and proper activity of those elements of the auditory apparatus which respond to regular vibrations being only occasionally called out, the sensational effects of such activity are proportionably remarkable and exciting.

§ 3. Tones and noises have no definite boundary line determined by quality of sound; and cannot be distinguished by the criterion of agreeableness.

It has been already said that these two classes of sound, which we have provisionally defined as tones and noises, merge into one another. The presence or absence of some slight degree of musical *timbre* in a sound is too hard to establish to permit the drawing of any distinct boundary line. A certain amount of musical *timbre* may exist in sounds which are generally accounted noises, and never thought of in connection with Music, as in the sound of wind, or in the tinkling of a fountain, or in piercing and distressing cries; while in musical tones, on the other hand, there is almost always a certain infusion of non-musical noise, as, for instance, in the rattling of the keys on the piano, or in strong consonants pronounced by a singing voice. Nor, in endeavouring to fix the amount of this or that element in any particular phenomenon, must we be led away by any notion that *agreeableness* will serve as a criterion. The *tones* of a cracked or screaming voice singing a song, may be as distracting as the noise of splashing water is soothing. Thus the terms *musical* and *unmusical* are somewhat ambiguous and misleading; it would be natural to call the singing voice unmusical, and the splashing fountain musical; so that the two words, used in relation to the quality of sounds, are in no way synonymous with capable and incapable of serving as material for music.

§ 4. Tones characterised by *certainty of pitch.*

This cross-distinction involves a modification of our definition of tones and noises: for it reveals that something quite different from what we understand as musical quality is necessary to constitute a sound a true tone. This something is certainty and distinctness of *pitch*; a certainty which is always possessed by, and is therefore generally associated with, sounds which have, besides, distinct and agreeable musical quality, as the notes of good instruments; but which very jarring and ugly sounds, as the notes of bad instruments, may equally possess.

At first sight, a difficulty may seem to be here involved. For it may be asked, how is it possible that this definite certainty in the pitch of a tone can exist unless as a result of regular vibrations and regular stimulation of the auditory apparatus? and these, as we saw, are the very conditions for agreeable musical quality or colour in the sound. The answer is that such regularity of vibrations must undoubtedly be present in every case where the pitch of a sound is distinctly recognisable; but these main vibrations, though succeeding each other with regularity, may each of them have a broken and uneven motion on its own account, so that a line representing them would have waves at regular intervals, but would be covered with minor jags and roughnesses; also each main wave may have superposed on it minor waves which fight and clash among themselves in the ear; and thirdly, in conjunction with the main regular elements, there may be all manner of irregular and jarring elements quite unconnected with them. To revert to our simile of the pond; the main set of regular circling waves might still be quite perceptible to the eye, even though their edges were chopped and jagged, and though the whole surface were lashed up into a number of shifting irregular elevations and depressions. So the ear is able to pick out and respond to the regular elements of the stimulus, which means that it hears a tone; but the irregular elements, which simultaneously affect it, may cause the tone to be utterly rough and disagreeable, or, in ordinary *parlance*, unmusical. Whether we consider this unmusicalness as harshness, or as absence of musical quality, is a mere matter of language; a substratum of *some* true musical quality there must be, since certainty of pitch and musical quality are necessary results of the same cause; but this may be so overborne by supervening elements, that while the pitch remains recognisable, the quality of the sound may be altogether on the wrong side of the neutral line.

It must be distinctly realised that the regularity we have spoken of is of elements far too rapid to count, or to perceive as discontinuous: physically, we know that they are regular, but in consciousness a multitude of them constitute one ultimate phenomenon, namely a tone. A thing may *sound* regular, may be represented in consciousness as uniform or monotonous, without any regularity of this kind in its constituent elements; for instance, the rustling of leaves in a forest affects the ear in a steady gentle manner, without shocks or jars, but also without any of the regular stimulation which constitutes distinct tone. There are many sounds from which regularity of vibration is almost or entirely absent, but where the irregular disturbances, though entirely in the ascendant, are not of a jarring kind. Yet such sounds, though agreeable, are noises, even as jarring notes, though disagreeable, are tones. The sound of a fountain, or of distant thunder, may be decidedly agreeable; but though we are conscious here of some slight blending of the tone-element, which distinguishes the sounds from the crackling of leaves or the rattling of a cab, yet it would be hopeless to attempt to assign to such sounds a distinct pitch in the scale; the tone-elements are far too much involved and swamped in what is merely noise, and far too uncertain and transitory on their own account, to be separately estimated and identified. Even sounds with a much more definite element of *timbre* than these may, nevertheless, be excluded by the criterion of clear distinguishable pitch from the class

*Many sounds are what we call regular, without having any of the special sort of regularity which constitutes tone.*

of true tones. Such sounds are those of common speech; for though we speak of a musical voice, with a far clearer conception of the implied colour-element than when we speak of a musical fountain, still the non-musical elements in speech are so prominent, and the sounds are often so uncertain, shifting, and spasmodic, that even a skilled musician may find it a hopeless task to track out the actual notes with anything approaching completeness.

It will be noticed that distinctness of pitch and positiveness of musical quality, depending as they both do on regularity of vibration, which may be swamped and hidden by simultaneous irregularities, naturally vary together as regards their prominence and the ease with which the ear detects them. The pitch of an extremely grating note is proportionably hard to identify; while if sounds are sharply clearly musical in quality, their pitch is recognisable even when they are extremely light and rapid. Now in the majority even of agreeable voices, the *timbre* (which must be carefully distinguished from clearness and refinement of pronunciation) is extremely neutral and inconspicuous. For sounds with so little true colour-quality to be definitely identified as to pitch, it would be necessary that each should be dwelt on for a very appreciable time; whereas in speech the shifting and sliding to and fro is as rapid as it is habitual. We need not dwell on the topic here, as we shall encounter it again when we come to consider the relations of speech to Music.

§ 5. Summary.

So far, then, our position is as follows. We have found that musical tones, sounds with a true and distinct colour-quality, are quite exceptional things, only slightly and dubiously represented in the ordinary course of experience in the world around us, and mainly connected with a quite special and isolated class of phenomena. We have further found that the word *tone* must not be confined to the sounds which are musical in the sense of being agreeable, but rather to the sounds which are musical in the sense of being available as material for Music, as elements of the recognisable combinations known as tunes; and that for this class agreeableness of quality, though so universally associated with the idea of musical notes, is a far less useful and accurate criterion than certainty of pitch. To this we may add, what indeed has been already implied, that in general this same certainty of pitch is, equally with distinctly musical quality, associated with an isolated set of phenomena: though we *can*, we practically seldom *do*, produce musical tones except in *music*. It was impossible to avoid here the notice of this fact, if only by way of contrast; but it will be perceived that we have *assumed*, without discussion, the existence of and necessity for certain and recognisable pitch in the sound-material of Music. To discuss this point would be to trench on the subject of Music itself, and to forestall a great part of our subsequent enquiry. At present we are more immediately concerned with sense-impressions regarded as unformed and independent phenomena: and our point is that for these, in the case of sound, we have what amounts to a *double* mode of sensibility, the ordinary and the extra-ordinary, responding respectively to irregular impulses and to regular vibrations of the aerial medium.

In this connection we may conveniently notice two points respecting the enjoyment of sound, which seem at first sight to present a certain incompatibility. On the one hand coarse and uncultivated natures seem capable of getting enjoyment from sounds which are especially distressing to others: and even without having resort to the coarsest natures or the most excruciating sorts of sound, we perceive that the firing of a gun on the stage must be a source of pleasure to a large number of the audience, or it would not be so constant a feature of modern melodrama; and that the ordinary style of after-dinner chorus must have charms for the majority of young Englishmen. On the other hand there is no doubt that a set of East End roughs would almost instantly discover the difference between, *e.g.*, a perfectly beautiful and a moderately good soprano voice; the better the voice the more they like it. That is, they show here, when they get the chance, a real discriminative delicacy of colour sense, un-paralleled in any other region of their sensations: for the same persons would certainly not pick out that particular flavour of wine which the connoisseur would most approve, as specially superior to others which he would despise; nor would their taste in visible colour satisfy a more artistic eye. It would be extremely interesting to know whether the same taste in sound would be found in savages; whose delight in what seem to us hideous noises can in no way be held to prove that they are incapable of enjoying what they have never had the chance of hearing, sound of really beautiful musical quality, in face of the fact that such sound *is* appreciable by many among our own roughest classes whose ears seem as obviously callous as theirs to violent usage. In the case of tones with any pretension to musical quality, I do not think the poorer and harsher are ever deliberately preferred to the richer and sweeter, though there may be any amount of differences of taste as to particular varieties of *timbre*. And as coarsely organised human beings seem com-paratively little behind their more refined fellows in detecting superiority of tone when they hear it, so also here they seem to be most distinctly removed from the brute creation. For in respect of the other senses animals often show a decided agreement with man, as in a liking for bright colours, for the tastes of various sorts of food, and in some cases apparently for fragrance; nor does the enjoyment by some of them of flavours and smells the very idea of which is to us disgusting, at all exceed that frequently found among savages. But, without relying for evidence on such facts as that dogs often howl at the sound of a fiddle

§ 6. Curious combination of coarseness and sensitiveness in many ears.

(prompted by feelings not perhaps wholly unknown even in human experience), I am not aware that, since the days of Orpheus, animals have ever shown any special partiality for distinctly beautiful musical tone, or even for tone which is so much as moderately satisfactory to us ; in spite of so often having a sort of music of their own, and occasionally even possessing a command of really sweet notes.

*This is to a great extent explicable by considerations of general physical stimulation,*

The remarkable coarseness and remarkable sensitiveness which seem to be combined in a large number of human ears, though strangely contrasted, each admit of a considerable amount of explanation. The love of coarse and violent sound is connected with the mere love of violent stimulation, and manifests the exceptional way in which stimulation of the auditory nerve overflows into the general nervous system; the discharge often finding vent in actual movements, and causing a general diffused excitement throughout the organism. This general discharge and need of a vent is shown in the fact that a person is pleasingly excited by sounds in the making of which he is actively participating, when passive endurance of them would be intolerable. The constant use by savages of instruments of percussion, which from the suddenness and sharpness of their sound are particularly effective in this way, exemplifies the same point; and the use is commonly accompanied by yells and dances.

*and of the distinction between noise and tone ;*

The perception of beautiful quality of tone, on the other hand, has no connection with general stimulation, and is entirely a matter of the more delicate and differentiated part of the ear : and the very contrast I am noticing would afford a strong *à priori* presumption for the truth of Helmholtz's elaborate theory that different parts of the ear are appropriated to noises and to tones. We observed in the last chapter what an extraordinary problem the development of the tone-portion of the ear presents : but once developed, there seems no special difficulty in the fact that it is regular and spontaneous in action, and that the sensations connected with it are well characterised and pretty universally possible and similar. And indeed there are grounds for regarding both the certainty and the general similarity of the enjoyment as specially natural in the

*tone being peculiar in two ways.*

case of tone. For in the first place, thanks primarily to Helmholtz, the objective conditions of beautiful tone can be referred with exceptional definiteness to comprehensible points of physical law and physiological function. The varieties of tone-sensation are connected in the most intelligible manner with a large number of actually differentiated elements, and the combined action of several of these, necessary for the production of a satisfactory quality of tone, takes place according to the most definite numerical proportions : whence, as long as the elements are there to be stimulated, it is not surprising if the sensations seem less liable to idiosyncrasies and divergences than do those of the organs which are less structurally differentiated, and where the various modes of nervous affection underlying the character of sensations are more remote and obscure. In the second place, the unique and independent position of tone in the world tends distinctly to the same result : beautiful quality of tone is altogether too exceptional a phenomenon for variable conditions, beyond the simple sensation of the moment, to have any appreciable effect on the kind and amount of enjoyableness.

These points become clearer through the contrast to them presented by visual colour. In its case, enjoyment and criticism perpetually have reference to other elements than the absolute quality of the tint. Associations with objects and textures, and with habits and fitnesses, are continually present in such overpowering force, that only by a strong effort can the purely sensory quality be detached and judged Numerous instances of this might be found in the various applications of colour to personal adornment, where anything unfamiliar naturally seems eccentric or extravagant ; and the style in which many savage customs are reported shows how habitually the eye refuses to recognise the quality of (it may be) beautiful colour in the wrong place. Often too the more refined pleasure, when it exists, is connected with gradations and juxtapositions which entirely remove the phenomenon from the simplest sensory class. So that even in the natural course of individual experience, we find far less fixity and absoluteness about the pleasing and displeasing qualities of simple colour, than of any other order of simple impression.

§ 7. Contrast of visual colour: the variety of taste in tints being partly due to references and associations far beyond their primary sensory qualities,

The contrast in the case of visual colour to the general certainty and agreement about beauty of tone-colour, cannot, however, be altogether, or even chiefly, referred to this cause; there is quite sufficient fixity in individual appreciation of individual tints to afford ample evidence of wide varieties of sensibility, quite apart from the more involved questions of application and juxtaposition in relation to which taste in colour is so often criticised. To realise this, we have only to compare a walk through a Manchester warehouse with a walk through a Cairo bazaar ; or to recall the popularity of the aniline dyes among people who would show themselves at a ballad-concert perfectly competent judges of harshness and sweetness of voice. Such facts certainly approximate the colour-sense, as regards the range of the variations in sensibility to which it is liable, rather to the senses of taste and smell than to that of tone. And we shall the more readily rest content with this variableness, if we observe the extreme obscurity of the physiological facts on which the variations are based. Even the most general formulæ which would connect coarse taste with pleasure in violent stimulation are exceptionally difficult to apply in the case of colour : for instance, the more luminous edition of a colour, which would be for all alike superior in pleasurable quality to a deader edition of the same tint, can hardly be held to fall short of the latter in violence of stimulation ; and a colour may be dazzlingly strong without giving to the

but in great measure also to a very wide range of variation in the primary sensibility.

most refined sense the slightest impression of vulgarity or crudeness. We certainly seem driven to choose roughness, or some other less definite word than violence, to express the special character of the nervous action which the coarser organ feels as pleasant or indifferent, and the more refined as offensive. But whatever word we adopt, the real place and nature of the physiological facts remain equally unknown to us; and this very obscurity completes the contrast with the case of musical tone, where the sorts of physical and physiological interruptions and shocks, connected with a jarring quality of tone, are as well understood as the conditions of richness and fulness.

§ 8. The neu-
trality or
colourlessness
of ordinary
sounds ;

It will be evident, from all that has been said, that the ordinary class of sounds, those met with in the normal course of experience, are the most neutral of all the impressions connected with a special organ; things heard can be neutral in a sense in which things seen, smelt, and tasted never can. All tastes, for example, are variations of a *single* mode of sensibility, and all have a *positive* character : any apparent exception to this positive character would only mean that the material in our mouths was affecting the nerves of *touch* in the tongue, but not those of *taste*. All visual sensations, again, are of positive colour, since colour is of the essence of light; absence of colour is blackness, which means absence of sensation. The colour may be dull and dingy, through poverty of light and an unfortunate mingling of its constituents; but it is none the less truly colour, and has for its physical cause vibrations as regular as those which generate purer and brighter tints. The grey sky and dull bricks which my eyes encounter as I now look forth, are certainly neutral enough as regards pleasure-giving quality, but what I see is still colour; whereas the scratching of my pen as I write, the sound of footsteps, and opening and shutting of doors in the house, and the distant clatter outside, are not only neutral in the sense of being heard with indifference, but in the sense of wholly lacking *timbre*, that is, of having no colour-quality at all. Wrong In the region of sound colour depends on exceptional physical conditions, on a mode of stimulation which is occasional, not habitual; so that the sounds possessing it in any conspicuous degree form a class quite apart. A practical experiment will show how real are the effects of this contrast. Daylight costs nothing; and the organ which is perpetually receiving colour-sensations of some sort, is sure of at least occasional gratification. No city is so steeped in smoke and ugliness as wholly to lack, in buildings or costume, bits of colour which may attract and arrest the eye; or even if it were, the face of heaven could not be entirely shut out. Flowers, again, present to the senses both of sight and smell the cheapest of all luxuries. But it would be quite possible to spend whole days in walking about a city, without receiving the slightest iota of direct satisfaction through the medium of the ear. The only bits of striking sound colour with distinct pitch and *timbre* that one would encounter, might probably be the shrill cries and laughter of children, which, though they may warm the heart, certainly do not exhilarate the sense.

We may even go further, and assert that the ear will not stand definite sound colour as part of its ordinary environment.   The most musical note, if prolonged continuously, would weary us in less than a minute; and formless successions of such notes would be more irritating still.   Compare looking at a sun-lit marble wall for half an hour, and listening to a tone or a few changing tones without form.   This shows the contrast.   The eye is always seeing lights and colours, and *rests* contentedly on agreeable masses; while the ear is peculiarly affected and *excited* by the occasional phenomena which present distinct sound colour.   Again, from a visual colour which wearies us, we can commonly turn our eyes; a fragrance pervading the place in which we are, cannot indeed be avoided by such simple means, but will soon cease to affect our consciousness; but in the case of the ear the sensibility of the organ is not deadened by the persistence of the stimulus, and the presence of true musical colour may make it as hard for us to become unconscious of a prolonged sound as would excessive and disagreeable loudness.

*such neutrality being even demanded by the ear.*

In spite, however, of the neutrality, the lack of colour-quality, which we find in the general run of non-musical sounds,[1] they have certain remarkable modes of affecting us; modes which we shall encounter, indeed, as prominent factors in the domain of Music, but which stand out as exceptional in the case of quite formless sense-impressions.   These modes may be distinguished as the soothing and the stimulating.

*§ 9. Yet non-musical sounds have certain very special possibilities;*

Where a *non-musical* sound has a soothing character, we shall find that this depends on the very condition which we have found to render a *musical* sound insupportably irritating, namely, that it shall be prolonged for a considerable time.   And this is the very reason that open-air sounds of a soothing kind are for the most part banished from cities, where all continuity of sound is swamped in fragmentary hubbub, and winds and waters get no chance; indeed, the only monotonous sound which can address the city-dweller with any soothing power is the distant

*in the way of soothing,*

---

[1] The word *non*-musical conveniently describes the sounds which, through the lack of any element or substratum of distinct and assignable pitch, are outside the region of *tones*, as above defined : *un*-musical is identified, according to common use, with harshness and disagreeableness of quality.  *Musical* is constrained to serve as correlative to both these negative terms : a *musical note* commonly means distinct pitch, which can therefore appear as an element in a tune, but which for all that may be very harsh and ugly; a *musical sound* commonly means an agreeable sound, like the splashing of oars, which for all that has no distinct pitch and could never appear as an element in a tune.  A further ambiguity lies in the word *tone* : in the singular it is constantly used to denote what I have called *timbre* or *colour*, as when people speak of one violin as superior *in tone* to another; that is, to denote not sounds, but a quality of sounds.  This ambiguity seems to justify the use of the French word, *timbre*, in preference.

roar of the streets, the effect of which is too easily destroyed by association, even when not broken in upon by some nearer noise. In the country or by the sea, on the other hand, the prolonged and gentle sounds of Nature have a markedly soothing, and even a soporific, effect on most organisms. There are, it is true, exceptional cases where the sound of the sea is distinctly objected to, and actually prevents sleep: this effect, however, may probably be referred to the rhythmic character of the waves, the attention being kept alert by a kind of unconscious counting, such as is often induced by the ticking of a clock. Where the general sound of the sea is found unpleasant, in the absence of any such special feature of annoyance, mental elements of association, or the melancholy connected with a sense of vastness and fate, are probably at work. I do not remember to have ever heard of a similar objection to the equally monotonous effect of a flowing stream; in connection with which I could much more easily conceive the 'beauty born of murmuring sound,' which will recur to every reader, to be a literal fact. Again, the lulling effect of a gentle voice reading aloud is well known. Here, indeed, the sound is not continuous in the sense of being quite unbroken; but the *timbre* of the separate parts is too diluted and inconspicuous for that annoyance to be possible which we saw would ensue from a formless succession of distinctly coloured tones.

In these soothing effects the sense of sight seems to come very far behind that of hearing. To a person who is sensitive to refinement of colour, daily peace of mind may of course be greatly promoted by a congenial *entourage* in this respect; but no specially lulling effect results from contemplation of any expanse of uniform colour, however mild and restful in tint. A soporific effect may indeed be produced through the sense of sight, by an amount of light which distinctly wearies the eye; but this happens more especially when the eye is actively employed, as in reading. It is the result of over-stimulation, but not of a gentle and unbroken uniformity of impression; and moreover as a rule darkness, that is, absence of all visual activity, is the preferable condition for sleep.

and in the way of stimulating; the stimulation being sometimes of a startling kind,

Still more remarkable are the effects of sound in the way of stimulation. Of all formless impressions, sounds can give by far the strongest shock to the organism. The phenomenon of starting is a common example of this fact. *Tastes* and *smells* cannot affect us with such sudden violence, nor can the stimulus in their case overflow with such rapidity into the general nervous system, as to produce a real instantaneous start; and though we start at the sudden *sight* of something unexpected close to us, it will be noticed that the something is usually either a living creature, or else an object in rapid motion. If we open the door and unexpectedly find on the threshold a ladder or some conspicuous inanimate object, we may recoil a step, but we do not start in approximately so violent a manner as if we

come upon a human being equally close to us; or, if we enter a room which
we imagine empty, and find some one in it, we often start, whereas the
sudden discovery of a new chair or table in the room will have no such
effect on us. Here, then, the phenomenon is due to elements beyond
the mere sensory impression, and connected with a feeling that the space
near us is occupied in a totally unique manner, when the occupying body
is a living creature. We carry about an habitual instinct of having around
us a certain amount of space in which we are alone, and any sudden violence to this instinct is very unnerving. That this is the true explanation seems to be shown by the fact that the gentlest possible touch, if it
gives the same impression of unexpected nearness to a living creature,
causes a similar start. The start produced by rapid motion in our immediate
vicinity has probably a different source, the instinct, namely, of self-pre-
servation: the start is invariably *from* the exciting object, and resembles
the recoil from a threatened blow. Nor are these causes absent in the
case of sound; identical instincts must certainly play a part in the nervous
shock produced by a sound which suddenly gives the impression either
of a living creature, or of some sort of violent motion close to us. But in
the starting caused by sound, there seems to be often a large element
which lies quite outside these instincts: a loud sound will startle us violently without being conceived of as due to anything close to us. There is
no sudden adjustment of ideas, as when we start at the sudden proximity
of a fellow creature; and no co-ordination of movements, as in the characteristic recoil from a threatening danger; only a uniquely disagreeable
shock to the organism.

But it is not in this painful way that the very direct effect of sound on
the organism is chiefly interesting. In the early and instinctive awe which
a single mighty sound produces, the sense of hearing has no parallel. No
case can be mentioned in which simple sensory impressions, of a sort of
which our personal experience would appear too limited to have originated
anything like an abstract idea, as of external or hostile power, nevertheless excite feelings which seem at least to touch the confines of such an
idea. Among the other senses, that of sight is the only one which could
even be mentioned in connection with such feelings; and in its case we
get far more definitely into a region where ideas have been clearly formed
from sense-material by an infusion of mental elements and associations,
and involve objects and occurrences of known experience. Roughly
speaking, a large object, like a mountain, impresses us with a sense of
tremendousness, partly because we have acquired a conception of space
and distance in connection with a long series of muscular experiences,
partly through associations of mighty movements, and even catastrophes,
with great height; but a mere blaze of light, the true analogue of a mass
of sound, conveys to us no such impression. The exciting and awe-

sometimes of
an awe-in-
spiring kind.

inspiring effect of sound, the sense of mystery and mightiness which it forces on us, may, indeed, for aught we know, be connected with events and catastrophes of the remotest past, but certainly does not seem due to any experiences of our own lives; and it is one of the most deeply seated and universal of instincts both among civilised and savage peoples.

§ 10. They also lend themselves readily to association.

As this experience of awe has already carried us somewhat beyond the region of mere sense, one more property of sounds may be noticed, which, though by no means peculiar to them, is still in their case very marked; the readiness, namely, with which they lend themselves to association in the experience of individuals. Mr. Spencer has adduced a very good example of this in the cawing of rooks; a sound which certainly has no intrinsic beauty, and yet which many persons hear with a certain pleasure and emotion. Mr. Spencer connects this pleasure with half-unconscious associations of early life, of holiday evenings and pleasant country-scenes among which the sound first became familiar. As a converse example of annoyance caused by a sound which on its own merits would seem to be agreeable, I sometimes imagine that a feeling of melancholy and distress produced in me, and I find in many others, by the sound of church-bells, may be traced to the dulness and confinement of childish Sundays. These effects of association often seem to bear an inverse ratio to the actual strength of the sound-impressions: they form in connection with the subdued murmurs of a summer-evening, with village-sounds and cries heard in the distance, with the faint tones of the Swiss herdsman's horn far away among the hills, rather than in connection with sounds which more directly force themselves on the attention. And indeed it seems natural that the favourable cases for such effects should be those where the original impressions blended with a general stream of agreeable experience, without themselves rising into special prominence.

§ 11. Form and Colour, both of them exceptional in the region of sound, are found combined in one set of phenomena,

We have now briefly glanced at the chief characteristics of sounds, regarded as impressions of sense, each of which constitutes (as a noise invariably *must*, a tone through isolation *may*, constitute) a perfectly simple phenomenon, having all its powers and properties there with it in the moment of its presentation, standing in no special relation to any other sound, and so calling up no exercise of any co-ordinating and combining faculty. But we saw, when we were justifying the high position of the sense of hearing in the æsthetic hierarchy, that there is a particular set of phenomena where sounds do come under the domain of a co-ordinating faculty; and we have since seen, in connection with the colour quality, that a certain class of sounds are marked off by certain characteristics as tones, and that there is also a particular set of phenomena to which these specially belong. It need hardly be said that the particular set of phenomena in the two cases is one and the same. The coincidence is not, indeed, absolutely perfect; as, on the one hand, there is one mode of combining sounds, the rhythmic mode pure and simple, which takes no account of their pitch or their *timbre*; and, on the other, definite pitch and *timbre* can exist in sounds which enter into no combination, as in the distant sound of a threshing-machine, or as when a person sounds a single note, or intones in monotone. But, neglecting such cases for the present, we may state broadly that for sound the region of Form is the region of Colour, and that while the eye is encountering form and colour at every moment of its waking activity, the ear practically identifies them with that unique order of experience, called Music, in which alone they are combined.

And this order of experience is not only exceptional; it is also purely artificial. Among the sounds of inanimate nature, though many of them are agreeable and impressive, there is not a vestige of form, scarcely even a vestige of the tone-material out of which forms are built. We shall find, in the sixth chapter, that a rudimentary sort of music is widely diffused in the animal kingdom, and even that it often holds a less exceptional position, in relation to the whole amount of sounds the animals can make, than with us; but that it is produced, like ours, with a distinct view to pleasurable excitement. With man, the production even of the material, of the tones possessing sufficient certainty and permanence of pitch to serve as elements of forms, requires a deliberate effort of the voice; while these tones would never, unless governed by a conscious aim, reach the stage of form. This, however, will be better appreciated when we come to discuss in detail the nature of melodic forms: for the present we may be content with the universal admission of the fact that Music is an artificial product. But universal admission goes further: according to it, Music is not only *artificial*, it is an *art*. And as, in reviewing the properties of sound, we discover one set of phenomena where alone the all-important factors of high æsthetic pleasure enter into combination, where alone, therefore, the supreme and peculiar *power of sound* could be imagined to reside, so now we find that in pursuing our enquiry we shall be engaged wholly with art, with sound as present in works of art. The very words may well put us on our guard, so charged are they with ambiguities and pitfalls: and since it would be impossible to proceed without a clear realisation of what is and what is not implied in these and other commonly associated terms, it will be convenient at once to clear the ground by a brief examination of the most general elements involved in a work of art, and of the relations which they hold to one another. This analysis will be the means opening out new points of comparison and contrast between the two supreme æsthetic senses.

*which is an entirely artificial product,*

*and constitutes an art.*

# CHAPTER III.

## THE ELEMENTS OF A WORK OF ART.

§ 1. Analysis and definition, in connection with emotional subjects, though an ungrateful is sometimes a necessary task. To many it is a disagreeable and difficult task to try to analyse the pleasure derived from beauty. To attempt this analysis in the actual moment of enjoyment would indeed often be quite useless, and would divert into speculative channels the nervous energy necessary for apprehension and appreciation. Nor in general is anything like detailed knowledge of the technical structure of works of art helpful as regards appreciation, any more than a knowledge of anatomy and organic chemistry is helpful for the appreciation of human beauty. There are, however, certain obvious elements common to all the arts, of which, obvious as they are, the existence and the nature seem in many cases not to be very clearly conceived. And of these broad elements, and of their relative place and importance in each of the arts, I cannot but think that a clear conception is necessary, at any rate for sound judgment, if not for vivid appreciation; while a comparison in respect of these elements between the various arts themselves with which such a conception naturally connects itself, is by no means unfruitful in suggestion and interest.

The process of definition and distinction cannot, I fear, be made very attractive. It is impossible to invest it with the charm of that higher criticism whose function is, by dint of the author's wider grasp and keener appreciation, directly to enlighten and guide the perceptions of others in the actual presence of the work ; and it is an ungrateful task to point out that this higher criticism occasionally gets so high as to lose itself in clouds and vapours, for the want of the ballast which a more rigorous definition of terms might have given. In proportion, however, as a critic of art avoids these dangerous regions, and really enlightens as well as delights his public, he will probably be ready to acknowledge the humbler service, if, in the more general and abstract region which surrounds the subject, the air can be somewhat cleared of the barren verbiage and meaningless analogies in which feelings of genuine admiration so often find vent. Few perhaps fully realise the difficulty of defining at what point the core of a true emotional experience begins to get involved in a subjective haze, where indistinct ideas are apt to betake themselves to the refuge of high-sounding phrases, whose reality and profundity it seems like profanation to question. Thus we are told that all beauty is a series of variations on one theme; or that all the arts are reflections of a single ideal; or point-blank that a musician is a poet. The oracular sound of such expressions is conventionally held to exonerate them from scrutiny: the Ideal, like Cæsar's wife, must be above suspicion. In reality an emotional ex-perience is seldom an isolated phenomenon; it is commonly surrounded by a swarm of accidental and evanescent images and verbal ghosts of images; and one who tries to demonstrate the adventitious character of the swarm may easily seem to be calling in question the central ex-perience, and to be impugning that which he himself presumably lacks the faculty to discover.

Perhaps, however, seeing that it is so hard to dissociate our feelings from our customary ways of regarding and expressing them, the question will occur, is it necessary or important so to do? What harm does the subjective haze do, if it surrounds a solid nucleus of appreciative enjoyment? Is it an occasion for heavy logical artillery, if a young lady professes that the im-pressions she derives from Wagner and George Eliot are precisely similar? If she can enjoy both, has she not in her the root of the matter? And truly, whatever the surrounding fog, it is undeniable that a natural capa-bility for enjoying any form of artistic work is something incommensurably more valuable than the mere faculty of perceiving extravagances and absurdities in the way of describing it. But unfortunately the above-quoted profession is hardly a caricature of views which are susceptible of being wrapped round in clever language and worked up into a very respectable semblance of profundity; and they act on production and on the opinion which creates the atmosphere for production. So that there comes to be real danger that valuable things and valuable instincts will drop out of sight, and that the mass of those who are capable of deep im-pressions from art, but lack strength and certainty of instinct, will be led away on false scents, and mistake the nature of their faculties.

The word 'art' has many uses. The most universal has probably been that which distinguishes art from science as being concerned with practical rather than intellectual results, with things done rather than things known; as when we speak of the *art* of medicine, and the *science* of abstract mathematics. With this meaning we have nothing to do. In such terms as 'high art,' however, the meaning is confined for the most part to æsthetic productions; nor is it always easy to realise how modern is the idea of Art *par excellence*, in the sense which restricts it to productions of a certain kind, nor how various within this region are the manifestations which have at different times assumed importance; and this not only in respect of detail and development, but of the main branches. For instance, among the Greeks (whom we regard as pre-eminently the artistic nation

§ 2. Uses of the word *art*.

of antiquity) dancing was fully as much of a high art as Music, and land-scape-painting was unknown.

§ 3. Characteristics of a work of art. It is made by man out of unformed material;

It will be useful first to consider what is now involved in the current conception of a 'work of art.' First we distinguish it from the works of Nature; it is a work designed and executed by man. And it must involve more than mere *arrangements* of beautiful and complete natural objects; for we should not, except in conscious hyperbole, say that a choregraphist or a landscape-gardener has produced a 'work of art;' in which some sort of domination of inexpressive and more or less intractable material seems to be implied. Similarly in the non-material region, we should never dream of applying the term 'work of art' to a collection or arrangement of ready-made literary productions.

it is a source of pleasurable emotion, consciously aimed at;

Next, it is through its beauty, or grandeur, or impressiveness of some kind, a source of pleasurable emotion to those who contemplate it. But many works of utility are this: an express train dashing by, or a vessel under sail, or a contemplation of M. Littré's dictionary, may give rise to such emotions. So we get another limitation: a 'work of art' is a work in whose effect (whatever else be included), at any rate pleasure is not only present, but consciously aimed at. Apparent exceptions may be adduced from the arts of Painting and Poetry. Pictures, for instance, have been painted with the distinct object of inspiring horror and dread of death: but just as there are people whose imagination is pleasantly stimulated by hearing of the terrible future consequences of their sins, so it is quite possible for horrible objects to produce pleasure, of however debased and distorted a kind; and these pictures would not have been painted had they not been calculated to fascinate some gazers. Again, the satires of Juvenal and of Hogarth might be quoted, and here certainly the great aim was moral and not æsthetic. Still, even when the humour is too grim for laughter, a certain glow from the perception of the evil and the wish to trample on it mingles with sympathy for the similar perception and wish in the satirist—indignation itself, where undamped by helplessness or hopelessness, having a certain infusion of pleasure: and this effect seems to gain pungency from the very irony of the employment of artistic forms.

it has permanence;

Again, we attach to a work of art the idea of permanence. An actor or dancer may delight us with *performances* in the highest degree artistic; but afterwards nothing remains to us but the impression, and no work has been created which will endure unchangeably, and whose effects are reproducible at will. It is hard to guard against all possible objections. It may be argued, for example, that an improvisation by a poet or a musician leaves no permanent work. But this failure is only accidental: the work might easily be written down at the time, or remembered and written down afterwards, and would then remain, quite independently of the personality of its creator; while a part like that of Rip van Winkle, as complete a creation of the actor as any creation of any artist, must necessarily cease to exist as an actual presentation with the cessation of the actor's activity.

So far, then, we have got as our definition a 'permanent work designed and executed by a man (or men) with a view to pleasure as at any rate one of his (or their) aims.'

Now things produced with a view to pleasurable emotion are *non-necessary*. It will be remembered that, in speaking of the simplest *it is not part of the machinery of life;* pleasures of sense, we noticed the view that the enjoyable activity of the higher senses had in it something of the nature of play, as compared with that of the lower senses, which had a special connection with life-serving functions. Though we hardly saw how this was in itself so clearly a sufficient ground for the superiority asserted, the fact itself was undisputed: and in the further stage at which we have arrived the non-necessary or *play* element is more striking still. For we are not now, as then, comparing two sorts of admitted pleasures: we are seeking to characterise those productions which do, as contrasted with those which do not, yield conspicuous pleasure in connection with the employment of our higher senses and our mental faculties. And we find by experience that such productions are remote from the necessary and mechanical part of life, and from all that is broadly comprehended under the head of utility; that a good grammar is less delightful than a good novel, and an engineering model than a statue. It may probably be a fact that our power to appreciate the region of higher pleasures depends to a considerable extent on the recognition of a region of work outside them, and on a certain sense of contrast: but the question what the pleasure-giving productions actually are is not thereby affected; and the answer is they are means, not of acting on our environment and adapting it to our needs, but of obtaining new kinds and possibilities of consciousness and ideal activities.

And this direct effect in increasing the range of our inner activity *it has vitality, and is an* gives an impression of *vitality* in the thing which produces it. The irre- *organism.* levance of the work to external and mechanical uses and appliances, the sense that its great function is just to occupy our imagination, that an additional element of emotional life has existed previously in the author and has now become part of ourselves, react on our view of the work itself. It seems like a living organism, not like a mechanical structure: we attribute to it vitality, through its effect in stimulating our own. This character is most closely connected with absence of utility, in the narrower sense. For where utility has been the object, the motive power in the author's mind has been directed to affecting our minds or bodies in some way quite external to his own inner life, as when he has written a book for our instruction, or invented a piece of mechanism for our convenience ; in the using of which things, however much we profit by them, our experience bears no resemblance and gives no clue to his state of feeling during the making of them. In the case of the work of art, the motive power in the author's mind acts by directly affecting and infecting our own ; we do not just benefit by what he knew or did ; we feel what he felt, that is, up to the measure of our appreciation we live what he lived.

§ 4. Definition of an organism,

In treating of the vital character of a work of art, I just now spoke of it as constituting an *organism*. This statement needs some further elucidation : and apart from its interest here, it is of great importance to our subsequent enquiry that the central idea of the word organism, and its various applications in connection with art, should be fully understood. A short examination of its meaning at this stage, besides adding completeness to our conception of a work of art as already defined, will lead up in the most intelligible manner to the next differentiating element in the definition, the element of form.

in Nature,

First, then, let us enquire how we distinguish an organism in nature. To begin with, it is something of which the parts present sufficiently distinct and permanent relations for the sum of them to be thereby recognised as an individual object or product. This provision excludes such a natural object as a mountain, which is not recognised as an individual thing by any essential relation between its parts, but merely by its size : but it would include crystals, the parts of which are arranged in definite manners with regard to the axis or axes, and each example of which is known and named in virtue of this structural symmetry. To proceed then, an organism is something which changes and developes without losing identity ; which we regard as the same individual, in spite of the addition to it of new material. But this, again, would include crystals, which grow by the accretion of new matter, adjusted conformably to their respective characteristics. Something, then, whose principle of being lies *in itself* ; which, by the exercise of functions, can react on external conditions without disintegration or loss of identity ; and further—since functions imply some differentiation of parts—something the relation of whose parts is not one of mere local accretion or symmetry, but of mutual interdependence. One further distinction may be made. The living organism is something which, after a definite season of growth, *ceases to grow* ; the cessation being due not to lack of fresh material, for this may be daily supplied, but to the internal necessities of the system. Growth and completion are governed, so to speak, from inside, inasmuch as nothing can enter permanently into the structure which has not been acted on by the inner digestive and assimilative processes ; the material has to be transformed, before it can be adjusted and locally arranged. It follows, then, that an organism is something which reaches what is recognised as its complete and perfect development. This entails in it an individuality of a special kind, as regarded from outside. The correlation of its parts, however complicated, is contained within a compass which is not only easily grasped, but is familiar to our apprehension as part of the idea of the object : whereas different specimens of the same sort of crystal owe such individuality as they possess to the mere accidents of breakage, and there is no stage in their magnitude which can be said to be more complete and perfect, or more essential to our idea of the object, than another.

Let us now see if we can profitably apply these distinctions to the products of the human mind. Among these we shall find, as among natural products, plenty which we can isolate as distinct objects, but which have no character of individual life. In many products of man's labour and ingenuity, there is such a relationship and adjustment of parts as results in a definite whole, recognised as a unity either in aspect or in purpose ; and these individual products or objects we at once distinguish from any purposeless and incoherent agglomeration of things which cannot be co-ordinated under one idea. But however complicated be the structure of these products, we should hardly think of calling them organisms merely on the ground of that complexity, unless indeed our imagination was so excited by the wonderfulness of the work as to justify a rhetorical exaggeration. We may say of Cicero's prose or of Mr. Tennyson's later blank verse that it is written in a highly organised style, meaning that the sentences are often complicated structures, in which many parts and clauses are duly subordinated and interwoven : but we connote some quality over and above this structural complexity ; we should not use the term of even complicated sentences which expounded the state of the share-market. Or, to take another example, a scientific treatise frequently presents a most complex arrangement and interdependence of parts : how, then, is this less organic than the arrangement of material in a work of the imagination ? The answer is involved in the special *differentia* of the imaginative work, that its life and growth is *from within* ; that it does not appear as an external result, bearing to its author's activities the relation merely of a manufactured article to a machine ; but as an actual picture of the activities themselves, of the author's living ideas and emotions, whose only result is to be reborn as part of others' lives. A scientific or mechanical work may, of course, have been laboured at under the influence of ideas and emotions of a lofty and even of a poetical kind ; but the result is a work of which, however much the excellence may be due to such ideas and emotions, the object and nature are external to them : the author of a mathematical demonstration may be all on fire for Truth, and worship her as a goddess, but the direct aim of his work is to prove his theorem. In the imaginative work the ideas and

*and in human productions.*

emotions are embodied *as such,* to be again and again reawakened as such.

Application of
this to con-
struction.
And the application of this to the question of construction is obvious. The arrangement in a scientific treatise is imposed, as it were, by the subject-matter; it is at the mercy of unalterable and perhaps intractable facts: while the dealings of the artistic worker with his subject-matter, whether in invention, selection, or treatment, are determined by his particular imaginative nature, and the whole fabric of his work is suffused with elements which have made a portion of his inner life. The development of the complete work of science or utility finds a true analogy in the growth of the crystal. All the material that is to appear is in actual existence, in the shape of facts and things already known or in process of being disentangled and becoming known; and the skilled arrangement of it may be compared to the striking and symmetrical form under which the material of the crystal is solidified and agglomerated. In both cases the supplies of the material, whether large or small, are *data,* independent of any individual activity or any modifying vital principle, and adjusted, but not conditioned or penetrated, by the forces at work. An imaginative product may also rest, it is true, and in many cases must rest, on a basis of facts: but these are assimilated in the mind of the author under the distinct influence of emotion, and the vital principle which governs their selection and co-ordination is of a wholly individual kind.

The same comparison holds in respect of the individual and self-conditioned completeness of the imaginative work. Any other sort of production depends, as in structural arrangement, so in growth and arrival at the final completion, on merciless physical and logical necessities. The size and scope of the whole are a result of these necessities, not of vital processes in the author's mind: its material and conditions are given it, and its completeness just means that it comprises and embraces them, as a crystal will comprise all of its material that is there for it. In imaginative production, the rounding into completeness, the conception of the work as a whole, and the pervading influence of this conception in the development of the subject-matter, are as much matters of internal and individual activity as any of the separate ideal or emotional elements. A true organic unity, not conceived as just comprising the parts or conditioned by them, but as the natural form in which their vital qualities find fullest realisation, is that towards which the whole process of development tends: and the artistic faculty must find the secret of such unity in itself. Slightness and fulness of detail are alike compatible with this perfect and independent completeness. The one condition which we attach to the scope of the imaginative work is one which, as it happens, we find to hold in the organisms of Nature, in spite of her very common indifference to our comprehension and pleasure; namely, that it shall not be too vast, nor the relations of its parts too complicated, for the sense and the mind to apprehend.

We may carry the analogy drawn from Nature one step further. Natural organisms seem practically infinite both in number and variety. Scientific reasoning teaches us, indeed, that the variations are intimately connected with environment, but the environment acts only by its suitability or unsuitability to modifications of structure which the accepted doctrine of evolution does not profess to explain, modifications which have and must have to us the appearance of accident. Given a certain deviation from the parent type, natural selection steps in and preserves it; but what account can we give of the primary deviation? We do not even hope ever to reach such a stage of comprehension as will eliminate this appearance of accident: our biological knowledge will always include events the necessary relation of which to their antecedents and conditions, however much we may believe in it, lies quite beyond our faculties of discernment, and which themselves therefore lie quite beyond our powers of prediction. Now with respect to those other natural objects whose structure is a mere matter of symmetrical arrangement, unconnected with function, as crystals, it is true that we equally little know, or expect to know, anything about ultimate necessities; the cause of their taking their respective forms is as much beyond our ken as any point in the history of organisms. But in their case the conditions, whatever they are, seem fixed once and for all, and the possible varieties of form are knowable. It is not only that the crystal which we find in the earth's crust to-day has dwelt there unchanged for long ages, during which organic Nature has been slowly modified: we do not need to consider long ages, or to go beyond our own individual experience, to appreciate the contrast. Thus we may observe the formation of crystals of many substances in actual process, and we can prophesy with certainty beforehand the exact shape they will assume; whereas in the case of a newly formed organism, all that we can prophesy with certainty is that, in the midst of a general resemblance to its parents, it will present differences which we *cannot* prophesy.

§ 5. Further analogy between natural organisms and imaginative works, in the element of the unforeseen.

It needs little straining of metaphor to connect these considerations with the sphere of human productions. Imaginative work is continually taking new and unforeseen directions, and producing new and unforeseen combinations of material. Environment has of course an immense influence on the development of the author's faculties, and often on the nature of his subject-matter; but within a certain region which is conditioned and marked out in this way, the play of originality has the air of being unconditioned and having unfettered scope. The feats of invention and expression seem like glorious accidents of individual imagination; and the modes of affecting us which a new genius reveals are often facts of which

the possibility was undreamed of till the reality was there. Thus his
work presents to us a newness of kind which no previous experiences
could lead us to foresee; it is in the most literal sense a creation. In
works of knowledge and utility, on the other hand, that stamp of individuality and fresh creation, which makes of the imaginative world a
perpetually new surprise, is necessarily absent. Not but that genius may
be at work here also, introducing its essentially indeterminate element;
and surprises of a sort may abound, as each year brings to our store fresh
facts about the universe and fresh means of utilising them. But through
all we have a sense that the facts, however novel to us, were *there*, to be
discovered or not as the case might be. And this applies to the facts
which still remain for us to know; others perhaps do already know them;
many may give a guess at them which some new invention may give the
means of verifying; at any rate they are already in existence: whereas
our future emotional experiences, and those of the perhaps unborn
author whose work will produce them, are simply variations in consciousness which have not yet taken place, and are as little knowable and
predictable as the primary unselected variation in an organic type.
Moreover, in the case of unimaginative work, the objective conditions of
environment do not just mark out limits within which originality may
work, but themselves make up the whole gist and burden of the work to
be done; they are the very things which have to be found out and
explained, or it may be contended against or utilised. And much as
newly found substances are found to crystallise according to the old
recognised geometrical methods, so newly ascertained facts and laws take
their place along with the old in one consistent and impersonal body of
truth. Once there, they are out of the range of surprises, and science
can do no more with them than classify them and generalise from them;
they themselves remain as persistent and unmodifiable as the recognised
crystalline types, and the ultimate generalisations which they yield are
perhaps almost as few.

§ 6. The
definition of a
work of art
narrowed: it
presents form,
either visual or
auditory, to a
*sense.*

In this discussion of the organic quality of imaginative work, we have
been doing no more than bring out what is involved in the idea of
production with a view to delightful emotion; and we have dwelt chiefly
on the vital and essential spirit, not on the outward aspect of related and
combined parts. We must now proceed a step. Our definition, so far as we
have brought it, is of a very wide kind; it will include, for instance, prose
works of fiction and oratory, among which we may undoubtedly find some of
the noblest and most artistic of human productions. If, however, we at
all try to follow the track of ordinary thought and language, we shall
have to narrow these limits, and mark off certain sorts of work as belonging
to the artistic domain in a more special and definite sense. For though
we may speak of the art of novel-writing, this is certainly not popularly

included among ' the arts ; ' no one, if asked which was his ' favourite art,' would consider prose-fiction as on the list to be selected from. And the differentiating characteristic, which marks off works of art in the stricter use of the term, is that they *appeal to a sense*; that they possess elements whose combinations present objects to a sense. This they can only do by dint of *form*, which, as we have seen, implies the special powers of co-ordinating impressions, possessed by us in connection with two only of the bodily senses; so that the form required must be one which makes a direct appeal to the eye or to the ear. The direct appeal is of course very different from a mere calling into activity; for these two senses are, as we have seen, channels for numberless things which make no appeal to them. Thus a person reading a proposition of Euclid uses one of them, that of sight, or having it read to him uses the other, that of hearing, and they are to him the necessary doors through which he obtains his comprehension of the proposition; but the proposition is addressed not to them in the least, but purely to his intelligence.

Generally, then, we may say that works of art, in the stricter use, are both imaginative works and objects of sense ; and as we formerly distinguished them from all other works, sensible or non-sensible, by their vital emotional quality, so now we distinguish them from all other emotional works by their sense-quality. The notion of *form* supplements the notion of *organism* in our definition ; or rather, as *organism* comprised the ideas both of individual vitality and of combination of various parts into a whole, *form* conveniently marks the essential feature of such combination as falls under the cognisance, and affects us through the medium, of a sense.

The necessity for both these elements, the emotional quality and the sense-quality, gives great distinctness to our definition, as it makes it easy to exclude in a moment the productions where one element is present but the other absent. The main conceptions which have occupied us in the preceding paragraphs are very readily applicable. For instance, a monument, if its form presented to the eye a distinct and permanent unity with some sort of pleasing symmetry, might be accounted a work of architectural *art*, though it might be of the rudest and most embryonic kind. But it is possible that a mere heap of stones might present an equally symmetrical form, and might even give an equally striking impression of size and strength. In what then does the superior character of the monument consist ? Its actual structure may hardly amount to more than a conglomeration of undifferentiated material. But it carries an idea ; its purpose lives in it ; it aims at awakening in others a certain strain of feeling similar to that which existed in its authors. The mere heap of stones, if put there for a purpose, is wholly *external* to that purpose, the purpose being to build a house or mend a road, while the heaping

*The above conceptions are very easy of application.*

is a matter of convenience carrying no idea; and this is just the sort of externality which we identified with non-organic and non-artistic things. Similarly, designs for mechanical and utilitarian purposes, or intended to serve as types and symbols, though they may chance to present graceful forms to the eye, will be excluded from the region of art. Photographs, again, are a good instance of productions which cannot as a class be absolutely excluded or absolutely included. One specimen may have been taken wholly mechanically, with no sort of idea or emotion in the worker's mind, and with a result therefore to which, though we might be able to call it a pleasing likeness, we should refuse the description of work of art; while another specimen may have been produced with loving and discriminative care in the arrangement of parts, over and above manipulative skill, and to this we should not be inclined to grudge the higher designation. It would be easy to multiply instances of branches of production where art and no art stand side by side; and also where they merge into one another in the same production, through the operation of the true artistic spirit in work whose more obvious *raison d'être* was utility.

§ 7. Form as perceived by the ear.    The meaning of form is perfectly obvious in the arts whose channel is the eye, as it is palpably involved in their very essence. The eye is always seeing productions the form or forms of which it takes in; and among them, any which satisfies the other conditions of our definition, which is a permanent work designed and executed by a man (or men) with a view to inspiring pleasurable emotion, as at all events one of his (or their) aims, is a work of art. That is to say, as the character of visual form marks off the productions of what are called 'the fine arts' from the whole region of imaginative work, so the character of imaginative work marks off the same productions from the whole region of visual forms. But in the case of the ear, form is not a matter of habitual experience, but (as we have seen) is confined to the region of art, and many find the notion of it here less easy to catch.

in Music,    As regards one, indeed, of the arts addressed to the ear, Music, the arrangement and combinations of sounds is too prominent and essential a feature for the general idea of form and order to present much difficulty.

and in Poetry.    But in the case of the other art, where the sense-element is of the auditory kind, Poetry, the place and scope of the form-element may seem less evident; and it is important at this early stage to notice an ambiguity in the word, or rather in the words order and proportion which are frequently identified with it, and to forestall sundry objections. Among what in the broader sense of art may be called arts of language, including fiction, oratory, &c., we shall, by applying the criterion of the sense-quality, mark off one as belonging to the narrow special category of arts. Poetry possesses in metre, or in something analogous to metre, an element of form or order which appeals with direct gratification to the ear. But it may be objected that metre is comparatively a small thing; that the insistance on the presence of a sense-element is here pedantic, and will exclude much of the loftiest poetical writing; that order may indeed be an element in art, but that it consists in broad proportion and harmony of parts or topics, in the *imaginative* structure which has to do with ideas and images, and so on, and not in a matter so technical as metre. Now waiving for the present the question as to the value of metre, and fully admitting the extreme importance of the characteristics just adduced, I must still maintain that, given poetical subject-matter and sentiment, metre (or some equivalent for it) is the element of order which *makes poetry poetry*; that is, which makes one special art of words an art in the strict use of the term. However essential be harmony and proportion in the *ensemble* of a good composition, (and it is essential to a good sermon, and to a good scientific treatise, and to many things quite outside the arts,) it is in virtue of sensible form, pervading the whole texture and substance, that a composition is a 'work of art' in the ordinary sense. It is of course perfectly legitimate to brand, as unworthy of the name of art, a metrical or a pictorial composition which is mean in subject or incoherent in arrangement; an exclusion of this kind would signify the absence of those vital qualities on which so much stress has been already laid; but this in no way nullifies the advantage and convenience of getting a working definition out of ordinary thought and language, which certainly bring *verse* of all kinds under the technical head of Poetry. Again, it may be objected that without any arrangement, either of words in metre or of parts in a harmonious and organic *ensemble*, the conceptions which we call distinctively poetical, are such, independently of any work of art into which they may eventually be worked up. But they may exist in the artist's mind, or be verbally communicated by him to kindred spirits, without being considered to come under the head of art; it is only through their investiture with form that their position as works of art (or parts of such) is assured.[1] One more objection may be made; the rhythm of fine *prose*, it may be said, gratifies the ear; how then can our distinction be made good? But if we really isolate the effects of the *rhythm*, of the *form*-element, in prose, its appeal to the sense is extremely faint ; apart from sweetness and resonance of voice (that is, of the *colour*-element) and grace of delivery, the amount of gratification to be gained from listening to prose in an unknown tongue can hardly be considered worth reckoning. The proper gratification of rhythm really depends on a feeling of continuous expectation continuously satisfied; and the definiteness necessary for this can

---

[1] The imposition of the form on the idea need not be a subsequent act; in the case of Poetry, which is independent of manual execution, the two will often well up together in the inventor's mind, in a union instantly expressible.

only be sought in metre, or in some such substitute for it as alliteration or the antithetical clauses of Hebrew poetry.

§ 8. Relation of parts to wholes in works of art;

The words just put into the objector's mouth about the broad general order and arrangement of parts in poetical work, introduces a topic of much wider application to the question of artistic organisms than appears in that special case. We shall encounter in the course of our enquiry two quite distinct sorts of combination of parts, two quite distinct relations of parts or elements to wholes.

first use;

If we use *whole* in its widest sense, signifying the entire work under contemplation, the *parts* mean naturally the main elements of which we perceive it to be made up, as the topics or principal divisions of subject-matter in a poetical work, the principal objects in a picture, the principal motives or sections in a musical movement, and so on. We shall find great differences in the importance of the relation of parts to whole in this sense ; taking the word organism to express the mutual adaptations of the parts in subordination to the total result, we shall find that some sorts of work present a closer and others a looser organism, or (if we prefer the phrase) that the structure is in some cases more, in others less, organic.[1]

second use.

In the second use, the parts, as they are in relation to the entire work, are *wholes* in relation to their own constituent elements; their completeness and individual character constituting them organisms on their own account. The constituent elements here are not formed sections or objects of any sort, but just crude unformed fragments, having no force or purport apart from their due combination. Such a whole may be a single stanza in a poem, made up of words ; a single figure in a picture, made up of features, limbs, &c. ; a single melody in a musical movement, made up of what in isolation are insignificant and unemotional sounds. Though *secondary* in a logical sense, in respect of their relation to a larger work, these smaller unities may be *primary* as regards actual importance ; and that they should possess complete and individual beauty is of course desirable in proportion as they are less essentially interdependent, and as their combination in a particular manner is less all-essential to the effect of the work. How entirely they may give the sense of complete and independent beauty is easily seen in the fact that in many cases, especially in the arts of Painting and Music, they are successfully isolated and presented in detachment ; photographs and engravings of a particular figure, special parts of long musical pieces, being frequently enjoyed not as quotations (so to speak) from a larger work wherein their surroundings have been known, but en-

---

[1] In considering *structure*, it should be observed that while the arrangement of various elements into a complex unity is the part of the notion of organism which is naturally most prominent, our right to use the word organism depends on its further connotation, and rests tacitly in every case on the vital and imaginative quality which has been discussed above.

tirely on their own merits. This of course implies that an entire work may consist of one, and not more than one, of these forms or organisms; as, for example, a sonnet, or an ordinary portrait, or a national melody.

In all the arts except Poetry, the large arrangement of the parts and motives into a complete work, as well as the separate parts and motives themselves, falls under the cognisance of the sense addressed; our eyes endeavour to grasp even the largest pictorial composition as a whole : the last bars of a musical movement may have direct organic relation to the first. In Poetry, on the other hand, it is the smaller combinations only that are perceived, in virtue of their *sense*-element, as distinct organic unities. For metre is not a thing which can embrace a whole long work in a *single* complex structure; metrically, such a work is necessarily divided up into small similar parts, either stanzas of some sort or merely lines of definite formation. So that while the work, as a whole, is an *imaginative* structure, an arrangement and development of certain subject-matter, of certain things to be presented—as for instance, in the organism of an epic, or the organism of a five-act drama—the scope of the small constituent parts, on the other hand, is naturally determined by *metrical* structure; and the poet's skill is shown in so arranging his matter under the metrical form that this shall seem its noblest and most appropriate investiture.

*Exceptional case of Poetry, where only the smaller combinations can present wholes or unities to the sense addressed.*

I have several times had occasion to use two words which represent necessary, though not distinguishing, elements of works of art, and which cannot but continually occur in the discussion of such works. One of them is *material*. There will be much to say of this hereafter; meanwhile the primary meaning of the word is sufficiently clear, as denoting the simple elements, whether material substances or physical units, which the artist employs and from which he builds up his work. The other word is *subject-matter*. The very fact of the unity of a work of art might be taken to imply some underlying bond, some title which would sum up and express its purport, and give the answer to such natural questions as ' What is it all about ? ' or ' To what does it tend ? ' We might seek this unifying principle in some central conception or purpose, to the carrying out of which the several parts were made to contribute, and which we should call the subject *par excellence*; but as a matter of fact we often find that there is no such very comprehensible central conception to be found, even in the arts where it is most natural to look for it; that the bond is of a much looser kind, and that the scope depends greatly on the amount which it is agreeable and easy for the *sense* to grasp at a time and to retain. In pictures, for instance, the only conceivable title would often be the collective name, or even a mere enumeration of the objects represented, as ' A group of three young women,' or ' A boy and girl in a boat.' That it is sensory rather than ideal considerations which in such cases impose the limits of a satisfactory unity, whether as to size or com-

*§ 9. Material,*

*and subject-matter.*

plexity, seems clear if we consider what happens when we get beyond the limits which the sense can easily grasp. Thus, we may contemplate a picture which covers a whole wall, which the eye has to take in and return on bit by bit, and which we have even to walk about to realise; yet we find nothing to complain of if only there be a central subject, if only the whole scene have a meaning for us: while a group of three hundred or even of thirty young women, sitting looking at each other or holding musical instruments, would be criticised as meaningless and absurd, though it would be hard to prove why in themselves they had not as much *raison d'être* as the former three. In landscape-painting, again, the unity is often pictorial; it is addressed to the eye and recognised as satisfactory or fine composition, but does not represent any central or combining conception discoverable in the actual things depicted. This is not the place to consider whether a fine imaginative subject be less necessary to the highest pictorial art than fine composition: I am only pointing out that even in painting, beautiful and imaginative work may exist without it: and in certain other branches of art we shall find that the very notion of such an all-comprising subject is inadmissible. Every art, however, necessarily deals with a certain class of things, one or more of which will be embraced in each work; and these parts or units must be in themselves sufficiently comprehensible and interesting to arrest the attention. It is difficult to find a single name for them which will apply equally well to all the arts: but *subject-matter* fairly answers the purpose.

§ 10. Tabular view of the arts, in respect of three main elements.

It will now be advantageous to arrange in a tabular shape the five main branches of art of which the works seem to be fairly embraced by our definition, under the three heads of subject-matter, material, and form, mentioning in what each element consists. In most cases the forms presented to the sense naturally either convey or constitute the subject-matter of the work; the case of Poetry being, as we have already seen, the marked exception. Many terms and remarks which are conveniently included in the table will be explained and justified afterwards.

---

*(Note to p. 55.)*

[1] I have said that the subject-matter of Poetry exists externally to and independently of *works of art*; this must not be construed into meaning that it could in all cases exist externally to *some imaginative faculty*. Such a limitation would be very inconvenient. We cannot but regard as fit 'subject-matter for Poetry' those many inward experiences which admit in Poetry of direct expression with a but slightly represented framework of external circumstances and objects, and which could of course have no existence independently of minds of emo-tional susceptibility. There is, moreover, that whole class of luminous conceptions, which, having already acted on subject-matter drawn from the universe, may then be worked up under artistic forms; thus being made themselves, in a secondary sense, subject-matter for works of art. So we may often distinguish two grades of subject-matter: first, the crude subject-matter of facts and things—for instance, the phenomena of sleep and death; secondly, this crude subject-matter as penetrated and selected and correlated by the imaginative faculty,

**ARTS OF REPRESENTATION.**

**POETRY** . . .

*Subject-matter.*—Objective and subjective phenomena of many kinds; arranged in groups, usually in subordination to some central conception or subject. This subject-matter exists externally to and independently of works of art.[1]

*Material.*—Words; differing in various countries, and changing slightly in every generation.

*Form.*—Metre, or something analogous to it; in any case abstract relations of sound.

**SCULPTURE** . .

*Subject-matter.*—Visible objects belonging to the organic world; but especially the one class of human forms; represented singly, or in groups usually with a central subject. (Sculpture of animal and vegetable forms becomes prominent chiefly in connection with architecture, and in such branches of art as ivory- and metal-work.) This subject-matter exists externally to and independently of works of art.

*Material.*—Marble, bronze, &c.; constant.

*Form.*—Implied in the subject-matter.

**PAINTING** . .

*Subject-matter.*—Visible phenomena of many kinds; represented singly or in groups with or without a central conception. This subject-matter exists externally to and independently of works of art.

*Material.*—Surfaces and pigments: theoretically constant, though liable to change from invention and losses.

*Form.*—Implied in the subject-matter.[3]

**ARTS OF PRESENTATION.**

**ARCHITECTURE**

*Subject-matter.*—Visible forms and arrangements of form of many kinds.[4] The central conception or purpose is usually in great measure utilitarian; and in many (not all) of the subordinate combinations utilitarian purposes, existing independently of art, underlie the art-forms which have no such independent existence.

*Material.*—Marble, stone, wood, &c., of various colour; each country is in this respect greatly dependent on its own products.

*Form.*—Abstract lines and surfaces and their proportional arrangements.

**MUSIC** . . . .

*Subject-matter.*—Auditory forms, i.e. series and combinations of sounds, wholly independent both of external phenomena and external utility, and having no existence independent of art. *Subjects* are the leading and recurrent phrases in a composition.[5]

*Material.*—Some system of notes; for us the notes of the chromatic scale, susceptible of various colour or quality according to the instrument by which they are produced. This material had a slow development, but has long been constant, and can hardly but remain so, except in so far as the invention of new instruments may add to its colours.

*Form.*—Abstract proportions of time and pitch.

**ARTS OF COLOUR.**[2]

---

[1] See pp. 54, 56, *for note to these words.*

[2]-[5] See p. 56 *for notes to these words.*

and brought together under some distinct idea, as when Sleep and Death are conceived of as twins ; finally, when such an idea is expressed under the forms of art it becomes a work of art or a part of one. But the mere existence of an idea, as we saw above, does not entail a work of art or even a fragment of one : it is only through artistic form that it obtains the stamp and seal of permanence. So that though we may, or at all events often do, say of a person to whom the world presents itself as a source of imaginative activity, in other words, who is rich in poetical conceptions, that he is a *poet*, this use of the word must not blind us to the fact that he may have never produced, and very possibly may be unable ever to produce, a single satisfactory poem.

These distinct poetical conceptions may of course occur to painters and sculptors as well as to writers of poetry ; but as they do not express them directly in words, but indirectly through visible forms, which are selections and copies (however idealised) from external realities, the description of their subject-matter as existing externally to their works can hardly be misconstrued.

[2] It would perhaps be more correct to say *arts of colour par excellence*. For the colour-quality is to some extent present in the vowel-sounds of Poetry, where, from the fact that the metrical element makes the ear attentive to the sounds over and above the sense, it is far more prominent than it would be in the self-same words unmetrically arranged ; and in its treatment here, though scope for skill is much limited by the actually existing words from which choice has to be made, yet general care is necessary, and special effects are possible. Works of Sculpture, again, in the days of the art's greatest glory, were frequently coloured, in fashions somewhat baffling to those whose ideas are derived from isolated specimens in modern galleries. This, however, would hardly constitute Sculpture an independent art of colour : such works, however conspicuous and important, were *decorative*, in the sense of belonging essentially and inseparably to a particular building ; and the effect of the colour more especially must have been entirely dependent on association with the surrounding coloured architecture.

[3] The forms of Painting commonly represent things as they *appear*, by perspective effects and the adjustment of size to distance. The forms of Sculpture represent things as

they *are*, in three dimensions, and can thus be looked at from many points of view, so that the greater simplicity of the work is compatible with a multiplicity of effects by a change of the spectator's position. The same feature is prominent in Architecture, and adds indefinitely to the effect of what, as unchangeable abstract form, might be monotonous.

Painting and Sculpture can of course suggest things and thoughts by something very far short of accurate delineation of form. There are, in fact, all degrees between such accurate delineation and either abstract ornament, or purely conventional symbolism acting as visible words to enforce a fact or an idea.

[4] For the sake of convenience, the sculpture and sculptured or painted details in which the chief glory of buildings may fairly be maintained to lie, will not be reckoned under the head of architectural forms.

[5] As regards Music, there is one misapprehension which is at once so common and so fatal, that though it involves a question which will be discussed in full later, a few words of caution at this stage cannot be altogether omitted. In cases where Music is joined to something else there is a natural habit of calling the subject of the something else the subject of the compound work. Thus the *Messiah* is called the *subject* of Handel's oratorio, and the included topics may be called the *subject-matter* of the special songs and choruses. This is intelligible and convenient : only it is important to remark that the sentiments and topics connected with the name are strictly and essentially the subject of the *words*, and only loosely and accidentally the subject of the *music*. For however valuable the union may be, and however inseparable its factors may now appear to us, we must remember that if any one ignorant of English heard the *Messiah* all he would infer would be that the words must be of a generally lofty character, with occasional bits of a more definite character, here pathetic, there jubilant. But the music might of course have been united perfectly well with other words of similar sentiment and rhythm. So the verbal titles which aim at summing up the expression of certain compositions (*e.g.* in Mendelssohn's *Isles of Fingal* overture, and many of Schumann's pianoforte pieces), however interesting, are so adventitious that they have often been suggested by instead of suggesting the music ; and a hundred auditors, if left to guess the title for themselves, would originate a hundred new ones.

There may seem to be a certain pedantry about tabulation of this kind; as to this I can only here say that I hope to convince any reader who will accompany me through the following pages of its usefulness for my purposes. But among other more specific objections which might be found, there is one against which, at the risk of forestalling subsequent topics, it may be well briefly to guard; as it is connected with a very common and mistaken method of approaching the main subject of this book, and exemplifies the necessity for just such distinctions as the table aims at supplying. It may be said, then, that *all* modes of using colour for the sake of beauty should be included under Painting; and that *all* fashioning of solid material into pleasing forms, whether imitative or not, should be included under Sculpture; and this may be even said with true advantage, if it is desired to impress on people's minds that, *e.g.*, so called decorative art is, or should be, art of a high kind, not mere manufacture; and that it implies faculties and instincts which cannot be dissociated from those employed in the production and appreciation of the two great arts of visual representation. Nevertheless even in respect of the visual arts, the ordinary popular view, which wholly differentiates Painting and Sculpture as *representative* arts, is in strict accordance both with the most valuable factor in the impressiveness of beautiful specimens of these arts, and with the formation and general nature of the faculties by which the appreciation of them takes place. Mr. Ruskin has said that ' Sculpture is essentially the production of pleasant bossiness or roundness of surface;' that is, of abstract and *un*representative form. Now rounded surface is clearly a necessary element in Sculpture: but to emphasise an abstract general quality to this extent seems only to confuse the subject. Mr. Ruskin's own example will suffice to show this. He refers to two engravings of Greek coins, representing human profiles, but regarded as abstract conglomerations of rounded masses made pleasant by gradation of light; which masses, he says, must be ' disposed with due discretion and order.' But in that little word *due* lies the whole gist of the matter. The question is how much would the discretion and order amount to on their own account, if presented, for instance, to a person of cultivated sensibilities, who had never seen a face? What *is* the order, apart from the combination into a face? Mr. Ruskin refers to the bossy masses of a distant forest as similarly delightful in surface, and to the spiral projections of a fir-cone as similarly delightful in order: but these references suggest the exact point of difficulty. A pleasantness of gradated surface in all three cases may be readily granted; but the forest-bosses have *no* order; the cone-bosses have a most *definite* geometrical order; what authority have we for saying that the profile-bosses, regarded as abstract unrecognised phenomena, have an extremely complex order, the same in kind but superior in degree to that of the cone-bosses, rather than that they have mere relative sizes and proximities

§ 11. Justification of the table by an example of a possible confusion;

of an accidental and unordered kind, like those of the forest-bosses ? and chance arrangements of bosses could hardly, as such, be matter for art. No one could have authority to pronounce positively on the abstract order of the profile-bosses, except a person to whom a profile was an absolutely un-familiar object ; for familiarity makes its own order. The fact is (as will be fully argued later on) that both the mode and the history of our ap-preciation of faces are in the main totally distinct from the mode and the history of our appreciation of bosses ; and if such terms as 'due discre-tion and order' above are not precisely and jealously scrutinised, there is danger (not to Mr. Ruskin, but to his readers) of confounding the scope which the two elements respectively afford to the exercise of genius, and the place they respectively hold in the value of Sculpture.

It is clear that for us, living not in a world of patterns or of mere gra-dations of light and shade, but among definitely known visible objects, the limits within which forms, and parts of forms, of objects can be regarded, appreciated, and criticised in true abstraction from what they belong to, must be very narrow : and to regard an art which deals with forms of known and recognised objects, as comprising a science of ' abstract relations and inherent pleasantnesses' of form, is to give a separate existence to what, as art, never can be separately or exactly appraised. Rounded surface in any object may be intrinsically pleasant ; a mere ball with its gradated shading may be as beautiful an object as Mr. Ruskin describes it to be ; but the popular view would be right in not regarding a ball or an arrangement of balls as Sculpture. And when we come to less definite figures and groupings the attempt at a separate abstract estimate is still more foggy. A painter may show consummate mastery in the arrangement of his points of light and masses of light and shade ; but blur all the forms till they are unrecognisable, and eliminate all the colours, and the ' inherent pleasantness' of the arrangement of points and masses will not do much to console us for the change.

*which is apt to act damagingly on the idea of Music.*    All this distinction, however, as regards visible forms, may seem very irrelevant to our main subject of sound : but in truth it is not so. For Art as a whole has been almost always treated of by writers whose speciality was *visual* art ; and whenever these persons, in the treatment of their subject, come across abstract relations and proportions and fitnesses, they invariably introduce the word *musical*, and other words connected with Music. Most rightly and legitimately, as long as the limits of the application are kept in view : otherwise, the application reacts very damagingly on Music itself, or rather precludes a true view of it. For instance, Mr. Ruskin, the author who of all authors that ever lived has been the most effective teacher of men's eyes, speaks of Music as some-thing essentially analogous to the harmonious adjustment of bosses ;[1] and

---

[1] Music is quite as often treated, among others by Mr. Ruskin, as analogous to the harmonious arrangement of *tints* ; and the very fact that writers on visible art are so

as he certainly regards the highest examples of form—beautiful faces, for instance—as much more than pleasantly bossed surfaces, the sound-art naturally falls, in his estimation, to a very subordinate position, as a sensuous delight, with a good deal of 'inherent pleasantness,' but only capable of being ennobled by conjunction with words. Apart from words, he holds, Music becomes degraded, and its 'senseless melodies harden the intellect or demoralise the ear.'

Now this seems a very natural view, where a person has never received from Music, pure and simple, more than a faint fraction of the emotion it is capable of causing; and where the pleasure it has given him is a mere drop in the ocean compared to the pleasure he has received through vision. As Music is undoubtedly an art of abstract relations, he will naturally refer the other abstract relations he knows to it, and it to them; and will think the art sufficiently honoured by being put in the same category as that general harmoniousness of abstract visible elements, that 'musical disposition' of masses and colours, which his eyes in certain cases find so pleasurable. The great arts of Painting and Sculpture, he will say, deal in such harmonious arrangements; and unless he clearly keeps in view how entirely the distinctive qualities of Painting and Sculpture lie in their *representative* character, it will naturally escape his notice how entirely his *rapprochement* leaves the distinctive qualities of Music out of account. The cardinal points thus ignored cannot be too early emphasised; namely, that Music, though dealing wholly with abstract proportions, is an art preeminent for the precision, individuality, and organic quality of its forms; that the component elements out of which the forms are built are not only not beautiful units, like curves or bosses, but in isolation are absolutely uninteresting, and, moreover, in mental reproduction may lose nearly all, if not all, of their *timbre* or sensuous colour-character; while the forms themselves present a vividness, a variety, and a depth of emotional impressiveness, unsurpassed in any region of beauty.

Returning now from this digression, if we examine our table, we may find several ways of subdividing it. Two of the arts, Poetry and Music, address us through the sense of hearing, the other three through the sense of sight: and this distinction naturally lies at the root of many points in connection with the main subject of our enquiry. Two again, Poetry and Architecture, impose the art-element of form on things conceivable as having a real meaning and existence apart from this element, Poetry often dignifying with it things expressible in prose, and Architecture things

§ 12. Various ways of subdividing the list of arts:

little careful whether it is relations of *colour* or of *form*, which they thus exemplify, might put any one on his guard who realised that these elements are as wholly distinct in the realm of sound as in that of sight. This distinction and the relations of sound-colour to light-colour will occupy us later: it is enough here to observe how specially wide of the mark is the comparison to arrangements of colour, of what is pre-eminently an art of form.

whose purpose is of definite prosaic utility, as of shelter; while in the other three the element of form is essentially involved in the subject-matter. Again, Poetry stands distinctly apart from all the other arts in its invariable use of symbols: *words*, that is, symbols to be interpreted by the mind, are its proper material. It is on this ground that Mr. Spencer has marked off poetry as the sole *re*-presentative art, in contradistinction to the others whose effect is so essentially bound up with the direct presentation of phenomena to the senses. We have already seen, however, that the sense-element, though external to the ideas conveyed, is necessary to a poetical *work of art*; and further on it will appear as a most integral factor of the whole results attainable by Poetry. So that though a true distinction is marked by Mr. Spencer's application of the words *presentative* and *representative*, I have used them as the only possible ones to express quite another, and as it seems to me a more essential, distinction. According to my view, Architecture (so far as it is independent of other arts) and Music are marked off by a most important difference from Poetry, Sculpture, and Painting. These three latter *represent* in various aspects things cognisable in the world outside them, and recognised on representation. This is obvious in the case of the two latter; and in Poetry, however new an idea may be, it deals with people or things that we have a knowledge of, and seems to us true by dint of its accordance with or interpretation of this previous knowledge. For idealisation is not an excursion in the clouds; ideal representation is of an imagined reality, and is founded everywhere on facts, by the selection and rearrangement of which the artist brings out fresh aspects and relations. Music, on the other hand, and Architecture (in the artistic elements which differentiate it from mere building by having pleasure, not utility, for their aim), imply no external fact at all. Their function is to *present*, not to represent, and their message has no direct reference to the world outside them. Their abstract forms and arrangements of forms appeal, in the one case to the ear, in the other to the eye, not as objects of recognition or as concerned with facts known elsewhere, but as something wholly unimaginable apart from the special manifestation. This last distinction is so important as to require a somewhat full discussion; the following chapters will therefore be occupied with the more general features of abstract form and proportion [1] in art, with the differences in

*the arts of presentation and of representation.*

---

[1] It may be well to point out a certain ambiguity in the word *proportion* which tends to conceal the essential difference between the two arts of abstract form and the arts of representation. Mr. Ruskin has poured scorn on those who would call Architecture an art of proportion, and in his demand for noble and significant ornamentation he has asserted an incontrovertible principle. But surely he momentarily mixes up two different notions of proportion in the following passage: 'Painting, Sculpture, Music, and Poetry depend all equally on the proportion, whether of colours, stones, notes, or words. Proportion is a principle, not of Architecture, but of existence. It is by the laws of proportion that stars shine, that mountains stand, and rivers flow. Man can

respect of this element between the two arts which are essentially concerned with it, and with the statement of the main problems which these very differences will help us to define.

hardly perform any act of his life, can hardly utter two words of innocent speech, or move his hand in accordance with those words, without involving some reference, whether taught or instinctive, to the laws of proportion,' and so on. Now this is all very true if proportion be taken merely in the sense of general fitness, of general adaptation and concurrence of means to an end, or of factors to a result. This sense, however, exceeds in wideness and vagueness even the wider of the two aspects of artistic structure noticed above, namely, the harmonious arrangement of integral parts in the production of a large complex whole. But we find proportions of a very definite and peculiar nature, pertaining to certain orders of impression in space and time which appeal with a seemingly direct and intuitive satisfaction to the eye and ear respectively ; and which, since they are representative of nothing in the external world, we call *abstract forms.* In so far, indeed, as Architecture depends wholly on such forms and proportions, to the neglect of noble representative ornament, it may be as inferior as Mr. Ruskin sometimes represents it to be : but the abstract element will always be prominently present, contributing its due effect ; and Mr. Ruskin himself has probably felt the effect more keenly, as he has certainly described it better, than any one else.

# CHAPTER IV.

## ABSTRACT FORM AS ADDRESSED TO THE EYE.

§ 1. The grouping or order peculiar to visual and auditory perceptions is either of co-existence or of sequence.

WE found in the first chapter that, out of all the senses, those of sight and hearing are the only ones which convey a sense of *beauty* ; and we connected this distinction more especially with their perception of *form.* To explain this latter peculiarity we dwelt, in the first instance, on the immense complexity of the two sense-organs concerned ; a complexity which, in the ear, takes the form of an immense variety of actual structural elements, differentiated as truly as the wires of a pianoforte ; and which in the eye consists partly in differentiation of elements whereby differences of colour are perceived, partly in an indefinitely large range of muscular movements. And arguing that this complexity means, on the subjective side, sensitiveness to an immense number of differences in the impressions received, we immediately connected such highly discriminative sensitiveness with the power, possessed in the case of sight and hearing only, to perceive an *order* in variety, and to combine separate impressions, separate units of colour or sound, into coherent groups or forms. We further found that such groups are presented to the sense of *hearing* only in the domain of art.

Order may clearly be either of *co-existence* or of *sequence.* In the case of sight, by dint of the eye's immense power of motion and adjustment, we can in an instant grasp and realise an enormous number of impressions of phenomena in space ; and we can also perceive such phenomena in succession, *i.e.* perceive motion : in the case of hearing, we possess a very limited power of grasping simultaneous impressions, but great retentiveness and power of perceiving the relations between successive impressions. Both senses obviously have in common a susceptibility to one kind of order in successive impressions, the effect of which, indeed, seems common to the whole nervous organism, namely, *rhythm* ; the case where this is most obvious to the eye being dancing. Dancing, however, does not rank among our fine arts ; and in the three of them for which the eye is the medium the impressions are all of phenomena in co-existence. As regards the two arts addressed to the ear, in Poetry the order of the sounds is entirely one of sequence. In Music, on the other hand, simultaneous sounds play a most important part : for though, as just remarked, the number of simultaneous impressions which the ear can appreciate is limited, the power to grasp this limited number opens up a quite unique range of phenomena, commonly spoken of under the head of *harmony.*

Now we have not yet at all considered the question *why*, in the case of each sense, certain forms afford such strong gratification ; *why* the arrangement of impressions in particular shapes or orders reveals a world the pleasures of which seem quite disparate with the pleasure of any sort of sense-impression taken in isolation. We cannot here connect the enjoyment with any directly sensuous basis ; the slight pleasure which may in some cases be referable to specially easy movements of the ocular muscles making (as we shall see later) an exception of small importance. We lose the appeal to simple nervous stimulation, such as is always our ultimate fact in explaining enjoyment of colour : what do we get in its stead ? It is easy to invoke, as in itself an ultimate source of pleasure, the sense of relation in the perception of the arrangement. For certainly the co-ordination and combination of units into what are recognised as wholes or groups involves a mental element over and above the instantaneous consciousness of the sense-impression : and as apprehension of order of some sort or other may be said, in a broad and general way, to be a characteristic of *all* satisfactory mental activity, *à fortiori*, it might be argued, should we look for it in the higher æsthetic pleasures. But this leaves us still in difficulties : for while the combination of *sound*-elements into coherent groups may seem to afford the mental element tolerable scope in the way of comparison and memory, the mental element involved in combining units of *sight*-impression into recognisable or recognised forms is, on the other hand, so slight that it is well within the scope of the most ordinary animal intelligence ; for very stupid animals know objects and perceive changes in them, while still we should not credit them with a sense of beauty. And moreover we, who can perceive forms as beautiful, can also perceive them as ugly. Although, then, we cannot but still look to some sort of infusion of advanced mental elements, having simply nothing else to look to for an explanation of the pleasurable qualities of form, it is at once clear, in respect of the visual region at all events, that such elements must comprise more than is involved in the mere perception and recognition of a form *as* a form.

§ 2. In what way or ways is the advanced mental element present ?

A fresh consideration will now be necessary. Forms, being combinations of an immense number of elements, are, unlike colours, as endless as they are distinct in variety. The number of possible combinations being practically infinite, there is no assignable limit to the number of forms which, if presented to us, we could distinguish ; and distinguish not in the vague and approximate way in which we may distinguish shades and gradations of light, colour, and tone-quality (these being in many cases quite *un*distinguishable except at the moment when they are actually perceived in juxtaposition), but with entire and absolute accuracy, and with a very

§ 3. Distinguishable forms are endless in variety.

great power of accurate representation in memory. And the importance of this power of distinction, which in itself has no direct bearing on pleasure, is at once seen if we consider that it is the necessary basis for variety of *association and suggestion* ; in other words, is the necessary condition for phenomena to derive any lasting character from circum-

and thus afford the basis for wide variety of *association.*

stances of whatever sort, or feelings from whatever source, which may accompany the perception of them. Wide range of association postulates that wide power of distinction and comparison which only exists in relation to form. For the present we may be content with the most familiar example ; namely, the immense variety of agreeable and disagreeable impressions which we receive from human faces, by association of certain qualities, events, and modes of behaviour with numerous slight, but perfectly distinct, variations of form ; so that even an infant will learn to invest its mother's smile with the agreeableness of things which have frequently accompanied it, such as food, soft touches, and cooing sounds, and to attach a contrary character to a frown or an angry tone. Here, then, in the principle of association (especially when extended to that of *inherited* association) we get mighty aid towards solving the problem of the pre-eminence of form. For in it is involved, not only the selection from the shifting chaos of impressions and feelings of groups which, in the very fact of their combination, become fixed as distinct and characteristic qualities of things ; but the condition for those extraordinary *transformations* which are as real in the chemistry of mental as of material ingredients. In the processes of association, feelings may often be wrought into products whose simple elements are as unrecognisable as those of water or of protoplasm ; and the sense of beauty is none the less unique and instinctive for having been built out of a variety of less ideal experiences.

§ 4. But how can association be present in the case of *abstract* forms ?

But again a difficulty presents itself. The example of faces just cited is of *familiar* objects, perpetually seen in connection with pleasing and displeasing circumstances : and with objects like these we have, it may be reasonably urged, daily and hourly opportunities of forming associations of the most definite kind. But we are capable of deriving pleasure from many visual forms whose power to affect us cannot be at all referred to such daily and definite associations ; for instance, from a graceful spiral : and as for sound, its combinations into forms are not material objects at all, but things of wholly isolated experience, lying apparently quite outside any definable circumstances of general life, and unable therefore to gather character from their concomitants. Must we not, then, infer some other and *special sort* of intuition to account for our pleasure in such cases

Must not the pleasure in these have its own independent conditions ?

as these ? Must there not be in abstract forms themselves, apart from any assignable associations, some special possibilities of exercising our faculties and appealing to our imaginations ? These questions will have to be subsequently considered : meanwhile it may be here premised that the scope of association will prove to be far wider than might at first sight be guessed; that we shall find its influence extending more or less indirectly over these remoter regions; and that it will be part of our subsequent task to examine, chiefly of course with regard to sound, in what ways the pleasure of abstract forms can be connected with a special sort of mental activity, and what parts of the whole ground are covered by this more special element and by the element of association respectively.

We shall, however, best approach the subject of abstract forms pure and simple, (that is, forms or combinations of elements designed and artificially produced by men, and presented on their own merits, without direct external reference), by rounding off our enquiry as to the main elements of effect, and especially as to the place of the abstract element, in forms which are *not* abstract; and we could not take a better example than our former one of human faces. For in these, as in all visible forms, there must be (potentially at all events) an abstract element: we always possess to some extent the power of representing to ourselves the lines in abstraction, of considering them simply as lines, without reference to the particular object into whose form they enter. In the immense majority of cases where we perceive objects with pleasure, it is of course the objects themselves, with the various qualities which past experiences have woven into our idea of them, which occupy our attention: the actual lines are often little more than symbols to us, the means by which the presence of the object is made known to us. But in the very notion of visible beauty is implied some more special and direct effect of form on us than this: and experience certainly seems to testify that forms may please us without any very perceptible suggestion of agreeable qualities in the object. Thus agreeableness of expression is by no means synonymous with facial beauty; and while, on the one hand, an ugly face may be agreeable to look at, owing to association with agreeable qualities, it is none the less true that an expressionless face is often described as beautiful.

§ 5. The abstract element in forms of objects,

Merely to recognise the frequent existence of an abstract element in our appreciation of the forms of concrete objects is, however, a very different thing from ascertaining either how far it is effective or how far it is indispensable. The attempt to isolate the effects by a simply mechanical isolation of this or that portion of form yields most disappointing results. The form of a beautiful cheek or chin, for example, may be thus isolated, and represented by a line on paper, or more completely by a piece of modelling; but though these representations when examined might reveal smoothness and delicate gradation of curvature, this could hardly give us any vivid sense of beauty, since we should perceive no special rightness or individuality about it; slight changes of the form, which would quite destroy its possibilities of serving as a cheek or chin, would be perceived with indifference; which means that on its purely abstract merits it would have

as of human beings.

little chance of being picked out for special commendation. So of the beautiful curves of the human figure at its best; which, if represented in an isolated way, would not be picked out from thousands of other abstract lines which the anatomy of the human body excludes. Nor will the idea of *symmetry*, though often adduced as an explanation of our pleasure in human beauty, contribute much to a solution of the difficulty. For symmetry really means only the similarity of two or more parts; and an ugly face or an awkward figure may of course have its two sides just alike, and so be equally symmetrical with a beautiful one. Perhaps the easiest and most striking way of realising how little abstract form and symmetry, taken alone, can explain our feeling of beauty in faces, is to consider a beautiful face upside down; to avoid any element of grotesqueness it will be best to lay a picture of such a face naturally on the table, and then go round and look at it from the opposite side. It will be found that though we may perhaps perceive the features to be well formed and regular, and *argue* that the face must be beautiful, scarcely any *direct* and pleasurable sense of beauty results. And this cannot be explained on the ground that the merits of the abstract forms in themselves might somehow be greatly affected by the change, as if we played a tune backwards; since we can scarcely doubt that if faces had always been naturally presented to us in that position, with the chin forming an elegant apex, our sense of facial beauty and ugliness would have formed itself quite regularly and completely on the given conditions, and the reversal of *that* position would then have given the unbeautiful result; that is to say, the *abstract* lines flow as well one way as the other.[1] Or, if any one objects to this statement, it will be amply sufficient to bring the eyes half-way down the cheeks; which cannot possibly be supposed to ruin the pattern as a pattern.

Influence of indirect association ;    The fact is that association of an indirect kind is really latent here under a great part of what we easily take for pleasure in abstract form. If pure boldly chiselled outlines, and finely gradated shades and curves, are admired in a face in a way they never would be on their independent merits, in a way they never would be, for example, if faces were quite new phenomena in the world, it is mainly because the faces which possess them appear to differ from the average in the direction of strength or

---

[1] The advantage of this experiment lies in its not being liable to an objection which might be brought against the isolation of a *single* part of a complicated contour. A person might conceivably maintain that the beauty of a face is mainly of the abstract sort, but that the virtue of the abstract lines and surfaces lies in the sum-total of their arrangement and combination : and such a view might seem hard to dispose of. For it is impossible actually to look at a complete face in the normal position and, wholly eliminating all notion of its being a face, and all associations connected with faces, to regard it as simply a pattern or congeries of lines : and as long as the two factors of face and pattern are inextricably interwoven, if any one asserted that his pleasure was due to some superlative quality of the pattern, his position would be as hard to disprove as to prove. But dissociate the factors by giving him his pattern upside down, and he will probably not even do it the honour of recognising it.

fineness of *type*: and the very notion of such characters of type is due to long trains of experience into which associated human qualities entered. Delicate modelling on a lump of clay representing no known object would mean almost nothing to us; the delicate modelling on human features, combined with a certain proportioning of them in matters of size and distance, mean to us the realisation of certain ideals which could never have been formed on abstract grounds alone.

This reference to types is exemplified in another way, which really brings in a third element distinct both from abstract form and association, the element of *habit*; the effect of which, however, is rather regulative than positive. The most approved outline, the most refined modelling, will not make up for even a slight overstepping of the limits of that norm which habit has set up; for all our judgments involve a latent sense of this normal type. Thus disproportion will mar the fairest features: the most beautiful adult nose on the face of a little child would offend us to such an extent that we should probably call the face ugly.[1]

*of habit;*

[1] Such an instance as this, it will be seen, implies the fact that ideal types may be of features and parts of faces as well as of whole faces; and if this be so, the importance of the controlling condition of a familiar standard in matters of size and arrangement is obvious. Perhaps, however, the notion of idealising *parts* at all may, at first sight, seem to ignore the harmony which is admittedly a large element in beauty. It is, of course, beyond dispute that there is such a thing as a special harmony pervading a whole face, that a special combination of lines and modellings may be accepted as a type *en masse*; as is sufficiently shown, for example, in the great distinctness of the types for which various painters have shown marked preference : yet in a large number of instances, it is easy to imagine such a harmony as more essential and more positive in character than it can be truly proved to be. Considering how many faces are called beautiful, to which we cannot in reason assign a type apiece, and yet which are too different and individual to be easily classified under a few distinct types, it seems that the process of selection and idealisation which gradually gives a stamp to our sense of beauty, must act in relation to parts as well as to wholes, and lend itself to a considerable amount of eclecticism. A certain degree of mutual suitability must of course be postulated : but the beautiful eyes of one face could hardly *contradict* the beautiful mouth of another ; and the same form of both features can certainly co-exist with many various modifications of the less mobile parts of the contour, without destruction of beauty ; the features when animated with one life, as by the painter's art, will, in a way, make their own harmony. And if we so far take our stand on parts as to look beyond the limited number of what could be truly called types of complete faces, we must admit, as clearly indispensable, the adherence to a normal and familiar standard in matter of the relative sizes and distances of the parts, under pain of getting an ugly result from even choice individual elements. It is easy to distinguish what belongs to the norm from the actual elements of beauty. Such factors as relative size and distance of parts are clearly too negative, too much the same in an immense number of cases, to be themselves the material from which ideal types are built : thus, they may be found practically identical in ninety-nine average faces and one beautiful one ; a clear proof that it is not they, but the actual individual lines and modellings, which make up the positive differentiating element. Given then the requisite subtleties of form in these lines and modellings themselves, and an absence of such gross contradictions as a tip-tilted feminine nose with a massive masculine chin, the essential and sufficient conditions of integration into, at any rate, some sort of beauty seem to be the observance of normal relations of size and distance, and the single life which shall control the movements and expression.

In many cases the result of wide departure from normal types gives the effect more of grotesqueness than of ugliness; indeed we may say that the slighter departure is the more general condition of ugliness, as in the case of monkeys, whose pre-eminence in ugliness depends on the approximation of their type of countenance to our own; and that the wider the departure, and the more glaring the incongruity, the more likely is the result to be grotesque rather than ugly, as in the case of centaurs. Our principle, however, of the limiting effect of habit on the sense of beauty will not suffer; for in the contemplation of the grotesque, however pleasurable, there must be a large dilution of the sense of beauty with other elements. Human limbs and equine limbs may both be beautiful objects; but the legs of a man on a horse's body, or those of a horse on a man's body, would certainly not reap the full benefit of their abstract grace of form and motion.

and of contrast. Habit tells on our sense of beauty in a quite different way through its necessary connection with the correlative experience of *contrast*. A meaningless fragment of delicately cut and shadowed marble conveys no vivid sense of *rareness*; but a beautifully chiselled mouth, for example, gives the impression of carrying fineness into a position where in thousands of cases it has been absent. Though a thousand mouths may all be different, this one has a mode of differing from them all which is wholly distinct from the modes in which they differ from one another, and makes it an individual and them a crowd. And the same applies to all beautiful things which are not isolated and unique, not too different in most of their attributes from a number of other things to be at once recognised as members of this or that class; the perception of contrast in the midst of general similarity being naturally most marked in connection with that pre-eminence of discriminative power which we found to characterise the perception of *form*. This half-latent sense of contrast, introducing a large positive ingredient of surprise and wonder, is probably a very main factor in a great deal of our delight in beauty; and just so far as its effects go, is it the case that, *e.g.*, beautiful faces would be considered less beautiful had they been the universal rule. Contrast thus takes in some measure the place with respect to beauty that the principle of intermittence holds in the case of the lower physical pleasures.

Direct associa-
tion. To conclude our brief review of the elements which enter into our appreciation of human forms and features: we shall probably find that after we have allowed the greatest weight to the points just mentioned—after we have demanded conformity to some ideal type or types in the fashioning of the parts, and a certain measure of reference to the normal type, if not to any special ideal, in their general relations to one another, and after we have admitted the emphasis given to any perceptible superiority through a sense of its rarity—still a very real and pervading influence must be commonly

exercised by that simple and direct kind of association which connects actual admired qualities with the actual object presented to us. In the case of figures such qualities are strength, ease of motion, swiftness; in the case of faces, the various elements of what we call expression, such as power, gentleness, dignity, and above all animation and mobility; for the admiration of barbers' blocks ought not to outlive childhood. If we call a face beautiful which lacks one or more of these qualities, or exhibits their opposites, we still are in all likelihood paying our tribute to others of them which are present; if, on the other hand, we prefer to call it disagreeable in spite of crediting it with beauty, it is more probable that our judgment of the beauty rests on an unconscious reference to admired types.[1]

It may be said, however, that in taking the example of human forms we have chosen just the case where association and habit are bound to be most prominent; that it is possible to grant the smallness of the part played independently by abstract form in that case, and yet to find it constituting a large factor in the effect of the contours of inanimate Nature. And in Nature it certainly does seem that lines of curvature, of beautiful force and flow, may be innumerable; Mr. Ruskin has given, in *The Stones of Venice*, representations of some specially beautiful ones from mountain and glacier. But then in natural scenery they are of course never seen in abstraction from the other elements of effect; associations of fertility or freedom, or ideas of size, strength, and distance, or the extremely important element of colour, probably contribute by far the larger part of the effect; and the abstract lines on paper, seen by a

§ 6. Abstract form in inanimate Nature.

---

[1] I have already pointed out how pre-eminently *direct association* is connected with form, as the constant and individualising quality of objects; and the same remark applies to *habit*. This point seems to be missed in Mr. Ruskin's criticism of Reynolds as to the influence of habit on the sense of beauty. Reynolds doubtless invites attack by the crudeness of his statement that 'if we were more used to deformity than to beauty, deformity would then lose the idea now annexed to it, and take that of beauty,' which ignores the element of abstract beauty and symmetry altogether, and also of association; for however much we were used to deformities, yet so far as they imply weakness and clumsiness, they could not reap the benefit of association with those pleasing and admirable qualities which pertain to the action of strong agile and symmetrical frames. But Mr. Ruskin introduces illustrations which are quite irrelevant, when he supports his view that 'beauty and ugliness are as positive in their nature as physi-cal pain and pleasure' by saying that *colour and sweetness* are inherently pleasant, and that no logic will enable a man to think the rainbow sombre or the violet scentless. Of course not. Colour and sweetness are matters of the direct nerve-stimulation of the moment; and habituation to darkness or to disagreeable odours of course could not give to non-stimulation or unpleasant stimulation the effects of pleasant stimulation. But a *form* is not appreciated through its mode of stimulating the nervous retinal elements; a scowling face does not act in this way differently from a smiling one; we like the one and dislike the other through experiences which have constantly connected the two with definitely known qualities—that is to say, our perception is steeped through and through with the elements of association and habit. And Reynolds is certainly so far right that, *e.g.*, if the corners of the mouth had always gone down instead of up in smiling, that downward position would have given us the pleasurable impression of a smile.

person who cannot associate them with the original, would hardly convey a shadow of what Mr. Ruskin felt in drawing them.

§ 7. Exceptional character of Architecture.

So far, then, our argument has seemed, if not to disparage the qualities of abstract form, and the extent of their operation in our visual enjoyments, at any rate to throw great doubt on our power of estimating that extent. There is, however, one region of visual phenomena which must strike us as extremely exceptional in this respect : for abstract forms are the very things with which one of our five arts, Architecture, is concerned, its distinctive element of form consisting, as we have seen, just in abstract lines and surfaces and their relations ; and the nobility of this art, and its right to take rank with the others, are matters which are never called in question. What then are the characteristics of such forms in this special art ? What sort of part does association play ? Architecture, if it present that element at all, must clearly present it in its vaguer and less direct character ; in contradistinction to Painting and Sculpture, where abstract form and direct association with the objects represented cannot but blend their effects as we have seen them to do in the actual objects. A brief examination of these points will prove helpful to us (though by way rather of contrast than resemblance) in gaining a clear conception of the special problems presented by the phenomena of Music, a conception very necessary to attain before passing on to our subsequent detailed examination of musical forms.

§ 8. Elements of effect in Architecture. Inadequacy of any physiological basis ;

Deferring for the present the more special and difficult question of proportion *as such*, of abstract relations of magnitude and direction, we will first enquire what more general elements of effect pertain to the characteristic forms of Architecture. The recognised laws of pleasurable nervous action will do a little, but a very little, for us. Thus the actual ocular motions are sometimes adduced as having an explicable pleasurable character ; and certainly the easy sweep of the eye in following an architectural line whose unbroken unity it can easily take in presents a quality which, in comparison with the fatigue and strain of following out jagged broken and angular lines, may be called positively pleasant. But then consider similar lines drawn in chalk on a black board ; the actual sweep of the eye is the same in following a curve on the board which is but a few feet from it as in following the line of an arch at a distance of many feet. That the conditions of pleasurable muscular activity in following lines may be stated with considerable precision, does not alter the fact that the direct muscular pleasure, so far as it is truly isolated from other elements, seems extremely slight ; nor have I encountered any account of the pleasurable conditions which would not apply quite as well to an ordinary wall-paper as to the Doge's palace.[1]    Moreover

---

[1] It must be allowed, however, that the more ideal pleasure in some of the points which are to follow, as complexity and symmetry, has a certain infusion of the physical element ; directly, in the ease with which the eye travels over and grasps the combinations ; indirectly, in the dim representation of the many possible paths the eye could

it would seem that in the works of man we do not get the pick of even such abstract lines as are to be had : Mr. Ruskin himself has pointed out in what slender degree the most beautiful of the ever-changing curves of Nature can be applied to buildings. Gradations of light and shadow, it is true, present means of enjoyment much more positive, and appreciable on a much smaller scale, than that of mere lines : but still less than lines are these amenable to the usual physiological considerations of nervous action, as that the condition for pleasure is exercise of function keeping short of fatigue, and with frequent rests and reliefs of the excited elements. For consider the pleasure in gradation of shade on a curved stone surface, the brightest parts of which are of the most moderate brightness. The nervous action at each instant, in such a case, is not like that involved in the sensation of bright colour, but is altogether too slight to be an ultimate ground of pleasure, and the eye could range for hours without discomfort over a plane surface of equal brightness with the brightest part of the gradated surface ; so that it would be absurd to base the pleasure physio-logically on active stimulation relieved in appropriate ways, or on anything but the special fact of gradual change. The principle of love of variation from uniformity which is here involved will be more especially noticed later ; but it is worth mentioning in the present connection, as the enjoy-ment of gradated surface seems so simple and ultimate, that *à priori* it might be guessed to be referable to some ordinarily recognised physiological condition of pleasure : whereas so far as there is a sensuous element at all, its physiological condition seems to be one utterly external to the ordinary formulæ about nervous wear and tear, and of a kind to which no such easily apprehensible notions seem the least applicable ; while in all pro-bability the pleasure has in its composition the most subtle and delicate mental ingredients.

*especially as regards grada-tions of light and shadow.*

At present, however, we are concerned with less intangible elements of effect : and, to begin with, in buildings we at any rate can have a *great number* of lines and shadows *conspiring* in ways which the eye cannot fail to perceive. To take one simple instance, the pleasure with which the mere line of an arch might be regarded is not only enhanced, but in a way transfigured, by manifold and deeply shadowed mouldings, where many lines and breadths follow harmoniously the same curve. This manifoldness, when it is so ordered as to occupy without puzzling or tantalising the eye, gives the specific sense of *richness* ; one of the most general of the notions involved in the admiration of visual abstract forms, and one which, since it is formed by abstraction from a great multitude of phenomena of very various kinds, reaps the benefit of vague emotional force due to many ex-

*§ 9. Multi-plicity of line and shadow.*

easily take, among a set of lines which it may be dwelling on with very little active movement. This part of the subject has been extremely well treated by Mr. Sully in a recent article in *Mind* on 'The Pleasure of Visual Form.'

periences.   In the given case the effect may be easily connected with a more general principle, which we shall encounter again and again—as a perpetual factor (though not in itself a sufficient condition) of beauty—namely, the love of the perception of *unity*, of a common uniting element, in the midst of and including a variety of parts : and when the unity is apprehended with ease and certainty, this principle in turn comes under the head of another still more general than itself, the delight, namely, in the exercise of *power*, in doing with facility a thing which seems to contain in itself the elements of difficulty.   The repetitions in painted geometrical patterns, the complex symmetry of elaborate tracery, afford other examples.   We cannot, however, confine the principle of multiplicity of line to cases which also present a unity.   With the proviso that the lines, or some of them, shall have a look of regulation about them which is not just the mechanical regulation of blank straightness and right angles, the mere multiplication of them seems sufficient to excite the imagination.   This would perhaps apply, for example, to rapid glimpses of Gothic interiors when we are not symmetrically placed, and cannot judge of the actual unity of the building ; side and fragmentary views comprising multitudes of crossing lines, which still present in themselves, however confused be their relations to one another, obviously regulated forms.   Nor, of course, is it to mere lines that these considerations are meant to apply, but to them and the surfaces and openings which they bound and control, including points and breadths and all sorts of gradations of rounded and receding masses.   Such points and surfaces and gradations, when multiplied and ordered in accordance with the ordering and multiplication of the various main elements of structure, are the most essential constituents in the impression of manifold richness, into the service of which they press all the changing mysteries of light and shadow.

§ 10. Multiplicity of conspiring parts in the larger sense ;

The moulded arch, which we just now took as our example of unified variety, constitutes of course only a single fragment or feature, not merely of the whole building but even of that possibly limited extent of it which, owing to the special position of the observer, can be taken in at a single view. But it is very noticeable in Architecture that the essential *parts*, however symmetrical and complete in form, have as a rule a less complete and individual effect, are more wholly subordinate in relation to the *whole*, or to large and complicated portions of the whole, than in any other of the works of art, whether pictorial, poetical, or musical, which present as parts complete and distinct forms or sections.   While Architecture is of all the arts the one which most lends itself to ornament, to matter which, however important as an informing element, is in some sense separately invented and superposed, at the same time there is perhaps no sort of work in which the organic combination of the more prominent parts is so close and cogent.   In recalling a picture we often recall first and instinctively a particular figure ; in recalling a poem, a particular stanza ; in recalling an overture, a particular 'subject' or melody. But in recalling any building to the memory, we naturally and primarily recall its *whole* aspect, its rows of columns and pediment, or all the mounting pile of window, buttress, and spire, or whatever the elements may be. However remarkable be the details, and however lovingly we may think of their individual graces, it is this *larger* aspect, or rather a whole set of larger aspects, which have made up the great mass of our impressions from the building; they are what the building as an individual has primarily *meant* for us. (I am speaking, it must be remembered, of the elements of abstract line and surface only, not of sculptured or painted ornament, which, in proportion as it is less abstract and more individual, may of course be naturally recalled in a more individual way.) We have then, in this close and delicate organism of buildings, an indefinitely various and glorified expansion of those characteristics of which we were just now considering a simple rudimentary case: the immense number of ordered lines may here raise the sense of richness and intricacy to its highest possible pitch.

And with this we may connect a further point. Apart from the simplest geometrical regularity, it is practically impossible that a *single* abstract line or surface should give a sense of cogency, a sense of special rightness in its own particular direction or gradation of curvature: while as to position there is of course no such thing as rightness in a line which is out of all relation to other lines. But when a number of such forms are combined, all sense of aimlessness in the individual elements is prevented; each reaps the benefit of the whole in which it is a necessary feature; the fact of its companionship makes it look definitely *right*, since a change in it would put the organism to some extent out of gear. When a considerable proportion of the forms possess independently whatever degree of merit their abstract character permits, this added stamp of congruence and rightness may well enhance the general effect a thousandfold. And if we consider the enormous number of abstract forms which are co-ordinated and interwoven in a large Gothic church—beginning with the simple correspondence of the two halves of the arch, further elaborated in trefoils and details of moulding and window tracery, and so carried through the whole range of mazy order, where the freeest lines are obedient and the most tangled combinations harmonious, on to the great fundamental features of structure—the exceptional effect of the phenomena will seem, to some extent at least, to receive explanation.

*and the resulting sense of cogency in the lines.*

All these elements of effect are more clearly realisable by contrasting the work into which they enter with some natural object. To make the comparison just, we must of course avoid selecting an object which has a number of exciting qualities over and above its particular form; as a mountain, in contemplating which the sense of its unmeasured mass and strength is mingled with latent notions of its character as a source of waters, as a barrier of peoples, as the lonely recipient of morning

*§ 11. Contrast with natural objects in these respects.*

and evening glows, as the home of mists and storms, and a score of others. We must take an object whose character and limited size will exclude these appeals to the imagination : we might, for instance, contrast a huge rock, not an obviously broken fragment, but grandly cleft and seamed in bold natural lines, with Salisbury Cathedral. In such a rock, though boldness and ruggedness may give it a beauty of its own, we shall look in vain for the qualities which we have seen that abstract lines may attain in art. The lines may be individually flowing and strong, but they are not regularly multiplied so as to give the richness of detail of which we had an example in arch-mouldings ; nor do the parts and divisions give more than a faint impression of conspiring together, in the interests of a whole to which each is not only subordinate but necessary. The extent of the irregularity precludes any vivid apprehension of unity, whether in minor divisions or in the whole ; it means an extent of independence which is inconsistent with mutual and harmonious action ; and the result is to preclude the special sense of cogency and of organic qualities. There are not enough lines and parts alike, to gain from similarity any objective character of rightness ; we have no sense that individually they are exactly what they ought to be ; and in the lack of strongly marked mutual control, of some decisive means to mark excrescences from essentials, we naturally have an impression of accident, as if the whole arrangement might be altered without paining us by the feeling that an *individual* beautiful thing had so ceased to exist.

It is not improbable that this sort of contrast between Nature and Art may serve as more than a mere means of making clearer to ourselves the architectural effect : they may actually represent an element in that effect. In other words, considering how fundamental a part the sense of contrast continually plays in the perception of beauty, we may perhaps assume that our pleasure in a large and imposing object, full of noticeably controlled forms, owes something to our common experience of similarly large and imposing objects which present no such special interest to the eye. Conversely, it may be remarked that in occasional cases, where Nature presents enough of order and seemingly purposeful arrangement of forms to arrest the attention, we perpetually exclaim at the resemblance of natural to human work in a way which implies some exceptional element of pleasure. Our eye dwells on groups of natural forms where it traces suggestions of architectural structure, as in the rich forest of fantastically moulded columns and groinings of a stalactite cavern ; or again, an avenue is thought specially beautiful if it recalls a Gothic aisle : and though in such instances the very act of association, and the sense of piquancy which resemblance in the midst of contrast involves, make up a mental fact of some complexity, we may discover a true element of added interest in the forms themselves, merely from their presenting perceptible relations.

We have found, then, a certain measure of reason for the pre-eminent position of abstract forms as presented in fine Architecture : but the reader may probably have felt, even in agreeing with what has been said, how much of the effect it leaves unexplained. This is sufficiently shown in the absolute inadequacy of even the most faithful pictorial or photographic reproduction to convey the full emotional effect of great buildings, though preserving with great completeness the forms and relations of line and surface. This mode of demonstration, ruthless as it may seem, is certainly justifiable ; as in a former case it showed the weakness of the physiological explanation of pleasure in abstract architectural forms—inasmuch as the physiological facts, the mere movements of the eye, remained identically the same, while producing hardly any pleasure, when such forms were re-presented on paper—so now it exposes the insufficiency of the ideal elements involved in appreciation of richness, complexity, and harmony of lines, to account for the impressiveness of buildings. It moreover suggests at once that the secret must be traced in great degree to actual *mass, size,* and *space*; elements in respect of which, as Mr. Ruskin has most successfully shown, the effect of a mighty building on the imagination may rival even that of Nature's vaster handiwork. And with these features are connected those notions of weight and resistance, in virtue of which forms obtain aspects beyond mere grace and flowingness, aspects of support and dependence, of satisfying solidity and springing force : thus the deviation from straightness in the lines is beyond doubt a main factor in the look of living and elastic strength which characterises the Parthenon.

And throughout this region of conceptions association is at work. Something may be attributed to direct, though vague, resemblances to Nature. Thus Mr. Darwin has suggested to me that the sense of sublimity excited by a grand cathedral may have some connection with the dim feelings of terror and superstition, experienced by our savage ancestors when they entered a great cavern or gloomy forest : to which might be added the sense of mystery and freedom which more distinct references, such as that of roof and aisle to forest-forms, may suggest. But it is in less direct ways that the influence of external associations is most important and pervading. It is indisputable that the effects on us of mere mass and strength reap the benefit of conceptions chiefly formed in the presence of Nature, and in connection with the daily exercise of eye and muscle. And the notions of support and dependence, again, are an abstraction from all manner of common experiences, where things have withstood pressure and maintained their form, and have so fulfilled their purposes, or else by yielding and falling have given us a shock, or at any rate failed of their end.[1]

§ 12. Further elements of effect in Architecture;

association with Nature,

---

[1] As to the general effect of environment on Architecture, there are two prominent views which, though perhaps not necessarily inconsistent, are at all events so opposite as

and with
human skill
and labour;

But architectural works possess another element of association, besides those of natural objects and events, which contributes largely to their effect: they possess a truly *human* element.   I am not referring here to anything so wide and general as historical or religious associations, but to characteristics more directly apparent in the actual forms which meet the eye; and among these must certainly be reckoned the incessant evidence of elaborate and conscientious human labour.   In no art is this element so strongly and persistently present to the mind : owing to it there exists in the imposing size, in the richness of detail, in the very weight and hardness of the materials which had to be lifted and worked, a peculiar emotional force profoundly affecting the whole nature of our admiration and delight.

adaptation of
means to ends;

In another element of effect, the *perceptible adjustment* of forms and materials to certain ends, there is often a concurrence of several of the elements already mentioned.   A column, or a supporting element of any kind, which looks neither unnecessarily massive for the work it has to do, nor dangerously and affectedly attenuated, gives at once the impression of enduring strength in the object and of skilful and accurate adaptation in the workman.   Such a simple instance shows how impossible it is in this region of phenomena to isolate the effects of form from mechanical and material considerations.

and reference
to well-known
types.

Nor is that reference to *types*, which we noticed in relation to faces, absent from our judgment of buildings.   Types of a certain kind are of course necessitated by physical and utilitarian considerations, by the prosaic realities of the builder's art, weight and thrust and so on, and by certain objects to be fulfilled.   A building cannot slope upwards from an apex, like an inverted pyramid, nor stand on its pinnacles, nor take at will the shapes of geometrical patterns that might be drawn *ad infinitum* on paper : and purposes of utility demand in almost all buildings some amount of internal space and of protection from weather.   But types of a more special kind.

to make their application somewhat doubtful : for when we can draw at once on opposite principles, it becomes a little too easy to explain anything so as to suit our own purposes.   Mr. Spencer has ingeniously connected architectural types with the external characteristics of Nature in the way of *resemblance*; alleging, for instance, that an irregular and castellated style of building is found appropriate in rugged mountainous scenery, while in towns we prefer architectural symmetry, because of the symmetry of surrounding objects, as men, horses, and vehicles.   M. Boutmy, on the other hand, in his excellent little book on Greek architecture, has dwelt rather on the principle of *contrast*.

He connects Egyptian temples with oases rather than with massive rocks; and conceives that when the natural environment is repulsive and poor, or when it has extreme and exaggerated aspects, Art tries less to reproduce these qualities than to supplement them.   In his observations on the relation of Greek landscape to Architecture, however, he recognises in a very general way the principle of resemblance; and in such characteristics as he there dwells on, unbroken contour, distinctness of line, smallness of scale, moderation in style and in amount of ornament, we find a subtler and perhaps truer relationship than in more definite features of actual shape.

connected with particular styles and particular classes of buildings, exercise a very great influence on most minds. The great difference from faces is that a degree of irregularity is common in buildings which is impossible in faces, and most unusual even in the most bizarre of living organisms. Whatever view we take of the irregularity, whether we refer it to association with the aspects of Nature, or to mere dislike of constraint and formality, or to both, the fact is clear that architectural types have a less fixed and objective footing than those of living organisms, and all manner of sentimental and historical associations colour the conception of them. Doubtless, the accepted types of human beauty vary and have varied : but, outside the savage preference for exaggeration of any feature which is already by nature strongly pronounced, there is and has been a sort of general agreement as to the elements which make up fineness of type ; at any rate such types are not subjected to the tremendous reversals of admiration and contempt, decline and rejuvenescence, which the history of Architecture can show. It would be curious to watch what would be the result, if a specimen of Queen Anne architecture, of a sort now commonly and justly accounted *piquant* and picturesque, could be suddenly presented for the first time, as a new thing, isolated from all remembrance of its fellows, or of the history of its style ; probably a storm of contradictory opinions, and hardly a single very deep and instinctive conviction. Comparatively few arrive at the power of judging Architecture with a reference either to mechanical or æsthetic principles ; and many never get over the stage of judging of fresh work by simple reference, very likely unconscious, to familiar and approved types and specimens. In the case of a monumental art this may be in the main natural and right : it is only noticed here as one of the conditions which affect the appreciation of architectural forms.

And here it will be well to pause for a moment, to consider certain general principles which underlie some of the points already noticed. For we have now arrived at the most convenient place for considering, in relation to sight, the *second* great characteristic which distinguishes the two privileged senses with respect to the pleasure they can derive from phenomena. The *first* great characteristic, it will be remembered, was the perception of form, with all that it involves ; this has been to some extent considered, as far as vision is concerned. The second is rather more recondite, and the actual statement of it was best deferred till some examples of its bearings had been given. It is the power, which exists only in relation to the two privileged senses, of perceiving a special impressiveness in certain general qualities presented by many external things, such as size, mass, complexity, force, swiftness. To understand how this is, we must examine what are the exact conditions for impressiveness in these notions ; what are their characteristics on the frequent occasions when they impart

§ 13. The *second* great characteristic of the two superior senses in relation to pleasure : the power of perceiving impressiveness in certain general properties of things ;

a distinct element of their own to the pleasure of our perceptions. For the notions themselves could be formed to a great extent through simple muscular and tactile experiences, unconnected with sight or hearing; and in all cases these muscular or tactile experiences play a most indispensable part in their formation. Thus we could get some conception of the size of a mountain, without ever having seen it, through ideas of distance and steepness gradually acquired through simple muscular experience. A blind man could realise the complexity of some elaborate piece of tracery by passing his fingers along the several lines; he could realise swiftness by the action of running, or by holding his hand in rushing water; he could gain a perfect idea of rapidity of succession by passing his hand quickly along some area railings. But none of the imaginative *pleasure* in size or swiftness, or any such general quality, seems possible without the supervention of one of the two superior senses. The case of hearing we will defer for the present: its effects of this kind will prove to depend very greatly on association with the phenomena of sight. It is in connection with sight, in the *seeing* of vast things, or richly complicated things, or things in strong and rapid motion, that we find the imagination most frequently and powerfully roused. It would seem then that the required conditions must be closely associated with some definite characteristic of the sense of vision. Now what special characteristics do we find in the eye? One we have already considered; namely, that power of discriminating an infinite variety of impressions which was so intimately connected with the perception of form. If we look beyond this, surely no characteristic is so prominent as the *ease and rapidity* with which the eye does its work: the muscles which direct it, so far as their normal use is concerned, seem almost absolutely untiring. The condition required, then, may be surmised to be that we shall take in and master with ease and rapidity and safety, as by the eye we are enabled to do, a set of impressions which in other ways are associated with exertion and physical stress, or even with pain and violence, as in the ideas of such sudden shocks and catastrophes as are involved in falls from heights and other rapid motion of external matter; which ideas in their turn owe their power over us ultimately to our direct physical knowledge, acquired partly by sight, and partly by direct bodily experience, of falls, resistances, crushings, and blows.

probably connected with the sense of power and the sense of contrast.

In this way we may connect our point with those two most general and fundamental factors of our supersensuous enjoyments, both of which have already been incidentally mentioned; the sense of *power* and the sense of *contrast*. To recur to our example of a mountain: a man who had never seen such an object would feel no imaginative glow from the mere realisation of its size by tiring himself in walking over it; but when we experience a sense of expansion and delight in gazing up its side, the two fundamental factors just mentioned are probably combined, in a pleasing feeling that we are, so to speak, traversing and surmounting with facile sweeps of the eye something the traversing and surmounting of which might be, in another way, a matter of time, toil, and danger, and whose very height suggests dimly the violence of a fall: while the very consciousness of this other way, so far as it is observed lurking in our minds, brings with it a sense both of power and contrast in the ease with which we avoid it.

That the eye can play the part here assigned to it, in the appreciation of size and succession, is primarily due to that same extraordinary power of distinguishing impressions which was involved in the appreciation of form, and which we have already connected with the extremely complex structure and action of the organ. In roving rapidly over a large space, or marking the rapid motion of objects, it can realise without effort the multitude and succession of the sensational elements. The tactile and muscular senses, as we saw before, agree with those of sight and hearing in possessing great power of distinguishing successive feelings, and we may add of acting for a long time together without any deadening of sensation; but then in their connection with the phenomena which yield the impressive conceptions we have been considering, the characteristics of effort and even pain become prominent. And it is to the engagement on the selfsame things of one or other of the two superior senses *and* of the muscular and tactile senses (these last acting of course as a rule through dim mental representation),—it is to this *interplay* of feeling, this *double line* of experience, this knowledge of the same external facts through such different and indeed contrasted means, that I have referred those stirring and impressive general conceptions which make so frequent an element in our æsthetic pleasures.

As regards Architecture, it is chiefly in relation to size and complexity that we shall find such an element prominent: but it probably would not be hard to extend the list of the conceptions to which the above principle will apply with more or less of explanatory power. We might connect with it our instinctive delight in the menacing aspect of overhanging tiers and frowning cornices. And in the mere apprehension of *symmetry* by the eye, there seems to be some reference to it: though several other elements of effect are certainly much more obviously present. Thus, symmetry is the natural condition of strength and stability for anything which has weight: in cases where this does not apply, mere habit has often an overpowering force, as in the sameness of the two sides which we consider normal in the human face; and even where habit has no such irresistible influence on our feelings, there is a sense of unreasonableness, when two things or two parts of a thing are identical in purpose and function, and yet different in size or form; as if we had one door-post square and the other round, or wore two boots of obviously different patterns   These considera-

*Application to Architecture.*

tions, however, on their own account are rather negative than positive ; they show rather why want of symmetry should offend than why symmetry should please. Nor perhaps can symmetry be really detached as an element of pleasure ; but where the elements of size and weight, and so of literal balance, become prominent, as often in buildings, I think that, combined with a latent consciousness that unbalanced things give way and fall, the love of power and of contrast may again be traced, in the sense of ease and rapidity with which we appreciate by vision facts otherwise ascertainable only by long and laborious measurements.

§ 14. Architectural effects are, in a large majority of cases, rather general than individual.

On reviewing, now, our account of abstract forms as presented in Architecture, one result to which we are led, and which seems confirmed by experience, is that effects of a somewhat *general* kind predominate. It is, of course, not denied that hundreds of beautiful buildings may stand out as individuals with as much distinctness as the beautiful productions of other arts. But such works must be exceptional among the buildings, whether really existent or ideally possible, from which the spectator should be able to derive true pleasure. To the ordinary apprehension there must always be many buildings which, however pleasing, will seem very like a great many others ; and even in the more remarkable examples of buildings similar in style and purpose, there will almost necessarily be many parts and points of view which will hardly impress the spectator as belonging to a new and individual utterance of the inventor. Not but that the humblest dwellings may have individuality of a sort ; no building which houses a human family should lack this ; but it must be rather in device or ornament or minor arrangements than in characteristic architectural forms. Such facts may of course be in part referred to the unchanging purposes of convenience and utility which, in the main, give to the art its *point d'appui* and opportunity ; a reference chiefly applicable of course to private buildings, where space and means are limited ; but applying also in a great degree to churches and more conspicuous buildings, the picked specimens where the art has wider scope, and in relation to which it is principally discussed. But the facts are connected also with the nature of the actual forms which are our present subject of consideration. Even those larger views which comprise at once a considerable portion of a beautiful work, the rows of columns round a Greek temple, the labyrinth of shafts and arches in a Gothic interior, present features which are admirable rather in their general effect of harmony and majesty than because we perceive in each particular case some altogether unique manifestation of beauty. And still more must this restriction of effect apply to the smaller elements and divisions : for according to our previous view as to the relation of parts to whole in abstract architectural design, individuality would be sought, if anywhere, rather in the complete than in the partial aspects of the structure.

To acknowledge this is not to charge even the subordinate parts or simpler elements of buildings with any want of power. On the contrary, portions of architectural design composed of the very simplest elements may be made most imposing through the enriching and informing of them with ornament, through the qualities of grand size and supporting strength, through the filling out of the framework they offer with forms of freer character or with noble masses of light and shadow. A simple form, such as a square, may be eminently suitable as an exponent of space and surface; the mere breadth being made impressive either by the natural beauty of the material or by the light of heaven and the 'wild signatures of time and storm.' But these points have nothing to do with individuality of effect. And it must be noticed that however much the formal elements of the art may gain in emotional effect from the various sources we have passed in review, they themselves are the objects actually presented to the eye; so that the possibility of a great variety of individual impressions from bits of architecture of at all the same kind would imply a distinctly recognised variety, individuality, and newness in the forms, or in their relative positions and proportions. And this is at any rate sufficiently rare to be noticed as remarkable, when it occurs, even by those most calculated to discern it. In the absence, indeed, of a definite *scale* of proportions, such as we shall find presented in Music through the element of pitch, abstract combinations seems to lack a main condition for complete individuality; since such a scale affords an obvious means for a form or arrangement to differ distinctly from its fellows, and so to appear spontaneous and free, while at the same time presenting recognised relations and limits which preclude any idea of chance or arbitrariness. Architectural structure comprises, of course, a number of most clearly marked varieties of *species* in the elements which it combines; but these will recur in building after building, in aisle after aisle, in façade after façade, with differences of form and arrangement which have to be regarded in their *larger* combinations, before the impression gets even the chance of being strongly individualised, for the majority at any rate of those impressed. I must repeat that I am excluding all forms of ornament where the representative arts, treated either in a direct or in a more or less abstract manner, are called into play; these may give life and distinction to every corner of the building, and are susceptible of any amount of variety and individuality of design and workmanship. I am speaking of purely abstract forms and arrangements. And though twenty different painted geometrical patterns, twenty different sections of moulding, may each be beautiful in form, and though in each a trained and loving eye might detect a quality which would escape the average admirer, each of them can hardly cause in even the most discriminative observer that peculiar delight and sense of possession which we associate with a new idea.

Nor is there lacking a certain sublimity to these very facts when duly considered; as when Mr. Ruskin points out that for one man who could compose first-rate foliated ornament, thousands could devise the abstract figures which, cut through the stone, would strike from the light out of the dark, or from the dark out of the light, stirring effects of power and majesty.

§ 15. Peculiarities in the development of the appreciative perception of architectural forms.

With many of the points noticed in our sketch of architectural effects may be connected peculiarities in the *sort of training* which the perceptive faculties here receive. It will be readily granted, in a general way, that the appreciative pleasure in buildings implies some considerable powers of perception and considerable training of the æsthetic sensibility. A boor may be astonished at a very big building, as he might be at many other unaccustomed sights, but his astonishment would have at best but a faint trace of artistic delight. A child's first impressions of fine buildings are generally merely of size and gloom, and of the colours of stained glass; it is only after an advance in perceptive power that the multitudinous order and harmony of parts attract notice and admiration. This in a general way may appear obvious and natural enough, but it is connected with a further point in which architectural work seems peculiar. In the other arts, parts are more obvious than wholes to the untrained mind; they are what are first picked out and noticed. Thus the child dwells on special figures and incidents in pictures; he has his pet verses in poetry, his favourite and familiar bits of tune in musical compositions, and it is long before he begins to take an interest in the organic union of these fragments. In architectural work, on the other hand, if we exclude the representative art used in its adornment, there is comparatively little of this gradual training of the faculties from the interest in more or less isolated bits to the more comprehensive appreciation of the whole. It is, in fact, the smaller bits which need the greatest discrimination and the true connoisseurship. *Noble* is a word which, as applied by Mr. Ruskin to the outline of a moulding or the proportions of a quatrefoil, must have puzzled many who would themselves apply it with genuine feeling to the majestic length of a Gothic nave. When the admiration begins, it begins with the whole, or at all events with such large aspects of the whole as a wide field of vision embraces. It is the effects where a number of parts, each independently of small emotional power, unite to create the characteristic impressions of multiplicity and harmony, it is these comprehensive aspects of richly varied order, which primarily strike the imagination; primarily, not only in the sense of being absolutely the most important, but also as being the earliest in their appeal to the individual. And their power to appeal at all, in a way which shall involve discriminative appreciation as distinct from mere vague wonderment and awe, depends on faculties of co-ordination and balance of a comparatively advanced kind. Nor is this all. The slow and hidden mental growth which leads to the more complete appreciation seems, here, in its earlier stages at all events, to mean less essentially an increase in the number of points on which the imagination can dwell, or a process in which one thing noticed and learnt acts as a stepping stone to the next thing noticed and learnt, than the development of certain somewhat abstract notions, which inform and give character to the lines and proportions, and which are gradually shaped and refined from their first dim and rudimentary condition in the untrained intelligence. In *Modern Painters* there is a surmise that changing gradations of curvature may move us by latent suggestions of infinity; and even those who may feel such lofty symbolism rather beyond them, must still be conscious that in realising those mundane qualities of spring and strength and adjustment of means to ends which were considered above, they are drawing on conceptions which are the result of considerable experience in comparison and abstraction. Thus scores will be at once struck by the mere bigness of the dome of St. Peter's, for one who will be keenly sensible of its superiority in form to the numerous other domes which the Pincian Hill commands.

Thus far, it will be seen, we have been able to survey at some length the more general sources and characteristics of impression, in the phenomena which we took as most prominently exemplifying abstract form, without dwelling on the most literally *abstract* element, the element of proportion *as such*, of actual *relations* of magnitude and direction. This more special element now claims closer attention. Our notice of it so far has done no more than throw doubt on its *individualising* power in respect of the smaller, at any rate, of the combinations Architecture may present to the eye : but this of course in no way affects the position universally accorded to it, as at the very least a positive and indispensable ingredient in architectural beauty. And it is naturally in relation to this element that any special mode of intuition would be looked for, and an answer be obtained to the question asked in the fourth section of this chapter. The points we have so far chiefly dwelt on have not suggested any such mode. Thus the elements of multiplicity and richness, though very prominent in many beautiful buildings, are not specifically connected with visual phenomena at all, being often admirably exemplified in the complicated fabric of polyphonic music : and the elements of support and strength, and the rest, we found to be distinctly associational; that is, the appreciation of their character is the result of manifold experiences in the external world. What further facts, then, does the appreciation of proportions in this rich and favoured region of abstract forms involve? Do we exercise in the appreciation of them any æsthetic faculty over and above those which have been considered ? and if so, how far is the exercise of the faculty peculiar to this range of phenomena ?

The most obvious way of realising the part our new element plays will

§ 16. Abstract proportion *as such*: how far does it involve some special mode of intuition?

be to take some case of beautiful architectural effect, to imagine some distinct modification of the proportions which, as far as we can see, leaves unaltered all the conditions previously enumerated, and then to ask ourselves whether the beauty remains or whether some of it is lost. If some of it is lost, our new element will be accurately identified, and the question as to its general or special character will naturally follow. Let us take, then, Giotto's campanile at Florence, which will serve the purpose very well. It will be seen at once how many of the already mentioned conditions are present in its effect: majestic height and mass, perfect unity, rich elaboration of detail, signs of patient and loving toil, to which may be added most delicate colouring, and most striking and beautiful contrasts of light and shade. And in its case, as it happens, we can specially easily imagine a change which would leave every one of these elements intact, though in itself most distinct: the separate segments or tiers can be imagined *equal* instead of *different* in height; with what disastrous result to the beauty of the building is instantly realised. Here, it will be noticed, we have not altered any harmony of curved lines; we have introduced no discordant element; we have not attenuated anything so as to make it look weak, or loaded anything so as to make it look clumsy or top-heavy, or done aught but just alter the abstract proportions of certain lines and surfaces; straight lines, moreover, primarily, and rectangular surfaces, that is, elements in themselves of the simplest and most mechanical kind; though naturally the relative proportions of the more complex elements contained within the rectangular boundaries would have to follow suit.

Principle of variation from uniformity:

Here, then, we have a specially perceptible case of a principle which is exemplified in subtle ways throughout the range of beautiful architecture, and which may be generically described as the principle of *variation from uniformity*. This principle must be distinguished from that of variety and multiplicity of parts perceived under an aspect of unity, which we have considered above. There the mind was concerned with the *number* of elements, many of which might be identical in form and size, and with recognising the order which embraced them: here it is occupied with a *few* elements or parts, different but sufficiently nearly uniform and equal to be comparable. The same principle is at the root of the pleasure given by changing curvature in a single line or surface, where the degrees of change are not so sudden but that the notion of uniformity may be considered latent in the very feeling of its being departed from; in such a case the variation occurs as *free form*, while in cases like that of the tower, where distinct and separate parts are perceived, perhaps it would be more intelligibly described as *free proportion*. Taken in either way, few who have received any sort of refined pleasure from buildings will doubt that, whether consciously realised or not, this element of effect has been very constantly present. Nor is it necessary or suitable to discuss here the various applications of the principle, in the face of the masterly exposition and exemplification of it in Mr. Ruskin's chapter on the *Lamp of Beauty*; where, by the way, he describes the tower of Pisa as the one thoroughly ugly tower in Italy, just because of its division into vertically equal parts. At present our less attractive task is to examine not artistic details, but psychological facts; to discover, if possible, whether or not the application of the general principle to architectural forms involves some distinct and peculiar mental process.

For it is clear that the principle itself is *general*; that it admits of much wider application than to a single art. The deadness of monotony is proverbial: the idea of it is common to all manner of experiences; and sameness of parts is not more alien to organic beauty than to all the higher forms of organic life. We might even connect the appearance of the principle in Architecture with the more prominent phenomena of organic life by something closer than the general agreement in differentiation of parts. In both cases the variations from uniformity are in the elements taken in the *vertical* direction, while the similar elements are *horizontal*: a tower or spire, like a man, or like a typical plant, is symmetrical horizontally, divided into unlike parts vertically. Further, as eyes and limbs and various pairs of similar organs are symmetrically arranged in animals, so in buildings those parts are similar which have a common office. We may even trace an identity of reason for this arrangement, where it is connected with facts of what may be called horizontal occurrence. Thus a space enclosed by walls or columns is usually wanted for proceedings which take place on a horizontal plane, viz. the floor, and indifferently over the whole of that plane, which is moved over in horizontal directions; the parallel vertical divisions, therefore, which all play an equal part in the surrounding of the space, naturally present similar parts at the same horizontal level; and they have all another function in common beyond that of enclosing, namely, to support the ceiling or roof, the weight of which is necessarily distributed in a horizontal plane at their tops, just as a man's weight is equally supported by his legs. So that over and above the fact that symmetry involves the notion of balance, and that balance is necessarily of things placed side by side, not one on the top of another, we may connect the relative positions of the unlike parts in the artificial works to some extent with the habitual presentation of the same relation in natural objects: and the look of organic vitality in beautifully proportioned buildings may thus be connected with our more general sense of organic structure.

Such grounds, however, as are thus established for the appearance of the element of variation in Architecture, are merely associational, as in so many of the previous cases: they do not lead us a step towards any *special* mode of intuition. And it may be asked, Why should we expect to find any such special mode involved in our sense of architectural proportions?

*its application in Architecture being specially connected with natural organic structure.*

*§ 17. Reason for seeking for some more special mental ingredient.*

Why should we not be content with recognising that sense as just a delicate exemplification of the wider principle which connects a feeling of deadness with utter sameness, and of life and interest with due variation? why should we seek to specialise it further? The question is so natural that it will be best to anticipate somewhat in order to answer it. We shall find, then, that the other class of abstract phenomena which it will be our business to consider, those of Music, present a unique and irreducible character, and that in their case the appreciation of free form *does* involve a special exercise, belonging to what I shall have to designate again and again as the *musical faculty*. I call melodic form *free*, meaning not that it is arbitrary and capricious, but that it is spontaneous; that no *à priori* exercise of intelligence could have deduced from the general principle of variation the smallest conception of what melody would be, and no clue is afforded by that principle as to why any specimen of it is just what it is; that each presentation of it which seems right seems so in a way peculiar to itself, and the sense of the rightness appears strictly intuitive. I call it *unique and irreducible*, because it is a matter settled, so to speak, between the sense of sound and the sense of form by a collusion which, with our limited intelligence, we can but describe as just a perceptive faculty for this particular class of phenomena, and which gives no handle even for such sort of explanation as analogies seem to afford. These statements will of course receive their justification later: I am *assuming* here, for the sake of clearness, and without argument, that whatever explanations of musical effect turn out to be possible, the exercise of the musical faculty will present an ultimate and inexplicable element. Now it cannot be considered unnatural to ask whether *visual* forms and proportions can be free and unique in this peculiar sense; whether the appreciation of these, like that of *auditory* forms, ever entails the *special* exercise of a faculty confined to that exercise; or whether, on the other hand, the *general* principle of variation from uniformity (supervening, of course, in the case of Architecture, on the numerous other elements of effect which have been more or less described) may be here regarded as a full and sufficient explanation.

§ 18. Special difficulty in determining the question in the case of Architecture:    The question presents peculiar difficulties. For it cannot be denied that in a great many specimens of architecture, and of good architecture too, we find variations from uniformity which are certainly *not* enjoyed by any special faculty for perceiving rightness of proportion, and where we can directly apply the general principle of love of freedom and dislike of formality. Such specimens usually fall under the category of what is commonly described as the *picturesque*: Elizabethan manor-houses, bits of street in Nuremburg, views in old cities at night with

> Towers that, larger than themselves
> In their own darkness, thronged into the moon—

these are things which most amateurs have enjoyed, and enjoy in retrospect, with a feeling rather of their fantastic, untrammelled, unconventional character, than with a sense of cogent rightness in the proportions of their parts realised by a special faculty. And a somewhat similar remark seems to apply to such deviations from regularity in comparatively regular work, as Mr. Ruskin has described in his chapter on the *Lamp of Life*; for example, in the west front of St. Mark's. The effect in such cases might, I imagine, be referable to the general sense of living freedom, as in the like yet freely differing members of a mighty forest tree: though of course I should bow to Mr. Ruskin, if he told me that his perception of the actual proportions was of something too positively and particularly right to be fully accounted for on such a basis. Again, the very simplicity of the notion of relative size is an added source of difficulty. Lines and surfaces are matters of measurement, and equality makes a standard from which variations are naturally measured; even changing curves can be mathematically quantified: whereas we shall find, when we come to melodic forms, that (owing to their resulting from two heterogeneous factors, those of time and pitch) they are complex after a fashion which precludes measurement or any quantitative notion of their variation from uniformity. The facility of imagining simple relations of form and size seems to create a constant possibility that what we call a sense of proportion (as in the case of the tiers of Giotto's tower) is nothing more than a direct application of the general principle of variation, with just the added proviso that the variation must be large enough to be quite perceptible, and not so large as to preclude all idea of comparison, not so large, that is, as to cease to be a true variation : while the perceptive faculty may be conceived to owe its *appearance* of specialisation to the exceptional amount and variety of exercise and interest which it happens to get in just this one class of phenomena, to the pre-eminence of this one field for its practice and development. Once more, the fact that the forms and proportions presented to the eye are grasped almost or quite instantaneously, makes the perception of them specially hard to examine, in contrast to the perception of melodic forms, which is a distinct *process* extending over a definite space of time. And again, our life-long knowledge of the external world, its lines, its weights, its mechanical facts, its living organisms, cannot be eliminated from our appreciation of proportions in buildings; which are congeries not only of visible forms, but of heavy and resistant matter. Equally hard is it, in many cases, to abstract the actual proportional element from the other features which are present to the eye without essentially entering into the proportional scheme, including not only such general ones as majestic size, but all the wealth of beauty in details of structure and in ornament and colour, which the controlling proportions (of the tiers, for instance, in Giotto's tower) embrace without in any sense necessitating. It thus seems hopeless to wonder what sort of power we should have of getting pleasure out of the lines and surfaces by what we now call sense of proportion, apart from all association and knowledge of these other elements; but it would, at any rate, be something infinitely inferior in distinctness of action and definiteness of results to the musical sense. For we might have exactly the main proportions of Giotto's tower in a high and narrow set of bookshelves, and prefer the variations in height of the perpendicular divisions to sameness; but the proportions would not impress us as unique, nor strike us vividly as being the same as those in the tower; whereas *Rule Britannia* is recognised as *Rule Britannia,* as one unique set of proportions, whether played on the tuba-stop of an organ or on a penny whistle.

Nor is it only in these ways, in the general difficulty of isolating it or of tracing its various concrete references, that a character of doubt here attaches to the sense of proportion: there is also a frequent difficulty in discovering how far its determinations are fixed for any special case, and with what degree of certainty and unanimity the feeling of peculiar rightness or wrongness obtains. We thus get back to the question of individuality which has already been to some extent discussed. It has been said that all good proportions are unique; but can they be said to be all *felt* as unique? How far is the impression individual in the sense that any change would impair it? Suppose for a moment that it were possible gradually to alter, before the eyes of assembled connoisseurs, the sizes of the various sections of some building, say the heights of the several segments of a tower and spire in a given position and of given material; would every stage seem wrong except at a few definite points in the change, at which all or many of the spectators would suddenly exclaim 'Stop!' with a relief, as from wrongness and ugliness? and would they carry away in their mind's eye a distinct vision of these few aspects as unique? Surely the gradual heightening of the spire might take place, within certain limits, without presenting a succession of aspects either so wrong as to be felt like wrong notes, or so right as to be felt as wholly individual. And, as regards the perceptions of the ordinary run of admirers, the very notion of such certainty and uniqueness becomes ridiculous.[1] The same applies to the forms whose abstract character is most unmixed and marked, such as beautiful spirals; many of which might be *seen* to be different from one another, but without creating the impression that each has an unmistakable and unchangeable individuality; for instance, we

---

[1] Even the much-quoted example of the 'Golden Section' has never received any sort of universal and intuitive recognition: while to insist on such a feature of proportion, which might figure in countless buildings, would of course only make it harder to claim free individuality for the abstract element of each particular building.

might pull one of them into another by imperceptible stages; but could never so treat two melodies. And in accordance with these facts, the number of harmonious visual forms and proportions in *total* abstraction, which we could keep in our heads as individually distinct, would be few indeed as compared with the thousands of musical motives which are easily and perfectly remembered.[1]

I am inclined to doubt whether any precise discrimination of the faculties we employ is here possible; and I can easily conceive that the very discussion of the question may seem a barren exercise in aimless and tiresome distinctions. My defence must be that it is impossible to devote any time and thought to speculation upon so unique a phenomenon as melody, without craving to get some view of an analogy in another field of experience, of some parallelism in mental process or mode of perception, if not in the things perceived. Sight and hearing occupy together too unique a position among our senses for a vista of comparison from the experiences of one to those of the other not to seem possible. And the possibility of the vista stimulates search: for that entirely ultimate and unanalysable nature, which we readily recognise in the case of simple sense-impressions, we find great difficulty in allowing to more advanced mental phenomena. In their case a *cul-de-sac* has a specially dispiriting effect; so dispiriting that, could it be fully realised, it might be regarded as complete punishment for impertinent curiosity, by those who hold as a sufficiently ultimate principle in these matters Mr. Ruskin's fundamental doctrine; namely, that we enjoy beautiful things because they have been made beautiful and we have been made to enjoy them. If the further analysis is fruitless and irreverent, these may say, it is well that it should be irksome. Nor can I, at this point, even so much as indicate the advantage to our main subject of treading these perplexing paths. In the face, however, of such statements as Mr. Ruskin's, that Reynolds, by those

*which suggests a discouraging view of the analysis of beauty.*

---

[1] On the whole, if the general feeling for variation from uniformity be indeed specialised in some peculiar and inexplicable manner in connection with the eye, it is perhaps easier to imagine the exercise of the specialised faculty in the case of the changing curvature of lines and the gradated shading of curved surfaces, than in relative proportions of lengths and sizes. I could imagine that a person of artistic sensibility who had always lived remote from buildings might have the Pisan tower with its equal tiers presented to his view, and might be brought to feel in virtue of the *general* instinct for variety rather than monotony, that at any rate some difference would be agreeable; that is, his faculty for appreciating variety of proportion would so far *lack* speciality, inasmuch as before it was actually exercised in this quite new case, the effect of its exercise could be realised. On the other hand, I can hardly imagine making a person who had seen nothing but uniform lines or ungradated surfaces feel the character of a changing curve or a gradated surface till he actually saw one: but then, here comes the difficulty, that he might not enjoy it when he did see it; that enjoyment of such curves and gradations may be entirely bound up with the perpetual past experience of them in the environment. And if this be so, most delicate and remote associational references may be supposed to be present; as, for instance, in the connection of a look of elasticity and spring with vital strength and growth in the organic world.

references to the influence of habit which were noticed above, betrays 'a doubt as to the existence of beauty at all,' it is worth observing in passing that the dully scientific procedure is truly not so much opposed as supplementary to Mr. Ruskin's principle; and that to attempt to trace the evolution of beauty is no more to deny or explain away its primary mystery (much less its existence) than to trace the evolution of physical organisms is to deny the mystery of life.

§ 19. Confirmation of previous remarks as to the cultivation necessary for the appreciation of Architecture, and the all-importance of wholes as compared with parts.

One positive result, at all events, from the foregoing argument connects itself with and confirms some of our previous remarks. Whether or not the faculty for fully appreciating visual forms and proportions contains a unique element, its exercise is at all events a late result of practice and culture: an uncultivated eye would be as unlikely to appreciate the refined variations of height in the tiers of the Florentine campanile as to feel delight in the moulding of an arch. We may go further and say that appreciation of the sorts of variation we have last considered is a more refined and later product, involving a more delicate discrimination, than the feeling of general majesty and of rich and complicated harmonies of form. Wrongness and contradiction in the fundamental lines will often distress the eye of the connoisseur, where that of the average observer may be roaming with admiration over the spaces which they bound, rejoicing in the expanse and the multitude of ordered forms, with the adornment perhaps of beautiful colour or the efflorescence of rich workmanship. And if this be so, a further fact of interest is thereby indicated; namely, that as in the earlier appeals of Architecture to the imagination, so in the last and most subtle appreciation of its beauties, it is on the whole, or very large aspects of the whole, rather than on the separate parts, that the faculties are principally and most effectively exercised. As we formerly found that a multitude of conspiring parts conveyed impressions the secret of which would be sought in vain in the forms and characters of the separate elements, so now we find that where the delicate perception of proportions becomes a prime factor of effect, it is pre-eminently in relation to the great elements which constitute the main divisions of the whole height and mass; the very simplest members, it may be, in actual form, but the controlling ones under the dominance of which the eye takes in all the varied detail of the organism. The bearing of these remarks will appear when we pass on, as we must now do, to the facts and problems of musical forms, considered briefly in relation to those views of abstract form which up to this point have presented themselves.

# CHAPTER V.

## ABSTRACT FORM AS ADDRESSED TO THE EAR.

THE relation between architectural and musical forms is, as I have premised, chiefly one of contrast. The saying that 'Architecture is frozen
Music,' is, for all its prettiness, exceptionally misleading; such resemblances as may present themselves hereafter being between the two arts
just *not* concerned with the elements of form and structure which seem
indicated in the word *frozen*. It may be said that such analogies are not
to be pressed; that there is a certain absurdity in taking such a phrase
seriously and pointing out its deficiencies in detail. But in reality the
phrase expresses in a picturesque way the sort of views to which I called
attention at the close of the third chapter, and which are all included
under what may be called the *external* conception of Music. These views
are seriously and literally held by many to whom ' Music' merely means
certain spaces of time filled with a large flow of agreeable and ordered sounds,
presenting certain impressive aspects of contrast and symmetry. They embrace all that mode of regarding Music which is apt to be implied in the
common talk about ' musical disposition ' of lines or masses or colours ; talk
which is perfectly legitimate as long as *musical* is accepted, on the authority
of its Greek original, as meaning in the widest sense harmonious and
fairly fashioned; but which naturally runs on into conveying the impression that the essential points in the *phenomena of Music* must be
connected with their kinship to these 'musical' phenomena. The misconception is fostered by the fact that there is in Music a definite element called
*harmony* ; and for that reason, if for no other, I cannot too early or too
emphatically state, what will become clearer as we proceed, that it is not
Harmony or notes in combination, but Melody or notes in succession,
which is the prime and essential element in Music ; nor for some time to
come shall we have anything to do with any other.

§ 1. As to form, Architecture and Music present little but contrast.

To begin with, supposing we are determined to find some visual
analogue for melody, a difficulty presents itself as to what is the right one
to take. Is it to be a *line,* or a *combination* of lines ? Melodies have often
been compared to arabesques, or wavy lines pure and simple ; not only does
their look on paper suggest this, but when heard they give an irresistible
impression of being things which we advance along steadily, of things

§ 2. Difficulty in finding where an ana-logue to melody, even of the most general sort, would lie.

which have to be followed from end to end, and whose nature prevents their parts from being regarded in an arbitrary or zigzag order, as when our eyes travel up and down and along, and glance and re-glance from part to part of, some large architectural combination. But then, on the other hand, in a melodic form the proportional element indubitably enters at every single note; every note-unit has definite relations of time and pitch to its neighbours; so that, reasoning on merely abstract grounds, we should say the analogy would be to some complete proportional arrangement of forms, rather than to a single line or surface, whose curve, though its degrees are measurable, in no sense consists of separate and distinct elements. As regards emotional character, again, we must certainly go to large and elaborate architectural structures before we arrive at effects as overpowering and enduring as are produced by many and many a melody only eight or sixteen bars in length; and this fact at once reveals the unreasonableness of connecting melody with some smaller piece of design, through measuring it by the paper it covers or the time it occupies. Here then the continuous line, or the minor arrangement of curves, seems put further than ever out of court by its unemotional character, contrasted with what is possible to melody; but then if we go beyond abstract structure, and come to æsthetic effects, we shall find that the combination hypothesis presents equal though different difficulties. This sort of doubt, and the reasons for it, sufficiently show at the very outset how empty and unsuggestive is either comparison, and how hopeless it seems to know even where we ought to look for any subtler and deeper affinities.

§ 3. Melody lacks simultaneous complexity of parts:

Again, in a melodic form there is no multiplicity or thronging of elements, no impression of conspiring parts all there at once. The elements are units succeeding one another in time; and though each in turn, by being definitely related to its neighbours, is felt as belonging to a larger whole, there is no simultaneity of impression. Thus the effect of a melody pure and simple is not in the slightest degree one of richness and number; nor though the number of its elements may be actually very considerable, do they exhibit anything analogous to the labyrinthine order presentable by a similar number of visual elements, which the eye would delight to thrid and master with a conscious realisation of their complexity.

but is preeminent in the sense it conveys of cogent and definite rightness in its elements;

As regards exact rightness and definiteness of the component units, on the other hand, melodic forms stand pre-eminent. The rightness here spoken of is of course not of that deeper sort which implies and is implied in a *good* melody with impressiveness of a distinctly individual kind; it is a general feature of melodies, good, bad, and indifferent. What is meant is that each unit falls definitely in its right place as an obviously essential part of the whole, such as it is; strike out or alter a unit here and there, and what was an organic whole is either broken into more or less incoherent fragments; or if in some exceptional instance it retains a satisfactory coherence, it is by becoming something else, recognised as another whole. If less marked notes be selected for omission, the melody may indeed retain a coherence as the ghost of its former self; but it would usually fail to give a notion of its true self to a person who heard it first in the mutilated form ; and this last condition would afford the true test, as the missing elements, if previously known, are easily supplied by the imagination. Even in cases where the melody is previously unknown, it often happens that certain notes follow so naturally on certain others (as, for example, in a phrase where some of the adjoining notes of the scale follow each other consecutively), that the supply of missing notes or the correction of wrong ones would be easy to any person of sufficient ear to catch a tune at all. But all who realise what melodies sound like, as played on a piano containing one or two dumb notes, or with still more marked results as played by a person who makes occasional wrong shots, will admit that to perceive what must be right is something so different from getting the appropriate effect of pleasure as to be compatible with an extreme degree of worry and irritation. And that the units can so easily be put so very definitely wrong implies that their rightness is very cogently and definitely right. The whole which they make up may perhaps be weak and silly, as (to use a very loose metaphor) a series of grammatical words may make up a weak and silly sentence ; but as in a familiar sentence words cannot be omitted or replaced (except by synonyms, and in Music there are no synonyms) without obvious destruction or alteration of the sense, so neither can single notes in a familiar tune be altered or replaced, except in very peculiar cases, without instantly producing this feeling of wrongness.

It is true that melodic forms have been altered in the making, and that the final result, though considerably different from its unelaborated predecessor, may manifest unmistakable kinship with it. But such alterations are of phrases or of bars, or at any rate of several notes together, most exceptionally, if ever, of single notes ; so that though the family likeness of the two forms, through identity of certain strong individual parts or pivots, may survive throughout, yet in each stage the units are fitted in, so to speak, and linked together in a close chain where each is indispensable in its place ; and when the tune is one on which the mind has dwelt with pleasure, any conceivable change will be resented.

But, it may be objected, this is no more than might be said of a loved piece of architecture : the eye, like the ear, would resent alteration in forms on which it had dwelt with pleasure. Not quite in the same way, however. The eye might resent the introduction of a downright wrong line, cutting across and marring the flow of other lines, somewhat as the ear resents a downright false note : but suppose that we saw a tolerably exact reproduction of a piece of architecture that we knew and admired, containing, however, certain differences not in themselves otherwise than good and harmonious; we should probably mark the resemblance and the difference, but should certainly not receive the shock of wrongness, as of our familiar object of contemplation disfigured, which we receive when we hear a favourite tune played with some new turn of phrase, or say an alteration of the closing cadence.

which is due to conditions of time,

The reason of this seems to be greatly due to the definiteness of the moment at which each element of a melody strikes the sense. The eye receives its impressions by its own free will at its own time, and wanders at its own pace over the parts of objects: whereas the ear is prepared for each particular unit of impression at a particular instant, and in proportion as the expectation is focussed on that instant, is a distinct jar felt when it is baulked.

and of pitch.

The other important cause of the definiteness of melodic form is the definiteness of pitch in the notes which are its material; and this is of course directly connected with the existence of a fixed scale of notes, deviations from which are instantly detected as errors of flatness or sharpness. The impression of unique and exact rightness, which is entailed in this peculiar power of notes to be *out* of tune as well as *in*, is most prominently brought out when a singer or player slides from one note through an interval till the sound reaches the precise point of rest at the next note. I will not anticipate the more detailed examination of melodic forms in a subsequent chapter by dwelling on this peculiarity; but it may be well to point out here that this actual division of the scale into elements at certain distances from each other, involves a definiteness quite beyond and distinct from the definiteness of pitch which we found, in the first chapter, to differentiate tones from noises. In that former sense we should have said that definiteness of pitch existed wherever at any moment a musical pitch could be assigned to a sound; wherever it would be possible to detect by examination, supposing the sound to be checked at any instant, that the last impression on the ear answered to some real position on or between the notes of a pianoforte. Definiteness in this sense is really tantamount to perceptible existence: it marks off certain sounds which have, from the general run of sounds which have not, a sufficient element of certainty to localise them in the scale. But sounds might be extremely definite in this sense quite apart from the division of the scale into fixed degrees. Thus a violinist who draws his bow across a string while he steadily moves the stopping finger up or down it, produces a shifting sound which is everywhere in the truest sense tone, which, if stopped and examined at any instant, would be recognised as having had at that instant a perfectly distinct pitch, but which is quite continuous and undivided.

§ 4. Definiteness in *whole* melodic forms:

The extreme definiteness of the notes, and of their mode of adjustment to one another, connects itself with the further fact of definiteness in the whole organic series which they compose. The one thing is really involved in the other. It follows, from the peculiarity in the elements of melody, as already described, that they present nothing analogous to an *outline* or skeleton of lines, capable of being presented or imagined alone and then filled in with subordinate lines and dividing forms or proportions. We saw that, if we consider the actual melodic notes (neglecting shakes and ornaments, if such be present, as being not structural elements at all, but pure excrescences), the structure or organism can only exist by dint of their all being there in their right places. Thus the ideas of outline and detail have no application: the proportions on which the form depends have no degrees of scope and importance; they are everywhere essentially present, and everywhere interdependent.[1] And this entire continuity of structure, this necessity for identifying each particular element as it occurs, under pain of missing any coherent conception of the form, cannot but entail a peculiar definiteness of individuality in the form itself.

[1] It is of course a frequent mode of producing a 'variation' to introduce unessential and ornamental notes between the cardinal notes of a melody; but this is analogous to dressing a complete figure in ornaments, not to filling in an outline with essential form, or filling out an inexpressive skeleton with flesh and blood. Thus, a 'subject' of Beethoven's beginning

subsequently reappears as

It naturally usually happens that such adventitious notes come *between* and not *on* the beats of a bar; but this fact must by no means be twisted into suggesting that, in a complete and unadorned melodic form, the notes on the beats of the bar are more essential than other notes, in the sense of presenting an outline from which the form could be judged. To a person unfamiliar with a melody, notes on beats of the bar, unless they constituted a large majority of the whole number of notes actually used, would convey as a rule not an *imperfect* notion, but *no* notion of the actual form; while to a person who knew and recognised the melody, the omission of the intervening notes would convert enjoyment into annoyance. Think, for instance, of 'I know that my Redeemer liveth,' as opening with

or of this, as a representative of 'Lascia ch'io pianga,'

Rousseau speaks of the *notes sous-entendues* in the Italian music of his day as not less of the essence of the melody than the actual written notes—which, so far as it was the case, is the best proof that the melodies had no true essence or coherence, and were a mere series of pegs for vocal gymnastics.

I must again guard against a misconception. The individuality is not necessarily at all of emotional and æsthetic character; but just as a hundred faces may all be quite uninteresting to us, while yet each of them is clearly perceived as a separate individual, so any tune, even a dull one, is apprehended as a clearly distinguishable form; identical, it may be, in certain of its parts with another tune, as one man might exactly resemble another in certain features, but individual in the sense that, after being once known, it is recognised again as itself and nothing else; and that if an intelligible change is made in it, such a change is instinctively perceived in relation to the whole; somewhat as a new nose on a man would make for us not so much a new nose as a new face, the change in either case being noticed not in detail, but in connection with the *ensemble*.

§ 5. And special importance of these as complete and semi-complete parts in any larger musical whole;　It must be especially observed what different things are involved in the entire interdependence of effect in the component units of a melodic whole, and in the fact which we noticed about buildings—that their parts are exceptionally subordinate to the whole, or to very large aspects of the whole, and that it is these large aspects which make up the most prominent effects of Architecture. If there is any liability to confusion here, it can only be traced to that old confusion as to what there is in Architecture which can be thought to represent a musical subject or melody; and the point will further show the futility of any attempt at such an analogy. For in Architecture the whole to which the parts were spoken of as conspiring with such marked effect was really the *whole work*, or a very large proportion of it, the eye being easily able to sweep round and embrace the larger aspects of a building and a multitude of its larger elements in their relation to one another. But the whole which the note-units make up—the only sort of musical whole which we have as yet considered—is a *melodic form*; and a melodic form is probably only a small fraction in point of size of any long whole into which it enters. No technical knowledge of musical structure is needed to realise that a musical movement, if it exceeds a certain length from beginning to end, is naturally divided into smaller lengths, with some sort, at any rate, of beginning and end and coherence of their own; that music runs down, or partially runs down, at certain places. We must defer the more detailed consideration of the varying looseness and closeness of sequence in larger and smaller segments, and of the frequent impossibility of marking a distinction between what shall be considered forms and what shall be considered parts of forms. It is enough here to realise in a general way that the amount which the musical apprehension will perceive and grasp under the most cogent aspect of unity, as having internal necessities of structure of the strictest sort, is limited in length; and though a close artistic coherence may pervade and bind together the several successive segments of form, so that, when the movement is familiar to us, one of them may seem truly to necessitate the next, yet, in proportion as the segments have their own unity, is it hard to recognise this larger order as at all parallel in kind to the order which dominates the note-units of the segments themselves, of the actual melodic forms. We shall find later that there are conditions in musical structure which cause one to shade into the other : but, broadly speaking, the closer order takes effect in the strictest organic evolution of a form out of mere sense-material, each unit of which in isolation is a nonentity; the laxer order of a longer movement is a series of parts which, whatever interdependence they may subsequently prove to possess, are anything but nonentities. Some of them may even be actually complete in themselves; while others, which are not thus rounded off and separable, may still often arrest the ear and haunt the memory in a detached and fragmentary condition. And, however organic the whole result may appear when fully known, the parts may here be said, in the truest sense, to be more important and primary than the whole ; for the whole being a combination of parts successively (and many of them to a great extent independently) enjoyed, can only be impressive so far as the parts are impressive; and the impressiveness can only be perceived by focussing the attention on each of the parts in turn, and cannot be summed up in rapid comprehensive glances. It would be unadvisable here, while we are engaged only with certain of the most general characteristics of melodic forms, to attempt to state or guard the above positions with anything like completeness : as regards general character I hope they have been made sufficiently clear.

*the parts being here in a true sense more important than the whole.*

One more feature of musical structure, comprehensible apart from technical details, may be mentioned as quite unique; namely, the existence and use of what are called *subjects*. These are leading musical phrases or sentences which recur, either simply or with changes, giving to a whole long movement a backbone and coherence which a mere string of quite unrelated paragraphs would lack. We find them treated in a great variety of ways—amplified, and subdivided, and inverted, and interwoven, and so on—and each mode of treatment in turn may give a basis to whole new members of the structure. This sort of recurrence with variations is practically confined to the arts of the ear. Such recurrence with differences as we may find in Architecture, if it is in parts seen *simultaneously*, is a matter of harmony and proportion which has no relation to the phenomenon of musical recognition : when it exists in subordinate elements which are examined *successively*, the differences are usually rather of small detail and ornament than of dominant form, abstract visual forms having too little individuality for one to recall another by being obviously a fragment or modification of it. The refrains of Poetry present a sort of analogy, but these are of course only occasional, and confined for the most

*§ 6. Uniqueness of musical subjects.*

part to short and simple productions; whereas the use of 'subjects' in music is a perpetual feature, and becomes most prominent in large and complex pieces, to which it is the great means of imparting organic unity.

This use of 'subjects' may perhaps seem somewhat hard to reconcile with what has just been said about the prime importance and frequent independence or semi-independence of parts in a larger whole. But, though it is true that, when a 'subject' is variously treated and developed, the enjoyment of the resulting members of the composition involves the recognition of the 'subject,' and is to this extent dependent on what has gone before, this sort of retrospective and serial relationship is clearly something different from the conspiring of mutually controlled parts to a single large effect. While our knowledge of the 'subject' enters essentially into our appreciation of the various uses made of it, at each fresh use our hearing is concentrated on the special bit of form then and there passing: and the relationship implied in recognition of our old acquaintance under a new aspect, though of the closest sort, is still between *two* parts (or, if two previous subjects be intertwined and developed together, between three parts), not between a whole multitude of parts, as in an elaborate building.

§ 7. In Music the remarkable effects are individual, not general.

If we turn now from these more objective facts of melodic structures to their effect on ourselves and our ways of regarding them, we shall find, while still confining our review to the most general characteristics, that the contrast with the facts of Architecture is quite as marked. It follows —partly from the extreme freedom and individuality of single melodic forms, partly from the fact that, as they are successive, we must be mainly occupied with one at a time—that musical effects are rather individual than general. In Architecture we found the opposite characteristics connected with the opposite result. Since the subordinate elements in buildings are necessarily limited in variety, and many of them recur in one building after another, we found, first, that it was rather to large combinations of these, to comprehensive aspects of a whole work, that we must look, as a rule, for striking individuality of effect; and next, that though sublime invention might thus appear, the art was too much bound up with unchanging external necessities and conditions, for genius to be perpetually finding vent in combinations which could be vividly felt as original and unlooked-for utterances; and that many beautiful presentations were recognised and welcomed as very like many of their fellows, and as belonging to a familiar type. In Music, on the contrary, the single pieces of formed structure are *un*limited in variety, and the shortest motive may produce a strong effect on us,[1] and stand out as a

---

[1] When I say *us*, I mean—may be in some special way impressive to some human being or beings. Such motives are happily common enough, but a multitude of tunes and pieces may be felt and spoken of as *just alike*, as streets or people may be spoken of as

spontaneous and individual utterance; while there are *no* necessities and conditions external to the essential nature of the art itself, whose forms in their free progress know no control save

Duty

To the law of their own beauty.

It is easy to see how the individuality of musical effects is related to the fact that musical forms present themselves one at a time, that the parts do not conspire to a single effect, but have their own special independence and unity. For parts must clearly be more numerous than wholes; so that the individuality of parts in larger wholes entails further a corresponding *multiplicity* of individual effects. It was not till the architect's plan was complete, till the last tier of Giotto's campanile crowned his work, that a result was assured whose individuality of beauty would cause it to be recognised as one of the exceptional buildings of the world. It was only after the conception had received its fullest due, and the vast and complex organism its perfect development, that the certainty arose of an effect on human emotion comparable to that which was born when the opening bars of the *allegretto* in Beethoven's Seventh Symphony had been played for the first time, and the idea of them was from that moment alive and abroad in the world. Nor of course need the musical forms be parts of larger wholes at all: they can not only be noticed and remembered on their own account, but they need have no sort of connection with any other forms; and many beautiful tunes of the length of eight or sixteen bars have never led any but an isolated existence.

It will be remembered that one of the considerations which led us to our view that architectural effects were, as a rule, rather general than individual, was that of the very habitual reference to structural types. It will not surprise us, then, that here again Music presents a marked contrast to the visual phenomena we have considered. Musical pieces may of course be classed under various heads, with reference either to the instrument or instruments they are written for, as a song or a string

§ 8. Reference to types is of an external and unessential kind.

just alike, where it is commonly implied that they have been regarded with comparative indifference, either through commonplaceness and poverty in themselves or want of appropriate faculties in the observer. I say commonly, not universally, implied, and the restriction is necessary. Streets and faces, even when they make no deep impression on us, are not necessarily mean and uninteresting, and may be even pleasing; and similarly, most of us will recognise the experience of listening to musical pieces with considerable pleasure, but with a sense at the same time that the æsthetic impression is on a par with what has been produced in us by fifty other equally meritorious and delightful pieces of the same kind, none of which have we sought to recall or in any way made our own. The larger class of march- and dance-melodies is rich in specimens which, without creating pre-eminent or individual impressions, are often listened to with passing pleasure. Nor am I saying that such experiences are not valuable and important; only that they are not what I am at present concerned with.

quartett, or with reference to certain general characteristics of arrangement of parts, as a rondo or an air with variations. But any one of these heads may comprise any number of pieces, each so distinct and individual as never to be thought of in relation to the others. Even in classes of pieces which we find distinctly conforming to a general rule of arrangement, as by division into several large sections connected with each other in certain ways, the kinship so established between the pieces is of the most external and nominal kind: the abstract type has no beauty or meaning for us, no ideal place in our imagination; it is nothing in favour of any piece that the mechanical part of it, its skeleton, so to speak, places it under one head or another. Our interest is in this, that, or the other particular series of beautiful forms which are arranged after this or that convenient and often conventional fashion: and the type itself, though it may have been gradually developed by the instinct of musicians and have proved its excellence as a mode of presenting musical ideas effectively, has so little essential connection with the individual beauty of the forms which it embraces and unites, that its nature and merits could be made tolerably plain to a person who had never in any single case had a clear perception of any one of the essential forms themselves. It may be added that the typical arrangement has been perpetually set at nought and defied by composers who still used the typical names to designate their pieces; and also that a multitude of pieces do not pretend to conform to any type of general structure at all, and ramble at their own sweet will. So that while the types of Egyptian beauties or of handsome Lombard peasants, of Greek temples or Roman basilicas or Elizabethan manor-houses, cannot but call up before us images of certain distinct concrete sets of contours, the type of a sonata or of a rondo represents not distinct concrete forms at all (for these could only occur so far as we recalled particular instances), but only certain abstract conditions for introducing and making the most of such forms.

There may be types of musical structure which have not reference so much to arrangement of sections as to the metre or some other element of structure, as if we speak of the type of a waltz or of a fugue. In such cases the idea is rather less abstract, and the word probably recalls the swing of triple time, or the sequence and winding in and out of parts. But here, too, when we are occupied with an individual presentation, the emotional effect owes nothing to any reference to the type.

The historical associations, again, which inevitably gather round types of buildings, are palpably absent from musical types. When a historical association does exceptionally attach itself to music in such a way as to make some appeal to the imagination, it is in connection with some particular piece of music, not with the class to which that piece may happen to belong. When we hear *Eine feste Burg*, or the *Marseillaise*, we do not feel, Ah! that is a psalm-tune, or, Ah! that is a march, and what delightful and suggestive things psalm-tunes and marches have a habit of being, with a rush of feeling such as we might experience in suddenly encountering a building of some beloved type or period: if we feel any associational interest, we say, 'Ah! that is Luther's psalm-tune,' or, 'Ah! that is the French revolutionary march.'

The element of more individual historical association was not dwelt on in connection with Architecture, as we were regarding only the general characteristics most directly connected with form. It will be enough here to observe that the contrast between the duration and the material of their respective presentations would alone set Music, in this respect, at the opposite pole from the great monumental art. Buildings bridge over the ages; while Music makes only occasional and temporary appearances on the earth, and builds there no permanent habitations or temples; being literally the 'queen of the air.'

§ 9. Lack in Music of historical associations;

But there is another class of association which we noticed as making a large factor in the emotional effect of buildings, and which musical structures lack. The latter bear no evidence of mechanical and material difficulties overcome by human skill, or of patient and multifarious human labour. We may admire the mechanical power of the musical executant; but his talent and practice are altogether unconnected with construction, and the actual forms which they enable him to reveal to us in a vivid manner, would have been there in the world independently of him. As regards the composer, we may of course know, as a matter of fact, that he found such and such difficulties in such and such parts of his work, that particular parts were gradually and laboriously developed and modified, and so on, and such knowledge may add the interest of personal admiration and sympathy to our delight in his work. But as little can any one contend that this chance knowledge makes up an integral factor in the peculiar æsthetic effect of the actual musical forms produced, as he can eliminate from the impressiveness of buildings instinctive suggestions of their makers; of the skill which has enabled frail men to rear on high mighty piles of stone and marble, and of the careful and prolonged manual labour which has gone to the fashioning of every part and detail.

and of vivid association with human labour.

The last two or three points of contrast we have considered connect themselves naturally with a marked difference between the stage of development at which the forms of architecture and of music begin to strike the attention and to be recognised with pleasure. As regards the former, we found that they were only appreciated with anything like discrimination after some experience and culture; that a little child might be awed by the size and gloom of a building, but would not be delighted with its forms. This we referred more especially to two causes; first, to the fact that the component elements of the whole lack striking and independent

§ 10. Early and instinctive appreciation of melodic forms.

interest, that such smaller and single parts as are not distinctly decorative are not impressive objects to the uninitiated eye nor nuclei from which appreciation gradually advanced to larger aspects, but that the admiration begins to a great extent with large and complex views of an immense organism, and in these such individuality as the building presents is chiefly felt ; and secondly to the fact that many of the conceptions involved, as of mass and strength and support, or of historical interest and human labour, are of a somewhat abstract character and are founded on considerable range and variety of association.   But a tune four bars long is an individual : to an undeveloped ear, a mere fragment of a tune is often a sufficient unity with no ulterior necessities : and it is simple snatches of this kind which first appeal to the child, whose powers of comprehension and appreciation spread quite gradually and normally to larger forms.   Children often show pleasure in music before they are three years old ; and at four or five they will very commonly demonstrate that it is not just the *sound* but the actual *form* which pleases them, by pricking up their ears at certain tunes and not others, and very commonly by humming and singing all manner of scraps quite correctly.   These phenomena are too common, even at that early age, to be justly accounted a mark of particular talent ; and a few years later the total absence of them would rank as a decided exception.   This early manifestation of pleasure in melody will prove later to have other much more fundamental grounds ; but it is worth noticing here in connection with the individuality of short tunes, and their effectiveness independently of cultivated perceptions and ideas.

§ 11. So far, no sort of explanation of melodic effect has presented itself.

Our review of the contrasts presented by architectural and musical forms, so far, seems all to the bad as regards getting an explanation of the æsthetic value of the latter.   When we were examining architectural forms, it will be remembered that certain grounds of explanation, insufficient indeed but positive as far as they went, presented themselves, before we arrived at association and the conceptions whose relation to definite external experience and knowledge we were able distinctly to recognise.   But the views which we obtained of melodic forms on this more circumscribed ground seem to yield not so much insufficient grounds of explanation of melodic effect, as no grounds at all.   In the other case we at all events got the elements of multiplicity and richness, and of a sense of mutually controlled rightness in the conspiring lines.   But in the case of melody the ideas of multiplicity and richness, as we have seen, do not apply : and though we found the word *rightness* convenient to express the definite character and position of the component units, and perceived that this also entailed definite individuality in the resulting melodic forms, it is difficult to see that such definiteness and individuality have in themselves any necessary connection with beauty or emotion.   And when we passed on to conceptions which could only have been gained by experience outside the special artistic manifestation, whether in realisation of size and distance as displayed in the aspects of external nature, or of the mental and manual qualities which have brought about the difficult subjugation of matter by man, or of our kinship with past generations of workers, the result was in every case to bring out emotional elements in Architecture which are absent in Music. In buildings we found the effect to be made up of a mass of association of which, even though to a great extent latent, it is not hard to trace the existence, nature, and history : in melody, association is so little perceptible that, for aught we can make out by conscious analysis, the effect on us would be the same if our only experience of sound had been just the music we have heard. So far, therefore, the elements of melodic pleasure seem all to seek.

The search will prove a long one : but one element at any rate meets us at the outset. If any one thing is suggested by any other, *physical movement* is continually suggested by melody. This doubtless looks at first sight as if it might do a good deal in aid of our explanation of melodic pleasure : for physical movement has admittedly agreeable possibilities. There is an attractive air of certainty about it, too, from the very fact that it is a thing which we realise as directly agreeable in our own bodies ; so that the suggestion of it stands on quite a different footing from the highly abstract notions of height and mass and support and number, which are too wholly ideal to have any direct physical effect on us. Those notions have of course been formed in the world of physical experience ; but we now habitually realise the height of a column without consciously thinking of climbing up it, and its weight without any idea of its falling on us or near us, and its supporting power without conceiving the notion of applying our own strength to a similar task. In melody, on the other hand, there is perpetually involved something more even than a suggestion of movement, namely, a direct impulse to move ; which is not only felt but constantly yielded to in varying degrees. We may notice by the way how intimately this fact of direct stimulus is connected with the early appeal of melody to the individual : it is in fact nowhere so conspicuously manifested as in young children, who are not burdened with conventionalities of behaviour or with weight of limb.

§ 12. Suggestion of physical movement.

The amount, however, which enjoyment of bodily movement can be held to contribute on its own account towards an explanation of the effects we associate with melody rather dwindles on examination. That when we are pleased with melody we have an impulse towards movement is clearly no proof that impulses towards movement or movements themselves are any sufficient reason for our being pleased with melody. The inadequacy of such a cause will indeed be palpable if we recall what is implied in the conception of beauty which we so instinctively connect with

But enjoyment connected with the muscular sense will not carry us very far :

melody.  Except in the minute movements of the eye, which in their muscular aspect scarcely ever reach the stage of even being perceived, physical
movement is not a characteristic of the differentiated senses at all, and
*à fortiori* not of the two pre-eminently artistic senses.  We do not conceive
of it as belonging on its own account to the æsthetic region at all, but, so
far as it is in any way pleasant, to that of the simplest and most universal
bodily gratifications, shared by us with the brutes.  Nor, looked at in its
own simple character, does it seem as if either emotional or imaginative
elements could be got out of it.  For, in the first place, the enjoyment

*it is unasso-
ciated with
emotional in-
terest ;*

of it is of a kind specially unconnected with desire, selection, passion, attainment, wonder, or any sort of emotional interest, and specially little
calculated, therefore, to supply the primary emotional factor of any
æsthetic phenomena into which it enters.  Not but that physical elements
of the most pronounced kind, as we shall find further on, may lie at the
root of pleasures wherein they have been modified quite beyond recognition ; but no pleasure could be thus modified into the emotional basis
of a special order of æsthetic presentation, which was physical after a
fashion so restricted and isolated, so utterly out of relation to definite and
desired objects, as this of muscular sensation.  Again, its physical completeness, so to speak, and the entire identification of the pleasure with

*and does not
imply a basis of
impressive con-
ceptions.*

the moment, puts it for imaginative purposes on quite different ground
from those more complicated masses of experience which lend themselves
to ideal transformation.  We have seen that transformed muscular associations are intimately mixed up with the conceptions of size and distance
which we found so important in connection with our admiration of visual
phenomena : but this only warns us carefully to distinguish the part
played by muscular experience in preparing the necessary material for
those abstract conceptions, from any physically pleasurable character which
the movements may occasionally possess on their own account.  However
true it may be that muscular movements have been at the bottom of our
conceptions of size and distance, and that these conceptions often take on
an agreeable imaginative character, yet for such an effect many mental
elements of a subtle kind are indispensable.  We may have formed our
sense of the size of a mountain-side through a multitude of muscular
experiences : but in our peculiar sense of expansion and delight in gazing
up it, we found that we drew, perhaps unconsciously, on mental elements
far beyond representations of crude physical facts.

*§ 13. Ideas
of force and
pace.*

It seems clear, then, that no mental chemistry can produce out of mere
pleasurable muscular experience any such imaginative elements as were
prominent in our enjoyment of height and size.  But it will be noticed
that so far we have been considering physical movement purely in relation
to our own bodies, as a source of direct enjoyment to our own muscular
sense.  We must pass now to another aspect of it, presented in external

things and in our perceived relations to external things : and in connection with this aspect certain general notions *can* be formed, which we shall find are often, though by no means universally, suggested by Music.   These notions may be summed up under the heads of *force* and *pace* : and here at last we seem to get well into the region of external associations, which afforded such help in the case of Architecture.   The power over us of the ideas of force and pace is undoubtedly due to a multitude of past experiences and associations ; either of our own muscular exertions, with the effects they have had on the aspects and conditions of external things, which we have in various ways encountered or opposed or overturned or escaped from or caught, or of external strains and motions, with all their striking and some-times startling or even catastrophic results ; these last, again, having been realised either with a sense of compulsion and violence in our own persons, or more commonly and on a more impressive scale in the vaster natural and artificial phenomena of the outside world, which we have perceived through the intervention of vision, not by direct contact.[1]

It will be remembered how, in the last chapter, we connected the im-pressiveness felt in certain general qualities of many phenomena, such as size, force, and swiftness, with certain characteristics of the two superior senses, and specially dwelt on the point in relation to sight.   We are now on the same ground as regards hearing, and *mutatis mutandis* the same remarks will apply.   As in the former case, the actual conceptions could be to a great extent acquired through tactile and muscular experiences only.   Thus a deaf person could realise the rapidity of the series of im-pressions caused by running a stick along railings ; or again, the extremely quick succession of clicks in some mechanical apparatus where a toothed wheel alternately retains and releases a spring, though normally perceived by the ear, could often be equally well appreciated by the finger.   It may very probably occur to the reader that such things, even when heard, are not particularly impressive ; and indeed it does seem to be the case that mere rapidity, either seen or heard, without a very decided element of force, is comparatively slight in its stimulating effect on the imagination.   This, however, is unimportant : we can easily have a sufficient body of moving tone for the idea of force vividly to present itself.   And now will appear the importance of the suggestion by Music of motion *outside ourselves,* of

Impressiveness of such general conceptions in relation to hearing.

---

[1] The notions of force and pace as com-monly conceived in relation to Music, are probably never so entirely removed from the primary physical experiences which lie at their root as were the notions of height, size, and strength, in visible objects.   For, how-ever far abstraction and transformation may have been carried, experience seems to testify that there is always a distinctly physical element ; that the first effect of the moving sound is an impulse to move, addressed directly to our own muscular sys-tems : and though it certainly flows over and passes on thence without an effort to vaguer and more general suggestions, we can hardly be aroused and interested by any idea of forceful movement, however remotely con-veyed, without some sort of imaginary parti-cipation in it.

motion of the sort that we realise by *seeing* (though probably with some degree of identification of ourselves with it), over and above the sort that we realise by *feeling*. For sound, as we know, does not give us a picture of events, but only leads us to infer they are happening: our true channel for knowledge of the outside world of matter is sight, not hearing. 'We observed, indeed, in the second chapter that the hearing of some mighty sound has an exceptionally strong effect on the nervous system: but so far as it truly excites the *imagination*, it is mainly through the stage of association with the phenomenon and its concomitants and effects as realised by *sight*, as in the case of a torrent or a storm or an express train; even the vaguest sense of awe betraying, as we surmised, the influence of bygone events of an imposing and startling kind in the external world. Now Music would seem to have less direct power of this kind than the sounds, *e.g.*, of thunder or water, since it only accidentally and momentarily contains the slightest suggestion of material things. But Music has the special character of being distinctly *moving* sound: it is not like the *single* burst of a thunder-clap, nor the *continuous* roar of a waterfall, but offers peculiar opportunities for marked changes and contrasts. And in the suggestion of movement, not confined to that experienced in our own bodies although not connected with any distinctly imagined external events, we may readily allow it the benefit of associations, powerful though vague and remote, with those mightier rushes, stresses, and shocks of past experience, for the complete knowledge of which in the first instance vision was indispensable, since direct tactile and muscular experience of them would have been overwhelming to the body rather than the mind.

Nor does it seem hard to imagine, in the case of such impressive general conceptions as Music presents, similar mental elements to those before suggested in relation to the expansive delight in a vast mountain-side; the sense of *contrast* and the sense of *power*. We should expect this similarity, since the rapid ease with which the ear does its work is completely comparable to that which characterises vision. There may be greater difficulty in applying the notions in the case of hearing, owing to the fact that the connection of sound with external facts, and with the tactile and muscular experiences which have a necessary part in the explanation, is indirect instead of direct. Still in any pleasure which is given by rapidity, as perceived by the ear, there certainly seems involved a sense of the facility with which, while sitting at ease, we take in and as it were master a multitude of impressions suggestive of haste, effort, or agitation: and a similar remark applies to the simultaneous grasp of the complicated lines of sound in polyphonic music. As regards more distinctly forceful sound, the sense of power in securely taking in a mass of impression suggestive of external might and effort is, perhaps, rather merged in direct identification of oneself with what is going on: and since, as a rule, no material object or event is in the dimmest way represented (unless it be through conscious subjective fancy), this identification goes to confirm the idea that in the case of strongly moving sound the overflowing of the effects from mere suggestion of muscular movement to the region of impressive general conceptions must carry with it all along a definitely physical element; so that what has been described as suggestion of motion outside ourselves is rather perhaps felt as suggestion of motion beyond our own limited physical possibilities; just as we might imagine flying through the air or overcoming resistances in a manner and at a pace which we have never actually experienced.

So far, then, our explanation seems progressing: for here in Music, as before in Architecture, we seem to have got ideal elements which must have a large share in its impressiveness. But again a more attentive examination brings disappointment. To begin with, there is the fact already adverted to, that these ideal elements are of by no means constant occurrence; a great deal of enjoyable music having no striking character of force or rapidity. But there is a more important point than this; a point which, constituting as it in fact does, the most marked contrast between visual and musical forms, will cause such analogy to Architecture as has so far appeared, in the frequent suggestion by Music of certain impressive general notions, to sink into insignificance. It may have been noticed that throughout the last section the word used was *music*, not *melody*: and the word *force*, in connection with the art of tone, has probably suggested to the reader some vast mass of sound from an orchestra or an organ; a perfectly legitimate application, so long as there is some perceptible movement in the mass, that is, so long as it is not simply continuous, in which case it might be deafening without giving any distinct impression of force. But it will be remembered that in this chapter we are not dealing with vast masses of sound, but with melodic forms presenting one note at a time. Now these can clearly be *rapid*, but can they be *strong*? And, if so, what are the elements of their strength? Can they be strong without being rapid? For force as conceived in the visible world depends on the factor of mass as well as on that of pace: it takes as much force to make a heavy thing go slow as to make a light thing go fast. Now the idea of mass is excluded from single notes produced with any moderate degree of loudness. Thus, as far as physical associations go, no element of force, save rapidity, seems possible to a melody. And yet the unhesitating answer of all who with any care examine the character of some of the melodies they know, will be not only that melodies may give the impression of force, but that they may do so while most moderate and unremarkable in pace; that is, when rapidity and mass are equally absent. And not only may melodies give the impression of force, but the impression of weakness, and that too in a

§ 14. But in relation to Music the idea of force has two applications, which must be carefully distinguished.

But in what way can associations of physical force apply to a mere melodic form?

manner equally unrelated to pace. Here, then, the door of explanation which the notion of physical force seemed to open to us is suddenly shut: in our very first reference to the special qualities of special melodies, we have come across something which is outside the obvious range of associations founded on physical movement. Nor clearly will any other sort of mechanical or dynamical facts help us here. In the world of visible phenomena all our external experience, as derived through touch and movement as well as sight, combines to explain the qualities we detect in forms. Thus in the case of visible objects we found no difficulty in connecting a look of strength or weakness with actual events; weak things cave in, lopsided things topple over, slender things give way: and as we associate ideas of danger and weakness with top-heaviness or abnormal tenuity, so we naturally perceive a strength in solidity and balance. But consider two simple strains of melody each four bars long, one from *Der Freischütz*, the other from *La Favorita*:

to which I will add the opening of a well-known English waltz:

In four bars Weber has carried us into a region where we feel there are forms as serenely and lastingly fair and strong as any temple of our outer world: the flaccid feebleness of the other strains simply irritates us with a sense that we cannot get substance into them or set them right, combined in the case of the waltz with a fear, only too well founded, that we may not for some time be able to get its deplorable existence out of our heads.[1] But what will any physical consideration do for us? What possible connection can the phenomena have with *events*? Thus we see that such a general idea as strength, which was a distinct aid in accounting for the impressiveness of visual phenomena, since there it could be clearly

[1] At this, the first instance in which any particular music has been described in special terms of praise or blame, I had better premise that the general views set forth in this book could for the most part be held perfectly well by a person whose opinions as to particular compositions were the exact opposite of mine. However, writing as a music-loving Englishman for music-loving Englishmen, I cannot pretend that I expect to have to fall back often on this apology.

traced back and connected with various sorts of past experience, becomes in melody one of the things most needing itself to be accounted for.

There is yet another aspect of physical movement which, though not concerned with things external to our own frames, carries us beyond mere sensory experiences. It is specially connected with *degrees of pace.* We have hitherto treated pace as tantamount to rapidity; but there are special characteristics of slowness as well as of quickness of pace, and both have a bearing on Music quite apart from the associational references of the last section. Everybody realises the extent to which mental states react on physical, and how this is most prominently exemplified in the muscular system, and especially in the limbs. States of excitement of various sorts cause an overflow of nervous stimulus which results in rapid and agitated movements: states of dejection or of tranquil meditation are usually accompanied by a relaxation of tension and a collapse of muscular energy. Thus degrees of pace, as far as we connect them with our own bodies, and so far as they deviate noticeably on either side from what is in any case conceived as a sort of normal mean, have a real connection with emotion. An obvious limitation of the effective part due to this element in Music, similar to one we found in the case of force, lies in the fact that a large amount of music is neither quick nor slow; while a large amount which is markedly one or the other has no emotional impressiveness of any sort. Still the point could not be omitted in a list of the more general elements of melodic effect.

§ 15. Relation of pace to various frames of mind.

To revert for a moment from these ideal and emotional regions, which so far seem only fraught with new difficulties, to movement in its more restrictedly physical aspect; there is one noticeable character it may take on, which, though by no means peculiar to it, is in its case especially prominent. It may be *rhythmical*; that is, it may present sensations at regular intervals of time: and in this is involved a perfectly new element of gratification. The more complete discussion of rhythm will be best deferred till we come to the detailed examination of melodic structure: at present it is enough to notice that we possess the appreciation of it in connection both with sight and hearing and with the tactile and muscular senses. These last assume in this respect, as before in the aid they lent towards the formation of general conceptions, a sort of importance superior to that of the slow-acting senses of taste and smell, with their purely sensuous and self-complete impressions; not superior, of course, in the amount of pleasure conveyed by the senses themselves, for as a rule the smell of a rose would give greater pleasure for the moment than beating time without music, or than mere rhythmical touches on the surface of the body; but superior in that the *multiplication* of the channels by which rhythm is perceived must enhance those æsthetic presentations of it which concern one or other of the two higher senses. The pleasure in rhythm

§ 16. Rhythm; in the appreciation of which there is a general consensus of the organism.

of the simplest kind, such as is sometimes experienced in tapping the table with perfectly regular up and down movements of the hand, or in swinging a foot to and fro, can hardly be said in itself to rise above the simply sensuous and unsuggestive stage; nor when this utter uniformity is varied and the movement is broken up into little regular groups, as again is frequently done in tapping the table, does the element of form, though it is certainly involved in the recognisable combinations of impressions, awaken any ideal or emotional interest. But for all that, any one who watches himself or other people as they listen to Music will perceive that the pleasure is often enhanced by the actual rhythmical movements, by the actual series of tactual and muscular sensations, which accompany the sounds; and the implied concurrence of large tracts of the nervous organism is not a matter merely of the moment, but must have tended through long ages to increase the mass and strength of the sensations involved, and to intensify the effect of rhythmical sound even where the rhythmic stimulus does not go so far as to excite visible movements.

§ 17. Total inadequacy of all the elements hitherto mentioned to explain melodic effect.

But after all, when we review such general elements of the effect of melodic forms as have presented themselves, their inadequacy in the way of explanation is almost ludicrous. It is only in the more distinctly physical characteristics, the elements of movement and rhythm, that we seem to have found any point which was absent in visual phenomena; while Architecture, on the other hand, presented many sources of effect apparently quite unshared by melody. And the degree to which rhythmical movement in itself will account for melody is fairly enough measured by the difference between our sensations if a beautiful tune is tapped to us on a table by a person who knows it, but who by such means can of course merely reproduce the rhythmic element of it, and our pleasure in realising it in its complete form. And yet melody is a thing which is every day giving varying degrees of pleasure of a most positive kind to thousands and thousands of people of every conceivable variety of class, character, habits, and mental and physical constitution; a pleasure, moreover, which is capable of seeming to many of these by far the most intense and perfect that they can attain through art.

The problem is but little realised.

The very extent of the phenomenon, the very fact that from babyhood we have enjoyed and seen others enjoy tunes as if it were the most natural thing in the world, prevents perhaps ninety-nine per cent. even of the more intelligent of those who so enjoy from noticing the extraordinary disproportion between the pleasure given and the amount of cause they can show for it. Much careful analysis of feeling it would of course be absurd to look for; but when an ordinarily intelligent person of not too philosophical habit of mind is asked why he admires a beautiful face or a beautiful building, he will certainly give some true reasons. He will say of the face that it looks strong, or refined, or kind, that the chiselling is firm and clear, the eyes bright, the mouth and chin free from coarseness and sensuality, the expression animated or kindly, and so on ; and he will very probably realise some of the associational grounds on which a liking for such qualities to a great extent depends. About the building he will probably say less, and the remoter psychological grounds for his pleasure in it may never have occurred to him ; but he will at any rate point to its size and height, its richness of decoration, its rows of stately columns, its look of mellow age, its picturesque irregularities, its history, and so on. But catch the same person whistling a tune of Mozart's with obvious gusto, and ask him why he likes it. Because it is sweet, he will say, or because it is beautiful, and will probably think you a fool for your question : if it is sweet and beautiful, why should he not like it ? it is an ultimate fact, a matter of agreeable stimulation of his auditory nerves ; you might as well ask him why he likes sugar. And yet, without troubling our un-philosophical friend with words like *form*, or with any abstract considerations, we can prove to him from his own experience that the problem presented by melody must be a very different one from that presented by sugar. We can recall to him the fact that he gets scarcely a vestige of pleasure out of sugar by merely thinking about it ; whereas numbers of people, including very likely himself, can get the quintessence of the pleasure of a tune by going over it in their heads quite apart from physical stimulus. And considering the immensely large ideal or emotional element thus left unaccounted for, it is surely odd how little curiosity it excites. People speak of the 'mysterious effects of Music,' much as they might speak of moonlight, meaning that the feelings roused have a mysterious tinge, that we feel transported by them into a new and unimagined world, and so on. But facts may be mysterious as well as feelings : and in the case of Music, it is not to the character of the effects, but to their existence, that the greatest mystery really attaches : how come there to be any particular effects at all ?

The very form of the question suggests that we should go back as far as possible to the origin of musical phenomena : association is the *deus ex machinâ* of too many psychological problems, and may be invoked from too remote a past, for us soon to despair of its aid. It may perhaps be thought that the better course would have been to take the phenomena of musical emotion as they are and as we know them, and to subject these first of all to as searching an analysis as possible. And truly of the two questions, how a thing came to be there, and what it is now it is there, the former can hardly but seem of very subordinate importance. My reason for attacking it first in this case is that to do otherwise would land us at once among the widest possible diversities of opinion, and the most conflicting records of experience ; that in spite of the general agreement in indifference as to the primary secret of Music's impressing us, there is a chronic con-

§ 18. Further arrangement of the subject.

troversy as to what the actual impressions are, and what they ought to be, and what relation they hold to other experience, and what are the signs and conditions of receiving them aright. It is hoped that by beginning at the beginning some light may be shed on this confusion; in what way could only be here indicated by anticipating the course of the argument.

Plan of the next four chapters. The immediate enquiry divides naturally into two main questions : in what new manner, by searching further back, can we connect the great principle of association with Music ? and in what does the special mental process consist, of the sort which was so hard to establish in the case of visual forms, but to the prominence of which, in the appreciation of Music, I then particularly adverted ? The subject of association can be entirely comprised in the next chapter. But the consideration of the special process, of the exercise of the special *musical faculty*, will necessitate for its comprehension a careful scrutiny of the structure of melodic forms; and even after that, such is the uniqueness of this peculiar faculty, that our comprehension of it will greatly consist in carefully making out what it is *not*, and so removing some very general misconceptions with regard to it. This will necessitate an enquiry into the relations between the æsthetic faculties and Reason; elements which, however much and however constantly combined in the appreciation of Art, will need to be carefully distinguished. By that enquiry I shall hope clearly to establish both the place and function of the musical faculty, and to explain its obscurity—to show, that is, why its action cannot be definitely described and illustrated nor its judgments accounted for; while, as a set-off against so disappointing a result, it may be claimed that the case of Music will afford an exceptionally good means of estimating the general question as to the relations of Reason to Beauty.

In pursuing the plan I have sketched, we shall make sure first of the more general ground, of the facts and processes which underlie *all* the distinctive pleasure of Music, and defer till afterwards the consideration of such special characteristics, ideal or emotional, as can be rightly or wrongly connected with it in particular instances; and in this way we shall keep clear of the most disputed topics till we have obtained all possible *data* for attacking them.

# CHAPTER VI.

## ASSOCIATION.

ASSOCIATION is a word which is apt to be used with considerable laxity. Thus people often speak of liking a thing from *old association*, when all that they really mean is *habit*; the thing is liked through having been long familiar, not through having been connected with something pleasant and different from itself. Association, strictly speaking, must clearly be of two or more distinct things, whether objects or feelings; and though it is perhaps possible to defend the laxer use by saying that we can make two things by separating the pleasure a thing has given from the thing itself, and so speak of associating the present object with the past pleasures it has yielded, the distinction should still be noted. The laxer association of habit in each case concerns one thing, or things of one kind; the stricter association concerns things of different kinds.

§ 1. Association and habit not always accurately distinguished.

Conversely, the word *habit* is continually used where the phenomenon is really one of association. Thus people are often said to enjoy some quality of their environment, very commonly its prevailing colour, or some form which has been continually before their eyes, from habit; especially in cases where the quality or form does not seem sufficiently striking, or the æsthetic sensibilities of the *habitué* sufficiently keen, for the enjoyment to admit of more direct explanation. But in such cases, what has really happened is generally that the environment, of whatever sort, has been there as the constant background to a conscious existence which has been in the main agreeable; and in this way the true cause of its being enjoyed is *association*, only the association has been with a whole indefinite succession of very various events and feelings, not with some particular sort of experience. This view of association, as the main source of the pleasurable feeling, seems confirmed by the fact that when the conscious existence of any individual has been on the whole disagreeable, the very environment which is enjoyed by others affects him in the manner corresponding to his melancholy experience. Precise experiments on such points are of course difficult to obtain, and the essential facts hard to isolate. For, in the first place, much both of the agreeable and disagreeable feeling will probably be connected with distinct

§ 2. With regard especially to a certain class of enjoyments, what is taken for habit is really association.

objects, having special associations of their own, and not with any general quality of the sensible environment : and, in the second place, such a general quality in itself is an experience which falls as a continuancy to the lot of comparatively few ; one would perhaps find it best exemplified as regards visual colour in monotonous northern landscape or high mountain scenery, and as regards sound in the neighbourhood of the sea or of running water. But in a minor degree most of us can probably connect vague likings and aversions, for things on which no special attention or feeling has been concentrated, with the general emotional hue of some considerable tract of existence.

That this sort of enjoyment, due actually to diffused association and commonly referred to habit, deserves careful distinction, will be clear if we consider what habit pure and simple really is in relation to sense-enjoyment. Gain of sense-enjoyment by *mere* habit can only mean that the organism has more and more adapted itself to a certain mode of stimulus ; for there is nothing in mere repetition to increase the enjoyment of a sensation, apart from such gradual modification of structure or function as shall entail new and more refined modes of nervous action. The habit here is a mere matter of past history, making the pleasure possible but contributing no elements to it : and to habit of this sort all primary sense-enjoyments might be referred ; though we more naturally restrict the term to cases where a sense has been subjected, within our knowledge, to some peculiar condition or set of conditions. Even in somewhat more advanced cases, as where an individual receives gratification from some familiar *series* of impressions, the habit, which results in expectation of the items of impression in their accustomed connection, does not imply more than extremely simple mental elements. The sort of habit, on the other hand, which is truly associational in nature, involves ideal elements and a large amount of self-consciousness ; for the enjoyment in its case is not merely a faint mental revivifaction of the various events and feelings which have stood out as enjoyable on a background of the general sensuous impression, colour or sound, or whatever it may be, but seems to involve in varying degrees a much more abstract and *recherché* element, a vague suffusive conception of existence as on the whole good. It follows that this latter sort of effect must be a matter of very late and refined development ; for we certainly do not conceive brutes to have any idea of existence as a whole, or any suffusive sense of enjoyment.[1]

This latter sort of habit cannot apply to animals.

---

[1] Animals are, however, sometimes represented as enjoying their general environment through habit which, if it is to account for the enjoyment at all, could only be of this kind. The primary assumption seems to be that if existence were not on the whole enjoyable rather than the reverse, it would cease ; and then enjoyment of the natural environment through habit is brought in to account for the enjoyment of existence in general, which, as we have seen, is just what would be needed to account for it. Even if we admit that the actual predominance of painful over pleasurable sensation would be

In an early stage of development, then, habit and association are entirely distinct; and we can imagine no other sort of association than that of a distinct impression, of whatever sort, with distinct concomitants. And this greatly simplifies speculation as to the dawn of association, and its effect on the development of pleasure; though the doubt usually remains, throughout every region of sensory pleasure into which association enters, as to the amount of the respective parts taken by it and by direct sensation. Thus we might imagine, as a simple case, that enjoyment of the bright colours of berries and fruits might be sensibly increased by association with the satisfaction of finding and eating food; but the sensation of brilliant colour can hardly but have been pleasurable on its own account: or we might connect our own enjoyment of green grass and green trees with the time when the one was the natural couch of our ancestors, and the other their natural shelter; but we cannot doubt that apart from such elements the eye must have been gradually adapted to dwell with ease and satisfaction on this most constant colour of its natural environment.

§ 3. Difficulty of separating the parts taken respectively by sensation and association in early enjoyments.

A large part of early associations with sensory impressions would naturally relate to the phenomena presented by fellow living creatures; and *colour,* so far as it played a part in sexual selection, might obtain thus an additional power of pleasing. *Form,* on the other hand, would stand on very different ground. In the first place, the amount of com-

§ 4. In the visual region association must have been pleasurably concerned chiefly with colour.

a sign of such hopeless want of adaptation to environment as would involve the cessation of existence, the fact that any existence which ceased would cease as a whole does not imply that it is enjoyed as a whole. On the contrary, the pleasures which are ordinary concomitants of advantageous activities are of a quite intermittent and particular kind. And we cannot assume that any *general* sense of pleasure in existence is possible to a creature which has not arrived at high powers of abstraction and self-realisation; for such a sense seems to depend on continuity in the stream of association, which would be impossible in the absence of recognised continuity in the stream of consciousness. If, then, in animals this general sense of enjoyable existence cannot be assumed, so neither can the sort of habit which derives a pleasurable character from that source be called on to account for the supposed enjoyment by animals of any familiar features of their environment. If the present argument be correct, we have no right to suppose that affections not in themselves directly pleasurable could ever become a source of pleasure apart from

high mental development; that habit could ever produce in an animal the enjoyment of some neutral and familiar element of experience. For we have no grounds for making any assumption as to the nature and existence of such enjoyment beyond our own knowledge of it—and that certainly seems to tell us that a familiar and little-noticed experience could not connect itself with a series of more or less agreeable feelings in such a way as to reap by association the benefit of their common quality, unless the series were bound together by a common bond, that of the continuous individual self-consciousness, with its power of taking rapid and highly abstract surveys of the general stream of past existence.

The only fact I am aware of which can be adduced as showing that animals enjoy any general quality of their environment is their occasional assimilation to it in colour, where sexual selection might be supposed to stamp the favourite hues. But even were this ground less uncertain than it obviously is, the objection as to the part played by habit, in rendering enjoyable what would otherwise not be enjoyed, retains its full force.

parison and abstraction which pleasure in form demands seems beyond the power of animals. A dog which can feel varying and sympathetic emotions at the varying expressions of its master's face may indeed appear to have at any rate the rudiments of the necessary faculty; but a vast number of instances must have been noted, and a large set of types must exist in the mind, before the gap is bridged over between an emotion at an expression and a disinterested pleasure in beauty. Still we might assume that size and strength would tell advantageously in the appearance of an animal for purposes of sexual selection, and that to this extent admiration of form might enter, quite apart from any sort of minute discrimination or comparison. Even so, however, the contrast with colour would be obvious. For colour has no operation except on the eye, no relation to external facts except as seen; in its passive appeal to the eye would lie its sole chance of special selection and preservation, and the conditions for that appeal are quite definite : whereas a multitude of relations to all manner of external uses and conditions would rule the preservation and development of the bones and muscles and various structures which take a perpetual active part in the struggle of life ; so that form would present no sort of definite or continuous standard of pleasure-giving quality in relation to a sense ; and in respect of it, till such time as experiences were multiplied and the faculty of minute discrimination active, association would be of a shifting and accidental kind.

§ 5. Origin of vocal manifestations.

But any sort of *visible* superiority, whether of colour or form, would be enjoyed in a passive fashion, with no instantaneous flash or stimulus, and, moreover, would produce no special sensory excitement in the *possessor* of it, but only in the eyes whose admiration he or she courted. So that the effect of sexual association in respect of visual impressions might be expected to be very slight, compared with its power of intensifying the emotion felt in some *active* display of eagerness and rivalry, some outlet of excitement involving strong and instantaneous stimulation in the organisms both of producer and percipient. A mode of such active display is provided in the *voice*: and the fact, noticed by Mr. Darwin, that almost all male animals use their voices more under the influence of sexual emotion than in any other circumstances, leads up naturally to his important theory as to the origin of vocal, and so of musical, phenomena. First, as regards the voice. To any creature which possesses a voice, utterance of sound affords a most natural outlet for nervous discharge under excitement. Mr. Darwin says that 'animals of all kinds which habitually use their voices utter various noises under any strong emotion, as when enraged and preparing to fight; but this may merely be the result of their nervous excitement, which leads to the spasmodic contraction of almost all the muscles of the body, as when a man grinds his teeth and clenches his hands in rage or agony.' Thus the utterance of sounds during the season of sexual excitement is quite in accordance with what we might have expected; and, with reference to the periodical swelling of the throats of stags, at the commencement of the breeding season, Mr. Darwin suggests as probable that the frequent use of the voice under the strong excitement of love, jealousy, and rage, continued during many generations, may at last have produced an inherited effect on the vocal organs of the stag, as well as of other male animals. So that, apart from any pleasurable qualities, we might expect that any voluntary production of striking sound, especially by a single individual, would reap the benefit of the exciting emotions with which in past ages such a mode of manifestation has been perpetually connected.

As regards the effect on the other sex, it may be that the primary use of the voice to the male would be to attract attention, to put himself *en évidence* as much as possible; and to this effect it would especially conduce from the natural effect of loud sound on the organism and from the rarity and individuality of the utterance. But, if the female found the sound pleasurable, it would naturally be turned to account and modified with a view to pleasure; and here we get beyond mere utterance, to the dawn of musical phenomena. Mr. Darwin not only considers that ' musical notes and rhythm' (*i.e.* musical notes and the habit of making rhythmical sounds) 'were first acquired by the male or female progenitors of mankind for the sake of charming the opposite sex,' but even that the requisite power of voice may have been primarily acquired with that view. It will be best to give the theory as far as possible in his own words. ' Although the sounds emitted by animals of all kinds serve many purposes, a strong case can be made out that the vocal organs were primarily used and perfected in relation to the propagation of the species. Insects and some few spiders are the lowest animals which voluntarily produce any sound; and this is generally effected by the aid of beautifully constructed stridulating organs, which are often confined to the males alone. Sounds thus produced consist, I believe in all cases, of the same note repeated rhythmically; and this is sometimes pleasing even to the ears of man. Their chief, and in some cases exclusive, use appears to be either to call or to charm the opposite sex. The sounds produced by fishes are said in some cases to be made only by the males during the breeding season. All the air-breathing vertebrata necessarily possess an apparatus for inhaling and expelling air, with a pipe capable of being closed at one end. Hence when the primeval members of this class were strongly excited, and their muscles violently contracted, purposeless sounds would almost certainly have been produced; and these, if they proved in any way serviceable, might readily have been modified and intensified by the preservation of properly adapted variations. The amphibians are the lowest vertebrates which breathe air; and many of these animals, namely, frogs and toads,

*Mr. Darwin's theory of the origin of musical phenomena. Sounds produced by animals during the season of courtship.*

possess vocal organs which are incessantly used during the breeding season, and which are often more highly developed in the male than in the female. The male alone of the tortoise utters a noise, and this only during the season of love. Male alligators roar or bellow during the same season. Everyone knows how largely birds use their vocal organs as a means of courtship; and some species likewise perform what may be called instrumental music.[1] In the class of mammals, the males of almost all the species use their voices during the breeding season much more than at any other time; and some are absolutely mute except at this season. Both sexes of other species, or the females alone, use their voices as a love-call.' Mr. Darwin quotes Mr. Waterhouse's account of the chromatic scale of the gibbon, *Hylobates agilis*, and Helmholtz's observation of the auditory hairs of crustaceans, which vibrate to particular notes; and refers to the well-known fondness of seals for music. He continues: 'With all these animals, namely, insects, amphibians, and birds, the males of which during the season of courtship incessantly produce musical notes or mere rhythmical sounds, we must believe that the females are able to appreciate them, and are thus excited or charmed; otherwise the incessant efforts of the males and the complex structures often possessed exclusively by them would be useless.'

The musical faculties in man.

After remarking that as neither the enjoyment nor the capacity of producing musical notes are faculties of the least direct use to man in reference to his ordinary habits of life, they must be ranked among the most mysterious with which he is endowed, Mr. Darwin goes on to observe that they are present in men of all races, even the most savage; and suggests that the faculties of producing and appreciating musical notes, similar to those of the before-mentioned gibbon, may have been possessed by our half-human progenitors. He then notices the capacity for musical development which the savage races, notably Hottentots and negroes, possess (it may be added that the very lowest races, the Fuegians, Anda-

---

[1] Mr. Darwin quotes from most careful observers that 'the males of song-birds do not in general search for the female, but, on the contrary, their business in the spring is to perch on some conspicuous spot, breathing out their full and amorous notes, which by instinct the female knows, and repairs to the spot to choose her mate:' and again, that 'the female canary always chooses the best singer, and in a state of nature the female finch selects that male out of a hundred whose note pleases her most.' He remarks on the 'intense degree of rivalry between the males in their singing,' and adds that it is not at all incompatible that birds should sing from emulation as well as for the sake of charming the female; as the two charac- teristics might have been expected to go together, like decoration and pugnacity. He also notices the very interesting fact that bright colours and the power of song often seem to replace each other. The following observation by Mr. W. H. Hudson (in the *Proceedings of the Zoological Society*, June 1876) may be added to the examples in the *Descent of Man:*—'Males and females of many species, in which the sexes are always faithful, sing and scream together in a jubilant manner at intervals during the day. This habit is most marked in the oven-bird (*furnarius*); these stand together facing each other, singing their shrill excited song, all the while beating their outspread wings in time to their notes.'

mans, and Australian aborigines, are remarkable for their love of music); and points out that though this cannot be reckoned a certain proof that some rude form of music existed in semi-human times, since it is possibly only an instance of the very common utilisation for one purpose of organs and instincts acquired and adapted for another, yet in this latter case the possession of some sense of melody has to be assumed ; and such a sense seems to be possessed by many animals, as in marked degree by parrots, which, though not belonging to the main order of singing-birds, can be taught to whistle tunes invented by man. Mr. Darwin then remarks on the power of music to excite emotions of tenderness, love, triumph, and ardour for war, adding that ' these powerful and mingled feelings may well give rise to the sense of sublimity,' and that ' we can concentrate greater intensity of feeling in a single musical note than in pages of writing. Nearly the same emotions, but much weaker and less complex, are probably felt by birds, when the male pours forth his full volume of song, in rivalry with other males, for the sake of captivating the female.' He quotes Mr. Spencer's remark that music ' arouses dormant sentiments of which we had not conceived the possibility and do not know the meaning,' and adds, ' the sensations and ideas excited in us by music, or by the cadences of impassioned oratory, appear, from their vagueness yet depth, like mental reversions to the emotions and thoughts of a long-past age. All these facts,' he continues, ' with respect to music, become to a certain extent intelligible if we may assume that musical tones and rhythm were used by the half-human progenitors of man, during the season of courtship, when animals of all kinds are excited by the strongest passions. In this case, from the deeply laid principle of inherited associations, musical tones would be likely to excite in us, in a vague and indefinite manner, the strong emotions of a long-past age. Bearing in mind that the males of some quadrumanous animals have their vocal organs much more developed than in the females, and that one anthropomorphous species pours forth a whole octave of musical notes and may be said to sing, the suspicion does not appear improbable that the progenitors of man, either the males or females, or both sexes, before they had acquired the power of expressing their mutual love in articulate language, endeavoured to charm each other with musical notes and rhythm. The impassioned orator, bard, or musician, when with his varied tones and cadences he excites the strongest emotions in his hearers, little suspects that he uses the same means by which, at an extremely remote period, his half-human ancestors aroused each other's ardent passions during their mutual courtship and rivalry.'

These ideas may seem at first sight somewhat startling ; but when we realise the extraordinary depth and indescribability of the emotions of music, the very remoteness and far-reachingness of the explanation is in favour of its validity. Till we come to examine the actual phenomena of

§ 6. Remarks on the theory : it goes to the root of the central characteristic of musical emotion ;

musical emotion, I cannot hope to show how admirably Mr. Darwin's theory fits in with them; and how it not only stands alone, among theories as yet suggested, in resting on a broad ground of evidence, but is apparently the only possible one which will the least account for present facts. It must suffice here to mention in the briefest way the prime characteristic of Music, the *alpha* and *omega* of its essential effect: namely, its perpetual production in us of an emotional excitement of a very intense kind, which yet cannot be defined under any known head of emotion. So far as it can be described, it seems like a fusion of strong emotions transfigured into a wholly new experience, whereof if we seek to bring out the separate threads we are hopelessly baulked; for triumph and tenderness, desire and satisfaction, yielding and insistence, may seem to be all there at once, yet without any dubiousness or confusion in the result; or rather elements seem there which we struggle dimly to adumbrate by such words, thus making the experience seem vague only by our own attempt to analyse it, while really the beauty has the unity and individuality pertaining to clear and definite form. Even when the emotion takes on a definable hue, a kinship it may be to laughter or to tears, it still has the character of directing down these special channels a high-pitched excitement having its independent source at the general watershed of unique musical impression. And it is just this characteristic of *fused and indescribable emotion* which seems explicable on Mr. Darwin's view: for a pleasure which was associated with the most exciting passions, would have correspondingly large opportunities not only for increase but for differentiation. As the power of differentiation is a most marked characteristic of *physical* life, in contrast to inanimate existence, so we may conceive that in proportion to the amount of *emotional* life with which an experience has been charged would be its liability to be differentiated and transmuted as the nervous basis of association developed; so that those primary experiences in connection with which the sense of vitality in past ages reached its highest point might prove susceptible, like primary physical organisms, of transformation into something unrecognisably high and remote from their original nature. At any rate, without pressing the physical metaphor, we know from individual observation how easily the recurrence of one element of an exciting experience recalls the intensity and general quality of the excitement, without involving any detailed memory of the concomitants; and the stronger the excitement the stronger the aid which inherited association would lend. And considering the strength of the passions involved in the present case, and the enormous period of time which we may allow for the supposed effects, we need scarcely doubt the power of Music to have become sublimated, as it were, out of the coarse definite passions and excitements, love, hope, emulation, hostile ardour, triumph, present during its early stages, and so ' to tell us of things we have not seen and shall not see.' From its employment ' during the season of courtship, when animals of all kinds are excited by the strongest passions,' what was primarily a simple ultimate pleasure which the organism was adapted to receive, might well become in time capable of opening the floodgates to mighty emotions, which, by the very extent to which they baffle analysis, might lead us to suspect their connection with the earliest and most universal of instincts.

Whether or not the theory commends itself on its own merits, there is no reason why it should seem derogatory to the art whose effect it would in some measure explain: for at any rate the differentiation in question is so complete that transcendentalists can easily afford to ignore the early steps of it. Surely, whatever Music is, they have only to suppose certain historical conditions and processes to be as necessarily the antecedents to our apprehension of it as the formation of a sense of space to our apprehension of geometry; and that, constituted as our race is, the manifestation to it in one case of æsthetic, as in the other of abstract, truth may have been possible only through the ὕλη of various and comparatively insignificant experiences. Those who believe in the expression of spirit through matter need find no difficulty in the sublimation of a spiritual language out of unspiritual associations. <sub>and cannot reasonably be considered derogatory to Music.</sub>

But fascinating as this theory is, it is necessary to mark at the very outset exactly what it is we want it to do for us, and exactly what is involved if we are to consider that it does it. We do not particularly need association to explain the vaguely pleasurable effect which may be produced by a mere sequence of musical sounds : that might be sufficiently accounted for by the direct effect of musical sound on the nerves, combined with a sense of movement in its changing progress. What we want explained is the indescribable and infinitely deeper emotional effect of certain ordered successions of sounds, perceived as ordered; and the theory comes to our aid by showing that in a primeval stage of existence successions of sound, containing presumably some rudimentary germ of order, were accompanied by emotions capable of transmutation into those we now experience. But then comes the fact that many ordered successions of sound yield us *no* such emotions. However individual tastes may differ, any one to whom Music is something more than mere vaguely pleasing sound, any one who distinguishes the various forms it presents to the ear, will recognise that he receives the indescribable and delightful emotion from some melodies, while he hears others with indifference, or it may be with positive dislike; which latter sort nevertheless are quite perspicuous to him, and as easily realised and recollected as the former. This fact must be faced, if we are to claim the right of invoking the associational element when we want it. <sub>§ 7. Mode in which the theory must be applied.</sub>

Admitting that, if all melody moved us in the same strong and mysterious way, the theory might seem to afford a tolerably satisfactory account of the effect, it certainly will not of itself explain the limits of its own application—in other words, explain the difference between what a person considers a *good* and what he considers a *bad* melody—and the fact that the one gives him extreme emotional pleasure, and the other none at all. For this difference must be bound up with *individual form*, though entailing, as will shortly appear, a complexity of proportion unparalleled in any other region of phenomena, and quite beyond the reach of conscious analysis. And it is impossible to suppose that of two modern melodies, each of which involves this singular complexity, one more than the other resembles any primitive succession of sounds: we might as well say that a beautiful person's expression reminds us more of an ascidian than a plain person's. Why, then, should one melody reap the benefit of primeval associations more than the other ? What is it which limits and supplements the effect of that element ? The answer is, that we must consider the physical and

**The door is opened to the associational element by the exercise of a faculty which is independent of it.** mental *process*, not any stereotyped successions of sounds, as at the root both of the primitive associations and of their present transformed and differentiated emotional result: that there is this fundamental distinction between the relation of association to enjoyment of form in the visible and in the auditory regions, that in the former it is prominently connected with *special forms* (notably, *e.g.*, with the contours of faces or figures), while in the latter it is connected with a *special mode of exercise*.[1] The melodic satisfaction of our semi-human or savage ancestors depended on some embryonic proportional and rhythmical element not extending, perhaps, beyond a few short and familiar recurrences; but I believe that in the hidden and unique processes by which the modern lover of music realises a melodic form, we have merely an infinitely elaborated and complex development of the same proportional sense. The startling difference may not seem greater than some which have been indubitably worked by evolution in other mental and moral operations: and it may appear quite legitimate to connect the present effect of the associations with the exercise of a faculty which, at the time the associations were formed, must have been in the most embryonic stage.

**Difficulty in this conception.** But the difficulty must not be blinked. If it were just in connection with the *exercise* that the associations were to be supposed to work, the idea would present nothing very exceptional: but the *exercise* is involved in the apprehension of the disagreeable as much as of the

---

[1] We have observed to what a comparatively late date the power of distinct enjoyment of *visual* form (apart from colour) must be referred; as late indeed in the case of *abstract* form as times of really high human development—whereas, there being a germ of form even in a series of rhythmical taps, the enjoyment of *auditory* form in embryo must be referred back to an incalculable distance, and had as great a priority in the evolution of the race as it so perpetually has in the case of individual human infants.

agreeable tune; we want to draw on the associational element only for the effects of *particular cases* of the exercise; while we have no way of discovering or characterising the *right* cases (right, that is, relatively to the musical faculty of the particular hearer), except through the very qualities with which the associational element informs them. So that the line of psychological facts with which the associational element must be supposed to have remained actually or potentially united is exceptionally recondite in nature and history. I seem driven to imagine that I find the legitimate linear descendant of perfectly rudimentary musical processes in the mental action by which I apprehend a melody of Beethoven, but not in the mental action by which I apprehend a melody of Claribel. Moreover, if the independent musical faculty [1] opens the door to the flood of associational emotion according to the amount of satisfactory quality it finds in what is presented to it, the ratio of the two elements becomes very hard to determine: we are left to conjecture how much that satisfactory quality would amount to on its own account, if there were no associational emotion to open the door to. Still, in spite of obscurities, I cannot but fall back on the emotional facts which are absolutely certain, and for the explanation of which the aid of the most profound and far-reaching associations seems to me indispensable. So I must assume that if the associations from the various passions were formed of old in connection with the *satisfactory* exercise of a rudimentary faculty, so with the developed faculty it can only be when the mind is *satisfied* by its hidden co-ordinative exercise (not where the proportions are either in some way defective or beyond the hearer's grasp), that the deep emotions, distilled from these passions through ages of inherited association, can be evoked. The special experience is bound up with an act or process belonging to the domain of a unique faculty, and of extremely variable nature: whence it is that to this day an Asiatic may enjoy a

---

[1] I must call special attention to the sense in which (for want of any other term) I am compelled to use the words *musical faculty*. The words of course are often used of *inventive* power, or some special sort of musical gift; a meaning entirely distinct from that we are now concerned with, which is limited to the ordinary power of perceiving and recognising tunes, of apprehending a melodic form as a whole by co-ordination of its parts. Now most of us go through life recognising the existence of such a faculty, and vaguely supposing that somehow or other its exercise is independently enjoyable and able to produce emotion, so that it does not occur to us to separate the exercise from the enjoyment: it is only after careful consideration that we perceive how inadequate any sort of perception of abstract form must be to account for the extraordinarily deep and passionate emotions of music, and so are led to refer for those effects to the most deeply seated elements of inherited association. But this reference clearly implies in the emotional experience, unanalysable as it appears, a *double* psychological process: and the difficulty is to realise that in this double process the musical faculty has its own particular part, and admits of all degrees of satisfactory exercise, from the most rudimentary to the most complicated, while at the same time that exercise, wherever it is truly satisfactory, by that very fact loses its separate existence in emotion drawn from the other source.

succession of notes which is hideous to a European, or (to take a case which cannot be referred to difference of scale-system) one European may enjoy a succession of notes which is trivial or annoying to another European.

A rough analogy may be found in the pleasure of watching the movements of an active and beautiful human form. Here, too, we may imagine for ages a rudimentary pleasure in mere symmetry of parts, and ease of line, so that, apart from any association, to look at a body with two arms would be pleasanter than to look at a body with one, and the smoothness of muscles or of flowing movements would be preferred to the angularity of bones or of jerky movements : still the pleasure we feel certainly has a great part of its roots in association which dates back to the primeval woods, and the days when bodily strength and activity were prime factors in the struggle for existence. And here again we, with our infinitely developed feeling for form, find the door unlocked to the strong emotions dependent on such association only in cases where our abstract sense of symmetry and proportion is satisfied : a very slight deviation from symmetry in the human form will so annoy us, as seemingly to close the channel of emotion ; and we derive no æsthetic pleasure from the gambols of a strong but clumsy creature, such as an elephant. The roughness of this comparison lies in the fact, already sufficiently emphasised, that the connection between proportions and physical properties and events is in the visual region so close and constant as to make the presence and effect of a strictly abstract element hard to fix and measure ; while this very connection affords frequent grounds for discussing the merits of visual proportions, which are lacking to the entirely and exclusively abstract proportions of Music.

I may add that in assuming the original existence of some amount of rudimentary musical faculty, independent of the intensification and differentiation of the emotions by the means suggested, we are completely borne out by Mr. Darwin himself; who does not profess to explain *how* or *why* the opposite sex was charmed, only how, *if* the appreciation existed to some extent, it might be gradually modified and enhanced. We may make some attempt, when we investigate the elements of melodic form in the next chapter, to conjecture in what the primary satisfaction can have consisted : here I only wish to insist on the fact that, if it was the necessary starting point for association *then*, its highly-developed descendant is the necessary condition *now*, for the emotions which association has bred—in other words, that the association-theory will do much to explain why melody *is* beautiful and emotional, but not why it so often is *not*; and that if that difference depends on the working of a special faculty, it can only be to the working of the same faculty in a rudimentary stage that we can refer the rudimentary satisfaction which lent itself to such startling emotional development.

There is another set of associations, the connection of which with musical phenomena is of great, though altogether secondary, importance. In anything which powerfully affects the organism through a particular channel, there will naturally be an ingredient of unconscious reference to other impressions received through the same channel; so that in certain qualities of musical effect we should expect to find a connection with qualities presented by other phenomena of sound. I need not further dwell on the very obvious occurrence both in Music and in Nature of special effects, due to overwhelming mass, or to startling suddenness, of sound; it has been already pointed out that such effects in Nature owe their power greatly to the rarity of impressive sound; and the same fact is exemplified in Music, which wearies instead of impressing us, if it is too lavish of its *fortissimos*. But we are at present concerned not with masses or sudden bursts of sound, but with melody, or successions of single sounds: and there is one and only one phenomenon which exhibits here the slightest parallelism, namely, *speech*.

§ 8. Association with other phenomena of sound;

The connection of speech with melody is only of the most general kind: apart from Mr. Darwin's theory, that the use of the voice for purposes of pleasure preceded its use as a means of communication, we shall find, when we come to investigate the nature of melodic forms and the nature of melodic emotions, how every argument based either on structure or on feeling confutes the idea of special relationships between the actual progressions of sounds in the two cases.[1] But the *general* bearing of speech on melody is none the less important; to it is due the vivid effect, which a fine melody produces, of being *something said*—a real *utterance* of transcendent significance. So prominent is this characteristic, that the instinct to project some sort of personality behind melodic strains seems absolutely irresistible. *Expressive* and *significant* are doubtless words which may be fairly called in question when the ideas and emotions conveyed have no assignable existence external to the phenomena so designated: however *im*pressive a phenomenon may be, it may be said, we have no right to call it *ex*pressive, unless we can say what it expresses; and to say what Music expresses except in music is essentially impossible. I admit the justice of this argument, and own that the complete fusion and transmutation of definable emotions in the most characteristic excitement of Music leaves us without any clear defence against it—except, indeed, by the adoption of transcendental formulæ, which after all do not deal with the peculiar facts of Music in relation to expression. Schopenhauer, for instance, considered Music an immediate objectification or *expression* of that cosmical will which he supposed to underlie phenomenal existence. But this has nothing to do with expression in the common and literal sense of *telling*— of *utterance*; and the fact that I seem to myself to use that word in a

and especially with speech, the bearing of which on Music, though of a very general sort, has exceptional importance.

[1] This subject will be treated in full in the chapters on *Song* and on the *Speech-theory*.

literal and not a metaphorical sense in respect of melody, is an instinct which I cannot get behind, and which can only be entirely realised by those who share it. A splendid melodic phrase seems continually not like an object of sense, but like an *affirmation*; not so much prompting admiring ejaculation as compelling passionate assent. The delusion, if delusion it be, seems quite explicable by the general association with speech; and as it certainly has a large share in the intensity and directness of melodic effects, the use of the terms *expressiveness* and *significance*, as opposed to meaninglessness and triviality, may be allowed, without the implication of any reference to transcendental views which one may fail to understand, or theories of interpretation which one may entirely repudiate.

We shall find later that there are other modes, besides this most general one of all, in which the phenomena of Music owe something to speech, though all are extremely general. For instance, features of pace, such as hurry or solemnity, are so markedly characteristic of emotional speech, that the corresponding features in Music will naturally owe something of their quality to the more familiar experience. Again, a certain pleasure in musical response, as in an alternation of phrases, perhaps sustained by two instruments of different *timbre*, may owe some of the interest with which it is followed, and in many cases a certain air of humour, to experience of ordinary vocal phenomena. And when several instruments are concerned at once, their relations may similarly afford semi-humorous suggestions: the violoncello may suddenly assert itself in the midst with what seems like a pertinent remark; a flute may echo an oboe, and be commented on by a clarionet. This sort of interest, however, the conditions of which may exist in the very poorest music, has clearly no relation to the essential impressiveness of melody with which we are at present concerned.

# CHAPTER VII.

## THE FACTORS OF MELODIC FORM.

MELODIC forms consist of notes in succession: and the succession has two aspects or factors, one of *time* and one of *pitch*, which we will first examine separately. § 1. Two factors of melodic forms.

Strict rhythm in its simplest form may be described as the quality of stimulation due to the production of a sound or movement, or of a small group of sounds or movements, at equal intervals of time. I say *small* group, because the most highly developed sense of rhythm that we know of can take in no more. If the group of sounds or movements to be repeated is too large, it will be impossible to grasp and retain it as a whole, and to expect its recurrence at a particular instant; and so the distinctive sense of rhythm, which depends on continuous satisfaction of expectation, cannot exist. And as the group must be small, so also must be the intervals between its recurrences: the mere repetition of a particular sound or group of sounds, even were it perfectly regular, might convey no strictly rhythmical impression to a human ear; as the interval of time before each recurrence might be too long for the memory accurately to measure, and an expectation can only be founded on accurate measurement. Rhythm.

It is worth noting that the *general* principle lies in getting a thing at the right moment—that is, at the moment it is expected—and that strict rhythm is a *particular case* of this, constituting the most obvious and natural way of fixing what the right moment is to be. It is, indeed, the only imaginable way of fixing the succession of right moments in connection with any wide variety of phenomena; but to creatures interested only in a very small number of experiences, habit might fix the right moment independently of rhythm. Thus very young children never tire of the little games consisting in repetitions of the same form of words—a series, it may be, of quite unmetrical clauses, accompanied by the same gestures, and leading up to a foreseen *finale*, which is received again and again with explosions of delight. And the same principle may perhaps apply to the notes and little subdivisions which make up the strains of birds' songs:

the smallness of the variety in each case seems to show that the mere repetition is agreeable; and, owing to this very smallness of variety in the strains, habit may well give to each element as it comes the cogency of certainty.

§ 2. Difficulty in determining the nervous conditions of the satisfaction in rhythm.

Strict rhythm, however, stimulation at fixed degrees of time, is naturally by far the most universal and important means for satisfaction of this sort. What the nervous conditions of the satisfaction are, it is very hard even to guess. It appears in connection with all the senses which are capable of sudden and rapid action—with sight and touch, as well as with hearing and muscular movement; but the two latter present it in much the most prominent form. Owing to this potential connection with a large proportion of the whole nervous organism, rhythm presented through any one channel has a tendency to excite an impulse towards the same rhythm in other channels; chiefly in those of movement and sound, which are not only its most conspicuous means of gratification, but afford to the individual specially natural and easy modes of self-stimulation.[1] The hearing of an *ir-*regular succession of sounds creates not the slightest affection in any other sense: but let the sounds become regular, and instantly the impulse comes to tap the hand or move the foot concurrently with them. And we cannot doubt that the pleasure of rhythm is due greatly to the wide range of the nervous discharge, and also to the associations of life and expansion which especially collect round the sense of muscular movement. But all this does not touch the peculiarities of nervous stimulation with which the primary gratification is connected. It may be suggested that the very mode of life of a nerve-cell is rhythmic, seeing that in it exhaustion and nutrition, waste and repair, succeed each other in regular order. But this order is only regular in the sense that between two exhaustions repair must intervene: there need be no sort of regularity of intervals; a nerve may be stimulated, exhausted, repaired almost instantaneously, then stimulated again immediately, or after a minute, or after an hour, and will equally respond in all three cases. The utmost this alternating mode of life would explain is the *negative* fact that violent stimulation, even though rhythmically repeated, might fail to give any satisfaction, through inability of the nervous substance to repair itself between the stimuli—as, for instance,

---

[1] The connection of rhythm with higher nervous centres than the special ones of the special senses, indicated by this tendency to discharge into other channels, is further shown by this fact, that a rhythmic character may be perceived in a series of *stimuli*, each unit of which is addressed to a separate sense. A flash of light, a sound, a tap, and a movement of our own, might by repetition be blended into a rhythmic series. Sounds and movements are especially often actually so blended, as we might expect from the generally close connection between the sense of hearing and the motor branches of the nervous organisation: thus in accompanying a regular succession of sounds with movements of hand or foot, it is as common to make the movements come *half-way between* the items of sound as *with* them.

if a *prestissimo* were played close to our ears on the bass drum : it does not touch the conditions of *positive* satisfaction in regularity, and positive dissatisfaction in irregularity, altogether disparate in character from the units of sensation which make up the series.[1]

Whatever be the physiological effect of regularity of stimulation on the nervous system, the resulting satisfaction on the subjective side must be accepted as an ultimate fact, as must the converse annoyance produced from the baulking of expectation by irregularity in stimulations which are sufficiently nearly regular to arrest attention. To us the satisfaction in many cases is extremely slight—so slight that it often does not counter-

§ 3. The satisfaction, though slight and sometimes overbalanced by annoyance, is the rule.

---

[1] In connection with rhythm, the notion of nervous waste and repair (with its suggestion of that dangerous formula ' maximum of stimulation with minimum of fatigue ' which professes to sum up the conditions for pleasurable nervous action) is so far from being explanatory that it presents a most special difficulty. We may certainly imagine in the most general way that a periodic mode of nervous action produces less wear and tear than an irregular mode, and that the failure of the stimulus or impulse to nervous discharge to come at the expected instant may cause the accumulated nervous energy to force a channel for discharge against some sort of friction or resistance, while the regular recurrence of the impulse enables the nerve-substance to discharge its energy with the least resistance, and so with the best chance of rapid repair; somewhat as we are able to impart the maximum of motion to a heavy swinging body with the minimum of resistance or fatigue, by timing the impulses we give to accord with the body's regular period of oscillation. Unfortunately, however, this is just one of the tempting metaphors which fail as soon as they are pressed in detail—for we are seeking for the nervous conditions of satisfaction in rhythm ; and rhythms *of the most various periods*, belonging moreover to stimulations which may widely differ in strength, are felt as having precisely the *same* satisfactory character. Thus the parallelism of the subjective and objective events seems to fail. A hitch or stop in an extremely gentle rhythmic stimulation may produce annoyance far more similar in amount to that produced by a hitch or stop in a far stronger and quicker series than would be warranted by the presumably large difference in amount of nervous wear; while a strong and rapid series (as in swinging the foot) may go on giving an even satisfaction without any of the gradual and increasing discomfort which might be expected, if the opportunity for repair between the nervous discharges were here as small as on proportional grounds it ought to be, and the amount of repair therefore increasingly inadequate. As regards repair after exhaustion, the one condition on which the nerve substance could be in the *same* state of readiness for stimuli of all rates and strengths would be if it could arrive at a state of *complete* repair in a time shorter than the shortest interval; an hypothesis which the fact of continuous satisfaction seems truly to necessitate. But then, on this hypothesis, it becomes hard to imagine how a sense of rhythm could be produced at all, if we are to recognise no other objective conditions for agreeable sensation than *degrees* of stimulation and of repair—for one would naturally suppose that for a succession of stimuli to produce a sense of rhythm, each must occur before the effects of its predecessor have quite disappeared, that is, *before* the condition of complete nervous equilibrium has been re-established ; and on the theory we are discussing, complete equilibrium seems unsusceptible of any other meaning than complete repair. On the whole, considering the sameness of subjective character producible by stimulations so widely differing in all those respects which we can connect with the idea of repair after exhaustion, we seem driven to conceive that some form of variation from equilibrium, or at any rate that certain *modes* of nervous action, over and above mere *degrees* of action and repair, may constitute the line of events which is more immediately connected with the character of the sensation. This subject is further discussed in the Appendix on Discord.

balance the disagreeableness of having something forced on the attention when we want to be quiet or to attend to other things. This especially applies to sound, which we so often hear involuntarily; whereas our muscular movements are within our own control: thus the ticking of a clock is often distinctly worrying. But such exceptions are clearly only apparent: everyone would prefer to have the ticking regular than just *ir*regular; and many lower animals, who are not liable to have their attention distracted from more important things, betray a marked interest in rhythm.

§ 4. Rhythmic movement under the influence of strong feeling.

As regards voluntary rhythmic stimulation, it is well known that strong feeling is apt to vent itself in measured movements: and this has been noticed as remarkable. Thus Mr. Spencer says that 'why the actions excited by strong feeling should tend to become rhythmical is not very obvious.' But if the principle of nervous overflow under excitement be recognised, it does not seem hard to see why the consequent movement should take the form most clearly adapted to enable it to continue easily for some time, especially when this form is productive on its own account of a certain amount of satisfaction. The satisfaction must be recognised as an element in all cases; and Mr. Spencer appears to me to have been misled by the examples he adduces of the swaying of the body to and fro under pain or grief, and of the leg under impatience or agitation—both instances of rhythmical movement under *painful* emotion. I cannot regard these movements as expressive of or as excited by the emotion, except indirectly: they are easily accounted for on the supposition that they cause a slight pleasure and distraction, which acts as a relief to body or mind. The need for some sort of extra nervous discharge which accompanies abnormal nervous excitement, the resulting effect on the muscles, and the consequent diminution of the original tension and the accompanying distress, have been admirably explained by Mr. Spencer himself; and in rhythmical movements the same relief is attained, *plus* the elements of easy continuance and of positive, though faint, pleasure. It may be added that on merely mechanical grounds a movement would often tend to become rhythmical, since a natural momentum may be set up which swingings and swayings, if irregular, would have to contradict. In cases of *pleasurable* excitement, while great strength or suddenness in the feeling may, as in the case of painful excitement, be accompanied by spasmodic and unrhythmical movement, a continuous rhythmic mode of affection is the natural concomitant of a steady and continuous emotional glow: and here it is often easy to pass beyond simply physiological ground, and to connect the phenomenon with mental conceptions—as, for instance, in the association of an idea of dignity with that of restraint, balance, and measure.

§ 5. Distribution of the sense of rhythm in the animal kingdom.

The distribution of the sense of rhythm in the animal kingdom presents difficulties; nor can we say with certainty where it begins, since the lowest animals cannot make voluntary noises. I have already quoted Mr.

Darwin's remarks that 'the perception, if not the enjoyment, of musical cadences and of rhythm, is probably common to all animals,' and that in the case of insects and some spiders the sounds made by the male to charm the female consist of one note repeated rhythmically. Birds may certainly be assumed to possess the sense, as some of them can pipe artificial tunès. Now mammals, if they possess a sense of rhythm, still do not seem to have any special enjoyment of it, as we may conclude from their not voluntarily making rhythmical noises or accompanying movements; for it is only with trouble and by adapting the music to their steps that horses and dancing-bears are made to keep measure; and pairs of horses in harness seem to have no instinct to keep step. It is certainly extremely curious if insects and spiders possess a strong feeling for rhythm in common with man, of which his fellow-mammals are destitute. A possible solution of this difficulty is suggested by the fact that many noises made by the lower animals are *naturally* rhythmical owing to the special way in which they are produced. Thus some insects make noises by rubbing the wing against the thigh, just as a boy runs a stick along a number of railings; when a movement of this kind has reached its termination, the wing is naturally withdrawn and begins again, and thus the sound will recur regularly. The same applies to sounds made by the regular process of inhaling and expelling air; just as with men the sound of moaning might become naturally rhythmical, being made when the air is expelled. We are not therefore compelled to suppose that the rhythm is the element in the spider's performance which is specially attractive to his mate; it may be the mere sound which is primarily agreeable: at the same time it is much more natural to suppose that the rhythm is agreeable, even though undesignedly produced.

The extraordinary specialisation and development of the rhythmical sense in man is a fact very hard to account for, but is doubtless connected with general development of nervous susceptibility, also (though these may be as much effects as causes) with the dawn of the practice of dancing, and with the power of making and handling instruments of percussion; which in themselves are far more suggestive of rhythmic use than the voice, owing to the fact, similar to that just noticed, that a withdrawal of the limb is necessary before a stroke can be repeated, and a to and fro motion is thus naturally set up. The same to and fro or alternate motion is also the natural one in many mechanical employments; and the natural instinct to make the work as easy as possible, through the utmost regularity of movement, would prompt a vocal accompaniment to mark the time, and thus intensify the association between rhythm and easy forceful movement. Thus in Burton's description of the East Africans, we read that 'the fisherman will accompany his paddle, the porter his trudge, and the housewife her

§ 6. Development of the sense in man, and its universal diffusion.

task of rubbing down grain, with song;' and it does not surprise us to
find that such people will sit for long hours at night 'repeating, with a
zest that never flags, the same few notes and the same unmeaning line,'
or that in their dances 'a thousand heels strike the ground simultaneously
like one.' So again we are told of the Chibchas of Central America, a
people who delight in rhythmical performances, and whose 'music and
motions never disagree,' that 'the same measure is kept when they are
dragging wood or stones.' So again the songs sung by the New Zealanders
in their canoes are described as having various measures, adapted for
pulling heavy or for pulling light. The fact of the love of mere rhythm
and repetition among uncivilised peoples seems nearly universal, and reminds one of what has been above remarked about very young children.
The one artificial instrument is often some sort of drum; and even where
a greater variety exists, the drum retains its independent effect. Thus
we read of the Gold Coast negroes, that 'however employed, whether
passing quietly through the street, or carrying water from the pond, or
assisting in some grave procession, no sooner do they hear the rapid beats
of a distant drum than they begin to caper and dance spontaneously.
The bricklayer will throw down his trowel for a minute, the carpenter
leave his bench, the corn-grinder her milling-stone, and the porter his
load, to keep time to the inspiring sound.' Similarly the New Zealanders are described as having a most accurate perception of rhythm; and
'while delightful music falls upon their ears without exciting emotion,
a noisy drum keeping time gives pleasure.'

§ 7. Con-
nection of the
dual basis of
rhythm with
bilateral sym-
metry.

There is, however, one fundamental characteristic of rhythm, especially marked in the superior musical development of man, which may, I
think, be accounted for on grounds which take us back to primeval
times; namely, the characteristic of *dual balance.* As soon as any differentiation at all supervenes on a simple series of equidistant accents, as
soon, that is, as such a series is divided off into parts, felt as having a
beginning and an end, the principle on which these parts are formed is
multiplication by two; thus, to take the simplest case, in tapping a table
or beating some percussive instrument, when an undifferentiated series
like this

 &c.

is at all developed, it becomes something like this :

 &c.

or,

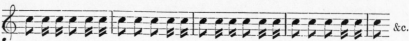 &c.

Melodic form of course involves such distinct and coherent sets of bars; and however simple or however complicated be the arrangements of the notes included in the bars, the number of bars is two or a multiple of two. To put it in another way, any complete melodic phrase stops after two, or four, or six component bars, and so on, but not after one, or three, or five.[1] A component phrase may consist of an uneven number of bars, as three or five; but then it will be answered by another of three or five. Nor must this be understood merely of melodies and subjects which can be reasonably presented alone; it applies to clause after clause in the longest and most elaborate musical paragraphs, bar answering bar, and pair of bars answering pair of bars, though linked into a series from which no independent bits could be detached. I am speaking of course of truly melodic passages; by which I mean not merely what

[1] Even apparent exceptions are rare. No one with an ear will need to be told that a bar of silence (filled up as a rule with accompaniment) may occur at the beginning or end, as well as in the middle, of a melody. For instance, the melody at the opening of Schubert's Sonata in B flat apparently ends at the seventh bar; but the ear would resent the idea of concluding there, or the starting of a new melody or phrase in the eighth bar, which therefore belongs rhythmically to what precedes. The opening subject of the overture to *Le Nozze di Figaro* is seven bars long in a far more uncompromising way:

here the odd thing is that the ear certainly feels at the end of the third bar as if it had had four, in the sense that it demands four more to correspond; and the extraordinary energy and suddenness of the opening phrase gives me, as far as I can analyse the experience, a kind of piquant satisfaction in making the first bar do duty for two, a piquancy which quite disappears if that bar be taken twice over. There are also cases where the same bar acts as a second term with the one preceding, and a first term with the one following, the ear fully comprehending and accepting the change of character. Again, Engel has pointed out that in some national songs one bar or phrase is repeated for emphasis, in which case the extra bar may be regarded as a kind of pause, keeping the ear a moment in suspense. Again, it may of course often happen that the melody extends into seven bars, while only six bars long. Thus the curious Russian theme, taken up by each instrument in turn in the trio to the scherzo of Beethoven's quartett, Op. 59, No. 2, has its first accented note at the beginning of the second bar, and the two notes in the first bar which make a sort of 'base' or 'catch' occur, when the repetition takes place, on the second and third beats of the seventh bar, whose first beat has just brought the tune to a conclusion: so that these two first notes and the last note of the tune account for just one bar between them, and the number of bars in any amount of repetitions of the tune will always be a multiple of six. It seems hardly necessary to notice such cases as where the dominant harmony is continued to the end of, *e.g.*, the eighth bar of a melody, and the actually final note delayed in order that it may coincide with the tonic harmony and the commencement of a fresh phrase on the first beat of the ninth bar.

It is worth noting in this connection, how habitually, in forms which divide themselves naturally into two main segments, if the exact symmetry of response is departed from, it is by the addition of *two* bars, not of one or three. As an instance of the extremely common response of six bars

would be ordinarily called tune or 'subject,' but passages where, however full and important the harmonic element, the main and decided movement is along a *single* line, and where the totally different interest caused by counterpoint, 'repetition,' and sequence, is absent or subordinate; though even in the most involved passages of 'carrying-out' and fugue, where these last elements are predominant, the dual basis will be found again and again reasserting itself.

This characteristic must, I think, have its roots in the simple fact of our being made symmetrically with two sides externally alike, which results in alternate motions with each side. A sense of rhythm is so essentially a sense of movement, that even without the evidence which we have, we could hardly have doubted the intimate connection of Music and dancing in the early stages of art: and as the enjoyment of rhythm must arise to a great extent from its association with the agreeable sense of vitality caused by motion, and especially by locomotion, so I think will the fact that all regular external movement is alternate or double, explain the characteristic of melody which I have mentioned: for naturally a series of alternate movements can only seem complete — so that on repetition of the series, whatever member had begun is ready to begin again—through an equal number of occurrences of each of the alternating actions, right and left, or whatever they may be. Thus if we had three legs and arms, our melodies would be based on the number three. Of course an enormous majority of our conscious actions are *ir*regular, but just on this account they make no impression on the attention or memory; while the experience of regular alternate movement which our ancestors have had, especially in walking and seeing others walk, is surely sufficiently large to account for the importance of the dual element in our sense of rhythm.

in the second segment to four in the first, the glorious melody which opens the slow movement in Beethoven's E flat Concerto might be given. Of the less common response of seven bars to five, the following specimen from the minuet of Haydn's quartett, Op. 76, No. 3, is worth quoting:

In connection with the wide distribution of the sense, and the fact that it is in no way confined to alliance with sound, but is bound up with large tracts of the whole nervous organisation, we may further notice that, whereas the arrangement of notes and intervals in the scale, and so the faculty for apprehending the relations of notes in respect of *pitch*, have proved to admit of many varieties, the fundamental instinct of *rhythm* on the other hand seems one and universal. Thus while such momentous changes as the invention of harmony and the development of the modern scale-system might seem to have revolutionised the very nature of the art, this one element of rhythm is as predominant with us as with the Greeks, and the most beautiful music in the world is written on a rhythmic basis as simple as that employed by the spider during courtship.

§ 8. Universal identity of the fundamental instinct.

But among the senses which take cognisance of rhythm, there is a very wide difference in respect both of keenness of apprehension and of power of appreciating complexities. Rhythm in its outline or skeleton is, as we have seen, of a perfectly simple and unchangeable character, and only means the occurrence of stimulations at equal intervals of time; but even in following rhythm of this most simple kind, the sense of regularity in a series of *flashes*, or of *touches*, is far less cogent and vivid and far less easy to recall than in a series of *sounds*. As regards the eye, supposing its muscles not to be called into play, and a rhythmic series of mere retinal impressions to be produced (a case which could hardly happen except in an artificial experiment), the sense of the rhythm might be tolerably distinct as long as the rate was not too rapid. But even in this most favourable case, the feeling would not be really vivid, and the passive way in which the phenomena would be watched would offer a strong contrast to the impulse which sound would cause towards some sort of accompanying movement; while if the rhythmic impressions were not specially brighter than the general field of vision on which they appeared, then the eye, which would not be shut or inactive in the intervals between the accents, but would be experiencing its normal amount of stimulation, would receive no very marked *stimulus* from the rhythmic impressions when they came; and a rhythm of this kind could not be observed, still less imagined or recalled with any keenness of apprehension.

§ 9. Great superiority of the ear in rhythmic sensibility,

Supposing, on the other hand, that the muscles of the eye are called into play, as in following movement, the very fact of having to follow here and there, and to adjust and readjust the mechanism, precludes absolute instantaneousness in the impression; while even apart from want of suddenness, the movements of the eye seem too deficient in strength to give in themselves the specific pleasure of rhythmic movement. In practice, of course, the two elements are usually combined, as in following with the eye a dancing figure, where the rhythmical stimulation is produced on the retina by marked movement, or marked pause, or change of movement at the accented beats; but even here, where the effect is powerfully aided by the nascent stimulation in the spectator of bodily movements corresponding to those observed, the actual sense of the rhythm, as betrayed by an instinct to beat or stamp time to it, would, in the absence of accompanying music, be far less keen than that produceable by the music without the dancing. Again, dancing may be literally *un*-rhythmical; and it thus affords a good means of testing the comparative want of keenness in the eye's sense of and demand for rhythm. For as long as the eye is only watching the uninteresting vibrations of a pendulum, its sensibility seems vivid enough; but let it be interested in other ways, as in watching graceful dancing unaccompanied by music, and it can be well satisfied by flowing motion [1] which, even supposing it to present a series of distinguishable accents through steps or movements of the arms, may present them at irregular intervals of time, thus lacking the true rhythmic character which becomes essential as soon as a musical accompaniment is added.

especially in cases of complex rhythm.

There is no doubt that one's own sensations of muscular movement come very much nearest to those of sound, as material for vivid impressions of rhythm. And the superiority in these two cases is still more clearly seen, if we introduce any complexities, by employing in our rhythm intervals of various lengths; as, in a simple form, by retaining the characteristic of regular repetition of one element, but making the element which is regularly repeated not a *single* unit of stimulation, but a *group*, presenting some variety in the intervals of time between its component single units. Clearly, if the steady repetition of such a group is to produce a cogent sense of rhythm, the group itself must present enough regularity to be grasped and recognised as a whole; and the natural method of obtaining a variety of intervals, while ensuring this necessary regularity, is to divide some standard interval into halves or thirds, and these again into halves or thirds, and so on; and an accurate instinctive comparison of the various lengths which are used will result in a distinct perception of the group as a whole. Now directly any very *short* intervals are introduced, the eye is heavily handicapped; since in the perception of movement the speed with which its muscles will act is very limited: and if we put movement out of the question, and imagine a mere series of retinal stimulations, as in a series of flashes, the eye is still very inferior to the ear in its power of separating very rapid impressions, and is so rapidly fatigued by the attempt as to lose the power of instantaneous response.

---

[1] It is singular that the original root of the word rhythm points more naturally to undivided flowingness of motion than to a measured series: but I am not aware that even in Greek the word was ever used without some notion of division by accents.

And even apart from speed, if we try to realise such a rhythm as this,

taken slowly, in any visual way, we shall find how little grip it gets on our attention and memory. The sense of touch will reveal the same deficiency in power to impress us with a particular rhythm, if we are careful to exclude the sense of muscular movement by shutting our eyes and getting another person or some external mechanical means to give the stimuli. And when we come to complexities involving frequent and rapid change, the ear outstrips even its constant friend and attendant, the muscular sense, at any rate in the ease and freedom from fatigue with which it acts, and the readiness with which its impressions are imagined and recalled, and also, I think, in its real power of exact and complete grasp at the time. One may, of course, exaggerate the superiority of the ear in this respect from the constant association of rhythm with music and verse, where the effect is indefinitely magnified; but at the same time the sense of rhythm may have been truly specialised in connection with sound by these very means.

It will readily be understood that the complexities of rhythm in Music are not only not incompatible with the simple regularity of the main rhythmic basis, but are really only possible through its existence. The spaces of time during which any note in a musical paragraph lasts, and the intervals of time or *rests* often intervening between the end of one note and the beginning of another, are proper fractions, usually quite simple ratios, of a constant standard;[1] and this standard is the length of the bar—that is, the length of time between two main accents, in relation to which every other time-length is estimated, and without which a variety of time-lengths would be perfectly vague and unintelligible. But though the ordinary subdivision of the bar by multiples of two and three makes the fractions as a rule tolerably simple, yet as, *e.g.*, one note may last for a

§ 10. Main facts of musical rhythms.

[1] The constancy is of course for each hearing or imagined hearing of the paragraph; the length of the bar is arbitrary to the extent that the composer may not have definitely marked it, and may be made slightly to differ according to different tastes. The nature of the musical passage also often necessitates slight changes of the pace, that is, of the length of bar; but the time-values of the elements in each bar are always of necessity definite fractions of the length of that bar, and the hurrying or retarding never obliterates the accents in such a way as to make the actual length of any bar doubtful. Liberties which, by suddenly distorting the time-relations, baffle the hearer's expectations, are always resented. One point is noticeable in connection with performance. A player who is quite susceptible to being teased by the nervelessness and capriciousness of other people's *tempos* will sometimes indulge himself in lallings and spasms such as recall Schumann's simile of the gait of a tipsy man: the reason is that the performer naturally has a sense of possessing control, of knowing himself exactly what is going to happen; so that any modifications of strict rhythm which he introduces keep in exact correspondence with his perpetual adjustments of auditory expectation.

whole bar and another for only the sixty-fourth part of a bar, we shall not soon exhaust the possible arrangements. Thus, not to take an extreme case, $\frac{15}{32}$, $\frac{1}{32}$, $\frac{16}{32}$, are the ratios which the three notes sounded in this bar bear

to the whole length of the bar; and as the $\frac{15}{32}$ and the $\frac{16}{32}$ could each be divided up in any number of ways which would retain 32 as the denominator of the component fractions, while each unit of the division may be represented either by a sound or a silence, the range of subdivision is clearly wide enough for a bar's length to give scope for an endless number of combinations; and every bar of a series may differ in its internal time-arrangements from every other. Such is the possible variety, that it scarcely occurs to one to call either the bars or any of the subordinate groups by the name of *feet*, which would seem to imply that the various sorts could be numbered and catalogued: at the outside, one would apply such a term to a few very simple and common examples. Thus *complete* musical rhythms—complete series of time-relations—are not fixed and general things, like recognised poetical metres, but infinitely various. The great distinction between one musical rhythm and another has no reference to these endless combinations, but to rhythmical *outlines*, which again differ from poetical metres in the *other* direction, of being far more general and less various. These are concerned primarily only with the *first* division of the length of the bar, which must either be into *two* parts or into *three*, giving respectively two and three main beats for a bar: this division into *double* and *triple* time is generic.[1] The next stage consists in dividing the halves in the one case, the thirds in the other, into two parts or into three parts; and this creates species for each genus, the original halves still constituting double time, even where subdivided into thirds, and the original

thirds still constituting triple time, even where subdivided into halves.

The main divisions being thus clear, the further subdivisions are readily and accurately appreciated by the ear; and even such exceptions as the

---

[1] I allow this word to stand, as it simplifies the classification: at the same time an equally true generic difference would perhaps be between those rhythms which admit the number *three* and its multiples, and all other rhythms. For though $\frac{6}{8}$ time is double

subdivision by three (or occasionally by five, or seven,) of a time-length which in the particular piece is normally divided by two and multiples of two, are extremely easily caught, through the absolute certainty of the simple accents which mark the first prime divisions of the bar.

It will be well to add that when in future I employ the word *rhythm*, I shall not confine it (unless expressly so stated) to the mere outline of main accents (double time, triple time, and their varieties), but shall use it in its fullest application to the value in time of every note and every rest in a melody ; that is, as representing exactly what a melody becomes if we neglect the pitch of the notes. Of a thousand waltzes, all written on a common outline (*i.e.* with three beats in a bar), each in this sense might have a distinct rhythm. The word *accent*, again, is ambiguous, being often applied specially to those notes which, in any particular phrase, seem to demand pointed emphasis, and which often fall quite irregularly, one bar containing perhaps more than one of them, and others none at all. Accent is, however, the most convenient term, and will often be here used, to express the *regular* strong places which occur normally in all bars, the places at which, in beating time, the marked down-stroke naturally comes.

The second factor of melodic form, *pitch*, presents the greatest contrast to rhythm both in nature and history. Rhythm, as we have seen, is a phenomenon which can be associated with several sorts of sensations ; pitch is absolutely confined to the sense of hearing. And, among the simple impressions of sense, differences of pitch present the absolutely unique peculiarity, that they are neither differences of *kind,* as between red and blue colours, or between bitter and sweet tastes, or between a violin-note and a clarionet-note ; nor differences of *strength* or *degree of intensity*, as between bright and moderate light, or between very sweet and slightly sweet tastes, or between a loud note and a soft note ; but they are differences of *distance and direction*, clearly and indisputably felt as such, and susceptible of the most minute shades of discrimination. The spectrum of visual colours affords, by contrast, the readiest means of appreciating this peculiarity. When a spectrum is thrown on a screen, the distances from each other of the various colours give no feeling of cogency or necessity. Presented as they are, the space-distance of any tint from any other could of course be mechanically measured for any particular adjustment of the screen and the prism : but such measurements would

§ 11. Pitch : its unique character, as regards perception of *distance* and *direction*.

time, presenting groups of three in pairs, music written in it could not infrequently be written as in $\frac{3}{8}$ time, which is triple time, by simply drawing a line down the middle of each bar, and so making each group of three a separate bar—for the fourth quaver, being in any case accented, may often seem susceptible, if we will, of as marked an accent as the first, and thus gives us the option of making an actual first beat of it by halving the bar. In such cases $\frac{6}{8}$ seems more akin to the class which comprises $\frac{3}{8}$ and $\frac{3}{4}$ than to the class which comprises $\frac{2}{4}$.

have no general or essential validity; by imagining the spectrum indefinitely lengthened or contracted at any point we can vary indefinitely the relative distances of the colours, so that distance in space is clearly quite irrelevant to their differences. The *order* of the spectrum, moreover, is, as far as our sensations go, perfectly accidental and arbitrary; we can construct or imagine other orders, presenting just as much, or rather just as little cogency, and whose gradation would look just as natural; for instance, we might make blue shade into red *viâ* purple. Again, if a bright spot of yellow (the middle colour of the spectrum) be thrown on a screen, and, by the gradual intervention of coloured glasses between it and the source of light, the colour be gradually changed to *red,* and a similar process be repeated so as to change the spot from yellow to *green,* we have absolutely no sense of having passed in *opposite directions* in the two cases; nor have we any sense of *going further* in looking from the leaves to the flower of a scarlet geranium than in looking from the leaves to the flower of a buttercup: whereas if we hear first a middle note on a piano followed by a bass note, and then a middle note followed by a treble note, the impression of opposite directions is irresistible; as is the impression of going further in the passage from a bass note to a treble note, as compared with the passage from a bass note to a middle note.

Reason why the directions of pitch are felt as up and down.

It is worth while, in passing, to notice the curious question why *up and down* is felt so instinctively as the natural description of the two directions which the scale of pitch presents. The reason must, I think, lie in the fact that since higher sounds are more penetrating and more conspicuous than lower ones, the higher register of the voice has been for long ages employed in all circumstances where an effort has been made to attract attention or to give force and wide reach to the utterance of vocal sound; and has thus become associated with elevation and dilatation of the physical frame, which are not only, in the case of the head and chest, directly connected with an upward strain of the voice, but are on their own account the natural movements, under the same conditions of desire to attract attention or impress a spectator. Thus the arms especially, which are ordinarily pendulous with the hands in a low position, are instinctively raised in passion and excitement, since the nervous discharge natural in such cases, if it is to affect them at all, can only do so in an upward direction; and similarly the head, which tends to droop forwards with relaxation of muscular tension, is liable to be sharply raised under sudden stimulus. To this we may add that bass notes have normally a volume and fulness which easily associates itself with the idea of mass and weight; and the connection of weight with sinking and depth is obvious.

Unique character of pitch as regards relationship of elements.

To return to the unique character of pitch. Fixity of order and distance are not the only peculiarities of the scale of tone: another is presented by the *definite relationships* existing between different points on it, the recognition of which is as distinct as that of distance and direction. To take the simplest case, if we start at any point and proceed up or down, we come in time to another point presenting a marked resemblance to our starting point, of a sort which, from the very uniqueness of the phenomenon, defies definition or description. This second point has the relationship of an *octave* to the first, and physics shows us that the ratio of the rates of aerial vibration for the two notes is two to one. Now the visible spectrum of colour, physically considered, constitutes about an octave; that is to say, the rate of ethereal vibration for the extreme violet at one end is about double of that for the extreme red at the other. But as regards sensation this fact has no significance; it is not represented by the slightest resemblance or relationship between the two colours. The only sort of resemblance possible to *tints* is that in which not any, or hardly any, shades of colour could be interposed so as to lead from one to the other; whereas any distinguishable *tones* between which it would be impossible to interpose any, or more than a very few, gradations of pitch, would be at an interval of a semitone, or less than a semitone, apart; that is, at an interval involving such discrepancy as would be fatal to their joint existence, or at best would constitute their relationship the most distant possible, in any tolerably satisfactory scale-system.

The contrast presented by tone-relationship to any visual phenomenon is more easily comprehensible, now that its physical and physiological basis is known to have no analogue in colour. This knowledge is due to the discovery by Helmholtz that on all satisfactory instruments each tone, though apparently simple, is a compound of many tones, a *prime* one and upper ones or *harmonics*. The various resemblances between notes result from their possession of a greater or less number of identical harmonics; or from common resemblance of this kind to some third note; and it is important to grasp the startling fact, that our keen feeling of the relationships is due to the presence in the notes of sounds which to most of us never become objects of independent observation.

Before we proceed to the further consideration of relationship, and of the actual fixed intervals, one remark may be made as to mere change of pitch on its own account. We have seen how, among changes of sense-impression, this is unique in giving the impression of passage from point to point. Rhythm clearly does nothing of that kind: however much it may suggest *movement*, it does not suggest *advance*: whereas no change in pitch can take place without involving this feature; and the most formless fragment of transition presents this fundamental attribute of what will be afterwards described as the Ideal Motion. To a developed musical ear indefinite transitions without the formative element of fixed degrees are quite devoid of interest; but in any embryonic use of the voice for purposes of pleasure, as among young children or in

§ 12. The fundamental pleasure in mere change of pitch.

the grown-up childhood of savage life, the mere change of note, differentiated from other changes of sense-impression, *e.g.* of colour, by the peculiar sense of advance, is very clearly enjoyable. The fundamental point seems to be the *change*: that the change should very commonly be to a related note, as the octave or the fifth, may be, in the earliest stage, a secondary and negative provision, due to the fact that if it were to some unrelated point of pitch, this last would be felt as disagreeably discrepant and unexpected. And much as the more advanced stages of the Ideal Motion may perplex us, this rudimentary pleasure in change seems specially easy to understand in the case of tone, owing to the peculiarly exceptional and intermittent, and therefore peculiarly exciting effect, of this form of sense-stimulation, as sufficiently described in the second chapter.

§ 13. Necessity of fixed degrees or intervals in the scale.　To definite melodic form, however, fixity of degrees in pitch, as well as in time, is of course indispensable : and we may go further, and say that, without fixity of degrees, changes of pitch if at all prolonged are positively disagreeable to moderately cultivated ears, unless the shifting be so slow that the ear has appreciable time to dwell on the various elements as they pass. Such slow transition may be sometimes heard in a wailing wind, and, where the *timbre* is not marked, may have a certain weird charm. But the sound made by the best violinist on the best violin in the world, if he passes by uninterrupted slides up and down the length of one of his strings, will inevitably recall midnight cats ; thus exemplifying what has been already said, that definite musical colour has its natural habitation only in the sphere of musical form. Whether the disagreeableness in such a case could be connected with any physiological grounds, or whether it is rather due to a mental sense of aimlessness and fatuity through the constant association of musical *timbre* with fixed degrees of pitch, is very hard to decide ; the latter hypothesis seems somewhat favoured by the fact that the slide, by a voice or on a stringed instrument, from fixed degree to fixed degree, is felt as distinctly pleasant.

But further, the fixity of degrees in pitch is really necessitated by the fixity of degrees in time, if time and pitch are to enter as factors into a form. Since the parts of time cannot, from their very nature, be compared contemporaneously, their variety would be chaotic but for a fixed scale of subdivision. Now time is limited to one dimension ; and though along this dimension rhythm can certainly produce formed groups which may be presented even in monotone, as on a drum, yet freedom and wide variety of form or curvature (to use the one conceivable metaphor) are clearly only possible through variations of pitch. Pitch, again, is only of one dimension, up and down ; and though in its case there are perceptible differences along the line, and so possibilities of contrast by sliding transitions apart from fixed degrees, yet as the changes can only take place in succession, time cannot be kept out, and will appear as chaotic unless regularly divided ; there is no *via media*. As, then, the changes of pitch, up or down, are stopped at definite instants, definite points of pitch must necessarily be presented at those instants ; and the actual points employed in the music of any place or time constitute a *scale-system*.

Even in the rudest forms of Music, there has been universal agreement as to the necessity of a separation, in some way or other, of certain degrees of tone from the range of continuous gradation ; but the separation has been carried out in the most various methods at various times and places. The obvious relationships presented by the octave and the fifth have made them constant elements both of melody and of harmony, and the third has had a natural charm for man as for the cuckoo. Thus the Sumatrans are described as confining their harmony to the octave ; while they and other tribes make more frequent use of the third in melody than of any other interval. And in the monotonous songs of the Ostyaks of Northern Asia, it is said that 'one hears little besides the fundamental note and minor third, and more rarely the fifth also.'

§ 14. Formation of scales.

In early stages the use of intervals less than a tone has often been avoided : but tones and semitones have been the prevailing steps of division in more civilised systems. By the adoption of these steps, the distance between a note and its octave can be divided into intervals at points each of which will present some perceptible degree of relationship with the extreme notes. This may be immediately realised by any one who knows the names of the notes, if starting on a piano with C, he will pass to the next C above by tones only, without using any semitones, thus dividing the octave into six tones ; he will then have to strike F sharp, a note unrelated to C, which by its odd uncomfortable sound, as contrasted with F natural, will show clearly what relationship and its absence imply. By the introduction of a semitone in each half of the scale, all such strange and unsatisfactory intervals are avoided ; but even when this is done, a good many varieties of arrangement are possible. For scales in which this condition is observed will be produced by passing on a piano, *by white keys only*, from each white key in turn to its octave : and if these various arrangements be compared, it will be found that the interval between the starting note and the next note to it, the interval between the starting note and the next but one to it, and so on, are each of them liable to differ by a semitone from the corresponding interval in some of the other arrangements. The same want of fixity affects the distance and relationship of the component notes of every possible interval in such scales, and is of course incompatible with the immediate and instinctive reference [1] of each unit in

Adoption of tones and semitones as steps,

---

[1] I have often found people professing a want of proper comprehension of Music, because, *e.g.*, they are unaware of referring notes to a key-note, and do not know the meaning of 'modulation.' In ninety-nine instances out of a hundred it is a mere case of M. Jourdain. Any one who knows two bars of 'God save the Queen' refers notes to a key-note in the only way in which it is possible to do so : that his apprecia-

any series of notes to a certain place in an unmistakable scale.  The result, therefore, of having all these arrangements in use would be not only lack of definiteness in the forms built on the notes of any *single* scale, but lack of the wide variety which is only possible by *change* of scale; that is, by clearly felt transference of the notes from membership in a scale with one starting-point to membership in a scale with another.

**and limitation of their modes of arrangement to two.**     This defect, inevitable on a system which recognises a number of modes of scale-arrangement, has been obviated by discarding all of them except two, the so-called *major* and *minor*; the effect of the limitation being that, whatever be the starting-point or key-note, the scale from it to its octave, while identical as regards steps or relations with the scale from every other note to its octave, contains two actual notes which exist jointly in no other scale (F and B in the scale of C), and which therefore, when both have been heard, unmistakably mark the key.  The feeling for these two modes has now become second nature to Europeans, though the process by which they were established was a very gradual one.  The history of this process has been admirably explained by Helmholtz, and does not fall within our scope: it will be enough to realise that the merit of the modern system consists in the absolute definiteness it has given to the sense of key, taking effect in the keenness with which not only notes in the key, but *accidentals* [1] or notes foreign to the key, and *modulations* or transitions from key to key, are apprehended and remembered.

**§ 15. Diversity of scale-systems.**     It is natural that people habituated to different scale-systems, especially if the diversity extends to the actual intervals employed, and not merely to their arrangement in the scale,[2] should find each other's melodies per-

tion of that bit of melodic form depends on the position of notes in the major scale

 and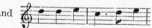

and seeing whether the latter seems to make a satisfactory start for the tune.  Similarly, any one who knows and approves 'God preserve the Emperor' has quite sufficient appreciation of modulation for present purposes.

he may convince himself by getting some one to play the two following strains,

[1] It is curious to notice the difficulty which young and untutored ears, even distinctly 'musical' ones, occasionally have in realising accidentals.  I have heard school-children sing a glee beginning

 &c.

perfectly *in tune*, but with the second G unsharpened; similarly I have heard street-boys whistle the waltz beginning

 &c.

perfectly correctly, save that the C in the sixth bar was unsharpened.  This is a different phenomenon from the frequent singing out of tune (*i.e.* taking the right note a little sharp or flat) by children; and

is rarely met with, I think, in an adult who can take notes true.  It implies a certain hesitation of ear or voice to launch itself beyond the track of the normal key-steps.

[2] As regards scales which agree with our

fectly unintelligible. The merit of our system is that, while taking a sufficient number of sufficiently varied intervals to admit of the production of endless forms from the notes of a single scale, it has rejected the minuter steps of subdivision; and by confining the notes comprised within an octave to twelve, which will serve for a whole linked series of keys (seven notes out of the twelve appearing in each), has opened out all the extraordinary possibilities of modulation. Other peoples have had, to their cost, an extraordinary sensibility to the minuter intervals, with the result that in their formation of scales the feeling for propinquity of note has overbalanced that of relationship. An Arab who derives keen pleasure from a melodic form in which he uses quarter-tones, naturally strikes a European as singing incoherent notes grievously out of tune; but that would be nothing against him if his system admitted of the abundance and variety of beautiful forms to which ours has proved itself adequate.

To realise the complexity of proportion involved in any use of the units of pitch which scales comprise, it must be noticed that the factors of distance and relationship are not only disparate in nature, but are wholly unparallel, so to speak, in the way in which their respective degrees appear in the scale. Thus the note most nearly related to C is another C, a long distance from it; the next in nearness of relationship is G, a considerable distance from it, while the nearest to it in distance is D, the relationship of which is comparatively remote; and the note between the two, D flat, is still nearer in distance and still more remote in the other sense. *A priori* we should have been quite at sea on these points: we could not have told whether it would not be necessary that order of propinquity should go with order of relationship, *e.g.* whether we ought not to take for the second and third degrees of our scale such notes that the former would be more nearly related to the starting-note than the latter; this being indeed

§ 16. Distance and relationship are utterly disparate,

own in the use of tones and semitones, but differ in the arrangement of them, as in the old ecclesiastic modes, the following facts may be noted. The actual relationships of notes to one another are of course something distinct from their particular position in a particular scale, though the reference to a key-note is now too instinctive for the other element to be independently appreciable in a melodic form. For instance, D, F, A, are notes of the scale of C, and when the intervals they form occur as constituents of a melody in C, the position of the notes in that scale is involved in the perception of the form into which they enter; equally when the intervals occur as constituents of a melody in D minor, or in F, or in A minor, or in B flat, the position of the notes in those scales is necessarily realised; but they possess certain independent relationships to

one another, which belong to them in their own right without reference to any special scale; and it is this fact which makes it possible for music written in an old mode, especially with a certain amount of artifice in the harmonies, to seem intelligible to modern ears. For instance, we may take the old mode which is represented by the scale of D, played all on white notes; and though we could not refer the notes used in that mode to a key-note D in the way in which we refer notes to the major and minor scales which are, so to speak, in our inmost musical fibre, we may still find them consequent and even agreeable; only not cogent or possessing. Still even this much would only be possible where, as in the instance given, the scale differed but slightly in arrangement from our own major or minor.

the condition we actually find to hold with respect to the fifth, sixth, and seventh degrees, G being more nearly related to C than A, and A than B. As a matter of fact, propinquity and relationship have both acted in the formation of the scale: the remote B, for instance, was adopted as the seventh degree of the scale of C in preference to the nearly related B flat, owing to its propinquity to the C above it, which is so naturally reached from it as to have obtained for it the name of *leading note*. But though these elements are actually so distinct, their presence does not involve any feeling of a double character in the notes, as presented in an intelligible melodic series.

Though each note in such a series has the two things, its particular degree of propinquity and its particular degree of relationship to any other, this analysis is not involved in our melodic perception. The note's value is as an element in all sorts of different forms, essential in each place of its occurrence: but it cannot be used in virtue of degree of propinquity without carrying with it its inalienable relationships, or *vice versâ*.[1] We find by experience that our scale-system affords a suffi-

---

[1] Notes may be used, however, which present no appreciable relationship; as often in the case of 'accidentals.' Even in simple melodies notes foreign to the key, and yet not leading into a new key, frequently occur: and these, though sometimes mere ornaments of the truly essential notes, may in other cases be entirely essential to the form. To take a couple of instances, everybody who knows the opening of Spohr's 'Rose softly blooming,'

or of the invocation to the evening-star in *Tannhäuser*,

will recognise how impossible it would be to dispense with the G sharp in the former or the C sharp in the latter. Relationship in the case of such notes is in abeyance, and their place in the form is wholly due to close propinquity, since they are instantly followed by one of the notes of the key from which they are only a semitone distant.

As regards the true notes of the scale,

perhaps the easiest way of realising how degrees of distance reckon, over and above relationship, is to take a case where a very distinct skip is made to a note as nearly as possible identical, in point of relationship, with a nearer note, which, however, when we try it instead, is found to spoil the form. For instance, in the second 'subject' of Chopin's *Funeral March*,

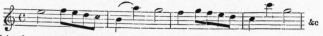&c

the interval in the second bar from B to the A above clearly could not be replaced by the

smaller and more obvious interval to the A below, thus

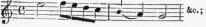&c.;

similarly the replacement of the tenth in the opening of Schumann's violin romance,

&c.

cient variety of elements, sufficiently numerous degrees of distance and relationship, to make up by rhythmic adjustments of the notes, and by transference of their allegiance from key to key, an infinite number of distinct forms : but how far a note seems right and necessary in a tune because it is at such and such a distance from the one before it, and how far because it presents such and such amount of relationship to that note or to the key-note, it is idle to enquire. We cannot alter one property without altering the other. The note with those relationships *is*, and cannot but be, at that particular distance : the note at that distance *has*, and cannot but have, those relationships ; but it has no dual character as regards the form, in which we feel its presence as that of a single un-analysable unit.

The fact is that though in judging of note-material apart from form, it is easy to realise the ' naturalness ' of the modern scales, and the compara-tive strangeness of accidental notes (as any one may see by playing such a series as this,

§ 17. Natural relationship in its deeper sense.

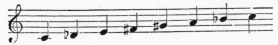

and then trying to sing it from memory), yet when the notes take their places in a melody we get a naturalness of quite a different kind. The natural relationship of each note in a melody is to the note or notes *next it in the melody*, its proper and necessary associates at that particular part of that particular form. As to what shall be accepted as natural in this deeper sense, the musical faculty justifies itself to itself alone ; its only interest is in the combinations it finds pleasant, for the supply of which, happily, the variety of material has so far proved amply sufficient ; as, to use the roughest of metaphors, a considerable variety of bricks might be necessary for certain architectural purposes, since no curved form could be constructed of simply square bricks : but the whole interest would be in the form and its gradations, not in the bricks. A person ignorant of written notes, and who had not studied singing, might encounter a very well-marked interval, occupying the same place in the scale, in fifty different melodies, of each of which he had perfect apprehension, without ever noticing it to be the same ; and in many cases considerable attention

by a third, thus,

&c.

gives an odd sense of repression and tame-ness. Similarly we might easily exemplify the importance of *direction*, over and above relationship, by cases in which melodies end either by an *ascent* from the dominant to the tonic above, or by a *descent* from the dominant to the tonic below ; each seeming right in its place, while in a form that was worth anything either would be resented as a substitute for the other.

and ingenuity would be necessary to enable him to realise the identity, even after his attention had been drawn to it. It is amusing to play a harsh detached interval to such a person, and immediately afterwards to introduce it in its place in a form (for instance, the major seventh from C sharp to D, in the second bar of the phrase to be immediately quoted); he will almost refuse to believe the two to be identical, even though only a few seconds has separated them. With chords the experiment is still easier, as the harshness of a detached discord is more striking than that of any melodic interval. Helmholtz says that thirds and sixths are melodically and harmonically the most attractive of intervals, and gives an ingenious explanation in the fact that they lie at the very boundary of those that the ear can grasp, and thus occupy a middle position between the too obviously simple interval of the octave and the intervals whose notes have the minimum of intelligible relation. But it is only when the intervals are detached that such terms can be applied. Harmony which dealt in thirds and sixths and avoided discords, would very soon pall ; and a melodic phrase can only be judged as a whole. We may indeed have our culminating and favourite points, but they will not turn out to be oftener connected with thirds and sixths than with any other interval. And in no case can such single intervals have any independent value. We may take a case where sixths are a very prominent feature, as in the beautiful tune from *Fra Diavolo*, which opens thus :

but here each pair of sixths is separated by a seventh, and the sevenths are of course a no less essential part of the continuous form. We do not first enjoy one sixth, and then wait and enjoy the next ; indeed, if we wish to make distinctions, there is something in the sweep down to the seventh in each case which makes that seem the more delightful interval of the two. It is as impossible to pick out special intervals in a melody, and say they are more attractive than others, as to pick out a certain square inch in a beautiful face and say the same of it. The interval and the square inch depend for their beauty and effect on the whole to which they belong, in which every part tells on every other.

§ 18. Further remarks as to the exceptional definiteness of the available points on the scale ;

Two more observations may be made before leaving the special topic of pitch. The first merely expresses the exceptional definiteness of the actual points on the scale which tone relationship involves; they permit absolutely no liberties. We have seen that liberties can be taken with the time-element; that rhythm is often to a certain extent elastic, and can be varied in pace without loss of the underlying sense of its regular accents, and regular scale of subdivision ; but with the pitch-element such liberties would mean the production of notes out of tune.   The extremely slight divergence from absolute truth of interval necessitated by equal tempera-ment,[1] is of course a constant, not an arbitrary or occasional, feature, and is perceived, if perceived at all, not as a liberty, but as a defect; though a defect which, on the pianoforte at all events, is scarcely noticed except by very exceptional and unfortunate ears.

The other characteristic to be noticed is a result of the above-men-tioned *sense of advance*, in combination with this extreme definiteness of the points to which the advance is made.   By this means the feeling of perpetually satisfied expectation gets a far keener edge than is possible through the mere occurrence of rhythmic stimuli at the expected instants ; and the excitement is heightened in the case of instruments which admit of sliding from note to note, by the mere act of following the rapid but gradual course of the transition.

and consequent keenness of the feeling of satis-fied expecta-tion.

---

[1] What this means, and how fortunate it is that there is a slight willingness to yield (or perhaps we should rather say a slight obtuseness) on the part of the ear, can be made clear to any one who knows the names of the notes and intervals.   To take a case on an instrument with fixed notes : if we tune a note as a perfect minor sixth from C, the sound made by it will be more than a true major third distant from E ; so that if we subsequently want to use the key of E, this same note, which now represents the third degree of the scale of E, will not bear an accurate relation to its key-note.   But this, it may be said, is an imperfection of the instrument; on an instrument which will give all shades of tone, the note might be a shade flattened, and the interval so made true in the new key.   Let us, then, take another case.   In this simplest of chord-sequences, if the A and G are per-

fectly tuned as regards C, then the D–A in the second chord, and the G–D in the third, cannot both be perfect fifths, and to make them so by altering the pitch of the D in the transition would be tampering with the common link of the two chords.   It is easy to see how in modulation, when several keys are used in succession, the occasions for

error which these two examples suggest are multiplied, and how, if our ears were per-fectly rigid in their demands, even perfect instruments could only get out of the diffi-culty by altering the pitch of some note or notes common to two consecutive keys ; whereby, so far as the ear *noticed* the altera-tion (which, on the hypothesis that it is offended by the errors when the notes are *un*changed, it ought distinctly to do), the very point which gives ease and naturalness to the transition, namely, the marked posses-sion of common notes by the two keys, would necessarily suffer.   The simplest way of obtaining identity of interval in such cases, as between any pair of keys, would be to *halve the error* and share it between the two keys ; a principle which, applied im-partially to the whole range of keys, means such a division of the octave as that from any note we can take any interval, a third or fifth, or whatever it may be, which shall be identical with the same interval taken from any other note : and this again clearly involves identity in the smallest available steps, or semitones, of which an octave con-tains twelve.   Octaves so divided make up the material of modern music, which may thus be said to owe its existence to a slight imperfection or elasticity in our ears.   I may add that the case as regards modulation has been put with admirable force and con-ciseness by Dr. Stainer in the two prefaces to his *Theory of Harmony*.

# CHAPTER VIII.

## MELODIC FORMS AND THE IDEAL MOTION.

§ 1. Fusion of the two heterogeneous factors of time and pitch.

So far we have considered the two factors of melodic form, rhythm and pitch, separately : and we have seen that such pleasure as each alone can afford is of a rudimentary kind, insusceptible of large variety or of development. We now come to their combination, to the fact which makes possible a seemingly infinite variety of form. The great cause for the uniqueness and complexity of proportion in the simplest melodic form, is this, that it is a *resultant* of two quite different proportional series, of rhythm and of pitch, whose work is at every moment, and through every variety of swing and poise, absolutely interpenetrative. The contrast with visual form is manifest. The impressions on the retina are of *space* in two dimensions : in these two dimensions all visual form is necessarily perceived, and, as they are absolutely homogeneous, the eye is concerned only with perfectly *homogeneous* impressions of line and surface. But *time*, in which audible phenomena take place, has only one dimension, capable indeed by metrical division of exercising our powers of co-ordination and so presenting formed groups, but groups which in isolation are of a very bald and unemotional kind, and entail but a slight advance on the facts of mere nerve-stimulation common to many of the lower animals : and what in Music takes the place of the second dimension is a totally different and unique element— the graduated scale of *pitch*. Thus the form of a melody is the product of two lines of perfectly *heterogeneous* impressions, each empty and insignificant alone ; a line of sounds and silences, each of a certain duration (arranged on a framework of accents), and a line of tones each of a certain pitch : [1] and each note-unit, in its place and function, stands to its neighbours in two totally heterogeneous ratios. The form is at every instant the

---

[1] This, for instance, is the pitch-line,

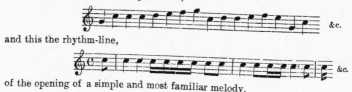

&c.

and this the rhythm-line,

&c.

of the opening of a simple and most familiar melody.

resultant of the two factors, and, the dimensions (so to speak) being incommensurable, it cannot be strictly compared even to the most elaborate curve with co-ordinates and an equation. Consequently no sort of true visual parallel is conceivable, and such analogies of curves and loops as occasionally suggest themselves merely tantalise by their feebleness.

This peculiarity of melodic structure is unaffected by differences in the history and nature of the two factors. The fundamental principle of rhythm, equal measurement, is, as we have seen, common to all Music : while a special rhythm may be common to several melodies, the identity being clearly marked and obvious to the ear. On the other hand, the systems supplying the note-material or available pitch-intervals have been many ; and confining ourselves to our modern scale-system, it is but a mere matter of curiosity, in no way capable of striking the ear, if we ever discover that some particular series of notes can yield two intelligible melodies, by association with two rhythms differing in the position of their main accents. Rhythm, again, when produced in monotone (as on a drum), has a character, though quite a slight and colourless one, of its own : and the fact that the rhythm of a tune is as clear and definite in the complete tune as if it were isolated, and tapped or given in monotone, will prove of great importance hereafter : whereas the notes of a tune taken irrespectively of rhythm will be totally meaningless. But for melodic purposes the interdependence of the two factors is entirely mutual : nor is the rhythm in any sense a framework or mould to be separately appraised, as the metre of a stanza may be considered the mould for the meaning to be poured into. In virtue of its detachable character, it may seem that the rhythm in a more special sense *forms* the otherwise incoherent sequence of notes, while the sequence of notes *informs* the rhythm : but both are in reality elements of form. A proof how indissoluble is the union between the rhythm and the sequence of notes into which it enters may be found in connection with the very fact, just noticed—that one rhythm may be common to several melodies, good and bad : for it is only from a melody which *in its total result* strikes us as good that we get the specifically and distinctively *rhythmical* pleasure, shown in an impulse to accompany it with real or imaginary movements : a tune in the same rhythm, if felt to be poor, awakens no similar impulse, or at best a very much feebler one.

The substitution of other notes in pitch for those which are found in any musical form so obviously leads either to incoherent absurdity, or to a new form, that it is not worth while to give instances of such changes ; but it will be well to give a few examples of the result to a musical form of a change in the factor of rhythm. For this factor is constantly treated as though it held in Music the position it does in Poetry, of something wholly external to the subject-matter, or at best as just a convenient means of supporting and exhibiting a melodic form, a set of suitable mechanical

§ 2. The interdependence is complete in spite of differences in the nature and history of the two factors.

Instances of change in rhythm.

pegs for hanging the form out on to advantage;[1] whereas of course it does not *suit*, but (with the other factor) *constitutes* the form, just as 5 multiplied by 6 constitutes 30. The following phrase, then,

with all the assistance of full harmony, and with the retention of the main accents on the first chord and the last but one, does not give much notion of the

of the *Pathétique* sonata; nor would

or

have struck any one as a supremely beautiful subject, though the changes from the

of the *Leonora* overture are very slight compared with what might easily have been made. As regards more self-complete tunes it is really so easy to make nonsense of any of them in a hundred ways by such alterations that the experiment soon palls: it is more amusing to notice occasional cases

---

[1] I need only quote two sentences from a treatise published in the most popular series of music primers. 'Rhythm will heighten the beauty of a melody.' 'Rhythm may be described as the art of the versifier—necessary, but yet only supplementary, to the genius of the poet.'

where the notes of a beautiful melody may be made to yield a silly and trivial, but still a coherent, melodic form.    Thus few would recognise in

the beautiful subject of the well-known movement in Beethoven's Sonata, Op. 90;

or in this wretched jig,

the fascinating opening of the rondo in the G major concerto;

or in this foolish ascent to the key-note, with no object but to come equally foolishly down again,

the dainty melody of the *Ruy Blas* overture,

nor will the phrase

gain much, even if its relation to *Ein' feste Burg* be perceived.[1]

---

[1] The enormous number of perfectly distinctive forms, good, bad, and indifferent—of tunes just as different from one another as tunes can be—which contain a number of successive ascending or descending notes of the scale, are worth noting as illustrative of the same point, or at all events as showing how irrelevant such isolated facts are to the

It may be well to give one example where the main accents and divisions are preserved, and where the melody is neither destroyed nor burlesqued, but is left in a perfectly recognisable and even agreeable form.    Let any

&c.

one play the following opening of a Barcarole of Rubinstein, and observe how utterly any rarity in its charm vanishes, when the triple time is altered to double, and the predominant pulsations cease to be distinguished by the alternation of a one-beat with a two-beat length, thus;

character of the complete melody ; since the same sets recur again and again, at the same parts, beginning, middle, or end, of melodies, while the fact, so far from being noticed, is a matter of surprise when pointed out.  The following cases where six or more than six such notes occur, not in a mere passage or run, but as separate and distinctly substantive units in the melodic form, have at once suggested themselves : they are mostly familiar and might serve as the nucleus for an interesting collection :—'Mandolinata,' the opening melody of the adagio in Beethoven's fourth symphony, the second melody in the allegretto of his seventh symphony, the tune in his sonata Op. 31, No. 3, quoted on p. 166, 'Robin Adair,' 'Pop goes the weasel,' 'Angels ever bright and fair,' the deplorable 'Spring' waltz quoted on p. 108,

the 'Blue Danube,' the great tune in the finale of Beethoven's first piano sonata, the second 'subject' in the first movement of his violin concerto, the opening 'subject' of his trio in D quoted on p. 167, the music-hall horror quoted on p. 220, 'Ein' feste Burg,' 'Tommy make room for your uncle,' Schumann's 'Des Abends,' quoted in chapter xiv., 'He shall feed His flock,' Schubert's 'Des Mädchens Klage,' 'Tom Bowling,' the second part of the *Tannhäuser* march, 'Durch die Wälder,' 'The Bailiff's daughter of Islington,' Mendelssohn's andante in E preceding the 'Rondo Capriccioso,' the leading theme of the allegro movement in Beethoven's great E flat trio, Ortrud's tune ' O du bist glücklich ' and Elsa's 'Lass mich dich lehren' from *Lohengrin*, Lord Mornington's vulgar chant, 'He was despised,' 'Rule Britannia.'

It is true, as we shall see, later, that, owing to the development of another element of order, Harmony, coherence of a sort can be supplied to successions of notes even in the absence of distinct rhythm. But the point and importance of Music, with its power of getting into the blood and clinging to the memory, are so dependent on the certain guidance of the ear in its cardinal expectations, that occasions on which this can be dispensed with must be comparatively rare: and when, as in an advanced state of the art, the varieties of form are infinite, when Music no longer consists of a limited number of strains endeared to childish or savage ears by perpetual repetition, the constant sense of such certainty implies that distinctness and completeness of melodic structure to which the factor of distinct rhythm, based on an outline of regular beats, is indispensable. For all vivid pleasure, for any individual and possessing motive of whatever sort, this definiteness of time is (save in the most exceptional cases) as truly essential as variety of pitch; it is present in nine hundred and ninety-nine parts out of a thousand of the Music which on any given day gives delight to the human race; and without it a prolonged succession of the most beautiful sounds is no more melody than a block of Parian marble is a statue.[1]

§ 3. Definite rhythm is not less indispensable to melody than variety of pitch.

[1] We cannot count such relaxations as, *e.g.*, in the reciting note of the ordinary English chant as true exceptions; for here the rhythm is quite strict as soon as it really starts, and the ear is merely held for a time in suspense, waiting for it to start. The principle of a marked-pause is the same, the ear being kept waiting in suspense for the next phrase: and such relaxations could only occur at the beginning or end of a phrase. The suspense is never so long that the ear loses its sense of the strict time-relations of the rhythm, of the exact satisfaction which is to follow. Sometimes, again, even in instrumental works, short interludes of irregularly accented strains occur, more or less resembling irregular recitative; but these are really less marked instances of suspense; no piece could end with them, and the suspense enhances the enjoyment when the music settles again into regular rhythm.

I must specially warn the reader against confounding definite rhythm with anything like metronomic and mechanical divisions of the time. For when insisting on the place of the rhythmic factor, I have been sometimes met by such examples as performances of national music by Hungarian performers, which, it was alleged, are *not* in definite rhythm. But definite rhythm, in my sense, is perfectly compatible with a large amount of swayings and humourings of the *pace*. The sense of its strictness consists, not in perceiving a mechanical identity of length in the bars and in their corresponding subdivisions, but in perceiving that the music has ribs, and where they are; in the absence of doubt as to how the bars and their accents lie, and must be perceived to lie under pain of missing the form; in the clear assurance that the notes can be beat time to in a definite way, and have, there-

§ 4. Speci-
men of the
reasoning
which leads to
a denial of the
true position of
rhythm.
Schopenhauer's
theory,

The entire essentialness of definite rhythm to melodic coherence (which means to the existence of impressive melodic form), needs to be specially dwelt on, inasmuch as modern metaphysical speculation is by way of denying, and modern musical practice of ignoring it. It is disappointing to find even Schumann, who certainly never ignored it in practice, writing that in a certain composition Music 'seems to have sought to return to its origin before it was confined by the laws of time;' and quoting with approval anything so remote from truth and sense as this,—'When it becomes possible to render the tyranny of measure in Music wholly imperceptible and invisible, so that this art is made apparently free; when it attains self-consciousness' (whatever that may mean), 'then it will possess the complete power of embodying lofty ideas,' and so on. As if the rhythmic sense had not been interwoven in our very substance for ages, lying at the very root, and alive in the very fibre, of melodic form. We might as reasonably expect a higher enjoyment of Architecture if we could escape from the 'tyranny' of line and surface. But it is in our own time that the error has assumed dangerous proportions; and it will be well to give a specimen of the sort of reasoning employed. To begin with, Wagner, as is well known, adopts as the ideal basis of Music Schopenhauer's theory; to wit, that the 'Will of the World,' the real essence of existence, first manifests itself 'in the ideas in Plato's sense, that is, in the archetypal forms which fashion the cosmos.' (I quote from one of Wagner's ablest exponents.) 'It is the aim of all arts to express the eternal essence of things by means of these Platonic ideas; only Music takes in this respect an exceptional position,' being, in Schopenhauer's words, 'as immediate and direct an objectification or copy of the Will of the world as the world itself is, as the ideas are of which the universe of things is the phenomenon. Music is not the copy of the ideas, like the other arts, but a representation of the cosmical Will co-ordinate with the ideas themselves.'[1] The basis being thus given,

fore, a definite form independent of any swayings and humourings which may supervene. That music may (suitably and beautifully in some cases, unsuitably and distressingly in others) be played with retardations and quickenings, in no way affects its objective possession of ribs in the right places; which implies similar definiteness in all the subordinate time-lengths.

[1] The last clause might give one the impression that this was merely a fantastic way of expressing the difference between presentative and representative art; at the same time I cannot profess to understand it, even from the metaphysical standpoint. For Music is expressly treated not as a presentation, as something parallel to beautiful real faces or landscapes, but as parallel to the ideas of which such visual things are supposed to be the embodiment or raiment. I should have thought that even a transcendentalist would have to accept a melody, like a face, as a *phenomenon*; it would surely be rather crude philosophy to exclude it from the sphere of phenomena on the ground that it cannot be touched and handled: and I fail to see on what principle it is to be put, genealogically, a step further back than a face or a landscape, and why in the case of one particular order of beauty the intermediate step of archetypal ideas is to be dispensed with. Why should not a melody embody an archetypal idea as much as a face? I suppose the reason would

what are the deductions from it ?  I will quote from the same source as before.  We start with a gem of *à priori* reasoning.  Music, being of an entirely supernatural character, '*ought to be*' likewise independent of space and time.  In an art of sound, space is altogether out of the question ; but even time can to a certain extent be dispensed with ' in that which is most musical in Music—harmony.'  As if the commonest and most striking effects of harmony (those of discord and resolution, where a desire is created by one note and fulfilled by another) did not depend precisely on the succession of notes *in time* : for in the sense of fitness with which we recognise the correspondence of things *simultaneously* perceived (as by the eye) the peculiar excitement of *expectation and satisfaction*, the importance of which, whether in melody or harmony, it is impossible to exaggerate, can have no part.  Rhythm is naturally treated as ' an intruder in the realm of absolute music,' and we are told that the essentially rhythmical nature of Greek compositions could not be favourable to the flow of melody : ' a remark, I will add, which must in consistency be extended to the greatest works of Beethoven, fathered by Wagner, with perfect justice, on the dance-melody ; as indeed all impressive melodic form must be, seeing that physical movement is the original and instinctive way in which the impressiveness shows its effects.  Wherever rhythm is perceived with enjoyment, there is implied a nascent stimulation of the dance-instinct : and however much Music *ought to be* independent of time, I am afraid that in listening to it, with our present physical organisms, we shall retain a prejudice for rhythmical *phenomena* in preference to unrhythmical *noümena*.

To return to Wagner's views: 'compositions which, like dances, are exclusively founded on rhythm must be of a lower order than where the melody grows out of harmonious relations.'  Now what is meant here by 'harmonious relations' ?  If the harmony is to be understood in a non-technical sense, and yet the relations are something external to rhythm, they can only be the pitch-relations of the notes ; but then pitch-relations of some sort are present in the poorest tune, for ' music founded exclusively on rhythm' could only be written for the drum ; and they can have no inde-

---

be that Music is a direct human creation, while faces are natural growths ; but this hardly seems a valid answer, for till we obtain some cognisance of archetypal ideas apart from phenomena, we have no right to say that they are not presupposed in human as much as in natural creations. And anyhow the melody once created, there it stands a beautiful object made out of given crude material, just like any other presentation. I cannot help thinking that my first impression was right ; and that the confusion had its source in the very obvious distinction between

the *arts*, namely, that while imitative arts represent things known outside them, Music presents things not so known—true and perfectly phenomenal facts implying in Music the relation of *a step further back* in the sense that melodic forms, like faces, are real independent things, while sculptured forms are representations dependent on the prior external existence of real independent things ; and that this relation has been shunted a stage further still, into a region where its meaning disappears.

pendent merit in the most beautiful tune, seeing that in the absence of rhythm such a tune would fall into tuneless incoherence. So that we are driven to ask why, in comparing a superior and an inferior form, each of them the resultant of two essential elements, is the pitch-element, meaningless alone, to be credited with the superiority of the one, and the rhythmic element, meaningless alone, with the inferiority of the other? This very common error seems due to the fact, already mentioned, that the rhythmic element of a melodic form remains perfectly distinguishable on its own account; we can tap the rhythm of a tune in monotone: hence when the form is silly and unemotional, the rhythm, being an obvious thing, is blamed; and it is forgotten that the very same rhythm might be a factor in a divine form, and that rhythm just as absolute *is* a factor in *all* divine forms. If, however, the above-quoted phrase is technical, and *relations of harmony* are intended, the reply is obvious that, however much melodies have gained in vividness and variety from the development of harmony and its assistance in fixing the sense of key and modulation, yet the cases where a beautiful melodic form has been actually suggested by a chord-progression are quite exceptional; and that melodies which do not modulate, or where the modulation is simple (conditions which include the vast majority of the best tunes in the world), do not necessarily imply, for their invention or comprehension, any suggestion from or reference to their harmonic accompaniment, beyond such reference as is naturally involved in a sense of the modern key- and chord-system, latent and presupposed, however little consciously recognised, in the most untutored perception of music. We shall have to return to this point in the chapter on Harmony; a single example may suffice here: of the two tunes quoted a little further on, beginning

and

one from the Choral Symphony, the other from the London pot-houses, one does not grow out of 'harmonious relations,' in the technical sense, either more or less than the other. I need not enumerate, on the other hand, the various beautiful melodic forms which have been known to *grow out of* the rhythm, in the sense that the simplest rhythmic outline, often given by some external accident, has set the melodic invention to work. The great point is that in *all* impressive melodic form the rhythm is not something superposed, or more or less consciously suggested or referred to, but is essentially *there*. Few, perhaps, who see 'three elements, harmony, rhythm, and melody,' assigned to Music as its 'means of expression,' would at once detect in such a natural-seeming list the germ of a far-spreading and disastrous error ; yet in this innocent-looking phrase, in the implication that melody can dispense with rhythm in the same sense that it can, and till comparatively recently did, dispense with harmony, is involved what if fairly pressed amounts to a denial, not only of the magnificent achievements of modern music (including much of Wagner's own), but of the facts of ages.

Wagner shows again and again in his writings how little he recognises the deeply-seated nature and artistic place of the rhythmic impulse, though too good a musician, or rather though too much made as other men are, to act consistently on his theories. That he should consider Beethoven's symphonies *limited* by their being in what he calls idealised dance-form, is of course in accordance with what has been already quoted. 'Dance-form' in an elaborate instrumental movement, merely means regularity of rhythm and formation of phrases by multiples of two : I have tried to show reasons for recognising, as Beethoven did, the musical necessity of such elements, but the actual feeling of them is of course an unchangeable and incommunicable instinct.　Elsewhere, in a connection where it suits him to refer to the dance for the sake of its *dramatic* element, Wagner actually ignores that prime characteristic which nevertheless, since it alone originated dance-form, must (according to him) be important enough to have cramped Beethoven's symphonies.　As the *Symphony* is a development of the dance-melody, so he treats the original *dance* as nothing but the germ of the dramatic action of the *Opera*, as if such a feature as rhythmic movement had never been heard of in connection with it. 'The original people's dance,' he says, 'expresses an action, mostly the mutual wooing of lovers.' The original people's dance has nothing to do with lovers,[1] and is exemplified every time a child of three years old nods its head or stamps its foot to music.

*Wagner's constant failure to recognise the deeply-seated nature of the rhythmic impulse.*

But among those who admit that for melodic coherence some continuous groundwork of satisfied expectation is a necessity, there are some who maintain that new kinds of rhythm can be based on new elements, which a subtler and more specialised sense will apprehend.　I have even been asked how Music is to advance except by some such means.　But why should I or anybody else be bound to say how Music is to advance ?　Who knows if it is to advance at all ?　And at any rate as regards rhythm, though I can conceive that the limits of grasp and retentiveness of the human ear might be increased, I cannot conceive, looking at the physical basis and history of the instinct, that it can be altered in *kind*, unless we get new limbs and modes of motion.　Meanwhile, it is worth remarking that

*§ 5. The idea of new kinds of strict rhythm has no relation to present facts.*

---

[1] It is curious how often among uncivilised peoples the dances of the men and women are kept separate.

the word *specialised* must be used with caution : for any clique, who admired things not admitted as admirable by the great mass of those interested in the subject, might claim to be the *élite* in whom a peculiar exquisiteness of sensibility had become developed. And specially in relation to a quite unique range of impressions, appreciated through a quite unique and very widely diffused faculty, such terms must be barren, except where the verdict of the *élite* is in time endorsed by an ever-increasing number, and the minority are as it were pioneers in sensation. Of course those who differ from me have a perfect right to regard themselves in this light, and to prophesy that in time the human race, when rhythmically disposed, will forget that it has legs and arms and throw itself on the infinite.

§ 6. The melodic result of the two factors is perceived without analysis, but with various degrees of completeness.

The perception of any melodic organism as the fixed resultant of the particular *dual* relation of each constituent note is, of course, a matter of common musical sensibility, not of analysis. That it admits of great varieties of degree is shown by imaginary resemblances found in melodies where such coincidence as exists is confined to one of the two factors, and the two results are therefore really quite distinct ; as well as by the fact that melodies in which some find a strong and enduring charm are pronounced commonplace by others, a criticism especially frequent in cases of obviously catching rhythm. Correctness and dexterity of ear with respect to the material employed in no way implies sympathetic apprehension of the evolved form : and there are expert musicians in whose views about ' transformation of themes,' identifying strains that utterly differ, and replacing simple and infallible art-perception by tortured and unnatural ingenuity, a want of keenness and completeness of melodic sensibility certainly seems to me to be implied.[1]   At the same time, musical sensi-

[1] I have known true lovers of Music capable of saying that the two following passages contain 'the same idea,' and that one must have been copied from the other ; the second 'subject' from a well-known movement of Beethoven, beginning

and the opening phrase of 'Robin Adair,'

When one demurs, they point out that 'the first six notes are identical ; ' identical also, it might be pointed out, with the concluding phrase of ' Tommy, make room for your uncle,'

The same persons might probably hold that the two melodies for a bass voice, the prayer in *Mosè in Egitto* and the invocation to the star in *Tannhäuser*, beginning respectively,

bility lends itself, as we shall find further on, to such variety of kind, and to such vagaries of verbal expression, as to make judgments of this sort dangerous.

Finally, it is most important to notice that the technical conditions of melodic beauty are really as much to seek as a satisfactory analogy; and that fewer explanations would have been attempted had the absolute interdependence of the factors of time and pitch been fully realised. For instance, we see a characteristic of one of the factors—pitch—taken as though it covered the whole ground, and we are told that good melody depends on frequent use of the successive notes of the natural scale, or that the skips are from one note to a nearly-related note. Now, neglecting the continual exceptions and granting the perpetual occurrence of such progressions, any musician will perceive, on reflection, not only that they are as common in bad tunes as in good, but that for each intelligible melody or succession of notes in which they are exemplified we can, while still employing them, make a million of formless and meaningless ones. So with the factor of rhythm : though metrical balance is as essential to a tune as symmetry to a face, we see that notes may be metrically strung together without presenting anything we could call a melodic form.

§ 7. The fusion of factors explains the inadequacy of the usual attempts to fix the technical conditions of melodic beauty.

A few simple instances will again be useful. Perfectly formless specimens would not be interesting; but the following trivial and worrying melody,

might be compared with Schubert's wonderful *Forelle*, a tune whose imperishable freshness no amount of repetition can affect,

conveyed in their opening phrase the same ' idea,' one composer having given it an upward and the other a downward ' expression.'

The former tune keeps more to the successive notes of the scale than the latter; in simplicity of structure the two are about on a par; not a single point can be adduced as exemplified in the *Forelle* and other tunes of its quality, and as absent in *Kemo Kimo* and other tunes of its quality: yet the difference of quality may be fairly called infinite; it is as marked as that between the *Blue Boy* and a figure in a tailor's advertisement. Or again, compare this sickly hymn-tune—

with *Dove sono*—

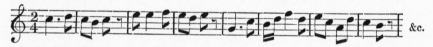

to which, owing to the fact that in both cases there is a circling round the C for the first phrase and round the E for the second, many would doubtless trace the origin of the preceding melody. Similarly the following tune,

which used to be the nightmare of my childish Sundays, might be compared with the 'subject' of the glorious movement known as *Le Retour*,

or a quickened edition of the boring melody which has lately been so much in the air, beginning,

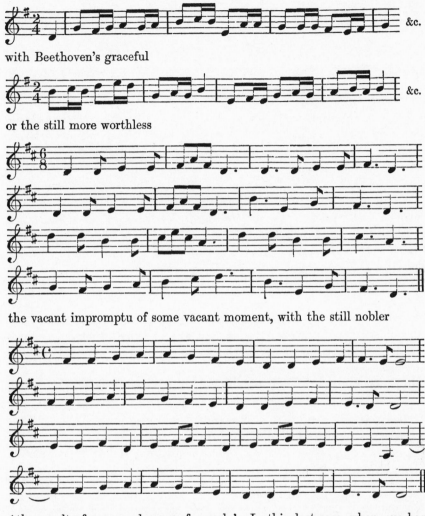

with Beethoven's graceful

or the still more worthless

the vacant impromptu of some vacant moment, with the still nobler

'the result of years and years of search.' In this last case, when one has the strong even rhythm of the second melody in one's head, the one-and-a-half measure of the other may seem mean and jumpy; but we have seen the futility of trying to estimate a melodic form by looking at either of its factors alone; and in one of the variations of Beethoven's tune this very measure is used,

which we may compare with *Pop goes the Weasel*, dignified by transposition into minims and crotchets. Or this latter in its original form might be compared with what is certainly its equal in point of jumpiness,

one of the numerous proofs that might be given that the greatest works of
Beethoven are the place to go to for 'catching' and 'popular' tunes.
In not one of these instances (and they might be multiplied *ad infinitum*)
is a single technical point presented which could be for a moment mentioned as differentiating the good from the bad, or forming the slightest
basis for any induction on the subject.[1]　Nor are the words *good* and *bad*
here meant to refer to any acknowledged classification.　Any individual,
whatever his taste, who among the tunes he knows discriminates those
which give him pleasure from those which do not, will find it entirely
hopeless to form any generalisation of structural features which are present
in the former and absent in the latter.

§ 8. The Ideal
otion ;

So far we have been occupied with the more external aspects of
melodic structure.　We must now turn to the actual *process* by which
Music is followed, to the facts connected with the evolution of melodic
form moment after moment in time.　The translation which this will
involve of the phraseology of *form* into the phraseology of *motion* will
make clearer the essential difference of this experience where form and
motion are blended—where form is perceived by continuous advance along
it—from perceptions both of visible form and of physical motion.　It is
the *oneness of form and motion* which constitutes the great peculiarity

---

[1] Even where it happens that a special
point *can* be picked out as definitely bad, in a
particular melody, it will continually be found
that the self-same point may be perfectly
agreeable in another place, while no reason can
be assigned why it should make a necessary
element here in a good form, there in a bad ;
so that even in these most favourable cases,
very little scope is afforded for generalisations as to melodic characteristics.　Thus,
the interval F–B, known as the tritone,
has a bad character, and is often said to be
unsuitable to melody, and I have heard the
considerable spice of vulgarity and cloyingness in the opening of the *Guards'* waltz
attributed to its presence :

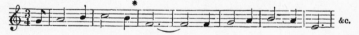

but in the *Leonora* overture, the passage quoted above is immediately succeeded by
this series of tritones,

where the notes, for all they are supported
by a single chord, are by no means a mere
arpeggio of the chord, but make an indispensable piece of genuine melodic form.

of melody and of the faculty by which we appreciate it. As we derive our primary ideas of sensible form from visible objects, a *form* which presents the character of *motion* in that it advances or is advanced along, in one order at one pace from end to end, is a novelty; as we derive our primary ideas of motion from physical motion, a *motion* which presents the character of *form*, in that bits of it separated by other bits and by wide distances are yet felt as indispensable parts of one unity, is a novelty. When a melody is familiar to us we realise it by a gradual process of advance along it, while yet the *whole* process is in some real manner present to us at each of the successive instants at which only a minute part of it is actually engaging our ears.[1] Melodic form and the motion in question are aspects of the same phenomenon; and no confusion need attend the use of the two sets of terms, as long as it is recognised that our sense of the characteristics of melodic forms cannot be abstracted from the continuous process by which alone we perceive them, or rather which constitutes our perception of them. I can think of no better term to express this unique musical process than *Ideal Motion*; ideal not just as giving a refined and idealised and glorified version of something already known, in the sense that a painter may often be said to glorify and idealise the objects he represents—not an idealised quintessence of any sort of *physical* motion—but ideal in the primary Greek sense of ἰδέα, ideal as yielding a *form*, a unity to which all the parts are necessary in their respective places. The common use of the term *idea*, in relation to Music, to express some special bit of striking form is thus entirely accurate, in spite of the extraordinary bungling to which it often leads, as though the idea were one thing and the music another.

*its oneness with melodic form.*

It may be well to give one rough specimen of a description of this process by which the course of musical forms is perceived, if only for the sake of realising how essentially indescribable it is. The melody, then, may begin by pressing its way through a sweetly yielding resistance[2] to a

*Melody is as little expressible in terms of physical motion as in terms of visible form and structure.*

---

[1] The indispensableness to one another of the different and separated parts of a melodic motion, essentially involved in all perception of coherent music, may be brought home at once to any one with ear enough to remember a simple tune after sufficient repetition. Let him hear some beautiful slow melody which he does not know; the first bar or two, heard for the first time, will probably be felt as quite neutral by the waiting ear; whereas, when once the tune is known and liked, the full pleasure of its beauty will be felt in going over those very bars, so that the apprehension of them must be entirely dependent on the consciousness of what is to follow. The concluding bars may afford a similar

illustration; music-lovers will realise how a perfectly familiar cadence, so ordinary as to be reckoned the common property of composers, may be entirely glorified by occurring at the end of a fine melody, while capable of sounding quite *banal* elsewhere.

[2] Expressions of this kind are unavoidable in description, and I should think that most lovers of melody would recognise the feeling which the words represent. At the same time different people may receive this and kindred experiences at quite different places in Music, and the same melody may certainly be felt in different ways even by people who all keenly enjoy it. For instance, I myself receive a certain amount of the impression

gradually foreseen climax; whence again fresh expectation is bred, perhaps for another excursion, as it were, round the same centre but with a bolder and freeer sweep, perhaps for a fresh differentiation whereof in turn the tendency is surmised and followed, to a point where again the motive is suspended on another temporary goal; till after a certain number of such involutions and evolutions, and of delicately poised leanings and reluctances and yieldings, the forces so accurately measured just suffice to bring it home, and the sense of potential and coming integration which has underlain all our provisional adjustments of expectation is triumphantly justified. One such piece of description (which to a person without melodic experience means about as much as a description of the sensations of figure-skating to a person who lacked the muscular sense) serves as well as a hundred, to show in what sort of remote way the Ideal Motion lends itself to terms of physical motion; somewhat as we have already described certain characteristics of melodies, regarded as forms, in terms of physical bodies and forces, by the help of such words as strength, weakness, balance, support, and so on.

§ 9. Apparent evolution of melody within ourselves.

There is one characteristic of melody which attention to its aspect as motion brings out with special clearness; and that is our sense of entire oneness with it, of its being as it were a mode of our own life. We feel in it, indeed, an objective character, inasmuch as we instinctively recognise that it has for others the same permanent possibilities of impression as for ourselves; but our sense of it nevertheless is not as of an external presentation, but of something evolved within ourselves by a special activity of our own. Thus it would be a very fair description of this opening subject of Beethoven's trio in D,

in question from the descending passage in the second phrase of the following exquisite tune of Beethoven's; no distinct *rallentando* would be possible in it, and yet each note towards the close seems just too good to leave; but to many persons I have no doubt the phrase would convey a sense rather of grace and *insouciance* than of intensity—

to say that it was left poised in suspense at the end of the fourth bar ; but the poising and suspense are entirely matters of our own experience ; it is *we* who are momentarily left to hang, and *we* who come toppling gently down again with the bass against us.

One more point, which was mentioned above, should be noticed again in connection with the Ideal Motion, namely, that in it the characteristics of purely *physical* motion remain undisturbed. The fusion of the rhythmic and the pitch-elements which is essential to the melodic form in no way disguises the rhythm pure and simple ; that is to say, the rhythm of a melody is as marked as though the pitch-element were eliminated, and the notes produced correctly in all that regards their time, but in monotone. The result is that the physical stimulation, which one sees so perpetually indicated during the performance of music in gentle tappings of feet and fingers and unconscious swayings of the head, seems woven into the very substance of the musical motive ; and a similar delight is given by watching good dancing (when it accompanies fine melody instead of being accompanied by trivial melody), the value of another sense here relieving as it were the pent-up yearning for motion. These physical events of course have not the slightest power to *express* melodies ; precisely the same movements may accompany melodies of the highest and the lowest rank. Physical motion can no more express ideal motion than the movements of a dancer or of a conductor as watched by a deaf person could convey the individual impression of the particular music as heard. But when the ideal motion is surging and swaying through one's head, the accompanying of it with rhythmical physical motion, real or imagined, seems to fuse the sense of the physical movement into the essence of the other ; the body seems as if itself endowed with the power of expressing perfect beauty, in a mode comparable to that experienced in the actual delivery of beautiful music by the voice ; or, if a very risky expression may be pardoned in the

§ 10. Distinctness of the rhythmic element and impulse towards accompanying movements.

description of what is indescribable, body and spirit seem literally one. Owing to the physically stimulating power of musical sound and the extreme distinctness and determinateness of the physical sense of rhythmic motion, our corporeal life is brought before us in the most direct and striking manner, while at the same instant raised into a new region by its fusion with a quite incorporeal activity.

§ 11. Danger of ignoring the essential and unique character of musical forms, by unduly emphasising those external aspects which have their analogues in movements in space.

It is necessary now to point out a special danger which the very use of the word motion in connection with Music involves. The danger is of forgetting that the essential characteristic of the complete Ideal Motion is an absolutely unique beauty perceived by an absolutely unique faculty, and of unduly emphasising the *external aspects*[1] of musical motion, the aspects of it which physical motion *can* follow and imitate, and which therefore may seem to follow and imitate (or, as it is more usually put, to idealise and improve on) physical motion; aspects which include not only matters of pace and rhythm, but of range in pitch, such as the steady and quiet keeping within comparatively narrow limits, sudden changes and jumps over a wider space, and so on. In other words, *motion* naturally suggests motion of bodies in space; whence people are led to attribute the effect of Music to those points in which a parallelism to motion in space is undoubtedly presented, forgetting that the complete Ideal Motion has *no* parallel outside Music, and that these points may be just as much presented in compositions which produce no pleasurable emotion as in those which produce the maximum of pleasurable emotion; that such features, indeed, are in themselves no more adequate to account for the beauty of any particular music than the possession of a nose and a mouth and two eyes to account for the beauty of any particular face. Thus Helmholtz says, ‘The incorporeal material of tones is much more adapted for following the musician's intention in the most delicate and pliant manner for every species of motion, than any corporeal material, however light. Graceful rapidity, grave procession, quiet advance, wild leaping, all these different characters of motion and a thousand others in the most varied combinations and degrees, can be represented by successions of tones. And as Music expresses these motions, it gives an expression also to those mental conditions which naturally evoke similar motions, whether of the body or the voice, or of the thinking and feeling principle itself. Every motion is an expression of the power which

---

[1] I am compelled to use the word *external* in a sense which can only be understood by the reader's meeting me half-way. Nose, eyes, and mouth are not external to a beautiful face; but the mere fact that such features are present is external to the quality of beauty, inasmuch as they are also present in ugly and unimpressive faces. So any particular music which presents features of pace, amount of range, &c., suggestive of a parallelism with physical motions and measurements, presents them as an inseparable part of itself; but the mere possession of such features, as in the other case, is external to, and in no way implies, the quality of beauty or musical impressiveness.

produces it, and we instinctively measure the motive force by the amount
of motion which it produces.' The degree of truth in these remarks
makes them the more misleading if they are taken as the whole truth.
For they ignore the *differentia* of melodic form, the unique proportions
which are as remote from anything suggested by movements in space as
from anything suggested by forms in space, and which cannot be in the
remotest way penetrated by the finest appreciation of mere physical
motion, or of the external aspects of motion presented in Music: they
treat musical motion just as an idealisation of physical motion, as a more
delicate and manageable way of doing the same things, and as emotional
simply in virtue of those modes in which it resembles physical motion.
On this view, a set of flashy variations, or four octaves of scale played
*fortissimo* up and down with both hands on a grand piano, varied with
occasional skips over wide intervals, should convey the maximum of force;
and that such melodies as the great subject of the adagio in Beethoven's
fourth symphony, or *Ein' feste Burg*, should seem the strongest and
most irresistible things in the universe, would be a simple impossibility;
both these melodies being confined within narrow limits of pitch, and
consisting almost entirely of the successive notes of the scale, following
each other at a slow pace, and in the case of the former played *pianissimo*.
Again, what can be quieter, judged on any external grounds, than the
movement in the following paragraph? If we 'measure the motive force
by the amount of motion which it produces' we ought to perceive infinitely more motive force, and so infinitely more emotional impressiveness in
a study of Czerny's, than in the following measured melody from the
*Pastoral* sonata; which, in spite of its simple progression of tones and
semitones and its perfectly deliberate and unbroken accompaniment, affects

the inner sense with a compulsion, a concentrated passion of movement, so overpowering that I scarcely know its parallel in Music; the four bars' break in the middle making the swing of the motive as it recurs, seem more than ever resistless.[1]

There is doubtless a physical reference in our measurement of the force of a melodic movement, in the sense that the *ictus* of strong melodies produces an impulse towards some strong accompanying movement: there are tunes which I never think of in the street without wanting to knock down a lamp-post at every accented note. But such physical suggestion for our own bodies (which is an effect, not a cause, of the character of particular Ideal Motions) has obviously nothing to do with 'amount of motion' as measured by pace, suddenness, width and variety of interval, or any other of the external characteristics which Music itself may present.

I do not wish to trench on the topic of emotion as expressed by Music, which will occupy us later. It is enough here to remark that while we shall find that some of those external characteristics which we have just noticed do connect themselves to a considerable extent with certain emotional aspects of Music, they never truly do so, in the cultivated stage of the art, apart from that beauty of form which they in no way guarantee or constitute, and which may be at its maximum in their absence; and that there is no essential relation between amount of force as musically perceived, and those features in which a parallelism to motion of bodies in space can be traced.

[1] There is always a danger in giving special instances, since they may always turn out to belong to the cases, so numerous in Music, where different people feel differently. Thus some one may tell me that he agrees as to the beauty of this passage, but does not feel it as specially characterised by force and passion; I have no answer; he may even support his view (though to this argument I should certainly demur) by pointing out that a large part of the movement in which the paragraph occurs is rather of a naïve and rustic character. Still the effect of the paragraph on me is a fact which, so far as any one believes I tell the truth about it, he must accept as a true example of the principle I wish it to exemplify. And as to the principle, the non-amenability of the Ideal Motion to such measurements as pace and width of jumps and other analogues of motion in space may suggest, I am not afraid of contradiction from any lover of Music who will think over some favourite passages. The intensity of many chromatic passages, where the motion is by the smallest possible steps (as partially exemplified in the last four bars of the above passage), would afford instances in point.

In this connection it is impossible to avoid some mention of a theory which has recently received some prominence, that the motion of bodies in space can be so regulated as to create a sort of visible music. The idea has long been entertained in relation to pyrotechnic displays; but Professors Perry and Ayrton have given it a new form by devising an ingenious machine, whereby a round shadow cast on a wall may be moved at all paces in all sorts of graceful curves, with all manner of variations of the size both of itself and of its shifting orbits, while the wall may be coloured and variegated with changing tints.[1] It is probable that a very attractive and impressive spectacle might be thus presented; the mistake lies in the view of its relation to Music. The Professors conceive that though Music has got a start as a means of producing emotion, the means they suggest might in time produce a worthy companion-art. They treat the emotions producible by art as existing in a kind of reservoir to which various taps may be applied, with the same issue in each case. And in fact we have certain broad and general modes of feeling to which this view applies: there are many aspects of force, for instance, which give rise to the same sort of wonder and awe; and the emotions caused by the things which the Professors adduce in illustration of their point, the rush of a train, the rolling of waves, the rhythmic motion of a large engine, may find true analogues in mighty moving masses of rich musical tone. But the special and characteristic emotions of Music belong to special and characteristic musical form. (The Professors seem indeed to have little conception of the characteristic virtues of individual forms in other arts; 'a piece of sculpture,' they say, 'is but suggestive—it merely introduces some simple emotion which acts in a controlling way upon the human mind; so also a fine picture induces a dreamy state and sets one a-thinking.') The emotional side of the subject as regards Music must, as I have said, be deferred; but it is little more than a restatement of what was said in the last paragraph to remark how radically distinct are those aspects of changing sound whose effect can be paralleled by that of forceful visible motions, from the essential characteristics of individual objective form. The progressive form, the Ideal Motion, of which each step is necessary to the whole— which is organic by dint of the relation of each component part to others, some of them separated from it by a very appreciable interval of time and, it may be, by a large number of intervening units of tone—is wholly due, as we have seen, to the fusion with rhythm of the pitch-element in which tone-relationship is the all-important feature. This is the sort of form, unchangeable in each case, along which we pass in glad compulsion. No similar necessity, no true organism, could ever be discerned in the sequence of movements of the Professors' ball, however graceful and

§ 12. Criticism of the idea of visible Music;

which entirely ignores the nature of musical forms.

[1] The paper on the subject by Professors Perry and Ayrton will be found in the *Pro-* *ceedings of the Physical Society,* vol. iii. Part I.

various. The eye might have its negative requirements, and resent irregular angularities of direction and violently sudden changes of pace; but the positive faculty of linking a long series of the swiftly vanishing impressions into a unity, that faculty which the unique sense of tone-relationship alone makes possible in the case of the ear, has no possible analogue in the case of vision, in the absence of any similar means of correlating the elements of a visual series.

I need not repeat what has been said more than once about the fact and the reasons of the cogent definiteness of musical forms, connected as it is with the arresting power, the ease and exactitude of reproduction in memory, and above all the distinctness of individuality, which so completely differentiate them from visual curves; but I should have thought the mere fact that the Professors' ball could be mechanically made, as they themselves say, to go through a million different graceful figures, would have brought home to them the difference of such phenomena from beautiful musical forms, which even to a Mozart and a Schubert were not by any means matter of daily inspiration, and which Beethoven had often painfully to fight towards, and to hew out like a statue from a rock.

*The mistake is perhaps partly due to the word harmonic;*

I fancy that the word *harmonic* has something to do with the notion of visible music as a possibility of the future. The fact that the *harmonic* curves traced by vibrating bodies are visibly graceful lines, combined with the fact that the word is particularly associated with Music, suggests a Pythagorean idea of a sort of parallelism in any phenomena into which something 'harmonic' enters. But in Music harmonics are of course a mere matter of tone-material; melodic form has absolutely nothing to do with 'harmonic' proportions.

*partly to regarding Music as of recent origin.*

As regards Professors Perry and Ayrton, however, the theory seems in great measure attributable to their view of Music as a recently invented 'vehicle for exciting emotion in us.' They consider that the special power of Music is the result of 'the accident that Western nations have more assiduously educated the emotional side of their minds in certain particular directions;' and that the differences in the music of different nations prove Music, unlike Painting, to have been 'a creation of each individual people;' they distinctly imply that the use of the ear rather than the eye as the channel for the emotions which appear to us characteristic of Music, is a conventionality parallel to the employment of different scale-systems by different peoples. No reader who has accompanied me so far will need to be reminded that we traced the power of Music in large measure to associations in comparison with which Painting and the more distinctly intellectual arts are things of yesterday; and that the differences arising from variety of scale-system have absolutely no bearing on the essence of Music and of the musical faculty.

We may now conveniently review our position. In the first place the more *general* characteristics of melody with which we were mainly occupied in the fifth and sixth chapters may be better appreciated, and the list somewhat extended, by the light of our recent more detailed examination. They may be summed up as follows: 1. The mere material out of which melodies are formed, i.e. musical tones, is unique in our experience, quite apart from the use made of it. The sensation of musical tone is not presented to the ear by any natural phenomena, even the natural voices of men and animals containing but little of it: it is a sensation produced on exceptional occasions by exceptional means (primarily of course by the 'singing' voice), and in early stages of development is probably extremely exciting in itself. That is, the mere producing and hearing of sounds and cries with some musical *timbre* would be exciting and enjoyable, without any formal connection, or with the slightest and most rudimentary connection, between them. 2. With Music, even in its most rudimentary stages, is associated the sense of motion, with all its powers of physical stimulation. These two heads alone do something to explain the fact that, while anything more than the most rudimentary enjoyment of abstract visual form is a late product, whether in the individual or the race, keen enjoyment of successions of musical sounds is a frequent characteristic—both of young children and of low savages. 3. Precision and definiteness is a marked characteristic of musical forms: this is due to the employment of fixed degrees both of time and pitch, and makes possible an extreme distinctness of individuality. 4. The continuous looking forward and expecting (exemplified in a very simple form in watching the approach to the key-note or some other landmark) affords a partial explanation of the *excitement* of Music, as marked off from anything that could be given by the impressions perceived *simultaneously* in space. 5. The forms, when they occur, and so far as they are impressive, are each new and unique things, not like new expressions or postures, or alterations and reminiscences, of known things: each fresh melodic presentation which is profoundly felt is felt as till then *wholly* unknown. 6. There are the mighty associational elements connected with the primæval use of musical sounds under the influence of sexual emotion; and (7) probably some instinctive reference to the phenomenon of speech, owing to the identical feature of a succession of changing sounds, contributes to the effect which melody produces of being *something said*, an utterance of imperative significance.

§ 13. Review of the general characteristics of melody;

Subsequently we passed beyond these general grounds, and examined the *special* peculiarities of actual melodic structure, the special characteristics of those proportions which the musical faculty (active alike in the expert's grasp of a symphony and the baby's recognition of some familiar ditty) perceives and balances with such instinctive ease. We saw how great was the complexity involved in the *pitch*-element alone, through the joint features of

and of the special work of the musical faculty;

degrees of distance and of relationship present in the notes; and we subsequently saw that the simplest melody throughout its course is the resultant of
*two heterogeneous factors*, rhythm and pitch, which further complicates the
proportions in a way quite unexampled in any other region of experience;
in a way too which makes it impossible to refer degrees of pleasing or displeasing quality to distinguishable points of technical structure. And the
phenomena are of course neither more nor less peculiar than the faculty by
which we apprehend them. Remembering what a marvel of cleverness the
ear is, both in its conscious and unconscious operations—how it appreciates
tone-relationship through harmonics which it does not separately detect, and
in distinguishing a chord as made up of component elements does unassisted
what the eye needs a prism to do for *it*—we may certainly feel that, if we
were to be endowed anywhere with a definite and perfectly unique sense of
abstract proportion, it might be expected to be in connection with *hearing*:
but no examination of the faculties of the ear apart from developed forms
could have revealed to us the possibility of such forms, and every fresh
application of the proportional sense involves a process which is a law to
itself. For such rudimentary facts as the change from a tone to a related
tone, the final rest on a key-note, the dual balance of phrase—the barren
elements or conditions which are common both to pleasurable and un-
pleasurable melodic forms—we can conceive such a justification as that
neglect of them would clearly lead to incoherence: but when we come to
actual forms, and to the startling differences of merit which the very
simplest known to us present, the musical faculty defies all explanation of
its action and its judgments. The only conceivable explanation indeed
would be an analogy, and we know not where to look for it. Since sight
and hearing are the only senses by which we perceive abstract forms at
all, we are in speaking of either reduced at best to a single line of things
for illustration or contrast. If we had a few more senses, yielding such
impressions as could be co-ordinated and unified into wholly new kinds of
forms, so that the inadequacy of curves to express melodies was paralleled
by several other examples, we might find it easier to realise that the
contemplation of the various forms involved an exercise of faculties
special for each class of phenomena, irreducible therefore under any such
general rule as we could call an explanation; and that what we loosely call
a sense of proportion is of a Protean character.

Finally, we proceeded to consider melody in a further aspect, not
merely as form or structure, but as *formed motion*; and again we noticed
the peculiarity of the process by which the motion is followed, and how
little clue to it is afforded by the phenomena of physical force and motion.
Here again, too, in relation to physical force and motion, we encountered
a general theory of musical impressiveness, which betrays its failure really
to reach the heart of the matter in much the same way as did the references

to more particular points of technical structure; namely, by proving applicable to music which is followed with feelings of indifference and annoyance as much as to music which is followed with delight. We are thus amply warned against the common sort of account of musical effect which ignores the simple fact that two series of notes, similar to one another on all the adduced grounds, may present the whole difference of possessing beauty and *not* possessing it; that the suggested conditions of effect are continually present when there is *no* effect; and that the problem presented by this variety of quality is altogether distinct from any *general* considerations of emotional power in Music. It was in ourselves facing this problem, as the central one of the whole subject, that we saw how unmistakably it points to a uniquely isolated faculty, whose decisions can no more be justified than they can be impugned by any law or from any standpoint external to the impression in each case.

We must now pass on to an idea, or rather a medley of ideas, which embraces and underlies an immense amount of the prevalent confusion on this subject, and the consideration of which will, I hope, mark off still more clearly the true position and scope of the musical faculty. The central conception is often held in the most unprecise way, and its applications are exceptionally hard to track out and examine : but, broadly speaking, it is the conception of *reasonableness*, as a source to which our feelings of beauty have essentially some sort of reference, explicit or implicit ; the conception of *order*, which is of course the natural expression for any combination of elements into a distinguishable form or series, as connoting features which must be logically defensible and have clear relation to the scientific (as distinct from the intuitional) faculties. The analysis necessary for a due examination of these ideas and the deductions from them must extend considerably beyond the sphere of Music, and will take us back to topics which have already been to some extent discussed : but the subject could only be made intelligible by treating it as a whole, and such treatment will not, I hope, involve any inconvenient amount of repetition.

*the scope and relations of which need still further elucidation.*

# CHAPTER IX.

## THE RELATIONS OF REASON AND ORDER TO BEAUTY.

§ 1. Ambiguities in the words law, order, regularity.

THE words *law, order, regularity*, are the key-notes of all scientific discussion; and we naturally come across them whenever attempts are made to treat æsthetic problems on a scientific method. There seem, however, to be special dangers and ambiguities connected with their use in that particular region; special facilities for sliding imperceptibly from one sense into another, and so adding extra confusion to branches of enquiry which are in any case sufficiently obscure.

Beauty is said to be subject to laws dependent on the nature of the intelligence : in what sense is this true ?

' Beauty,' says Helmholtz in the last chapter of the *Ton-Empfindungen*, ' is subject to laws and rules dependent on the nature of the human intelligence.' This, though sounding most reasonable, is just the sort of statement which is liable to be misunderstood and misapplied : and some of the points I wish to discuss in the present chapter may be conveniently introduced by enquiring in what sense and within what limits it is true. That there are limits is soon manifest. For instance, it is a law that regular rapid stimulation of certain nervous organs produces the sensation of a musical tone : in other words, the subjective impression of beauty of tone is subject to a certain rule of nerve-stimulation which in no way depends on the nature of human intelligence, and the relation of which to the sensation of pleasure is an ultimate simple and non-reasonable fact. So a piece of red coral presented to an infant, or a piece of blue sky vacantly gazed at by an adult, affords a pleasure whose conditions may certainly be generalised into a law, but a law expressed in terms of physics and nervous organs, not of human intelligence. And a large part of the beauty perceived in the *colour-qualities* of sights and sounds is clearly of this ultimate character.

When, however, we pass on to *forms*, to regions of perception where the mental faculties become active, Helmholtz's statement about laws and rules seems at once applicable. But a confusion is still possible : *subject to* laws and rules often slips into meaning *consisting in subjection* to laws and rules, clearly a very different thing. For instance, if we take works of art, with special reference to which Helmholtz is speaking, we see that a painter must not represent in one picture a number of heterogeneous and quite unconnected objects, because it is a law that the mind is puzzled and distracted by total aimlessness and want of unity ; a composer must not repeat exactly the same passage twelve times running, because it is a law that the mind is wearied by prolonged and objectless monotony ; neither painter nor musician must introduce grotesque incidents or episodes into solemn compositions, since it is a law that the mind resents pointless incongruity. But the laws and rules which can be thus formulated have, so to speak, an external sort of relation to the beauty : they are controlling conditions, not essence : no such formulæ will account in the slightest degree for the central face in the *Cenacolo* or for *Dove sono.* So again, it is quite true, as Helmholtz goes on to observe, that we may ' seek to enhance our enjoyment and interest by tracing out the suitability, connection, and equilibrium of all the separate parts' in a work of art. But still we shall be dealing in great measure with the conditions, the framework, the means of setting forth and focussing the essentially expressive forms. The necessary regularity of the composition in the *Cenacolo* would disappear, and we should instantly see the mistake, if the divine face were in a corner instead of in the middle, and an indispensable rule is observed by at any rate putting it in a conspicuous position : but this is the arranging, not the informing, element ; it is the expression that moves us, not the position.

*The laws are often related to the beauty only as conditions of its most effective presentation.*

Nor need we take such extreme instances. The selection and treatment of the subject-matter may not be irrational, and yet may fail to be imaginative or interesting ; and its success or failure in this respect falls naturally under our intellectual cognisance. Thus a painter introduces as many objects as he likes into a picture, and groups them as he pleases : he could to a great extent verbally explain and defend his arrangement ; and though the presence of an abstract or *pattern* element in a pictorial composition, embracing objects which in themselves and in their relations are independent of such an element, makes the appreciation of the arrangement a very hard thing to analyse, still we can discover, or a more appreciative spectator could discover for us, various ways in which the eye is led and helped and the mind satisfied, aspects of order both of the abstract and of the reasonable kind, and the various causes why the arrangement was powerful and suggestive, or (it might be) weak and theatrical. But it is not in any way demonstrable that one nose is more orderly than two, or two eyes more conformable to reason than four. The expression of a face, the strength of a mountain, and freedom of Turner's clouds and waves, the magic of his distances, are not revealed to us by any reasoning process. However characteristic of the artist's genius, however necessary to the completeness of the effect, be the features of rational or imaginative combination and arrangement, they stand distinct from the qualities in virtue of which the subject-matter is primarily selected for development or idealisation : and considerations which can be set forth to the intelligence in words cannot penetrate to the essential forms and effects, whose appeal (as I hope further to show) is to our immediate consciousness special and ultimate, and only presentable in the proper materials of the particular art.

§ 2. Considerations of reason, as applied to representative art by Lessing ;

The representative arts naturally give special scope to Reason, inasmuch as their subject-matter, in its selection and treatment, involves the constant exercise of distinctly intellectual faculties, and admits the propositions and arguments attaching to known objects and events. Thus Lessing points out that ' Timomachus has not painted Medea at the moment in which she actually murders her children, but some minutes before, while maternal love was still struggling with jealousy ; ' and that Ajax was not represented in the act of slaying the herds, but sitting remorsefully afterwards. Many reasons could doubtless be given why these were the wiser moments to choose : but how much does the mere choice imply ? How much does it guarantee in the way of excellence in the work ? The very fact that the intellectual side of the imagination is so prominent, and reasoned criticism therefore so possible, in the case of the representative arts, involves a special danger of substituting ingenuity for intuition, and of evolving reasonable ' laws and rules ' which bear no relation to the true *differentia* of beautiful works. There could not be a more effective means of realising this danger than a perusal of the *Laocoon*, where the *whole* merit of works of art is throughout found in things which a person without the slightest artistic genius could and would think of as naturally as an artist. A great painter is differentiated not by *common sense* but by *vision*.

It is strange that while Lessing has been considered the special champion of beauty for its own sake, his criticisms rarely or never contain the slightest indication that he had used his eyes as eyes, or received any thrill through so using them : if the fact was otherwise, he certainly has done himself injustice by the frigid emphasis with which he dwells on external conditions and considerations, and on general features in themselves quite empty of beauty. A few instances will make this clear. Thus he says, ' Rubens in his *Resurrection of Lazarus* has chosen the moment when Lazarus comes forth already alive from the grave. I believe that this is the proper moment : it obviates the necessity of holding the nose, for the stench could not have continued with the living Lazarus.' His admiration of an *Annunciation* by Tintoret rests on the fact that the angel is entering through a breach in the wall, the painter being unable, he says, ' to express the spiritual essence of the angel,' but having succeeded in showing ' that such a being cannot be excluded by anything.' Again, ' the painter who, in imitation of the description of a Thomson, has represented a beautiful landscape, has done

to Painting ;

more than one who has copied it directly: the latter out of a lively impression on the senses creates something beautiful; the former out of a slender and feeble representation of arbitrary signs produces the same result.' We may grant that a beautiful landscape produced entirely in a studio would be a very remarkable phenomenon: but in the imagined relation between painter and poet we find the old mechanical and external view. The points out of Thomson's description which could be transferred to canvass might of course be enumerated in a dry catalogue which any one with ordinary eyesight and observation could draw up, and of the like of which any landscape painter could draw up a hundred a day. Yet a painter who embodies them is said to have imitated Nature through the medium of the poet: as if supposing a painter to be able to paint landscapes in his studio, such mediumship could be of the slightest use to him; as if an enumeration of objects could be the means by which in his mind's eye he beheld, not the mere fact of their presence, but their essential visual beauty and pictorial value; as if the painter was enabled to express distance and light through the mediumship of Thomson's saying there was a distant sun-lit hill, or as if Thomson's saying that the sky was mantled in fair and fleecy clouds gave the painter the clue to the expression of cloud-beauty and fleeciness. We might as well say that Shakespeare represented human nature through the mediumship of the authors who suggested some of his incidents. How completely Lessing was satisfied with barren reflections, and with characteristics in no way involving any essential and informing charm, seems indicated by his being quite as rapturous over pictures he imagines as over anything he has ever seen. Thus he conceives a favourable subject for a painting from Homer: ' The banqueting gods at council; the open golden palace. Groups of the most beautiful and dignified figures, placed according to the will of the painter. Hebe, eternal youth, ministering with a goblet in her hand. What architecture! What masses of light and shade! What contrasts! What manifold variety of expression! Where shall I begin? Where shall I cease to feed my eye?' It is of course easy to write and to understand such a passage as this without knowing the difference between the feeblest daub and a Veronese; but to Lessing the mere mental survey of the subject-matter seems quite sufficient satisfaction. It would be unfair to infer absolutely that he would not have discriminated between a good and a bad delineation of the scene he proposes; but one cannot resist the impression that he failed to see how little the charm of the picture, if it succeeded, would lie in the mere fact that the subject-matter was such and such. Only a born painter has a right to smack his lips over an unborn work, the essential artistic excellences of which (as distinct from the vague visions any of us can summon up at a moment's notice) are, for all but him, non-existent till they are actually presented to the eye.

to Poetry ;

Nor does Poetry fare any better. With respect to the representation on the Shield of Achilles of two scenes from the same city, one in the streets and one in the market-place, Lessing laboriously argues, on the ground that the laws of perspective could not be understood in Homer's time, that Homer must in imagination have contemplated the city 'from so raised a point of sight that he thereby opened a clear view simultaneously both of the streets and of the market-place.' Having been struck with a certain absurdity in pictures where the Homeric cloud was introduced as a screen behind which the spectator saw the hero lurking, he is careful to tell us that when Homer uses mist or night to conceal his personages it is only 'a poetical mode of describing invisibility :' and again, when Poseidon darkened the eyes of Achilles, Lessing warns us that they were not *really* darkened ; it was a metaphor to express how extremely swiftly Æneas was withdrawn from their sight. He attributes Milton's more elaborate descriptions, as contrasted with Homer's single epithets, to Milton's having lost the power of quickly imagining what things look like, through blindness : he surely ought to have noticed the vulgar idea that Homer was also blind, if only to confute it with the converse argument. Equally mechanical is the chapter which professes to expound the beauties of the *Philoctetes* ; where the proposition that screams are out of place in tragedy, put forth on the very disputable ground that we do not adequately sympathise with physical pain, is treated as constituting a difficulty which nothing but supreme genius could overcome : and we are made to dwell on such points as that Philoctetes had a *visible* wound in his foot (not a stomach-ache) ; that he was solitary ; that, after all, people *do* sometimes scream without incurring contempt, and so on. Supreme genius would hardly thank its expositor. Nor are these occasional or isolated lapses : almost every page of the book gives the same impression of a man laboriously striving from outside to discover reasons for admiring approved works.

and to the relations between the arts.

As regards Lessing's more general views about the relations and differences of the arts, it is but fair to remember when and where he lived : and to give him credit for the discovery of such laws as that a sculptor may not, though a poet may, represent a man screaming, because it would distort his face. But in reality the famous dictum of Simonides that Painting is silent Poetry, and Poetry speaking Painting, which it is Lessing's chief aim, put in the forefront of his treatise, to expound and modify, took him in not less fatally than other people. 'The poet should always paint,' he says : and his cardinal thesis is that, as the poet has to use words *in succession,* he must confine his painting to physical *action,* the parts of which take place *successively.* It seems almost incredible that a poet should have found the basis for an essay on Art in a doctrine which debars Poetry, first, from attempting to describe external scenes and objects, and secondly, from attempting to depict the inner life of the soul; a doctrine perhaps as radically delusive as any fundamental tenet in any book of equal reputation. Lessing most characteristically supports his view that Poetry cannot be effectively employed in the description of scenes and objects, by quoting, as a *reductio ad absurdum*, a mechanical and detailed description of a bouquet of flowers, and calling it a 'masterpiece of its kind.' How radically he confuses the functions and possibilities of the very arts he is professing scientifically to distinguish is shown by his expressly stating the poet's great business to be the *creation of illusion* : and poetical descriptions of scenes and objects, he says, ' must necessarily lack the power of creating illusion,' ' because the co-existence of bodies thereby comes into collision with the consecutiveness of language.' Such blindness in so honest a writer can only be attributed to an irrelevant delight in mere schematism; to a feeling that it is *logical*, if representation of movements is forbidden to painting, that conversely representation of objects should be forbidden to poetry. Equally singular is the absence from the *Laocoon* of any hint that beyond material phenomena, whether objects or actions, Poetry possesses, in large tracts of the inner world of feeling, an altogether special sphere, and a true monopoly of subject-matter, since it is only by words that many inward facts can be expressed as directly and definitely as any other; and that in sounding the depths of human experience, and setting forth in all its myriad relations and aspects the image of the world on the individual soul, lies a mightier task than in ' the invention of incidents,' which seems to be Lessing's one idea of poetical imagination.

I have dwelt thus on the *Laocoon* because it is a typical instance of the failure of logical analysis to penetrate to the essence of beautiful work; because, of all the books I have ever seen which deal with beauty, it most constantly provokes the exasperated feeling that the points it lays stress on might all be there, and all the given laws and conditions be observed, and yet the beauty be entirely absent. Nor is the popularity of the book hard to explain, when we remember how apt we most of us are, in reading criticisms and explanations on matters which we have never independently considered, to be extremely prepossessed in an author's favour if we find we follow him easily. There is never a doubt what Lessing means : and it is natural for those who are more readily appealed to by literature than by art to repay such a writer for the pleasure of comprehending him, for the glow that accompanies an easy dip into a great and presumably difficult subject, by accepting as luminous and profound anything that they find at once new and intelligible. Perspicuity and erudition were certain, for instance, to impress a mind like Macaulay's, in the absence of strong artistic instinct; but that such criticism should have acted as a powerful intellectual stimulus to a man of Goethe's calibre might give one pause in

*Reason for dwelling on the Laocoon.*

attacking it, were it necessary to go much beyond quotations, and simple statements of the leading views, which admit of no double meaning.

§ 3. The laws which generalise the facts of mental processes are quite different from the imagined laws to which Beauty is said to be subject.

But, it may be urged, granting that in some at least of the things presented or represented in a beautiful work there is an inherent impressiveness and significance, which no intelligent reasonings about the choice, the conception, and the treatment of the subject-matter will penetrate—yet we feel that impressiveness, we enjoy that instantaneous and unreasoning, and yet thoroughly non-sensuous and ideal quickening, on grounds which may surely be classified and defined: granting the general arrangement of the subject-matter in elaborate works to be a more distinctly intellectual and describable affair, still our knowledge of mental constitution should surely afford us *some* principles about the more essential elements of beauty. Certainly: such principles, so far as they go beyond the mere laws of sensory stimulation and extend to the intellectual region, will be the general facts of our mental processes, as regards, *e.g.*, the pleasure of imitation, or the love of type and metaphor; but far above all, the laws of association, hereditary and individual, which are deeply involved in most if not all of our enjoyment of form. But here the 'laws and rules' are of a totally different kind from those we have hitherto spoken of: they are general facts about the development and characteristics of mind itself, not about relations which the mind desiderates in phenomena, and to which therefore beautiful phenomena are bound to conform. They are general as applying to all

---

[1] And surely reverence for a great name may go a step too far. For instance, in the preface to the translation of the *Laocoon* from which I have quoted, a gentleman of ability and eminence tells us of Lessing's not being able to endure music, which obliged him 'to rush out into the air in order to breathe freely;' and naïvely continues, 'How far, if at all, this curious physical fact might have influenced his opinion on the subject we cannot tell. . . . It is probable that a treatise by Lessing on the science of sound and the art of Music would have given us another occasion for admiring his immense erudition, the vigour of his criticism, and the clearness of his conclusions.' There is an innocence in this which disarms indignation; but can the same be said of the following? Lessing 'knew that from a keen perception and critical observance of the mutual affinities of the arts had been derived the doctrine both of the beautiful and the ideal which had animated the unrivalled creations of the great philosophers, poets, and artists of Greece.' To such a sentence as this a really heavy responsibility attaches, inasmuch as unsuspicious people who do not happen to know anything about Greek literature and art might naturally believe it. The next thing will be to wonder how the sculptor could have produced his *Laocoon* group, or Virgil his description of the same scene, without having had the advantage of studying the true 'doctrine' of such performances under Lessing. It would of course be equally untrue to find the secret spring of the great artistic works of *any* age in a doctrine based on critical analysis: but the idea is peculiarly startling in connection with the childlike growth, and the utter spontaneity, free alike from self-consciousness and from pedantry, which so specially characterised the great art and literature of Greece. It is to be doubted whether any Greek before the time of Aristotle would have had sufficient interest in 'mutual affinities' between the arts, to detect even the amount of deficiency which Lessing did in the above-quoted dictum about silent Poetry and speaking Painting: and we certainly have no record, among their works, of symphonies in brown and amber, or of façades in the Phrygian mode.

minds, not as applied by the mind to all phenomena; their regularity is not a logical order demanded by the mind, but the mere historical regularity wherein the evolution of mind resembles all other gradual natural processes. So that, if we try to apply this new conception to the quotation from Helmholtz with which we started, its sense is wholly inverted and it becomes a barren truism. From meaning that phenomena, to be beautiful, must first prove themselves to be reasonable by subjection to general rules of the intelligence, it would have come to mean merely that the mind perceives and feels a particular thing, beauty of this or that kind, as it has been by nature constituted to perceive and feel it.

In an artistic work, then, it seems as if we may perpetually discriminate an element of law and order, an element of reasonable, striking, and purposeful arrangement, which can be formulated and recognised as within the domain of the general intelligence, from an element of beauty and impressiveness which, in the case of form no less than in that of colour, is beyond the scope of reason and of reasoned analysis and argument; and the intuitive perception of which in each special kind of presentation seems often connected with some special range or ranges of association, dating back, perhaps, to the very dawn of emotional life. This element is specially characteristic of the units, which, while entering as parts into some larger composition, are themselves more completely and essentially organic, inasmuch as further reduction or analysis of them would mean absolute mutilation and loss of all characteristic impressiveness; as, for instance, if we divide a face or figure into its separate features or limbs, or a theme from some musical piece into detached notes or bars. At the same time it is impossible to lay down hard and fast limits: we have already seen that different sorts of work differ greatly in the extent to which they concentrate the chief interest on any such complete or semi-complete units. We could not isolate a piece of delicately gradated light as a form; and yet the sense of free and sunny space, or of endless aerial perspective, which it might suggest, would come distinctly under the head we are considering. Both in landscape and buildings shifting effects and general effects are often more essential to the emotional result than the more permanent characteristics of particular forms; and in landscape especially, the frequent impossibility of the more definite references is easily explained, if we remember that the various associations from which our enjoyment of Nature has been evolved have had quite as much to do with broad qualities of views embracing a multitude of objects as with objects individually considered. Even in the case of Music, which does, as we have seen, in a remarkable degree concentrate attention on each part in turn, and where any melody or 'subject' or phrase which can be thought of and enjoyed in detachment has enough completeness to constitute a form in the sense meant, we shall see in the next chapter that it is useless to attempt to

§ 4. The intuitive element of artistic enjoyment is often especially connected with such parts or units in a larger work as have most organic completeness of their own;

but often also with more general qualities.

draw any distinct line, dividing off what shall be regarded as complete organisms from the clauses, themselves organic, which combine into larger forms.

§ 5. The notion of *sym-metry* is often unduly pressed.

But, again, it may be urged that though there has been pointed out one sort of law and order which does not explain or constitute beauty, we have no right to assume that reason does not penetrate beauty in some other way. Is not *symmetry* perpetually an essential factor in the individual and irre-ducible forms? and surely this commends itself as reasonable to the in-telligence. Now the main source of confusion between general intellectual processes and special perceptions of beauty, is the very fact that one of the simplest relations which the mind perceives and grasps, is that of sym-metry and regularity, combined with the further fact that this relation, being often present in beauty, is often perceived with pleasure : whence, by taking the factor for the whole, and then mixing up the ideas of regu-larity and rationality, a sort of relationship seems to be established between beauty and recognised laws of mental activity ; and such a statement as that the reasoning mind requires and enjoys symmetry and order, becomes one of the laws and rules to which ' beauty is subject.' In other words, it *sounds* more rational to say ' the mind is so ordered as to enjoy order ' than to say ' the mind is so ordered as to enjoy disorder.' And yet the latter statement would serve quite as often as the former, if we could at all rest in either as an adequate explanation : for if, on the one hand, Westminster Abbey is beautiful, so on the other is the tangled luxuriance of a tropical forest. But we continually find such facts, for example, as that the human face is normally pretty symmetrical, and in case of beauty often very completely so, and also that beautiful faces do not present wide divergences from a norm, taken as a basis for an explana-tion of human beauty ; which is referred to ' the mind's love of symmetry and regularity,' and dislike of things exaggerated and abnormal. When we examine such a particular case, we of course see at once that many faces which are quite regular and have no exaggerated feature, have no beauty ; and that beautiful faces and figures, seen in profile, have no symmetry, which, had we always seen each other in that position, would never have occurred to us as a necessary element ; so that, even when seen under conditions of symmetry, the beauty must lie essentially in minute details of free form and curvature, the unanalysable effect of which on us is mainly due to vast hidden stores of association and an extraordinarily developed power of comparison, *regular* only in the historical sense that their existence is not an unconditioned ' fluke.'

§ 6. Exami-nation of the view which identifies

The conception of regularity and conformance to reason as the primary factor in beauty, if legitimately pressed, naturally leads on to an actual identification of æsthetic with scientific perception, of the intuitive with the discursive action of the mind; an identification which appears in the æsthetic perception with scientific cognition. ideal schemes of both Plato and Comte,[1] and which often turns up under some form or other in æsthetic discussions. While engaged on this chapter I have been so fortunate as to find an especially clear and courageous statement of this view in an ingenious paper on the 'Evolution of Beauty' in the *Quarterly Journal of Science* for July 1878, some sentences of which I cannot do better than quote and condense.

'Beauty,' says the writer, ' is an abstract idea of the same nature as Goodness, Truth, Power, Charity, &c., and that which causes this idea to present itself in the human consciousness is the *perception of relationship among a number of diverse sensations*, of unity co-existent with variety. When the attention of the mind is focussed upon a variety of points in rapid succession, and the intellect is able to recognise *relationship* among all these points as members of one group, there arises the idea of Beauty. It can only present itself under the conditions of mental activity co-existent with the perception of relationship, proportion, unity.' Acts of attention, if absolutely repeated, are monotonous; hence the primary condition under which any object can appear beautiful to the human mind is that it be compounded of sufficiently varied parts. ' Every object in nature is so compounded of various parts, but human minds are not equally sensitive to small shades of difference.' ' Every object in nature is a group of parts related to each other in ways more or less complex and subtle. If any mind were absolutely sensitive to all degrees of relationship in all its aspects, nothing would appear chaotic. A mind absolutely sensitive to all shades of difference and to all degrees of relationship at the same time, would see everywhere throughout creation variety bound up in unity, would find neither monotony nor chaos, discord or ugliness, but only a universal Beauty.' The mind, however, is ' sensitive either to variety or unity only within narrow limits.' No difference is perceived between seeds of the musk-plant, no relationship between the numbers 264, 330, 396, 462 ; whereas the stones on a gravel-walk present sensible differences, and 2, 4, 6, 8 are obviously related. ' The closer the relationship, the more

---

[1] Plato considered that the wisest and cleverest people should not only be the best judges of music, but the best performers of it. Comte did not demand that his directing class should be themselves active musicians, though they were to supervise production in this as in other spheres ; but he expressly held the separation of speculative and scientific from artistic activity to be unnatural ; and that the faculties by which problems are solved and art is enjoyed are, and in an ideal state of things would prove to be, fundamentally united if not fundamentally the same. Fortunately for the unscientific and unspeculative majority, the apportionment of the susceptibilities with which human beings are actually born into the world is more natural than any ideal ; and we shall see more and more as we advance, how and why Music is pre-eminent in setting at naught the laws and restrictions which would connect it with intellectual education and activity, including even education and activity of the imaginative faculties in other directions.

easily is it recognised.' A pentagon, hexagon, circle, square, equilateral triangle possess beauty; a dodecahedron is scarcely beautiful except to a mathematician.

The size of the whole, and the number and arrangement of the parts, must not be beyond our powers of perception.

Now here the identification of æsthetic perception with cognition is so fundamental, that all reference to our actual senses seems to be dispensed with. To *see* ' everywhere throughout creation' beauty in place of chaos, a change of eyes would certainly be necessary: for those we now possess see, except in rare cases, only outsides. Moreover extent, as well as opacity, would make universal beauty hard to get at. Suppose, then, we give up such inconceivable regions and select some very large object, say the desert of Sahara. It is probable that no two grains of sand there are identical in size and shape, so that with sufficient magnifying power we ought to get a splendid notion of unity under variety; but then unfortunately the disproportionateness of the parts to the whole is so enormous that the differences of the parts seem to have absolutely no relation to the individuality of the whole, which would remain unaffected if the position of every part were altered.

We have, then, to come down with a run to limited and clearly defined conceptions, and to what in the visual region we know as forms—to audible phenomena the writer makes no reference—and in considering the view in relation to these, we must do what he has not done, and carefully distinguish *two modes* of relation between the parts and the whole. (1) Definite points of identity are perceived in the parts, and the relation between the parts is at the root of and explains our perception of the whole; as, for instance, in a geometrical figure, whose regularity and unity are perceived by a comparison of similar lines and angles, or in an arithmetical series, seen to be a regular one by the perception of the common difference. (2) The sense of the whole is the primary and fundamental fact, and the only point of identity perceived in the parts is their common character of belonging to the whole, the exercise by each of a function impossible to it in isolation: as in the profile of a face, or in some irregular natural object, or in a line of changing curvature. Often, indeed, the first of these modes of relation seems partially present with the second, as in a human face and figure seen from the front; but here, though the relation of symmetry between the two sides is perceived, the effect of this element is not so essential but that it could and would have been dispensed with, if human beings had been naturally and habitually unsymmetrical in some definite way. In the first mode, pure and simple, the recognition of the common characteristics and the relations of the parts seems scarcely able to get beyond the satisfaction of mere scientific cognition: and the writer I have quoted would surely have to admit some such distinction as we have drawn, if he would avoid the conclusion that a complicated but intelligible geometrical figure is as beautiful as a statue; since the perceptible

Two modes of relation between the parts and the whole.

points of identity and relation in the parts of the statue might well not exceed in number and variety those of the figure. And, indeed, though most of his statements and examples point to the first mode of relation, he does himself say that ' the point of identity which must be perceived in order that the group may appear beautiful is that all those phenomena belong to that group,' and take a necessary part in its formation : which is a statement of the second mode.

If, then, we examine his position on this side, it is of course obvious that the perception of beautiful form does entail the perception of unity under variety. We have already dwelt on this point, and on the fact that it is through the delicate and rapid sensibility of the eye and ear to variety in the impressions they receive, and the consequent opportunities for comparison and co-ordination, that seeing and hearing are *par excellence* the æsthetic senses. For not only is the mental activity, which is a necessary factor of the highest pleasure, intimately connected with this exact and subtle sensibility to the arrangement or order of impressions, but the immense variety possible in forms is the necessary condition of any wide variety of association and suggestion. Thus it is only in connection with *forms* that the higher and more complex mental faculties come into close and habitual relation with sense-impressions ; whence their æsthetic superiority to *colour*, the purely passive and sensuous enjoyment of which is shared with us by many animals : for though an animal may *recognise* objects, may take this or that shape as a symbol of known attributes, it lacks the mental development necessary for æsthetic enjoyment of their form.

The perception of beauty in form does entail the perception of unity under variety:

But the perception of unity under variety, merely as such, and failing any independent ground of interest whether in the elements or in their combination, cannot make good its claim to a truly æsthetic character. There are indeed instances of which some presented themselves when we were considering the sources of architectural effect, and others might be found in polyphonic music, where the complexity and unity are both so striking that the sense of ease and power with which we grasp them becomes an important element of our enjoyment ; but even here the effect would be impossible in the absence of all other elements of interest in the things combined, and such cases are quite exceptional. Unity under variety is a characteristic, or rather is the definition, of all form, not specially of beautiful form. On the above-quoted theory a prize-pig is as beautiful as a peacock, the Wellington statue as the Venus of Milo. The spectator is treated as though he were a sudden importation from another sphere, gifted with the perception of relations of fact, but without any emotional history or nature ; not as the product of slow development in a certain environment, a being whose perceptions in certain directions are saturated with emotion, and whose feelings, how-

but this characteristic is in no way peculiar to beautiful form, the differentia of which must be sought elsewhere.

ever interfused and transformed, have their primæval roots in simple experiences, and in associations whose ingredients are usually easy enough to surmise. I might quote Mr. Spencer's admirable divination of the strains of experience which enter into the enjoyment of landscape; or if we want a case of more definite and self-complete unities, we may recur to our former instance of the human face and form. Here the acts of attention in which we and our ancestors learned the minute and infinite varieties of shape and adjustment have been associated with countless experiences of safety and comfort in connection with smiles and kind looks, of strength and security in connection with healthy limbs; the qualities of power and gentleness would be sufficiently manifest even in the pre-human stage, and the eye would note their visible signs, while such more complex qualities as dignity and refinement, or meanness and vulgarity, would need more advanced powers of abstraction and generalisation; grace easily associates itself with the pleasure of smooth motion; the visible appearances of weakness and clumsiness have had various failures and discomforts as attendants; and so on. Thus in the acts of contrast and comparison characteristic of the sense of sight, differences would be perpetually not only *known* but *felt*; and the complete impression would be quite incommensurable with the perception that arms differ from legs or a pentagon from a hexagon.

§ 7. Helm-holtz's view as to the relation of reason to beauty in works of art;

We may now pass on to the more important view referred to at the beginning of the chapter, which seeks to establish a special relation between Reason and Beauty in the sphere of art, and which we shall find to be specially connected with our main subject of Music. The view in question, while differing fundamentally from the one just noticed, in recognising that our senses, with their given powers and limitations, are for us the channels of beauty, still involves in a certain form the first mode of relation above-discussed, though again it differs by representing the *rationale* of relationship in the parts as something not consciously apprehended but instinctively surmised. It is the view drawn out at considerable length by Helmholtz in the last chapter of his *Ton-Empfindungen*, and it appears to me decidedly less sound than the masterly physical exposition to which it is appended. His reason for its introduction is his opinion that 'there are probably few examples more suitable than the theory of musical scales and harmony, to illustrate the darkest and most difficult points of general æsthetics.' Postponing the musical point, I will briefly epitomise his statement of the problem itself.

Works of art (he says), though subject to laws and rules, must *appear* undesigned: if anything proclaims itself a product of mere intelligence, we refuse to accept it as a work of art. The very fact, however, that we subject works of art to a critical examination and trace out the suitability and connection of the parts, shows we expect it to be *reasonable*, 'shows that we assume a certain adaptation to reason in works of art, which may possibly rise to a conscious understanding.' Yet the beauty must be such as to be recognised by the immediate taste without any such deliberate reference to reasonableness. Nay, this unconsciousness is essential : for it is through the imperfection of our perception, 'through apprehending everywhere traces of regularity, connection, and order, without being able to grasp the law and plan of the whole,' that we get the ennobling conception of the existence in the work of a mighty permeating order, visible to us only by fragmentary glimpses, and that hence we divine a something infinite and transcendent by virtue of which a work of art seems to represent the infinite and ordered universe. 'It is precisely from that part of its regular subjection to reason which escapes our conscious apprehension that a work of art exalts and delights us, and that the chief effects of the artistically beautiful proceed, *not* from the part which we are able fully to analyse.' The difficulty is to understand how, without consciously feeling the regularity *as such*, we nevertheless appreciate by our own tact and taste an amount of 'order, connection, and equilibrium of all internal relations' as conscious thought could only accomplish with infinite time and labour.

Such is the view : and, again, those unfortunate words *order* and *regularity* seem to me the real culprits, leading on, as they do, to the position that because beauty is *ordered*, it *is order*. The element of an elaborate work which we are *not* able to analyse and reason about, the element which I have described as the inherent significance or impressiveness connected specially with the irreducible individual parts, is treated as though it was a further and more complex carrying out of the same kind of order as that which we *are* able to analyse and reason about, which I have described as the general laws and features of composition and congruity in the whole. Helmholtz says that 'through apprehending everywhere traces of regularity, connection, and order, without being able to grasp the law and plan of the whole,' we get the idea that the design is something transcendent, illimitable, and so on. That is, essential beauty is treated as continuous and identical in nature with rational and striking arrangement; supposed conformity to general rules of balance, variety, and coherence is credited with the vital beauty of a face or a melody. This 'law and plan of the whole,' which is what Helmholtz says we cannot grasp, represents to my mind the necessary conditions, the combining order, the *rationale* and significance of the general treatment, which are, I hold, just what we *can* grasp and connect with recognised facts of our mental operations : such regularity as is so presented is consciously perceived *as such*, or may become so with further acquaintance. What we *cannot* logically grasp or analyse is not the plan of the work, but the *essence* of the impressiveness and individuality in the forms, visible

which seems to present the old confusion between the conditioning order and the essential beauty.

or audible, which make up its subject-matter. To this element law and regularity can only apply in the barren *historical* sense that our perceptions of it came regularly about by natural laws : its *nature* is out of all relation to regularity or irregularity, to reasonableness or unreasonableness, and the intuition of it would not be reached by the most intimate knowledge of ' equilibrium of parts ' and internal relations.

§ 8. In respect of the presentative arts, the theory seems at first sight specially attractive.

No more need be said about this with respect to the imitative arts : but as regards the two arts of presentation, our discussion in the fourth and subsequent chapters may be usefully supplemented by examining them in the light of Helmholtz's theory. It is to these arts that such a theory would, at the first blush, seem specially applicable. However rooted in the conditions of our environment be the enjoyment of the forms of concrete objects, it may be said, must not the pleasure in abstract proportions and forms be in some way a pleasure in order and regularity ? for, since they are in their very nature representative of nothing in the external world, it is not very obvious how their effect on us could have been built up out of simple associational elements ; and does not the very word proportion imply subjection to some reasonable law ?

In enjoyment of Architecture intellectual elements and a sense of reasonableness have an important part :

Now as regards Architecture, we found that much of the effect produced by impressive buildings could, after all, be very distinctly traced to associational sources. Caves, for instance, and forest-forms must have been connected with some of the deepest feelings of primitive man : and in the ornamentation which is often the informing spirit of a building, many of the forms, though stopping far short of direct representation, are more or less distinctly founded on those of organic nature ; so that the recognition of their look of living strength and freedom clearly involves some element of association with open-air life. In the pleasure given by mass, size, and strength also, we found that Architecture owes its effect to conceptions in the formation of which natural phenomena have had a large share. At the same time it is indisputable that in Architecture even the associations are often of a more reasoned and less immediate and instinctive kind than those, for instance, which enter into our sense of human beauty or of natural landscape. We need only refer to the evidences of elaborate and conscientious human labour, to the sense of historic interest and of the relation of buildings to successive generations of men, and to other points mentioned in the fourth chapter. And, over and above this more distinctly imaginative exercise of the intellectual faculties (which clearly has nothing to do with subjection of the work to reasonable ' laws and rules '), there really are many points in Architecture, where our satisfaction, however instinctive it may seem, may in great measure be traced to conformity with reason, to a sense of adaptation of means to ends, and so on ; the notion of the workman and his problems and difficulties being in this art so exceptionally prominent. Thus, in the symmetry which is so prominent a fact of many buildings there is a considerable element of external reference: for architecture rests on a basis of utility; and the end or purpose of the building being apparent, as well as the amount and sort of material with which it had to be realised, a large amount of symmetry seems both rational and in many cases necessary, as in the arrangement of the walls and the proportions of the roof. Similarly with the rule that equality is suitable to the horizontal divisions but not to the vertical divisions of a building; the horizontal divisions standing in general on a par as regards the work they have to do. Again, in Mr. Ruskin's rule that, the smaller the building, the more necessary is it that its masonry should be bold, we see reason and adaptation: for a cottage, lacking in itself dignity of size, may gain from huge stones what bricks could not give it; while a building of imposing size would be to some extent dwarfed if built of obviously large stones. So again with the rule that delicate carving should not be put where it cannot be seen; or that the bounding lines of spaces meant to impress by their size should be distinct and unbroken. In these last rules, however, we have rather simple recognition of the facts of visual experience than reasoned conclusions; and in every such case the true element of pleasure, size, or ornament, or whatever it may be, is independent of reason. The instances are, perhaps, more in point, where our consciousness that the eye is being treated in a reasonable way is of such a kind as to make the physical and mental elements very hard to separate; as, for example, in the easy leading of the eye by means of parallel lines, perpendicular groovings in columns, and so on. It is this sort of reasonableness which M. Boutmy expresses in a very French way by calling the Parthenon 'une supposition de syllogismes.'

But giving its full due to the element of rationality, whether connected with orderly and perspicuous arrangement of parts pure and simple, or with a further reference to convenience and mechanical conditions, we find *but free form and free proportion are quite beyond their scope.* that when we trace down the complexity of forms to the simple constituents, and arrive at such a fact as subtle curvature of line or surface, in structure or ornament, we have passed the point where apprehension of reasonable order can be at all adduced in explanation of beauty. To the lines of nature Mr. Ruskin attributes 'the universal property of ever-varying curvature in the most subtle and subdued transitions, with peculiar expressions of motion, elasticity, or dependence,' and all beautiful lines may be said in a sense to be borrowed from nature, though they are of course fairly called *abstract* if they do not suggest any natural object; just as, conversely, we may attribute to objects beauty of abstract line if the lines are such as would appear beautiful even in abstraction. Constant variation then, and not regularity, is the essential feature; otherwise straight lines and circles would be the most, instead of the least, beautiful of the lines which the eye can easily follow: and similar considerations apply to what, if we call the curves free forms, we may term free relations and proportions of forms ; otherwise the absence of truly parallel perpendicular lines on the Acropolis, and the irregular angles at which the buildings were placed, would be indefensible anomalies. I mentioned Mr. Ruskin's suggestion that ever-varying curves are in a way typical of infinity ; but it would be hard to lay much stress on this point, and their expression of action or force is probably more truly at the root of the matter. We saw in the fourth chapter how, in that case, subtle elements of association would be involved : though the pleasurable effect certainly presents marked differences from that produced by human and natural beauty, in that, beyond a slowly gathering accumulation of simple experiences, it involves advanced habits of observation and abstraction. But it has the same negative characteristic—remoteness from any idea of order or plan associated with processes of the discursive reason ; nor could any rule about it have been suggested *à priori* by even the most complete knowledge of those processes.

§ 9. As regards melody, the pleasure in it has been traced back to the exercise of an embryonic faculty, acting as a nucleus for extraordinarily exciting associations ;

If now we turn to the other sort of abstract forms, those presented by Music, the difficulty seems in every way greater, since for these not only is there no sort of foundation or suggestion in the phenomena of nature, but all reference to the external world in the way of utility and convenience is also absent. What then is left, it would be naturally asked, except proportional relations ? and does it not seem that the secret of our pleasure, so far as it is more than simply sensuous, must be in large measure connected with divining (or, according to Helmholtz, half-divining) the complicated plan of their adjustment ?

As regards the fundamental fact of Music, the enjoyment of a series of notes perceived as forming a connected group, those who have followed me so far will have no difficulty in answering this question. We have traced that enjoyment to the simplest elements, direct pleasure in rhythmic stimulation and in change of tone in pitch, the two factors of melodic form ; and we have seen how the utterly unique nature of the forms postulates a faculty equally unique and unable to give an account of itself ; but supposing that faculty to have existed in an embryonic stage and to have given pleasure in the remote past, we have surmised how it became linked with the deepest and strongest emotions ; the sublimated quintessence of which, so to speak, is evoked by the infinitely developed exercise of the same faculty, now possessed in considerable perfection by an enormous mass of mankind. And so far, in these all-essential and characteristic forms, the general intellectual faculties, whether imaginative or logical, seem to have no place at all : the unique faculty of co-ordinating the notes and perceiving the group as a whole may be possessed by the most dunderheaded boor ; whose pleasure in a melody which keenly touches him is wholly impossible to distinguish in kind from that of a cultivated person in the same or some other melody which keenly touches *him.*

Now taking part in these free and unanalysable musical forms there are present, as we have seen, the most marked elements of order and regularity, analogous in some measure to those we noticed in human beauty and in Architecture. The ever-changing evolution of a melody takes place on a basis of regular accents as natural as the two eyes, two arms, and two legs of a human being, or as the symmetrical columns which support a springing arch, and, apart from other elements, as little able as they to account for the beauty into which it enters. For in Music, too, as in the other regions, the self-same regularity is compatible with weak and ugly forms : bar corresponds to bar, as eye to eye, but, whether it be face or melody, the beauty essentially depends on gradations of form of which this fact is no more than a single condition. The special varieties of the element of regularity in Music may be resumed under three heads. They are (1) fixity of degree in time and pitch ; (2) a regular succession of main accents : (3) dual balance of phrase. And if the order here be thought to have some connection with reason, some community with facts on which our general intelligence is exercised, on the ground that equality and regularity are things which in many kinds of experience are defensible on reasonable grounds, our answer is plain. For we have seen that pleasure in regularity of rhythmic stimulation is a most pervading fact of nervous organisation ; as regards fixity of degrees in pitch, we have seen that notes produced at a certain instant cannot help being at some definite pitch or other, while as regards the actual degrees used, they are the empirical result of shifting instinct, Helmholtz himself having struck the most powerful blow at the Pythagorean idea that the connection of note-relationship with simplicity in the ratio of the numbers of the vibrations rested on the fundamental reasonableness of things ; and as regards dual balance, we found that it resulted naturally from the facts of our physical symmetry.

*and the elements of regularity in it are wholly unrelated to reason.*

When we go beyond single organic groups of notes to larger combinations of musical periods and paragraphs, advanced elements of memory and comparison become more distinctly involved ; and in the sense of balance and contrast of sections, of the economy of special effects, and of the judicious disposition of the material which the various themes supply, we certainly recognise mental action of a kind which is familiar to us in application to other lines of experience. We may perhaps consider, then, that our general knowledge of mental processes might have suggested some of the ' laws and rules ' to which long musical combinations are ' subject.' Such negative conditions as that perpetual repetition without change or advance, or that perpetual violent contrast, is to be avoided, naturally approve themselves to the intelligence ; and we might go further and say that the general arrangement of matter in, *e.g.*, the first movement of a sonata may be made to sound ' reasonable ' in description. But conformity

*And even in larger musical combinations the rules of ' rational ' arrangement come to very little.*

to reason is here even more markedly of the external and conditioning kind than in the case of the works of the representative arts noticed earlier in the chapter: such 'laws and rules' might be observed in the dullest and most mechanical as well as in the most inspired composition, and merely concern the most effective presentation of forms which must have their own essential and independent freedom and beauty. In the mention of these essential musical forms I am constantly sensible of a certain liability to misconception, as a casual reader might take me to mean merely lengths or phrases of eight or sixteen bars. I have already said that in Music the line between subsidiary organisms and larger combinations may be, and often is, a very indefinite one ; that cases are abundant of long paragraphs or movements where independent or even semi-independent forms can- not be marked off, and where the linking of phrase to phrase through a whole series of periods is too close and organic for anything short of the whole to give at all a satisfactory notion of completeness. But then in such cases, at every point of transition, of contrast, of insistence, of repe- tition with a difference, and so on, it is as distinctly the pure and simple musical faculty which penetrates and perceives, as in the shortest melody. Reason might say, ' Follow a fiery paragraph with a calm one,' or, ' Follow a major with a minor,' or, ' Having invented a fine subject, introduce it on various instruments and with various developments and accompaniments: ' but the individual paragraphs, the individual instances of ' development ' as much as of ' subject,' cannot be appreciated or criticised from any stand- point external to themselves : and in proportion to the amount of organic connection and continuity musically perceived, we may safely infer the absence of any rule or order which our general notions of rational arrange- ment could have enabled us to lay down.

§ 10. Manner in which Helm- holtz connects what he con- siders the main æsthetic pro- blem with his discoveries about tone:

We do not, then, even *primâ facie*, find much foundation for a theory like that of Helmholtz, which tries to follow the ' order ' right down from the general arrangement of the work to where it is lost to view, and divines a ' plan ' pervading the domain which we have seen to belong to free form. The subject will receive further elucidation if we now examine the special manner in which Helmholtz connects what he considers as the main æsthetic problem with the results of his work on Sound. His diffi- culty, we saw, was the supposed existence in a work of art of a reasonable plan, which nevertheless eluded observation : he considers that this difficulty is relieved by the fact that in the subordinate sphere of musical tones and harmony the enigma is actually solved. The relationship of consecutive tones has been found to depend on their possession of some common har- monic or harmonics, not consciously perceived as such except by careful scrutiny and practice ; and somewhat similarly the close relationship of consecutive chords depends on their possession of some common note or notes, which again may be quite unperceived by an uninitiated hearer in spite of his perfectly apprehending the natural and easy sequence of the chords. By the presence, then, of these links, essential though so commonly undetected, ' the æsthetic problem is referred to the common property of all sense-perceptions, namely, the apprehension of compound aggregates of sensations as symbols of simple external objects, without analysing them.'

If, then, the ' suitability and connection of the parts ' were followed continuously down, as Helmholtz seems to imagine that higher perceptive powers would enable us to follow it, from the general plan of arrangement to the essential forms, we should arrive, in the case of Music, at the relations of tone in a melody ; and this Helmholtz thinks specially instructive, inasmuch as here certainly the exact mode of relationship, presence of a common tone-element, *does* escape notice and *is* in a way reasonable. But unfortunately in the very act of throwing light on Helmholtz's ' æsthetic problem ' as to the hidden ' order, connection, and equilibrium of all internal relations,' this favourable instance reveals how irrelevant that problem is to the real question of beauty. If this particular case of ' subjection to reason which escapes our conscious apprehension ' is to enlighten us as to the beauty of works of art in general—as, on the above-quoted view that it is just from such subjection to reason that ' the chief effects of the artistically beautiful proceed,' it certainly ought to do—it ought at any rate to begin by enlightening us as to the *particular* beauty, that of melody, into which it immediately enters ; and this, as we saw in the last chapter, is precisely what it will not do.

but this only reveals the ir-relevance of the problem.

The *rationale* of relationship of notes in pitch is known, thanks mainly to Helmholtz ; that is, it is known generally in what way notes present links of connection with other notes. But this goes no further in accounting for the beauty of the free form than the possession of convenient stones and plenty of cement would go in explaining Giotto's tower. The relation of note to note is parallel to the fact that one stone rests naturally on or is firmly bound to another ; such facts of course make the form possible, but they do not account for it. You may analyse the structure of an arch or of a tune by pulling it to pieces ; but you cannot so analyse its æsthetic character. The *reasonableness* which underlay the gradual formation of our diatonic scales (and so gave us our stones of convenient sizes and angles) fails helplessly when we try to read it into a free melodic form. We have dwelt sufficiently on the all-important fact that the notes-in-pitch would be formless if the lengths-in-time and the rhythmic accentuation were altered ; but even neglecting this, if we look only at the pitch-element, no view of *reasonable* connections will cover a single one of the existent melodic forms, infinite as they are in number and variety of merit. Apart from the difficulty, which we noticed, that degrees of propinquity are perpetually crossing degrees of relationship, the degrees of relationship, if stated numerically, would

The *rationale* of tone-relationship in no way explains free melodic form.

present to the mind no kind of plan or order; more and less distant relationships seem (as far as *reason* goes) jumbled up promiscuously; and till the unique phenomenon of the formed series, the unity, presents itself to the musical sense, no guess could have been made as to whether it would be sense or gibberish. We may exemplify this even with an exceptionally regular melodic sequence, such as the series of ascending sixths and descending sevenths in the tune from *Fra Diavolo* quoted on p. 148; the one interval means a tolerably close relationship between the two notes composing it, the other a distant one; yet the sevenths of course enter as essentially into the form as the sixths. If we make each relationship nearer, and substitute fifths for sixths and sixths for sevenths, it looks as if we ought to get something more *reasonable*: but the beauty will unfortunately be found to have vanished.[1] The *contrast* was essential, some one may say. Clearly it was *here*: but then we take another tune and equally ruin *it* by just the opposite sort of change in its intervals. Reason must give it up. The power and method of co-ordination is not something abstractable from the phenomenon: we do not know we can co-ordinate tones into forms till we perceive a melodic strain as a unity; we can make no prophecy about its composition till it is there; and whether or not the problem of its impressiveness receives a satisfactory solution in the theory of primæval associations of an exciting kind, gathering round a particular order of exercise and impression, at any rate divinations as to its structure, and surmises of relations and adjustments supposed to be penetrable by a more complete and powerful intelligence (even supposing we were generally conscious of such events), would do very little to explain our pleasure. It is of course begging the question to call a form reasonable because we first find it beautiful: that is an argument drawn from our own sanity, not from the nature of the phenomenon. When we examine the parts we may find reasonableness in the same sense as we find it in a chemical formula, which we construct on paper so as not to contradict the atomic theory; and beauty of form is as little a necessary result in the one case as an actually existent substance in the other: it is

[1] It may perhaps be said that the latent element of harmony cannot be here neglected, and that the proposed progression would suggest an accompaniment of consecutive fifths, which, it may be urged, is just an instance of what *can* be *rationally* forbidden; seeing that the fifth is so prominent and definite an interval, that a succession of fifths might be expected *à priori* to be felt as hard and oppressive. The fact as regards modern European ears is undeniable, though I cannot but regard it as purely empirical. However, that point is not worth arguing: the objection can be obviated by inverting the accent of the suggested phrase, and taking the notes as follows:

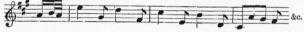

This progression would admit the very same accompaniment as Auber's, but nobody is likely to be much impressed by it.

in virtue of something beyond such conformances that a tune is a tune, and sugar sugar.

The application of the idea of *plan* to single abstract forms seems in fact to involve a radical confusion. A plan implies an end in view. An architect plans the arrangement of his building with a view to certain effects, and ordinarily to certain uses. A composer, though untrammelled by utility, has still his object : and in writing any composition longer than a single melody, arranges it so as to introduce his themes with due emphasis and contrast, to develop and interweave them, and to round them off into a larger sort of completeness. The end is to combine a number of impressive things into coherence, so that each shall seem in its place and stand out at its best; but when we come down to the impressive things themselves, the purely musical forms or ideas, no *end* can be imagined until it has ceased to be an end and is *there*; a thing which is essentially new, free, and individual, is out of all relation to *intelligent* adjustment of parts. A plan by which parts are grouped implies laws with a generality of application extending beyond the particular art, or at any rate beyond the particular manifestation ; it cannot underlie the essential individuality of the parts, and all our efforts to penetrate this only make it recur again and again to account for itself; no fiction of adaptation or conformity will turn it inside out for us. The same fact appears in the process of *invention* of melodies; if they do not suggest themselves in a flash, the struggle is towards the *whole* form, or at the very least whole organic phrases of it, surmised as through a veil ; they gradually clarify into distinctness and are seized; but the process is not of adding brick to brick, but resembles rather the freeing of a statue from a rough semi-shapeless block. It appears to me, indeed, that if we ignore the positive effects of abstract forms, and if, remembering merely their negative character of not representing objects, we set to work to imagine *à priori* some plan which shall underlie them and shall be justifiable to the intelligence, we are tied up to symmetry more or less complex, and nothing else. For symmetry is entrenched, as it were, and could call on any divergence to defend itself; and if no intelligible end or aim is proposed, divergence could never make good its cause to our reason. The justification of *freedom*, the certainty of the *right* irregularity or ἀσυμμέτρεια as distinguished from a million possible *wrong* irregularities or ἀσυμμέτρειαι, is only given in the particular non-reasoning act of co-ordination. And though an invisible and transcendental *plan* pervading a work of art is an idea that may momentarily pass muster, we can scarcely say the same for an invisible and transcendental *symmetry*, in the face of the fact that *actual* symmetry and sameness of parts is precisely what free form shows its freedom in departing from.

If, then, we abandon the notion that the essential beauty of a work of

§ 11. Confusion in the application of the word *plan* to single abstract forms.

§ 12. Such *reasonableness* as the facts of tone-relationship may seem to present is quite external to beauty.

art lies in conformance to an order which impresses us in spite of, or rather because of, our only catching intermittent and imperfect glimpses of it, we see that Helmholtz's comparison of the unperceived reason of simple tone-relationships to the unanalysable element in æsthetic impressiveness, instead of being an instructive analogy, is only the loosest of metaphors. And even in those simple elements, though the possession by the notes of a common factor does constitute a general rule of connection which may be called reasonable, the reasonableness seems to stand outside æsthetics. If the progression, *e.g.*, from G to C *does* seem to possess any æsthetic character, it is owing to its presenting the faint rudiment or suggestion of a free form. The mere fact that two things possess a common element, whether consciously apprehended or only felt, contains in itself no ground of beauty. If we apply the same perception of relationship in some other region of phenomena we get not the slightest sense of beauty—we receive no satisfaction, for example, from contemplating a square on one side of which is inscribed a triangle, though the two figures are similarly related by possession of a common element. Nothing could à *priori* have led us to expect that in connection with one set of sense-impressions a string of such resemblances more and less distant would be a factor in an absolutely new phenomenon—a free form. And if any further proof were needed that the relationship of the notes is a necessary characteristic of the material of Music and not an explanation of its beauty, it would be found in this, that just as the same bricks may be used over and over again to build many different forms without its ever being discovered that they are the same, so instances of the same notes occurring in the same proximities occur in melody after melody, but the forms being wholly different the fact never obtrudes itself. Nor can we feel the following illustration which Helmholtz gives as anything but delusive. He says that 'when a father and daughter are strikingly alike in some well-marked feature, as the nose or forehead, we observe it at once, and think no more about it ; but if the resemblance is so enigmatically concealed that we cannot detect it, we are fascinated ;' and that if a painter in drawing the two heads combined a difference of expression with this indefinable resemblance, we should prize the effect as a high proof of his skill. But here our pleasure (1) would not be evoked if the faces were not intrinsically more or less interesting ; (2) is dependent on most complex human emotions. In the supposed case, not only would our imagination be occupied with the human relationship of the persons, but we should be comparing two highly organic forms or units, whose interest to us is connected with a prolonged course of varied experience and association : and the right musical analogy would be two organic melodies, different, and yet intuitively perceived to be by the same composer ; not two simple and ultimate sensations, the perception of whose resemblance or relationship

Helmholtz's comparison of the resemblance of two faces is delusive.

involves the very minimum of mental elements. We seem, indeed, to find in this rudimentary phase of co-ordinative action fresh support for our main position. Just because the principle of tone-connection, the principle of the perceptible connection of two things through their joint possession of a common part, *is* reasonable—is applicable, that is, in many different ways, thus implying some *general* mode and habit of apprehension—it is easy to show from other instances that such a general mode of apprehension no way entails æsthetic pleasure. Down in this elementary region of what, to revert to our old metaphor, we must call the masonry, not the architecture, of Music, as formerly in the symmetry which was seen to be in so many directions a necessary and conditioning attribute of beauty, we have found an element of order which is in a sense reasonable. But underneath and compatible with such conditioning order and attributes we have found everywhere an essence and a freedom inexplicable by and unconnected with reason: the mental processes involved, whether connected with imaginable and definable suggestions or with obscure and transmuted associations, seem to lead us in every case into a sort of *cul-de-sac*, where the phenomena, however linked together by their emotional effect on us, appear in themselves as ultimate as the simplest sense-perceptions; and in the case of Music this æsthetic 'order' falls under the supreme and sole cognisance of a wholly isolated faculty.

In conclusion, I would suggest that the indefinable ideas of expansion and infinity which seem so often to be a feature of the highest æsthetic emotions do not necessarily connect themselves with the grounds laid down by Helmholtz. It appears to me that the surmise is not of infinite arrangement and order in the work contemplated, objective facts to be more and more comprehended and appreciated by increased intelligence, but of infinite potentialities in one's own being, subjective facts, to the apprehension of which in special experiences the windows of the soul seem momentarily opened. Such unity as is surmised in connection with the subjective exaltation is not a unity of law or plan, supposed to lurk hidden in the special work, but is a general unity in the whole range of the phenomena which cause us lofty emotions, corresponding to the persistent unity of our own *ego*; for this *ego* is inevitably led dimly to divine hidden relations between things which are akin in having deeply impressed itself.

§ 13. Surmise of infinite potentialities in one's own being.

# CHAPTER X.

## FURTHER REMARKS ON MUSICAL FORM AND 'SUBJECT.'

§ 1. Some further explanations are necessary on the topics of the last two chapters.

I WAS unwilling to encumber the exposition in the last two chapters with subsidiary points, or with more than was absolutely necessary in the way of controversial matter or of musical examples. As, however, the topics there discussed constitute the most difficult part of our subject, it seems better to encounter the charge of tediousness than of obscurity with regard to them; and there are still certain explanations and illustrations which may, I think, help to define and support the positions laid down.

The main principle of *two sorts* of unity embracing variety;

One of the main contentions of the last chapter which is not hard to grasp, may be put in this way: that, while unity under variety is a conception to which we are accustomed in relation to form and to works of art dealing with form, and which at first sight seems simple enough, there are in most works of art of any elaboration *two sorts* of unity under variety; that which is involved in the arrangement of independently impressive or expressive parts, and that which is involved in each one of these parts on its own account. And these sorts differ *in kind*; their nature and laws are wholly distinct. Thus in a picture the conceptions which enter into our appreciation of rational or artistic arrangement of figures and faces, could not give us any clue to the essential beauty and expressiveness of a figure or a face, nor any idea as to what figures and faces are superior to others in these respects. We gain that perception by a process of experience and association in which no conscious reference to any sort of principle of arrangement is made. Here, then, we have a principle of a general sort of rational and artistic unity in variety, characteristic of large combinations, to be distinguished from the unity involved in each of the independent essential forms which constitute that variety.

which presents certain special difficulties in application to Music,

Now the application of this principle to Music presents special difficulties; while at the same time a failure to perceive how and in what cases it can be applied, and where the difficulties lie, may entail important misconceptions as to the nature of essential musical form.

though in simple cases this may not appear.

In a quite simple case the distinction may seem clear enough. Thus an air of Handel's very commonly contains a major paragraph, then a minor paragraph, then a repetition of the major paragraph. Here we have unity and variety, a pleasing sense of contrast in the minor bit, a pleasing sense of recognition in the repetition of the major bit, and a more complete and satisfactory piece of musical experience than if either of the bits had been presented alone. Or again, the rondo of a sonata starts with a melodic phrase which is repeated again and again at intervals throughout the movement, the several departures and recurrences again producing a sense of variety bound together under unity. As Mr. Sully has well expressed it, 'provided only that a melodic subject is striking and worthy of the prominence thus given it, the treatment of it as a central point from which the successive waves of melody may all radiate, and to which they may finally return, opens up possibilities of a high degree of pleasing variation and of artistic symmetry.' This is the sort of unity embracing variety which is rational and comprehensible; it represents just what a person without the slightest sense of music would admit to be a good way of arranging certain beautiful things which have to be presented in succession; though of course such a person could not enjoy the mere fact of the arrangement, lacking the power to perceive that the arranged things were beautiful. But when we leave this artistic and satisfactory method of arrangement, and come down to the arranged things themselves, then we can give our unmusical friend no rational account of their beauty; we find, moreover, often that they are *not* beautiful, but are thoroughly weak, twaddling, or even ugly; and, as we saw in the eighth chapter, we can point out no objective characteristics of the beautiful ones which may not also be exhibited in the unbeautiful ones. Here, then, in these elements or forms which may be either beautiful or unbeautiful, but whose qualities are detected entirely by a special intuitive faculty, we have a unity under variety of a quite different sort; we have not a combination of impressive forms (supposing them to be impressive) into an effective whole of convenient length, but a combination of sense-units of next to no independent value into impressive forms.

But though this may seem pretty clear in a rapid survey of simple cases, a more attentive survey of musical compositions will reveal a peculiarity which must be examined. In Poetry the formal element of metre marks off a number of distinct and complete units, stanzas, or lines; in Painting we have no difficulty in deciding as to which are the complete units of form, but perceive at once that this is a man and that is a tree; but in Music we often lack a criterion for this sort of completeness. We may perceive *form* and coherence throughout a long paragraph, but we should often find it hard to regard the paragraph as in any way a series of separate and distinct *forms*. Smaller combinations of bars often merge into longer ones without presenting any marked sections with beginnings and ends, while still the paragraph may hardly give the impression of a sufficiently cogent sort of coherence for it to seem natural to call it a

§ 2. In Music complete units of form cannot be always marked off.

single form, in the sense we should apply the term to a shorter melodic 'subject.' As a fact, however, a paragraph, if it is to be musically valuable, cannot arrive at any great length without being provided with some clear principle of unity ; for example, the frequent reiteration of a recognisable phrase, as in the development of a ' subject,' or in the persistence of a certain kind of figure or rhythmic group. A long succession of phrases which exhibits nothing but perpetual differentiation will escape the grasp of the ear, and will seem rambling and aimless. But whether or not unified in some such special manner, any paragraph which is to be musically valuable, must satisfy the test that each bit shall necessitate, as it were, and so enter into organic union with the *one next to it* : a test which will be found practically to necessitate reference at each point to parts considerably further removed from it, whether behind or in front, than the points which are absolutely contiguous to it ; and in proportion as this test is unsatisfied, while at the same time we detect no bits of sufficient length and coherence to be impressive as individual forms, is the music felt as shiftless and unarresting. Nor, indeed, is the application of such a test confined to long paragraphs : we can divide a more compact passage, with its distinct beginning and end, into subordinate groups of notes ; and in proportion as we feel nothing cogent in their union, and could hear changes and substitutions in them with indifference, is the series one which fails to give us the characteristic delight of a melodic form. If its limits and self-completeness were obvious, we could not deny it the name of ' a form,' which we should not apply to the shiftless longer paragraph : but the point to notice is that the cardinal idea of organic form in any musical sentence or paragraph is not to be connected with this length or that length, but with *cogency of sequence* at each point : a long series of periods may exhibit it throughout, and the shortest fragment may lack it.

Various degrees of cogency of sequence.

But there is a further point. Between the passages which have definite beginnings and ends there are all degrees of cogency of sequence, which we might figure to ourselves as colons, full stops, divisions of paragraphs, and so on. We may go further, and say that the bond which links together the shortest phrases capable of awakening any sort of interest and desire to have them supplemented, admits of all gradations of stringency, down to the loosest and sometimes almost accidental conjunction of two elaborate and complete sections ; which is of course compatible with absolute stringency throughout the whole of every one of the component parts or clauses. Moreover, beyond the loose sort of union realised in the mere easy following of one larger section on another, there

Links of transition ;

are special sorts of connection which may also differ greatly in strength. The link, for instance, may be a pure link of *transition*, an interposed passage of more or less intrinsic interest, and perhaps containing references to some phrase or figure in what has preceded; but the far more important case is where it consists in some such backward references in the new paragraph itself, when we might call it a link of *reminiscence*. And these links of reminiscence may present every degree of closeness, from the most obvious re-presentations of whole pieces of form, with, *e.g.*, a new accompaniment, or with ornamental variations, or transposed into the minor, to the mere recurrence of some single recognisable feature, some marked fragment of rhythm, or a piece of melodic figure which is made to appear with all sorts of developments throughout whole new reaches of form. <sub>and links of reminiscence,</sub>

It is natural that this latter sort of link should play the most important part in prolonged musical structures; not only on account of the aimlessness which might be felt in a mere string even of beautiful sections, but because a sentence in music passes so quickly that it is natural to desire its repetition; and because new forms in which some previous form is recognised as varied and transfigured, or it may be only as faintly suggested, constitute the most obvious mode of extending a movement or combination of forms to a convenient length, while preserving a marked element of unity. Convenient length, however, is clearly the vaguest phrase, and there is the widest latitude as to extent and stringency in the employment of this sort of unifying principle. As a matter of fact, except in the very shortest and simplest pieces, we usually find more or less recognition of *each* of the two plans under which musical forms and sections can be put together; that of quasi-independent and serial juxtaposition, and that where different sections are distinctly connected by the possession of recognisable common features. For even in movements which are too extended to dispense with recurrences and perceptible organic bonds, through a large part of their course, it is common to find passages which are strictly *episodes*, and justify their existence purely by their independent beauty; and these too present no fixed rule of length. On the whole then, in the conjunction of complete paragraphs as in the conjunction of smaller divisions, we see that mere considerations of extent have very little to do with organic unity. Quite short paragraphs in juxtaposition may have so little vital connection that one of them might be easily replaced by a kindred paragraph out of some similar work, which to a new hearer would seem perfectly in its place, as might be exemplified very often in the case of minuets and trios, and in the paragraphs of dances; while much longer movements may be in a true sense organic throughout. <sub>which last are of prime importance.</sub> <sub>Considerations of extent have little to do with organic unity.</sub>

The various degrees of cogency with which musical segments are united are the more liable to escape due recognition, from the fact that the same word, 'form,' is indiscriminately used in relation both to the closest and the laxest combinations. I have confined the word in the previous chapters to such single organisms as are palpably grasped as <sub>§ 3. Indiscriminate use of the word form.</sub>

unities whose elements are entirely interdependent, and in the strictest sense necessitate one another; and I have explained in the present chapter how the idea must be extended to include all true cogency of sequence. But the word is often used (and it is hard to substitute any other) for larger combinations or 'movements' into which several of these complete unities enter as parts, with often little of that strictly vital interdependence which is tested by the ear's strongly and instinctively resenting any change or omission. Thus we speak of minuet-form, rondo-form, variation-form, and so on. It is even possible, though less accurate, to extend the use of the term still further, so as to include a combination of several of these movements; the contrast between form in this sense and the essential form of a melodic subject being roughly comparable to the contrast between the 'form' of a five-act drama and the metrical form of a sonnet. The reason that it is thus allowable to speak of the form of composite instrumental works, such as sonatas and symphonies, is that the severally complete movements are few in number and have each a more or less marked and understood structure (the minuet-form, rondo-form, &c., just mentioned), while the contrasts of pace and character by which they supplement one another make a sort of bond of musical relationship, rapidly tightened by association. A looser use is when the word is applied to some more fortuitous or exceptional conjunction of movements; as when people speak of the form of the *Choral Fantasia,* which is simply a pianoforte fantasia followed by a chorus; or reckon as a case of inventiveness in form the starting of a concerto with the solo-instrument instead of the orchestra: while to talk, as is very commonly done, of the 'form' of an oratorio, is much like talking of the form of a ballad-concert, or a penny-reading, or any other miscellany.

§ 4. No general rule is possible as to what shall be accepted in Music as self-complete sections. As the result of these considerations, we may say that unity in variety, the combination of various elements into definite organic units or wholes, does not in the case of Music admit of very distinct division into two sorts, as represented, *e.g.*, in Painting by the combination of the elements of feature, limb, &c., into one organic unit, a human being, and then the combination of several human beings into a larger artistic whole, a pictorial composition. Rather there are in Music all degrees of closeness and laxness in the unifying bond, all degrees of organic coherence, from that which may bind two separately meaningless fragments into a division of a short melodic 'subject,' to that which may bind together two or three very complete sections into a movement; and this implies the widest differences in the degrees of enhancement of effect afforded by one part to another.[1] It is impos-

[1] The following melody from Schubert's octett, if we imagine it heard for the first time, may afford a simple example of several distinct degrees in the necessity of one part to the apprehension of another; though as it is really only a single form, all the parts are really essential, and when once known can hardly be thought of separately:

sible to measure definitely the various strengths at different portions of
the thread of continuity, or to lay down any rules of general application
as regards the extent in length of the matter presented which should
be supposed to rank as a tolerably self-dependent section: but that
the extent does actually admit of enormous differences is shown by
our finding ourselves in some cases dwelling contentedly in memory on a
melodic subject of two bars' length, and in other cases being as it were
driven to reproduce, if we can, a whole long paragraph. It admits also
of very wide subjective differences, in accordance not only with varieties
of musical habit and facility, but with the changing extent of our individual acquaintance with an individual work. The more complete the
acquaintance, and the more vivid the association of the various parts with
their place in their relation to one another, the less power we have of
judging about such points. Nor is this shifting and uncertain character       *Reasons why*
of our own experiences the only reason why they are here specially difficult   *even our own*
                                                                               *experience is*
to examine. The keen sense of that closest bond which unites the actual        *here uncertain*
note, heard or imagined at this or that instant, with its more immediate       *and difficult to*
                                                                               *examine.*
neighbours, quite prevents us, at the moment when we are thinking through
the form, from analysing or realising the gradually decreasing ratio in which
the effect is due to continuity with further parts of the chain ; especially
since, as we have seen, degrees of organic union depend not merely on rela-

&c.

Here the first two bars are clearly nothing
in themselves, though they are over too soon
to cause any appreciable sense of waiting
for the beauty to reveal itself as the form
develops; the interdependence of this pair
of bars and the next pair is of the closest
kind, and these four together make a phrase
which already has true beauty. But when
once the succeeding phrase has been heard,
the effect of the difference it presents in the
ascent to the A and the following bars up to
the close on C, so obviously depends on the
remembrance of the first phrase, and reveals
in that first phrase so much more purpose
and significance than at first appeared, that
the two become henceforth indissolubly
linked. The connection of this sentence in
the minor key with the following one, which
is nearly all in the major, is clearly less close,
since either could have existed in very complete beauty without the other ; at the same
time the enhancement of the effect by the
contrast is so striking that after a little
acquaintance it is hardly possible to avoid
feeling it necessary.

tive distances but on all manner of points of parallelism and resemblance of phrase, so that our metaphor of a chain, stronger and weaker at different parts, is after all a most imperfect one. Again, music passes so quickly, and the amount which can be grasped altogether in the closest way so very quickly, that small bits, though they may be thought over and enjoyed in detachment, may still seem too short to be able to be presented alone. And in this way our realisation of the facts of set performance, together with a natural desire for more, and in music that we know an inevitable association between things which have always been presented to us together, may give us an impression of actual incompleteness even in units of form which are quite organic enough to recur to the memory independently, or accompanied by only the most shadowy reminiscence of parts before and after. For instance, no pianist, still less a band, would think of sitting down and playing the following passage from the overture to *Egmont*, and then stopping :

A person who recalls this passage without exactly recalling its *entourage*
will still feel that it *has* an *entourage,* and that it is not and could not
be the opening phrase of the piece ; nevertheless, it is in itself a very
complete little bit of most beautiful form, fully enjoyable in detachment.
On the other hand, it is often extremely difficult to make sure of the
amount which we *can* at all thus enjoy in detachment ; since when we
once know a musical sentence, a phrase of it which suggests itself vividly
to the mind, as though on its own account, will as a rule entail some
faint ideal representation of the rest, and indeed could often not be at
all appreciated except as a recognised part of the form to which the
rest is indispensable.  We have a consciousness of the remainder, hidden
as it were behind a veil, but still there : and even when such positive consciousness does not make itself prominent, we still have a feeling that our
phrase is a fragment and is bound to have some sequel, and we enjoy it
under that kind of impression ; as is shown by the fact that if we actually
heard it played and immediately succeeded by some other piece of tune
with which it had no organic union, we should at once resent the incoherence.  For instance, after first hearing *Durch die Wälder*, all I
could exactly recollect was

It may easily
escape notice
how far a
phrase which
seems to be en-
joyed in detach-
ment really re-
calls parts be-
yond itself.

which haunted me for days ; but this bit of form could certainly not have impressed me as it did in the first instance had it not had its due pendant in the

which follows ; nor could I have received my pleasure in the reminiscence of it but for a latent sense of its being balanced in some such way. And the same thing practically occurs with parts of much more extended pieces of composition. A person of ordinary musical intelligence, hearing the first movement of Beethoven's symphony in A for the first time, might appreciate to some extent the grandeur and originality of the few slow bars at the opening, and then the overpowering advance of the ascending scales, but he would probably be only thoroughly arrested and feel that he had got something to take away with him when the scales lead on into

This passage is really very much less self-complete than that quoted from the overture to *Egmont*; taken in pure isolation, its beauty is only half apparent. Nevertheless its form is so tangible that to many hearers it must have stood out prominently in recollection ; and if it has so haunted them as to recall the full delight it gave in its place, there certainly must have gone with it a latent suggestion of its mode of occurrence, of the marvellous stir, the resistless measured march of sound, which ushers it in, even though nothing outside itself can be remembered except as a vague impression.

But though it is thus impossible, in treating of Music, to lay down any general line of distinction, in kind or extent, between formed units and larger arrangements of formed units, our own experience does enable us to draw very clear lines in the large majority of particular instances ; for the various coherences of parts may exhibit only a few of the possible grades of strength, and those at the markedly opposite extremes of the scale. Let us take the case of some movement which is divided off into very definite paragraphs, such as the andante of the *Pastoral* sonata. The three first paragraphs begin as follows :

§ 5. Still we practically do continually draw a line for ourselves between single forms of the strictest sort and looser combinations.

We see here a link of resemblance between the second section and the first, a link of contrast between the third and the other two, and we feel that their juxtaposition much enhances their effect : but a man who said that he could perceive no beauty in any one of the three independently of the others—in other words, that he could not have seen any merit if his first introduction to the respective sections had been through hearing each played in detachment from the others, and that he is as unable to get pleasure from realising one of them alone as he would have been if a single note or chord or a detached half-bar here and there had been all that he had ever known of them—would clearly be talking nonsense. And this difference between the relation to one another of the small and separately *formless elements*, notes or half-bars, and the relation to one another of the *formed sections*, this difference between the *presence* and the *absence* of absolute indispensableness and interdependence, may be said to constitute a distinction in kind. Though chains of musical continuity may present links differing merely by gradations of strength, we practically make the difference one of kind and not of degree, so far as at certain places and variously at various times we break the chain for ourselves, or accept it as broken, and get enjoyment from detached pieces of form, in every one of which the principle of the indissoluble coherence of *its* elements is recognised. And the same fact must constantly characterise our enjoyment of successive portions in an actual performance, however much it may be there disguised, or reduced to mere potentiality, by the uninterrupted continuity of the whole presentation.

§ 6. Application of the foregoing remarks to general laws of rational arrangement in Music ;

The statement in the last chapter as to the extremely slight and general nature of any general laws of rational arrangement that could be laid down for musical composition may now appear in a clearer light, after this notice of the manner in which the unity of a long piece of composition is attained. We have seen that ‘essential form’ is not connected with the limitations of extent which the term might suggest, or with special lengths of four, or eight, or sixteen bars; but represents a *principle*, that of close coherence at a very large number of points, as tested by the feeling of resentment or of indifference with which the ear, after sufficient acquaintance, would receive changes or omissions at those points. We have seen that this principle may be exemplified not only in a compact melodic ‘subject,’ where we very distinctly recognise not only form but *a* form, but throughout a long paragraph, which can only be keenly apprehended and enjoyed in proportion as its successive parts seem to necessitate and justify one another. We have seen how the less extended forms and their parts may merge, so to speak, into the more extended, persisting and recurring at point after point in all manner of different aspects, and often acting as starting-points and suggestions for new pieces of form, the appreciation of which involves a recognition of their origin. Thus the larger sort of organism often results less from happy juxtaposition of smaller organisms than from the domination and penetration of a long succession of periods by single threads or motives of 'subject,' which present not rational arrangement but musical amplification. In other cases where a 'subject' is not thus 'worked out,' the simpler juxtaposition of formed and satisfactory sections may seem less alien to the notion of reasonable rules of balance and arrangement; but not only must the number of such sections be very small if the series of them is to be construed as a unity, but the links of purely musical connection (whether consisting in points of parallelism and reminiscence, or in the growth of one section out of another by actual steps of transition) are still, like the amplification just mentioned, matters in which the unique musical faculty acts with as sole and supreme an intuition as in the appreciation of the shortest and simplest melody.

And, indeed, when things have to be arranged which not only represent no external realities, but conform to no external or mechanical facts, and arranged almost entirely in a line of sequence, it seems hard to imagine any rational laws of arrangement, bound to approve themselves to any person with a general artistic sense, beyond such barren generalities as sufficiency of *iteration* and sufficiency of *contrast*. As to what shall be considered a sufficiency of either, the musical faculty is again paramount, since the decision entirely depends on the actual content, the actual things to be disposed, which differ in each case; nor will induction from any amount of particular instances, or from the sorts of plan or order observed in various classes of composition, land us in any less general or barren laws than just these of iteration (including variations and reminiscences) and contrast, which of course contain no description and imply no vestige of beauty or vitality, and are as compatible with worthless and dreary contents, and so with a worthless work, as they are conducive to the highest effect of beautiful contents in an inspired work. *which reduce themselves to sufficiency of iteration and sufficiency of contrast.*

And this brings us back, with increased power of appreciating it, to a point mentioned in the fifth chapter, namely, the all-importance of the *parts* in a musical composition. It will, I think, be clear how thoroughly this is enforced, and not contradicted, by our recent discussion of the extension of organic unity into a large movement. We have seen that the central principle of form, entire mutual interdependence of elements, admits of gradual relaxation as the size of the elements increases; up to the point where it becomes absurd to attempt to apply it, as when we take as elements the separate movements of a sonata.[1] And though the *§ 7. Reassertion of the all-importance of the parts in a musical composition.*

---

[1] I lately saw in a leading newspaper the following remark, *à propos* of a new symphony of which only one movement had been performed: 'The first movement of a symphony conveys but a vague idea of the design and the merits of the whole work.' The first movement conveys of course a *perfect* idea of its own design and merits, and *no* idea at all of the design and merits of the other movements. One might as well say that an acquaintance with one member of a family gave one but a *vague* idea of the merits of the whole family. This, however, was probably only a convenient way of

question of this gradual relaxation is somewhat complicated by the variety in the sorts of connecting links, transition, reminiscence, and so on, and by the different sorts of completeness which we exact in actual performance and in mental representation, nothing touches the central simple principle in its stronghold, in its typical and closest application, which is to the successive notes and smallest fragments, as they turn up moment after moment, throughout any piece of music which is keenly and characteristically enjoyed. Thus the point I am urging does not merely mean (what nevertheless is perfectly true and well worth dwelling on) that the smaller bits—mere fragments, it may be, in relation to a whole long structure—are in Music of quite exceptional independent value, as being often the only things which an ordinary person can at all carry away from an elaborate work, and the pivots on which his further acquaintance with the work will have to rest. It is characteristic of the whole apprehension of Music, of all grades of perception of it from the highest to the lowest, that the attention is focussed on each part as it comes; and that we never get our impressions of a long musical movement, as we commonly do those of a great architectural structure, through views which sweep over and embrace the whole rather than dwell on the parts. Even though one part of a movement may owe its point in great measure to another, either through a contrast involving some faint sort of ideal representation of the other, or through actual similarity and reference to the other, that definite relation is at most to another *part*, not to the whole, and its effect is to increase our pleasure *at a part*. The whole may be, or may become through familiarity, so truly organic as to make each part seem an unalterable phase of the continuous motion : but for all that it is in our enjoyment of the parts, one after another, that that quality of close and vital organism takes effect; the subtle relationship of part B to part A being one of the qualities of part B which makes the moments it occupies peculiarly delightful. Thus pleasure in the whole has no meaning except as expressing the sum of our enjoyments from moment to moment ; a sum which will be increased in proportion as the organic principle pervades the whole. In fact, to say that the parts are all-important is merely to assert our inability to do what involves a con-

filling up a paragraph. But consider the astounding impudence of such an assertion as that of Lenz, that the unity of the Choral Symphony has been vindicated, and 'the whole placed in a perfectly new light' by the detection of an 'identity' between the following phrase in the first movement—

with the theme of the last movement—

&c.

tradiction in terms—to enjoy something the essence of which is a *succession* of impressions by a *simultaneous* review of all the impressions. We may doubtless think through the work in much less time than would be needed for its performance, but our thoughts are still of its successive portions. In the representative art of Poetry, where, as in Music, the element of form is realised in successive portions, but where the subject-matter and ideas are completely distinct from it, we can often take an almost instantaneous general survey, and omitting details can summarise the whole under a very rapid concatenation of a few fundamental ideas; the subject *embraces* the subject-matter and its relations as the general embraces particulars: but in Music, though we may have our 'subjects' or leading phrases, we cannot summarise under them all the various matter which, though they act to it as starting-points and supports, they in no sense embrace, and into every part of which the element of measured duration essentially enters.

Difference of musical from poetical 'subjects.'

These last points, the slightness of rational rule or order, in the absence of distinctly-outlined and discontinuous objects to arrange and of distinct mechanical and utilitarian problems to solve, and the residence of the essential beauty in the successive parts, which make up a pleasurable whole by dint of the pleasure they each in turn convey, and cannot be embraced in a simultaneous view, may seem hardly obscure enough to deserve such insistence. But they are really to a great extent ignored in very much that is said and written as to the 'architectonic' aspects of Music, in vague references to the 'design' of the composer in this or that instrumental work, and in all phraseology implying the existence of some grand primary scheme, filled in with detail in the process of production, and capable now of being abstracted and admired apart from the actual bits of form which moment after moment engross the ear. It is naturally to the larger combinations, which embrace a number of parts, that such a conception would, if anywhere, apply: and phrases about 'symmetrical proportions,' and 'manifold aspects of parallelism, variation, and contrast,' and 'subtle harmonies of structure,' and the like, are accepted, not just as descriptive, if anything, of the more or less obvious aspect of *unity* under which the succession of various and variously related parts presents itself, but as in some way expressing the *essential beauty* of the work. One reason of this seems to be that we only feel impelled to launch out into such language in cases where we perceive a large amount of beauty, since we do not seek to justify enjoyment till the enjoyment is there, and do not dwell on the features of music we do not care about: and then the fact that the features described are truly there, that the beauties of a movement reveal themselves in recognisable modes under the general scheme of the movement, and the convenient vagueness of words like harmony and proportion, are apt to blind us as to where the essence of our enjoyment really lies. It is forgotten that such general characteristics as are described in the above

§ 8. Undue emphasis is often laid on the 'architectonic' aspects of Music ;

phrases, the 'architectonic' aspects of structure, the general plan on which a number of parts are built up into a large movement, and the general features of recurrence and development, may be common to a hundred pieces of all degrees of goodness and badness, and are compatible with the most barren and mechanical work; just as in the last chapter we found it was not always observed how in the visible world the ugliest things may resemble the most beautiful in the amount of variety they present under an aspect of unity. In Music the notion of a larger and *more* essential design, in reference to which shorter individual strains are *details* in the sense of being *less* essential, has no application. The scheme has no value apart from the bits.

*as though the virtue of a musical work could lie in any large general scheme, apart from the individual content of the successive moments.*

Thus, while it may seem a matter of indifference whether we talk of the beautiful proportion and symmetry of parts, or of the proportion and symmetry of beautiful parts, yet really, so far as the former phrase is meant to imply something different from the latter, it is extremely misleading. It conveys an idea that the composer's inventive act is primarily rather of some grand dominant scheme of combinations, like the vaguely dawning vision of a cathedral, than of individual bars and phrases. It suggests that a melodic 'subject' is something parallel to a single architectural element, a column or a buttress, right in its place and serving to support and supplement other similar things by combination with which it becomes an element in a large beautiful effect; instead of being what it is, a form bound to absolute beauty on its own account, and constituting the gist and centre of growth of all manner of further beauties. The word *symmetry* seems particularly inappropriate in an account of the nature of the larger musical structures, as the utmost irregularity of length and arrangement of sections may be and perpetually is exemplified in the greatest and deepest works, the utmost regularity in the poorest and lightest: nor can the word *proportion* be applied to such structures in any way which will the least differentiate the good from the bad, the living from the dead.

*Difficulty of realising the unique conditions of musical structure.*

The difficulty of seeing this lies greatly in our familiarity with the idea of proportion of entirely interdependent forms—of impressiveness due to complex arrangements of comparatively unimpressive but distinct and separate units—as applicable to the larger sorts of unity in variety which delight our eyes in Architecture. But for this we should realise much more easily that, while the abundant wealth of beautiful form in a movement of Beethoven constitutes, on due familiarity, a unity of the truest kind, and while association will soon rivet the connections in much less truly organic structures, the significance belongs to each part of essential form in turn; that where the forms present recurrences and imitations and variations and amplifications and all the interweaving and unifying features which may be classed under links of reminiscence, they still do this by dint of *being just what they are,* note after note, bar after bar, not by dint of

carrying out any pre-existent or separable ' design ;' and that the distinguishing point of Beethoven, as the great master of large organic structure, was not a power to conceive grand schemes or outlines, which could
have *no* grandeur apart from successive bits of content, but the extraordinary manner in which one bit of form acted in his mind as a germ for
new but related forms ; so that his most characteristic movements are
often absolutely pervaded by the principle of reminiscence. The fact is
that the unifying bonds of large musical structure, especially as regards
this subtle element of reminiscence, though instinctively recognised by
the musical sense, are so unlike anything else as to be specially hard to
analyse from outside and describe in general and untechnical language.
And as the disappointing character of movements in which the parts
seem irrelevantly tacked together is patent, while yet the parts themselves in such cases may possess true beauty, it seems natural to lay
the blame on the whole *as distinct from* the parts ; and to refer the
defect to the absence (and the converse merit to the presence) of some
grand general outline imaginable apart from details, of some large scheme
analogous to the first impression one might receive from some mighty
building, in which only general proportions and large features of combination would find place. It doubtless requires some little attention to
perceive how those ordinary features of larger organic structure, those
various links of relationship which bits of form, perhaps at some distance
apart in different paragraphs, may so conspicuously present, are not
specimens of ' proportional arrangement ' or 'harmonious adjustment '
supervening on or embracing the parts as units, but are as much a matter
of the essential form and the actual individual notes of the parts, of their
going just as they do and no other way, as the simplest presentation of an
isolated melodic ' subject.'

Thus however *organic* through and through a musical movement may
seem, so that every transition and every contrast comes as a divinely
ordained necessity, yet so far as the word *architectonic* suggests some
scheme to be more or less appreciated apart from the details it embraces,
or some large *single* aspect to which the parts are regarded as *contributions,* instead of being what they are ('subjects' and links and transitions
and developments and all), the *essential* things on each of which in turn
the attention is engrossed, just so far is it misleading. The term ' essential
form,' then, has everywhere its most literal meaning ; the strictly *essential*
' proportions ' in Music are none other than those of time and pitch which
belong to essential form ; and the parts presenting them are none other than
the crude and shapeless elements of tone-material, cast by their means into
groups which, as we have sufficiently seen, are alike invented and appreciated by a wholly unique and intuitive faculty. And we may here recognise the full importance of our previous conclusion ; that while objectively
complete organic units are often and in various ways hard to mark off in

Music, a true generic difference must be recognised between combinations of such parts as are sufficiently organic to be beautiful even when heard or thought of on their own account, and combinations of the unformed notes and smallest fragments, which have absolutely no value till fused into a larger and apprehensible form or bit of form.

§ 9. Many describable aspects of variety in unity are presented by *single* melodic forms, and equally in the good and the bad.

We perhaps obtain the clearest view of the character of expressions like those above quoted, as mere *descriptions* of certain common aspects of unity and variety, and not *explanations* of beauty, by noticing that they are in great measure applicable to the separately insignificant and unintelligible clauses of those less extended themes, those compact melodic organisms, whose enormous difference in merit is the most striking fact in Music. That is to say, over and above the recognition of such entirely general characteristics as the presence of bars of equal length and of the notes of the familiar scale-system, we can often specify certain points which constitute the unity in variety of single melodic forms, and at the same time perceive clearly how utterly such points fail either to supply a clue to their beauty, or to differentiate the beautiful among them from the unbeautiful. In the case of such distinctly single organisms, the analogy of the features in question to those points of structure which would be included in the description of an antelope and a rhinoceros, of Hyperion and a satyr, is markedly apposite. The parallelism really holds throughout; for the great general principle of organic development—increased differentiation of parts combined with increased integration and mutual interdependence—applies to Music as much as to the organisms of the visible world, and in both cases is equally external to æsthetic effect. Thus the principle is as truly exemplified in the difference between a savage or infantine chant, with its endless iteration of a single strain, and a developed modern melody, as in the difference between an invertebrate creature, with its row of similar segments, and some highly developed vertebrate structure; but neither in the musical nor the visible region of form is it in any way a principle of beauty. Where a high degree of beauty exists it will naturally be in connection with the more developed organisms: but in both cases thousands of the more developed organisms may be found with no beauty at all; though in Music, where beauty is the only true *raison d'être* of the organisms, and has been the aim with a view to which the gradual development of melodic structure has taken place, the fact is less strikingly presented.

*Parallelism* in the direction of phrases.

First, then, we may take the sort of resemblance of phrase to phrase given by *parallelism* of direction. Mr. Sully, in speaking of what he calls the geometric characters of Music, says that 'the ear is able to trace out a number of half-hidden resemblances in the direction of a movement, to note how a melody, amid all its seemingly free wanderings, moves through a certain order of curve, alternately rising and falling through greater or lesser intervals in a graceful serpentine line.' [1]  Our examination of the factors and nature of melodic forms has, I hope, made sufficiently evident the hopeless inadequacy of any visual analogue for them; at the same time, as their clauses do exhibit these parallelisms of direction as a marked characteristic in a vast number of instances, curvature of a more or less orderly kind is a notion which may naturally suggest itself.  But to introduce this melodic curvature as an 'aspect of beauty,' and to dwell on the

---

[1] Mr. Sully's chapter on 'Aspects of Beauty in Musical Form ' in *Sensation and Intuition* seems to me an admirably clear description and classification of the various ways in which form or unity in variety is presented by Music.  My only difference from it lies in the fact that the features of structure which are described are treated as though they necessarily were 'aspects of beauty ; ' that the title and mode of expression throughout seem to show that the descriptions are held to *account for* any beauty that may be found in the forms, so that where they are applicable, such beauty would be bound to exist : whereas the actual account of the forms, apart from adjectives, would apply to all sorts of musical presentations which I am certain Mr. Sully would agree with me in regarding with indifference or aversion.  Mr. Sully says that 'the *beauties* of musical form ' are susceptible of exact study and definition ; but he would surely admit that, as regards single forms or themes, his account (where it goes beyond details of mere *anatomy* to more general aspects) deals only with features of coherence, one or more of which must be exhibited in any sequence of phrases which is to present any sort of structural unity ; while as regards larger and looser combinations, it at most describes the conditions of effective presentation of subject-matter whose essential beauty must be presupposed.  Such features as alternations of prolonged and staccato notes, or a *crescendo* rise to a climax and a *diminuendo* descent to repose, may be quite worth pointing out as general methods of variety, under which musical form may be exhibited ; the former may be pointed out as entering into the constitution of this or that form ; the latter may be essential to the effect of this or that paragraph ; but both are features which the poorest musician can introduce into the poorest composition at a moment's notice. Again, Mr. Sully says that passages from perfect to less perfect accords 'afford elements of variety and artistic relief,' whereas 'sequences of chords of similar harmonic character manifest a certain æsthetic unity.' But such considerations would apply to many quite formless, though very likely harmless, groups. Any sequence of chords which is felt as characteristically impressive, is so felt by dint of presenting a certain form, whereof the various elements (as in an impressive melody) are important as elements of a unity intuitively appreciated, not as each affording 'artistic relief' to the one before it. Once more, he says that alternations of lighter passages with sequences of full harmonies 'impart a fine æsthetic character to the composition : ' but, again, it surely all depends what the passages are ; the mere alternation of lightness and fulness contains no guarantee for beauty in the forms which exhibit it. Again, Mr. Sully remarks that 'amplitude, freedom, and variety' convey 'a rich picturesque beauty' to operatic arias.  But amplitude, freedom, and variety of what?  I do not see how such qualities could be denied to many compositions whose contents are altogether unbeautiful ; or, if they were denied *because* the contents were unbeautiful, all I am contending for would be conceded.  Thus modern pianoforte music is rich in 'fantaisies' where little tinkling, tuneless tags of tune alternate in the freest way with squirts and cascades and tricklings and skurryings of all varieties, diversified with ample noise and extended to ample length.  From some of them I should imagine that no one has ever received a moment of characteristic musical enjoyment ; but whether or not this be the case, it is enough for my point that many, like myself, perceive in them 'amplitude, freedom, and variety,' and are wearied and sickened by the lack (to us) of beauty.  But though in these respects Mr. Sully's expressions seem to me unsatisfactory, my objections in no way touch the real merits of his excellent essay.

gracefulness of the linear curve, is surely to ignore the fact that any number of worthless and annoying sequences of notes could be made whose linear representatives would 'alternately rise and fall in a graceful serpentine line.' So represented, the well-known bars which close a paragraph of the andante in the *Pastoral* sonata—

do not yield a 'serpentine line' a whit more 'graceful' than the following horrible Music-hall fragment,

*The grace of the visual curves adduced in illustration of melodies is itself extremely questionable.*

Even as regards the grace of the visual line itself, it is very delusive to take a melody where the notes are all of equal length; as in that particular case the time-element in the musical proportions causes no trouble, and since lines in space are competent to represent the lengths and directions of intervals, a tune whose clauses exhibit a tolerable amount of parallelism can be represented by a tolerably symmetrical and orderly-looking curve. Even so of course the great *differentia* of the musical elements, tone-relationship, is necessarily ignored, and the analogy of the line is totally barren and uninstructive; but neglecting this fatal objection, it is perhaps worth while to point out what ugly and *bizarre* lines we get by merely taking a melody where inequalities of duration in the notes force us to take some account of them. This can only be done by such an artificial convention as that horizontal length shall represent time-duration and perpendicular length pitch-distance; on which convention the following clause from *Batti batti*, as sweet as it is simple—

might be pourtrayed somewhat in this way by a line which looks like a temperature-curve:

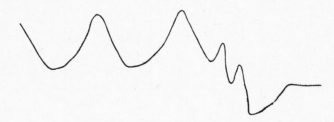

It would perhaps be hypercritical to say that we really have no right to use curved lines at all (unless indeed to express sound without fixed intervals, as in the aimless and wholly unmelodious sliding up and down on a fiddle-string), and that the literal representation on the above convention would be

though, after all, there is not much to choose between the two diagrams in point of beauty. No one, however, will seriously contend that a curve which has no definiteness or cogency, and may be just as well looked at from right to left or upside down, can really represent the fixed and unique proportions of music : the more important point is that the relation of parallelism of different parts, which may be fairly held to go towards giving to a changing line a character of graceful waviness, contains no guarantee of grace or any other character in a melody.

The case with respect to *contrast* at different points and between *Contrast presented at different members of a melodic form is simpler still, so obvious is it that ferent points in there is no merit in the point itself apart from the individual form in which a melodic form.* it is merged : though, owing to this very fact, it is not easy to take what would be admitted as the *same* contrast and exhibit it in a good and in a bad tune, as we did with the more palpable feature of parallelism of phrase ; for we cannot look at the contrast apart from our musical perception of the form ; whereas parallelisms of phrase could be seen and testified to by the eye. We may, however, take the common change from major to minor, or *vice versâ*, as affording a marked contrast which may obviously be a mere tricky feature in a wretched tune, as in so many drawing-room ditties, and may equally enter into the essence of a perfect form, as in the conclusion of Schubert's *Leise flehen—*

For an instance of a no less striking point of contrast, not describable under any such general head as major and minor, we may take a form of, if possible, still more transcendent beauty, the same composer's *Du bist die Ruh—*

If one desired to direct attention to the special beauties of this melody, so far as they can be separately dwelt on at all, the first item would natur-

ally be the simple intensity and intense simplicity of the repeated motive
at the opening ; and then in the following phrases one would point to the
contrast depending on the A *natural* key-stone of the one, and the A *flat*
key-stone of the other ; the uncertainty and change of direction towards a
new landmark given by the A natural, with the diminished seventh and
modulation, causing an intensity of satisfaction when the A flat arrives on
a strong chord of the original key, and bears us on towards home ; while
the combined originality and simplicity of the final bars, as they swell on
into perfect rest, leave one marvelling whether any cadence as lovely yet
remains to be discovered. Now in such an account, anything that we say
about the beauty of the *contrast* is just as much *descriptive*, and just as
little *explanatory*, as all the rest. We may direct attention to that point
as an item in the form, as an exemplification of variety in unity, as one of
the facts which constitute this whole series of notes a single intelligible
melody. But the beauty is not a matter of contrast, but of *that* contrast,
of those two individual bits of contrasted motion. As far as harmonic
progression goes (and this is the only way in which the relation of the contrasted portions could be looked at apart from the actual melody) the same
contrast has been used in hundreds of cases without seeming specially interesting or necessary ; and we can but accept it as a fact of musical
intuition that these two particular bits of melodic motion, resting on this
simple harmonic foundation, do by their mutual reaction merge into an
organism of incomparable beauty, in which, conformably to the true nature
of an organism, each of them is indispensable to, and each reveals the
necessity of, the other.

Another marked case of contrast on which no sort of judgment can be
passed apart from the motive into which it enters, is that which appears in
the repetition of a phrase with the tonality altered (or giving a momentary
impression of being altered) by a single step, usually upwards but occasionally downwards. An example of the ' lifting of the musical horizon '
by the raised tonality is afforded by the repetition in C minor of the phrase
just heard in B flat, at the opening of Schubert's trio in the latter key
quoted in Chap. XIV. § 6. This kind of contrast is specially susceptible of
commonplace and vulgar use. The downward change is exemplified in the
effect of the chords of B flat in the well-known opening of the *Waldstein*
sonata—

*Modulation* has no intrinsic and independent virtue.

Finally, the general phenomenon of modulation may be adduced in illustration of the same point; since such change constitutes one of the commonest aspects of variety, whether in a single melodic form, or in a more diffuse paragraph, or in the conduct of the successive transitions in a long developed movement. And in no case does the fact of the transition contain the slightest guarantee for beauty. A modulation which strikes one as beautiful in a melody does so not through any general virtue in the passage from such a key to such another, but in virtue of using those precise notes in that precise rhythm. I was once admiring the second part of a melody where a beautiful sentence, already heard, was modified on repetition by advancing into a new key: the composer remarked to me that the effect, though doubtless good, was 'a trick;' but the point was to have invented a sentence so arresting that the trick 'came off.' Exactly the same modulation, *quâ* modulation, may occur as a constituent of essential form in the best and in the worst melody: while the customary formulæ about natural and related keys are perpetually being set at naught. We shall no more get a man to write us a *Forelle* by telling him it is a good and natural thing to modulate to the key of the dominant, than we shall get a genius to refrain from writing down passages like that from the overture to *Egmont* quoted on p. 208, or that from *Nell Gwynne* quoted on p. 252, if they occur to him, by telling him that transitions to the harmonies of 'remote keys'[1] are to be avoided in simple single forms. When

---

[1] It is worth noting that this phrase is apt to mislead an untechnical lover of music; a transition to the harmonies of a 'remote key' sounds as if it ought to be either something very odd and startling, or something very scientific and esoteric. The two

modulation occurs in longer movements as a mode of transition and junction, it may either be purely transitional; that is, whether presented in a supplementary connecting passage or in the progressive direction given to an integral division of the structure, its avowed object is to get somewhere else for the sake of starting again in a new key; or it may present distinct and individual beauties of its own, either through links of reminiscence or by the presentation of quite new matter. In the first case, it is unnecessary to point out how mechanical and undistinctive must be any rules laid down for it. 'To modulate,' as Piccini said, 'is not difficult in itself: there is a route for that as well as all other trades;' and the lamest and feeblest movement may present such 'architectonic' features as are involved in progression through an approved cycle of keys. A scheme of modulation is like a metre, ready for any one to use. But when a great composer changes his key, whether by keeping to the beaten tracks of modulation or by transitions and episodes which are a law to themselves, beautiful Ideal Motion is apt to spring up along his path, just as in his more self-complete single themes; and as a theme is not good because it modulates, so the whole work is good not through wealth of modulation in the abstract, any more than through wealth of bars or wealth of crotchets, but through sustained beauty and individuality of essential form.

We may conclude our review of the nature of essential form in Music by noticing two special dangers, the importance of which will be most evident in connection with the topics of the present chapter. The first is of a decline either in the quantity or the quality of musical 'subjects,' of short individually impressive pieces of tune; the second is of a decline in the impressiveness of those forms which are now felt as impressive. The former danger is clearly peculiar to Music, among the arts: the very isolation which is an advantage as regards perils from without exposes her in an exceptional degree to perils from within. The subject-matter of the representative arts is practically unlimited; and architectural works can be grasped in their larger aspects while the eye still embraces a multitude of independent and semi-independent details, so that a vast amount of individual characteristics can be seen if they are there, while, as has been pointed out, very much less individuality is actually demanded than in Music. We have seen that though minor points of individuality may be

§ 10. Danger of a decline in musical 'subjects.

---

instances quoted would alone show how easily such transitions may enter into forms from which the most naïve hearer receives a vivid and instantaneous impression of perfectly unstrained and coherent beauty. I may remark by the way that the constant occurrence of harmonies of alien keys, with no distinct modulation or view of staying in those keys (as, *e.g.*, in the cases referred to, the passage in A flat comprises harmonies belonging to the keys of A major and D minor, and the passage in E comprises harmonies belonging to the major keys of F sharp and D sharp), seems somewhat overlooked in the talk about 'cycles of keys' and 'conduct of modulation,' so common in connection with the 'temperament' controversy.

demanded in all buildings which claim to be works of art at all, the most strikingly individual buildings must necessarily be somewhat few and far between; while the fact that two or twenty beautiful buildings were extremely alike would not detract from their value if they were suitably situated in different places, one of which could not reap the benefit of a building in the others, and in buildings a very large amount of resemblance may exist without entailing any sense of dead and servile copying. The primary requisite both in simple and elaborate musical work, on the other hand, is that it shall contain motives of individuality as well as beauty; for of music more truly than of anything else may we say with Bacon, 'there is no excellent Beauty that hath not some strangenesse in the proportion.'[1] If the leading phrases are echoes of others already known, annoyance and a sense of weakness rather than pleasure are apt to result from the resemblance; partly because a beloved motive will so little suffer change that reflections of it are often as charmless as that of a face in a convex mirror; partly because in Music there seems no reason for saying again what has been once said well, inasmuch as the conditions of musical presentation oppose no barrier to the production of the same work in a thousand different places.

The important bearing of the *shortness* of the successive bits which the ear will grasp, illustrated in one way by the contrast in the immensely rapid and comprehensive sweeps of the eye, may be seen in another way by comparison with Poetry, the other art in which the sense has to grasp bits in succession, and where the element of form must be present in bits of a size suitable to being grasped. But in Poetry, where the ideas and subject-matter are matters purely for the mind, it is *they* which constitute the organism, it is in them that originality and coherence are demanded. It is entirely in the relations perceived by the intellectual faculties that the constituent portions must approve their fitness and their bearing on each other and on the whole, under pain of seeming rambling and nonsensical; while the metre or form which

---

[1] I have found that the experience of many others tallies with my own in the following respect: that a common (though very far from universal) feature of a simple melody which is strongly approved on first acquaintance is that, while it seems perfectly natural and easy to catch, one cannot quite get hold of it afterwards; there is some point where it baulks one's efforts, some special rarity in the Ideal Motion, any substitute for which seems *banal* and charmless; and this though the intervals may all be of a simple kind, and the right notes when supplied are often quite close to our futile attempts, so that when once the progression is familiar, the only puzzle is how it could ever have puzzled one. Different instances will occur to different people: I am at this moment being tormented in the way I have described by the beautiful tune in waltz-measure in Auber's overture to *Haydée*; the notes seem all in my head, but when I try to whistle them they will not come quite right. Some may perhaps recognise a shorter and more striking example in the subject of the Rondo in Beethoven's G major concerto, quoted on p. 153; it would argue no lack of ear, if a person to whom this passage was new failed to whistle it through, even after it had been played to him half a dozen times; yet how innocent it sounds! In this particular case the start on the subdominant chord makes an obvious little trap; but as a rule no such special cause can be assigned.

addresses the sense is something in a manner superimposed, and the same metrical forms may be used thousands of times. In a musical presentation the *whole substance* is apprehended through the sense, consisting as it does essentially of form; and owing to this entire dependence on a sense, the faculty of viewing as a whole the relations of affinity or contrast which different parts of a musical movement [1] present, has a much shorter tether than the free intellectual faculty which is concerned with literary work. One may comprehend the unity of a poem which takes many hours to read; whereas the furthest limits to which it would be possible to extend the comprehension in the other case would be reckoned by minutes. And the mode of structure within these limits entails, as we have seen, organic forms very much less extended still, these last being the elements whose character is all-important. Though the duration of a complete musical paragraph may very considerably exceed that of any verbal stanza or strophe, still the more extended and elaborate a movement, the more necessary is it that it shall rest on shorter themes and progressions, which, though they pass too quickly to be actually presented alone, are in a way self-complete, and which will recur and be recognised in various forms; this perpetual reassertion of 'subject' being the cardinal feature of musical development. The very fact that the organism of a long movement is loose enough to admit episodic forms, whose *raison d'être*, provided they be beautiful and offer a pleasing contrast and relief to what surrounds them, is not rigidly enquired into, and that a short acquaintance with the resulting whole soon cements it into perfectly satisfactory coherence and unity, exemplifies the same point, the all-importance of the individual bits of form, the individual lengths of Ideal Motion, or whatever we choose to call them. And a shorter work, such as a song, often consists wholly of one or two complete pieces of tune, and is really therefore all 'subject.'

Now the question presents itself whether the mine of good 'subjects,' of beautiful short self-complete forms, is practically inexhaustible. Though the length of each is very limited, still the variety rendered possible by the two factors of time and pitch seems as if it might be endless; but experience alone can decide. As an answer to the assertion that the possible combinations are to a considerable extent exhausted, it is sometimes pointed out that, *e.g.*, unpublished works of Schubert come to light containing quite new and simple ones, redolent of the old indescribable charm. But this is not an altogether conclusive argument. For the fear of cessation in the creation of first-rate 'subjects' depends, perhaps, not so much on the actual exhaustion of the mine, as on the

*Is the mine inexhaustible?*

---

[1] I am perpetually obliged to avoid the word *work*, as this is very commonly applied to a *collection* of the larger sort of musical organisms, as to a symphony or sonata, consisting of several movements, or to an oratorio, consisting of many distinct solos, duets, choruses, &c.

following consideration: whether the musical atmosphere in which a composer is now necessarily nurtured is adapted to stimulate his actual melodic inventiveness as distinct from his ingenuity; whether the elaborate involutions through which his faculty is always being led, may not affect his direct and intuitive power of striking on combinations of materials the simple arrangements of which have at all events been to some extent used up. And no elaboration of treatment could make up for a decline in this respect. Whatever the larger plan of the structure, whether continued on the accepted lines of chamber-music and symphony, or on any other lines which shall embody the essential conditions of iteration and contrast, musical composition can be rendered vital by new and beautiful themes, and by nothing else; failing that, it would lose the popular element which is the mainstay of its existence, and would become the ingenious amusement of a clique.

A composer's melodic inventiveness is singularly subject to the influences of the Music already in existence, and may conceivably be swamped by it.

Nor is the outlook brightened by the following consideration: that while Music enjoys the advantage of not being dependent on outside currents of thought and feeling, and so is unaffected by conditions under which other arts may languish, yet in the musical region itself the talent of new-comers is in a pre-eminent degree subject to the influence of their predecessors and elder contemporaries. A child of musical genius is absolutely impregnated with the music of his time; the motives of elder composers are perpetually going through his head; and the greater abundance of existing motives of very high quality may appreciably narrow the field of remaining possibilities, not only because those particular ones have been invented once for all and cannot be re-invented, but because their number and variety may so possess musical minds, may so monopolise the springs of musical impulse, as to prevent any but the very highest genius from striking out new paths of Ideal Motion, sufficiently individual to seem in their turn first-rate. They may even be first-rate and yet lack that genial quality, that extraordinary popular freshness, which is the very life-blood of Music in its most important aspects. Prodigious, for instance, as is the genius of Brahms, simple and strong and magnificent as are many of his melodies, no one, I imagine, can expect that a great deal of his work will ever be anything like the tremendous popular force in the world that Beethoven's is.

§ 11. With this danger is connected that of incoherence.

There are many signs of a present danger that elaboration is tending to swamp melody; but in the opposite direction there lies perhaps a still greater danger, that of simple incoherence, of a loss of the feeling for true unity of sequence and development. If these isolated and irresponsible sound-structures may, on the one hand, easily degenerate into complicated patterns and ingenious mazes, still more easily, on the other, may they dissolve into a formless chaos of flying fragments. And this latter danger, like the other, is really connected with that of a lack of impressive themes;

since if a theme be not in itself impressive, it will not be apt to lend itself to noble and loving development, or to suggest new beauties. Links of reminiscence fall naturally into disuse when there is nothing sufficiently arresting to be particularly worth remembering: and the very lightness and elasticity of the control which the laws of effective structure in long movements impose, make it seem possible to discard them, and to put the ear off with a phantasmagoria of restless and unrelated progressions, carried down perhaps by the childish sop of some accompanying verbal programme. Perpetual transition and modulation, perpetual differentiation without integration, are the natural resources of uninspired ingenuity, which may produce a thousand series of showy fragments, but never a single piece of first-class form. The germs from which a large movement grows, as we have seen, may be, in proportion to its length, the merest fragments; but they are centres of growth, not parts of a medley : and the fact that there are ' subjects ' in the world whose magnificence is revealed in a very few bars in no way precludes organic sequence and amplitude in the sections of the subsequent development. It is an insult to the ear to treat it as if it could not spread its perception over these more extended reaches of form, and as if the only way to keep it going was to give it perpetual fresh starts and jogs in unforeseen methods and strange directions ; especially since it is the almost invariable rule that the greater the variety of modulational twists and turns, changes of *tempo* and pace, and so on, the less impressive are the individual fragments themselves; beautiful pieces of form not being such everyday occurrences that a composer willingly leaves one when he has got it, or breaks it off at the fourth bar with a diminished seventh for fear of being thought vulgarly straightforward.

This fact is ignored in a retort which is very commonly made to complaints of incoherence and formlessness in some particular composition. People point to some fine melody, some piece of truly noble form, by the same author, and say, ' See what melody he can write *when he likes*;' implying that since he hasn't liked in the particular case complained of, some still higher beauty must necessarily be supposed to lurk there. The fallacy is obvious. Schubert himself, whose productiveness in relation to the brief term of his activity stands wholly without parallel in the history of art, could not write a noble melody whenever he chose. Such melodies are jewels, which may indeed occasionally flash forth on the composer's path, but which must often be long and diligently searched for ; and in neither case does he command them at will. And apart from this, so unique and overpowering is the effect of beautiful melody, that it is as little believable that a person endowed in any abundance with melodic inventiveness has ever refused to exercise that power and has wantonly chosen to write unmelodious music in preference, as that any person, having actually invented a noble melody, has cast it aside as a thing of no account.

Tokens of the danger may be found among the hearers and performers as well as the composers.

Nor is it only among composers that tokens of the danger are to be found; a considerable section of the musical public evinces the same tendency to accept strange and cloying sequences of tone in place of definitely organic and apprehensible form; as though beautiful tunes and 'subjects' admitted of any conceivable substitute. It is to be feared that some of the present vagaries show the feverish craving for novelties which is a sure sign of disease. I hear that there were members of the Wagner Society in London who expressed a strong longing for *quarter-tones*. Now as it is impossible to suppose that these persons want all existing music to be suppressed, and as the relations of notes in modern European music, depending on a system of tones and semitones, are even more definitely fixed than the proportions of the human form, the desire shows as much æsthetic imagination and perception as if a devotee of sculpture, in the interests of his art, were to pray for a time when the arms and noses of half the human race (say, the female sex) should be of half the usual length. The fact that scale-systems are to a certain extent arbitrary, and admit of many varieties, is quite irrelevant: for it is of course only in relation to races and generations, not to individuals, that this is true. If any tribe had been used to nothing but arms and noses of half the present length, their sense of the beauty and expressiveness of the combinations into which these elements enter would have been formed naturally on the given materials; but that noses and semi-noses should go together in any individual's ideas of facial expressiveness is simply impossible; and the case of the elements of melodic form is precisely similar. Whether the disease to which such signs point is chronic or acute it would be premature to decide. Serious it undoubtedly is, as appearimg in just those sections of musical society whose influence ought to be powerful in guiding and leading on the popular taste: but its direct effects are not likely to spread far, and we may rest secure that the musical perceptions of the majority are incapable of being permanently warped.

§ 12. We have a vast heritage in the music of the last two centuries;

As regards composition, it would doubtless be easy to point out that there has been no interval of unproductiveness, and that plenty of beautiful and healthy music is perpetually appearing. But, after all, the question of the future of Music is perhaps too exclusively considered in reference to the production of new works; and it seems to be sometimes forgotten that in the truest sense the music of the future will be, to its hearers, just the music that they hear and think about, whether written in their own time or centuries earlier. Nothing can deprive them of their heritage; in the music now existing both we and they have an inalienable possession. The education of the musical sense to maturity was a slow process, and in the development of the art waves of indifference swept over many successive strata of music whose effect in its own age was most fresh and powerful. But much of Handel's work (to say nothing of many isolated productions of much earlier date) stands out now as young as on the day it was written, and was never so well known as in our own time; and from him and Bach onwards the chain of great composers much of whose work is in the most literal sense popular is quite unbroken.

At the same time it would be but a superficial view which refused to recognise within what limits these latter remarks are applicable. Even of the music written since the beginning of the last century, a large amount which seemed first-rate in its generation has become in a very real sense obsolete; not merely crowded out by fresh accumulations, but unable when heard to give the delight it formerly did. Nor does this apply only to operatic works, of which both the contemporary and the posthumous popularity depends greatly on elements and chances external to the music. This subject of obsolescence in Music is too intimately connected with questions as to the future, not to deserve special consideration; and fortunately its wider aspects may be to a certain extent illustrated by reference to individual experiences. In the absence of any reference to those stable external facts to which the representative arts owe allegiance, the history of the various fortunes of musical productions has been, in the normal course of things, entirely controlled by that ever-alert musical instinct, so wholly autocratic in its own domain, so willing to try, so prompt either to accept or to reject, any new path which is presented to it; so irresponsible both in its fidelities and its infidelities. When the ear tires of known forms, there is an end of them; they have ceased to give the pleasure which it is their sole function to give: when the ear accepts and welcomes new forms, their position, for a time at least, is assured, however much they may set previous theories at defiance. And that perpetual demand, which has been already noticed, for individuality in any new forms that present themselves, a demand which merely means that if the individuality be absent, the forms will not impress people or stick in their heads, has naturally occasioned great vicissitudes in the history of various features of form as they have in turn presented themselves. Thus when the feeling for the major and minor modes, to the exclusion of all others, was in its earlier stages, and the fixation of key by the 'full close' of dominant and tonic chords was a comparatively new feature, neither composer nor hearer could have too much of it, and in some of the music of the seventeenth century half a dozen full closes may be found in a single half-page. After a time this naturally palled; an effect which was everybody's property was felt to be cheap; and its perpetual recurrence, breaking up a movement into definite short lengths, was of course incompatible with prolonged development. Similarly the effect of mere transition and modulation seems to have been much more decided in the last century, before such things were so much a stock-in-trade. Rousseau speaks with great admiration of the passing suddenly from one key to an-

*though it is important to notice the limits within which this is true.*

other, or from major to minor, in Italian melody ; features which to us, apart from the motives involved, seem very cheap thunder. The same sort of fact may be paralleled by many a childish experience, in which some sweet cadence or effect of harmony has seemed, on first acquaintance, to reach the very *acme* of beauty, and has afterwards come to be recognised as right and necessary in its place, but not in itself an extraordinary piece of musical invention.

Now, when we leave special points of this kind and come to complete tunes, and when we consider what seem to us the less remarkable specimens of some past generation of music, though here of course it becomes impossible to put into words the reason of their seeming to lack individuality and special charm, though in all the points which can be examined from outside, they may seem as different from one another as other tunes which *have* for us the necessary individuality, yet the inner musical sense admits of no contradiction. The exquisiteness of those particular Ideal Motions has vanished for us, like the exquisiteness of perpetual full closes ; and we may be inclined to call the melodies second-rate, forgetting that they may have caused in their contemporaries the maximum of melodic pleasure. And here again most of us will be able to parallel the facts in the history of our own childish partialities. This sort of obsolescence is less noticed than it might be, for several reasons. First, the picked specimens from these earlier generations have *not* lost their freshness and are always *en évidence*; but their survival is of course just owing to the fact that they *are* the picked specimens. Secondly, different sorts of music have had their pre-eminence at different times. Thus, not to go further back than the last century, Bach preceded Haydn ; but while the polyphonic music of Bach is still wholly unrivalled in its kind, the instrumental works of Haydn, in spite of their marking one of the great eras of music by their extraordinary advance on preceding examples, and in spite of the wealth of undying beauties which ensure their continued popularity, still contain scores and scores of melodies which no one will maintain to be capable of giving the same pleasure now that they did at the time of production. Thirdly, no generation of music-lovers is homogeneous : each contains, so to speak, representatives of several preceding stages, and epitomises a variety of tastes which have had their day of predominance. The truly predominant taste can only be roughly judged by a very wide view of a very gradual process, and any generalisation about it will always be open to a thousand contradictions resting on individual cases ; thus there are still plenty of people, and very likely always will be, who prefer the quartets of Haydn to those of Beethoven.[1]

*The obsolescence is very real of much even of this modern music.*

---

[1] It is a remarkable fact that musical children of twelve years old will now so commonly accept at once, as perfectly natural and as profoundly beautiful, passages in Beethoven's works at which some of the trained musicians of his own day were

But, it may be said, can this loss of power in so much music which has doubtless seemed imperishable to those to whose ears it was first addressed, be other than a very ominous fact? As long as Music was clearly advancing, and advancing not only in large development and elaboration, but in the sense that the melodies and 'subjects' invented during a space of ten years seemed superior in beauty and vitality to those produced in the same space of time fifty years earlier (as, for instance, if the period about 1730 were compared with that about 1780, and the period about 1780 to that about 1830), the fact that much of the older music slipped out of knowledge would not seem of much account: but the same fact might well appear in a different light to those who hold that from 1830 to 1880 there has been no such advance, and that in spite of the immense amount of beautiful music produced in that period the greatest music in the world by a good many degrees was written before the former date. But there is really plenty to reassure us. Work which in the third generation remains absolutely pre-eminent has sufficiently proved its lasting power; and as regards the mere proportion of the part which lives and spreads to the part for which no genuine revival can be expected, the music of the popular giants of the previous generations, Handel, Haydn, and even Mozart, will stand no comparison with the achievements of our own century.

§ 13. This may appear ominous for the future;

but there is much to re-assure us.

It is an interesting question how far the decline in the charm of a good deal of past music has been due to an inevitable though unconscious comparison of it with what succeeded it; how far certain things would have palled, or at all events got to seem a little commonplace, but for some experience of new and profounder modes of Ideal Motion. That this has been the case to some extent is certainly suggested by individual experiences; [1] and the fact would involve the comforting belief that we are not likely to suffer any appreciable loss in what we have got till we get something better.

It is not improbable that some of the charm which has faded might have survived but for the appearance of more stirring forms.

aghast: for the interval of time is of course far too short for any hereditary influences to have been able to act. The fact may perhaps be taken to indicate that in some cases training and perpetual practice of music tend rather to set and stereotype the perceptive faculty than to give it elasticity and receptivity.

[1] As an instance I may perhaps be allowed to mention a personal incident. There was a time when, as a child, I thought *Ah che la morte* a divinely beautiful tune. It happened that when I was in a state of great rapture and excitement about it, I made my first acquaintance with Beethoven by hearing one or two of the movements from the earlier sonatas. I fully realised, even at the moment, that this was one of the most extraordinary experiences that would ever fall to my lot: but for about a fortnight I tried to keep up my belief in *Ah che la morte* as well; and I have the most vivid recollection of the sort of struggle that went on in my mind, till at last I had to admit that, to me, the two things were incompatible. I need hardly add that I attach no objective value to this fact. *Ah che la morte* is a melody which has been a source of immense pleasure, and I should be nothing but a gainer if I could now enjoy it as I once did: it only happens that I cannot.

# CHAPTER XI.

## POLYPHONY AND HARMONY.

§ 1. Melody only has been hitherto considered, the priority being in every way justifiable.

So far we have been engaged entirely with melodic sequences. Melody is the fundamental fact of Music, not only in the sense that homophony, or a succession of single unaccompanied notes, is the primary form in the historical development of the art as well as in the tentative efforts of every individual, but in the sense that throughout the most highly developed music the melodic element, however adorned and supported by other elements, is displayed in full pre-eminence. (I need hardly explain again what was made so abundantly manifest in the last chapter, that by the melodic element is not meant lengths of eight or sixteen or any particular number of bars, with a distinct ending, but simply the phenomenon, in whatever length of series exemplified, of continuous and coherent Ideal Motion.) I am aware that in treating separately of one element, and especially in illustrating the treatment (as one cannot but do) by examples from music in which the other elements are also present, one runs the risk of seeming to under-estimate the place of these last in the total effect. Not only, however, did perspicuity absolutely demand this separate treatment in the present instance, but in a general attempt to trace the sources of the power of Music and the place and nature of the musical faculty, it can hardly be deemed unnatural that the facts and experiences of ages should take precedence of those to which, as in the case of Harmony, the most liberal estimate could not assign a history of more than a few centuries. Nor when we examine, as it is now time to do, the nature of the contributions made by these more recent elements to the total of musical effect, shall we find the melodic element to be at all disturbed in its position of pre-eminence, however much its effects may have been enhanced and its scope enlarged by the appearance of the others on the scene.

§ 2. The two heads of Polyphony and Harmony distinguished.

The elements in question may be classed under two heads; Polyphony, i.e. simultaneous presentation of two or more distinctly separate parts or series of notes; and Harmony, which in its most distinctive aspect is an agreeable succession of chords, each regarded rather as a *compound* unit in a *single* series than as a mere concurrence of superposed notes each belonging to its own separate series or 'part.'[1] No distinct line can be drawn separating these two modes of presentation from one another : thus in harmonised chorales and many pieces of modern part-writing the progression of the separate parts, taken by different voices or instruments, technically the *counterpoint*, is quite distinct, while still their combination makes a complete chord-series ; and even where no distinct chord-series of this kind is presented, yet as every case of modern polyphony conforms to the laws of harmonic progression, it is based on an outline which might be drawn up as a simple chord-series. But while harmony in our day thus dominates polyphony, it has a domain of its own where polyphony in the technical sense does not at all enter ; namely, where in the course of a harmonic progression the ear recognises no series of single notes, or only *one* such series, as specially prominent and continuous ; and thus receives the harmonies either as an agreeable succession of compound units without reference to any separate voices or 'parts' at all, or as an agreeable support and adjunct to a *single* melodic voice or 'part.' Between such a case where the polyphonic element is entirely absent, and that of some distinct piece of four-part harmony where it is prominently present, many degrees of prominence are possible to it : for instance, an early stage of its appearance might be exemplified in a case where a melodic 'part' is accompanied by a set of chords the bass of which forms a distinct 'part' of its own, and has sufficient independence of movement in relation to the melody to give 'contrapuntal' effect. Counterpoint, the simultaneous appearance of parts whose motion relatively to one another is distinctly singled out and watched, really enters to some extent into the large majority of written compositions, down to fragmentary bars and half-bars of it in the piano accompaniment of the simplest songs. We shall find moreover that the *principle* of polyphony, the pleasure of hearing several distinct things going on at once, applies to many cases where there is no sort of separate progression of 'parts' in the technical sense.

*The principle of the former extends beyond what is technically included under the term.*

Polyphony in its more accurate and restricted sense need not detain us long. For though its place in musical effect is of the highest importance, and though the account of the various forms of it and of the devices used in its treatment constitutes a chief part of what is usually called the 'science' of Music, and though an enormous amount of ingenuity was lavished on it for several centuries before true harmonic

*§ 3. Polyphony :*

---

[1] It is sometimes said that in harmony it is the *perpendicular* aspects of the notes concerned—in polyphony or counterpoint the *horizontal* aspects, which are specially prominent. But though harmony can doubtless be exemplified in a single chord which is wholly perpendicular, and counterpoint can only be exemplified in parts containing a certain number of consecutive notes, which are therefore horizontal, the distinction is very inaccurate ; since all the power of harmony depends likewise on *succession*, on a horizontal order of compound units.

progressions obtained an independent footing, its effects (so far as we can separate them from interest either in the *melodic* aspect of one or more of the 'parts' or in the *harmonic* basis of the progression) may be referred

its principle;
to that general principle just noticed, the love of hearing and following several lines of things simultaneously. This might seem to be just one form of detecting unity in variety; but it has clearly a speciality which enables us to point to it confidently and without reservation as a source of pleasure; in contrast to those cases of unity in variety (comprising graceless geometrical figures, rhinoceroses, and ugly or trivial melodies) where we have found the mere exemplification of that principle to be no guarantee

it produces a
pleasing sense
of power in the
perception of
unity under
variety.
of æsthetic character. The speciality in the case of polyphony is obviously that the variety is not of elements which have to be co-ordinated into a single form, but of things having each its own definite completeness; for even if a separate 'part' lack independent melodic impressiveness, it is still an independently coherent series of notes. And here the sense of *power* which was noticed several times in the earlier chapters, the pleasure of thridding and unravelling with ease and certainty what nevertheless presents an aspect of high complexity, comes distinctly into play. We remarked how, so long as the forms had some independent aspect of strength or grace, this easy grasp and mastery of a number of them at once entered prominently into the pleasure derived from Architecture; and though the 'parts' in Music are necessarily few, this fact is more than counterbalanced by their precise individuality (so much emphasised on several previous occasions in contradistinction to anything obtainable by abstract visual lines), by their immense varieties of motion, and by the clearness with which the common rhythmic outline, and in modern music the harmonic basis, stamps and confirms their true union through all their meetings and partings and fightings and embracings. This vivid sense of grasp and power has of course no place in the perception of unity under variety in those cases where there is no sense of complexity, as where a number of elements, insignificant or meaningless in isolation, make up a single form, whether beautiful or ugly: we do not feel actively *clever* in perceiving or appreciating a single face or figure, or a single arch or dome, or a single series of melodic notes. These may give us their own distinctive pleasure, but not that particular glow of doing a thing easily, in spite of its seeming to have the elements of difficulty, which we experience as our eye sweeps through a complicated interior, or as our ear follows the tangled order of a fugue.

§ 4. The
chief features
in the early
history of
polyphony.
Three points in the pre-harmonic history of polyphony should be distinctly realised: (1) it started (about the commencement of the twelfth century) with the discovery that two independent melodic parts could be followed agreeably at the same time, provided their synchronous notes were not harshly dissonant: (2) it led gradually to the important devices of

'imitation' and 'canon,' one part taking up what had recently been sung by another, and thus originated in a way those 'links of reminiscence' which have proved so prominent a means of developing prolonged musical tissues : and (3), though the interest centred essentially in the motion of the parts, yet the perpetual concurrence of notes, producing chords so to speak accidentally, 'accumulated,' as Helmholtz says, 'a mass of experiments' for the development of the true chord-connections of harmony.

Now the gradual development of the sense of harmony and of the sense of key with which it was so intimately associated, naturally imposed more and more stringent conditions on the polyphonous parts; for the negative condition that synchronous notes must not clash, or produce isolated disagreeable moments, was gradually substituted the necessity that the synchronous notes should present combinations coherent in harmony and key with the neighbouring combinations. And there is one result of this which has not been sufficiently noticed; namely, that it must now be an *exceptional* piece of good fortune if two melodies of decided independent impressiveness can be directly combined as two parts ; though when such a case does occur, our modern sense of actual harmonic fusion, over and above that of independent motion in the two parts, must produce a greater intensity of pleasure than could have been felt in the much commoner combinations of well-known melodic themes, possible to the Flemish burghers in the pre-harmonic days. This point is worth noting as throwing some light on the confusion which has existed respecting the relations and comparative merits of *polyphony* and *melody*. It reveals the germ of truth which lurked at the bottom of Rousseau's absurd theory that several 'parts' could not be enjoyed at the same time, which he carried to the length of saying that a vocal duet ought to be simply a dialogue ; an absurdity fully equalled by musicians who, in moments of scientific enthusiasm, maintain the inherent superiority of contrapuntal writing to naïve tune, on the ground that it gives two or three '*melodies*' to be enjoyed instead of one.

*Noticeable effect of the sense of strict harmonic connection on polyphony.*

Very little analysis is needed to distinguish to some extent the place which independent melodic impressiveness of one or more 'parts' holds in various specimens of polyphonic composition, and the manner in which, where this particular feature is more or less lacking, musical effect of another sort is supplied. The different stages may be roughly classed as follows.

*§ 5. The relations of polyphonic to melodic effects may be classed in several stages.*

It occasionally happens that two motives of distinct independent beauty admit of immediate combination without any change or compromise ; with a result which, in amount of beauty, is more like the product than the sum of the constituents. The trio in the Choral Symphony affords a simple and splendid example, the effect there being heightened by the inversion and different instrumentation of the two motives when they are repeated :

and then later—

This stage may naturally be realised with varying degrees of completeness, as when one of the motives has true independent impressiveness, while the other, though complete and melodically coherent in form, is not suffi-

ciently striking to have been worth presenting on its own account; a head
to which pieces of noticeably free and melodic bass might often be referred.
Schumann's little song, *Wenn ich früh in den Garten geh'*, may serve as
an instance, though there a person who has heard the song once, and half-
unconsciously recalls it, is almost as likely to begin humming the bass as
the treble:

Again, the primariness, so to speak, of one of the motives may often
appear mainly in its greater *continuousness*: it may be perpetually fused
in effect with pieces of counterpoint which appear along its path, whose
independent merit as melodic strains may or may not be manifest, but
which would be but fragments alone.

Another class of combination is where a theme is *modified*, whether by
actual alterations in its rhythm or notes, or by breaking it up into fragments, so as to fit another theme or take part in a piece of more prolonged

polyphonic development; as continually in the interweaving of 'subjects,' in the 'carrying-out' of instrumental movements.

Next, we may have melodic motives, more or less completely appreciable on their own account, ruling, so to speak, over the contrasted *entourage* or support of some other 'part' or 'parts,' which, as isolated melody, would have *no* point or impressiveness: a simple example of this is supplied by the ascending bass in the theme from Beethoven's trio in D, quoted on p. 167. This stage is perhaps the commonest mode of the appearance of counterpoint in Music. It includes a great deal of strictly fugal composition, where such melodic interest as is present attaches to *single* fine themes given forth again and again, but where the interest of the surrounding complexity, and the distribution of the themes among different 'parts,' indefinitely enrich and vary the effect; while the harmonic progression fills the interstices of the more prominent melodic motives, as well as binding together the whole tissue by its own continuity. A similar enrichment and support of melodic motive, with every shade of importance in the less prominent 'parts,' may be traced through all sorts of compositions, ranging from those written on the strictest conventional lines to the freest movement in which a stream of dominant melodic phrases manifests itself amid varying aspects of polyphonic dispersion.

The next stage will be where there is less independent interest in any particular theme, or bits of theme,[1] and the ear is rather saturated with the sense of a rich and changing concourse than arrested by individual beauty of motion; where therefore what has been described as the characteristic aspect of polyphonic intricacy is presented in its most unmixed form. Not, however, by any means necessarily in its most delightful one; for prominent melodic interest, when we get it asserting itself through the waves of polyphony, seems able, without in the least interfering with the stirring sense of multitude, to lift the whole effect into the region of its own peculiar glory.

Finally, every one of these stages may be exemplified in a single page of music.

This sketch, though necessarily very brief and general, could hardly be made more precise without copious musical quotations, which after all might only prove how widely modes of perception and appreciation differ in this particular region: such as it is, it may serve to indicate the various sorts of alliance and mutual accommodation to which melody and counterpoint lend themselves. That the two phenomena may appear as be-

---

[1] The reader may recall Mr. Browning's most powerful and humorous picture, in *Master Hugues of Saxe-Gotha*, of an organist whose faith in a fugue he has just been playing needs confirmation; especially the passage beginning—

'First you deliver your phrase
  —Nothing propound, that I see,
Fit in itself for much blame or much praise—
  Answered no less, where no answer needs
    be:
Off start the two on their ways,' &c.

longing to different regions of effect, that there is a *difference in kind* between melody and anything so remote from melody as part-writing in which no separate ' part' is individually impressive, may seem, when thus stated, to be a truism. That the difference in such cases does not mean natural *antagonism* between polyphony and melody is equally a truism to those who realise the width and importance of their common zone. But for the sake of subsequent observations on the varieties of musical suscep-tibility and of the practical necessity of recognising those varieties, the fact that a sense of antagonism has been felt,[1] and the modes and reasons of that feeling, are worth consideration. The divorce which existed in the middle ages between the scientific contrapuntal compositions which had degenerated into mere Chinese puzzles, and the popular music which never was and never will be other than melodic, has still its lessons. We may smile at Rousseau's wild talk about ' l'usage des fugues, imitations, doubles dessins, et autres beautés arbitraires et de pure convention' with no other merit than their difficulty, and invented in the infancy of the art to make science look fine while genius was out of the question : but the most learned musician would have no right to smile at Metastasio's less sweeping view, that the music of the era previous to his own ' was in general too full of fugues, of parts and contrivances, to be felt or understood except by artists,' and that ' all the different movements of the several parts, their inversions and divisions, were unnatural, and by covering and deforming the melody, only occasioned confusion.' Of all celebrated literary men Metastasio perhaps lived in most intimate contact with musicians, and took the most intelligent interest in their art; and his opinion is thus the more valuable, as an em-bodiment of the verdict which will always be passed by the great public, cultivated and uncultivated, whom Music addresses, against the music which only musicians can understand. That both during and after Metastasio's lifetime all the resources of the art should have been blended in a series of works of ever-growing popularity, may somewhat blind us to the truth which was patent to backward-looking eyes in the still uncertain dawn of those events; namely, that the failure of melodic genius or (according to the argument of the last chapter) of the opportunities of

*Melody and polyphony, while capable of appearing separately in totally different regions of effect, are not antago-nistic;*

*though they have often ap-peared so.*

---

[1] A latent sense of this antagonism, at all events as between anything like strict coun-terpoint and tune, is often revealed by the special welcome accorded to some piece where it seems to be overcome. Thus I read lately in a newspaper that in the madrigal *As Vesta was descending*, by Thomas Weelkes, ' charming melodiousness is com-bined with scientific depth, all the more re-markable as it never intrudes upon the attention of the hearer, who may imagine he is listening to the simplest harmonies while the most complicated contrapuntal devices are being worked out with unfailing accu-racy.' No one can really complain of this criticism; but it must be observed that the combination in question is a single whole, to be duly appreciated in proportion as the whole is (not technically but musically) grasped ; not a mixture of ingredients, ' graceful melodiousness' to please the vulgar, ' scientific depth' and ' contrapuntal devices ' to please the learned.

melodic genius, must inevitably leave mere ingenuity, as for centuries it did leave it, in possession of a barren field.

§ 6. Harmony. The pleasurable effect of coincidence of impressions is by no means confined to the sense of hearing.

We have seen that Polyphony in modern music is entirely subject to harmonic control; and Harmony [1] is really much the more remarkable phenomenon, though its uniqueness in Music may not immediately appear.

[1] The word Harmony, as used in the text, includes both concord and discord : it is sometimes rather unfortunately restricted to concord, a usage due to the mode of its employment outside Music, and to the peculiarity of Music in presenting *discord* as a prominent feature of *beauty*. The physical and physiological conditions of harmony lie outside the compass of our general enquiry; there are, however, certain points in which the accepted theory seems to me incomplete and misleading, and the discussion of these will be found in the Appendix on Discord at the end of the book. The great distinction between the old and the new view of harmony may be stated here in a very few words. It had long been known that consonance is produced by notes whose rates of vibration stand to one another in a simple ratio, 2 to 1, 3 to 2, 5 to 4, and so on ; that the capacity of two tones to flow on simultaneously without interference or jar is connected in some way with such ratios. This led to the view that the æsthetic pleasure was essentially bound up with the *perspicuity and orderliness* involved in this simplicity, with the obviousness in the mode of arrangement presented, *e.g.* by the coincidence of every second vibration in one series with every third in the other. Now if sound-vibrations were things present *as such* to consciousness, this view might have been defensible, in so far as the simplicity of the ratio would imply ease in following and connecting the two lines of sound : but as the vibrations are not distinguishable as such, and their effect merges in what is felt as a perfectly continuous tone-sensation, the supposed connection between the agreeableness which *is* perceived and the simplicity or orderliness which is *not* perceived becomes a palpable figment.
Helmholtz set the matter in an entirely new light by an explanation in which discord is the prominent positive phenomenon, and concord is the absence of discord. He showed that discord arises from a rapid series of breaks in the even continuity of the two streams of vibrations, due to the very close proximity in pitch either of the actual notes sounded or of some of their respective harmonics ; that these breaks or 'beats,' when rapid enough to merge in an apparently simple sensation, produce the jarring effect of dissonance, which disappears, however, when the rapidity passes a certain limit. Notes which, when sounded together, produce none of these breaks, are perfectly concordant ; and the various degrees between perfect concord and the harshest discord depend, broadly speaking, on the varying amount in which this feature is present (though it should be noticed by the way, as showing how fallacious physical and physiological explanations of æsthetic matters often are even in the most elementary regions, that the parallelism of the objective and subjective facts is here very far from complete, and that the intervals which from the physical point of view are the more *perfect*, fifths and fourths, are far less agreeable in isolation than the less perfect thirds and sixths). Remembering now that the harmonics of any tone are the notes whose rates of vibration are twice, three times, four times, &c., that of the original tone, we easily see that pairs of notes which stand to one another, as regards vibration-rate, in a simple ratio, are just those which will be free or comparatively free from closely adjacent harmonics. Helmholtz has thus shown the precise point of connection between the capacity of two notes to flow on simultaneously without interference or jar, and the presentation of simple ratios by their rates of vibration ; that it lies not in the obvious *positive* fact which the simplicity of ratio involves, viz. the repeated coincidence many times a second of particular states of one of the nerve-fibres concerned with particular states of the other ; but in the *negative* fact of absence, in these special cases, of certain irregularities in the vibrations ; an *absence* which could only be realised when the *presence* of the said irregularities was indisputably proved in all cases where simultaneous notes *fail* to produce a smooth concurrent flow, or, in other words, present the phenomenon of dissonance.

For the production of an agreeable compound effect through the coincidence of several impressions on the same sense-organ is not a peculiarity of Music: the ear is by no means alone in susceptibility to such a compound effect. Thus the eye perceives colours in juxtaposition by what are practically simultaneous impressions; and finds them 'harmonious' or 'discordant;' the sense of taste can distinguish onion, celery, and turnip in a good gravy soup, strawberry and vanille in a compound ice, and many more components might be distinguished by a skilled person in a made dish; and the sense of smell possesses a considerable amount of the same power. The two higher senses might indeed seem to be distinguished from the lower, with respect to these compound effects, in that the elements of impression in their case are not only different but *outside* one another, colours in space, tones in pitch. This distinction, however, is by no means so invariably marked in the case of the ear as in that of the eye; and the actual individual elements of a compound are perhaps less often distinctly realised in sound than in any other mode of sensation. If a person who had never heard tones except singly were listening to one continuous tone, and meanwhile a concordant tone were started so softly as to be all but inaudible, and then gradually increased in loudness till it equalled its fellow, the hearer would be very conscious of a new sensation, but I doubt if he could be at all conscious of two elements in it, much less of an interval between the two. This is of course an extravagantly violent instance; but chords may be at any rate perceived with comparatively slight consciousness of their presenting several points of pitch, by very many persons who are in the truest sense musical, but whose ears have not received any special training. To analyse a chord in the sense of picking out and singing its several notes is, it need hardly be said, a matter either of exceptional acuteness or of considerable practice; but even the perception that several notes are present (unless they are specially individualised by being taken by different voices) is often but faint, and would be fainter still but for the external knowledge of the state of the case, due, *e.g.*, to habitually seeing several keys of a piano struck at once.

*and the perception of the out-sideness of the impressions to one another is not always at all marked in the case of the ear.*

Wherein, then, does the fundamental difference between a single chord and, *e.g.*, an agreeable combination of tastes consist? If we confine ourselves to the impressions of a moderately trained ear, the answer is plain. The elements of the taste combination are perfectly simple things; each of them has *one* aspect or character and one only, viz. its own particular taste, that self-complete unrelated aspect of sensation which is, according to the explanations of the first chapter, entirely analogous to *colour*-quality: whereas the elements of the sound-harmony have *two* aspects or characters, that of *timbre* or colour-quality, and that of *pitch*, whereof the former may be changed without changing the latter; thus if we play a chord first on the piano and then on the harmonium, the character depending on pitch

*§ 7. The great diffe-rentia of sound-harmony: its elements have to one another distinct rela-tions, owing to the unique cha-racter of the scale of pitch;*

remains and the harmony is thus recognised as identically the same, in spite of a complete change of colour, while an alteration in either direction of any of the pitch-elements at once alters the harmony. And there is a similar difference between musical harmony and *visual* colour-harmony; as, though colours are external to one another in space, they have no definite and unalterable relations of position identified with particular harmonies. In a word, the musical chord is unique in having essentially an element of *form*, however directly sensuous may seem the pleasure which it gives. Whether or not this form can truly be said to be present in the impression produced by a single chord on hearers who have never specially marked the existence in such a chord of separate notes and intervals, is perhaps hardly worth disputing: I myself should certainly say it was; that the difference to such hearers between a single note struck and a chord struck is a difference of kind expressible in no other way, and that the sense not only of the compound character of the chord, but of distances or intervals in it, is practically seldom entirely latent in an attentive ear.[1] This becomes clearer when we imagine one chord struck after and compared with another, provided they differ by more than the very slightest amount of interval: thus the difference between

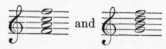 and

is, I find, naturally described by casual hearers as a difference in *shape*, one such hearer adding that the second chord 'had a corner in it.' But at any rate it is a sufficiently safe statement that the difference between the sound of C and the sound of C E G is in some way generically distinct from the difference between the taste of strawberry and the taste of strawberry vanille and cream; whether we call it a form or not, the chord is a new individual, not the mere mixture or sum of its constituents.

and these relations distinguish tones from colours as much in harmony as in melody.

It is in contrast to phenomena of visual colour, that the presence of form even in a single chord needs emphasising: since the *physical* resemblances between light-vibrations and sound-vibrations continually induce an idea of some analogy between the spectrum of colours and the scale of

[1] In noting the generic difference between a chord even when not very definitely felt as compound, and a single tone which is definitely felt as simple, we need not fear being confronted with the fact, that a single tone is really also a compound, depending as it does for its *timbre* on the presence of 'harmonics' of various pitches. For these harmonics which accompany the fundamental tone are so merged in the single effect that not only is special apparatus necessary to examine them thoroughly, but only by practice, and by the closest attention in the most favourable cases, can even the more salient of them be detected. On the other hand, the fact that chords are made of parts is patent at once to everyone if the notes be far enough apart, and can in all cases be made patent instantly by playing the notes one after another and then together. The faculty of realising chords as compounds lies always as it were close to the surface, and a very little attention establishes the habit of so realising them unchangeably for life.

tones, and so between combinations of colours and of tones. The delusive-
ness of the idea will be sufficiently manifest after our observations on the
nature of the scale of pitch in the seventh chapter : [1] if we want an analogy
to colour-harmonies, we must seek it in the *colour*-region of sound, in the
various combinations and contrasts of *timbre* presentable by different
voices and instruments.

So far we have been considering a single combination of notes. It
need hardly be said that in musical presentation chords do not occur in
this isolated condition ; though, owing to that very multiplicity and relation of elements which makes of each chord a sort of form, the shortest
series of chords may present a completeness unattainable by an equal
number of single notes ; and as a chord may be agreeable or disagreeable
in a way in which a single note cannot, so two or three chords may be
definitely right and satisfactory, or definitely wrong and distressing, in a way
in which two or three notes cannot. The specially unifying effect of
discord and resolution makes the dominant seventh and tonic of an *Amen*
as welcome as a pair of bald consecutive fifths on an accordion is the
reverse. We must now, however, pass on to the consideration of longer
series, and examine the mode in which harmony enriches melody, and the
various relations of the two elements.

§ 8. Frag-
ments of chord-
combination,
being richer in
elements, may
also be more
distinctly satis-
factory or un-
satisfactory
than fragment-
ary groups of
single notes.

This brings us instantly into the region of form. As long as we are
speaking only of single chords and single tones the harmonic superiority
may be argued to be a mere matter of fulness and richness of clang, a sort
of colour-beauty. But the effect of chord-accompaniment on a melody
clearly does not just consist in making each sound as it comes fuller and
richer,[2] immense as is the service which is thus rendered : the harmony,

§ 9. Effect
of harmonic
accompani-
ment on
melody :

---

[1] See also chap. xii. § 3, last note.

[2] The point of sweetness and richness of
separate clangs is important in connection
with the dispute about just and tempered
intonation. The aspect of harmony which
would gain by increase of justness in the
intonation of intervals is that which, though
the fact of independent parts (so far as present to consciousness) seemed to differentiate it from the class of simple sensations
analogous to colour, appears nevertheless
almost purely sensuous ; the aspect of chords
as *single* individuals each making its own
sensuous appeal to the ear. It is true that
just intonation has a certain effect on
chords regarded as a connected series,
and so on any melodic form they may
support, through affording a more marked
distinction of effect between the various
positions or inversions of the same chord,
and between major and minor chords ; but
against this improvement we may certainly

set the facts, stated by Helmholtz, that the
chord of the dominant seventh with just intonation is no more discordant than the
common chord with tempered intonation,
which means that by employing the just
chord of the seventh we should sacrifice the
characteristic effect of the commonest discord and resolution ; and that diminished
sevenths, none the less a prime necessity of
music that they are liable to abuse, are almost unbearable with just intonation. But
in any case the superiority of the just intervals is comparatively of little importance to
chords *quâ* support and definition of melodic
progression ; even as it is comparatively of
little importance to melodic progression itself, a fact admitted by Helmholtz, and exemplified in the production of ill-sounding
chords in a quartett by players whose intervals heard melodically in solo-playing are
never complained of.

Increased beauty of chord-clang is, then,

this is something utterly beyond mere enrichment of *clang*, the harmony supporting and defining the melodic form and immensely increasing its organic coherence.

with its own varied and connected tissue, supports and defines the form, and intensifies the sense of its coherence and the satisfaction in following it; the difference made being really as unique as are melody and harmony themselves, and defying therefore attempts to describe or

undoubtedly the great object of just intonation. To call this beauty sensuous is in no way to deny its desirability: and so far as just intonation can be applied to chords without injuring their bearing on the connected series, this increased beauty of clang is nothing but an advantage, and any mechanical means for giving keyed instruments the power which voices have of producing it will be warmly welcomed. But the truth remains that Music has become what we now know it through the ease and scope of modulation, due to the use of tempered intonation; that the element in Music which makes it something more than a series of sweet clangs, something more than a mere sop to the ear at the moment of presentation, the whole world of form which exercises the active musical faculty, and stores the memory with undying treasures, has received its astonishing modern development on that system. And this fact, that the modern scheme of key-relationship and transition depends on, and supposes tempered intervals, would remain untouched even if mechanical facilities for rapid enharmonic change should enable us to play with the maximum of justness in any key at which we had arrived. The desirability of the added beauty so attainable is disputed by none; but a protest is needed against the notion that what Beethoven readily dispensed with can be a matter of cardinal importance to those to whom his music speaks unchangingly; and that such loss as we have sustained in respect of this sensuous feature can be named in the same month or year with our gain through free modulation and the use of 'doubtful' chords.

On this point even Helmholtz seems to give a somewhat uncertain sound. He says, 'We cannot fail to recognise the influence of tempered intonation upon the style of composition. The first effect of this influence was favourable. It allowed composers as well as players to move freely and easily into all keys, and thus opened out a new wealth of modulation. On the other hand, we also cannot fail to recognise that the alteration of intonation compelled composers to have recourse to some such wealth of modulation. For when the intonation of

consonant chords ceased to be perfect, and the differences between their various inversions and transpositions were, as a consequence, nearly obliterated, it was necessary to use more powerful means, to have recourse to a frequent employment of harsh dissonances, and to endeavour by less usual modulations to replace the characteristic expression which the harmonies proper to the key itself had ceased to possess.' He goes on to deplore the modern predominance of dissonant chords, and of perpetual modulational change, as threatening to destroy the all-important feeling for tonality (a danger which no reader who followed me through the closing part of the tenth chapter will accuse me of underrating), and argues that tempered intonation has been a blight on vocal writing, adducing the superiority of Beethoven's instrumental to his vocal works. It is worth suggesting that the whole bent of Beethoven's genius was instrumental, and that Schubert and Schumann, who lived no less than he in the atmosphere of tempered intonation, have left us an unequalled legacy of song. But justness of intonation is truly so indispensable to satisfactory part-singing, where the music presents only few and simple modulations, and indeed to any series of tolerably slow chords with sustained notes (to say nothing of the inspiring effect on musical composers of habituation to the sweetness of perfectly true intervals), that every step towards facilitating that condition, *compatible with preserving the music we have got*, is well worth making. I presume the importance of the italicised words would be admitted even by those who, like Helmholtz's English translator, look forward with a light heart to 'great changes in the conduct of modulation from the acceptance of just intonation by composers.'

This being granted, however, there remain several points in the above-quoted view as to the effect of tempered intonation on composition, past and future, which, to say the least, suggest a confusion as to the relative importance of *clang* and of *form*. What is the sweetness, the 'saturated harmoniousness' of clang, the pleasure which can only be enjoyed when the sounds are actually in our

illustrate it.[1]  This difference is of course due to the greatly increased
amount of tone-relationship which is introduced into the same length
of form, and the marking of various aspects presentable in various
conjunctions by one and the same melodic interval.   In the key of
C, for example, G-A is always an interval of a tone at a particular part of
the scale ; as such it is capable of appearing in all sorts of melodies ; but
the respective parts it plays in them may gain indefinitely in distinction
and individuality, and the Ideal Motion at the point of its occurrence
obtains a new choiceness and completeness, if its various appearances are
differentiated by other relations.   Thus the A might be accompanied by
the same chord as the G, thus,

ears, compared with the wealth of form
which free modulation made possible ?  The
new means were really the wings for undreamed of flights of invention, without them
absolutely impossible ; whereas Helmholtz
seems to treat them as a *pis aller* to which
composers were driven in order to produce
the *same effects* as were previously attained,
by dint of just intonation, in a narrower
sphere.   But so far as those effects depended
on just intervals, what kind of relation could
they bear—what relation can the very maximum of evanescent sensuous delight ever
possibly bear—to the impressions of a great
instrumental movement, impressions un-
paralleled in power and individuality, and
some measure of which all music-lovers can,
on sufficient acquaintance, revivify for themselves, while to many they are as much realities in silence and solitude as in the actual
hour of performance ?  *So far*, I say, as the
effect depended on just intervals : justness of
interval is of course no bar to beauty of
form ; but to suppose that this beauty of form,
this essence of the composer's message, can be
bound up with perfect justice of interval seems
to me like supposing that all sense of visual
form would be lost if the outlines were the
least bit blurred.  Why, essential form can be
detected through an amount of dissonance
which is torture to the sense, as on a piano
grossly out of tune ; to say nothing of the
fact that the shades of difference between
just and tempered intervals sink into non-
existence while the act of invention is going
on in the head.  That modulation and tran-

sitional harmonies may be abused is a point
I have sufficiently dwelt on, and a thorough
training in pure vocal music with just intonation might be a very wholesome corrective to some modern tendencies ; but surely
Beethoven and his great contemporaries and
successors have satisfactorily shown that the
abuse is not a necessary result of the means
through which they worked their wonders.

[1] It is this indescribability which excuses
the habit of calling the effects of harmony
on melody *colour*-effects, as when it is said
that 'the same melody is presented with
different harmonic colouring ;' colour being
naturally thought of as an element which
supplies various modes of enriching the
same form.  It is useless to dispute over the
word, as long as the fact is realised that the
effect, like that of the melodic form itself, is
a matter of relation and coherence of successive parts, by the evolution of which the
melodic form may be, in all degrees, defined
and supported.  Two points may, however,
be specially noticed as bringing out the character of *form* in the harmonic support of a
melody : first, the exactness and unchange-
ableness with which the chord-effect is perpetually recalled with the melody, and often
*must be* recalled, with however various degrees of vividness, for the melodic effect at
all to recur : secondly, the fact that the
phenomenon of discord and resolution is
markedly alien to the immediate and self-
complete nature of mere formless sense-
impression.

or by a chord of which one note was common to the chord which accompanied the G, thus,

or by a chord all whose notes were different from those of the chord which accompanied the G, thus,

or in other ways; each of which would seem right in its place, and while impressing its own characteristic difference on the interval, would multiply the sense of cogency and rightness in the melodic step by the momentum, so to speak, of its own contributions. That one mode of supporting the melodic motion should seem right and another wrong is a matter for the most part as outside explanation and argument as the motion itself; like that it is a matter for the musical faculty alone to decide; and as a melody is judged, so its adequate or inadequate harmonisation is judged, in the sense that the latter compared with the former gives an impression of something amiss, by multitudes without a vestige of technical knowledge.

*The right and wrong of chord-support is a matter entirely in the domain of the musical faculty.*

It is true there are far more *rules* as to the progression of chords than of melodic notes. This is partly because, while there is no interval (within ordinary limits of compass) which does not occur as right in its place in melody, many harmonic progressions can be forbidden as invariably and inherently disagreeable. But the chief reason lies in the very nature of the two phenomena. Melody aims at individual beauty, and every successful melody is a new free form which must be created, not manufactured; whereas, apart from rhythmic motive and in their merely harmonic aspect, pleasing sequences of chords, in nine hundred and ninety-nine cases out of a thousand, aim at no individual beauty at all, and may be almost mechanical things. Nor does this lack of distinctive beauty apply merely to students' sequences or the random modulations which are sometimes called 'improvising,' but equally to the most beautiful works if their timeless harmonic basis be presented alone. It is not of course meant that genius cannot appear in the harmonisation of melody; only that melodies can be quite satisfactorily harmonised without it; and even in cases where he melodic motive really needs and would not suggest itself without its tparticular support, or where melody in the narrower sense is absent and the motive consists essentially in the rhythmically arranged chords, the harmonic basis in itself is perpetually such as any one who can string together chords and modulations might have written down. The general rules for

*There are, it is true, far more definite rules for chord-progression than for note-progression:*

smooth harmony, for attaining sufficient freedom and fulness while avoiding but the rules would be quite inadequate in the absence of the definite musical faculty. over-rapid changes within too short a space, and so on, may in fact be learnt and applied by any one with an average amount of ear.  And a person who wrote correctly according to the rules, as he would not produce anything impressive, like a good melody, so would not produce anything definitely disagreeable and trivial, like a bad one.  But no one could harmonise tunes satisfactorily by the mere light of the rules.  If we take a tune at random we may probably find one or more modes of harmonic support which violate no rule, are smooth and consistent in themselves, and introduce no extraneous or preposterous notes, and yet are recognised by an ordinarily good ear as wholly unsuitable—spoil the tune, in fact ; while others seem to enrich it satisfactorily, and one in particular may fill up all the gaps, so to speak, and stand out as pre-eminently right.  And all this is perceived by musical instinct alone ; so that the rules are not explanatory even in that most external sense in which conformity to a general law is an explanation of rightness, since they stop far short of discriminating what satisfies from what irritates the ear in the actual cases : we cannot say such and such is the right harmony *because* it obeys the rules, seeing that what in that place would sound wrong may also obey them.

Before passing to the more detailed account of the relations of harmony § 10. Examination of the so-called *dependence* of melody on harmony. to melodic forms, it will be well to consider a phrase which is connected with important misconceptions, the *dependence* of melody on harmony. The debt to harmony, the part played by chord-connections in the fixation of the major and minor scales and in the development of the sense of key, and their prime importance as a means of defining modulation, are well-understood facts which in themselves lie outside our enquiry : the point we have to notice here is that these facts do seem to imply, in a certain sense, the dependence of modern melody on harmony ; while yet, as a matter of experience, cases are frequent where melody appears truly as independent of harmony as in the ages before harmony was ever dreamed of.  The nature and varieties of the dependence and independence, as matters of actual musical experience, will occupy us in the next section : but in its crude form the seeming contradiction may be at once cleared away.  'Dependence on harmony' may mean two quite different things, and the trap lies in not distinguishing them.  It has a true and universal application to the part played by harmony in strengthening generally the sense of melodic relationships, through heightening the feeling for key with all that it involves, a part continued through the whole childhood of every modern European's musical faculty.  But the phrase is continually used in a much more special sense, as though it necessarily included specific reference to some set of harmonies (actually present or imagined) in the invention and appreciation of modern melody : and the very fact that such reference does undoubtedly take place in many instances only makes it the more necessary to observe that in many instances it does *not*. As regards the *invention* of tunes this may perhaps be for a moment disputed, since most people who make set melodies possess enough musicianship to imagine their accompanying harmonies almost mechanically. Still there are plenty of exceptions, and the fact that Rousseau was probably to a great extent one himself does not make his question to Rameau at all less cogent; ' cette basse fondamentale qui lui a suggéré son chant, et qui n'est ni dans son entendement, ni dans son organe, ni dans sa mémoire, où est-elle donc ? ' And as regards *appreciation* of melodies the facts admit of no doubt. Even where tunes have been first heard with harmony (and very often this has not been the case, many a tune passing from mouth to mouth without ever getting or needing an accompaniment) they are perpetually dwelt on and reproduced in their simple melodic state, without the slightest power or wish to recall the harmony. None the less has that important constituent of the modern musical sense, the keen feeling for tone-relationships, which the hummers and whistlers of such tunes inevitably possess, been formed, however unconsciously to themselves, under the guiding influence of chord-connections. Thus the practical independence of the particular melody is fully compatible with the influence of harmony as a pre-existent and educating influence, acting unconsciously on the hearer's faculty and conditioning the mode of his perception.

§ 11. The various relations of harmony to melody.

The various relations of harmony to melody may be conveniently realised by considering four cases : (1) When the melody can stand perfectly well alone, however susceptible of harmonic enrichment ; (2) when the melody is not only generally enriched by harmony, but demands a special harmonisation, at least in certain places, to bring out its point and character ; (3) when the melodic progression demands a special harmonisation, at least in certain places, under pain of seeming inane or incoherent ; (4) when the effect, which in this case ought not perhaps strictly to be called melodic, but which is at any rate distinctly included under Ideal Motion, seems to lie in the chords themselves, rhythmically disposed, and not in a special single set of melodic notes. We might find all these classes exemplified within a very short space in a developed movement. Moreover they do not represent precise distinctions, but shade into one another, from the case where a child who has been perfectly content with humming a tune to himself is gratified by hearing it played with chords, to the case where the whole significance of some elaborate instrumental passage depends on the definition of its modulations.

Cases where the harmony can be readily dispensed with.

Under the first head, cases where harmony, though not needed, is more or less desiderated and is felt as an improvement, might be distinguished from cases where its addition would be more or less cumbrous and detrimental. A tune like the *Old Hundredth* perhaps sounds noblest in unison. In such a theme as this, from Schubert's octett—

&c.

unison seems perfectly adequate to give its complete character, however delightful be the filling in of the harmonies in the second clause. A good many popular airs, new as well as old, would probably fall under the same category: but in the written music of this harmonic age such cases are naturally a minority, unaccompanied and unison-passages being as a rule short and chiefly used as effective by contrast.

Even with regard to this first head, however, there are several reasons why the classification must be of an uncertain and provisional kind. The importance of harmony in relation to melody cannot be treated, even in a particular case, as an altogether unchanging fact; it depends partly on degree of acquaintance. Thus on a first hearing one may quite fail to catch a tune which lacks the advantage of harmonic definition; and this failure rightly to grasp the connection of the melodic relations is to some extent answerable for a feeling with which many of my readers must be familiar, a certain desire to get under the carpet when a fellow-creature is singing an unknown song, or indulging in vocal reminiscences, quite out in the open without any accompaniment. Yet on due familiarity the strains in question may appear perfectly self-evident.

The effect of the harmony is to some extent a shifting and subjective factor.

Another difficulty of judging how far a melodic form can dispense with harmony lies in the fact that, after becoming familiar with it in its full harmonised presentation, no one can quite decide how far some image of the harmony may not be accompanying the re-presentation of it in its simply melodic aspect. A skilled or practised faculty will indeed summon up such images whether the melody has been actually heard with harmony or not; and the phenomenon admits of all degrees, from that where the complicated accompaniment of a long melodic progression suggests itself to the musician with irresistible clearness, down to the mere dim recur-

It is difficult to say how far the sense of harmony may not be latent, even where not particularly observed.

rence of the effect at some single salient point; as, for instance, at the
final cadence, where some shadow of the invariable dominant and tonic
chords probably recurs to many who whistle a tune through with no more
conscious thought of harmony than a parrot. Nor is technical knowledge
or skill necessary for a much more complete harmonic re-presentation than
this last: for we must remember that thousands fully appreciate the
effect of harmony on a melody, and would recognise and resent changes in
it, who could no more isolate and sing its component notes than fly; and
as the effect is felt so it can be more or less recalled. All music-lovers
will testify to the addition which even imperfect re-presentation of
harmony may make to the enjoyment of melody in memory; the imperfection consisting merely in dimness, not in any sort of wrongness. I may
give one instance from my own experience, useful also as an illustration of
the impossibility of knowing how far one has got a melody isolated from
the support which has once been associated with it. The following passage
is from a *rataplan* chorus in Mr. Cellier's *Nell Gwynne:*

This ran in my head for days without my being able to get exact hold of what underlay the melody. The effect of the melodic progression, with the beautifully free ascents to the A sharp and B sharp in its second division and the perfectly easy subsidence into the original key, could hardly have been realised in the first instance, apart from the complete harmonies ; yet afterwards, in spite of an amount of uncertainty as to the harmonies which must have implied that my re-presentation of them was of the faintest, I was deriving keen pleasure from whistling the melodic notes, the special charm, moreover, lying in just that part of the motion which without harmonic assistance presents some difficulty, the launching oneself up and poising accurately on those audacious accidentals. At the further point of transition to the original key, however, I discovered my need of harmonic support by getting melodically lost without it. That enjoyment of a melodic sentence containing so wide an excursion from its key should be even to this degree independent of harmony (so that the case falls rather under the second than the third of the above heads), may be accounted for by the close resemblance in the movement of the second clause to the first, whereby the points of contrast are easily marked. A much simpler instance of the second head is supplied by the theme from Beethoven's trio in D, quoted on p. 167 ; the opening phrase of which one cannot imagine as entering any one's head without the point given by the chord on the pausing note ; or as being recalled with any real satisfaction without at any rate some revivification of that harmonic effect. Another simple instance may be found in the familiar *Leise leise* from *Der Freischütz*:

after one hearing of which, the third melodic note carries its diminished seventh with it for the rest of one's life ; and does so even to the least instructed lover of the tune, in the sense that if he hears it with that chord changed, he will be conscious of some distinct loss to his pleasure. An instance depending less on a single point may be found in the splendid ' subject ' of the movement called *l'Absence*, in Beethoven's sonata Op. 81 :

The upper part of this can be perfectly hummed or thought through melodically, and even so is truly impressive ; but no one who had only so heard it could guess at the force of its complete motion, the reiterated separation of the upper and lower parts making here a polyphonic as well as a harmonic effect.

Instances of the third head, where the harmony, whether heard or remembered, is most strictly and entirely indispensable to the significance or coherence of the music, will naturally be found chiefly in more extended passages than definite single melodies, in progressions which entail numerous or wide excursions beyond the notes of an established key and of which the modulational course needs the most complete definition ; and this might lead us on to the general sense in which all modern prolongations and developments of music beyond the limits of single well-defined forms depend on the harmonic element, as making an extended groundwork for the looser tissue of melodic phrases and responses, and affording the basis of all polyphonic and contrapuntal effects. Here, however, we are considering the more particular relations of harmony to special melodic motions : nor is it hard to find, even in quite simple melodies, instances of points which bring them at any rate upon the borderland between the second and third heads. If any one unfamiliar with the following melody of Lassen's, *Mit deinen blauen Augen*, will play through the melodic notes, he will probably feel that at the point where an asterisk is placed, the point where the ear naturally expects a climax of some sort, the melodic motion becomes tame and pointless : let him play the chords, and the climax will certainly not disappoint him. The example may also illustrate the way in which harmony survives its actual presentation, even in ears whose owners would disclaim the power of truly imagining chords :

Cases where
the harmony is
more or less
indispensable.

The fourth of the above heads, where the Ideal Motion seems to lie in the rhythmical series of chords as chords rather than in a single prominent part which the chords accompany, is again difficult to divide off by any hard and fast line; so ready often is the ear to accept the re-presentation of the upper line of notes as an epitome of the whole effect. No better instance of this class of effect could be given than the passage from the overture to *Egmont*, quoted on p. 208, a perfectly complete and wonderfully vivid piece of Ideal Motion, but not presenting any detachable melodic part; nor are chords necessary here merely to explain the transition to and from a remote key: the motion throughout is wholly bound up with them. The same may be said of the simpler and still more magnificent motive of the allegretto in Beethoven's seventh symphony:

Cases where the Ideal Motion resides entirely in the chords, rhythmically disposed.

in the latter part of which passage the various lengths of the notes make
a distinction among the parts sufficient to constitute a polyphonic element.
Another beautiful instance may be found in the funeral march from the
sonata Op. 26 ; or again in the following motive from the *Eroica* symphony :

In this class of Ideal Motion, which is of perpetual occurrence, the factor
of *rhythm* is of course as indispensable and unchangeable as in a purely
melodic progression, and the factor of *pitch* is merely presented in a
succession of chords or compound units instead of a succession of tones or
simple units. To the same head must be referred musical sentences and
paragraphs of all degrees of individuality and beauty, from the incomparable motives just quoted to the often agreeable, often neutral, but for the
most part undistinctive and unarresting passages of the rhythmical chord-
accompaniments to many vocal melodies. A good instance of a rhythmical
string of chords which it seems really delightful to play alone, though they
are only meant as accompaniment, is afforded by the two lower lines in the
passage from Schumann's quintett quoted on p. 266 : but in all such cases
any knowledge of the melody is fatal to finding out what the chords would
amount to in its absence.

Harmony then, so far, has appeared under the following aspects :—as
almost universally an invaluable means of *enriching* melodic form ; as very
frequently a necessary means of *defining* melodic form, and to be
considered a vital part of the complete form in so far as the particular
point and beauty would disappear, or could never have appeared, in an *un-*
harmonised sequence ; as able, *by metrical arrangement,* to give rise to
what are in any case coherent *chord-forms,* and in such cases as the above
might fairly be termed *chord-melodies.* The principles which have been

best illustrated with quite simple and definite melodies and motives, may be easily combined and applied so as to cover (with certain exceptions to be immediately mentioned) every sort of appearance of the chord-element in music.   Those clear and typical cases where it is possible to consider that a melody (in the ordinary narrow sense) has been harmonised in such and such a way, or where a series of mere chords stands out as sufficiently individual to constitute a 'chord-melody,' are constantly, of course, but portions of developed musical movements, and may be interspersed with all sorts of other portions to which such descriptions would be quite inapplicable.   But amid any amount of dispersion or attenuation of the melodic element, from the elaborate evolutions of a 'carrying-out' to mere passage-writing on a harmonic basis, the use of chords may still be referred to the same heads :—enrichment of motions intelligible without them ; participation in motions of which they have, from the first, been the essential and inseparable foundation ; and production on their own account of coherent chord-tissues, exhibiting all degrees of organic vitality.

§ 12. None of these relations have the slightest connection with the false view of the harmony as containing the germ or essence of the melody,

It is hardly necessary to point out how entirely the relations we have considered, even when the dependence on harmony has been most entire, differ from that relation which is presumed in the theory that the harmony contains in some way the essence or germ of the melody, and that the melody is evolved from it.   We encountered this idea in the chapter on melodic forms, where we noticed how a kind of opposition was set up by certain writers between rhythmic melody and melody evolved out of 'harmonious relations.'   Three undoubted but vaguely apprehended facts— the place of harmony in fostering the sense of tone-relationship and of the modern scales, the place of harmony as the branch in which intervals and their relations are chiefly studied (due of course simply to the possibility in its case of a tolerably complete body of applicable rules), and the actual omnipresence of harmony in modern music—have contributed to a not uncommon notion that harmony is at any rate the most fundamental if

or the primary source of effect in modern music.

not the sole originating source of impressive musical effects in our age ; a misconception far more disastrous in its results than the old idea of phantom harmonies and basses as an essential ingredient of melody, to which Helmholtz gave the *coup de grâce.*   A single example is really enough to show the true state of the case ; the principle being identical for any simple single form and for the most complex conjunctions of the melodic and harmonic elements.   Let any one play these chords :

a perfectly smooth and harmless progression, such as might be paralleled from thousands of books of exercises written during the first month's study of harmony. Now compare the opening 'subject' of Beethoven's move-ment called *Le Retour*, of which the above is the harmonic basis:

In what conceivable way can the harmony here be considered to contain the source, or germ, or essence of the melody? A germ developes into one thing and one thing only; but a single harmonic progression of this sort might serve as a support for a score of perfectly distinct melodies, good and bad. Call it *essential* to all of them, if you will; they may be melodies which really need the support and definition of harmony; but how can the same harmony be *the essence* of all of them? I have chosen this melody purposely because it keeps quite close to the notes of the chords, and is little more than the chords spread out in arpeggio, so that if ever a tune sprang straight out of 'harmonious relations,' without in-dependent melodic excursions, this does; yet how much did the 'har-monious relations' come to, till seized as material and pressed into the service of melodic form? Numbers of melodies, again, admit of several modes of satisfactory harmonisation; and among them are naturally in-cluded many of those which are appreciable apart from any harmonisation at all, and which thus present what Schumann and many others have held to be a marked characteristic of the highest class. In such instances the absurdity of the derivation-theory would be the converse of the previous one : instead of different forms evolved from a single embryo, we should have different embryos evolving a single form.

The vital dif-
ference be-
tween mere
harmonic pro-
gression and
the Ideal
Motion.

The case can really be summed up in a single sentence, which is but a restatement of a point in the last section. Harmonies, which are as wholly and restrictedly *pitch*-elements as single notes, are as unable as they to make up striking and individual sequences, apart from the factor of definite *rhythm*. Harmonic progression, as such, knows nothing of rhythm, while Ideal Motion, in its arresting and possessing aspects, has rhythm as one of its two essential constituents ; whence it follows that the harmonic element, even where most indispensable, can never be more than *a single factor* in such Ideal Motions ; that it in no way epitomises or holds in embryo the complete forms, or evolves them as phases or manifestations of itself; and that therefore the application to it of expressions like *germ* or *vital principle,* or whatever other phrase or metaphor be adopted to express such essential priority of nature, can never be anything but misleading.[1]

The phrase
*harmonic out-
line,* though
perhaps un-
avoidable, is
misleading.

Nor can we account as much more fortunate the phrase *harmonic outline,* specially often used in respect of long pieces. For outlines in

[1] This is equally true on a general view of the phenomena, and in relation to the inventive springs of a particular composer at a particular instant. Cases where a melody has had its start in a chord-fragment might no doubt be found, though very far less frequent than the case of direct rhythmic suggestion exemplified in the story of the hammer and Beethoven's violin concerto : the difference being that rhythm by its very nature is prone to run in the head, often in a most monotonous and boring way, and the melodic invention may spontaneously begin to work along the given line ; while a mere harmonic fragment has hardly enough individual force to run in the head alone ; and any chord-series which has that amount of vitality will be found to have fallen into some sort of rhythm, thus owing its chance of becoming a true germ for further melodic development to the supervention of the essential formative element which it has in no way originated. And the same remark really applies to the case of a fragment which might be at first regarded simply in its harmonic aspect—till melodic motion begins, till the chords begin to be thought of in relation to some sort of rhythm, it would be absurd to say that even the embryonic life of the future form had commenced. By way of example, let us suppose, what is most unlikely, that in the composition of the opening theme of the overture to *Tannhäuser,* the chords

suggested themselves first as a purely harmonic progression ; but these chords are no more than anybody who put his hands on the piano in a moment of abstraction might naturally strike : the origin of the melodic form would be *after*, not *in*, the chords, its germ would be created, not derived, by the accentuation of the first and third chords, simultaneously with which an E would probably flash to the top of the first. Again, if we made the still wilder supposition with regard to the tune of Lassen's, quoted on p. 255, that the harmony of the marked transition was the starting-point of the whole, still in that mere point, in the simple

the visual region are generally conceived as giving some considerable idea of the distinctive and essential form. But the harmonic ' outline ' of an elaborate movement could be written in a string of rhythmless chords, which, in the case of many most beautiful and original movements, might contain not a trace of anything beyond the power of hundreds and thousands of exercise-writers to concoct; while so far as any rare and extraordinary feature was there presented, it would be something which did not occur to the composer, and will not impress us, as mere abstract harmony, but in indissoluble connection with the Ideal Motions into which it enters.

The words *in its arresting and possessing aspects,* a few lines above, were used advisedly; and it is in this connection that it will perhaps be best to consider the opposite case of music in which true strictness of rhythm is *absent.* The statement in the seventh chapter that, while no series of single notes could present a coherent series without the rhythmic factor, harmony possessed a certain independent binding power, will at our present point appear plainer. Both the amount of binding and formative power in the harmony, and the amount of departure from strictness in the rhythm, admit of most various degrees. Rhythm may be perceptible without being precise, and in the absence of compact metrical sections: the overlapping of part by part, for instance, so common in the music preceding the modern era, which precluded division into definite lengths, was quite compatible with rhythmic motion in the individual phrases and rhythmic balance in their adjustment. Thus some measure of the rhythmic element is present in compositions of Palestrina, which are very commonly called unrhythmical, though often certainly it is sufficiently relaxed for these works to afford the most notable examples of what harmonic progression and polyphonic variety can effect between them. But however enchanting to the ear be Palestrina's harmonic tissues, there are many of them which it would be absurd to represent as arresting the attention and haunting the inward ear like the more definite and closely organic forms of later composers. So far as any one fails to perceive in them some degree of connected rhythmic motion, so far as alterations in their time-relations would pass unresented by him, if not unnoticed, so far will they fail to haunt *him* save as the vague memory of certain minutes filled with a rich stream of exquisite sound. Acquaintance and attention may often bring

§ 13. The binding and formative power of Harmony in relation to comparative laxity of rhythmic structure.

The music of Palestrina.

there is no invention, no birth of anything, any more than in the strokes of the hammer heard by Beethoven; such a progression is really a piece of musical material ready for all to use. But let the six-eight rhythm begin to swing through the first chord and alight with an accent on the second, and the Ideal Motion is started.

out a greatly increased measure of definite melodic motion in the parts, and reveal an individuality of beauty in many of the harmonic progressions themselves: but still the element of appeal to the sense as sense, to the ear as an organ for transient and indeterminate though exquisite sensations, will remain a large one.  Such strains were for special occasions rather than daily companionship; they were meant to be heard in their place, sung by beautiful voices, and their effects, depending thus greatly on colour-beauty, can be only faintly enjoyed in silent re-presentation. How essentially their life was, and is still, bound up so to speak with the actual moments of their presentation, is even indicated by a point which has been regarded with special admiration—the delicacy of the feeling for harmonic clang which they reveal, and the prominence in them of chord-effects depending on the utmost purity of intonation.  They were exactly calculated to excite at the proper moment the general emotional susceptibility appropriate to religious service; and to say that they do not in general present sufficiently distinctive forms to be utterly possessing, to survive individually in all varieties of lengths and fragments in the musical memory of hundreds of thousands, is merely to say that they are not what it was impossible they should be and what they did not aim at being.

Harmonic series of a less organic kind.    There are other harmonic progressions, very different from the rich tissues of Palestrina, which in various degrees lack strictness of rhythm. Such are the chord-supports of recitative, which will be better considered later, in connection with Song.  We may, however, notice here the sort and the amount of laxness which such a simple chord-series, free from polyphonic variety and enrichment, may present.  We have seen that a pair of chords, partly by the independent fulness and agreeableness of each of them as compared with a single tone, partly by the number of their tone-relationships to one another, can give a satisfaction which is perfectly impossible to a pair of tones; and a longer series may in a similar way present the sort of coherence which comes not from the perception of the whole as organic throughout, but from a sense of pleasantness in each chord as it appears in connection and contrast with its few more immediate neighbours.  Examples *ad libitum* might be given by any one who possesses the trick of stringing chords together on the piano.  If the ordinary productions of that order could be thought of as having any vital unity, it would only be in the lowest invertebrate sense that its parts do just present themselves naturally one after another; but their combination utterly fails to satisfy the test of wide interdependence of effect and perception of each point as in necessary relation to other and distant points of an extended form.  This is the extreme case.  Such series may of course vary greatly in harmonic point, from aimless fragments linked together by diminished sevenths to a really fine progression.  The absence of rhythm, again, is, as before, a matter of degree. That element may suddenly appear and bring a certain number of consecutive harmonies into a sort of form; melodic phrases and passages may likewise be interspersed, but nothing which is rhythmic or melodic by fits and starts can make a coherent whole. We shall encounter mongrel series of this kind, decked out with instrumental ornaments, when we come to discuss a certain class of modern recitative, where a string of formless vocal notes is supported by them. The Wagnerian theory of derivation of melody from harmony, may seem in such cases rather more applicable, since the vocal notes may naturally be said to be derived from the only thing which seems at all to account for their going one way more than another; but then, unfortunately, so far as they lack rhythm, they lack one of the two factors necessary to constitute them melody.

To return to the relations of harmony to melody proper: one often encounters expressions which, without implying the derivation theory, assume nevertheless a more general dependence of good melody on certain points in the accompanying harmonies than experience will at all warrant. On the other hand it is often said that the best melodies are those which are apprehensible apart from harmony, a view which certainly needs limitation. For the characteristic is of course not distinctive, since it is found in no end of bad and vulgar melodies; the more distinctive sign would perhaps be that the good melody, though it can dispense with harmony, will yet, if it is susceptible of harmonisation, gain most from it; beauty being there, we get new delight from emphasising and enriching it, while harmony cannot make an insignificant tune beautiful. But apart from this, though the number of strong and beautiful tunes to which the remark applies is legion, it still seems too general; in face of those other melodies of the highest class to which the definition at any rate of a chord or two here and there is more or less indispensable. The statement would be safer in the converse form, that the tunes which sacrifice stability of key to a superfluity of restless and cloying transitions, and so demand perpetual harmonic explanation, have their inferiority stamped thereby.

Another frequent characteristic of good melody, which is still less capable of being elevated into a criterion, is a free and more or less melodic bass. This is just one of the cases where the presence of a thing is noticed, and not its absence: even three or four notes of melodic bass in independent or 'contrary' motion will arrest attention, and one feels inclined to attribute the merits of the tune to this noticeable element. The merits of that particular melody of course may not be abstractable from that particular supporting and blending movement, but hundreds of other beautiful melodies present no parallel feature. What are we to say of that wonderful *Forelle*, with its simple alternations of tonic and dominant, such as might support the feeblest drivel of a theatre-hack? It is

§ 14. It is impossible to find a criterion for good melody in considerations of harmony;

either in the power of the melody to dispense with harmonic support,

or in special features of the harmony when present.

worth noticing, moreover, that these two criteria tend to be mutually destructive, since a melody to whose effect the bass very appreciably contributes is to that extent not independent of harmony.

Similar considerations apply to particular single points of chord-support, where the chords are often held accountable for the beauty which may seem to culminate at their occurrence. Thus when listening to a song, people will say at a particular place, 'What a beautiful chord,' or 'What a beautiful change of harmony;' allowable expressions enough, provided those who use them realise that what is really beautiful is the form to which the chords at that point contribute, and that precisely the same chord-progression might occur in a melody they did not care about, without being admired or perhaps even noticed. The idea of the harmony as having an independent beauty with which it illuminates and transfigures the melody (an idea very common among those who have never themselves harmonised melodies, and to whom harmony appears as an endless store of magical effects capable of being turned on almost anywhere at a moment's notice) is really an inversion of the truth; for the melody being new and the chords old, we must say, if anything, that the melody transfigures the chords; and indeed nothing in Music is more striking than the power of a good melody to make a simple chord or juxtaposition of chords seem utterly new.[1]

[1] Almost equally noticeable is one's inability to derive pleasure from an effect which depends on some such harmonic feature as I have been describing, if the melodic part in some way annoys one. The prayer in *Mosè in Egitto,* with the modulation into B flat at the conclusion of the first part, and the subsequent repetition in the major, is an instance in point as far as I am concerned; which I do not regard as its fault, but as my misfortune.

Nobody will deny the striking quality of this tune, or quarrel with De Stendhal's account of its sending women into fits. Nevertheless to my ears it has such a ring of coarseness and pretension as to preclude any sense of pleasure in it: consequently all I can personally feel in the vaunted resumption of the strain in the major key, is how fine it would be if the strain itself were finer; and the effect of the transition to B flat merely seems trying by its indisputable cleverness to extort admiration which—the melody being to me what it is and this being only a point in the melody—I cannot give. It is worth noticing that the same transition to the harmony of B flat (though with different positions of the

Harmonic accompaniment perpetually assumes the shape of a 'figure,' that is, the extension of the constituent parts of the chords into a certain rhythmical form, sufficiently often repeated for its continuance to be a noticeable feature.[1] The groups may naturally take many varieties of rhythmic shape: an instance of the very simplest kind would be the presentation of

§ 15. A *figure* is often produced by separation of the harmonic notes;

What can be done by such a figure, presented in the very simplest rhythmic form, may be seen in the irresistible swing of the passage from the *Pastoral* sonata quoted on p. 169. An example of a different kind, where the harmonies are not 'broken' or presented in successive parts,

or by distinct rhythmic groups of chords.

chords) constitutes the remarkable feature in Lassen's *Mit deinen blauen Augen,* as quoted above, where, however, its effect is so different that one seems to recognise the sameness only as a curious and irrelevant fact.

[1] The characteristic of a 'figure' is this repetition of a group of a certain shape: the groups are not in any way confined to the notes of a chord, and by the interspersion of other notes may approximate more and more to a true melodic character; through a stage like that exemplified in Schumann's *Traumes-wirren*—

where an outline of the melody is given by the first notes of each group, however necessary be the notes of the 'figure' to the complete effect—to such a case as the second motive of Chopin's waltz in C sharp minor—

where every note is definitely melodic. When used as harmonic accompaniment, 'figures' are naturally more confined to the notes of the chords.

but where the regular appearance of the chords in distinct and similar rhythmic groups is essentially a 'figure' effect, may be found in the accompaniment to the beautiful motive in the first movement of Schumann's quintett:

These two cases are types of an immense number of accompaniments : but of course the very nature of an accompaniment implies a second line of sounds, whether it presents any noticeable feature of figure or not.

The principle here exemplified is in fact what, by an extension of the term beyond its technical application, may be called the broad principle of polyphony, the delight in tracing two (or more) distinct lines of sound agreeing amid their difference. But there is nothing to confine the application of this principle, in a case of 'figure,' to a melodic part supported by an accompaniment of 'broken chords;' the supporting 'figure' itself may assume a melodic aspect, while the other melodic part (which may be too fragmentary to have been presented alone or with a more neutral chord-accompaniment) mingles its contrasted stream. A magnificent example of such fusion of a melodic figure with another melodic or harmonic motive may be found in the finale of the *Appassionata* sonata :

*This is really an application of the broad principle of polyphony ; which may be exemplified in other ways besides figure.*

Another good example is Chopin's prelude beginning as follows:

&c.

The same principle of two distinct lines of sound agreeing amid their difference has various other particular applications which deserve remark, apart from its general application to part-writing. I may mention as one salient example the use of 'pedal,' that is, of a single note, always one of the most fundamental in the key, prolonged or repeated to such an extent that its persistence becomes a noticeable feature, and often enables it to be carried through harmonies in which it has no natural part, and to justify the passing conflict to the ear.[1]

[1] Under the same broad principle may be reckoned all *special* cases of accompaniment and of combination of parts. Such, for instance, is the use of 'syncopation,' the oc-

§ 16. An-
other relation
of harmony to
melody is as a
background
rather than a
distinct line of
support.

One further mode of relation between harmony and melody may be found in the class of cases, almost wholly orchestral, where the harmony has the effect rather of a background of continuous and slowly changing sound, on which melodic phrases are presented, than of a distinctly marked line of support, rhythmical or unrhythmical; though the difference after all is only of degree, since where a melodic phrase appears on this background the chords necessarily have their proper relations to it. This class of effect very soon cloys, and often owes its character more to the beauty and mystery of instrumental colouring than to anything particular in the actual harmonic progression; but such spreading orchestral murmurs may give a peculiar charm to the entrance of a new contrasting voice, where, for instance, some conspicuous solo-instrument presents a melodic passage in marked relief against them.

§ 17. Par-
ticular chords.
The distinction
of character
between major
and minor.

We pass now to a quite new topic, the peculiarities, namely, of particular chords; and especially the great distinction between *major* and *minor*. At the opening of our discussion of harmony we noticed the general mode in which a sound-harmony differs from a combination of tastes or colours. This feature of major and minor marks a special and equally striking difference. If the triad

be struck after the triad

no one with any ear or any power of describing his sensations will describe the first chord otherwise than as *melancholy*: [1] and that single word sums up one of the most puzzling facts in the whole subject of Music.

Helmholtz's
explanation;
the slight
obscurity of
clang in minor
chords:

The account of the phenomenon given by Helmholtz presents very decided difficulties. He attributes the veiled or sad effect of a minor chord to certain notes foreign to the chord which physical reasonings

currence of one motive on the unaccented beats of the bars, while the sense of the accented beats is kept up by other parts or by an accompaniment. A very pretty effect of this kind may often be heard in waltzes, where the melodic notes occur alternately on the first and third, and on the second, beats of bars, so that practically a melody in $\frac{3}{2}$ time swings through an accompaniment in $\frac{3}{4}$ time. Amateurs will recall the magnificent instance of the kind in Schumann's pianoforte concerto in A minor. The various other ways of individualising

simultaneous parts by special rhythmic differences, as in combining double time with triple, fall naturally under the same head.

[1] I may warn the untechnical reader to distinguish between major and minor full chords or *triads*, consisting of a note with its third and fifth, and intervals containing only *two* notes, to which the names major and minor are also unfortunately applied. For instance, the major triad of C contains a 'minor' *interval*, E–G, and the minor triad of C contains a 'major' *interval*, E flat–G.

prove to accompany it and which a skilled ear can in favourable circumstances distinguish. ' The foreign element thus introduced,' he says, ' is not sufficiently distinct to destroy the harmony, but it is enough to give a mysterious obscure effect to the musical character and meaning of these chords, an effect for which the hearer is unable to account, because the weak combinational tones on which it depends are concealed by other louder tones, and are audible only to a practised ear.'

But what is the direct effect of these foreign notes? Simply to add a slight element of dissonance. Now degrees of dissonance are due to degrees of a certain kind of nervous disturbance; and as on the physical and physiological side there is one gradual scale of degrees for this disturbance, so on the subjective side there is one gradual (though not absolutely parallel) scale of simple sensation-qualities, from the agreeableness recognised when the disturbance does not exceed a certain degree to the disagreeableness recognised when it reaches an extreme degree. There is, however, nothing unreasonable in saying that at certain points on the subjective scale other special sensation-qualities, beyond agreeableness or disagreeableness, may present themselves; and *obscurity* may be one of these : but the theory that a sense of obscurity, caused by a certain slight amount of dissonance, accounts for a sense of *melancholy*, brings us at once face to face with a difficulty. For the same slight degree of dissonance as exists in the *minor* triad may be made to supervene on a *major* triad, by adding to it a certain extremely faint amount of discordant elements : it would seem then that this major triad thus slightly dimmed or confused ought to sound melancholy ; but it does not in the least. So that instead of an explanation, we merely have the old problem in another shape : why should it be in the case of the minor chord alone, that the obscurity produced by a certain slight amount of dissonance is felt as melancholy? Dissonance, as Helmholtz has himself taught us, is the result of a particular mode of nervous disturbance ; a certain amount of this disturbance sets up equal obscurities in two chord-sensations ; where does one of these obscurities obtain a monopoly of stirring up the psychological connection between obscurity and sadness?

Nor can I think that the above theory would be satisfactory even apart from the difficulty I have suggested. Let us treat that difficulty as non-existent, and imagine the melancholy character which the minor triad presents to be the constant result of a definite slight amount of disturbance of consonance. But in the immense majority of cases where the melancholy effect is felt, the disturbance does not reach consciousness as disturbance at all, any more than the ' beats ' of which a rapid succession produces harsh discord reach consciousness as ' beats.' This is practically admitted by Helmholtz, when he says, ' Modern harmonists are

and the difficulties which that explanation presents.

unwilling to acknowledge that the minor triad is less consonant than the major. They have probably made all their experiments with tempered instruments, on which, indeed, this distinction may perhaps be allowed to be a little doubtful. But on justly toned instruments, and with a moderately piercing quality of tone, the difference is very striking and cannot be denied.' Granted: but since Helmholtz can hardly mean to deny that the melancholy effect of a minor triad, as compared with a major, can be perceived on a tempered instrument, what becomes of the theory? How can the sense of melancholy essentially depend on the sense of disturbance and obscurity, if it is present where that is absent? For I will undertake to say that the melancholy effect will be perfectly well perceived by ninety per cent. of the children of any national school, when the two chords are struck one after the other on an ordinary piano. I have just tried the experiment successfully on a child of nine, with a piano where the chords were not only tempered but very distinctly out of tune into the bargain; which would render it practically impossible to differentiate the two consonances by the contrast in their respective amounts of disturbance. A single instance is really enough to prove the point; but as a matter of fact it is probable that to most ears a minor triad with its melancholy tinge is, as generally presented, a perfectly pure and unclouded sound.[1] This argument becomes still stronger if we remark how easily and completely we recall the contrasted major and minor triads in memory, and certainly should be able to do so if our only acquaintance with them had been through a piano. Nor can I feel, even taking the case most favourable to the theory under review, the case where a sensitive ear does actually and clearly perceive the disturbances as obscuring the consonance, that we have got a satisfactory explanation of the very decided impression of sadness; the psychological passage from obscurity to pathos being very far from certain and self-evident.

Suggestion of another explana·ion in the character of the *characteristic notes* of the major and minor scale.

A new and quite different sort of difficulty presents itself in certain considerations which, though they concern melodic features, were best deferred till the harmonic problem was before us. The features in question are those of the *characteristic notes* of the minor scale as compared with the corresponding ones of the major: and their examination may possibly suggest another explanation of the remarkable character of the minor triad. We have sufficiently seen the impossibility of penetrating the

[1] I need hardly point out what a totally false analogy would be involved in the argument that as in discord we get a sense of unpleasant jar from disturbances which we do not perceive as such, but as a single unanalysed sensation, so in the minor triad we might get an impression of *melancholy* from disturbances which we do not perceive as such, but as a single unanalysed sensation. For the unpleasant jar of discord is a simple sensation, the result of nervous processes whose objective characteristics (*intermittence* in this case) are not copied in the sensation or reproduced *as such* in consciousness, while melancholy is a *recherché* mental state, to which disturbances and obscurities would present no relation unless actually existent *as such* in consciousness.

dividual character of any complete melodic form by any analysis of its structure ; but there are certain isolated rudimentary points where the connection between structure and a rudiment or fragment of Ideal Motion can be just traced ; some of which, since they belong to the notes of the scale as presented in order, are more conveniently remarked in the bare scale itself, in which the supervention of form on note-material is of the most embryonic kind, than in actual melodies containing some of the scale-notes in order, where the points in question would be minute and inseparable constituents of a complete and complex whole. These points are found where the *semi-tones* occur in the scale. We have already noticed how the proximity of the leading-note to the key-note conveys to the ear so decided an expectation that the motion will rise, that its fulfilment is accepted as a satisfactory close. Let us now consider the other semitones presented in the major and minor scales. If we ascend the scale of C and strike E natural, its nearness to F gives the motion a similar tendency to rise ; hence the E seems able to supply the strength for the rise, to have got far enough from the D to be sure of its ground, to have its own balance and the power of making an independent spring, which naturally gives an impression of *confidence.* If, on the other hand, we strike E flat, the sound keeps close to the D and seems dependent on it and willing to sink back to it ; if we still advance to the F we seem to press our way through the reluctant E flat, not to be sped onwards as by the E natural ; and this dependence and reluctance to advance give an impression of diffidence, a character which at any rate seems more naturally suggestive of pathos than uncertainty and obscurity were. Similar remarks apply to the F G A as compared with F G A flat in the second half of the scale : the A natural of the major scale is not quitted, it is true, by the step of a semitone, but it leads on securely and confidently to that step at the final stage ; while the reluctance of the A flat to advance is even greater than that of the E flat, inasmuch as the instinct to use the B natural as the seventh degree of the scale, in view of the approaching keynote, is so strong that, if the A flat is used as the sixth degree, the motion has to make the long and difficult step of a tone and a half. The same considerations, *mutatis mutandis,* apply to the descending scale, the pathetic character in the minor descent always attaching to the note which is only a semitone from its lower neighbour : not of course that the pathos lies in the mere fact of the close proximity (for at that rate C B and F E in the descending *major* scale would be pathetic), but in the close proximity occurring in the two cases where there is a *choice* ; where the confident and independent A or E might have been used instead of the diffident A flat and E flat.[1] Descriptions of this kind

[1] The melodic passage containing the distinctively minor notes need not of course be in diatonic steps. In the opening to *He was despised,*

in relation to the unique and instantaneous musical experience, necessarily seem the most ponderous and clumsy things, as though one were using one's hands to unravel a cobweb; and I can only ask the reader to take the two scales and make an analytical effort of his own.

Now the fact of this *melodic* pathos is indisputable; and the alternative to such an explanation of it as I have suggested could only lie in attributing it to the pathetic character of the two *chords,*

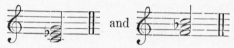

It will probably not be disputed that an explanation of a pathetic effect which would refer it to *motion*—to a process where our own musical activity comes in, where the motion seems our own and the conceptions of reluctance and dependence our own, and the consciousness of those feelings may lead on to that of pathos through natural though hidden associational channels—offers in itself less difficulty than an explanation which would refer the effect to a certain disturbance and obscurity in that which, like a chord in its mere clang-aspect, is little more than a unit of passive sensuous impression. And on examination the untenability of the latter view becomes still clearer. It is impossible to imagine that an unsophisticated ear perceives a sadness in these notes,

*It seems impossible to explain these characteristics by the chords;*

the pathetic effect in the sixth bar, of the G flat or minor third of E flat, as distinguished from the major G natural which might have been used, is instantly recognised; and is not aided by any minor clang, as the E flat which would complete the minor chord is omitted.

Similarly in the first bar of Schumann's *Imploring Child,* quoted in Chap. XIV. § 5, the flattening of the B, the major sixth of the scale, into B flat has a distinctly pathetic expression though the accompanying chord is not a minor clang at all.

or in the introduction of the G flat in the passage from *He was despised* quoted in the note, through a dim suggestion of slightly disturbed consonance in an imaginary chord, even if we neglect all the previous difficulties we found with regard to that disturbance and its supposed emotional effects; it is equally impossible to doubt that similar impressions must have been produced by similar means in preharmonic music, though the fixation of the two contrasted scales, and increased sense of key and tone-relationship, has probably made them more distinct.

But the question now arises, since the chord-effect will not account for the melodic effect, is it not possible that the melodic effect may account for the chord-effect? for there is a oneness of character in the pathetic minor tinge which seems to preclude the idea of different explanations for the two cases. I cannot pretend that the view I suggest is free from difficulty. When we hear the minor triad, we certainly have no distinct feeling of running melodically up and down the notes it comprises. Still, must not the notion of a potential passing from one note to another lie at the root of the perception of *distance* as a relation which they present, just as a similar notion of passage and movement is at the root of the perception of two points as outside one another in space? and some faint perception of distance or interval we found reason to suspect was practically always present in the impression of a chord. If this be so, the faint suggestion might suffice to recall by association the feeling with which the relations of the notes [1] in actual melodic progression have been so constantly and vividly connected. And it is much in favour of this view, and an additional argument against the derivation of the melodic effect from that of the chord, that while uncertainty and disturbance of consonance must be felt, if at all, more prominently in the actual chord than in any mental representation of the chord which we might supply to the melodic notes, the pathetic character (to my ears at all events) is decidedly more vivid in the melodic than in the harmonic presentation of the intervals.

Another argument for the proposed view may be found in the following fact. The minor triads of D and of A are of perpetual occurrence among the harmonies of C major; and yet they do not seem then to convey the

*and it therefore seems natural to explain the character of the chords by them.*

*This view presents difficulties,*

*but has much in its favour.*

---

[1] Neither in melodic progression nor harmonic clang is the G necessary to the production of the characteristic effect, all that the above description of the motion requires being realised in

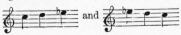 and

provided only we feel ourselves to be in the C minor key; if we once imagine E flat as the key-note, the whole progression

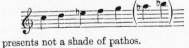

presents not a shade of pathos.

distinctly pathetic impression [1] which we have been discussing, and which is instantly produced by the appearance of the triad of C minor. Now if the pathetic tinge were a mere matter of a slightly disturbed consonance, how could it fail to present itself wherever that consonance occurred? This consideration seems clearly to mark the relations of the notes to the whole scale, only ascertainable by motion within the scale, as at the root of the phenomenon: we do not feel

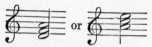

as distinctly melancholy when we are definitely in the key of C, because we do not feel the unbracketed notes here,

or here,

as melancholy in that key. Finally, this limitation of the distinctively pathetic effect to intervals (whether melodic or harmonic) occurring in those positions in the scale where the corresponding major scale would substitute the characteristic *major* intervals—that is, to places where an implicit contrast with the major is involved—leads on to one more observation. For we see how infinitely easier it is to conceive of such an implicit

---

[1] This may be disputed: and any direct experiment on the point tends to defeat its own object, since as soon as we pause on a chord and begin to consider about it, it will assume the most familiar and prominent aspect of a minor triad, just as it would if we struck it in isolation. If, however, we play straight through or recall our experience of such a progression as this:

we shall realise that the second and fourth chords give us no such characteristic minor effect as, *e.g.*, the fourth chord in the following:

and that even here the effect is quite changed if we add the two concluding chords, and play the series through again with the knowledge that the fourth chord is going to be understood, not as the characteristic triad of the key of C minor, but as the chord on the second degree of the key of B flat major.

contrast in respect of phenomena which are truly on the advanced mental stage—as in the following of melodic motion, where opportunity is given for expectation and doubt, and the remote sense of an alternative between the confident and the diffident note, decided one way or the other—than to conceive that one unmoving sensuous clang, owing its character *ex hypothesi* to a definite disturbance of its consonance, can further owe its character to the suggestion of a contrast which there is nothing to suggest, with another unheard sensuous clang.

In discussing the ethical character of major and minor scales and chords, I have had somewhat to anticipate a subsequent branch of enquiry, which will deal with the whole subject of Music as expressive of definable emotional states: and in that place, and later in connection with Song, it will be seen in what further ways and senses harmony may affect musical expression. Meanwhile, it may be safely asserted that the major and minor triads (and these to a great extent only by contrast with one another) are the *sole* chords to which a distinct ethical character can be ascribed. We have just seen how completely, even in their case, the character which is perceptible when they are heard and contrasted in isolation may be swallowed up in a connected series, the critical question being at what part of the scale their intervals fall ; while even the *mode* (major or minor) which decides this, has, as we shall find later, but very limited control over the character of the various Ideal Motions produced in it. But other chords have in isolation no definable character at all : and in respect of these the fact that definite musical expression does not, any more than musical beauty, result from isolated units, but from *whole* pieces of Ideal Motion into which they enter, is doubly palpable. So that Rousseau, when he says that 'every chord has its distinct character, a manner of affecting the heart peculiar to itself,' and then instances major and minor chords, and adds that all others must obviously act in the same way, makes a double blunder ; first not perceiving the special peculiarity of major and minor chords ; and next implying that the heart is touched by the separate meaningless items instead of by the motive which results from their combination in a series.[1] The latter mistake, which is a very common

§ 18. The major and minor triads are the only chords to which, in isolation, a distinct ethical character can be attributed.

---

[1] Take the case of discords, which, by creating expectation, may be said to have at any rate a definable sort of *mental* effect. But first, even this is not a property of *single* chords, but is dependent on our experience of their resolution ; for if discords had never been resolved, they would have been simply more or less harsh sounds, rousing no expectation whatever. Secondly, if we waive this and consider the discord and its resolution as a single effect, still the mental fact of expectation and satisfaction, being common to *all* resolutions of discords, could not differentiate their characters into distinct ways of 'affecting the heart.' Thirdly, the isolated mental fact does not reach the emotional level of affecting the heart at all ; as if it did a single harmonised melody might change its emotional expression at every half-bar of its course, and keep 'the heart' in a perpetual see-saw. Again, a discord, say a diminished seventh, poises us in a sort of doubt from which we get relief : but the discord, *carrying this character with it,* may occur as

one, is the more important, and is in fact a confusion of the heart with the ear. Every chord produces of course a distinct effect on the ear; but, from an æsthetic or emotional point of view, we cannot go much further in discussing single *chords*, or even, as a rule, isolated fragments of chord-combination, than in discussing single *notes* or groups of two or three notes together. There is more volume of tone and a larger element of form, but scarcely more characteristic impressiveness, in

*Isolated chords or fragmentary groups of chords can scarcely have more character or value than formless groups of single notes.*

than in

A person unused to chord-analysis might learn this fragment by heart, yet might listen with perfect appreciation to the adagio of the *Pathétique* sonata—

&c.

and never perceive the progression in the sixth and seventh bars to be harmonically identical with it. Why should he? He might as well be bound to recognise the tip of a particular nose cut out of a picture. Such absence

a constituent in the most glorious and the most paltry form in *Leise leise*, quoted on p. 253, and in *O mio Fernando*, quoted on p. 108. The whole view is curiously at variance with other passages in Rousseau's musical writings, where he goes to the other extreme of regarding harmony as an unemotional sort of decorative *colour*, and fails to recognise its frequently essential relation to the significance of melodic motive.

of recognition would only go to prove the most literal truth of what we have already remarked, that it is the privilege of a fine motive to *transfigure* a special feature with its own individuality.

There are, however, certain single chord-effects which, while equally able to enter as constituents into fine or indifferent Ideal Motions, strike the ear so individually as to be much more generally recognisable by ordinary hearers of Music. Such *par excellence* is the sudden occurrence, in a major key, of the major chord borne by the note a major third below the key-note, as of the chord of C major occurring in the key of E major, or of the chord of E flat in the key of G. This feature is so easy of introduction, and in its way so striking, as to be a sort of commonplace of Music: and it is all the more interesting to compare its conventional appearance in the noisy wind-up of an overture, as thus—

§ 19. Certain chord-effects have sufficient individuality of sound to be very easily recognised even in very different connections.

&c.

with its splendid effect, three times repeated, on the word *Tremblez* in Auber's *Voyez sur cette roche*; where the contrast it makes with the fresh *naïveté* of the melody gives exactly the tone of alarm and warning needed by the words, with a tinge of mock-heroic exquisitely appropriate to the verse where the disguised Fra Diavolo takes up the air—

The effect of this harmonic feature is entirely one of immediate contrast. Another sort of very individual and recognisable chord-fragment, involving indirect rather than direct contrast, may be found in those fragments of *cadence* which stand out, by their comparative rarity, in marked distinction from the universal dominant-and-tonic cadence of modern music. It is possible to regard these occasional cadences, from their very shortness, as remnants of those older 'modes,' which gave place to the major and minor owing to the impossibility of connecting their chords in any prolonged and coherent series. Take the following cadence from *And with his stripes* :

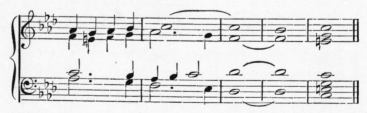

Helmholtz considers the real key-note of this chorus to be C, and the cadence a Doric one,[1] with the D flat as a descending leading-note. I should say that, so far as a piece which oscillates between several keys can be said to have one 'real' key at all, it would be better to select F minor, in which it starts, and on the dominant of which it concludes: but disputes on such matters are perfectly barren; the effect of the concluding chords is the same to all, and is instantly recognised as a familiar one in solemn music.

Another very special and noticeable chord-feature is the appearance of the major chord of the note a semitone above the key-note, as of the chord of D flat in the key (usually minor) of C,[2] thus—

or with melody, as thus in the sextett in *Don Giovanni*—

[1] It should be noticed, even if we adopt this nomenclature, that the notes of the Doric mode in C, are C, Db, Eb, F, G, Ab, Bb, C: so that the E *natural*, which the modern ear absolutely demands in such a cadence as the above, is not a note of the mode.

[2] I describe the chord by the sounds that are in it. Harmonists may derive what comfort they can from looking outside it for its 'roots;' but to all ears it makes one indisputable sort of clang, which, in the case mentioned, is that of the first inversion of the chord of D flat.

These two last cases are strongly confirmatory of the view taken above, that the primary source of mournful effect must be sought in *movement*, in succession of notes, and not in obscurity of harmonic *clang*. The cardinal point in all the examples given is the D flat, the occurrence of the degree next above C at the distance from it of a *semitone* instead of a tone; giving a sense of lapse and depression quite parallel with that which we noticed in respect of the characteristic notes of the minor scale. And in the second case, which is much most distinctly mournful, the D flat chord is a simple major, with no disturbance of clang at all. It is true that Helmholtz has, beyond disturbance of clang in the separate chords, a second principle for explaining distinctively minor effects; namely, the inferior power of the harmonies in the minor scale to fortify the relationship of the several notes to the key-note, and the less clear and intelligible connection of the chords; inducing a less decided character and an inclination to modulate. I doubt whether these features would be at all adequate to produce a melancholy expression but for the character of the individual minor chords, as to the source of which I have ventured to dissent from the accepted view. But in any case this principle of inferiority of tonic predominance and obscure chord-connection does not seem available for the cases on which we are now engaged. The verdict of direct consciousness is that the connection of chords, in these mere fragments containing the D flat, is perfectly clear and natural. When we come to analyse, we see that the clearness does not indeed result from harmonic connection, but from another equally legitimate source; the close proximity, namely, of the D flat (the 'descending leading-note,' as Helmholtz has himself well termed it) to the C in which it takes refuge. This gives naturalness to the unrelated D flat, just as, in the case of the ascending leading-note, the step B-C is made natural by a similar closeness of proximity in spite of a similar want of relationship.

A striking example of this harmonic effect will be found in Schubert's *Die böse Farbe,* quoted on p. 323.

It would be possible to give other specimens of special chord-combinations, sufficiently distinctive to be easily recognisable amid very various surroundings even by quite unpractised ears: but seeing that the very point to be observed about them is that they are but fragments of material, and that their value in any particular place can in no way be abstracted from the larger form which they help to constitute, it seems scarcely worth while to extend the list.

# CHAPTER XII.

## MATERIAL AND COLOUR.

So far we have been dealing entirely with the element of Form; with the peculiar nature of those coherent groups of sounds which produce the characteristic impression of melodic motion; with the manner in which the essential principles exemplified in the shortest and simplest piece of intelligible tune are connected with prolonged organic development; and lastly with the phenomena of Polyphony and Harmony, and their several relations to that great central fact which, in order to exclude the narrower associations of the words *melody* and *melodic*, we elected to call by the more comprehensive name of *Ideal* Motion, motion which is perpetual *form* by dint of the perpetual interdependence of its successive parts.

§ 1. We now pass from the element of Form to that of Material.

We now come to a quite new topic; the variously coloured material, the sound-quality or *timbre* of the notes, in which the forms of Music are presented.

And first, the relations of the various arts to their material present remarkable differences. Music has the special peculiarity that we must reckon under the head of its material not merely sounds in reference to their colour-quality or their mass, but sounds in reference to their arrangement in a scale. The scale of available notes is ready for the composer's invention to work on, simply in virtue of their pitch-relations, apart from any colouring or weight of sound given them by particular instruments. This bare material thus already comprehends elements of form and proportion, and has arrived at the stage in which he finds it by the previous working of these elements into true forms; while we might regard in the same light many ordinary fragments of combination and effect, susceptible of use in all sorts of forms. I need not repeat how this peculiarity affects the forms produced at various times and places; so that they become to alien ears not anything analogous, *e.g.*, to buildings of timber and buildings of marble, the varying characteristics of which a sympathetic knowledge of the respective materials may soon enable an artistic eye to appreciate equally; but structureless and uninteresting juxtapositions of sound.

§ 2. Differences in the relations of the various arts to their material.

This peculiarity of musical material having been noticed, we shall for the future be concerned only with its aspects of mass and colour. Under these aspects it presents a decided resemblance to the material of Painting, as distinguished from that of the other arts. Neither in Painting nor Music is the mere material calculated to excite much independent interest : no special associations or strong feelings of pleasure are excited by even the fairest tints on a painter's palette, or by scales or fortuitous successions of notes played on the most beautiful instruments. In the other three arts the material has more independent importance. The verbal material at the command of the poet is the partly spontaneous, partly artificial growth of centuries, and he finds it ready charged with shades and associations of all sorts. In Sculpture and Architecture the material, though not a product of human development, is commonly beautiful in itself, and always carries with it a delightful sense of obedient strength and durability, which makes a most sensible factor in the completed work. It is to its simple and homogeneous material, to the elimination of the element of colour and the imperishable aspect of the pure marble (features which to modern eyes, used to seeing statues in detachment from architecture, become specially characteristic of the art), that Sculpture owes much of its peculiar dignity and its monumental character. In our latent consciousness the expressionless block has lent its own endurance to the emotional image which it seems to have had concealed within it. And this is in entire accordance with the spirit of the art which, accepting a comparatively limited range of subject-matter, attains extraordinary intensity within that range by abstracting secondary and emphasising primary characteristics, and, through the concentration of the beholder's attention on these, presents him not more with individual objects of beauty than with eternal types. The mass of association and sentiment which is summed up and concentrated in the expressive aspects of ideal human or even animal form, the feeling that in a single look and attitude our imaginations find epitomised the attributes and essential spirit of a whole existence, seem to demand inherent worth and dignity in the vehicle of representation. And in all branches of the sculptural art, whether in the working of rougher stone than marble, or in pottery, or in glass- and metal- and ivory-work, the character of the material and the workman's loving obedience to its conditions are essential features, to be recognised in any true appreciation of the result.

With these features we may contrast the only possible analogue to them in Music, namely, the composing with a just regard and skilful conformance to the special capabilities of special instruments, in respect both of actual sounds and of mechanical difficulties. Here a person without technical knowledge, though he may notice failures, as when an instrument or a performer is set to do unsuitable and awkward things, will take no particular account of successes. When the music goes all right, and the instruments or voices seem perfectly adequate to present it, there is nothing

*Characters of the material of Sculpture and Architecture,*

to suggest any special problems or niceties in the mere management of the material: and while the most ordinary knowledge and intelligence will reveal in great measure how the nature of stone or metal has been considered and conformed to, only connoisseurs will perceive the composer's care and thought for the compass and tone and special mode of producing notes of each of his instruments, and for the mechanical peculiarities which make some sorts of passages suitable and effective in one case and impossible or ineffective in another.

But it is in Architecture that the element of material assumes the most prominent and independent position, and this in virtue of characteristics peculiar to this art. We have already noticed the part played in architectural effect by weight and mass, that is, by sheer amount of material presented in a single effect, and instinctively contrasted with the feeble physical strength of the men who nevertheless have thus reared it at their will. Again, in the natural objects employed colour is given ready made, and of a kind permitting extraordinary variety and latitude of treatment. Mr. Ruskin has said that he has scarcely ever seen an offensive introduction of the natural colours of marble and precious stones, whereas he has never seen a painted building which seemed to him quite right: and among the natural colours of architectural material we may include the stains of time and weather, with all their wealth of emotional suggestion. Besides this, the material of magnificent buildings has also the strongest suggestiveness in respect both of preciousness and of the labour of moving and working it. The æsthetic effects due to these two sources have been most luminously explained by the writer just named; and everybody must have had evidence of their reality, *e.g.* in the revulsion of feeling caused by learning that some beautiful and delicately cut tracery he had been admiring was only a sham. It is noticeable too of Architecture, that since in many places magnificent material is supplied to it direct by the earth, the art in its infancy naturally became a means of magnificent display. The decorative art of Homer's poems consisted in casings of costly materials, silver and gold and ivory and amber. And this exhibition of nature's treasures remains a prominent feature throughout the history of Architecture; constituting a marked distinction from Music, whose fine and costly material, specially contrasted with that of Music. in the shape of highly-cultivated voices and elaborate instruments, is an artificial product and for the most part of very modern manufacture: nor does our knowledge that many hours' work a day has given to a voice the power and elasticity we admire contribute, except very occasionally and indirectly, to our pleasure; for the work was not devoted, like that of the graver or inlayer, to the patient fashioning of the beautiful thing we see or hear, but to wide practice on all sorts of matter, often of a quite neutral and unbeautiful sort. A further contrast may be found in the nature of *ornament*, which in Architecture often appears as colour, natural or painted, not applied along the lines and over whole surfaces of the buildings but in independent spots, lines, and patterns: whereas the only meaning of ornament in Music is in shakes and turns and diverse variations and efflorescences of essential *form*; and any *colour* which appears can only do so on the lines of a form, the form being necessarily presented *in* such and such a colour, *on* such and such an instrument.

The subject of architectural material will recur again, in connection with the ethical bearings of that art as compared with Music: but for the present it is from the face of Nature and the art of Painting that we shall derive most aid (though still rather by points of contrast than of affinity), in the special consideration of coloured tone-material to which we must now pass.

§ 3. Confusion between musical colour and form is very common.

After our full discussion of musical *form,* and after the definition (which can hardly be simplified or amplified) of musical *colour* as consisting in the various sorts of *timbre* or quality of tone which various instruments can produce, it might seem hardly necessary to begin the detailed discussion of the latter element by more particularly marking its distinction from the former. As a matter of fact, however, the confusion in the use of the words and in the ideas connected with them is so common, and is so much unconsciously fostered by the language of art-critics whose paramount interest lies in the arts of the eye, that a brief notice of it, and of the sort of expressions in which it takes shape, is unavoidable.

The confusion is only a special form of one which has been already noticed. Reference was made in the third chapter to the habit of using terms derived from Music to describe visible phenomena; a habit quite legitimate for the purposes in view, but apt to react very unjustly on the art which

We have seen that the use of musical terms in description of visible phenomena tends to conceal the essential peculiarity of Music;

supplies the metaphors. We noticed how such phrases as the *musical* disposition of masses, the *harmonious*[1] arrangement of, *e.g.*, the leafy bosses of a distant wood, are apt to induce the view that Music itself just consists in pleasing arrangements of pleasing things, *i.e.* of agreeably-toned notes or chords; arrangements enabling the ear to trace a sort of connection and balance in its various sensations, but capable of little more decided individuality than is perceived in, *e.g.*, several distant woods, in each of which the fortuitous massings and bossings of foliage would of course as a matter of fact be different, but without making any vivid difference of impression. We saw later how little, even in more ordered and deliberate combinations of lines and masses, the element of mere abstract form and proportion could be thought of or estimated as an independent factor; and how rich multiplication of line and feature, mass, material, ornament, colour, breadth of light and shade, consciousness of

---

[1] Music can of course claim no monopoly of the word *harmony*: still the word is so prominently connected with Music that it much facilitates sliding into the looseness of view I am speaking of.

labour, and various other considerations, all inevitably entered into our sense of architectural effect.[1] In contrast to which, we saw that a set of musical proportions, making up a few bars of perfectly skinny tune, and not only not presented in massive or beautiful material of sound, but thought of in silence without any definable sound-quality at all, might produce a sense of individuality as distinct and unmistakable as that of a well-known face, and a sense of force and beauty as overpowering as any it is given to man to know. That is to say, for a pleasing arrangement of nicely gradated bosses we get a phenomenon with an equally small number of ultimate elements, and yet bearing the stamp of the rarest and most inspired invention no less than the roof of the Sistine chapel or the Florentine campanile.

But we now go on to observe that the misconception frequently takes another form ; and that it is not in the comparison of Music to arrangements of lines or bosses or any sort of proportional shapes, but in the comparison to arrangements and harmonies of *colour*, that its essential character as a perpetual presentation of perfectly organic and individual form is most apt to be lost sight of. And with the notions that Music is a sort of kaleidoscopic affair is connected a converse notion that kaleidoscopic or pyrotechnic effects might be developed into producing ' the same sensations as Music ; '[2] which they will do when they produce

*and the case of colour is a most prominent instance of this.*

[1] As happily illustrative of the way in which the sense of visible proportions is interfused and informed with all sorts of concrete associations, I cannot forbear quoting some remarks of Mr. Ruskin's on Prout's rendering of the proportion and grace of Gothic spires and towers :—' Everything in grace of form depends on truth of scale. You don't show how graceful a thing is till you show how large it is ; for all grace means ultimately the use of strength in the right way, moral and physical, against a given force. A swan no bigger than a butterfly would not be graceful—its grace is in its proportion to the waves, and power over them. A butterfly as large as a swan would not be graceful ; its beauty is in being so small that the winds play with it, but do not vex it. A hollow traceried spire fifteen feet high would be effeminate and frivolous, for it would be stronger solid—a hollow traceried spire five hundred feet high is beautiful ; for it is safer so, and the burden of the builder's toil spared.'

[2] A sufficient criticism of this notion is contained in the remarks on the ' music of colour and visible motion,' towards the end of the eighth chapter. I was there explain-

ing the total irrelevance of the proposed visible effects to that which is the essence of Music—organic form : the points now under discussion, that there is such a thing as *musical* colour, and that its distinction from musical form is absolute, may further illustrate that argument.

*A propos* of colour, however, I must quote one more passage from the theory I before examined. It is there said that certain persons, when they hear music, ' see beautiful changing mosaics, the patterns of which have definite connections with the musical chords.' Now I would ask the reader to turn to the example on p. 278, of three chords first given in a single group, and then as they occur in a melody from the *Pathétique* Sonata ; showing how absolutely chords and fragments of chord-progression are, like melodic notes, subordinate parts of organic forms, apart from which they have no artistic individuality or significance. Therefore if (which one may take leave to doubt) anybody has a definite change of mosaic patterns answering to these three chords on their own account, (and the ' definite connections ' can imply nothing less), the very fact would prove the entire irrelevance of the pattern to the indi-

the same sensations as the Venus of Milo, and not before. Further on we shall see a good deal of the danger of analogies between the arts; and a considerable part of this danger lies in the loose application of terms which are common to more than one of them. The word *tone* is a notable instance of the kind, and has a special connection with the present point. In application to Painting, it refers to the preservation of the true colour-qualities of objects under the various degrees of illumination or shadow which are produced on them by a homogeneous light. But in Music the same word is used either of the *quality of sound*, the element of musical *colour* (as when we speak of the tone of a first-rate violin or violinist), or of the *sound itself*, regarded as notes capable of use in Music, the element of *form* without emphasis on quality (as when we speak of the tone-art), or more definitely still of a certain accurately measured degree in the scale of such notes (as when we speak of tones and semitones). The consequence is that such a phrase as *gradations of tone* may lead to most important misconceptions. I have heard an art-critic of the highest authority maintain that Painting has a superiority over Music, because its gradations of tone are infinite, whereas those of Music are limited by the fact that the degrees are at fixed distances. The question as to the superiority of one art over another becomes worse than useless when involved with what is nothing less than a total confusion between colour and form. The gradations of tone which are infinite in Painting are of course gradations of light and colour: we shall examine afterwards to what extent Music admits of analogous gradations, but the only possible place to look for them must be in *quality* and *mass* of sound—tone, in the sense that a violin has a penetrating tone, or an oboe a nasal tone or a trombone a loud tone—the varieties of which are called, even in ordinary *parlance*, musical colouring.[1] The gradations of tone in Music which consist in fixed degrees

*An example in the use of the word tone.*

viduality of this melody of Beethoven, and to every other individual form which this special chord-progression helps to constitute: and in the same way the irrelevance of *every* such colour- and pattern-effect to *every* actual and possible specimen of organic form in Music.

[1] I may remind the reader of what has been already explained, that no *physical* analogy between the coloured spectrum and the range *in pitch* of musical sounds has any bearing on our perception of the two sorts of phenomena. The scale of notes presents intervals and proportions of the most definite kind: the coloured spectrum presents not a single definite interval, not the most rudimentary germ of proportion. The mere fact that vibrations producing rays at the blue end are about twice as quick as those at the

red, *i.e.* that the *physical* relation is that of an octave, has absolutely no counterpart in sensation; to us the difference merely means two different *colours*. Differences and relations in the elements of the spectrum are matters of *colour* pure and simple, and have no connection with *form*; the perception of visual form being due to a process which is quite independent of the colour-sense and has no parallel in the ear, namely, the mechanical shifting of the eye in rapidly carrying it along the lines and over the surfaces of objects. Differences and relations in the pitch of notes, on the other hand, are an indispensable factor of musical *form*, in whatever colour presented, and the sensation of *colour*-quality in sound knows nothing of them; the proportions present in the harmonics which are the *physical* basis of such are the notes of the scale, the *formal* elements of melody and harmony, just as much as faces and limbs are the formal elements of figure-painting, and lines and surfaces of Architecture. And this mistake led naturally to a still more fatal one. Musical colouring having been confused with, and put in the place of, musical form or 'subject,' this latter had to be accommodated with some *habitat*; and this was found by identifying it with the verbal statements or sentiments with which the music might happen to be connected—a confusion due perhaps in its turn to an ambiguity in the word *subject*, and equivalent to identifying a Gothic cathedral with the Apostles' Creed. As a legitimate consequence any music which is not set to words was supposed to have no subject (all it had being colour), and the enjoyment of it to be as purely sensuous as the enjoyment of mere colour without form in the fold of a piece of drapery. It is this same identification of melodic 'subject' with mere sonorous and sensuous beauty which we shall see implied in Wagner's view, that Music, to be complete, must express some preconceived poetical idea. Fortunately, however, it is a law of our being that in the apprehension of form we find a sense of active grasp and self-realisation entirely distinct from sensuous enjoyment: while in form lies the possibility of a permanent and solid nucleus for the associations, of the stuff of which our sense of beauty has been so largely compounded, and the power of vivid and fruitful reproduction in memory. The fixed degrees and proportions, which were objected to as limitations, are of course as essential to form as they are alien to colour: to them is due

colour-quality being as little represented in normal sensation as the particular number of physical vibrations which go to constitute a particular visual hue.

The essential relations of musical *harmony* to form have also been explained. But it is very common and permissible to speak of *harmonic colouring*, in reference to the effect on a melody of harmonising it, perhaps in various ways. Even regarding harmony in this light, however, we should notice that it is quite unique, and presents a common difference from both pictorial and instrumental colour. In colouring subjects and forms with the two latter, considerable variety of treatment is possible: but the ways of harmonising a melody are limited, and one or two are almost sure to be decidedly better than others; while often a particular chord or set of harmonies appears, not as one of several possible adornments, but as an unalterable means of defining the form, and a necessary element in its significance. In contrapuntal writing, where the harmony is formed by several distinct and continuous voices or parts, it becomes of

course still more obviously identified with form.

One further use of the word *colour* in connection with Music is worth mentioning. Music is often said to have some sort of *national* colouring, if it presents resemblances of effect to other music associated with special localities. Thus, *Hope the Hermit* might be said to have English colouring, through a certain strong and straightforward musical character which is common to it with many other of the older English airs. Tunes, again, which, by avoidance of the seventh, are playable on the black keys of a piano, a well-known peculiarity of Scotch music, will be said to have Scotch colouring. When we come to such instances as Rubinstein's 'Persian' songs, and generally to music supposed to have *oriental* colouring, it is not probable that there any particular resemblance is involved; but melodies may easily have that sort of strangeness which gets considered oriental when once that convenient description of a certain indefinite unusualness of character has been suggested.

the power of musical motives to exist and to be to us as divine utterances. That musical sound of a formless and indefinite kind should give us this sense of importance and individuality is as impossible as that we should get the impression of a human face from something without definite or recognisable proportions of line and surface, or that a picture should strike us as religiously expressive which represented only clouds and jelly-fish.

The colour-qualities of musical material are thus as entirely distinct from musical form, as the redness of a cherry is distinct from its spherical shape. We shall find in the next chapter that there are certain musical effects of true value, where colour is completely in the ascendant, and form hardly if at all discerned ; as is also the case in many impressions

In the auditory as in the visible region, colour is a *secondary* quality of phenomena.

received from Nature through the eye. Meanwhile we find that in auditory exactly as in visible phenomena, form is the *individualising* element by which things are known and recognised ; and that as in the outer world the same forms are perpetually invested with different hues, whether by their own nature or by the hourly changes of light or by the passage of years and seasons, and different forms with the same hue, so in Music the same forms may be presented in many varieties of sound-colour ; and one and the same sound-colour may invest any number of forms ; in brief, that in Music, no less than in Nature, form is a primary and colour a secondary quality of phenomena.

§ 4. The characteristics of visible and auditory colour.

This being settled once for all, we may go on to consider the various related and contrasted characteristics of auditory tone and natural visible colour. In the first chapter we saw that it was not easy to make out that a perfectly simple ungraded impression of visible colour gives for the moment a superior pleasure to a delightful taste or smell ; the standards of superiority usually employed being external to the simple impression, as, *e.g.*, power to give pleasure to an indefinite number of people without being possessed or consumed, or facility of being frequently repeated without loss of effect or detrimental consequences. We might perhaps add that pleasing colour reaps the benefit of its association with our whole external outlook on the world, in some power of vaguely stirring the imagination with dim suggestions of freedom and expansion. But in any case the view has little practical importance ; for in our sense of the beauty of colour in the visible world, such perfectly simple impressions have little part.

Various elements of constant occurrence in visible colour,

The feature of large extent, or of large variety with many elements of contrast and harmony, is very commonly present ; and above all, the element of gradation, necessarily involved in all curvature of coloured surfaces. There is no greater mystery in that whole mysterious region where higher mental elements begin to mingle with sense-impressions, than the extreme pleasure producible by gradations of colour. We have seen that it cannot, like the pleasure in complementary colours, be based on any physiological ground, as that the change in the amount of stimulus, while the eye travels from the lighter to the darker parts of the colour, relieves the nervous elements employed and gives them opportunity for repair; for the pleasure is felt to the full in colours which, if throughout as bright as their brightest parts, would not be sufficiently bright to cause any fatigue or need of quick repair. Apparently we must be content to accept this pleasure in mere graduated change of sensation as an ultimate fact, parallel with the equally ultimate pleasure in gradation of curved form : at any rate we need not solve the problem in order to compare the experiences of the ear with those of the eye in this respect.

As regards sound, then, gradations of *pitch*, which might have been expected to present some analogy to *curvature* of visible form, do in fact present the strongest contrast to it; sliding changes of pitch being un-bearable in any strong and bright sound-colour, as on a violin, unless the sliding sound passes swiftly from one perfectly definite point of the scale to another intelligibly related point; and even with such fortuitous transitions of pitch as *have* a certain agreeable character— as, for instance, the shifting tones of a sighing and moaning wind, which are naturally dim in musical quality and are further tempered to our ears by the non-musical sounds of rushing and rustling—the association of cur-vature is inexpedient; since by suggesting form it tends to conceal the cardinal fact that true melodic form depends essentially on fixed degrees. In application to sound-*colour*, the general meaning of gradation would be in reference to degrees of loudness and softness. For in sound no merging of actual tints is possible; the tone of a violin cannot gradually shade into the tone of a flute, as blue into green; and the modifications of a single species of tone which are possible on the most perfect simple instruments, and of which an exceptionally fine performer may make very refined use, are too much bound up with variations of loudness and softness, and features such as suddenness and shortness of note, which do not strictly belong to *timbre*, to count as a separate class of colour-gradations analogous to the merging of visual tints. Graduated degrees of loudness and softness are of course often an immense en-hancement of musical effect, and are very necessary elements in the pre-sentation of certain forms; but such gradations in Music have nothing approximating to that universality of occurrence which is ensured, by the very nature of light and shadow, to the gradations of hue on visible objects.

So much for gradation. As regards other features, our compari-son of visual and auditory colour can, for the most part, only be an extension of that general comparison of the impressions of the ear and the eye which suggested itself very early in our enquiry. The ear agrees with the eye, as opposed to the lower senses, in its clear appreciation of quantity or mass of colour-impression, and in its accurate power of

and in various
other ways.

distinguishing many simultaneous elements. But we found sound-colour of a distinct kind to be impossible as a continuous feature of daily environment, partly because it is naturally more wearing to the nerves than the quieter pleasures of the eye, partly because it cannot be shut out or turned away from : we may now give as additional reasons that there are no *complementary* sound-colours, that is, various sorts of *timbre* do not afford to the ear the rest which the eye is perpetually receiving from the variety of colours in its range ; [1] and that musical colour is the natural and perpetual investiture of forms, and of forms which demand *attention*, so that it can never be musingly regarded like the blue sky, purely on its own account. We found musical colour, however, from the very rareness of our experience of it, to be of a particularly arresting and exciting kind ; while the visible colours even of a beautiful environment are often from their very commonness disregarded : similarly we may consider that the exceptional occurrence and comparatively limited variety of distinctive combinations and contrasts of sound-colours in an orchestral or choral performance is compensated by an exceptional susceptibility in the ear to vivid delight from them. On the other hand it may be said on behalf of the eye that it is people's own fault if they neglect the beauties of visible colour because they are common : against which again we may put, if we like, the point previously noticed, that there is naturally a very far more *general* sense of fine sound-colour than of fine visual colour; partly as a mere fact of nerve-stimulation ; partly because beauty of visual colour depends so much on the subtler elements of gradation and harmony; partly because beautiful visual colour so often appears merely in a fragment or patch amid neutral and commonplace surroundings; whereas the sound of a beautiful voice stands out in isolated and unmistakable predominance, and compels recognition even from the coarse and careless. Unfortunately, however, though the susceptibility to great beauty of sound-colour is common, the beautiful sound-colour itself is exceptionally hard to get at and command ; and a large majority of our people go through life without ever hearing a perfect voice or a perfect instrument.

I have referred to the general agreement in appreciation of fine sound-colour. This remark may be much extended in a way which opens

---

[1] Change of colour pleases the eye by giving comparative rest to one set of retinal elements, and throwing the main work for a time on a new set. The most effectual source of similar relief to the terminal nervous elements of the ear would be alterations of *pitch* rather than of *timbre* : but formless successions of tones, even when so varied as to exercise different sets of terminal elements, will rapidly cause strong irritation, which seems hardly diminished by the fact of this variety : so that the fatigue must apparently originate in some nervous centre beyond the differentiated terminal elements of the ear. Tone-stimulation, whenever so orderless as to preclude the relieving exercise of any higher faculty, seems to have, in its purely sensory character, exceptional power both of compelling and wearying the attention.

up a striking contrast between visible colour and sound-colour. For in sound the degrees of merit in each class of colour are in a very great measure absolute: while as regards visible colour, though certainly the shapeless hues in a prism may be called absolutely good and the aniline dyes absolutely bad, it is impossible in our ordinary visual experience to separate the sense of mere colour-beauty from other elements, or to compare colours in the abstract; it is difficult perhaps even to determine how much of our dislike of the cheap manufactured hues may not arise from the way they are presented, from the ugliness of crude ungradated and unharmonised masses of them. Of Nature's colours, at any rate, which make up the enormous majority of our most delightful colour-experiences, it is often hard to say with any definiteness that one shade is inherently superior to another shade, this blue inherently more beautiful or more right than that blue; the beauty and rightness being so much matters of place and harmony, depending on association with known objects and conditions, and on the influence of surrounding tints. In Music, on the other hand, the comparison is absolute: we can perpetually assert with the utmost definiteness that one soprano voice *is* preferable to another, that the tone of this violin or of this piano *is* superior to the tone of that. Differences of taste doubtless exist in respect of *different classes* of musical colour, some people preferring tenor to bass, or a clarinet to a flute, in the sort of way they may prefer blue to pink, or crimson to orange. In variety of susceptibility to these definitely distinct qualities, the eye and the ear are pretty much on a par with the nose and palate; such general preferences seeming to be quite irrelevant to the higher perceptions, and in sound, for instance, presenting no relation to differences of musical taste or proficiency.[1] But in respect of *varieties of the same class*, the scale from bad, through indifferent and pretty good, to excellent, is exceptionally well marked, and the widest unanimity will be found to prevail as to the various degrees. Hardly any one would fail to tell the rounder and richer from the poorer or coarser or more wiry quality: and though some ears seem little liable to suffer from harsh and screaming tones, I have never heard of their really preferring such sounds to sweeter ones of equal power.

Two more points may be reckoned to the account of sound-colour. First, it is not dependent on accidents of light and climate, and is undimmed by the conditions which starve the eyes of men; so that Music can find adequate presentation just where other beauties fail. Secondly, while a new and beautiful visual colour, the like of which has never been

---

[1] It is curious how taste alters with regard to *timbre* from time to time. As lately as the beginning of this century *contralto* was not in vogue, and the most beautiful voice of that order passed for some time with little recognition. At the present time, so far as I have watched popular audiences, I should say that contralto is perhaps the most naturally moving of all qualities of voice.

seen before, is an impossibility, new and beautiful sorts of *timbre* are perfectly possible, and, judging by the past, even probable.

and their number, if not absolutely very great, is at any rate unknown.

This difference is connected not merely with the fact that the most beautiful visual colours are natural, and the most beautiful sounds artificial; it depends on the fundamental differences of the two sense-organs. For there being (according to the most accepted view) only three different sorts of retinal elements, by the stimulation of which, in various degrees and combinations, the sense of various colours is produced, the number of actually distinct and independent tints is very limited, and the range of colour-impressions is *un*limited only in the sense that the gradations, and the varieties producible by degrees of light and shade and by texture, are numberless. But the number of individually different nervous elements which tones affect is far greater; and as varieties of *timbre* are due to the simultaneous stimulation, in various degrees and combinations, of a good many of these (being produced by the *harmonics* which accompany the vibrations of the fundamental note, and stimulate each of them a distinct element of nervous structure), a large number of quite distinct sorts of *timbre* are theoretically possible, and any day may witness the invention of a new instrument with a new one. The course of improvement, however, is more likely to take the form of enrichment and purification of existing sorts of *timbre* (as notably exemplified in the recent history of the pianoforte), than of frequent discoveries of novel sorts; while it is most improbable that the colour-quality of the best stringed instruments or of the best voices will ever be surpassed.

§ 7. Visible and auditory colour in their relations to form.

This may conclude our comparison of the two sorts of colour, so far as they can be at all considered independently. We have next to compare them in respect of their connection with form, and of the degree of necessity and importance attaching to that connection. Colour, it has been said, is a secondary and more or less accidental quality. The first consequence of this is, that beauty of colour is compatible, both in the world of the eye and the world of the ear, with neutral and with low and worthless forms.

Beautiful colour is compatible with neutral or worthless form;

First, as regards neutral form. There are plenty of things and fragments of things in the visible world, which are what is called shapeless, or at all events which lack individuality or beauty of shape, while covered with lovely colour. I have seldom seen a more beautiful tint of blue than in the gall-bladder of a frog; and less bizarre examples, stones, bits of lichened wall, low aquatic organisms, and hundreds of others will readily occur to the mind. The only kind of musical parallel to such forms, which we do not dislike or despise simply because they have not enough definiteness and individuality to pretend to beauty or expression, would be certain exercises and study-passages; which similarly make no pretence to beauty of form, and yet may so bring out the colour-genius of a fine instrument as to produce, at any rate for a short time, a pleasing sense of sonorous beauty even in ears to which the nugatoriness of the form is palpable.

Far more important is the case of shapes which may be said in a positive sense to be worthless and despicable. In the visible world these consist, broadly speaking, of two classes; first, those which directly suggest moral or physical degradation, as certain sorts of face and form in living beings; and secondly, artificial products, and especially those which have aimed at beauty; an ugly vase or an ugly piece of ambitious architecture being more offensive to the eye than the ugliest square box or warehouse. Both these classes are susceptible of the irony of beautiful colour; the second, or artificial class, permanently, by being made of beautiful natural material; and the first, or natural class, occasionally, by the impartial play of warm light. In the case of the natural class, however, though debased forms may take part in a scene of glowing colour, it is not commonly as themselves exponents of any specially beautiful tints. It is rarely, for instance, that a despicable face arrests our attention by very great beauty of colouring: and though Jordaens may bathe in sunny light a scene of low revelling, the beauties of tint lie in the dresses and wine and fruit, rather than in the bloated faces of the revellers. It is doubtless a fact of interest, in connection with the primary and permanent chararacter of *form*, that the glories of *colour* may impartially visit scenes whose true character we find in the intimate association of their more noticeable forms with conditions of vice and misery. But though the sun, with his transforming hues, rises alike ' on the evil and on the good,' Nature herself is perpetually, in a thousand directions, stamping the association between beauty of colour and beauty of form. Nor is it common in Painting to find representations of distinctly coarse and despicable forms in the midst of a wealth of beautiful colour; for a painter capable of producing the latter would naturally eschew the former: though if his forms are simply poor and weak through bad drawing and falseness to Nature, beauty of light and colour will doubtless sometimes get his work believed in.

On this head it is unfortunately not to the works of Nature, but to those of man, and especially to the class of production which can present worthless and ugly abstract forms in porphyry and alabaster as easily as in clay, that sound-forms must be compared. Music differs from Nature and from Painting, first, in its arbitrary and unfettered power over its tints; for whatever a painter's command of pigments, and however much he may admire sky-blue, he cannot enlist admiration for his faces and limbs by painting them of that colour, while a composer may set perfect voices to sing what wretched melody he likes: and secondly in the fact that vulgar forms cannot, like the faces of Jordaens's boors, be made mere accessories in a brilliant composition, but are necessarily brought out one by one in prominent colour. So that *in which respect Music is specially liable to suffer.*

while we cannot think of blaming sunlight and colour as delusive for visiting coarse and squalid scenes, or feel that a painter gets vulgar forms into repute by any hues he can shed around them, in Music we find the actual bad and trivial forms themselves presentable in the most beautiful sound-colour the world affords. And so far as they are accepted and approved on that ground, so far, for instance, as shakes and flourishes and roulades are applauded by people capable of appreciating tunes, and weak tunes by people capable of appreciating strong tunes, on the ground of their being presented by a beautiful voice, we must reckon that an absolute wrong is done to men's powers of enjoyment, and that they are persuaded to accept the less for the greater : and in a manner all the more deplorable that the available stock of beautiful sound-colour is always limited. It is hard, perhaps, after our recognition of the very general and true preference for the purest and most beautiful sound-colours, to call any enjoyment of such colours vulgar and vicious in the sense that such terms might be applied to the eye which preferred crude tints and violent contrasts : but it is none the less a fact that willingness to accept sound-colour at all, even the best, apart from distinction of form, or to accept form merely on the ground of the quality of tone in which it is presented, is a condition as alien from deep and lasting artistic enjoyment as the preference of the most glaring Manchester fabrics to a Titian.

*Beautiful sound-colour is treated with peculiar unfairness.*

*§ 8. Colour can be abstracted from visible forms,*

The next consequence of the fact that colour is both to the eye and the ear a secondary quality of phenomena, is that it can be by both dispensed with ; representations of objects in white marble, or in black lines on white paper, being accepted with pleasure by the eye ; and musical forms, though necessarily presented to the ear in some kind of sound-colour if presented at all, being reproducible in memory with the very minimum of realisation of any actual sound-quality.

*and to a very large extent from auditory forms when they are recalled to memory.*

It might seem, from the fact that there is no means of presenting forms to the ear absolutely without *timbre* of some sort, that the colour-quality of musical forms would be less liable to be abstracted in the mind than that of visible forms. As a matter of fact, the reverse is the case. Though the eye can rejoice in the uncoloured forms of things in works of art, and certainly in the case of Sculpture never thinks of supplying in imagination the natural tints, we never recall any objects or scenes of the real visible world without recalling them in approximately their true colours. With Music it is very often quite otherwise. People probably vary greatly in the distinctness with which their memory of musical forms carries with it the revivification of the actual *timbre* in which those forms were presented ; but except with actual experts, the revivification is commonly, I think, very slight; so slight in pleasure-giving quality that the crudest and most imperfect presentation, by humming or whistling, that is, with a perfectly different and most inferior *timbre*, is perpetually preferred to mere silent imagination; though it would seem impossible but that such sounds, being actually there in the ears, should interfere with rather than aid the imaginary sensation of the true sound-colour. Thus if we compare visible colour and sound-colour merely as regards the respective parts they play in the enjoyments of the inward eye and the inward ear, the value of the latter sort sinks into comparative insignificance; the beauties of the auditory region being recalled, so far as they are recalled, with perpetual elimination of distinct colour-qualities.

Again, so far as *timbre* is actually imagined, it will not necessarily be the identical quality which has been actually heard in performance, but very likely some shadow of the best imaginable quality of that order. Thus while a person who recalls trees and flowers will not recall them in the fairest greens and reds he can imagine, but as far as he can in their own greens and reds, a person who recalls music, or who reads it by the eye, may imagine it to himself in the *best* violin-sounds and the *best* voice-sounds, and so on, that his imagination can command. While Music is far less absolute than Nature as to the connection of this or that colour with this or that form, we have seen that there is a quite unique absoluteness as to the degrees of merit in each order of musical colour-quality: and no one would have music in the worse tone if he could get it in the better, whether in real or imagined presentation of it. *Sound-colour may be not only abstracted in imagination, but changed;*

We have seen, then, (1) that a special *timbre* or colour can be almost or altogether eliminated in memory, and (2) that by experienced persons at all events it can often be more or less replaced in memory by a superior *timbre* of the same order. A third point is that it may be often effectively replaced, in actual performance, by a quite different order of *timbre*: so that, *e.g.*, orchestral music and vocal music can be presented on the pianoforte or on the organ, or with various combinations and arrangements of instruments, whereby the essential significance of the forms is preserved in spite of a complete change in the colouring associated with them. These statements must not be misunderstood. It is not of course meant that, *e.g.*, a pianoforte presentation [1] of an overture chorus or symphony can, as a rule, approximate in exciting quality to a complete performance, nor that there are not often features in such works which the best ' arrangement ' in the world would be incapable of even suggesting to a person ignorant of the original; but only that the *main* portions of works with strong motives and clear developments can and do stand such treatment with success; that the most valuable and enduring part, that *and may be changed not only in imagination but in reality.*

---

[1] Pianoforte arrangements may fail to do justice to an orchestral work, not owing to the substitution of monochrome for varied colouring, but by simple inadequacy to present the notes; certain passages which are easily playable on orchestral instruments being perhaps impossible or indistinct on a pianoforte. Many difficulties arising from multitude and complexity of notes may naturally be best overcome by eight-handed arrangements.

which must be justly called the essence, of the various beauties is so presentable and recallable ; and that the special bits of instrumental effect which present no charm or individuality of form, and are wholly lost in abstraction from their particular colour-qualities, are, in great music, a small minority.

Great import-
ance of this .
last point.

But after all possible reservations have been made, the importance of the main fact is difficult to over-estimate : it simply means the thousand-fold multiplication of the knowledge of musical works, and the more than thousand-fold multiplication of the hours and minutes during which they can be enjoyed. It is by foregoing special rights as to colour that all sorts of beautiful music, from a simple chorale or canzonet to whole large portions of oratorios and symphonies, can be brought home to people's own firesides, and made a feature of ordinary domestic life.[1] While good orchestral and choral performances are necessarily confined to special times and places, a few early years of pianoforte practice, with average musical taste, on the part of one member, or far better two members, of a family, will give, not indeed great mastery over the instrument, nor even the power of thundering and squirting at admiring friends in the most approved and accomplished manner, but for all that the key to many chambers in the great treasure-houses ; opening them both in the way of absolute enjoyment of many of their beauties, and not less in the way of preparation for hearing occasional complete performances, and of power to possess afterwards and perpetually the impressions there received ; opening them not only to those whose fingers do the work, but to all who care to hear, and especially to the unconsciously awakening ears of children.

§ 9. The
irony of the
comparison of
the real and
the apparent
success of many
musical com-
positions.

In the combination of two of the main points which have been noticed as to the relations of musical form and colour, namely, the frequent association of the finest colours with the poorest forms, and the power of recalling forms either with some imaginary association of fine colour, or (as I think is far more common) in the abstract notes, with a sense of any amount of force and ictus but with little suggestion of definite colour-quality—in this combination, I say, lies a curious irony, if we compare the real and the apparent fortunes of various musical compositions ; from the point of view that the real fortune and success of music is to be alive, and that its life is to be measured simply by the keenness of the delight it can give and the permanence which that delight can attain. An opera on which every device of rare and expensive colour has been lavished, which fills the air with its vibrations for four weary hours, and obtains favourable notices in

[1] I am far from saying that fine colour is not of extreme importance, even for the popularising of Music. On the contrary, it will be seen later that I regard it as of great importance to excite people's attention and get them to hear beautiful forms by presenting them in as beautiful and arresting colour as possible.

scores of newspapers, may enjoy an apparent success, without having really lived for a single instant of its course, or done more for any ears to which it may have proved acceptable than gorge them with hues which are as little to them now as last year's rainbows. The motive which occupies a quarter of a minute on a cottage piano, the air of Mozart or Schubert played on a cheap harmonium or truly sung by an untrained voice, the familiar chorus of Handel, snatches of which may be heard among the din of a Yorkshire factory, the *Volkslied*, which three-fourths of the children of a village may render for themselves without a bit of colour worth the name, these act as ever-recurring source of pleasure and count their life by hours and hours of happiness, the more precious that it may mingle its stream with the most prosaic employments. And even in one's own private experiences the irony I have mentioned may have a cheering as well as a saddening effect. As one walks home, perhaps, sick and weary with hearing brilliant sound-material and elaborate performance lavished on uninventive and joyless work, where voices and instruments and trained skill have been combining to persuade men's ears that the garment is the reality and that richness of colour can dispense with beauty of form, the sudden memory of some great melodic ' subject ' may come across one with an effect which is half-amusing: so easy and ample is the revenge which form takes in that tremendous power of assertion when the voices and instruments are silent and the trained skill at supper, and when a few dumb bars of bare notes will swamp and wash away the sonorous inanities of a whole evening.

We may now pursue our comparison of the colours of sight and of sound to the actual employment of them by artists in their works. And from all points of view the musical composer's colouring is evidently a less important and less difficult element in his work than is the painter's in his. In a painter's colour-art nothing is given him absolute and ready made. In external nature he finds every conceivable gradation of hue under every conceivable condition of distance and *chiaroscuro*, and each tint he puts down must bear a relation to the truth of these external facts and to the key into which he transposes them, and necessarily also to every other tint in his work ; nor can he transfer a grain of colour in careless independence from his palette to his canvas. A musician sits down with no external nature to consider, and with a certain number of absolute colours or qualities of sound, incapable of gradating insensibly one into another. First-rate instruments and skilful playing may beautify and clarify these colours ; but such modifications of tone as under a skilful touch become in a sense differences of kind (*e.g.* between brilliant and *cantabile* pianoforte passages) are not things invented by the composer, or superimposed on his forms with a delicate perception of all manner of relations, but are simply the well-known means of presenting certain forms

§ 10. Musical colouring in relation to the labour and talent of the composer.

most effectively, and applicable alike to the best and the poorest. More-over as the composer in writing may imagine ideal performance, he may be considered to have all his tints at their very best given him ready made. Very often he only makes use of one of them : long series of the very greatest and completest works, as the forty-eight preludes and fugues of Bach and the pianoforte sonatas of Beethoven, were written for a single instrument : so that the greatest composers have not only asserted their superiority, but have produced works which rank in splendour and perfection with any in the world, without any manipulation of colour whatever, and, curiously enough, with far less notion of beautiful colour associated with them than is natural to any concert-goer of the present day : Bach especially would have been considerably astonished could he have heard one of his fugues on a modern ' grand.' In other chamber-music there is but a limited range of quality of sound and small scope for colour arrangements. In the orchestra of course he has a wider field, and here he may indefinitely heighten the effect of his forms by adaptations and contrasts of colour.[1] But the looser and non-simultaneous connection of parts in a musical work naturally excludes that pervading harmony of a painter's colour which consists in the clearly-felt relation of every atom to the whole ; a fact which alone would imply the subtler and less mechanical character of this element in the pictorial art. And as the colours are ready to the composer's hand, as their main relations to each other are obvious and constant, as many beautiful combinations of them are a stock-in-trade, and as the form of melodies and passages often suggests almost inevitably some special mode of orchestral treatment, it would seem that though supreme genius in this particular line may indeed make startling revelations, these are not necessary features even of great instrumental works. It is not too much to say that for every musician who could write a fine symphony, there are probably a thousand who could score one from a pianoforte arrangement with very adequate success : effective streaks and masses of colour, and due balance, contrast, and emphasis, not exceeding what natural taste and fancy and trained musicianship may be well adequate to attain.

It is somewhat difficult to represent colouring as occupying a subordinate position in relation to the composer's genius without seeming to underestimate the part which colour plays in the actual impression of his work : but there need be no confusion between the two things. Beethoven said that his melodies and motives naturally occurred to him in some instrumental voice or other : but of course the great inventive fact

---

[1] If we rank under the head of colour such qualities as the brightness of a higher register, fancy and ingenuity are of course concerned in the most effective uses of them. But these uses, like gradations of loudness and softness, will continually almost suggest themselves unsought when the forms are worth effective investiture ; and their special effect is, as it were, an absolute and permanent known possibility.

was the occurring to him of those particular melodies and motives ; the occurring in particular colours is only what might happen in the case of quite inferior melodies and quite uninspired composers, the available colour-qualities being a limited set of known things. The wonderful enhancement of musical effects by fine orchestration and the manner in which the various instruments and their groupings wed themselves to the forms they present, so that special passages seem identified once and for ever with special orders of *timbre*, still do not affect the fact that the essence of music and musical invention lies in melodic and harmonic combinations ; that the instruments assume beautiful individuality through the beauty and individuality of the forms they clothe ; and that the significance of these forms is an unchangeable reality, which certainly did not depend on the colour for its occurrence to the composer, which will in the majority of cases be perceptible even with quite new associations of colour, provided only the notes be duly rendered, and which may assert itself with overpowering force to the inward ear where the memory of the actual colours survives only as a dim echo. If, on the other hand, the forms are weak and empty, no amount of attention to their coloured investiture will give them importance or individuality ; except indeed in such a style as Meyerbeer's, who seems always calling attention to his instruments by making them attitudinise. But while the full glory of varied colour will lend itself only to the composer who is capable of dispensing with it, and whose forms can, to the extent described, survive its removal, to him it will lend itself easily and lavishly. When we get a man whose invention is adequate to the production of large and noble musical organisms, we may be pretty certain, not only that he will apportion their colouring suitably, but even that striking and magical effects of colour will, as it were, spring up on his path : and it may be readily granted that just because musical colours are artificial and only heard in Music, while each instrument has its own definite and familiar colour-quality, the charm of a beautiful combination may be felt, in its place, as more wholly distinct and arresting than is perhaps possible in any minor group of the more relative tints of Painting.

One point with respect to instrumental colouring, not always sufficiently noticed, constitutes a disadvantage which seems in great measure unavoidable. It is that colour, in the masses and varieties in which orchestras or organs frequently present it, is apt to *swamp* form ; in other words, that the actual forms are often hard for the ear to discern, in the way that visible forms are hard for the eye to discern when flooded with too dazzling a light. This difficulty disappears when the music becomes to a certain extent known, and is much diminished in the case of those who can follow a printed score : but a very large number of persons genuinely capable of appreciating a particular work may at first be completely unable really to

§ 11. Musical colour is specially apt to hide form.

*hear* it, except in the most fragmentary way.   Even on a pianoforte, where the notes and passages are so clearly presented that there is no physical difficulty in making out what is going on, the structure of an elaborate movement, with 'subjects' and 'workings out' and episodes and all the rest, is not always immediately obvious, and such a movement on an orchestra receives a new element of complexity from the mere multiplicity of voices, now leading, now accompanying, interweaving with and echoing one another in various ways; but the present point is that, in addition to all this, the actual passages in course of presentation are liable in many places to get swallowed up in the general blaze of sound.   For instance, the central motive for some bars may be presented by a flute or an oboe, with quite sufficient prominence for an ear which knows it is there, but yet really so little distinguished in amount of tone from its concomitants that it may easily pass unnoticed.   Thus it may perpetually happen that an average amateur, unless he has learnt what to listen for, what to focus his attention on from point to point, quite loses sight of the thread of development, and only catches occasional themes interspersed among the sonorous waves; so that even in a well-constructed movement, as clear as the day when once familiar, he may find a good deal which, for aught he could tell at a first hearing, might be the mere cloak of showy noise covering musical emptiness.   It may be said that an amateur who does not care to extend his acquaintance with a symphony beyond a single chance hearing is not to be pitied if he fails to get much out of it.   But as a matter of fact many in whose lives musical enjoyment is a most valuable feature cannot command either their own time or the occasions of performance.   Musical works are not, like pictures, contained in a national gallery which can be walked round once a week, and it may be necessary to wait a year for a repetition.   It must thus be accounted a misfortune that when the real stuff is there which, and the like of which, can address quite unskilled ears in the clear monochrome of a pianoforte, the conditions of strong and varied colouring are apt decidedly to increase the difficulties of true apprehension: and this is one of the strongest arguments for giving orchestral and choral works the advantage of domestic study.

§ 12. Danger of the prominence of colour, in respect of the chance it gives for imposition.

It is impossible to avoid adding that the habituation of a large number of concert-goers to finding a good deal even in first-rate works which does not reveal to them its true beauties, and their failure to ensure any such adequate acquaintance with those works as should make the beauty manifest, reacts very damagingly on composition.   The variety of ready-made hues in a modern orchestra, and the natural desire to turn them to account, are alone enough to offer strong temptations to abuse; the more so that the actual performers are likely to be unduly prepossessed in favour of music which gives them, from a mechanical point of view, novel and amusing work, and to find more entertainment, for instance, in Meyerbeer than in Mozart. Mr. Prout, in his excellent little treatise on instrumentation, says that 'it is at least an open question whether, with all our modern fulness and richness, the science of instrumentation has made much real progress since the scores of *Figaro, Fidelio,* and *Les Deux Journées* were written.' But the opportunities, and I fear the taste, for finely-toned noise have none the less increased and may yet increase; and it is, and always will be, infinitely easier to use any amount of such noise than to write a single piece of noble tune. If, then, the majority of the concert-going public have no safeguard against imposture, if they habitually give such cursory attention to orchestral works as leaves them ignorant to what extent fine motives are present or absent, and thus put themselves out of court for demanding fine motives and refusing to be put off with fine noise, the composer is only too liable to give them what they will take; to forget, in his search for novelties of colouring, how shallow is its nature apart from distinct and beautiful form, and, in his delight at the kaleidoscopic effects which he commands, to be dazzled over the boundary, in Music so dangerously indefinite, between sense and nonsense.

# CHAPTER XIII.

## THE TWO WAYS OF HEARING MUSIC.

§ 1. The definite and indefinite ways of hearing Music: their relation to perception and non-perception of form.

It now becomes necessary to define and distinguish two ways of hearing and enjoying Music; which, though they shade into one another, and may each of them in various degrees be realised by a single individual in listening to a single composition, are for all that in their typical states radically different. They may be called the *definite* and the *indefinite* way. Music may be described as having a definite or indefinite character, for any particular person on any particular occasion, according as the individuality[1] of what is presented is or is not perceived; according as the person does or does not grasp something which can be recognised as itself and nothing else when the presentation is repeated, and can be reproduced in memory not as the mere knowledge of a past fact, but with some vital realisation of the actual experience. This definition at once recalls the distinctions already drawn between form and colour. It is indeed obviously natural that any matter presented to the higher senses should exhibit the definite æsthetic character just described, in proportion to the degree in which striking *form* is perceived in it. It is only another way of stating the same fact to say that the mind naturally assimilates and makes completely its own that on which it has brought its own activity to bear; and activity of mind, whether appearing as unconscious and semi-conscious comparison, contrast, and association, or in Music as a unique process of active co-ordination, demands an order of some kind in the matter on which it works. And just as we have seen form to be a primary and constant and colour a secondary and shifting quality of objects—for 'a dahlia is a dahlia whether it be yellow or crimson,' and *God save the Queen* is *God save the Queen* whether played on an organ or a Jew's-harp— so we

---

[1] Definiteness and indefiniteness of a certain kind may of course belong to mere *species* of sensation, under which head the formless taste of a strawberry or the formless tone of a bassoon are as definite and unmistakable as anything in the world. But the definiteness of *individuality* described in the text is confined to the domain of the higher senses; to the visible and audible phenomena which are peculiar in constituting not mere sorts of sensation, like strawberry-taste common to all strawberries and bassoon-tone common to all bassoon-passages, but an infinite number of separate and persistent groups of coherent sensations.

may say that form or relation of parts gives permanence to our own impressions of objects, and is the element which the mind makes its own and retains; while most people will find that colour (to which may be added the qualities of size and mass [1]) demands for its appreciation the actual presence of the object or scene, and is apt to become comparatively ineffective in subsequent reflection. Thus for one person whose inward eye can dwell with prolonged delight on a vanished sunset, a hundred will find pleasure in recalling a face or even a photograph or engraving. The rule, however, as we saw to some extent in the last chapter, applies very much less completely to the visible objects of Nature than to Music; partly because the refined enjoyment of visible colour, being so much a matter of harmony and gradation, often does demand a large amount of the mental elements of comparison and co-ordination, and reaps the benefit of these in memory; partly owing to the constant association, in the visible world, of the same familiar colours with the same familiar forms; but chiefly on the more radical grounds that visible colours are, as a pretty universal fact, easier to recall, and also that they are very often actually seen and enjoyed apart from distinct or noticeable form, which facilitates the habit of recalling them on their own account. Sound-colour, on the other hand, we have seen to be almost always presented in connection with form which at any rate claims attention *as* form, as having an individuality of its own which is foreign to many fortuitous and unordered contours of the outer world. And the mere musical colours are practically never recalled by themselves with independent enjoyment, the enjoyment of them, apart from the form they should clothe, being too purely sensuous to lend itself to any sort of continuous after-meditation; while a person whose lack of musical ear leads him habitually to hear them as mere agreeably-toned sounds, with no perception of the form they invest, is if anything specially incapable of reviving the sense of them. It is thus in the case of Music that the two modes of effect, as above defined, connect themselves most

---

[1] Size and mass in visible things are *primary* qualities, and are essentially involved in the impressiveness of any object in which they are noticeable features, so that a mountain or a pyramid would lose in proportion as these qualities were reduced: their effect, however, not being essentially connected with *form*, is very hard to reproduce strongly in memory. The natural representative of size and mass in Music might seem to be mass of sound, amount of sonorous clang filling the ear: but this, it should be noted, is a *secondary* quality of Music, and one which, though often greatly enhancing the splendour of presentation, can be reduced or abstracted without destruction to the essential value and significance of the forms. Loudness or mass of clang belongs, in fact, properly to the *colour-*region, excess of it overpowering the ear as disagreeably as excess of light dazzles the eye: and the nearer musical analogue to impressions of visible mass and size, the musical experiences which prompt words like *vast* and *stupendous,* lie far more in true musical magnificence, in some superb motive, however presented or imagined; but this, being in its very essence *form,* is most vividly reproducible in memory, unlike the vaguer impressions of glorious size in the visible world.

clearly and conveniently with perception and non-perception of form ; the *definite* character of Music involving the perception of individual melodic and harmonic combinations, the *indefinite* character involving merely the perception of successions of agreeably-toned and harmonious sound.

§ 2. Nature of the indefinite pleasure ;

This variety of *kind* in musical receptivity complicates the normal relations of comprehension to pleasure in a very curious way. A 'musical ear,' in the sense of an ear which distinctly grasps, recognises, and remembers music, so that any particular music becomes familiar to it after sufficient hearing, is a faculty so specially isolated and so easily tested that the degree in which it is possessed might have been expected to afford an exceptionally good criterion of the value of the art to any individual. As a matter of fact the criterion breaks down, chiefly indeed because quickness of ear is no guarantee for keen emotional susceptibility, but partly owing to the point now under discussion. While it is natural to consider as *unmusical* those persons in whom a 'musical ear' is lacking or is only imperfectly developed, and who therefore cannot at all reproduce or perhaps recognise melodies, such persons can often derive extreme pleasure of a vague kind from fine sound, more especially when it rushes through the ear in large masses. They will be apt to find their own meanings in the music, which merely shows that the sound has a stimulating or a soothing effect on their nerves, and acts as a congenial background for their subjective trains of thought and emotion. The organ in particular,

its connection with *timbre*,

with its great waves of sound and varieties of *timbre*, is a specially effective instrument in this respect ; a quality, by the way, which particularly adapts it to places and occasions where the main objects are not artistic but devotional or meditative. To a trained ear a rapid and loud fugue on the organ, if previously unknown, is apt to be ' full of sound and fury, signifying nothing,' and the same may often be said of elaborate polyphonic choruses : but to many persons who are capable of being strongly moved by Music in a vague and mysterious manner it is a matter of indifference what is being played or sung, so long as the volume of tone is full and the quality agreeable. Apart from the fulness of *timbre*, the most fundamental source of the indefinite effect is doubtless harmony. We saw in the

and with harmony and polyphony.

eleventh chapter how the richness of the separate chords, or single items of harmony, and the mere sense of change from one to another, may give satisfaction from moment to moment to ears whose tether is too short, or (as we may now add) which are too much overpowered by loud and intricate sound, to co-ordinate prolonged groups of notes into coherent motives and passages : so that to such ears the difference between a succession of harmonies and a succession of single notes is like the difference between waves and pegs to a man who wants easy and encompassing support. The dim sense of answering and interlacing parts, again, may be a large ingredient in this indefinite pleasure ; so that the contrapuntal compositions whose beauties few musicians would pretend to unravel or appreciate till after some little acquaintance, are often just those about which others who do not profess to be extremely musical will go into perfectly honest raptures at once.

That the pleasure arising from any series or combination of sounds which conveys no distinct musical meaning should be lower and less than that attainable through more definite apprehension, scarcely requires proof. First, there is the evidence of the majority of those who at all enjoy listening to Music, and who have experienced at different times both sorts of pleasure. Next, we have the right to identify the higher pleasure with the more specialised, that which is appreciated by the more developed and differentiated sense; and which of course belongs to the distinct exercise of the musical faculty, as opposed to the nearly universal nervous susceptibility to the effect of rich and powerful sound. Next, while the impression of mere beauty of sound-colour is exceptionally sensuous and passive, not admitting of any of the indirect æsthetic effects given (as we have seen) by the material of Architecture, nor of the associations of space and freedom which a painter's most formless hues may gain from the blue sky and the other coloured spaces of nature, the apprehension of musical motives, on the other hand, constitutes a specially active kind of self-realisation. And lastly, there is the point already sufficiently insisted on, the power of, in some measure at least, permanently possessing forms which have once become familiar, in contrast to the utter transience of all form-less sound-effects. At the same time, the indefinite pleasure is rarely or never a matter of *mere* sensuous impression, like the quite unintelligent enjoyment of a taste or smell. Even where the true melodic and harmonic forms are not in the least discerned, either through lack of musical ear or because the mass of sound really renders them undiscoverable, tangible frag-ments of them may appear, and there is at any rate the perception of change and movement, and constantly also of rhythm: so that the impression of mighty waves of measured sound is often something much more unique and positive than the general exaltation or the soothing and attuning of the organ-ism, such, for instance, as the subtle formless influences of a summer-evening or a dose of opium might produce. Under fortunate conditions the vaguer emotions induced by Music may rise to extraordinary power, as when some mighty polyphony, in its resistless blending of tumult and order, calls up deep indefinable associations of the mightier stream of lives and fates. Still whatever their value may be, such effects are obviously very indirect, quasi-accidental, and subjective; they are not the composer's message; they cannot be presented to the inward ear when the orchestra has vanished, and though combinable with perception of form they can never replace it.

The effect described is naturally exemplified most typically in those who have not a ' musical ear,' but is by no means confined to them. We saw in the last chapter how mere amount and sonorousness of clang often

§ 3. Various reasons why the indefinite effect must rank as lower than the definite;

though it is capable of arousing a great mass of emotion.

§ 4. The effect of Music is constantly indefinite even

to people who
have a per-
fectly good
musical ear,
though the
vaguer
pleasure is
often com-
paratively
small in their
case.
interpose distinct physical hindrance to the clear discernment of form : and apart from this, persons with plenty of ear may constantly fail to detect the points of an elaborate composition with which they are unfamiliar, or after a time their attention may flag ; so that either enforcedly or volun-tarily they resign themselves to the indefinite mode of affection, catching at any fragments they can, but for the most part letting the stream of sound flow by without seeking to individualise its parts.[1] The amateur mode of listening to a fugue is very commonly a mixture of the indefinite way with definite welcome of the returns of the opening 'subject.' But though lapses into this passive attitude are common enough to all but the exceptionally gifted, I fear that the power of deriving *pleasure* from it must be rather in the inverse ratio of the actual amount of the special faculty, and must recede as a more definite musical sense develops itself. An ear which has become accustomed to searching for coherent melodic and harmonic meanings cannot easily throw off this seeking attitude, or make itself sufficiently passive to derive satisfaction from beauty or mass of mere changing sound. Just as it will be soon offended by poverty and conventionality, however splendidly presented in the way of mass and colour, so it will be wearied rather than delighted by Music which it fails to penetrate and follow. And the result is often very literally that ignor-ance is bliss, and that the non-musical hearer enjoys what puzzles the ordinary amateur. The sense of bewilderment is indeed far more often a sign of *presence* than of *absence* of ear, and it would be well if this were

Few ears can
really at all
master intri-
cate music till
it has been
repeated
several times.
more widely understood. If the real difficulty of many musical composi-tions were more of an accepted fact, difficulty not in the sense that an average ear cannot comprehend them, but in the sense that an average ear cannot comprehend them at a glance, both sentiments and expressions of

---

[1] The gradations from the indefinite to the definite reception of Music are the same in kind for the least and the most skilled ears, though of course the immensely larger part of what is indefinite to the former is clear at once to the latter. The test of *reproduc-tion in memory* may seem to press unduly on quite unskilful ears ; but not that of *recog-nition* ; if any passage, be it only two bars long, be picked out as specially agreeable, the very act of preference implies that after a limited number of presentations the com-bination of notes will become familiar.

It must be noticed that *enjoyment* is neces-sary to the test of recognition. Music may be so utterly commonplace, or so utterly un-interesting to a particular hearer, that his mind retains no traces of it even though his actual perception of it at the moment may have been clear enough ; just as a face in a crowd may appear for an instant as an indi-vidual, not quite the same as any other that has ever met the eye, but would not be known again on another occasion. The analogy of faces may help in another way to illustrate musical recollection. The memory of some particular music is often even to a musician too dim and fragmentary for him to be able at all to get it right or piece it together in his head, and yet may haunt him persistently ; similarly a face which has been once seen may haunt the memory, while yet so dimly realised that no detailed descrip-tion of its features could be attempted. But in both cases the mental object is the dim image of what has been definite, and is it-self definite in the sense that the actual phenomenon will be instantly recognised if it recurs, and will stamp its image further on the mind, while a false substitute would be certain of detection.

admiration would gain greatly in intelligence and sincerity. I do not suppose that many of Bülow's London admirers had any acquaintance to speak of with Beethoven's great B flat sonata: and I used to wonder, if, instead of repeating the last movement, he had played something else equally long, fast, and elaborate, what proportion of the audience would have been the wiser. It is of course hard to certify such points by direct experiment: but there are persons to whom enthusiasm about most difficult works seems to come with such enviable facility, that it is impossible not to wish occasionally to test it, by advertising a repetition and having other music of the same external character substituted.

In respect of indefinite æsthetic effects, it is impossible to help comparing Music with Architecture. Such a comparison would be suggested by the mere identity of place and occasion in which the service of religion associates the two arts, much at any rate of their value in that relation being indisputably due to the more general sort of impressiveness which does not concentrate or absorb the worshipper's attention. From several points of view these two presentative arts are naturally the ones in which indefinite and subjective effects might be expected to assume prominence. In the arts of representation, persons who in various degrees lack keenness of perception have still the definite stimulus and interest of recognition, and their ideas are directed along the various lines of thought which the subject-matter may open up; but in the presence of abstract form and colour, those who either habitually or temporarily are not actively percipient have, from the nature of the case, no such special guide to their thoughts, and may follow at will any fancies or meditations in harmony with the exalting or calming influence of the impressions which meet the senses. Again, Music and Architecture are the only two arts which are able constantly to present any vast and overpowering *mass* of impression to the senses; colossal pictures and statues being rare exceptions; and mere mass and amount of impression is a quality specially favourable to the suffusive feeling of awe and the vaguer imaginative stirrings. And with the same feature of mere extent and quantity is connected the power to encompass and affect large numbers at the same time, by which again these two arts are peculiarly adapted to solemn ceremonials.

§ 5. Comparison of Architecture to Music in respect of indefinite effects.

If, however, the two arts be compared as to the place their less definite effects can be held to occupy in the sum of their value, the comparison at once becomes a contrast, and Architecture is left in a quite unique position: for the indeterminate and subjective order of impression which is quasi-accidental in the case of Music, and arises there greatly from a simple failure to penetrate and grasp the forms, is connected with some of the essential features of buildings, and the power to produce it must be esteemed one of their most constant and substantive functions. Music is *par excel-*

*lence* the art whose occasions are brief and definite, and its appeal to the hearing ear arresting and peremptory : Architecture is as emphatically the encompassing art permanently linked with human occupations, and to which therefore we should especially look for such emotional conditions as will mingle with and colour varied streams of thought and feeling.   These streams are often, indeed, less fortuitous and subjective than those which the unperceptive hearing of Music sets in motion : nor, in the case of Architecture, does the less determinate quality of impression fall altogether under the definition given at the beginning of this chapter, since it does not necessarily imply inability to recognise or recall what has been presented.   Often it is rather the result of extreme familiarity ; buildings being from their very nature so habitually seen and used that their actual contours, for a large proportion of the time that they are in the field of vision, are not specially noticed, while yet they may pervade the life they shelter with a subtle sense of ordered grandeur or of quiet and abiding harmony.   But I am here not referring to effects so remote as this from actual observation of the work, like the dimly felt influence of a cathedral on an intent worshipper ; but rather to experiences in which the eye is truly receptive and awake to any architectural beauty it may find surrounding it, like an ear truly listening to Music ; and it is in these circumstances, in what may be called its normal impressions, that Architecture presents the indeterminate sort of effect with such exceptional prominence.

The grounds of the difference in the case of Architecture.

The grounds on which this character rests are not hard to trace. We have already sufficiently remarked the less striking individuality and variety of abstract visual forms and proportions as compared with those of Music : but while in Music, when once the element of individual form ceases to be definitely and engrossingly attended to, nothing is left to the account of less definite impression than so much moving and coloured sound, Architecture, as we have seen, is specially rich in other elements of effect.   Not that the eye in ranging over a building can ever fail to perceive form, or get into the mazed condition which we have noticed as possible to the ear ; but though the other elements must thus appear under the dominance of form, they are really what charge the whole with its emotional character.   The mass of matter and number of features capable of striking the spectator simultaneously, yet allowing the eye to grasp at the same time a multitude of detail, or to trace it at leisure with the perpetual background of the larger magnificence, preciousness of material, the signs of human labour, the look of strength, the look of age, the sympathetic gloom and mystery in the broad massings of shadow, all these are things which fit a great building rather to be an environment for the musings and aspirations of individuals or for social or religious gatherings than an immediate and overmastering object of attention. They are conditions eminently fitted to encourage the widely diffused associations proper to a monumental art, and to give it a character which, while often lacking strong artistic individuality, may be ethically and socially most powerfully effective. For beautiful buildings are not like other works of art, burning messages from soul to soul, too pregnant and often too rapid to allow thought of other things: rather their office is to lend grace and dignity to the outer uses of life while harmonising with its varied inner phases, and to stimulate every strain of worthy emotion by enabling men to breathe at times an atmosphere that belongs to other generations, charged with the memories that turn to hopes or the hopes that shall turn to memories.

We need not extend further our notice of the indefinite way of hearing music. Though its existence, its commonness, and the sort of value attaching to it, are extremely important points, there is from its very nature little to say about it. In the following chapters it will be understood that I am dealing entirely with the definite way, the mode of hearing which follows and distinguishes the motives as they pass.

§ 6. There is naturally little to say about the indefinite way.

# CHAPTER XIV.

## MUSIC AS IMPRESSIVE AND MUSIC AS EXPRESSIVE.

§ 1. The two aspects of impression and expression.

WE now pass on to quite a new branch of our enquiry. So far we have been considering Music almost entirely as a means of *im*pression, as a presentation of impressive (or, as too often happens, unimpressive) phenomena. We have now to distinguish this aspect of it from another, its aspect as a means of *ex*pression, of creating in us a consciousness of images, or of ideas, or of feelings, which are known to us in regions outside Music, and which therefore Music, so far as it summons them up within us, may be fairly said to *express*. The chief difficulty in getting a clear view of this part of the subject lies in the vagueness and looseness of thought which is apt to run in the track of general and abstract terms: and this being so, I can only make my argument clear by insisting on the clear separation of the sets of conceptions which come under the heads of *im*pression and *ex*pression respectively, or at any rate may be justifiably so classified after due definition.

The distinction is made very simple by considering that expression involves *two* things, one of which is expressed by the other. The expression may take the form of imitation, as when an appearance or a movement of anything is purposely suggested by some aspect or movement given to something else. Or the thing expressed may be an idea, as when a fine idea is expressed by a metaphor; or a feeling, as when suffering is expressed by tears; or a quality, as when pride is expressed by a person's face or demeanour. As regards expression of qualities, some preliminary explanation is

Explanation as regards expression of qualities.

necessary. When a quality is so permanent and general and familiar an attribute of anything that our idea of the thing comprises the quality, the latter does not seem separable enough for us to conceive of it as expressed; and thus we should not naturally say that a tree expressed greenness, or a dark night darkness, or a church-steeple height. In a word, a thing is expressive of *occasional* attributes, not of the essential attributes of its class. There is a doubtful region where such phrases might be used even of very general qualities with reference to some special idea in the speaker's mind: thus a Platonist might say that the face of nature expressed beauty, conceiving of beauty as a single principle, which is one thing; capable of manifesting itself in this or that form, which is another thing : but we should not, in an ordinary way, say that a flower expresses beauty, or a lion strength, but that the flower *is* beautiful and the lion strong. So with respect to musical forms or motions ; they are so familiarly conceived as aiming at being beautiful and vigorous, such qualities are so identified with our idea of their function, that we do not naturally think of them as *expressing* beauty and vigour. So with qualities identified with the most general effects of impressive sound on the organism ; we do not conceive of any sounds, musical or non-musical, as expressing soothingness or excitingness. But we do not quarrel with the description of music as having a romantic or passionate or sentimental expression, even though the analogy of the effect to modes of feeling known outside Music may be of the dimmest and most intangible kind ; and when some more special and distinctive quality appears, such as agitation or melancholy, when a particular feeling in ourselves is identified with a particular character in a particular bit of music, then we say without hesitation that such a particular bit *expresses* the quality or feeling.[1]

It is true that there is a very important method of using words like *expressive* in relation to Music, in the absence of particular describable qualities or particular suggestions of any sort ; a usage which has been more than once adopted in this book, and which it seems to me impossible to forego. Thus we often call music which stirs us more *expressive* than music which does not ; and we call great music *significant*, or talk of its *import*, in contrast to poor music, which seems meaningless and insignificant ; without being able, or dreaming we are able, to connect these general terms with anything *expressed* or *signified*. This usage was explained, at the end of the sixth chapter, as due to the inevitable association of music with utterance, and of utterance with something external to itself which is to be expressed,[2] as our ideas are external to the sounds in

§ 2. Another manner of using words like expression and significance,

---

[1] The necessary connection of quality and feeling should be noted : for there being no personality in music, the qualities it can be in itself expressive of must be identified with some affection of ourselves. Thus we should not say that quick or slow music expressed such impersonal qualities as speed or slowness, but possibly hilarity or solemnity. Music may present even decided qualities which are not suggestive of any special and occasional mode of feeling in ourselves. Thus a melody may be *simple*, but as it does not make us feel simple, and as we have no definite mode of feeling identified with the contemplation of so general a quality, we should not naturally say that it *expressed* simplicity ; unless there were some simplicity external to it, in some words or person associated with it. The feeling in ourselves need not necessarily be the *same* as the quality attributed to the music : the special feeling corresponding to melancholy music is melancholy, but the special feeling corresponding to capricious or humorous music is not capriciousness or humorousness, but surprise or amusement : clearly, however, this mode of feeling is sufficiently identified with the contemplation of the quality.

[2] Quite apart from the notion of such a something to be expressed, our habitual projection either of the composer's or of the performer's or of some imaginary personality behind the music we hear may naturally lead to such phrases as that some one expresses himself or expresses his personality or expresses his soul in the music ; in the

which we utter them. But even those who take the transcendental view that something *is* so expressed or signified by all beautiful music—whether the something be the 'Will of the World,' as Schopenhauer taught, or any other supposed fundamental reality to which our present conceptions are inadequate—may still perfectly well accept the following proposition : that there is a difference between music which is expressive in the sense of definitely suggesting or inspiring images, ideas, qualities, or feelings belonging to the region of the *known* outside music, and music which is *not* so expressive, and in reference to which terms of expression and significance, however intuitive and habitual, could only be logically pressed by taking them in a quite peculiar sense, and postulating an *unknown* something behind phenomena, which the phenomena are held to reveal or signify, or, according to Schopenhauer, to ' objectify.'

*which need lead to no confusion.*

*§ 3. Music cannot be truly expressive without being impressive ;*

The distinction as thus stated does not altogether coincide with that conveyed by the words *expressive* and *impressive* ; since there is nothing to prevent music which is *ex*pressive in the former and tangible sense from being also *im*pressive by its beauty. As the true distinction involved in the words is between two different *aspects* of Music, both of these may naturally be presented by the same specimen ; and indeed we shall find that no music is really expressive in any valuable way which does not also impress us as having the essential character of musical beauty ; an unpleasing tune may be lugubrious but not melancholy. But the great point, which is often strangely ignored and for the sake of which the distinction has been thus pedantically emphasised, is that *ex*pressiveness of the literal and tangible sort is either *absent or only slightly present* [1] in an immense amount of *im*pressive music ; that to suggest describable images, qualities, or feelings, known in connection with other experiences, however frequent a characteristic of Music, makes up no inseparable or essential part of its function ; and that this is not a matter of opinion, or of theory as to what should be, but of definite everyday fact.

*but a great deal of impressive music is not definably expressive.*

The immense importance of this truth, and of its relation to the facts of expression, will further appear when expression has been separately considered ; but this independent impressiveness is so entirely at the foundation

*The foundation of Music's independent impressiveness.*

same sense, *e.g.*, as a theist may hold the Creator to express himself in the beauties of Nature : such a use need not at all confuse the distinction in the text. The word expression, again, in such a general phrase as 'playing with expression' does not mean the signification of any thought or feeling external to the music, but merely the making the utmost, the literal squeezing out, of all the beauty which is there *in* the music.

[1] It is hard to word this so as to obviate all possible objections. In modern music it may perhaps be the case, more often than not, that some one out of the category of descriptive adjectives may seem at any rate more appropriate than most others : words like energetic, peaceful, solemn, and so on, may be made to cover an immense amount of ground. But the qualities may be said to be slightly expressed if they excite no special remark ; if one's impression, if it runs at all into words, is far more vividly 'how beautiful,' or ' how indescribable, how utterly a musical experience,' than 'how extraordinarily solemn,' or ' how exceptionally peaceful.'

of the argument that it will be best to start by briefly recalling its root and groundwork. We found these, it will be remembered, in the fusion and sublimation of those strongest elementary passions and emotions which, according to Mr. Darwin's view, were associated with the primeval exercise of the musical faculty, the primeval habit of following tones and rhythm with pleasure; and in the light of generally admitted principles of hereditary association, we found no extraordinary difficulty in connecting what are now some of the most profound stirrings of our emotional nature with those crude elements which were yet the most profound emotional stirrings possible to our progenitors. In this connection it is well worth noting that at every stage which comes under our observation, Music seems capable of stirring up the strongest excitement that a being who musically typifies that stage can experience. This enjoyment to the utmost of the best that can be got is exemplified equally in the case of singing-birds, and of the gibbon, moved with rapture at his own performance of the chromatic scale, and of the savage repeating over for hours his few monotonous strains and maddened by the rhythmic beat of the drum, and of the ancient Greek spellbound by performances for the like of which we should probably tell a street-performer to pass on, and of a circle of Arabs sobbing and laughing by turns in ecstasies of passion at the sound of their native melodies, and of the English child to whom some simple tune of Mozart's reveals the unguessed springs of musical feeling, or of the adult in his loftiest communings with the most inspired utterances of Beethoven.[1] And it is all-important to observe that these emotional experiences are essentially connected, throughout the whole long course of development, with the distinctly *melodic* principle, with the presentation of a succession of single sound-units; such series being exemplified in the percussive drummings of the spider and in the song of the gibbon, as well as in the distinguishable lines of tune indispensable to the emotional character of modern composition. So that our general theory entirely bears out the view which in the fifth chapter was deduced from simple musical experience, that the ground for the essential effects of the art must be sought, not in any considerations connected with large or elaborate structure, or with rich complexity of parts, or with splendid masses of tone, but in the facts of mere note-after-note melodic motion.

*The strength of musical emotions at very different stages of development;*

*and always in connection with the melodic principle.*

---

[1] What is said here may be connected with what was said in the tenth chapter as to the rapid obsolescence of music. The newer and apparently more original kinds of Ideal Motion often make older music seem tame and trite. But it would certainly be most unfair to think of comparing, as regards amount of enjoyment, our own musical experiences with those of a person in the middle of the last century, by comparing the pleasure *we* derive from Beethoven with that which *we* derive from, *e.g*, the earlier works of Haydn. Evidence entirely confirms what *à priori* we might have guessed, that that earlier music stirred its hearers to the very depths, in a manner which we can only realise by recalling some of the strains which have had a similar effect on ourselves in childhood.

Striking cor-
respondence of
the theory
with the facts
oi musical
emotion.

And while the theory, in its invocation of the strongest of all primitive passions, as germs for the marvellously sublimated emotions of developed Music, seems not only adequate but unique in its adequacy to account generally for the power of those emotions, it further connects itself in the most remarkable manner with that more special peculiarity of independent impressiveness which is now under review; with the fact which attentive examination of musical experience more and more brings home to us, that Music is perpetually felt as strongly emotional while defying all attempts to analyse the experience or to define it even in the most general way in terms of definite emotions. If we press close, so to speak, and try to force our feelings into declaring themselves in definite terms, a score of them may seem pent up and mingled together and shooting across each other—triumph and tenderness, surprise and certainty, yearning and fulfilment; but all the while the essential magic seems to lie at an infinite distance behind them all, and the presentation to be not a subjective jumble but a perfectly distinct object, productive (in a thousand minds it may be at once) of a perfectly distinct though unique and undefinable affection. This is precisely what is explained, if we trace the strong undefinable affection to a gradual fusion and transfiguration of such overmastering and pervading passions as the ardours and desires of primitive loves; and it is in reference to these passions of all others, both through their own possessing nature and from the extreme antiquity which they permit us to assign to their associative influence, that a theory of fusion and transfiguration in connection with a special range of phenomena seems possible and plausible. The problem is indeed a staggering one, by what alchemy abstract forms of sound, however unique and definite and however enhanced in effect by the watching of their evolution moment by moment, are capable of transformation into phenomena charged with feeling, and yet in whose most characteristic impressiveness separate feelings seem as fused and lost as the colours in a ray of white light: but at any rate the suggested theory of association is less oppressive to the speculative mind than the everyday facts of musical experience would be in the absence of such a far-reaching explanation of them.

§ 4. The
activity of the
musical
faculty,

The more serious difficulty, we found, came later. When we merely ask why are melodic forms emotionally impressive, and why are they emotionally impressive after a fashion which defies analysis or description, the association-theory comes to our assistance. But the further question, why one melodic form is felt as emotionally impressive and another not, reveals in a moment how much any such general theory leaves unaccounted for ; and our further examination of melodic forms showed that the faculty of discernment, the faculty in which the cognisance of them is wholly vested, is one whose nature and action have to be accepted as unique and ultimate facts, and whose judgments are absolute, unreasoning, and unquestionable.[1]  It is not necessary to repeat what has been said in the preceding chapters as to this extraordinary and independent faculty of co-ordinating a series of time- and pitch-relations into forms or notions, and of deriving various degrees of satisfaction or dissatisfaction from the proportions so progressively contemplated; nor as to the somewhat difficult but still warrantable supposition that the *satisfactory* action of the faculty, the concentration of it on such proportions as give it adequate scope and exercise, is the only mode whereby the flood-gates of emotion from the associational region are opened, and the perception of the form transfused and transfigured; the transfusion *ipso facto* preventing our knowing what the mere perception, the simple musical impression as it might be if the informing associational elements were non-existent, would in itself amount to.

But we now come to the consideration of certain points in musical forms and in the exercise of the musical faculty which are new; these being specially connected with Music in its *expressive* aspect.  As long as Music is regarded only as a means of *impression*, as productive of a sort of emotion which, however definite and crude may have been its unfused and undeveloped germs, has been for ages so differentiated as to convey no suggestion of its origin, and is unknown outside the region of musical phenomena—as long as the forms, however various and individual to the musical sense, still present a musical character undistinguished and unpervaded by any particular definable feeling of joy, gloom, triumph, pathos, &c.—no examination of their structure from outside (as we abundantly saw in the seventh and following chapters) throws the slightest light on that musical character and its varieties: no rules can be framed which will not be so general as to include the bad as well as the good. The exercise of the musical faculty on such and such a form is found pleasurable and emotional, its exercise on such and such another is found neutral, or unsatisfactory and irritating; and that is all: a mode of perception which is unique defies illustration, and on this ground the only answer to the questions which present themselves is the showing why they are unanswerable.  But when we come to the *expressive* aspect of Music, to the definite suggestion or portrayal of certain special and describable things known outside Music, whether images of objects or ideas or qualities or feelings, we should naturally expect to be able to trace in some degree the connection of any special suggestion or shade of character with some special point or points in the musical form and the process by which we follow it: and we have now to examine the various modes in which such connections may present themselves.  None of them, it will

*as connected with differences of musical expression.*

---

[1] Absolute and unquestionable, not of course as final or competent judgments of merit or anything else, but in reference to the power of a particular bit of music to affect a particular individual at a particular time.

now be evident, can be held accountable for any musical *beauty* which may be present : a tune is no more constituted beautiful by an expression, *e.g.*, of mournfulness or of capriciousness than a face is. The impressiveness which we call beauty resides in the unique musical experience whose nature and history have just been summarised : but in proportion as the beauty assumes a special and definable character or aspect, it does so in virtue of features in the musical form which are also special and definable.

§ 5. The several ways by which definite expression may be produced.

It will be convenient to consider first the expression of qualities and feelings ; the suggestion by music of objects and ideas being of a much more external and accidental kind. In our ordinary experience the natural mode in which qualities and feelings are expressed otherwise than by speech [1] is of course physical movement of some kind ; thus human beings express confidence and good spirits by rapid and decisive movements, solemnity by measured movements, agitation by spasmodic movements, and so on. Now the Ideal Motion of Music gives us an aspect of physical movement ready made ; the aspect, namely, of pace and rhythm ; which can be presented without any sound at all by movements in space, and the correspondence of which with movements in space we perpetually exemplify in our own persons, as we follow and in any way keep time with Music. Moreover the Ideal Motion regarded in its completeness, without such particular reference to the rhythmic element, will be found to present certain faint affinities to external movement and gesture. But while it is naturally in motion that we should look for the signs of definite emotional states, or, as we commonly say, the *expression* of such states, in Music there are three other features connected with expression, two of which belong especially to the tone- or pitch-element apart from peculiarities of motion ; the use, namely, of the major or the minor ' mode,' and of occasional noticeable harmonies ; the other being *timbre* or sound-colour. And we may take these first, as there is less to be said about them.[2]

---

[1] The relation of Music to Speech will be discussed in succeeding chapters, with results which will supplement without otherwise affecting the arguments in the present chapter. The emotional elements which music may gain by association with definite words and scenes will also be subsequently treated of ; and certain extensions of the senses in which Music can be considered expressive will present themselves in connection with Song and Opera.

[2] Particular *keys* are sometimes credited with definable emotional powers. That certain faint differences exist between them on certain instruments is undeniable, though it is a difference which only exceptional ears

detect. The relations between the notes of every key being identical, every series of relations presenting every sort of describable or indescribable character will of course be accepted by the ear in any key, or if it is a series which modulates through a set of several keys, in any set of similarly related keys. But as it must have a highest and a lowest note, it will be important, especially in writing for a particular instrument, to choose such a key that these notes shall not be inconvenient or impossible ; and also the mechanical difficulties of an instrument may make certain keys preferable for certain passages. Subject to correction from considerations of this sort, the composer probably

The expression which can truly be attributed to mere *timbre* amounts to much less than is generally supposed. When we consider the cases commonly adduced, we shall find that it is the pace or the manner of beginning the note, or something else beyond the mere colour-quality, which gives the sound its peculiar character. For instance, when we speak of the plaintive sounds of a violin, we are thinking of slow, long- First, *timbre* or quality of musical sound.

generally chooses the key in which the germ of his work first flashes across his mind's eye; and when the music has once been seen and known, written in a certain key, the very look of it becomes so associated with itself that the idea of changing the key may produce a certain shock. But the cases are few indeed where, had the music been first presented to any one's ears in a key differing by a semitone from that in which it actually stands, he would have perceived the slightest necessity for alteration; and as a matter of fact, when a bit of music is thought over, or hummed, or whistled, unless by a person of exceptionally gifted ear, it is naturally far oftener than not in some different key to that in which it has been written and heard. Even the difference most commonly alleged, between C major as bright and strong and D flat as soft and veiled, comes to almost absolutely nothing when a bright piece is played in D flat or a dreamy one in C. The view of Helmholtz, which seems unassailable, is that the differences, so far as they exist, result from features of certain instruments; *e.g.* that on the piano the method of striking the short black keys produces a somewhat different quality of tone, and on bowed instruments the bright strong notes of the open strings will distinguish the keys in which those notes are prominent: and that thus this alleged character of keys differs on different instruments. He observes that on the organ and with singing voices the differences are not discernible, and even on the piano (it may be added) they would hardly be discernible except in chords.

That a variety of emotional characters can be definitely attributed to the various keys is a notion so glaringly absurd that I would not even mention it, were it not that it is very commonly held; that I find it asserted and exemplified in the gravest manner in a popular manual by a well-known musician; and that such doctrines are really harmful by making humble and genuine lovers of Music believe that there are regions of musical feeling absolutely beyond their powers of conception. What I shall quote may also

serve as a sample to indicate that, as regards the whole matter of this and the following chapters, I am not fighting the air, but that the exactly opposite views to mine are what are practically in possession of the field. In the manual referred to, the following statements occur:

'*C major* expresses feeling in a pure, certain, and decisive manner. It is furthermore expressive of innocence, of a powerful resolve, of manly earnestness, and deep religious feeling.

'*G major*, that favourite key of youth, expresses sincerity of faith, quiet love, calm meditation, simple grace, pastoral life, and a certain humour and brightness.

'*G minor* expresses sometimes sadness, sometimes, on the other hand, quiet and sedate joy—a gentle grace with a slight touch of dreamy melancholy—and occasionally it rises to a romantic elevation. It effectively portrays the sentimental,' &c. (Another author, quoted by Schumann, found in G minor discontent, discomfort, worrying anxiety about an unsuccessful plan, illtempered gnawing at the bit. 'Now compare this idea,' says Schumann, 'with Mozart's Symphony in G minor, that floating Grecian Grace.' He quotes from the same writer that E minor is a girl dressed in white with a rose-coloured breastknot.)

'*A major*, full of confidence and hope, radiant with love, and redolent of simple genuine cheerfulness, excels all the other keys in pourtraying sincerity of feeling.

'*A minor* is expressive of tender, womanly feeling; it is at the same time most effective for exhibiting the quiet melancholy sentiment of Northern nations, and, curiously enough, lends itself very readily to the description of *Oriental* character, as shown in Boleros and Mauresque serenades. But A minor also expresses sentiments of devotion mingled with pious resignation.

'*B major*, a key but seldom used, expresses in fortissimo boldness and pride; in pianissimo, purity and the most perfect clearness.

'*B minor*, that very melancholy key, tells of a quiet expectation and patient hope. It drawn-out notes, taken very gently without percussion or anything to give them a strongly-marked catch at the beginning. Nor does it occur to us to call sound of the same quality plaintive when, instead of being divided into these long gentle notes, it is produced continuously, nor when it is divided into short notes begun with more sharpness and suddenness. Association with particular sorts of Music and particular occasions may produce a somewhat erroneous impression in this respect. Many people perhaps vaguely regard the organ, which has an immense variety of *timbre*, as an essentially solemn instrument, just as a Greek who had commonly heard the flute in connection with pathetic and effeminate melody would identify its natural tone with that character : but both the organ and the flute will of course lend their colours to all sorts of music. Mr. Prout, in his excellent primer on instrumentation, justly remarks that the oboe, which has a very peculiar *timbre*, ' is equally useful for the expression of melancholy, tenderness, and gaiety ; ' and he might have added for the colouring of music which does *not* particularly present any of these characters. The horn is described as having a dreamy or melancholy character ; but is eminently suitable for lively and hunting strains. The bassoon, which is unrivalled for humorous and grotesque effects, was described by Piccini[1] as sad and melancholy ; and, as Berlioz remarks, when Meyerbeer

has often been observed that nervous persons will sooner be affected by that key than by any other.

' *F sharp major* sounds brilliant and exceedingly clear ; as *G flat major* it expresses softness coupled with richness.

' *F sharp minor*, that dark, mysterious, and spectral key, is at the same time full of passion.

' *A flat major* is full of feeling, and replete with a dreamy expression.

' *F major* is at once full of peace and joy, but also expresses effectively a light, passing regret : a mournful, but not a deeply sorrowful feeling. It is, moreover, available for the expression of religious sentiment.

' *F minor*, a harrowing key, is especially full of melancholy, at times rising into passion,' &c. &c.

These are but extracts, and a good deal of the humour is lost by selection. For the ' characters ' of several of his keys the author gives a list of examples ; the choice of which, inasmuch as every possible character might be exemplified from compositions in every single key, cannot have been very difficult. It is something like proving that Monday is a day ' especially full of melancholy,' on the ground that some individual lost a relative on it, or that the characteristic of Thursday

is ' confidence and hope,' on the ground that on it an individual came in for a fortune. Subject to the above-mentioned qualifications, anything can happen in any key, as anything can happen on any day, or as any motion can take place in any part of space. With a dim perception of this the author explains it, and innocently confutes his whole theory by saying that ' one composer detects in a certain key qualities which have remained entirely hidden from another ; ' so that one finds cheerfulness and another mournfulness in the same key ; which is like explaining the difference between a joyful and a sombre picture by saying that one painter detects in his canvas qualities which have remained hidden from the other. The author tells us that the German professor on whose work his own is founded, evolved his theory ' *from philosophical principles* ; ' some further principles might perhaps have been obtained from the work of the Chinese philosopher who traced the five tones of the old Chinese scale to the five elements, water, fire, wood, metal, and earth.

[1] Piccini's views on instruments represent the sort of laxity which is still very common. Thus he considered that ' the oboe has an expression which does not belong to the clarinet ; and it, in its turn, differs totally

wanted ' a pale, cold, cadaverous sound ' for the resurrection of the nuns, he obtained it from this instrument. There are, however, less malleable instruments with the *timbre* of which a particular emotional character does seem more identified. It is something in the piercing and peculiar tone of bagpipes, over and above association, which produces the stirring and martial effect attributed to them in their native country : and among re-cognised orchestral instruments, the sounds of the trumpet are too brilliant and sudden not to occur more frequently and prominently in joyous and triumphant strains, than in a peaceful or pathetic style of music. But even here, if we consider a sufficient number of instances, we shall find the only rule that can be laid down is too general to allow us very closely to associate even a *timbre* as marked as that of trumpets with definable expression : the most we can say is that they belong rather to the strong and exciting than to the smooth and quiet passages. Trumpet-sounds perpetually occur with splendid effect in most various motions ; often in places where no particular emotional tinge of triumph or joy is produced, and where brilliant and forcible colour seems entirely appropriate to the musical passage without thereby doing more than make it musically more arresting and exciting.

*Mutatis mutandis,* similar remarks would apply to other instruments ; and also to the effects of marked *fortes* and *pianos*, which suit all sorts of musical motions, without its being possible to class them as belonging to, much less as constituting, separate and definable emotional characters. *Fortissimo* passages may be sombre as well as gay ; and *pianissimo* is often as appropriate to passages full of passion, hurry, and excitement as to the gentlest lullaby.

The major mode demands no special notice. The expression of con-fidence usually attributed to it really belongs to the cases where it is contrasted with the minor. Major music is not perceived as confident in virtue of its ' mode '· alone, or clearly more than half the music we possess would have to be considered definitely expressive of this character. Music in a major key may be profoundly mournful ; and it would often be impossible for any description to touch the musically felt difference between such music and mournful minor music. The minor mode has a somewhat more constant range of effect. The main fact, the impression of melancholy and want of confidence conveyed by the characteristic notes of the minor scale, whether used melodically or harmonically, was sufficiently dwelt on in the chapter on Harmony. The character of the minor mode, as com-

*Secondly, major and minor 'mode.'*

from the flute. The horns change their cha-racter according to the key in which they are employed,' and so on. Here not only does the unfortunate word *expression* tend unwarrantably to identify difference of musical *timbre* with power to suggest different states of extra-musical feeling, but not a word is said of the forms or motions presented by the various instruments ; so that colour is represented as usurping the *whole* sway of the expressive element.

pared with the major, must rest primarily on the melodic and harmonic character of those particular notes : but it is very possible that the effect of trouble or mystery is aided by the general want of certainty in the harmonisation of the mode, as pointed out by Helmholtz. But in reality the extent to which we can identify the use of the minor mode with definable emotional experience is but slight. Out of a hundred minor bits of music, only a few may be at all distinctly melancholy or elegiac. Features of pace and rhythm may be connected in some with an agitated, in others a majestic expression ; some may be marked by intensity, others by *insouciance*, others by caprice ; none of which characteristics have any special connection with the minor mode. Many, again, may wholly lack extra-musical character : or if even among wide and marked differences of musical individuality a certain tinge of trouble, pathos, or complaint may be traced (as compared, for instance, with the effect of similar motions in the major), such a tinge is too intangible and general to be easily thought of as definable expression. It is just in such a case that the error would be made which we shall have to notice later as of very common occurrence ; the error of supposing that *because* we perceive a great variety of musical forms, of forms which in their musical aspect are entirely distinct from one another and individually impressive, and *because* a few of them correspond with or express some mode of emotional experience known outside music, *therefore* the others must express shades and varieties of such extra-musical experience.

**Thirdly, particular harmonic features.** The definable expression given sometimes by a single harmonic feature (apart from major or minor effects) is chiefly connected with the use of discords. The effects of discords and resolutions, as of harmony in general,[1] are generally, of course, bits of purely musical satisfaction, occurring in their proper places as elements of all varieties of form, and in music of all shades and no shades of definable character. But a particular expression may be occasionally traced to discords in marked positions. Thus in Schumann's *Imploring Child*, beginning thus—

&c.

---

[1] Harmony is so often called the great 'means of musical expression' (with perfect truth in the wider sense, that it enormously intensifies and varies musical effects, making them go further into us, so to speak, and tell us more of those unfathomable things which Music alone reveals), that we should the more carefully note the limits of its expressiveness in the more precise sense here used, of its power to bring musical emotions into the definable zone.

the special accent of trouble is given by the unusual start on the ninth;
it is increased by the flattening into the minor note, B flat, as was noticed
in the chapter on Harmony. Another simple instance of expression
conveyed by a simple chord may be found in the use of a diminished
seventh in the bar which immediately precedes the cadence of *Auld
Robin Gray*, thus—

As this is the only place where the melody goes above C, the ascent to the
F would alone produce an expression of strain and yearning, to which the
troubled chord gives a strong additional shade. Such effects, however,
easily get an exaggerated air; and, in the present case, the unstable,
unsatisfied sound of the chord of the dominant seventh without the dominant, thus—

is all that is really wanted, and is on the whole preferable. A beautiful
example of distinct expression, from a single harmonic feature, occurs in
Schubert's song, *Die böse Farbe*—

the feature being one already noticed, on p. 281, as one of the most distinctive in music. In its present position, on the last syllable of the line, ‘Ich möchte die grünen Gräser all’ weinen ganz todten-bleich,’ it has a most passionate accent of sudden wailing.

It is clearly impossible, however, to lay down rules assigning such and such harmonies to such and such emotional effects, as the same actual harmonic features, in connection with different forms, may intensify quite different sorts of expressiveness. Even when the harmony seems not so much to intensify as actually to produce an effect, impossible without it, it must still be in virtue of some relation to the general musical motion into which it enters. Thus I described the E flat chord in *Voyez sur cette roche*, quoted on p. 280, as suggestive of alarm and warning; but that character results purely from the sort of contrast it produces occurring in the midst of a naïve and debonair melody. In the crash of the finale to an overture the same harmonic change, as we saw, though it may be impressive, has no assignable expression.

§ 6. Expression produced by characters of motion. First, by pace. — When we come to considerations of *motion*, the ground is much clearer. First as regards *pace*: the expressive character of anything noticeably fast or slow is evident; for pace, to be expressive, must deviate noticeably one way or the other from some normal standard. If we see a man running at the rate of nine miles an hour, we consider his movement expresses eagerness or sportiveness; if we see him walking at the rate of one mile an hour, we consider his movement expresses solemnity or depression; but if we see him walking at four miles an hour, it does not strike us that his pace expresses moderation. Similar remarks apply in great measure to Music. It is impossible, however, to lay down any very precise standard of moderation for musical pace; partly because there are no physical conditions such as correspond to three or four miles an hour in walking; partly because the outline of a slow or moderate *tempo* may comprise passages formed of a number of short quick notes, which may produce the most energetic effect. Pace, moreover, in musical as in physical motion, is far too wide and general a feature to mark the character with any certainty: but we may at any rate safely say that a very slow movement is often solemn, and never gay or agitated, and that a very quick movement is often gay or agitated, and never solemn ; and that unwarranted liberties with pace are as destructive of the definable character, if such exist, as of the essential musical beauty; witness Meyerbeer's treatment of *Ein' feste Burg* in the overture to the *Huguenots.* Positive moderation and calmness may seem more distinctly expressible by Music than by degrees of physical motion which are too habitual and unnoticed to be thought of as expressive. In Music, however, the quality of calmness is connected rather with evenness of flow, with the absence of strongly marked groups and of wide variety in the time-values of notes, than with mere moderation of *tempo*: nor is the connection by any means constant, inasmuch as we have already found, and shall find again, that extreme musical passion is compatible with an even and moderate rhythmic flow. And even in normal cases, when a musical motion is interesting us by its beauty, the expression by it of anything so neutral as calmness, is hardly calculated, as a rule, to strike us in a more positive way than the quality of moderation in the average pace of a walker.

We find the connection of *rhythm,* as distinct from pace, with musical expression chiefly in features of metrical outline and of strong marking of accents: in the more detailed structure the rhythmic element presents no features which can be dwelt on apart from the Ideal Motions into which it enters only as a single factor.

The crowding together of strong accents, as in the 'subject' from the movement *L'Absence,* quoted on p. 254, is connected with an expression of passion and vehemence, which we might compare with the similar expression given by frequent strong gestures to passionate speech. We see the essential connection of the *ictus* with the passion in such an instance as that quoted, in that it goes to constitute, and does not result from, the force and stir of the Ideal Motion. We do not conceive the motion as passionate, and then put an *ictus* on such and such notes; the passion has no true existence until the *ictus* is there, and a person who played the passage without the *ictus*, would simply show that for him its passionate character did not exist. Similarly it would be impossible to conceive the energy of the opening subject of Schubert's B flat trio—

Secondly, by abundance of strong accents.

without feeling in it a tremendousness of *ictus* which would seem extravagant in actual performance, and which therefore makes all earthly performance appear inadequate.

An expression of *confidence*, again, is very commonly connected with a strongly marked rhythmic outline at a certain somewhat quick pace ; and especially in double time, since there we easily get an association with the movement of marching, which is impossible in a measure where the bar cannot be halved.   Triumph, again, of the clear, direct kind which may be suggested by a firm and buoyant step, is similarly often connected with a strongly marked rhythmic movement ; though naturally such expression only rises into the stage of being noticed or defined in cases where the music has beauty enough to be arresting and stirring ; as, for instance, in the opening of Mendelssohn's *Lobgesang*.   It would be ridiculous to attempt to extend to music in general the distinction between double and triple time,[1] which the greater physical confidence of the former in certain cases might suggest.   But it is possible to trace in many simple instances a certain very indefinable character which seems dimly to connect itself with that distinction.   Thus, if we compare a waltz with a quadrille or galop, there is something in the triple beat of the former

*Thirdly, by strongly marked rhythmic outline,*

---

[1] The idea of forcing emotional characteristics on things so empty in themselves, and so capable of the most various sorts of content, as the several rhythmic *outlines* of Music, is not less preposterous than the notion about keys discussed in a former note.   I may quote a few pieces of information from the same source as before.

'The common time expresses the quiet life of the soul, a solid earnestness, an inward peace—but also strength, energy, and courage.' It 'lends itself readily to the representation of passion,' but 'is also expressive of quiet meditation.'

'The three-eight time expresses joy, a bright and sincere pleasure, which less affects our feelings than it carries us insensibly along in an unpretending and agreeable manner.'   It is also, we are told, expressive of suddenness and impulse, which are liable soon to degenerate into the expression of a frantic excitement ; but its best characteristic is innocence and simplicity.

'The three-four time is expressive of longing, of supplication, of sincere hope, and of love.   It lends itself also very effectively to the description of sincere devotional feelings.   The six-eight time is the natural interpreter of a spontaneous joviality and pleasure ; but it also unites gracefulness with dignity, and may sometimes be used as expressive of

a mournful sentiment ; yet the sorrow it indicates is rather that of young persons.' And so on.

It would be interesting to hear from this writer what happens when any one composes a piece in common time, which ' expresses the quiet life of the soul and inward peace,' and in the key of E minor, which 'represents grief, mournfulness, and restlessness of spirit.'

After the previous discussion of rhythm, I need hardly warn my readers against the totally false analogy of *poetical metres*, to which, within very wide limits, certain characteristics *may* be attributed ; in English verse, for instance, anapæstic metres might be said to be swifter and more stirring than iambic.   The difference between word-metres and rhythmic outlines in Music is obvious. In the first place the word-metre to a great extent controls the pace, while every rhythmic outline is compatible with the most various paces.   In the second place, the word-metre is *the* rhythm, the *whole* rhythm ; while every rhythmic outline used in Music will embrace an indefinite number of rhythms or sets of time-relations, and a different set (the number being indefinite it would be absurd to call them feet) may occur in every bar even of a single piece.

which seems to give more chance for delicate leanings and poisings in the Ideal Motion, for movements whose half-tantalising caprice and grace is shown in the way one wants to humour them, to dwell for an infinitesimal time on this and that note, and so on. The outline of a galop or quadrille seems less elastic and less adapted to such small impassioned impulses; and thus we often find in good waltzes a tinge of passion and romance, which we do not associate with dance-music written in double time.

which, however, we must not think of in abstraction from the whole Ideal Motion into which it enters.

I have said advisedly that the expression of confidence and triumph is often *connected with* strongly accented rhythmic movement: to say it was *given* or *ensured* by such movement, would be quite incorrect. The rhythmic element always remains a single factor of the form or Ideal Motion; and if the Ideal Motion in its completeness is not satisfactory or striking, no amount of accenting of its rhythmic outline will redeem its poverty, or make it seem expressive of any emotional quality. The boldness of expression is bound up with the *whole* musical motion; and it would be easy to give instances where features beyond those of rhythm, such as pieces of ascending and descending scale, might also be specially associated with the bold effect: but such features could not really be reduced, like those of rhythm, under any wide general head.

**Fourthly, by undecided rhythm,**

The opposite sort of expression, that of doubt and hesitation, is perhaps even more markedly connected with features of time-relations and rhythm. There could not be a better instance of this than the passage in Beethoven's pianoforte sonata in E minor, Op. 90, which is said to have been humorously connected by the composer with the indecision in the mind of a certain noble lover whose passion for an actress had been expressed in a preceding theme—

Even tapped on a couple of drums, this, so far as it was not absolutely in-coherent, would have an air of uncertainty, owing to the confused accents and varying time-values of the notes; but the effect is clearly a hundredfold clearer and stronger when the actual phrases are heard, catching each other up, and less and less able to get on, till at last they are mutually jogged, so to speak, into making up their minds. The importance of not attempting to detach the rhythmic factor from the whole musical motion is thus again illustrated. But though the expression of uncertainty may be connected *to which a similar warning applies.* in various cases with various melodic and harmonic features, we may safely assert that the most general feature, the one which is almost essentially present, is some pause, hesitation, or retardation in the rhythmic flow, as the analogies of physical motion, gesture, and speech would have en-abled us to predict.

Other special points of musical motion may be connected with the *Example of other special points of motion.* rarer and more definite character of actual despondency, as expressed, for instance, in the air *He was despised*, quoted on p. 274. The effect of the minor intervals in this melody was noticed in the chapter on Harmony; but the character is really set in the opening six bars of the piece, before any such interval has occurred. Here the motion, grave throughout, owes its character of absolute dejection mainly to the two groups of three descending thirds in the middle; these receive a special intensity from the accent's falling on the second of the three chords; and the pause after the first group emphasises the effect of the reiteration, as though the power of movement were gathered together again only to sink to a still lower depth of depression.[1] The effect is borne out further on in the piece by the reiterated longer pieces of descending scale. These features present a clear affinity to physical movements of drooping and collapse; and somewhat similar ones might usually be found in similar cases of ex-pression. Such explanations, it must be again observed, are concerned only with the *special character the beauty wears*; they do not attempt to

[1] *All* these points have to be considered before the peculiar character of the motion can be at all accounted for. The crude *rapprochement* made by a popular English writer on Music, of mental elation and de-pression to mere up and down in pitch, is wholly unreal, and is in fact a mere verbal juggle. Is the writer himself really kept in a see-saw of elation and depression by all the various ascents and descents of an ordinary melody?

account for the beauty, for the delight given by the exercise of the musical faculty on the whole melody. A hundred melodies might be written which would seem to embody the same features of motion, but there being no special beauty in them, there would be no special pathos. In the explanation of the expressive character of the phrases their musical value is, so to speak, presupposed: the reason why they fill up their place in the form to such divine issue lies hid in the instinctive perceptions of the musical faculty.

§ 7. Means of expression in the less obvious processes of Ideal Motion. Yearning and Intensity.

In pace and rhythm, and such a feature as slow yet emphatic motions of drooping, we have considered modes in which musical motion corresponds in the most obvious way with expressive physical movements; but our search for the means of definable expression in Music may carry us beyond these obvious features into the more inward processes of the Ideal Motion. Consider, for instance, this tune of Schumann's, the opening of a little piece called *Des Abends* :

which may be simplified as follows:

The characteristic expression of this melody is certainly *yearning* and *imploring*; and as it is in a major key, moderate in pace, and in perfectly even rhythm, none of the more obvious sources of expression are present. The general style of the harmony may perhaps be adduced in explanation; the accented notes several times constituting discords which are resolved on the next unaccented notes, and the prevalence of diminished sevenths aiding the expression of unrest. But these features, though they intensify the effect here, occur elsewhere without any similar result; and, moreover, the simple melodic form conveys the expression without any accompaniment at all. The yearning character can, I think, only be due to the fact that, in a large part of the process of following this Ideal Motion, we are yearning, not for inexpressible things, but for *the next note*, or at all events for some foreseen point beyond. Take the place of junction of the second and third bars; in leaving the A (in the simplified version) we seem to be stretching out for, straining towards, the F sharp, with a desire which results in an almost imperceptible dwelling on it when we have once arrived.[1] Then in the ascent to the upper F, we have a gradually growing excitement in the approach and the same final strain towards the longed-for point, in arriving at which our satisfaction is again expressed by a momentary dwelling, or as it might be on the violin by a thrill. The

---

[1] Such *nuances* in the Ideal Motion are to be remarked as very frequently connected with the character of intensity and fervour in Music; and the connection is rather the converse of what is generally imagined. The general view would be, ' You feel the impulse to dwell, to emphasise, to humour, to indulge in slight hurries and retardations, because the melody has emotional intensity.' Rather it is the fact that any particular specimen of Ideal Motion makes these demands, that the musical sense feels itself constrained in these sorts of ways, which constitutes the motion a yearning or passionate instead of, *e.g.*, a confident one.

accessory C sharp and D sharp again yearn upwards, and the C sharp in the final cadence downwards. Contrast this sort of motion with our activity in following the *Forelle* (quoted on p. 161) or the *Old Hundredth* ; where we feel no yearning or strain, but pass in easy confidence or in solemn confidence from one note to another. The gesture and attitude of straining, of stretching out towards a thing, is of course the common mode of expressing yearning and entreaty ; so that we have here merely a subtler form of expression through the indication of known signs of feeling. It must be observed that I am not attempting to explain *why* the musical process is of the kind it is, *why* such and such a combination of notes makes one yearn for such and such a starting point for such and such another, and so on, matters which belong to the inscrutable musical faculty : I am accepting this as a fact, and showing how it is connected with the particular expression of the melody, which in the above case many would describe as shadowing forth all the indefinable aspirations of their lives.[1]

Or take the first sentence of Schubert's *Leise flehen*—

[1] There is always a danger in quoting examples, as one can but choose the things which are powerfully affecting to oneself. If any one does not appreciate *Des Abends*, he will not perceive it to yearn, or rather will not yearn with it. As I was debating this point, it happened that some one passed the window whistling an Italian melody which I especially dislike, with a certain manner of making his way to the notes, a yearning 'expression,' which showed its power over *him*.

Here the slightly troubled rhythm given by the triplets, the reiteration of the movement of the first two bars, the falling back for a moment
with relaxed energy, and then the straining towards and attaining a point
beyond in the higher note, &c. &c., are features of melodic motion which
help to explain the passionate and yearning character of this serenade, as
compared with the more serene and confident flow of Handel's *Love in her
eyes.* And here again the facts of the motion and of our satisfaction in it
are the *data* on which the explanation proceeds. No amount of triplets
or reiterations or fallings back or straining upwards would have any emotional result if the particular motion as a whole were not musically delightful; no description of such features would convey to any one who did
not know the melody the slightest shadow of its rare and individual
beauty; but the melody and the musical beauty being there we can to
some extent connect the features with its more special emotional tinge.

Cases of expression depending rather on the general tenor of the Ideal   Tenderness.
Motion than on distinguishable points might be exemplified by such a
character as *tenderness*, expressed by melodies in which (beauty again
being presupposed) the motion is smoothly and gently gradated. When,
again, the gradualness is connected with chromatic harmonies, which introduce the feeling of uncertainty by suspending for a time the definite   Mysterious-
sense of key, *creepiness* may be the word which the sort of groping motion   ness.

suggests. I need only refer to the effect in its place of the famous passage in the andante of Beethoven's C minor symphony—

And a *mysterious* character may often be connected with somewhat similar features.

A somewhat different instance of definable expression may be found in Carmen's song *Presso il bastion*—

**Caprice with a touch of sadness.** The characteristics of this melody are undoubtedly melancholy and caprice, of a sort which association with the person in whose mouth it is put may readily enable us to define as girlish. The predominance of the minor key, combined with the easy swing of the tune, may be connected with the air of melancholy without earnestness. The caprice may be traced both in the alternations from minor to major and major to minor, and in the marked change of motion presented by the second phrase of four bars, with its two emphatic little triplet groups, clinched by the delicate impetuosity of the octave-spring—features which have some faintly perceived analogy with familiar gestures of wilfulness; while in the following part this character is further confirmed by the sudden breaking off of the half-pathetic vein with the little upward rush and final decisive step of the cadence.

In this last case we have traced the expression in great measure to relations between parts; and a peculiarity in this respect is not less frequently at the root of it than some *single* pervading feature, such as minor ' mode ' or strongly marked confident rhythm. Given unity of beauty in the whole, we shall continually find that aspects of passion and romance may be connected with lapses and renewals of effort, and marked points of contrast and climax. Even the strictest sort of composition may be thus coloured with a romantic character, as, for example, the fugue in D minor in the second division of Bach's *Wohltemperirtes Clavier.* Passion and romance.

Humour is another quality in Music which is often connected with comparison of parts and marked features of diversity and change. The simplest possible case would be the slackening and pause immediately before a cadence (as in the third figure of the *Lancers'*), succeeded by a quick wind-up; which is quite parallel to things that make babies laugh; and this tantalising and surprising of the expectant ear has many more delicate varieties. Another sort of fun in Music depends simply on the watching of a race, as in the minuet of Haydn's quartett, Op. 76, 2. But there are also less simple effects, especially common in the works of Beethoven, where the most comprehensive definition of humour is realised in the simultaneous presentation of subtle aspects of congruity and incongruity. Humour.

So far we have been able to connect the character with actual features in the music which there was no difficulty in distinguishing. But it is not hard to see that in a world peopled with so vast a variety of very distinct forms as that of Music, varieties of character may arise which are perceived in less special and direct ways than those we have been considering, and greatly by unconscious comparison of the phenomena among themselves; that is to say, by judging any special one in reference to its fellows, and with a latent sense of a variety of effects which have made up our previous experience, we are sensible of many qualities with which we cannot at all identify any special peculiarities of the musical motion. Thus one melody seems on the whole *prononcé* without being original, and we call it *vulgar*; another is pretty without being *prononcé*, and we call it *innocent*; or perhaps *delicate*, if its motion, while unemphatic, strikes us as having a sort of indefinable rarity. Again, we have connected *humour* with certain distinguishable features; but if we take the more intangible quality of *quaintness*, all we can usually say is that certain bits of music present to our musical perception that amount of divergence from familiar types, that sort of unexpectedness and oddness in relation to their fellows, which is analogous to the character described as quaintness in other regions of phenomena. Similar remarks would apply § 8. Other sorts of expression which cannot be connected with such special features in the Music.

to many other qualities which Music may occasionally present. But on such ground we have evidently got beyond the characters which correspond with any definite conditions of our own feelings, or in virtue of which any value could be assigned to Music as expressive of our emotional life: and once on this ground, we may give our adjectives the freest play. In the attempt to describe music—an attempt as hopeless as to write English with the letters x y z—we are often driven from the recognised category of æsthetic emotions to terms such as tantalising, uncompromising, persistent, *insouciant,* and even stranger expressions. It would be hard, for instance, to describe, except as a piece of divine folly, the 'Jill came tumbling after' effect of the scherzo of Beethoven's sonata in F for piano and violin: but it would be absurd to say it *expressed* folly or inspired the feelings with which we commonly regard folly.

§ 9. The very act of cataloguing a few of these definite emotional characters makes one feel how transient and uncertain they often are ; how little they sum up the substance of the thing which is actually delighting us.

It has been necessary to go through a certain number of samples of the special emotional characters which Music may without absurdity be said to express. But the very act of giving them this amount of definition oppresses one with a sense of unreality when one stops and realises what the impression of most of the music one cares about truly is. Half a dozen such tinges of expression may be presented by a single melody, which, as musically apprehended, is a perfect coherent unity. And if one forces oneself to try to give a name to the character of the successive sentences or phrases in a page of a sonata, though this one as compared with that may be more confident, or more relaxed, though we may find an energetic phrase here and a pleading phrase there, a capricious turn in close proximity to a piece of emphatic reiteration, and so on, our interest seems to lie in something quite remote from such description, and it is only by a sort of effort that we perceive whether or not the musical current has been coloured by occasionally floating into the zone of describable expression. The more general and undistinctive the character the more chance is there of its being kept up for some time: and an air of cheerfulness or peace or solemnity may pervade entire pieces of a moderate length. But we surely have only to look, to perceive that in hundreds of the most emotional instrumental movements [1] the effect is rarely, even for so much as a few bars, the suggestion of a recognisable emotion, and is

---

[1] *Instrumental* music is of course the ground on which the subject of Music as expressive must be first and mainly studied. Till we have obtained perfectly clear views on that ground, we have no power at all of fairly examining the nature of the expressiveness of Music as connected with words and persons ; for in the music which is so connected we cannot possibly eliminate the factor of association, more or less unconscious, with the sentiment of the words or the character of the persons. Words and scenes may seem to a dozen people to be satisfactorily and even remarkably 'expressed' by music of which, if they heard it first apart from the words and scenes, they would have given a dozen totally different versions. We shall return to this subject hereafter.

*never* essentially that, but rather like a revelation of self-evident and wholly untranslatable import.

Nor is it only with respect to this piecemeal and haphazard sort of application that the suggestion of definable characters seems tantalisingly remote from the essential effects of Music. If we take various musical motions, the definable seems to pass into the purely musical and indefinable in the most impalpable and unaccountable way. For certain of the features of musical motion which, when sufficiently prominent, may be connected with definite character, such as yearning or triumph, are really to a great extent present in *all* beautiful music ; or at all events there are characteristics of the Ideal Motion which, if we attempt the hopeless task of putting them into words, can only be so described. Thus to take the word *triumph.* The deep satisfaction felt in winning our way from note to note, or phrase to phrase, continually gives us a sense of inward triumph in music whose general expression, so far as it is describable, would not be called triumphant, but solemn it may be, or intense or passionate. In poor music, note after note and phrase after phrase seem to present themselves trivially and pointlessly ; but in music we enjoy, as we progressively grasp the form, the sense of absolute possession, of oneness with it ; the cogent and unalterable rightness of every step in our progress, may produce the most vivid impression of triumphal advance. If we attempted in such a case to translate the Ideal Motion into terms of physical motion (and this is allowable if we are careful to remember that they are distinct things and that the result is the faintest metaphor) we might say that we were inwardly elated at the certainty, strength, and success of our steps, without at all feeling that our outward and obvious gait and aspect were of a confident and triumphant character. Again, take the word *yearning.* The points in the Ideal Motion which seem in some way to suggest it, are found in all sorts of music quite outside the region where, as in the *Des Abends*, quoted above, the quality of subdued yet straining pathos seems predominant. The feeling of stretching out longingly to a foreseen note, indicated sometimes by actual movements of the hands, may exist in cases where the very slightest variation of pace or attempt to give musical emphasis to the rendering would be impertinent or impossible.[1] Again, the still more obvious feeling of *passion*, which seems more or less a definable expression in cases where music presents

*Sensations of triumph and yearning are constantly present in music which we should not dream of describing as* expressive *of those qualities.*

---

[1] A faint sense of irony may often be felt in passing by without special outward recognition or emphasis notes pregnant in musical importance ; and to some performers it is a matter of real difficulty to play such notes with the requisite ironical indifference. It is dangerous to attempt to exemplify so delicate an effect from personal experience, as any one who happens not to appreciate the example will complain of the description as over-fanciful ; but I will risk some of the inner notes in the latter section of the allegretto of Beethoven's seventh Symphony, as quoted on p. 256. The C sharp, for instance, in the fifth bar from the end of the quotation, could not possibly be in any way emphasised : yet one has a sensation of wanting to hug it as it passes.

marked features of agitated motion, is perpetually felt in music which suggests no external signs of passion at all : and though we may excusably call such music *expressive* of passion, by imagining it a vent for some external condition of excitement and exaltation, we must still recognise that the particular sense of excitement belongs to a state of consciousness known only in the realisation of music, and not essentially referable to any mode or exhibition of feeling belonging to times when music is not being realised.

§ 10. The definitely expressive element is far less constant and essential than is usually imagined.

Such descriptions as the above can only be arrived at by considerable attention to one's own sensations : I can but hope that as they represent my own experience truly, however inadequately, others may find them to correspond in some degree with theirs. And the result is certainly to relegate the definitely expressive element in Music to a much more subordinate position than that commonly assigned to it.

These words must not be misunderstood. The element of expression is not subordinate in the sense that, when present, it is slight or shallow ; on the contrary, it may reach the very extreme of intensity and profundity, since the whole mass of musical feeling which is stirred up appears steeped in the colour of any special emotion it may suggest. But it is subordinate (1) in the sense that it is far from being a constant element ; (2) in the sense that not in it, but in the independently impressive aspect of Music, must be sought the explanation of the essential effect of the art ; and that the very intensity of which musical expression is capable, so far from being explanatory, is one of the prime mysteries to be explained. Both these senses are commonly ignored. In ninety-nine per cent. of the current talk and writing about Music and composers, it is implied (even where not definitely stated) that Music is primarily an art of expression ; that it is 'the language of the emotions,' *i.e.* of modes of feeling familiar in the life external to Music (which for convenience I have called *extra-musical* modes of feeling); and that its great function, either with or without the association of some external words or subject-matter, consists in the evocation of these emotions. And this view is connected, either as cause or effect, with the idea that in mentioning the expressive aspects the problem of Music's power has been solved. To many the question never occurs *why* mournfulness or exultation should be held as any more explanation or guarantee of overpowering beauty in a tune than in a face. The chain of error may be traced partly to the fact that those who theorise on the subject are apt to consider cases where Music is associated with definite words or scenes, or at all events cases where definable characters of feeling *are* more or less suggested, so that they do not feel driven to look beyond for some more fundamental source of effect ; partly to the natural difficulty of fully recognising the unique and independent impressiveness in Music, in the lack of some such expedient as the application of Mr. Darwin's theory attempted in this book. But however the view may be accounted for, its bearings on theories of musical art are none the less disastrous ; and its importance must be my excuse for presenting the various objections to it at some length and in precise order.

First, we have the fundamental fact that in an immense amount of beautiful music the element of definable expression is absent ; or present only in such vague and fragmentary ways that, in describing the phenomena under that aspect, we seem to get about as near the reality as when we attempt descriptions of things in the vocabulary of some unfamiliar foreign language. The bearing of this on the cases which *do* present definable expression is obvious. Taking a *single* specimen of music with a definable expression, we might find a difficulty in proving to any one that it did not owe its value to its expression, for the simple reason that it is impossible to present that specimen without its expression. A beautiful face can change ; it is capable of being neutral or of wearing many different expressions, under each of which the form is so slightly modified that the face remains obviously one and the same : whereas a pathetic melody, a triumphant melody, and an undefinable melody are necessarily three and not one, and one of them cannot become either of the others. But clearly if I find twenty bits of music beautiful and indescribable,[1] and one bit beautiful and pathetic, it is unreasonable to say I enjoy the last (which I don't enjoy at all more than the others) *because* it is pathetic.

Secondly, the very features which may be often indisputably connected with definable expression are perpetually present in cases where, the music not being perceived as impressive or beautiful, they produce no effect on us. The essential conditions of musical beauty, of the satisfaction of the musical sense, must therefore be quite outside these special features of effect. On the other hand, if any music expresses distinct feeling, it expresses it *better*, we say, the more beautiful it is ; that is, the more profoundly it exercises that sense of musical impression which, in the cognisance of *all* music, is felt as one in kind.

Thirdly, it is often found that music which wears a definable expression to one person, does not wear it or wears a different one to another, though the music may be equally enjoyed by both. For instance, the great 'subject' of the first movement of Schubert's B flat trio, the opening of which was quoted on p. 326, represents to me and many others the *ne plus ultra* of energy and passion ; yet this very movement was described

Reasons why it will not at all account for the essential power of Music.

---

[1] *Indescribable* must not be confounded with *indefinite*. However indefinite Music may often be in its *ex*pressive aspect, in its *im*pressive aspect it shows its virtue in being definite. (Cf. Mendelssohn's remarks quoted in § 9 of the next chapter.) Apart from the definiteness of individuality due to the actual perceptible difference of one musical form from another, we can often feel in Music a general character so definite as to make us certain of the author of the composition. But as this character, which is so certainly perceived by the musical sense, has no sort of extra-musical existence, it of course cannot be described.

by Schumann as 'tender, girlish, confiding :' and the reiteration of the bass figure in the adagio of Beethoven's fourth symphony, which has always seemed to me quite tremendous in its earnestness, appeared to Schumann as a *humorous* feature.

Fourthly, take twenty bits of music, each presenting the same definable character, such as melancholy or triumph. Now if the stirring of this emotion is the whole business of any one of these tunes, how is anybody the richer for knowing the other nineteen ? for in respect of this stirring character they are all on a par, and one of them would do completely all that could be done. In reality, of course, each of them is an individual, with a beauty peculiar to itself, and each is, to one who loves it, a new source of otherwise unknown delight. The mistake, as thus regarded, connects itself with the inward nature of the sense of hearing : as we cannot touch what we hear, the fact that we perceive a piece of music as an individual object is apt to be lost sight of in theory, however universally exemplified in the whole practice of musical appreciation.

Fifthly, even if definite bias of expression did really belong to all enjoyable music, there is the *à priori* impossibility that abstract motion of any sort should produce the extraordinarily vivid and individual effects of Music by the mere suggestion of emotions, apart from some independently based beauty, some independent means of powerfully affecting us. Why should the mere expression of some mode of feeling by an abstract musical motion be more adequate to stir us than the expression of it by the gestures of some uninteresting concrete personage ? Apart, indeed, from some independent source of impressiveness, it would seem far less adequate. For a melancholy look, a pleading gesture, an energetic gait, may set our imaginations coursing down a score of interesting avenues connected with the subject or object of that particular human manifestation : but in Music our attention is centred on forms which are for us the unique inhabitants of a perfectly unique world, disconnected from the interest of visible things. How should the mere suggestion of emotions suffice to transfigure these abstract forms with individual life and beauty ? On the contrary, it is the life and beauty which the forms draw from their own peculiar spring in our organisation that enables them to transfigure any definable emotional character they may perchance suggest. The extraordinary intensification which known emotions undergo in musical expression, the movingness of the pathetic, the jubilance of the exulting strains, might alone suggest the problem how one method of motion should possess such a monopoly of expressive power ; and might have led to the answer that the particular expression is a phase in an independent mode of deep and mighty impression, whose depth and might it thus makes its own.

One special form of the error we are discussing demands separate notice. The question asked in the last paragraph, why is the effect of expressive music so infinitely greater than that of the corresponding physical motion, by resembling which [1] it suggests definite conditions of feeling?—why is the effect of an agitated presto of Beethoven superior to that of a man excitedly waving his arms in the air? why is *Des Abends* more delightful than a series of imploring gestures? why is Carmen's *Presso il bastion* more pleasurable than any copy or accompaniment of it by capricious physical movements?—such questions, I say, are often answered by saying that Music presents an infinitely greater *variety* and more delicate *nuances* of motion than physical movement. But this answer, when connected with the theory that Music is effective by the expression of extra-musical emotions, becomes absurd; as will be obvious if the argument as to the relation of musical to physical motion be briefly but connectedly restated. The three main facts are as follows;—

§ 11. Nor can the view that *expression* is the source and secret of musical effect find any support or relevance in the number of *varieties* and *nuances* of musical motion.

A. Musical or Ideal Motion has infinite varieties and *nuances*, which constitute the whole body of musical forms.

B. Musical Motion may present a certain number of very general features which resemble and suggest definite physical motions in space; sometimes presented in an obvious way by pace, rhythmic outline and emphasis, and width of intervals; sometimes connected with the more inward processes of the Ideal Motion, as when the musical straining towards a note dimly adumbrates some corresponding physical gesture.

C. Human or extra-musical emotions, so far as they are expressible otherwise than by language, are normally expressed in a rough and general way by physical motions: and musical motion, by its resemblances to physical motion, can in an extremely general way suggest the conditions of feeling with which definite features of physical motion are thus connected.

Now if Music's power consisted in the expression of extra-musical emotion, the greater variety and *nuance* in musical motion could only give it a superiority over physical motion by enabling it to express a greater variety and more delicate shades of extra-musical emotion. But such a theory (not to mention its inapplicability to the beauty presented in single homogeneous passages of limited length) at once brings us into collision with C. Musical motions express extra-musical moods and feelings through their resemblance to physical motions: how then can it be maintained that an infinite superiority in variety and *nuance* makes them infinitely superior in this power of expression to that, by resembling which it is that they express at all? [2] The varieties and *nuances* of course exist; but they belong to the essence of the Ideal Motion, as musically perceived in its numberless manifestations; which may reach the maximum of im-

---

[1] For simplicity's sake I neglect here the more occasional elements of expression found in *timbre*, 'mode,' and harmony; which may be done without injury to the ensuing argument.

[2] The criticism, in the eighth chapter, of Helmholtz's view that the effects of Music are sufficiently accounted for by mere consideration of motion, may now be supplemented and completed. He dwells especially

pressiveness in the absence of any features suggestive of extra-musical moods and feelings. A single instance is stronger than any argument. Take two musical movements, alike in agitated pace and rhythm, and in what we may call physical character: both equally express, if we will, an agitated state of feeling: but will any one seriously maintain that the varieties and *nuances* of Ideal Motion, which make every phrase and bar of the one totally different from every phrase and bar of the other, correspond with varieties and *nuances* of extra-musical mood? Such an instance is alone utterly subversive of the hypothesis that musical motion is effective by doing *more delicately and minutely* what physical motion does roughly and generally.

§ 12. Extreme broadness and generality of the feelings Music can express.

The theory about shades of emotion becomes doubly absurd when we notice what the largest general qualities really are, which may be included under some comprehensive mode of feeling, and how utterly any mode of motion lacks the power of following and expressing even these broadest distinctions. Under the general head of pathos or melancholy, for example, may be included a multitude of large qualities, which can be expressed either by the verbal representation of persons and characters or by visible forms, but which mere motion, musical or physical, could never the least touch or suggest; patience, for instance, and pity. Sculpture can depict patience, because it can make a patient-looking figure; but what means has Music of giving us a patient-sounding tune? Pity may be itself subdivided into many kinds; we feel one sort for Antigone, another for Lear, another for Hamlet: but Music cannot even get so far down in definition as the broad attribute of pity itself, nor differentiate it from regret or any other of the qualities which a general pathos of expression might cover. Earnestness, agitation, are differentiated in life in a score of different ways, not one of which can be marked out by any special peculiarity in the expression of the general character by motion. And indeed when we realise the essential distinction between presentative and representative art, the wonder is not so much that the expression of emotions by Music should be comprised for the most part under extremely wide and general heads, as that even that amount of definition should be possible.[1]

on the variety and delicacy of musical motions, and does not seem to perceive the inevitable dilemma, as stated in the text. If the superior delicacy and variety of musical motions involves no improved means of discriminating and expressing extra-musical feeling, *that* source, which is what Helmholtz ultimately relies on for their effect, is unavailable to account for it. And since mere variety of motions does not help us unless we can say why any one of them should be su-

premely pleasant, it follows that their power to awaken deep and unique feeling must be derived from some *other* independent emotional source; the possibility of which, in the connection of the satisfied exercise of the musical faculty with hidden channels of primæval association, I have attempted to explain.

[1] Some may find a certain difficulty in catching the notion that many different and individual presentations, each loved with a special love, and all emotionally stirring, do

The want of definiteness in musical expression is sufficiently obvious to have been recognised even by some of those who, with great inconsistency, assign no ground for the power and value of the art save its expression of extra-musical emotions: and the recognition usually takes the form of saying that the expression is not of definite emotions, but of some general mood, *Gemüthsstimmung*, capable of taking many channels; such a general emotional disposition, for instance, as might equally appear in the ardour of the lover and the ardour of the saint, and might therefore be differently interpreted according to the subjective fancies of the hearers. These emotional states seem to be just those extremely general ones [1] which we have noticed as corresponding with certain known physical conditions and modes of motion, and so as naturally expressible by Music. And as regards the question where the essential effect of Music lies, we need scarcely fear that any sane person will seriously attribute it (however much his language may imply such a view) to characters like these; characters so broad and undistinctive and which so little strike us as being deliberately or definitely expressed, that one of them may pervade a hundred different pieces without seeming to constitute the slightest kinship between them. No one who has any musical appreciation is likely to think that the *raison d'être* of a tranquil or a lively piece is the expression of liveliness or tranquillity, or to attach any vital importance to such

Impossibility that a *Gemüthsstimmung* should be the source of definite musical beauty.

not awaken distinct sorts and shades of feeling. And especially when two bits of music present a certain character, but a character which cannot be described more particularly than by saying, *e.g.*, that both bits are melancholy, it is very natural to conceive that the melancholy of the one is different from that of the other. A moment's thought will, however, show that the sense of difference concerns the two individual forms or motions, not the melancholy which they express; just as if two children of different physiognomy be told a piece of bad news which affects them exactly alike, the same sentiment will be expressed by their totally different and individual faces.

It is disappointing to find how loosely even Schumann, whose position about the general undefinableness of musical feeling is often firm enough, can sometimes speak about shades of emotion. 'Half-educated people,' he says, 'are generally unable to discover more than the expression of grief and joy, and perhaps melancholy, in music without words. They are deaf to the finer shades of emotion—anger, revenge, satisfaction, quietude, &c.' As if, on the one hand, satisfaction and quietude were fine shades, instead of the most general and undistinctive

characters possible; and as if, on the other hand, Schumann or any one else could distinguish between anger and revenge as 'expressed' in Music. Elsewhere, after disclaiming all artistic value for the titles of his pianoforte pieces, he adds 'the different soul-states only are interesting to me.' Now the soul-states are either things possible and known apart from Music, or they are not. If they are *not*, the words used are very misleading: if they *are*, how many of them are there, and how many pieces of music belong to each? If each of them is only an extremely broad *Gemüthsstimmung*, like those treated of in the following paragraph, how can it be the interesting or distinguishing element in a number of vivid and different individuals?

[1] It is strange that Helmholtz, after correctly pointing out the extreme vagueness and generality of these states of feeling, and how one of them, such as 'the dreamy longing for transcendent bliss,' may represent the broadest common element in a number of more distinct feelings, such as love, piety, &c., should in the same paragraph directly contradict himself by adding that Music expresses extra-musical emotions '*exactly and delicately.*'

attributes. But though this *Gemüthsstimmung*-theory is thus less of a trap than the theory of 'shades of emotion,' we must notice how far it is from being generally applicable. For, in the first place, in hundreds and thousands of cases it is as impossible to name any general mood as to name any more definite emotions; the mood is simply that unique one which we can but describe as the mood of musical exaltation, by whatever music produced.[1] And, in the second place, it is just in connection with a *Gemüthsstimmung* that a difficulty already noticed is at its maximum: if we try to assign corresponding moods to the passages of some long and exciting instrumental movement, we often cannot stick to one for a dozen bars together. So far as they can be conceived as existing at all, they are perpetually changing, sometimes at a moment's notice. There is surely a sort of unreality about the notion of playing football in this irresponsible way with what are represented as very deep and pervading emotional conditions; and those who imagine they dignify Music by calling it a reflection of life, forget that neither does life consist in pitching oneself without rhyme or reason from one definable mood into another, and would be very unpleasant if it did.

*Moreover it perpetually happens that not even an assign able Gemüths- stimmung is present.*

[1] The customary phrases about depiction of moods are deceptive only by their vagueness. To see what they come to, we have but to scrutinise them in direct connection with a few specimens of music we care about. Take for instance the two following beautiful tunes, each completely appreciable in its unaccompanied melodic form: the first is from Beethoven's *Serenade Trio*—

the second is a song, *Willst du dein Herz mir schenken*, attributed to Bach—

In spite of a certain superficial similarity, these melodies are to the musical apprehension as different as different can be. But any one who thought he could define the difference as a difference of two particular moods, might fairly be called on, within a limited range of music, to find names for many hundreds of moods, to correspond with differences equally patent to the musical sense and equally inexpressible in known terms of emotion. The most conclusive experiment would be to take twenty such persons, if they could be found, and ask them to write down the difference of mood in a particular case like the above, and then to compare their descriptions.

So far we have been considering emotions as awakened, or not awakened, in ourselves. We may now briefly consider the same topic in relation to the composer. Of course the doctrine that a composer expresses his emotions is subject to all the modifications entailed by the absence of continuous and definable emotional expression in perhaps the greater part of his work: on this we need not further dwell. But the doctrine is sufficiently faulty even for the cases where definable expression is most clearly present. Suppose a painter is depicting 'Night' or 'Autumn' as a melancholy female: is he expressing his own melancholy all the time? if he paint a death-scene, is he mournful during the whole of the working hours of a month or six months? Similarly a musician may be a month in working up a funeral march, without at all losing his good spirits. Indeed he would naturally be much less under the dominance of the mournful emotion than the painter. For the latter has the middle term of his own intellectual representation; in depicting a scene of sorrow he must constantly realise to himself the mood and its concrete embodiment; his own emotions may be only artistically pumped up, but still he is face to face with mournful realities. But the musician is not kept in the presence of external realities; and no one can keep a mood going for the mere purpose of expressing it. The painter again, having the world to choose from, deliberately chooses such subjects as he prefers to dwell on himself; and as many of the forms and objects which he depicts might be known and imagined, and might show their beauty, in several moods or aspects, his choice of a special mood may seem characteristic. The germ of a musician's work is very different. His 'subjects' are not aspects and relations of things deliberately chosen, but fragments of musical inspiration, independent of views of life and habits of sentiment. It may be readily granted that if, without conscious aim, he sits down to his piano at one of those times when there is a sense of pause in the more vigorous pulses of life, he is more likely to fall into a melancholy and rhythmically quiet *andante* than into a tumultuous *presto*; and conversely, when a mood of confidence reflects the exhilaration of joyful surroundings, the humour of the moment may flash forth in more impetuous strains. But his longer works, with their solemn adagios and sportive minuets and so on, can be no sort of reflection of his from-day-to-day existence. His musical activity may be to him the natural vent for (or refuge from) all sorts of emotional conditions; but to suppose that it was bound to expression of those conditions to us would be to suppose that sonatas and symphonies were short gushes of impassioned impromptu, instead of works of prolonged labour. The exciting music which is held to indicate the pre-existence of some emotional storm in its author, may equally have been the result of the most peaceful and ordinary work-day.

The history of musical composition is so clear on this point, that

§ 13. Expression of emotions in relation to the composer.

people can only have been driven to find in what they hear the expression of the composer's emotions at the moment, by supposing that Music must express something and not seeing what else it could be. For anything so wrapped up with the physical organism as Music, it is rather in the *physical* conditions of the composer that we should naturally look for some assignable connection with musical workings in his brain.   There is a most interesting account by Mozart of the manner in which his music came to him, when he was comfortable after dinner, or lying peacefully in bed: Auber's ideas were set in motion on horseback, and Beethoven's in his rapid walks, enlivened by strange hummings and shoutings, about the environs of Vienna.   But emotions (real or imagined) external to the music, though they may act generally and indirectly by quickening and attuning the mind to a sense of beauty, are far oftener wholly latent or irrelevant.   A melody composed for an instrument in a neutral frame of mind might afterwards be set to religious words, of which it might then seem to breathe the very spirit; music written without a thought of death or any solemn subject might turn out to make a first-rate funeral march and be adopted as such; and a gifted child who had never personally realised the existence of such a feeling as mournfulness might appreciate and even invent a deeply pathetic melody.   We can yearn, triumph, and so on in purely musical regions; and where we find in music a mood describable by some adjective thus drawn from the category of the emotions, to say the music was composed as an expression of the composer's emotion would as a rule be as true as to say that the interior of St. Mark's was designed as an expression of a previous mood of gloom on the part of its architect.

When for special purposes, as in writing for occasions or for words, a man has obviously turned his musical faculty into a special vein, as of tenderness, or sportiveness, or solemnity, it may seem cynical to imagine him entirely absorbed in his unique creative region.   But as a matter of fact, his faculty may set itself on the inventive track, so to speak, in a slow rhythm and a minor key, or in quick capricious snatches which gradually flash into a vivacious 'subject,' without any swayings of his conscious moods.

**Relation of a composer's temperament and circumstances to his work.**
It is of course quite another question how far a musician's *permanent* temperament and circumstances, or some long and abnormal affection of body and mind, may be perceptibly connected with his artistic work. Different answers might probably be given in different cases, and we might doubtless find instances where a predominant tone of struggle and despondency or of serenity and gladness seems in sufficiently striking correspondence with external characteristics and conditions.[1]   The most general attribute of physical intensity, so prominent in the organisation of many

---

[1] Schumann says of his C major symphony, 'I sketched it out while suffering severe physical pain; indeed, I may call it the struggle of my mind, which influenced this, and by which I sought to beat off my disease. The first movement is full of this struggle, and very peevish and perverse in character.' We see here the same sort of connection

great musicians, is certainly often accompanied by strong affections and emotional fervour.  But it is dangerous to try to press more special points. Nothing, for instance, in Beethoven's music is more striking than the variety and delicacy of its humour : as a man, his sense of humour could of all things be least relied on, and the jokes he preferred were of a very rough-and-tumble description.  And even on the more general ground we shall perhaps be safer in tracing the connection to the most fundamental inborn bias of disposition than to the emotional conditions which special circumstances might affect.  I believe that Mendelssohn's work would have remained in general flowing and *rangé*, through any amount of external or internal tumult ; that the sublime pathos and stormy energy of Beethoven would not have been stifled by comfort and happiness ; and that as a rule the springs of musical creation, even where strongest and most abundant, dwell singularly apart, and have for their very own the hues they are thought to reflect.  The fashion of imagining and overstraining connections between a man's music and his life is due to a tendency, amiable but in Music especially ill-advised, to make heroes of artists.

In conclusion, I can imagine that a reader who has given assent to the various propositions and arguments which have been presented in this chapter, may still feel that, after all, there is a sense in which Music may be truly considered a reflection of the inner life.  I am far from denying that such is the case : the error is in not seeing that so far as the idea has any sort of generality of application, the reflection itself must be of the most general and indefinite kind ; very different from the definable expression, with its dubious and fragmentary appearances, which we have been discussing.  Characters far too wide to be regarded, without absurdity, as what the pieces were written to express, or as what their merit and individuality consist in their expressing, may still make a sort of undefined human atmosphere under which the distinct musical forms are revealed and the distinct musical impressions received.  Moreover, if the following and realising of music be regarded as itself *one complete domain* of inner life, we may then perceive that it is large and various enough, full enough of change and crisis and contrast, of expectation, memory, and comparison, of general forms of perception which have been employed in other connections by the same mind, for the course of musical experience, as felt under these most abstract aspects and relations, to present a dim affinity to the external course of emotional life.  In this way we may feel, at the end of a musical movement, that we have been living an engrossing piece of life which, in the variety and relations of its parts, has certain qualities belonging to any series of full and changing emotions : and this feeling may impress us with much more of reality than

§ 14. The sort of sense in which Music may be considered a reflection of the inner life.

between physical states and musical stirrings, between the restless, sudden, and impatient movements of the sufferer and the music which kept time to them in his head, as was less painfully exemplified in Beethoven's striding walks and Auber's ~

any attempted ranking of the several parts and phases of the music under particular heads of expression. It is easy to distinguish general affinities of this kind from anything referable to the more definite categories. Such qualities, *e.g.*, as evenness and continuity, or interruptedness and variability, of musical movement, may suffice to suggest a sort of kinship between musical and other trains of feeling, while far too abstract to define or guarantee the character of the pieces where they occur, and able equally to cover the most various content : the slowness and sustainedness of an *adagio* movement, for instance, often described as typical of a peaceful flow of consciousness, we have found to be as compatible with the undefinable stirrings of musical passion as with the definable expression of calm. Another instance of abstract relationship, equally remote from definite suggestion and expression, may be found in the faint analogy of mingling currents of music to that mingling of various strains of feeling and idea which is so frequent a feature of our ordinary life : it would be absurd in the vast majority of such cases to attempt to represent each musical current as typifying some distinguishable train of known feeling, so that here the quality common to the musical and the extra-musical experience seems so abstract as to be little more than harmonious concomitance of several elements in each : yet this mere parallelism of complexity seems enough to open up in Music faint tracts of association with extra-musical life. A similar affinity has been attributed to the predominance of a single melodic theme in relation to its accompaniment ; where the mere relation may possibly suggest our general experience of prominent strains of feeling as standing out from the general stream of consciousness, whose other elements make for it a sort of dimly-felt background.

And Music condenses a very large amount of inner life, of the sort of experience which might lend itself to such general associations, into a very brief space of actual time. The successions of intensity and relaxation, the expectation perpetually bred and perpetually satisfied, the constant direction of the motion to new points, and constant evolution of part from part, comprise an immense amount of alternations of posture and of active adjustment of the will. We may perhaps even extend the suggestions of the last paragraph so far as to imagine that this ever-changing adjustment of the will, subtle and swift in Music beyond all sort of parallel, may project on the mind faint intangible images of extra-musical impulse and endeavour ; and that the ease and spontaneity of the motions, the certainty with which a thing known or dimly divined as about to happen *does* happen, creating a half-illusion that the notes are obeying the controlling force of one's own desire, may similarly open up vague channels of association with other moments of satisfaction and attainment. But these affinities are at any rate of the most absolutely general kind ; and whatever their importance may be, they seem to me to lie in a region where thought and language struggle in vain to penetrate.

# CHAPTER XV.

### THE SUGGESTION BY MUSIC OF EXTERNAL OBJECTS AND IDEAS.

In the last chapter we considered the subject of expression in direct rela- § 1. The present topic is closely con- nected with the last. tion to the feelings, to the perception of musical beauty as coloured by more or less manifest tinges of definable emotional character. We have now to enquire into the power of Music to suggest external objects and events and intellectual conceptions, and into the amount of value which can be attached to such suggestions. This topic is naturally bound up most closely with the other; but may be much more easily and shortly treated, owing to the precedence of the other and the recognition of its more fundamental nature. Both the necessity and the difficulty of dis- tinguishing definable emotional expression in Music from the aspect of unique and independent impressiveness were due to the fact that in a great deal of music such expression *is* actually present as an important and inseparable feature. But the connection of suggestions of external images and conceptions with the essential effects of Music will prove to be of a much looser and more mechanical sort; while inasmuch as the con- nection is possible, for the most part, only through the medium of emo- tional expression, the conclusions of the last chapter will be immediately available without repetition of the argument.

The suggestion of objects and events, the awakening in the mind of § 2. The suggestion of objects and events may take place by *particular* resemblances; definite concrete images, may take place in two ways. First, the actual sounds and motion of the music may perceptibly resemble actual sounds and motions of other things. If we look down any list of titles of musical pieces, we are certain to find examples of this. Brooks, cascades, storms, bells, hammers, rides, gondolas, sources of sound, and moving things of all sorts are laid under contribution, while such titles as *Restless Nights* have a more remote but still real connection with concrete images of movement. This kind of direct resemblance, aided greatly of course by actual association, has a place in dances and marches: and amid the variety of scenes and objects which these words might suggest, the mind may be easily led more or less to define the image either by the pervading cha- racter of the music or by certain special points in it. Thus of two dance- pieces, one might be appropriated to nymphs and the other to giants, by flowing grace in the one case, and by more emphatic phrases and perhaps bass effects, like heavy steps, in the other : and we can easily realise the quaintness of turn or the solemn advance which would indicate a marionette or a hero as the subject of a funeral-march. Such features, again, as blending or as hurry and confusion of strains easily suggest external analogies. It is obvious that such resemblances as these may present all varieties of closeness and remoteness, of reality and fancifulness. The fountain may truly suggest itself in the trickling passages of the music ; the confusion of the carnival, though not thus self-evident, may be accepted as an image which at any rate keeps easily parallel with the changing maze of musical sounds : Purcell's indication of the fall of Troy by a descending scale, on the other hand, is not less uninteresting as illustration than as music.

or by *general* resemblance of character.

The second way in which images of external facts may be suggested by Music is by general qualities. Here again we might procure our examples from almost any list of musical titles : the sea, evening, moonlight, sunny landscape, any scene or season with which we associate a distinct emotional colouring, may find in Music its faint reflection. These more general analogies are often combined with the more distinct resemblances ; as is natural, if we consider that definable qualities in Music are mainly connected with distinct features of motion : the same calm and steady musical flow which might suggest a quiet succession of waves has naturally an expression of tranquillity corresponding with the same idea.

§ 3. The suggestions are for the most part very indefinite ; apart from verbal assistance the same music might suggest quite different things to different people ;

These suggestions, however, remain in almost all cases extremely indefinite. This is sufficiently clear when we have only some very general quality to fix our image by : but even the more special points of motion or sound leave almost always a very wide latitude of choice. Given the title, of course all who are the least interested in having an image at all will have the same image ; but left to themselves they might each select a different one. We will defer for the moment the disputed subject of what is known as programme-music, where the musical illustration which is attempted is of a much more elaborate kind, and where high æsthetic value is claimed for the perception of the correspondences. As regards the simpler suggestions which can be summed up in a title, there can be little dispute. They belong naturally rather to the slighter category of musical sketches and impromptus than to works of prolonged labour and elaborate construction ; and however unessential, they are at any rate convenient, inasmuch as the number of technical designations by which musical pieces can be distinguished is small, and persons who do not themselves perform the pieces cannot be expected to burden their memories with keys and *opus* numbers. The interest of the imagined resemblances, even where strong enough to be worth taking into account, is not likely to be identified with the excellence of the work. The interest, for instance, which any one may derive from reading the remarks on Mendelssohn's visit to Italy, often found in programmes as an introduction to his *Italian* symphony, is the interest not of musical interpretation but of personal sympathy with the happy composer of the happy music. At the same time, the confusion of the essential and the accidental is so apt to creep in, and to pave the way to further fallacies, that even on these outskirts of expression the independent impressiveness of Music is worth defending. The very ease with which Music lends itself to subjective association makes it the more necessary to notice how entirely subjective the association usually is: and when a composer lovingly or humorously connects some musical product with the outward occurrence or the inward vision which, acting through hidden channels, may have stimulated his fancy, he sometimes innocently gives a handle to a misconception he would often be the first to disown. For instance, Schumann tells how a composer had been haunted, while writing, by the image of a butterfly floating down a brook on a leaf, with the result that his composition was characterised by a kindred simplicity and tenderness. Very likely it was: but Schumann would not have denied that in the range of Music hundreds of equally simple and tender compositions might be found, written by writers who, as it happens, had *not* any such particular vision floating before their eyes; and in conceding this, he would concede all for which I am contending.

*and the convenience of a title, or the interest of any external association connected with a piece, does not make them matters of substantive importance.*

Similar remarks apply to titles and pieces of suggestion of a less concrete kind. Schumann's own works present many titles drawn both from visible realities and from more abstract conceptions, which are considered most happily characteristic, but which were actually thought of after the composition of the respective pieces. And his written criticisms are specially emphatic in respect of this very point. His imagination, indeed, suggested as humorous and interesting flashes of allowable subjective interpretation as can be anywhere found; and one is specially tolerant of such fancies when they come from a master: when wine is of fine flavour, one does not quarrel with the froth. But while his images run riot in most graceful fashion, we feel that he is always estimating them at their true value;[1] and he often puts in a word to warn us against mistaking the dream for the reality, the dim mirror of metaphor for the veritable region, 'which,' as he says, 'we have never explored, and consequently can have no recollection of.'

As regards ideas unconnected with concrete images and events, it might be at once surmised that the only ones Music could be thought capable of expressing or suggesting must belong in some way to definite

[1] I have invariably found, in musical discussions, that the most vivid and penetrating similitudes have been thrown out impromptu by those who are furthest from taking them *au sérieux*.

qualities of the music and its emotional expression, such as were discussed in the last chapter. For example, that while the idea of fervour and insistence, which is a distinct mode of feeling associated with motion and gesture, is expressible in Music by emphatic reiteration, there is no similar way of expressing an idea so withdrawn in the abstract intellectual region as perseverance. I believe that such is the case, and that any analogies attempted outside this emotional class of ideas are of the most barren kind. A single example of an attempt of this kind will suffice. Professor Macfarren, in his critique of Brahms's *Requiem*, says that in a pedal bass, continued with beautiful musical effect for a long period, we must conceive the composer to have ' set down his thought of the Divine permanence.' Such a *rapprochement* seems exactly as mechanical as that of the fall of Troy and the descending scale, noticed above. The perception of something *going on* for a considerable time neither makes us feel permanent, as, *e.g.*, triumphant music makes us feel triumphant, nor wakens any feeling which corresponds with it in the way that, *e.g.*, the feeling of amusement corresponds with the perception of caprice or pursuit. The connection of the abstract quality of the musical feature with the Divine or any other permanence must be a totally irrelevant and deliberate mental act: and Brahms here as much or as little expresses his ' thought ' of anything beyond his splendid musical effect, as we should express our ' thought ' of the bottomless pit by playing a shake on the lowest notes of the piano.

It seems, then, that the abstract ideas which Music may naturally suggest must not lie outside the region of definable emotion. We saw, however, in the last chapter, what wide affairs the definable emotions usually were: and as a pervading air of joy or peace or struggle left us a wide choice among scenes and objects, so they will leave a wide field for our subjective fancies in respect of more abstract conceptions. The field too may be extended by combinations of two or more conceptions, corresponding to relations of the parts of the music to one another; and expression or quasi-expression may thus be carried somewhat beyond the stage we have as yet considered. For instance, two passages, neither of which would suggest any particular extra-musical idea on its own account, may present such a contrast that the idea of despair struggling with hope, or of darkness dispelled by light, or of the subdual of death by life, when once suggested, may all seem to have a vague sort of applicability. And here we are launched on the region of ' poetical ideas,' which we are now so authoritatively told that it is the great business of Music to express.

Perhaps the best introduction to the subject will be to see what the ideas come to, in connection with some first-class piece of modern instrumental music: and I will take as an example a short ' analysis ' of the first movement of Schubert's unfinished symphony, from the programme of a Philharmonic concert. I select this analysis because it is not in any way ridiculous, and does not contain specially overstrained and fanciful comparisons, or expressions which did not strike one in following the music as sufficiently appropriate. Disentangled from musical terms it stands as follows :—We begin with deep earnestness, out of which springs perturbation ; after which almost painful anxieties are conjured up, till the dissolution draws the veil from an unexpected solace, which is soon infused with cheerfulness, to be however abruptly checked. After an instant of apprehension, we are startled by a threat of destruction to the very capability of rest, which in its turn subsides. From the terrible we pass to the joyful, and soon to playfulness and tenderness ; a placid character which is quickly reversed by a tone of anger, continued till it leads up to a repetition of all that has gone before. Then comes the unfolding of a tale of passionate aspiration and depression, which works up to a culmination; after which some more repetition of the already twice-heard perturbation and what follows it leads us to the final part, where, after being led in an unearthly way to abstract our thoughts from the present and its surroundings, we at last conclude in the strange mystery with which we set out, though just at the very end there is an effort to shut the mind against its incertitude.—Now, the work in question (as was stated in the programme) is not more remarkable for its beauty of detail than for its general structure, which, as one follows it, impresses one with a cogent sense of coherence and completeness. Yet the verbal ideas seem to bear to each other the relation of the events in the time-honoured tale of the 'old she-bear ;' and surely in seeing what an uninteresting and inconsecutive jumble this really respectable piece of criticism looks, in the unfair light of a statement of 'poetical conceptions,' we see how impossible it would be for a musician deliberately to work it up, and in what total independence of it Schubert must have invented and developed the music. As a figurative *description* of certain effects and transitions (which was doubtless what the writer intended), the remarks may fairly pass ; but as an interpretation or elucidation of what Schubert had in his mind, they would be meaningless ; for they as little reveal or explain the essence of his utterance as a heap of loose garments on the floor reveals or explains the breathing beauty of face and form.

*Even in descriptions which are quite free from absurdity, the verbal ideas do not the least penetrate into the essence of musical effects, which have been evolved in total independence of them.*

It would be pedantic to quarrel with such descriptions : so far as they assist and interest any auditor, they are worth having. But the danger of attaching objective value to them has been conspicuously illustrated in these latter days. Those who agree with Wagner that henceforth every composer with high aspirations is 'to consider it his task to express a preconceived poetical idea by means of sound,' cannot of course ignore the past achievements of Music, nor their own reverent appreciation of them : and the instrumental works of Beethoven are too gigantic a fact

*Danger of attaching objective value to such descriptions, and of considering them in some measure as interpretations.*

in the musical world, their beauty is too overpoweringly evident, for any subsequent theory which proclaimed an absolutely new departure to have a chance of acceptance. So the 'poetical ideas' have to be found in Beethoven: and the only way in which this can be done is by giving objective value to just such subjective and accidental associations as were exemplified in the above description, and by proclaiming that the difference which indisputably exists between the music of Beethoven and that of his predecessors is to be traced to this element. It appears to me that the advocates of this view can be put at once in a dilemma. Suppose, for instance, that I and a thousand others declare to Herr Hüffer, an able and candid exponent of the modern theory, that the most exquisite and overpowering effects we have ever experienced in Art have been through music which conveyed to us *no* idea, poetical or unpoetical, external to itself; and in relation to which such descriptions as that above quoted (though we perceive in what way they are applicable, and may even take occasional interest in them) contain for us no vital truth and suggest nothing of what is really there. He would perhaps say that the music we refer to cannot be that of Beethoven: but when we reply that, on the contrary, it is the works of Beethoven of which we are specially thinking, he would seem driven either to give up the objective value of the 'poetical ideas,' or to maintain that he gets more out of Beethoven than we do; and as we have told him that Beethoven represents to us our very deepest æsthetic emotions, he could only adopt this latter alternative by assuming himself to be markedly superior to all of us in artistic sensibility. A further point could be urged by those of us whose most rapturous musical moments take place as often in silence and solitude as during an actual performance: for Herr Hüffer does not only deny the loftiest impressiveness to music which suggests no idea appreciable in other ways, but he treats such music as presenting mere 'sonorous beauty;' that is, describes it as I should describe a scale or a chord played on a beautiful instrument.

§ 7. Conscious embodiment of extra-musical ideas throughout a long movement is out of the question;

As regards any conscious embodiment of changing ideas throughout a long instrumental movement, no one perhaps will seriously contend for it. Even if a strain of analogy somewhere suggests itself, it has to follow like a shadow in the independent steps of the musical development; and as musical development (especially in Beethoven's own beloved sonata- and symphony-form) has organic necessities wholly of its own, the shadow is apt to become extremely shadowy before long. In other words, 'poetical conceptions' imaginable in details do not penetrate complex musical structure. Any one in listening to a symphony may invent his own phantasmagoria, and the doing so may be as interesting to some people as it is superfluous to others: but at any rate the notion of the composer's sitting deliberately down to depict a shifting set of emotional ideas, unsupported and unjustified by any nucleus or guide of external subject-matter, falls hopelessly to pieces. How little the best descriptive analysis of Beethoven's instrumental music at all represents what he was aiming at in the several parts of a movement, will be plain to any one who reads his own account of the struggles with which he got his musical ideas into shape : and to try to grasp the import of the work by such analysis would be to apply a wrong and totally inadequate mental organ ; exactly as though one who had never seen should try to judge of the beauty of a face by passing his hand over it. The matchless structures stand out to the musical sense as unalterably right and coherent, and any one who musically appreciates them knows as much and can tell as little of their secret as Beethoven himself. The process by which we follow such music as this is as different from that by which we follow the development of a poem as from that by which we follow the steps in a proposition of Euclid ; in fact, the three have nothing in common beyond the mere abstract sense of *following*.

But the reading of the 'preconceived poetical ideas' even into single features is hardly less opposed to reason and evidence. The typical instance is the remark of Beethoven about the opening notes of the C minor symphony, 'It is thus that Fate knocks at the gate,' often quoted as if it were a revelation ! No one would complain of the expression : such fanciful associations may be striking when thrown out in conversation, or useful as safety-valves for excitement. But there seem to be those who believe that Beethoven conceived a desire to ' express Fate,' and then struck three quavers and a minim. If this is not beyond a joke, the joke it is not beyond must be the late Mr. John Parry's musical representation of a boot-jack on the pianoforte. I once heard a first-rate musician say of the magnificent effect produced, at the opening of the *Waldstein* sonata, by the fresh start in B flat of the phrase which has just been heard in C, ' That B flat chord is like getting into a new world :' one may surely enjoy the happiness of the expression without perceiving in the music a preconceived poetical idea of heaven or America. With Beethoven in all his work, no less than with Haydn and Mozart, the musical impulse came first ; the motive might or might not turn out to present describable affinities, but it was first and foremost a musical motive, and often of superlative merit, because Beethoven was Beethoven. Nor would Wagner's own assertion make us believe that he was himself dependent on pilgrimages and heavenly bodies for the *Leitmotiv* of *Tannhäuser* and the glorious invocation to the evening-star.

*and the notion is often hardly less unfortunate in respect of single features.*

No reader who has followed me with assent through the main arguments of this book will find any difficulty in grasping the true relation of the composer's inventive faculty to other things. As a matter of fact, certain people are so constituted that the germs of forms which strike themselves and others as beautiful are continually occurring to them,

*§ 8. The true relation, or absence of relation, of the composers' inventive faculty to extraneous things.*

coming as it were unbidden and demanding presentation ; [1] and a great natural facility in developing and arranging these melodic and harmonic ideas, so as to build them into an organic work, is commonly connected with the gift of originating them ; though composers have differed greatly in the ease with which the more mechanical work of setting and interweaving their combinations has been done. The delight is so strong and the impulse so overpowering that all sweet and noble emotion, and many extraneous trains of thought, are likely, in one thus gifted, to connect themselves subjectively and intangibly with the prominent train of ideal conceptions. And it is by no means impossible that the composer may himself be deceived as to the sort and amount of objective embodiment which in one case or another he may imagine he has given to these : for a person quite unused to psychological analysis may easily get confused between the immediate cause and the actual result of his artistic impulse. But it is a simple matter of evidence that the power of creating beautiful music may be as independent of any conscious sense of these interactions as of a definite prior and external aim or standpoint. And whatever be the author's subjective state of mind, he is able to delight the world only through the welling-up in his mind of forms of objective and self-evident beauty, which may dimly reflect nationality and temperament, but which convey by themselves no tangible reference to experience or environment or external conceptions of any sort, and are in a quite unexampled degree the simple result of a unique and self-absorbed activity. When once he is engrossed in his work these musical ideas will have it all their own way, and in proportion as the world is genuinely delighted, will it trouble itself little about ulterior suggestions. The inventive faculty, once set, so to speak, for a largo or a scherzo or whatever it may be, works on in the given vein. Not in one case in a hundred has any definite image or conception been suggested for the more important class of instrumental pieces ; [2] and it would clearly be absurd to say that such indefinite ab-

---

[1] Apart from questions of analogy and interpretation, people often speak of a composer's musical thought or idea, and his presentation or expression of it, as different things. This is either a truism or a confusion. The musical idea in his head is different from the notes written on music-paper ; and the germ of the idea struggling into shape is different from the idea as completely evolved. But of course there is no *investiture* of the idea in music : it is music from the beginning. If a composer has in his head an impression of something musical which is yet totally destitute of shape, he merely so far resembles the people who seem to hear beautiful music in dreams ; music which is of course inexpressible, inasmuch

as no true musical form or idea is involved in those vague mists of imagined sound.

[2] An amusing instance of the danger enthusiasts for a theory run in catching at straws of suggestion from the original source, is afforded in connection with Beethoven's sonata, of which the three movements are entitled *Les Adieux*, *L'Absence*, and *Le Retour*. The work has been delightfully commented on and gushed about as a pourtrayal of passages from the life of two lovers. Unfortunately, however, on the original copy Beethoven wrote :—
'Farewell on the departure of His Imperial Highness the Archduke Rudolph, the 4th May, 1809,' and 'Arrival of His Imperial Highness the Archduke Rudolph, the 30th January, 1810.'

stractions as tremendousness, or tenderness, or sportiveness, were what any movement was written to express. Such qualities are not the result of any conscious direction of the faculties, but are simply inherent in forms which present themselves to the composer as independent and ultimate phenomena: and in the working up of these there is a considerably larger proportion than is commonly supposed of semi-mechanical skill, acquired by sound musical education, not inspired by views of the universe.

But the words of great composers are the best statement of the truth here set forth. Beethoven's complaints of his interpreters and expounders were frequent and bitter; but it is naturally in the writings of the more literary musicians, Mendelssohn and Schumann, that we should look for coherent expressions on the subject. Mendelssohn wrote, 'What any music *I* like expresses for me is not *thoughts too indefinite* to clothe in words, but *too definite.*—If you asked me what I thought on the occasion in question, I say, the song itself precisely as it stands. And if, in this or that instance, I had in my mind a definite word or definite words, I would not utter them to a soul, because words do not mean for one person what they mean for another; because the song alone can say to one, can awake in him, the same feelings it can in another—feelings, however, not to be expressed by the same words;' a passage which pretty satisfactorily disposes of the essentialness of extra-musical ideas and feelings, to Mendelssohn at all events. Schumann's position as regards verbal readings of music may be gathered from such passages as the following:— 'Critics always wish to know what the composer himself cannot tell them; and critics sometimes hardly understand the tenth part of what they talk about. Good heavens! will the day ever come when people will cease to ask us what we mean by our divine compositions? Pick out the fifths, but leave us in peace.' 'Different ages select different bases for their texts and pictures; where the youth of eighteen hears a world-famous occurrence in a musical work, a man only perceives some rustic event, while the musician probably never thought of either, but simply gave the best music that he happened to feel within him just then.' Speaking of Bennett's *Musical Sketches*, he says that the composer himself might be unable to tell whether the impulse came from within or without. And again, 'Beethoven understood the danger he ran with the *Pastoral* Symphony. How absurd is it in painters to make portraits of him sitting beside a brook, his head in his hands, listening to the bubbling water.' Once he even goes so far as to object to the very titles of the *Heroic* and *Pastoral* Symphonies; and there is one passage of special indignation at a mob of chatterers who, after a performance of the Choral Symphony, professed to find in it 'all forms of poetry,' and interpreted it as the history

§ 9. Remarks of great composers on the subject.

of the origin of man, containing the entire first chapter of the Pentateuch. 'Must a great man always find a thousand dwarfs at his heels?'[1]

§ 10. Pro-
gramme-music.

Only one important paper of Schumann's shows a certain confusion and inconsistency of thought on this head; and it is worth noticing, as it introduces the subject of *programme-music*. In speaking of the verbal programme which accompanied a symphony of Berlioz, he marks the exact distinction between æsthetic perception and superficial amusement, when he says that 'all Germany greeted it with the declaration that such signboards have an unworthy and empirical air;' but that 'a Frenchman, reading the programme as he listens, would applaud the countryman who so intelligently treated the whole.' But he seems to lose the point, and to confound essence and accident when he goes on, evidently influenced by the beauty which as a musician he found in the work, to find some defence of its plan in such obvious but irrelevant considerations as the following:—'Involuntarily an idea sometimes develops itself simultaneously with the musical fancy;' and, 'Why is it not possible that the idea of immortality occurred to Beethoven while extemporising? Why should not the idea of a fallen hero excite him to composition?' Of course such things may and do happen, and the creative activity is thereby quickened; but creative activity may be quickened by lofty thoughts in dozens of directions where the objective results of the activity will still have no intrinsic connection with the thoughts: and, moreover, an inspiring thought is not a programme. Schumann himself suggests a doubt 'whether the listener, unaware of the composer's intention, would see similar pictures in his mind's eye to those which Berlioz has designated;' and this is really a complete admission of the vague and

---

[1] My only defence for such prolonged insistence on the argument of this and the preceding chapter would be to increase their length and tedium by copious quotations, showing the extraordinary prevalence of the fog I am attempting to disperse. Such phrases as that Music 'is the reproduction in tone-language of the feeling in the mind of the composer,' and that a composer has 'to dive into the psychological mysteries of the human heart' to get at the feeling, the description of a movement as 'seemingly having nothing to do with the rest of the sonata, but doubtless having a profound signification in the mind of the composer' (and these examples might be multiplied by the thousand) —all point to the same figment of the necessary pre-existence of some extraneous and independent feeling or idea for which notes have to be found. Even such expressions as that with Beethoven in some of his latest works the *idea* became everything, the *form* of expression nothing, though containing a perfectly correct meaning, are apt to give countenance to the fallacy. It may be true that the works in question lack clear intelligible evolution and connection of the parts in the larger organism of a movement. It may be also true that to many ears the parts, the melodies and motives, the forms in the stricter and more organic sense, appear incoherent, *in*organic, form-*less*: but just in proportion as any individual finds this to be the case must musical ideas be non-existent for him in what is presented. Every true musical idea, to everybody who apprehends it, *is* a form, an ἰδέα, an organic piece of Ideal Motion: and so far as any composer presents pieces of motive in a germinal and *un*formed state, so far are valuable ideas, not loosely and ungrammatically *expressed*, but *not there* in the notes, however much potentially resident in the future workings of the composer's brain.

subjective character of musical phenomena regarded in the light of symbols. We have seen that the interest of some single simple suggestion may be vivid enough to last through slight and short instrumental works, where the whimsicality of the connection is often half the charm. Even in more elaborate works, the fact that there is no evident cause for the order in which movements of various pace and character succeed each other, gives a certain *raison d'être* to a few external suggestions in respect of the very broadest attributes. The suggestion of *Les Adieux, L'Absence,* and *Le Retour,* for instance, over and above the convenience of a title, affords a sort of completeness and justification to the succession of parts. No one would complain of the adjunct of headings to the *Pastoral* symphony, as long as it is recognised that the essential beauty and significance of the work might be realised by a person who had never left the centre of a city ; that if that beauty be truly perceived, the additional interest due to having been in the country cannot be put at more than one per cent. of the whole ; and that however truly the impression of the music, with its calm and storm and rustic dance, may be said to 'resemble' emotions evoked by pastoral scenes, the emotions they far more vitally resemble are those evoked by the other symphonies of Beethoven. Deliberately to force a string of more detailed analogies on a long instrumental work is to trifle with the sources of inspiration, and to endanger the musical ideas at the risk of merely exciting after all an empty, transitory, and mechanical interest. In proportion as the suggestions are minute will they become childish or grotesque ; as when a midnight ride through a goblin-haunted forest produces a cantering figure in the bass and an orchestral cacophony of cries, shrieks, and groans : while a parallelism which is loose and general, and to that extent harmless, is still a snare in proportion as stress is laid on it ; in proportion, that is, as persons are led by the programme to concentrate their attention on the sort of external characters the music ought successively to present, and then to think it very clever if only it presents them, forgetting that an appropriate air of solemnity or sentiment or agitation is as easy to assume as it is irrelevant to intrinsic coherence and enduring charm. It is distinctly detrimental to the musical perception and education of many hearers to have this obvious stage of extraneous comparison to take refuge in. They cannot all be expected to perceive of themselves with Schumann, that 'the main point is still whether the music is anything in itself without words and illustrations : ' that is what it is the business of composers to prove to them by taking them captive. ' People err,' says Schumann, ' when they suppose that composers prepare pens and paper with the deliberate predetermination of sketching, painting, expressing this or that.' But unfortunately this is just what Berlioz *did* do, and what many would extol him for doing.

# CHAPTER XVI.

## MUSIC IN RELATION TO INTELLECT AND MORALITY.

§ 1. The view of the isolation of musical impressions has now to be extended in several directions.

IN the last two chapters we have been considering the *rationale* and limits of Music's power directly to express and suggest definite emotions, images, and ideas, as exemplified in the best music of our own era. We must now take a rather more comprehensive view of the position in which the art stands, or has stood, to life in its various aspects, to the individual, and to society. The central view of our discussion has been the uniqueness of the impressions in which the essence of musical pleasure consists, and this has been now presented both as a deduction and a fact. Our next task will be chiefly to extend the conception of the uniqueness and its consequences in various directions. I feel too strongly the general fascination of the ideas of kinship and solidarity between lofty emotions, I realise too vividly how delightful it would be if those who appreciate Shakespeare were *ipso facto* in a condition to appreciate Beethoven, and *vice versâ*, not to be aware of the prejudice to which this idea of uniqueness and isolation is liable ; a prejudice which is perhaps more likely to tell in connection with what follows than in connection with the drier arguments on which the view itself was founded. That Music should seem to lose in dignity by isolation is the result of what to all non-musical and many musical persons is the natural way of regarding the subject. Nor, on the other hand, is this independence and uniqueness a thing which devotees who do not disown it can fairly appeal to *per se* as a sign of the loftiness of their art ; for the high and the low, the raptures of devotion and the taste of olives, may both affect us in very unique ways. The appeal can only be to experience : when this is rightly interpreted, the incredulous will have no right to look down on impressions as sensuous or trifling, which are declared to be something else by those who show in other ways a capacity of self-analysis ; nor again will musicians be reduced by jealousy for the dignity of their art to prop it up by unreal supports and connections. And it is this latter tendency which I am most concerned to resist, inasmuch as Music, like many other things, suffers most from its friends.

§ 2. The isolation is foreshadowed

The barest statement of the earliest facts of Music, as here conceived, suffices to foreshadow the subsequent relation of the art to the world of ideas and feelings outside itself. If its simplest elements can be referred in the earliest dawn of musical phenomena. to the mere functions of nerve-cells, and for ages before logical processes were possible it was building up its groundwork in the organism and summoning to its aid, through association, by far the most powerful and exciting feelings of primitive times, we shall not be surprised at finding it ruling mightily in a sphere whence we seek in vain to trace back the infinitely long and subtle trains of past feeling ; or at seeing its emotions swayed in apparent independence of the rest of our nature, and, if at one time harmonising with other things, at another soaring off among heights and depths which are wholly their own. We see at once the distinction between this art and the arts of representation ; and how completely inapplicable to it, though true of them, are Comte's *dicta* that 'Art begins at first with simple imitation, which becomes raised into idealisation,' that 'Art may be defined as an ideal representation of fact,' and that 'the contemplations of the artist begin with the simple objects of the external world.' We see that Music lived ages ago, as it lives now, quite aloof from imitation, and how the germ of the æsthetic faculty, in the sense of the *association of order with emotion*, existed independently in the apprehension of its earliest and most rudimentary utterances : for while the other arts find order in, and impose order on, external facts, Music finds it in her own essence. It is curious to observe how the metaphysician Wagner and the positivist Comte, who, though on different grounds, agree in considering the germs of song to have preceded speech, have missed in different ways the essentialness of form or order to the idea of art. Wagner considers that man's first utterances came nearer to the *noümenon* or true reality ; Comte that 'the first things we express are those which move our feelings most,' so that primitive utterances were more *æsthetic* than subsequent more conventional ones. The latter view is the more intelligible, but equally with the other ignores the element of order : primitive instinctive cries are neither more nor less æsthetic, in the accepted sense of the term, than subsequent conventional ones, because neither are æsthetic at all. Whether the wailings of an infant express *noümena*, or (as seems more probable) the infant's private feelings, they have no connection with art : and the above views have as little meaning when applied to the development of Music in the world as when applied to the vocal efforts of a future *prima donna* at the age of three weeks.

No clear conception can be gained of the true relation of Music to the § 3. The essential characteristics of Music must be carefully distinguished from the facts of its historical employment in connection with words ; rest of our faculties, and no sort of explanation can be given of its position in the world, unless we are careful to separate what may be termed the accidents of its history from its essential characteristics. As a matter of fact, its employment by civilised man was, till comparatively recently, almost entirely in connection with words. This was to be expected, until the development of the art and its instruments should have reached an advanced point. The voice—man's first and most natural instrument —is also the organ of speech, and speech arrived at high (in Greece the highest) development while Music's full powers were wholly undreamed of. What wonder that the hymn should 'rule the lyre'—that speech called on the budding art to add charm and emphasis to words and held it under an imperious sway ? But the historical connection between Music and Poetry has led many to suppose that this is the ideal condition, and will be more than ever realised in the future. The view that Poetry and Music should unite, each at its highest, and that the period of possible independence is the passing and less valuable stage, is almost invariably connected with the idea that the germs of the two arts started together. My view is of course the reverse, that the musical instinct existed long before coherent intellectual conceptions were possible, and that Music, having passed through a long and imperfect stage of tutelage, breaks forth in the fulness of her unfettered strength, still indeed a possible ally of Poetry, but insisting everywhere on her own inalienable rights. I will not trench here on the subject of the actual objective union of the two arts, which we shall consider in the chapters on Song and Opera : but this will be the place to examine somewhat further the question of the general relationship between these so-called sister-arts. It is here I think that the question of origin becomes of extreme importance. If the germs of musical emotion are traced back through thousands and thousands of organisms to ages far beyond the more distinctly intellectual conceptions of Poetry, we shall be led to regard very differently the attempted connections and mutual interpretations of the two arts in their developed forms. I am not claiming greater intrinsic value for musical emotions, only a longer history ; and in this respect their position among our artistic feelings may be compared to that of the deep sea-currents, part of the same ocean as the waves above, but not in obvious close connection with them or a guide to their pace and direction.

Not that I would ignore the immense scope of the sense of analogy in the emotional region. Even in the absence of inherent connection, the fuller vitality resulting from a powerful stirring of one part of our emotional nature seems often to quicken all the higher faculties and susceptibilities, and in this way might well give rise to associations between them. But though subjective affinities of course exist between many deep impressions and emotions of the same being, it is not enough realised how different these are from interpretations or translations. Words are, in a general way, so closely interlocked with ideas, that it seems a kind of necessity of thought to crystallise all impressions by their means : and Poetry, being the art of words *par excellence*, is vaguely regarded as a natural mine of conceptions and metaphors suited to all emotional experiences, and able to embody all lofty reality. The very

*which has greatly misled speculation.*

*§ 4. One may admit a large amount of subjective analogy between different orders of impressions, while entirely repudiating attempts to give these objective value, and to explain or interpret one order by another.*

attempt to express one thing in terms of another often seems to give the kind of relief that one gets from bodily change of posture ; for the dwelling on anything wholly within its own region is apt to produce a kind of mental pins-and-needles. But there is a distinct danger of mistaking this sort of mental relief for fresh knowledge, and of ignoring the point at which impressions become ultimate through a true differentiation of our faculties. A man who calls Milan Cathedral a marble poem, or conceives of his *fiancée* as a female poem, does what is quite justifiable but not instructive ; for he does not really judge these objects, either as a whole or in detail, by reference to Poetry. The secret of the uniformities he is dimly conscious of lies in the furthest depths of his own being, and is not penetrated by imaginary identifications of widely varying impressions ; young ladies and cathedrals not being really poems any more than cathedrals are young ladies. Similarly there is no harm in calling a picture a symphony,[1] as long as it is recognised that such uniformity as is

---

[1] A good deal of what one hears about 'subtle affinities' between the arts is connected with the old trap, the failure to distinguish between Form and Colour. We saw in the first chapter that between the *colour*-impressions of the eye and the ear there *is* an occasional affinity, extremely inferior in degree but still remotely comparable to that between the impressions of taste and smell. The resemblance between trumpet-tones and scarlet may be called subtle, in the sense that the feeling of it, while perfectly distinct, is still very peculiar and indescribable. Between a visual and an auditory *form* there can of course be no affinity at all, except such most broad and *un*subtle ones as the being both of them impressive and beautiful, or unimpressive and mean. If any one should assert an affinity between Painting and Music on the grounds, *e.g.*, that partial repetition of line may be compared to parallelism in the direction of contiguous phrases, or that the principle of contrast is perpetually observed by both arts in the arrangement of parts, we may leave him to extract such illumination as he can from his *rapprochement* ; only remarking (what was sufficiently dwelt on as regards Music in the tenth chapter) that these features are as common in the worst compositions as in the best ; and that therefore unless he goes the length of comparing some actual embodiment of them in a beautiful picture with some actual embodiment of them in a beautiful musical piece, the abstract fact that they are presentable in both arts does not seem charged with much emotional power.

The representative arts naturally possess more ground for affinities among themselves, since they have a large amount of common subject-matter, and may express common ideas and sentiments. But even in their case the agreement is often unduly pressed. A poet indeed is not often called a painter, except in relation to some special bit of description ; it being pretty obvious that sensitiveness to visible beauty is a quality which even a great poet might conceivably lack, and which several great poets have possessed in no greater degree than many other persons of artistic perception and taste. But one often hears a painter called a poet, in a way which is misleading precisely in proportion as a definite meaning is attached to it. We cannot dispense with the word *poetical*, as applied to that way of regarding things which seeks to draw out from them such beauty and emotional power as they possess. But if every producer who delights in poetical aspects of things is to be considered *a poet* and a producer of *poems*, these words lose all distinctive meaning. A poet is a creator of a certain kind. And if a painter cannot create after this kind, he is not at all differentiated from his fellows in virtue of certain ideas and sentiments which he shares with a poet, this being broad common ground shared by thousands of others : he shows his difference from those others not by doing what a poet does, but by doing what a painter does. That is to say, as soon as poet and painter begin to occupy the common ground of thought and feeling, or to occupy new ground of their own, with their own individual creations—as

felt consists in the most general attribute of harmonious beauty, the manifestation of which in the one case throws no light on that in the other, and may be fully appreciated by one who is totally blind or deaf to the other. Though one hears people talk of such and such a picture as being ' like music,' no one, I suppose, was ever so bold as to say that a picture, or a part of a picture, was like a particular modulation from C into E minor ; [1] and it is this, and things like this (not technically known, but felt), which give the true artistic musical pleasure, as distinct from general and suffusive feelings of admiration, excitement, or awe.

The 'instrumental poems' of Beethoven. And these remarks will apply at once to the ' instrumental poems' which we hear so much about. On this subject the modern theories, as we saw in the last chapter, have made Beethoven the inevitable centre of dispute. It is a real distress that the bone of contention should be the music in love of which all are so profoundly one. When I read anything written with so much insight and reverence as the paper on that music contributed some years ago by Mr. Dannreuther to *Macmillan's Magazine*, I vividly feel, ' *Amicus* Dannreuther ;' but again some of his remarks in that very paper—as that Beethoven's later music preaches ' depreciation of self and negation of personality ' [2]—compel me to add ' *major amicus* Beethoven,' and to recognise that any attempt at mutual comprehension is hazardous. It is not necessary to repeat what has been already said as to the supposed poetical basis of great instrumental works. The ' poetical conceptions' have almost always to be guessed at ; for to say, as Mr. Dannreuther does, that where not avowed they are implied, is simply to beg the question. But even had Beethoven always, instead of extremely seldom, hinted at such things, and even had he never, instead of frequently, complained of the discovery of them by others, I should say the same. The reference to some analogue in another region may, as we saw, have been occasionally an interest and a convenient verbal outlet to Beethoven as to others : two melodic parts may seem to sustain a dialogue or a dispute, storm and struggle may yield to calm and sunshine, Fate may knock at the gate : but the whimsical absurdities which result from attempts to press home and

soon as they set to work in the fashion which constitutes them poet and painter instead of poetical and artistic persons—their activities diverge ; and the intellectual qualities called into play are hardly if at all less distinct from one another than is the process of casting thought into metrical language from the process of putting colours on canvas. It is worth noting that this is the case even in places where the two sorts of art seem to have most common ground. The opening of *Œnone*, for instance, differs from a mere catalogue of objects by dint of something which a painter no more keenly perceives, and could no more himself produce, than any other true appreciator of the poem.

[1] Perhaps, however, I underestimate the possibilities of human audacity : for since writing this I have heard of a dispute between a master and pupil as to whether a particular modulation in a sonata of Mozart meant ' but ' or ' if.'

[2] It is curious to find this phrase quoted with approbation by an able critic who himself truly describes Beethoven's later works as ' full of intense personality and a wild unimprisoned spirit.'

follow out such fancies, even in the comparatively few cases where they seem momentarily obvious enough to be interesting, show what an unessential luxury they are. And are we poorer instead of richer if our worlds are multiplied? Are we bound to catch the echoes of the visible world in all we hear? For it must be noticed that even such descriptive analogies as can be plausibly adduced are not in any special sense poetical, but only of some external or human significance: there is no poetry in such isolated conceptions as grief and triumph, appeal and response, storm and calm and moonlight, and the rest. And indeed the tendency I have been discussing seems to me as damaging to the idea of Poetry as to that of Music. It would almost seem as if those who so speak conceived of Poetry only in unformed and unrelated streaks and patches, and not in its truly artistic aspects. Poetry differs indeed from Music in drawing its subjects from life, but that does not mean that all life is Poetry, any more than all sounds are Music: and the greatest poetical artists, in discovering and drawing forth the latent harmonies of human and natural relations, exercise an imaginative faculty as much beyond the crude suggestions of programme 'analysis' as the composer who draws forms of unparalleled beauty from his meaningless six octaves of notes.

The idea that instrumental music is, or can or should be, a sort of transfigured poetry, is too preposterous to be steadily and consistently kept in sight by any one: but there is another common misconception as to the intellectual bearings of Music, of a quite different kind. And as the former idea seemed to be more or less vaguely connected with the long dependence of Music on Poetry, so the idea we are now to consider is connected with the complete breaking of that dependence, and the tremendous assertion of Music's unique predominance in the last century and a half. The recession of that phase of Music in which its independent emotional power was less recognised theoretically (though practically, of course, exemplified in every case where any melody spoke to any human being), and in which the great business of the art was supposed to be to emphasise and beautify the enunciation of verbally-expressed doctrines and sentiments, has considerably misled speculation on the subject; and we are always hearing modern music, in its principal instrumental developments, connected with the complexities of modern sentiment and the self-consciousness and introspectiveness of modern life and thought, as though the same causes had effected in both cases a gradual modification.

§ 5. Weakness of the attempt to make out a close and definite correspondence between modern music and modern thought.

The synchronism can, I think, be shown to be of scarcely any real significance. Nobody can have paid the slightest attention to the history of Music without observing how entirely its advances depended on its material, under which must be included both the instruments presenting it and the prevailing scale-system, the set of notes and relations out of which its forms have to be constructed. As long as the presentation of

Music was almost confined to the voice, a musician would not be likely to imagine forms which the voice was wholly incompetent to execute : and if he had, his compositions would have had no existence except on paper. Still more important and fundamental, in respect of musical possibilities, is the scale-system. The actual set of notes, the uninteresting and un-emotional stuff which lies ready for all to build from, differs from the material of all other arts in that it is itself gradually modified and de-veloped *pari passu* with its use. Each musician inherits a material which has become what it is by being tried and worked up into forms, a set of relations which have gradually established themselves in the very process of artistic invention and success.[1] And any being born with any musical faculty, with any power, that is, of perceiving a succession of tones as a coherent group, leaps straight into the conditions and possibilities belong-ing to the system which prevails around him. The feeling for the modern elements of tonality and harmony can be awakened in an organism which has certainly not received them by inheritance : even were there not suffi-cient evidence in the small number of generations during which the modern system has prevailed, this has been abundantly proved in the case of negroes and Hottentots, and (as regards melody at all events) of parrots. A negro is not more complex or introspective than an Athenian of the great age ; and it seems therefore pretty certain that our music would in a very short time have been quite comprehensible and delightful to an ancient Athenian could he but have lived among it. A Greek had the suggestions for perfect sculpture in the forms he daily saw : and his marble lay ready to his hand : his music was limited by the limitations of his meagre instru-ments and of his system of notes and note relations, which afforded material indeed for heart-stirring melody, but (in the absence of harmony and mo-dulation) gave little chance for wide variety and development. The fact that he did not discover anything like the modern system is precisely on a par with the facts that he did not discover the planet Neptune, or the steam-engine, or photography, or Cremona violins. Accident has always played a large part in the history of discovery : and a single nation in a limited time cannot do everything. The complete foundation of modern music was a very difficult thing to arrive at, and required a long experimental process, carried on by generations of writers, performers, and listeners. Once found out, the coherence and variety of the structures based on it, and the convenience therefore of the basis, commend themselves to the human ear as readily as the adaptability and convenience of prominent architec-tural elements to the human eye. Having obtained at last mechanical facilities, and a suitable material in the tempered scale-system with all its

---

[1] This of course applies to all manner of combinations and fragments of progression which are of perpetual occurrence, and have become as much the common property of musicians as the notes and common chords of the scale.

possibilities of harmony and modulation, Music advanced naturally and rapidly to its great achievements; which, be it observed, are connected for the most part with the names of singularly simple and one-idea'd men,[1] and which in many cases have belonged to the very earliest manhood of artists who had lived from babyhood absorbed in their one pursuit.

In speculating on this point it is beside the mark to argue from such facts as the simplicity of Greek drama, or the absence from their literature of analytical works of fiction; for in accordance with our theory of Music's peculiar history in relation to the organism, we constantly find persons quite incapable of appreciating and unravelling complexities in other regions, to whom in music the faculty is natural. Music is thus specially calculated to illustrate the danger of over-centralising—so to speak—the springs of emotional enjoyment, and of forcing correspondences among the æsthetic faculties for the sake of a factitious symmetry and unity. The metaphors in which one line of perception is illustrated by another are in this way often misleading. For instance, M. Boutmy, in his excellent little work on the architecture of the Greeks, illustrates by a brilliant metaphor that especially Ionian dislike of marked contrasts, and preference for flowing and easy transitions, wherein he thinks the people's characteristic love of ease and calm, of an orderly and peaceful life, was translated into their buildings. Consonances, he says, abound in this architecture; dissonances are almost unknown: the harmonies of Beethoven, profound and mournful, with their resolution constantly deferred, give place to the short and simple modulations which Cimarosa brings perpetually to rest on the perfect concord. This illustration is admirable for its purpose: but just because illustrations of the sort are possible, it is important to beware of deducing any vital affinity between different orders of impression from such extremely abstract principles as, *e.g.*, dislike of contrasts and complexities. Among the Greeks, for example, the architectural transitions might be simple and flowing; so might the approved dance-movements: but if we turn to poetry, the metrical structure often presents most sudden turns and contrasts; and in the arrangement of long strophes and antistrophes, the ear is constantly kept waiting very long for the resolution of its expectation by the symmetrical balance of the answering verse. Again, it might be easy to argue from characteristics of their sculpture that the Greeks lacked that special modern sense of melan-

*Speculation with regard to the Greeks, and danger of crude conclusions.*

---

[1] It is odd to notice what minute things in a man gifted with genius in one direction are taken as signs of genius in all. Mozart's widow said to some English visitors that 'Mozart loved all the arts, and had a genius for most of them. He drew a little and excelled in dancing. Indeed, he was an angel,' she added, 'and is one in heaven now.' We may hope he is, without considering that drawing a little and excelling in dancing are signs of special genius. So one has heard it said of Mendelssohn (who no doubt was a man of more than average culture), on the ground of his having made a little sketch on one side of a leaf and written a few verses on the other, that had he taken seriously to Painting or Poetry he would have excelled in them no less than in Music.

choly which is connected with conflicts of material and spiritual forces and a generally less harmonious life : but we know that they had pathetic music, and in the opinion of Plato appreciated it only too well.

Whether or not the Greeks, as a nation, would have appreciated such music as Beethoven's, had the modern scale-system and its results appeared two thousand odd years sooner, is of course a doubtful question : but if not, it would have been simply because their musical nature had not sufficient vigour to lend itself to such mighty and often complex kinds of Ideal Motion ; which is just what may be said of the Latin races of the present day.  To say they would not have liked it because of its passion and profundity would be quite misleading, if it were meant that they would have found in it a suggestion of new and unwelcome conceptions or emotions. Music among us is perfectly and profoundly appreciated by thousands of men, women, and children whose habits of thought and sentiment bear no characteristic stamp of a restless and analytical age.   A musical child may feel the overmastering magic of Beethoven before the shadows or conflicts of life have any existence for him ; and his circumstances and temperament may be such that in point of emotional and imaginative experiences he remains pretty much of a child in adult years, while Music retains the monopoly of stirring him to the depths.  The Greeks might not have apprehended Beethoven : their musical faculty might have refused to grasp his forms. But if they had apprehended, they would certainly have enjoyed : for where the range of impressions is self-contained and there are no definable external references, apprehension and enjoyment of beauty are virtually synonymous.  We may apprehend a poem, and while appreciating its artistic merits may be pained by its images and suggestions : not so a musical piece.  Whether the Greeks would altogether have approved of their enjoyment is another matter ; and here really lies the doubt as to the value they might have assigned to our music, in its striking dissociation from politics and religion.  Their intense feeling for ἁρμονία in life might have inclined them to be sceptical as to the goodness of a quite differentiated range of emotion, however delightful ; and it would have been extremely interesting to watch the ethical conflict which might have ensued.  But a radical misconception is involved in the attempt to connect modern music directly with modern introspectiveness and ' subjectivity :' any beautiful musical form is as objective a phenomenon to the people who care for it as a beautiful face, and probably produces on all of them equally similar impressions.

The connection between the present position of Music and the intellectual facts of the age is a negative one.

The position of Music as the popular modern art can only be truly connected with general facts of contemporary intellectual life in this negative way, that the uprooting of beliefs and blight of satisfying ideals has made many men the more thankful for a region of pleasurable emotion whose reality gives no possible handle for question or attack.  This is a reason for its being a specially fortunate circumstance that Music is now what it is, but clearly is not at the root of its extraordinary and self-engen-dered development.

We have really but to think of the people we know or have heard of, *Argumentum ad hominem.* to realise the generally isolated and accidental position of musical suscep-tibility among the mental faculties and habits. Music is no more loved by clever people than by stupid ones; no more by the poetical and imaginative than by the prosaic and matter-of-fact. Bentham loved it deeply, Lessing was driven out of the room by it, and such instances might be multiplied to any extent. The only *set* of people to whom the taste has ever been attributed with the slightest plausibility is mathemati-cians. There can hardly be anything more in this than so far as a taste for symmetry and neatness may give a person a certain pleasure both in figures and formulæ and in the more external aspects of precise and symmetrical musical designs, as, *e.g.*, a two-part invention of Bach's, or a canon.[1] But the view, as usually stated, is always found to rest on a certain number of known instances, which could be instantly paralleled from any other class. As regards performers, again, to whom as a class we should unhesitatingly look for a special 'taste for Music,' how often will Pomfret's couplet recur to the mind—

> Melania dotes upon the silliest things,
> And yet Melania like an angel sings!

a poetical exaggeration which needs modifying in the second line quite as often as in the first; and which at any rate suggests the truth in so far as musical talent, being an isolated gift, may be possessed by the most or-dinary people, and is a sign of nothing beyond itself.

Having considered Music in its relation (or want of relation) to the § 6. Music must be judged by the amount of *pleasure* it gives or is capable of giv-ing, and is only *indirectly* con-nected with morality. intellectual side of life, we may pass on to the ethical. The second great fact involved in the general view of Music's singularly independent nature is that what is partially true of all the arts is wholly true of this one—that it must be judged by us directly in relation to pleasure, and that pleasure is the only criterion by which we can measure the relative worth of different specimens of it. The pleasure, from its peculiarity, its power of relieving the mind and steeping it as it were in a totally new atmosphere, its indescribable suggestions of infinity, and its freedom from any kind of deleterious after-effects, is of an extremely valuable kind; and moreover, since indirect effects may be to the full as strong and important as direct, my argument would not affect the fact, but only the grounds, of

---

[1] One of the most eminent mathematicians in England connects mathematical and mu-sical culture as 'similar in their habits and affections.' He calls 'Music the Algebra of sense, Algebra the Music of the reason; Music the dream, Algebra the waking life— the soul of each the same!' It is not won-derful that the same writer should say Horace would have been a senior-wrangler, on the ground of his having used the alcaic stanza with metrical skill.

This is opposite to the ancient view, as represented by Plato.

the connection of Music with morality. Still the view, as here stated, is at palpable issue with that which is commonly maintained: and the opposition to it is generally supported by references to Plato, the great representative of the ancient view, who very rarely relaxes his tone even to the extent of saying that he does not mean wholly to exclude pleasure, and that ' songs may be an amusement to cities.' We cannot enter on the subject better than by considering the grounds on which that ancient view rested.

We find the reason of the difference in the extremely simple character and the completely subordinate position (already noticed) of Music as conceived by Plato. In those times the true independent power of Music was almost latent, and, as a mere accessory to other things, it might in various ways receive an ethical import. How elementary was Plato's view of melody, and how dependent on external associations, is shown in his weighing the merits of rhythm, not in connection with the *notes* of a melody, but by simple reference to the kinds of *physical movement* which accompanied them in the dances he knew.[1] More important, of course, would be the direct association with *words and occasions*, which in the music described by Plato would always be present, especially as he was exceedingly anxious to limit it in amount and to prevent novelties. In the dialogue of the *Laws*, the Athenian stranger tells how in Egypt all art has remained unchanged for 10,000 years, during which time the ancient chants composed by the goddess Isis had received neither alteration nor addition ; and remarks, ' How wise and worthy of a great legislator !' while, on the other hand, he regrets that ' in other places novelties are always being introduced in dancing and music at the instigation of lawless pleasure.' The bard of versatile poetical and histrionic talent, who deals in variety of melodic and rhythmic transitions, is to be anointed indeed and crowned ' as a sacred, admirable, and charming personage,' but to be promptly sent away to another city. It could only have been association with the words of the song or the gestures of the dance, which made Plato so invariably represent Music as simply representative and imitative : for while he sees no difficulty in the analogy between the copy of a human form in sculpture and the copy of virtue and vice in Music, and speaks, as if everybody would comprehend him, of ' the natural rhythms of a well-regulated and manly life,' he nevertheless expressly says that ' when there are no words it is difficult to recognise the meaning of harmony or rhythm, or to see that any worthy object is imitated by them.' Some of the

---

[1] The dances of the Mexicans and Guatemalians have been described as having always a particular melody suited to their purpose, and as often becoming scenical. Such melodies would obviously assume an ethical character which would intensify a hundredfold their natural emotional colouring, and which would be confirmed on every occasion of their use.

lengths to which he pushed his views on the ethical bearings of Music are very curious. No instruments of wide compass are to be permitted: the lyre and guitar will be used in the town, the pipe in the country.[1] Not only is the use of instruments otherwise than as accompaniment to be eschewed, as leading to every sort of irregularity and trickery—'for,' says he, 'we must acknowledge that all this sort of thing, which aims only at swiftness and smoothness and a brutish noise, is exceedingly rude and coarse'—but different classes and sexes are to keep to distinct styles, and the grave and wise elders will not only be the best arbiters of Music, but the best performers. 'The Muses,' he says, 'would never fall into the monstrous error of assigning to the words of men the gestures and songs of women, nor combine the melodies and gestures of freemen with the rhythms of slaves and men of the baser sort.'[2] Grand melodies are to be sung by men, those which incline to moderation and temperance by women. Judges of not less than fifty years of age are to make a selection from ancient musical compositions and dances, and may consult poets and musicians, but are not to allow them to indulge, except in some minor matters, their individual fancies. But the most amusing notion is that which concerns the chorus of elderly men; these, by reason of their larger experience and intelligence, have the greatest influence, and therefore are bound to sing the fairest and most useful strains; but as, owing to the sourness of age, they may be expected to entertain a dislike to public artistic appearances, they are to be made slightly intoxicated, in which condition they will greatly edify the public by their performance.

It is of course hard to say how far, in many respects, Plato represents the ordinary Greek views; but he fully corroborates the other evidence which we have of the extreme simplicity of the emotional element in Greek melodies. We have proof of this in the very existence of several well-known styles of melody, each connected with a particular 'mode,' and so definite in character that the name of the 'mode' was sufficient description; somewhat as if we could sufficiently describe the expression of our music by saying a piece was in the major or in the minor, as though a special air of gladness or dolefulness were thereby implied as a matter of course. They had also fixed themes on which different composers made

§ 7. The fewness and distinctness of the styles and absence of elaboration in Greek music must have much facilitated definable expression, which would be perpetually stamped by association.

---

[1] We may compare the remarks of Prynne in the *Histriomastix*, to the effect that 'cymbals and dulcimers are instruments of fraud; that pipes and flutes are to be abandoned from a sober feast; and that chromatical harmonies are to be left to impudent malapertness in wine.'

[2] There is one sentence in the *Laws* which fairly puzzles me. 'Common people are ridiculous in imagining that they know what is in proper harmony and rhythm, and what is not, when they can only be made to sing and step in rhythm by sheer force.' It is not wonderful that Plato should be ignorant as he was, of any musical perception in animals: but the above remark, at all events in respect of marching in time, seems to contradict universal experience, and inclines one to imagine that Plato was not himself musically perceptive.

variations, and fixed melodies to which fresh words were from time to time fitted; all facts indicating what we should naturally have expected, that the very smallness of scale and lack of large variety in their music facilitated a very clear and definable expression in the different specimens of it. And while this characteristic might probably be very perceptible apart from verbal and other associations, the small number and the definiteness of the styles would make it impossible but that such associations should always add their effect. The character of the music was doubtless emphasised by the *timbre* and pitch of the instrument with which it was allied : the effects, *e.g.*, of the shrill Phrygian pipes might find a modern parallel in the pibroch. Only those strains are approved by Plato which represent the tones of men in a courageous or in a temperate mood; plaintive melodies are to be discarded, ' for they are useless even to women that are to be virtuously given, not to say to men.' It is especially forbidden to excite the citizens or make them weep with sorrowful melodies during a sacrifice : such songs should be sung by choruses of foreign minstrels on some polluted and inauspicious day. In the age of subservience of Music to Poetry, as of Art in general to Religion, it is easy to see how one single and obvious emotion at one time, and another at another, would be definitely and deliberately appealed to. Moreover, amid a greater simplicity of outward and inward life, all emotion found much straighter channels to action, so that artistic as well as other appeals to feeling might have far more visible results then than now. We can readily imagine that the Achilles who wept and lamented at an insult might be unnerved by a dolorous chant. If then Music had remained in tutelage, a blighting effect might certainly have been produced on it by the greater repression of individual feelings, the increased self-consciousness and artificiality, and all the restraints of a more complex civilisation, and we might have had reason to lament both the ethical and the æsthetic loss. Luckily, however (and as argued above quite independently), the art itself has undergone still greater revolutions : and melody nowadays, if through external conditions it has little opportunity, so through internal transformation it has still less need, to act as a nucleus of associations, and can pass into popularity without owing anything to occasions or adjuncts.

§ 8. Immense difference entailed both in the external conditions of the modern world, and by the developments of modern music.

I would not willingly forego the advantage of Plato's authority as to the effect of Music on the masses; for this has in no way ceased or decreased, nor have the endless elaborations of modern music by any means outstripped or rendered obsolete the simpler elements whose utterance reaches at once to the comprehension and the heart. Even in modern times Music has lent itself—not, however, by such definite ethical influences as Plato imagined, but by its generally spirit-stirring power—to important ulterior purposes. We are told that in the German Reformation ' the people sang themselves into enthusiasm for the new religion, and many who were hostile to the name of Luther were converted to his tenets by the irresistible charm of the simple and touching Protestant church-psalmody ; ' and that ' the first conversions of some of the Slavonian peoples were due to the sacred melodies of the Church of Constantinople.' Parallel facts are recorded in connection with other missionary enterprises, and with the Wesleyan movement in our own country. But the increase in the population and area of states, and the thousand complexities of modern life, preclude any connection between the popular benefits of Music and the discipline of the *Republic* and the *Laws*. In relation to the sum of Music's present value in the world, its importance in giving zest to the harmonious movements of numbers, or in adding point, force, and una-nimity to verbal sentiments outside the domain of artistic pleasure, from which it in turn receives the benefit of association, has been reduced to a minimum. Whatever ethical influence may still be found in unanimity of movement or of verbal expression, such a result is usually quite indirect and secondary as regards the actual music, not belonging to the essence but to the adaptation of the strains employed. And owing to the growth of the art in extent and intricacy, to its instrumental develop-ments, and to the cosmopolitan character consequent on its release from words in special languages—facts completely beyond Plato's power of prevision—the portions of the whole bulk which carry permanent asso-ciations or are pervaded, like ancient melodies, by a simple definite character, plaintive, orgiastic, triumphant, or whatever it may be, have become an insignificant fraction. Ethical interpretations appear as forced and absurd as naturalistic ones, now that the time is past when Music can be docketed off into a few classes, each connected with a special range of emotion. Military music seems almost the only branch to which it can be pretended that such a character attaches : and even here I for one feel that, if I were inspired to bravery in battle by music, it would be not because I perceived it to be martial, but because I perceived it to be beautiful—in other words, because it gave me an indefinable sense of exhilaration : there is a great deal of martial music which from its in-herent dulness and triteness would make me much more inclined to run away. And it is to be remarked that the very term suggests not a special sort of *melody*, but a special sort of *timbre*, the penetrative and percussive sounds of instruments adapted to the open air. The general effects thus produced on the nerves are wholly different from special appeals to the melodic sense, and belong really to what we have regarded as the *in-definite* way of hearing music.[1] Our previous discussion of that subject

---

[1] I am inclined to think that such *direct* ethical influence as can be at all attributed to Music in our experience is truly to be sought rather in the indefinite than the defi-nite mode of impression. The suffused feel-ing which is perhaps best described as a *sense*

suggests another category of a similar kind in what is often described as *religious* music; where the prominent motion is of slow and massive waves of sound which float beneath a vaulted roof as sweetly and almost as vaguely as incense. But in fact all occasional effects are now as nothing in comparison with the permanent bearing of the art on those in whose lives it forms an important element; and I run no risk of contradiction in saying that for these its value lies not in its sometimes soothing them when they want soothing, or stimulating them when they want stimulating, but in its own special and indescribable revelations.

Music has passed from the stage of drill and use to that of pure and lofty enjoyment.

The case of Music may be compared to the instances, so common in the history of organic life, where things once useful in the struggle for existence have gradually become merely ornamental; for it must be remembered that it was chiefly as fostering warlike habits and aptitudes that Plato considered Music so important a branch of education. This utilitarian stage stands, as it were, midway between the primary use of song as a gift of vital importance to the possessor, calculated, like bright feathers, to allure the opposite sex, and Music's present lofty æsthetic employment. Nor can any but the narrowest view of life and progress conceive as a degradation of the art a transition from the region of struggle and drill and use to that of θεωρία and pure enjoyment. All beautiful things and all healthy emotions tend to dignify existence; and if such power as Music has over life is not by direct suggestion and teaching, but by stimulation of the vital powers which is bound up with the pleasure it gives, this in no way interferes with the tremendous social influence which it can exercise, through sympathy, in swaying a multitude with a common awe and gratitude.

§ 9. Failure of the attempts to force moral significance on modern music.

Those who are unwilling to accept this hedonistic view should notice that the acceptance of the criterion of pleasure will make little practical difference, unless it is maintained that of two musical works one may be in the sum of its effects the more moral, but the less pleasurable. I think, however, that but for the fascination of the ancient view, especially in its connection with Plato's general scheme of education, it would have been more generally remarked how completely the relation of Music to other things must change with its development, and with the consequent cessation of the possibility of associations universally felt and known. It is matter of the commonest experience that in listening to modern music the complex process of attention and emotion perpetually raises the mind to a state of elevation as remote from moral as from immoral suggestions.

*of multitude,* produced by vast masses of sonorous impression—especially in connection with actual delivery by a multitude, as in a great chorus—may involve true though very vague and intangible social associations. But if this be so, it only brings out more clearly the distinction from the ancient idea; since the direct ethical influence, as conceived by the Greeks, was not a matter of overpowering nervous stimulation, but of definite melodic forms.

No amount of such analogies as, *e.g.*, Mr. Haweis has attempted in *Music and Morals* between Beethoven and morality, in point of balance, restraint, reasonableness, and so on, will bridge over the gulf or turn artistic impressions into ethical promptings. Nor even where certain describable emotional states may be plausibly said to be produced by special kinds of music, as the languorous, the triumphant, and so on, can these be accounted less external to the general character of the hearer. For while we can understand the relation of purity and humanity to the appreciation of other arts—how pictures of carnage are likely to be popular when a people are brutalised by much bloodshed, and how highly-coloured literature may have a distinctly deleterious effect on the mind—it is hard to see how that which only produces, according to Mr. Haweis's description, a special emotional atmosphere, uncharged (according to his own admission), either naturally or by association, with any idea applicable to life, can in any direct sense have force to mould conduct. The emotional states where a mind receives a bias are those which depend on some working idea, and which can therefore be summoned up by recalling the idea. An atmosphere can only permanently affect our moral and mental habits when we can make it surround some more definite nucleus. However languorous music may be, its languors cease for the most part with the performance: or, if it be objected that where it haunts the memory the effect is more permanent, and that the prevalence of a particular stamp of melody, like opium or a hot climate, might gradually enervate individual or national character, we not only have an obvious appeal to the absence of physical results, but it is easy to point out a clear difference, and a proof of Music's independence of the movements of the practical reason, in these two facts: that a person may be haunted by music in the midst of and without interruption to the busiest and most opposite avocations; and that the musical emotion may actually produce a feeling of a character the reverse of its own; for the most mournful music, if sufficiently beautiful, may make us happy, and the most jubilant music may leave us mourning over its evanescence.

In contrasting Music with Painting and Sculpture in this respect, we need not at all confine ourselves to questions of directly and deliberately elevating or debasing suggestions. We may easily see the entirely distinct relation of the representative arts to regions of impression from which ethical ideas cannot possibly be excluded, by merely considering what is involved in the daily experiences of the eye and the ear. As we noticed very early in our enquiry, innumerable phenomena are continually meeting both senses: but most of those that meet the eye, through presenting many permanent distinguishable points, are *forms*, and an immense number are the very forms which visual art uses; while those that meet the ear are *formless*, and have no relation to the definite pro-

§ 10. The contrast presented in this respect by the arts of Painting and Sculpture,

portions on which the melodic and harmonic presentations of auditory art depend. Thus, from the moment when as infants we smiled at a kind face and cried at a cross one, association, entering into our experiences of human expression (real or depicted), has largely identified beauty and ugliness with a sense of right and happiness and with a sense of wrong and wretchedness respectively, human beauty being in the main incompatible with surroundings of vice and misery; while musical forms, inasmuch as they are artificial and wholly isolated exceptions among the crowds of unshaped successions of sound (including even kind tones and pleasant words) which our ears naturally receive, have an exceptionally independent and direct relation to the organism, are wholly unconnected with the stream of external life, and could only gather associations from that life by conscious use in certain connections, never by inherent

*and of Architecture.*

necessities. Architecture stands, of course, on quite different ground from the representative arts, but in other ways it has most distinct ethical bearings. The power which ' could not rest in the expression or seizure of finite form,' and took its imagery ' from the shadows of the storms and hills,' is a power inspired by sympathy with Nature and association of man with his dwelling-place. The glooms and lights of Architecture are literally sympathetic; and they come not as the shifting characteristics of transient and occasional sound-forms, but as belonging to that which really encompasses and shelters our lives, as brooding companions, the daily visitants of familiar spots. And apart from these and other general means of influence which are noticed elsewhere, ethical ideas enter in respect of many minor features. Thus it is the moral taste which is offended by the falsifying of the qualities of material, as in making stone look soft and flexible instead of firm and elastic, or by the deceits of inadequate supports; and in questions about the disguising of material by paint or gilding, and many other points, there is a similar reference to instincts of sincerity. And it is the moral sense again which specially condemns slovenly workmanship, and is specially gratified by signs of loving toil in that which is primarily meant to endure. All which considerations are entirely alien to musical works.

*§ 11. The effects of Music must not be confused with the causes that bear on its production.*

On this question of morality it is important to avoid confusion between the effects of Music when produced and the causes that bear on its production. Morality tells in the *production* of all work; and of course a naturally-gifted musician is failing in duty if through a failure of earnestness he shirks his responsibilities and writes down to his public, as though a schoolmaster should bring up his pupils on fairy-tales: but the fact that his public are satisfied is the result of their being children, not the cause of their being naughty children. So again a deep moral fervour, as in the case of Beethoven, may accompany and inspire the composer in his work; and it is doubtless the greater earnestness of character, as well as the larger and stronger musical grasp of the Teutonic race, which has led to the marvellous development of modern instrumental music in their hands. But Mr. Haweis contends that the symphony of Beethoven stands in direct relation to the *morality* of the *listener*; while I maintain that it is in the greater *beauty* of the work, and the consequently deeper and more enduring *pleasure* of the listener, that Beethoven's strenuous labour, patient self-criticism, and general moral superiority to Rossini (in combination of course with his immeasurable superiority in genius), take effect.

If really legitimately pressed, the moral view would mean that if, *e.g.*, some Italian of strongly national musical taste received a sudden moral elevation, that is, if he became to-morrow more earnest and unselfish, he would soon see the difference between Beethoven and Rossini in the light in which Mr. Haweis sees it. It seems to me that any one might safely contradict this from his own experience. I at all events have never found a partiality for modern Italian, or modern German, or any other style of music, to be at all more an indication of moral effeminacy, or moral grandeur, or moral anything else, than a partiality for mathematics or sponge-cake. We see, as a matter of fact, all sorts of people, good, bad, and indifferent, caring about all sorts of music; the good turn this, like all other enjoyment, to good moral purpose, the bad do not; but the morality is concerned with the use that is made of the pleasure, not with the stage of receiving it. Plato defines as the best music ' that which gives pleasure to the best and most learned people : ' the converse view that to admire Palestrina, Handel, and Beethoven is a proof of special excellence and learning, though it might be very delightful to many of us, would, I fear, hardly be convincing to our acquaintance. To me the hearing of a great orchestral work may seem as bracing as a walk by the sea, and the endless cadences of an Italian opera may rather suggest hours spent amid the sickly fragrance of a hot-house : but there is nothing in either one or the other to affect directly the current of my outside life ; and for a modern being at all events it is quite possible to conceive noble designs in a hot-house and mean ones by the sea. And as I know that in listening to Beethoven I feel my moral inclinations and capacities enlarged and strengthened only in the indirect ways I have mentioned, from the added value and dignity given to life and from the glow of sympathy, so I conceive I have no right to accuse one who admires what seems to me feeble and effeminate music of having his moral nature enervated thereby : for I do not believe in a *direct* effect, and the *indirect* effect in the shape of a vital and sympathetic glow may be as genuine in his case as in my own. I call my music better than his simply because I believe my pleasure to be greater and more enduring than his.[1] Mr. Haweis is very happy in his

§ 12. *Argumentum ad hominem.*

---

[1] It may be objected that at any rate the more sensuous and passive pleasure of listen-ing to mere successions of sentimental strains cannot be as bracing an exercise as the fol-

description of the spasms and languors and the want of middle-tints in modern Italian opera-music; but after three hours of them do I who dislike or another person who likes them issue forth in a languid or spasmodic frame of mind ?  Such analogies are purely verbal.  The view from the Görner-grat on a sunny day is utterly wanting in middle-tints, and is as violent in its contrast of black rock and dazzling snow as can well be imagined ; but would six weeks spent in pretty constant contemplation of it result in violent and unmeasured habits of mind and conduct ?  or would the daily hearing of a rapid and crashing overture have a tendency to make people loud and fast ?

§ 13. Music must not be judged by association with things external to itself, its con-nection with which is accidental.

Another common source of misconception is the very natural habit of judging Music in connection with words and scenes to which it has been made an adjunct ; and thereby dispersing through a thousand channels the same faculty of association which, when concentrated, as in Greece, by a whole people on comparatively few and universally known forms of melody, pro-duced the ancient ethical view discussed above.  Without doubt the power of Music to lend itself to the aid and adornment of the good and the bad gives it still in such connections a strong ethical bearing ; but association must be eliminated if we wish to judge whether independently it has moral significance.  And while we call certain tunes vulgar in the first instance, perhaps, from their vulgar concomitants, and even after abstracting them from these feel no inclination to recall the term, seeing how dis-agreeable they are to us and how trivial and fleeting is any pleasure they are capable of giving, we may still perceive that they often *do* give a certain pleasure to children and to adults of small musical development, who show no inclination to vulgarity in other ways.  So that our con-demnation of such music must rest on its vulgarising the musical taste, and so tending to decrease the capacity and chance of superior pleasure : but (apart from accessories) we have no ground to consider it vulgarising to the moral character, any more than a taste for bad puns or for garlic, which are relished by numbers of most moral people.

On these points I shall hardly be accused of special pleading or a wish to undervalue the differences in Music, since personally I detest much of the inferior music which Mr. Haweis in a modified way admires and

lowing of a finely-built movement, which implies active grasp and memory.  Certainly not ; it approximates more to eating sugar-candy, which we despise not as an immoral but as a trifling pleasure ; and may doubtless be considered on an inferior *mental* (as distinct from moral) level, in a quite comprehensible sense.  But as the mental act is too unique and remote from any logical process for Music ever to have been valued as sharpening the purely intellectual faculties, this inferiority may be at once expressed in terms of pleasure : the sugary pleasure is not only as a rule by far the less in amount at the mo-ment, but even where it is eagerly sucked in is apt to cloy and lose its power ; while its almost invariable dependence on the adjunct of voice-colour confines its very existence to particular times and exceptional places.

approves. I am still more anxious not to seem to ignore the indirect moral and social power of Music, already enormous and capable of enormous increase. I believe as firmly as any one that if in life we may promote happiness through morality, in Art we may promote morality through happiness: but this belief will gain and not lose from a recognition that moral and æsthetic excellence are not Siamese twins, but ' twin-sisters differently beautiful.'

# CHAPTER XVII.

## FURTHER PECULIARITIES OF MUSIC'S NATURE AND POSITION.

§ 1. Certain qualities of the experience of hearing music which are in intimate relation with the uniqueness of the impressions.

THE conclusions of the preceding chapters receive yet further illustration from certain experiences in listening to Music which, though actually within the knowledge of every attentive auditor, have received little explicit notice. The message of Music is direct and unique. To the auditor, then, it is a matter of hit or miss ; and, if it misses, there is no intermediate range of ideas and associations to enlist his attention or relieve his tedium or act as a buffer to his dislike, simply because he is not made aware of any interesting impression or idea with which the artist was pleasurably occupied and which his work has more or less suggested. So that while in the case of a picture we may see all sorts of imperfections, but may still be able to eliminate this element of annoyance and take pleasure in the general spirit, or in the life depicted, or in a variety of other things, in the case of a musical piece we simply have a feeling of *ennui*, caused by looking for emotional beauty and finding none. If we find nothing outside to help to explain the interest Music often evokes, we equally find nothing to justify or excuse its imperfect and unimpressive utterances. It is inevitable that the mind, so differently affected at different times within the same region of experience, should ever and anon turn round on itself with the question 'Why?' without being able to extract from the actual experiences any sort of answer. This impossibility of getting any point of view from which to account for the existence and purpose of the phenomena, and for such vividly felt differences in their value, sometimes brings their unique nature home to one with startling force. For in the case of no other phenomena entailing anything like the same amount of mental and emotional activity are we thus helpless. Mere ultimate impressions of sense, a taste or a tone, may be unique. Many very various æsthetic and emotional experiences are unique in their way : a building is not a face, nor a face a landscape. But in Music there is this *unique sort* of uniqueness : that its success means to us a delight quite removed from mere sense-impression, a delight which is felt to be bound up with very active powers of grasp and comprehension, and to be stirring very deep depths of emotion, and yet totally, and at times it may be tantalisingly, isolated from the facts and interests of life ; while, conversely, its failure means to us the weary watching of phenomena which are in no relation to anything we know or care about, and suggest no sort of reason why they should ever have existed.

It is not strange, seeing how little this singular aloofness from external regions of thought and practice has been realised, that its further bearings on the experiences of the auditor should have escaped due recognition. The confusion on this subject is illustrated in rather an interesting way by some remarks of Wagner's. In his letter to M. Villot—where he gives a popular account, marked by great literary ability, of his theory of Opera—he speaks of the impossibility that the hearing of a symphonic piece of music should entirely silence the persistent and distracting question ' Why ?' which we are constrained to ask. When I first read this quickly through, it seemed to me to express a view which might be entertained or rejected. For my own part, though often finding the ' Why ?' a most real and oppressive question in some music where there seems no reason or necessity for the notes to go one way more than another, I am not conscious of it in music which seems to me utterly beautiful: but I thought Wagner's experience might be different, and that in accordance with it he was perfectly right to suggest alliance with drama as the way to silence the importunate question; because, in his own words, ' the dramatic interest raises the sympathetic sentiments of the spectator to a state of ecstasy where he forgets that fatal " Why ? "' and so on. So far then, apparently, so good. But a few pages further on I found the following paragraph :— § 2. Wagner's misconception on this point.

' The interest in *Lohengrin* rests entirely upon a process in the heart of Elsa, which touches all the secrets of the soul—the duration of a charm that spreads with convincing truth a wonderful happiness over all surroundings, depends entirely upon her refraining from the question " Whence ? "—the question bursts like a cry of despair from the deep anguish of a woman's heart, and the charm has vanished. You divine how strangely this tragical " Whence ? " coincides with the theoretical " Why ? " of which I have been speaking !'

I was somewhat staggered by this, as the comparison seemed to confound the discomfort caused by prolonged speculative failure in impossible regions with that caused by unsatisfied curiosity about an external detail. The ' Why ?' which we may ask during an instrumental performance is a continuous questioning as to the course and value and upshot of something which is not bound together and rendered intelligible by ordinary laws of logical coherence. Now if Elsa were a profound psychological study of a woman who, while in happy circumstances, was driven by her nature to be always examining and doubting the grounds of her happiness, and who was for ever attempting to read the riddle of her hourly life by getting to some imaginary external standpoint, there might be some reason in comparing her to a person whose pleasure in a symphony is dimmed and distorted by side-questions as to the secret of the charm and the internal necessities of the structure, and by a vain longing to seize the intangible or to get behind his impressions and see what they are made of; and such a character, though impossible in an opera, might in itself be interesting. But Wagner's Elsa has no secret self-questionings at all. She simply wishes, with female curiosity, to know an external fact which she has been told not to ask about; and in the external fact itself and the prohibition there is no more significance than if she had been told not to look out a particular word in the dictionary.

So far this may seem rather a criticism of the dramatic qualities of the particular play than of a confusion in thought about Music: but reverting to the first passage by the new light (or darkness) cast on it by the second, I found it had received my modified assent only because I had imagined the subject of the 'Why?' to be something quite different from what Wagner himself meant. I had thought the importunate question to be the natural one in an art which is peculiar in dealing with no external realities, and to be concerned with the points mentioned above and the import of the presentation—to be, in fact, the hopeless attempt of an individual to analyse and translate in his own person, and with no appeal to anything outside his own organism, impressions which to the consciousness are ultimate, and whose depth depends on countless accumulations of experience and association in the race. But I saw on reperusal that the question was one we were supposed to ask ourselves in the presence of *any* impressive phenomenon. Now I do not know of any such question, unless it be the utterly worn and barren one (which after all is less liable to distress the mind when occupied with impressive phenomena than at other times) as to the meaning and object of existence. When the question leaves the metaphysical region, and is changed from 'Why do I and this object exist?' to 'Why does this object impress me as it does?' it can almost always be approximately answered. In the case of Painting, for instance, though there remains a large unanalysable element, still, as the subject is independently comprehensible, and the elements in it are objects independently known, the main interest presents no urgent problem to the mind. In the admiration of a landscape, though distant ages have doubtless woven into our organisms a number of strains of feeling which we cannot disentangle, the main acts of imagination, the sense of freedom, fertility and strength, the recognition of streams and mountains as important elements in the dwelling-place of man, and a score of others, are quite simple and intelligible. And generally, in anything presented to the eye, the feeling of its belonging definitely to the world in which our whole life is spent, and being related on all sides to things of which we have familiar knowledge, makes its relations to our own senses and imaginations seem too natural for the admittance of analytical perplexities. The peculiarity of Music (as I must repeat *ad nauseam*) lies in the isolation of the pleasure it gives from life and social conditions, and in the extreme obscurity and remoteness of its first existence and gathering associations; the perception of it, moreover, not being a matter of rapid glances which can be discontinued if not repaid by pleasure, but an orderly act to which the ear is committed for a very noticeable time. This gives it a real 'Why?' of its own, which happily is often and often swallowed up and forgotten in the supremeness and completeness of its best utterances. But Wagner's 'Why?' which he considers appropriate in the presence of any impressive phenomenon, is a mere metaphysical puzzle, and has no connection with the musical difficulty to which his proposed satisfaction applies. Curiosity on such points may indeed be as idle and fruitless as Elsa's; but this was certainly not the *rapprochement* intended. I believe that Wagner, like everyone who has thought about Music, has been conscious of a certain mental reaction involved in the exercise of following a train of unique emotions, but that he has not perceived in what way it is peculiar to Music, much less the *rationale* of the peculiarity; so that his mind has simply got into a fog over his ' discovery of causality,' till he has confused the quite special feeling, which it is most desirable to recognise, with a fruitless bewilderment as to the grounds of feeling and existence in general; the result being that his proposed solution of the difficulty in the case of Music becomes entirely unmeaning. It involves no disrespect to such musical beauty as *Lohengrin* possesses, if we connect these reasonings with a mind likely to invest with factitious profundity and dramatic interest the main incident of Elsa's history, and to imagine in a shapeless and unsuggestive fragment of fairy-tale a deep and serious import.

The obvious conclusion to which these considerations lead is that in Music the perpetual presentation of actual beauty is of the most prime importance, and that works which lack distinct individual charm, have less *raison d'être*, and less chance and claim to survive, in this than in any other branch of art.[1] We have seen that, the utterance being direct, if it fails at all to arrest and impress us by its immediate appeal, it simply goes in at one ear and out at the other, without our ever wanting

§ 3. The perpetual presentation of beauty is in Music of supreme importance.

---

[1] This must be chiefly understood of works of some constructive pretension, which occupy time and claim attention on their individual merits. It would seem, moreover, very harsh to say that many 'popular' strains, even though they give but slight and shallow pleasure, have little *raison d'être*. I shall explain further on why, so far as they are trivial and vulgar, they may be esteemed of little account; not because they are not much better than nothing, but because they might so easily in many instances give place to something infinitely more delightful. As a matter of fact, however, any music which has the power to be in any true sense popular has *ipso facto* far more *raison d'être* than a vast number of more laborious works. The quite different sort of value pertaining to vague and undistinctive effects of beautiful sound has been sufficiently dwelt on in the thirteenth chapter.

to recall it. In these more barren tracts, if one cannot become simply inattentive, one is apt to turn restive and ill-humoured. In listening to works which, while musician-like and clever, nay even perhaps while tuneful and well thought-out, nevertheless are in no sense revelations, which we know we shall never either recall or in any way live on, the utter separation of Music from the ordinary regions of mental activity, and its independence of moral and social relations, seem to spread a blight over our views of the value and dignity of the art ; a blight which is as rapidly dispersed when the right moment arrives and once more a message is received from the mysterious infinite region which is Music's own.

The absolute necessity for beauty, the necessity that the auditor should be directly impressed, is of course not to be understood as meaning that nothing but the loftiest and rarest impressions are valuable. On the contrary, music may be what is called light, even lightest of the light, and still be of complete excellence ; the test, as we have already seen and shall further see, being the amount of delight produced or producible. But the point is that elsewhere a layman may be strongly *interested* in various ways by work which does not *delight* him with a sense of beauty : in Music the only interest possible as distinct from perception of beauty is, with very rare exceptions, of the purely technical kind confined to connoisseurs.

§ 4. Review of the various arts in this respect.

It is worth while to notice briefly to what extent the necessity for the actual exhibition of beauty applies in other regions of art. Poetry naturally stands pre-eminent, not only in being able to deal effectively with themes which rather rouse intellectual interest than delightful emotion, but in the power of presenting even ugly and mean subject-matter in such a way as to give keen pleasure. As a single instance we may take the lines from *Aylmer's Field*—

> His wife, a faded beauty of the baths,
> Insipid as the queen upon a card—

where the power of the description delights us in spite of the absence of any delightful quality in what is described. Such a power is naturally much less prominent in Painting, where the eye is compelled to dwell continually on objects, and where pleasure in the brief flash of poetical description is replaced by a sense of the painter's having spent time and pains on the minutiæ of dull and ugly things. Aristotle's remark—that 'provided objects be copied with extreme accuracy, the sight of the copies delights us even in cases where the sight of the realities would distress us ; as in representations of the meanest and most disgusting animals, and of corpses'—embodies a view so vulgar that few would openly endorse it : and the difference here between Painting and Poetry is brought out by this very fact, that, represented in *lines and colours*, what is mean or ugly cannot do more than look exactly like ; and can be suffused by none of that intangible atmosphere of association and suggestion which *words*, subtly used in ever fresh collocations, will carry with them. Sculpture, which represents not complicated scenes with a multitude of objects of various degrees of prominence, but at most a few prominent forms, can still less afford to introduce unimpressive or ugly objects. Nor in these two arts can beauty of sentiment ignore the direct claims of the eye : for instance, a young mother nursing her child may be taken as a subject of wide emotional appeal, but the emotion will be but slightly evoked if mother and child be both represented as ugly. But while Painting and Sculpture (under which may be included all representation in solid material) are thus in the main closely bound to beauty, or at any rate to subject-matter which is in a literal and direct way agreeable to contemplate, the beauty need not be of a striking and original kind to have true artistic value. Work in these arts may fall so far short of lofty and ideal excellence, as to display little more than average talent and artistic pleasure in its exercise, and yet, in their suggestion of much beyond what they actually embody, may excite true interest and pleasure. In Architecture, again, though the very name, as distinct from mere building, implies the aiming at beauty, utility and economy will of course justify innumerable works whose artistic features are of a very quiet and ordinary kind. But in Music the value to any one of any particular specimen must be reckoned by his gladness to recall it or to have it recalled, so that after sufficient recurrences he at least recognises and feels some possession in it : and this implies that it has *for him* some really striking and individual motion ; having which, it approves its excellence as far as he is concerned. We will not enter here on the question of differences of taste. We may admit that much very inferior music is enjoyed, and still see in the very fact of its *being* enjoyed, of its having that amount of individuality, a distinct difference from the greater part of the music which is and always will be thrown upon the world by craftsmen without genius. It is depressing to think what an amount of this fifth and sixth-rate music, whose analogues in Painting or Architecture may be pleasing features and adornments of daily life, simply runs its feeble course of existence without making any true impression on any single hearer.[1]

Nor is it only in respect of their most direct appeal to our senses and

---

[1] It would be beside the mark to argue that, *e.g.*, at the present day there is as much bad painting or bad architecture as bad music. If so, it is a misfortune of the time : but it cannot be denied that an immense deal of painting, and of architecture and decoration, good enough to give a pretty constant amount of quiet satisfaction, may be produced by men, who, if endowed with a parallel degree of talent for music, might be competent interpreters of the works of others, but would never affect anybody's happiness by their original creations.

§ 5. The
interest of the
other arts in
respect of
historical
association.

feelings, that the other arts reap the benefit of their direct connection with external realities. The distinction is equally manifest in respect of a whole world of ideas which may be classed under interest of historical association. The manifold interest of Poetry as a reflection of its age is too obvious to need a word. As regards Painting and Sculpture, a very slight knowledge of the history and civilisation of various periods and countries will enable an amateur to find a fund of enjoyment in early works which make but little direct appeal to his artistic sensibilities. Architecture is especially rich in this kind of interest, since the problems, the struggles with material and mechanical difficulties, the adaptations and triumphs, as well as more distinct records of national life, are ineffaceably traced in it. In more general ways, too, and apart from the direct contemplation of special works, these arts minister to our historical interest and imagination. Thus we trace in the unmeasured towns, temples, and pyramids of the East, in their immensity of scale and mass of material, the same reflection of the external aspects of Nature and of irresistible external forces as contributes so fundamental a factor to Oriental religious conceptions. We connect the idealisation, ever repeated and ever interesting, of corporeal beauty, and the change of Architecture to make a shrine for a human god, not a temple that should cover a plain or a tower that should reach to heaven, with the development of the Hellenic spirit, joyous and harmonious, knowing nought of asceticism or mutilation, and little oppressed with the mystery of the unseen or the deeper riddles of existence. And so on, through all the changes of the nations and the centuries.

The contrast of
Music in this
respect.

The contrast presented by Music is here most striking. The history of the art, is in itself by no means devoid of interest; but the interest is clearly not of a kind calculated to sustain enjoyment through the performance of a special work of some former age in which no beauty is detected. Practically such works are never presented, but are left to the musical archæologist: and even his interest must be very limited in range, unless association with words or with traditions of usage external to the actual music enliven the merely technical aspect of the study. In the first place, the changes and varieties of Music in different epochs and countries are perfectly distinct from those of any other art, owing to the fundamental differences of scale-system. People familiar with music in one system find music written in another (even though that other be the immediate precursor of their own), not odd or old-fashioned in any interesting way, but simply incoherent and unintelligible. They can extract as little artistic enjoyment out of it as out of literature in an unknown language. Whatever may be our archæological knowledge about such music, we are powerless to realise its original effect: for purposes of musical comprehension, our ears are simply *different organs* from those to which the music was first addressed : and it is just as well for our Hellenic enthusiasm that an ancient Greek performance cannot be revived for our benefit. But even apart from this special peculiarity, and supposing that we knew and could appreciate all the work which the musical art has produced, what could it tell us of its original surroundings ? What records could it give us of men and manners ? No attempt at connecting the resuscitated strains with the people who used them would take us beyond the emptiest generalisations—as that rude music appears normally amid rude conditions, and tends to develope with civilisation—in contrast to the manifold and exact information furnished alike by the archaic and the developing stages of other arts.

There are indeed cases where Music has retained a strong element of external interest, not by any information it could itself convey, but through our historical knowledge of its original employment. The Gregorian chants are still endeared to many, in spite of their uncouthness, by venerable memories; and the chorales of the Reformation are specially interesting, from the fact that the necessities of the time did actually in their case exercise a direct and most beneficial influence on the development of music. Now and then, too, a single melody, like the *Marseillaise*, has had an historical existence. But such exceptions only make the rule clearer by their rarity.

Other samples of the negations which leave Music in so singular a degree to its independent and immediate sources of impression have already been noticed in other connections. They are the negations inevitable to the art of immaterial forms. Thus in the arts of the eye we have the sense that the works have been actually touched and moulded, that they are the literal handiwork of the men to whom we owe them : whereas some of Music's divinest utterances have never even been heard by their composers except with the inward ear. But the distinction goes further than this ; it involves in Music an impossibility of embodying sacrifice or munificence, or of giving any outward symbol to social virtues. A rich man may support a choir or hold a grand musical celebration ; but in so doing he offers the performances, not the music. The material and the labour, in the shape of the instruments used and the acquired skill of the performers, are the transient means of presenting the work ; they are not spent on the making of it nor embodied in its substance. So that in the narrower as well as the wider sense, in reference to individuals as well as nations, musical works lack the monumental character : lacking which, I need hardly add, they belong not to a place nor to a nation, but to the world.

§ 6. Other negations of Music in point of external and indirect interest.

There is no indirect way, then, in which Music can make good that claim to our interest and attention which only its own actual beauty can enforce. Compositions which lack or lose distinct individual charm may be galvanised for a season by fashion, but in the end die irretrievably : for the fact that Music has to be deliberately performed, and is not put on a wall and looked at from time to time, makes doubly sure the oblivion of what has not true vital strength.    And of too much which perishes it may be affirmed that if it is worth forgetting it was never worth having : of the music of our generation, at any rate, it cannot be said that it gradually gets to look trite and obsolete owing to the perpetual advance of the art in scope and resources.    Inferior work simply takes the place of something better, and is produced mainly because those whose ears require a little pleasant tickling like to know that what tickles them has been recently manufactured, for their especial benefit.    Even in respect of compositions

But mediocrity, though here specially uninteresting, must be to a considerable extent endured.

of true artistic purpose, it must be admitted as unfortunate that, in the very art where mediocrity is specially uninteresting, one work is, as far as public presentation goes, exclusive of another, inasmuch as the two cannot be presented simultaneously.    And as there will always be a number of works written with enough earnestness and technical skill to seem to warrant production, as moreover composers would hardly write if their works were not to be performed, and we could not get our occasional genius except as the crown and crisis of considerable artistic activity before and around him, we must just be content to be a good deal bored.    Schumann's remarks on a certain symphony, which had obtained a prize at Vienna, while those of Schubert were lying on a shelf, will often recur to the mind : 'If it contained grave errors, weaknesses of form, extravagances, there would be an opportunity for improvement, encouragement : but, alas ! here we can only say " Very good," or " It is rather tiresome," or sigh, or think of something else.'

§ 7. The infinite distance which sometimes seems to separate the best and worst work of a composer.

We may connect with the fundamental peculiarity of Music another fact which must have struck many as remarkable ; the infinite distance, namely, which may separate the best and the worst work of a particular composer : so that sometimes we seem to find diamonds in the very gutter. In arts which deal with life, the way of looking at life, and to some extent therefore the way of living, must directly affect the art.    As a rule, a painter or poet will hardly do any first-rate ideal work unless he possesses, if not elevated habits, at any rate a certain elevation of aim and sentiment ; and this will so far act as artistic ballast that while at all the same man he will hardly produce any quite contemptible work.    This outer region of mental habit in relation to the penetrating art-instinct might be compared to the earth's atmosphere of air and vapour, suffused with warmth and colour by rays which they in turn tend to preserve from dispersion : whereas a melody of surpassing charm may dart into the mind without affecting or being affected by any such conditions, or entailing any sort of assimilation ; and from the relation in Music of 'theme' to development, such an isolated flash of melodic inspiration may act as the germ of much beyond itself. But it is not necessary to enter on this debateable ground of connection between artistic and other faculties and habits. The fact I am noting follows sufficiently clearly from the general hit-or-miss character of musical impressions. For this character may be exemplified as easily in the works of one composer as of many; and will often involve, as far as our perceptions and judgments go, the whole ungraduated difference between what is quite delightful, and what we simply want to get rid of as occupying time in an uninteresting way.

There is one more point of musical experience which cannot be passed over. It is, I fear, a necessity of Music's independent position in our æsthetic life, that nothing in it will stand perpetual iteration. The frequent hearing of or continuous dwelling on a particular set of notes is too apt to sate the ear or dull the perception, so that we look in vain for the old message. Those are indeed fortunately constituted who escape this altogether. In one way the better the music the less the danger: in fact, music that will last with him is the best subjective definition that any one can give of good music. But on the other hand the keener the first impression and the more haunting the first delight, the more chance is there, in music which is short of the best, of at all events partial or temporary failure. This may be called the defect answering to the quality of unique and possessing interest, to the power of actually running in the head over and over again without affording to the mind the scope of any wide and general region of conceptions. A short interval may suffice to restore the condition of receptivity, and in the case of the very best music, from a perfect *Volkslied* to a Beethoven symphony, the impression is never permanently injured. But in work of a just lower order, most of us know the feeling of some particular music as being at its *acme* at the second or third time of hearing, when it is new enough still to surprise us, and old enough for us to feel the triumphant sense of possession which is given by recognition. Most of us know how for the moment composition after composition has appeared to eclipse its predecessors, and then has gradually receded, till perhaps after lying dormant for a time it has resumed its old sway: and it would be absurd to condemn the pleasure whose only fault is to be somewhat intermittent and transitory.

§ 8. The degree in which Music will stand iteration is by no means unlimited.

So far the consequences which we have connected with the fundamental uniqueness of musical impressions have seemed to be rather to the disadvantage of the art. We should certainly be the gainers if Music could open a fresh channel to the past, and if mediocre music were less unredeemedly dull, and if all the music which gave pleasure in its day could give the same pleasure in ours, and if the freshness of individual beauties could be to us unchanging and perennial. But there is a very different side to the subject. When we turn to the actual position of Music in the

§ 9. In the isolation of Music lies one essential cause of its exceptional popularity.

present day, to the actual effect of those works, from a street-song to a symphony, which have any sort of true vitality, we shall find that the extraordinary power or popularity of the art is due to the very same isolation of its sphere, to the very fact that its roots have their place apart in our physical and spiritual nature, and know nothing either of the interest or the disturbances of intellectual social and political life. Taking the world as we find it, we must account it no less fortunate than it is certain that an independent nature entails an independent history. For that independence means that Music can flourish to the utmost in an age of the most feverish speculation and the most prosaic activities; where the confusion of beliefs and aims, the want of an atmosphere of outward magnificence and beauty, the lack of the very conditions under which the other arts have chiefly flourished, only bring into stronger relief the singularity of this one. It means that Music owes no allegiance to intellectual minorities or to social aristocracies, to the arbiters of thought or the arbiters of show; and that even the ebb and flow of national ideas and sentiments such as have often so powerfully influenced Art, can have little bearing on works which are already and increasingly cosmopolitan, and in their aloofness from views and creeds affect equally and similarly men of all views and of all creeds. It means that the art whose connection with social and political conditions Plato considered vital enough for a change in the one to entail of necessity a change in the other, can be connected with nothing less wide than the whole relation of popular life, both as cause and effect, to the quickening and diffusion of all healthy pleasures.

§ 10. The relations of the other arts to their environment.

It will be impossible to enter at any length on so vast and complicated a region of enquiry as the relations of the other arts to their environment and the public: but a brief notice of the subject is indispensable, as the singularity of Music's present place in the world can only be clearly marked out by contrast. The contrast will appear mainly under two heads: we have (1) the point as to *time*, the fact that the art has culminated in our own era, and flourishes to the utmost amid the conditions of that era; (2) the point as to *range* of influence, the enormous width of the popularity which the art enjoys. The former point, as it happens, can be best illustrated in relation to Architecture, which we will therefore consider first.

Architecture.

The case of Architecture is specially striking, not only because a comparison of its past and its present condition is of all such comparisons the most discouraging, but because in its practice and history it presents certain points of resemblance to Music, which only serve to strengthen the essential contrast. Music and Architecture present a common social aspect in that both give employment to large numbers of persons, in addition to the composer or main designer; and a common historical aspect, in that both have been pre-eminently linked with public worship. But the facts which have been of the very essence of the one art, and which survive as living ideas and memories in its actual products, have no sort of similar relation to the other. In the greatest days of mediæval building the workmen were themselves in a measure creators, and the complete work represented an extraordinary combination of inventive faculty. Architecture of course owes the peculiarity that its greatest triumphs have been civic and national rather than individual, to its being the only art of which utility forms the basis. It stands in direct relation to the practical facts of life ; and these facts being continuous, local and national history becomes embodied in the resulting works, to which often the hands of many generations have contributed. This gives the associative side to these works : as for their purely artistic side, since the world is to the majority a place of toil, we should naturally expect any strong popular artistic sense to manifest itself in the region where practical and religious necessities made work and workmen abundant, and in connection with things constantly presented to the senses of every member of every community. And not only do single buildings owe much of their beauty to the loving detail of the subordinate craftsmen ; for a Gothic cathedral was a social product, crowded with expressions of common religious beliefs and aspirations : but in Architecture, alone of the arts, can a number of works form themselves into a still larger unity, where, however loose the organism, part must most sensibly affect part ; and in some rare instances a mediæval city, depending as it did for its external aspect on a multitude of individual efforts under the guidance of a common instinct, formed in its impressive *ensemble* and varied details an ideal representation of the social organism which it environed.

In these modern days, amid the strife or wreck of ideals and creeds, when the sense of civic life is feeble and towns are human hives full both of the most dispersed activities and of the most monotonous labour, one need not indulge in vain regrets or one-sided hopelessness, to feel that such art, for the present at least, is impossible. We may doubtless see marked signs of progress and improvement ; but till there is a tolerably widely felt delight in beauty and hatred of ugliness, till there is a wakeful instinct in thousands and thousands of pairs of eyes, Architecture will remain the craft of a comparatively few individuals whose inspirations must be strong indeed if they suffer no blight from the absence or anarchy of public taste. In this art, of all others, the artist's heart and brain are at the mercy of social and civic conditions : and if beautiful house-architecture comes from ' the abiding wisdom of contented life,' if ' the architecture of a nation is great only when it is as universal and as established as its language,' we may have long indeed to wait. And moreover in this particular art the sins of the fathers are terribly visited on the children. Buildings once put up remain *en évidence*; and while beautiful structures could never be multiplied beyond their uses, nor can Amiens Cathedral be pulled down in order that Catholic France may build another, so neither will Gower Street disappear in our lifetime.

The contrast of Music, in being the very opposite of a monumental art.

And here Music reaps the advantage of its aloofness from the facts and uses of outside life. Demanding for its execution only healthy appreciation and technical skill, it depends for its invention on individual not national genius—happily a less uncommon phenomenon in the world ; and having no direct end but beauty, it exercises a social and uniting influence amid any amount of industrial and speculative dispersion, and needs none of the external concord and enthusiasm necessary for costly displays of civic pride and religious zeal. It can live the most vivid life in the present in virtue of the very facts which preclude it from being, like Architecture, a monumental art ; and the works we admire in it are none the less admired because they are presented to us not by still hands of other generations, but by living fingers of our own. The contrast is clearest of all in connection with religion. Architecture won its noblest triumphs in association with public faith and worship ; and those triumphs cease in days when the great temples are ready built, or when people do not care to build them. Music went through a natural stage of religious tutelage during the time when the Church was the chief patron of all the arts: but passing on from strength to strength, it almost forgets, in its free and independent maturity, the struggles and glories of its youth. Moreover the connection, even when in full force, was often of a kind very far from vital. In the later middle ages, when almost all serious music was written for Church purposes, the liturgical phrases formed for the most part a purely mechanical framework, often most strangely strained and distorted, for the scientific ingenuity of the composer to build on. And in much later and more developed music of this kind we continually find words of the utmost significance and of the most diverse sentiments used with sublime impartiality as so many vocal syllables, and doing duty for the exemplification of the most abstract and complicated musical forms.

Mazzini's idea of Music,

It is touching to see how this isolation of Music sometimes affects those who, with a deep love for it, cannot bring themselves to face the facts and necessities of its nature, or to see that its essential power, as the great modern art, rests on its independence of the very conceptions and tasks they would force on it. Mazzini, describing his sensations in standing at sunset before a Gothic cathedral, says, ' See how the very soul of Christianity has inspired the whole edifice ; how the spirit of prayer bends the arch, or threads its way upwards along the winding columns to mount to heaven on the spire.' . . . ' I see the red blood of the martyr blended with the hues of hope, offered up to God upon the lofty windows, and feel how the aspiration of the believer's soul towards the infinite informs the ample and mysterious vault of the roof, whence the spirit of Christ, descending from the huge cupola to the sanctuary, was diffused around the vast walls, surrounding and embracing in its love and benediction the entire church, which it peopled with apostles, saints, confessors,' &c. And then he adds, ' What! shall an entire synthesis, a whole epoch, a religion, be sculptured in stone ; shall Architecture thus sum up the ruling thought of eighteen centuries in a cathedral, and Music be unequal to the task ? ' It sounds hard. But what are we to say if, as a matter of undeniable fact, by far the greatest music the world has known has appeared within the last two centuries, and by far the greater proportion of it in the latter half of that time ; and if that music, so far from telling us about the ruling thought of preceding centuries, tells us nothing about the ruling thought of its own ? Does not the fact contain its own consolation ? If, on the one hand, the intricate Church-compositions which led up to the reforms of Palestrina were as absolutely unrepresentative of anything outside their composers' talent for putting together puzzles and labyrinths, as the glorious architecture of the same period was truly representative of the religious and civic life from which it sprung, is that not due to the very causes which enabled Handel in England and Beethoven in Austria to flourish amid national circumstances the very reverse of glorious ? We may surely set thoughts like these against Mazzini's dream of a ' musical expression of all the passions in an ascending series of sublime harmonies, wherein every instrument will represent an affection, every melody an action, every concord a moral synthesis.' *Parturiunt montes* : and the *maestro* who is destined to regenerate Music by the foundation of a European school is— Donizetti!

and the consolation for perceiving it to be a dream.

We turn now to the arts of representation. In days of transition and scepticism, and destruction or dispersion of ideals, Poetry has, in the universality of its range, a decided advantage over the other representative arts. For Poetry takes for its subject-matter the emotional aspects of all things, from the most abstract to the most concrete. It can deal with the most various and complex conceptions, with the intellectual and even the questioning view of life, as much as with the most direct and simple facts. Poetry may have its great ages, in the sense that only at a few points in history is a large amount of poetical work produced whose objective excellence ensures its prolonged survival : but as all the elements of life can be dealt with in words, and all that present any sort of emotional interest in poetry, upheavals and revolutions only multiply the facets in which this art reflects the world. The result may of course be a very wide diversity of taste in the public, and great uncertainty as to how much in the poetry of the age has the enduring vital quality : but for all that a generation of intellectual activity is likely to find for itself in its own poetry utterances as vividly

§ 11. The position of the arts of representation. Poetry.

delightful, and with perhaps as much of illumination in their broken lights, as in those treasures of the past which were born of some enormous bias or wide unanimity of life and thought, and have been carried down to us with all the prestige of a more homogeneous age. From this view, especially when thus briefly and crudely stated, there may be many dissentients: dissent will only leave my main point of Music's exceptional position the more impregnable.

Painting.

I think, however, it must be clear that the relation of Poetry to a restless and revolutionary age is at any rate very different from that of the other representative arts; of which we may take Painting as by far the most prominent. The regions of landscape, *genre*, and portrait, it is true, the painter has always at his hand : but in the selection and treatment of subjects outside these classes, in what may fairly be called the more ideal style of work, inasmuch as it comprehends the ideal and imaginative treatment of the human form, it seems impossible that an age of scattered views and complex emotions should not seriously cramp, if not his genius, at all events its popular results. A picture cannot shift its points of view or analyse its subject-matter ; it cannot extract interest or pathos from conflict, contradiction, and suspense ; its expression of ideas and emotions is adapted chiefly to single and positive ideas, to simple and homogeneous emotions ; where a massive background of belief or interest in the spectator counts for very much, and more purely intellectual habits and subtleties for very little. While Poetry, with its rapid glances down countless vistas of suggestion, image, and sentiment, easily fits itself to the intellectual and emotional conditions of a shifting, many-sided age ; Painting, in its conspicuous and permanent presentment of the single imagined scene and in the use of the noblest types of familiar visible forms, seems made for adding glory and stability to men's deep pervading views of the universe in which, be it chaos or kosmos, their own fates are bound up. While the painter's intellect does not, like the poet's, grasp a multitude of subtle relations, while he cannot, like the poet, draw innumerable separate threads of interest into the tissue of his work, there seems a special fitness in his more vivid, condensed, and objective exhibition of fewer and simpler aspects of existence, to embody profound and abiding conceptions of it. But in proportion as the wide prevalence of such conceptions may open up to him such a mode of influence, does the absence of them mar his chances. A painter desirous of making popular and effective use of the noblest types of beauty, cannot now presuppose any sort of general attitude towards any department of emotional ideas ; and missing the chance of direct and simple appeal, either to belief in a supernatural religion, or to such a strong body of feeling as was once the interest in antiquity, is reduced for his ideal subjects to abstractions and allegories ; in the investiture of which, though he may produce such loveliness as to

give to the few some of their very most exquisite experiences, he cannot
deeply touch the heart of his time. For the present, I think, it must be
admitted that the disagreements as to the very meaning of a spiritual
world, the clouding and confusion of those conceptions in the light of
which the world we know is something more than a riddle, have thrown
an air of unreality over much in art which does not actually trench on
religious grounds. Painting, on the very face of it, so claims to be dealing
with what *is*, to idealise not by deserting but by transfiguring reality,
seeing into the heart of it and collecting its scattered beauties and fixing
its supreme moments, the highest imagination, in Painting as in Poetry,
rests so thoroughly on penetrating vision and not on irresponsible fancy,
that in so far as a painter's world is dreamland, men whose feet are on
the earth will be apt to pass it by. If dreamland is the best we can get,
that surely is the strongest proof that the time is unfavourable to great
popular painting. It is not the painter's fault if he cannot presume in
his public a large common fund of sentiment or interest : nor is it mere
blindness and crassness in the public if they feel a certain remoteness of
subject, and a want of adequate reason for the idealisation of human
beauty and for the expressions given to human faces and forms, in a good
deal of the best contemporary work. Painting can never truly arrogate to
itself a separate kingdom, like that of Sound, wherein it may withdraw
men and cheer their life in the world by the simple process of taking them
out of it ; since for that which, in its very visibility, suggests a real relation
to a real outside world of facts and feelings, one possible mode of failure
must always be the seeming *un*real.

Nor can the responsibilities of representative art to its subjects be got
rid of in the way which the modern advocacy of ' art for art's sake ' seems
often to suggest. We hear it seriously stated that the subject of a picture
is to the essence of its effect as external as the words to the music of a
song. This of course can only mean that the essence of pictorial effect is
the production of a delightful pattern. But only through being naturally
short-sighted, or by more than half closing our eyes, can we get the effect
of a pattern without at the same instant recognising objects : the pattern-
lines cannot divest themselves of their character as lines of objects, and
the objects cannot be recognised apart from their associations and relations.
Even in work where the actual objects seem most accidental to the main
interest in the painter's mind, the effect is a far more complex one than
any mere pattern could produce. Thus a painter like Rembrandt, whose
main interest is often in the lights and shades he can throw around and
across his figures, might be said in a sense to care more for his pattern
than for his subject-matter. But he could never have moved us by the
pattern-element alone : the figures and natural objects have to be there,
if only for the sake of their quasi-ironical subordination to that brave im-

*The place of
the subject and
subject-matter.*

partial play of colour and shadow, which transforms and makes them what it will, sweeping them into accidents of its own manifestation. And with every increase in prominence of the forms, as a necessary part of the pictorial composition, must come an increase in the proportion to the whole effect of the ideas and associations they suggest : the more salient their place in the pattern, the less can their significance as forms of known objects be detached.

Mr. Pater's view.

Mr. Pater seems to have at any rate skirted the edge of this fallacy in his most interesting essay on the *School of Giorgione.* He says that the essential pictorial qualities—'the arabesque traced in the air by Tintoret's flying figures, by Titian's forest branches,' 'the magic conditions of light and hue in the atmosphere of Titian's *Lace-girl* or Rubens's *Descent from the Cross*'—must first of all delight the sense 'as directly and sensuously as a fragment of Venetian glass, and by this delight only be the medium of whatever poetry or science may lie beyond it in the intention of the composer. In its primary aspect,' he adds, 'a great picture has no more definite message for us than an accidental play of sunlight and shadow for a moment, on one's wall or floor,' and so on. But there is a great ambiguity in the words *medium* and *primary* aspect as here used. The *pattern* is not really the medium for any further conceptions of poetical meaning or anything else : no dwelling on the pattern *quâ* pattern would ever give us any insight into such conceptions, which belong entirely to the objects composing the pattern. It is true, of course, that the presentative or 'essential pictorial qualities' are the indispensable condition for the objects and ideas to be wrought into a transfigured and illuminated presentment, a unique and untranslateable work of art ; but equally are the representative qualities the indispensable condition for a colour-pattern to stir in us depths of imaginative joy.[1]

---

[1] Though I believe I comprehend and concur with the purport of Mr. Pater's introduction to his essay, I cannot think he has well summed up that purport in saying that 'all Art constantly aspires towards the condition of Music.' He explains that the effort of Art is to obliterate the distinction between matter and form, a distinction which in Music has no existence. But when he goes on to illustrate his meaning, we find he is using *form* in a very wide sense, as mode of handling, mood, emotional and informing expression, which the artist infuses into his work, and which so penetrates his objects and incidents that they are thus stamped for ever in their most imaginative aspect. Such a use of the word *form* departs widely from the accurate use of it in relation to the abstract shapes of sound presented to the ear by Music. Identity of matter with form, in the sense that a painter's subject is saturated with the spirit of his handling, has clearly no logical relation to identity of matter with form, in the sense of absence of any separably knowable reality from forms which are *abstract* just in virtue of that absence. So that though other art, where it presents a wonderful fusion of matter and spirit, may perhaps be loosely and metaphorically described as 'aspiring towards the condition of Music,' to call Music 'the true type or measure of consummate Art' seems to go beyond metaphor, and seriously to endanger the recognition of the insuperable distinction between presentative and representative art. However much form and matter in a picture may be described as 'presenting, in their union and identity, one single effect to the imagin-

One further distinction is necessary to complete even the briefest comparison of Poetry and Painting, in respect of their present chances of influence. The portion of the public in whose lives high imaginative work in either art holds a large place is a small minority : and it is only in reference to such work, and therefore to the effect on a small minority, that the above comparison of the scope of the two arts at the present time, and the concession of a wider chance of influence to Poetry, must be understood. As regards the mere sum of their appeal to the general public, pictorial art should naturally have a great superiority. For a poet's permanent audience consists, except in very rare instances, of the educated, of those to whom, through a special though perhaps unconscious training in thought and language, *words live.* Apart from questions as to contemporary production, Poetry may, in a sense, undoubtedly be held to flourish in an age when it is more read and meets with more general appreciation than ever before. But whatever its influence among the educated classes, it scarcely touches the people. On the one hand, lives which are too often starved of what is merely harmless and healthy, let alone what is beautiful and refined, can rarely themselves afford to the artist material by the poetical reflection of which they in turn may be delighted and ennobled : while, on the other hand, those intellectual conditions which give its chief interest to contemporary poetry are those which set it most aloof from broad popular sentiment. For a large majority of persons, then, it is not in verbal but in visible representations, that the yearnings and gropings after such beauty and sentiment as life and outward things can offer find their readiest satisfaction. So that it is even common for people to arrive at their conception of poems through pictorial representation of their scenes. In Painting consequently a large amount of conscientious work which never becomes famous may and does become a source of innocent though uncritical interest, in which enjoyment of mere imitation is blended in various degrees with more ideal elements : whereas a conscientious poem of parallel merit would be read by no one.

But it must be added that if poetical art touches the people hardly at all, pictorial art touches them in great measure by its most prosaic and least artistic examples. That any qualities by which fine contemporary painting produces a sense of unreality in the educated must necessarily put it still further from the appreciation of the vulgar is hardly worth saying ; so few chances have the vulgar of seeing it. But most of the cheap contemporary art they do see, even where true in sentiment and innocently pleasure-giving, is still, after all, vulgar like themselves. And all this is the more important in that representative art in general has its chance of reaching

§ 12. The positions of Poetry and Painting compared.

ative reason,' that effect is a very complex one, and all the ideas and associations which the represented and recognised objects sug- gest are inevitably part of what the imaginative reason is occupied with.

the masses mainly through *contemporary* productions, through the delineation of facts and ideas which are actually uppermost in men's thoughts and affections : this being the natural means of putting the less educated portion of a community *en rapport* with artistic modes of expression and idealisation.    An uneducated and busy person who cannot understand or finds little response to his experiences in the poetry of his own age is not likely to cultivate much serious interest in earlier literature : and an uneducated person with eyes fed perpetually on 'realistic' pictures and prints, and at the mercy of his natural surroundings for the chance even of appreciating landscape, will not be likely to seek ideal beauty from regions of the past into the atmosphere of which he could only bring himself by reading and thought, and will probably gaze half-doubtingly at nine-tenths of the treasures even of a National Gallery.

§ 13. The far deeper contrast presented by Music.    In the very terms of this last distinction between the two great representative arts is implied the far deeper distinction of both of them from Music.    The relation of Music to the public is so large a topic that I reserve its more detailed treatment for a separate chapter.    But what will be there further illustrated may be here briefly asserted ; namely, that Music not only speaks intelligibly to the masses, but speaks to them, when the rare chance is given, by its very choicest and noblest utterances. These are the facts which constitute the special uniqueness in its popularity ; and which are the more interesting in that they could hardly have been asserted with all possible confidence, or estimated at their true value in the history of art, until the present era.    It has been said that all the greatest art is essentially popular : but in respect of Art in general, how little in our day can such a phrase represent but regrets and desires ! How little comfort can it have for us, now and here, save as a noble aspiration ; a vision which at certain epochs has been so far realised that we cling to it and trace in it a true and stimulating principle, but any realisation of which must always depend on many currents and on varied chances of inward and outward life, on harmonious conditions which are rarely indeed thrown up amid the complicated developments of civilisation. And these rare conditions for the popularity of great Art are, it is almost a truism to say, conditions of the *populus* as much as of the art.    For Music, on the other hand, the one condition is that it shall be heard, and the necessary education consists in reiterated hearing.

There is a danger of being misunderstood if one marks this distinction by saying that appreciation of what is best in the other arts presupposes education : since education is apt to suggest consciously acquired knowledge rather than the spontaneous result of harmonious surroundings on habits and sentiments.    Not but that even the narrower use of the word has its application : for in respect of works which extract relations and harmonies from the external universe of facts and things, some knowledge of the nature and significance of the subject-matter must underlie enjoyment of the representation, and such knowledge must often imply a certain amount of general culture. But putting this aside, any wide popularity of representative art must at any rate presuppose a less conscious education, a natural training of the susceptibilities and the emotions, through the perceived presence of at least some beauty in the external aspects of life, and of at least some clue of harmony among its discords. It is not only that men's eyes, as mere percipients, are inevitably affected for better or worse by what they daily and hourly see, and that the faculty of observing depends on the presence of things which repay observation ; the training we desiderate would extend to all modes of thought and feeling which can find a body and a reality in the outward aspects of things, and by the sap of which alone can visible art become vitally real to common men. In other words, the popularity of the representative arts presupposes a set of conditions which need very much besides Art to bring them about, and of which Music is markedly independent. Only by realising these things can we realise the incomparable importance of the fact that the art-kingdom of the ear is inviolate ; that not even the unavoidable sounds of life (naturally of course not one-millionth part as representative of its realities as are the sights) have or pretend to have any relation to the forms which Music reveals. Without this independence no art in the present state of society could be at once great and in the literal sense popular. Music alone can take the world as she finds it, and make daily advances in popular favour, unaffected by a state of life and thought which she in turn makes no pretence of directly affecting ; though ruling in right of her own beauty, she exercises indirectly a social influence of the most far-reaching and salutary kind. She makes no complaint that men's ears are unobservant and their hearts dead : she simply takes ears and hearts by storm.

Nor need we dwell on anything so obvious as the connection of this final peculiarity with the various topics of the preceding chapters. Our whole argument as to the nature of musical impressions and the roots of musical pleasure, with their deep and separate place in the human organisation, our whole survey of that independence of intellectual, moral, and external conditions which specially characterises Music, tend to the same result, a unique width and depth of popular instinct for it. In its peculiar isolation lies its peculiar strength : in the fact that its utterances pass direct to the consciousness, without the chance of obscuration or distortion from vulgarity, ignorance, or prejudice, lies its power to awaken in thousands who are inaccessible to any other form of high emotion a mighty sense of beauty, order, and perfection.

Obvious connection of this with the separate origin and nature of musical impressions.

# CHAPTER XVIII.

## MUSIC IN RELATION TO THE PUBLIC.

§ 1. The essential characteristics of a 'people's art.'

IF we were asked *à priori* to imagine the characteristics of a ' people's art,' we should require (1) that some elementary instinct for it should be deeply ingrained in the human organism, so that it should be capable of profoundly stirring the most diverse natures ; (2) that it should be independent of logical processes and ranges of ideas beyond the ken of the vulgar and uneducated ; (3) that it should be susceptible of cheap and to a great extent of open-air presentation ; (4) that it should be capable of extremely definite re-presentation in memory (because the majority have no time or opportunity for perpetual fresh presentations); and (5) that it should admit of wide, rapid, and cheap or gratuitous diffusion. It is surely matter of congratulation that every one of these requirements is satisfied completely by Music. The last point includes facilities for obtaining both published music and musical instruments : but it is well worth while to dwell on that more universal sort of diffusion which is independent of both, and is a mere matter of common human faculties. This connects the fifth head intimately with the fourth : for the power of a melody to get into the air and traverse a country and a continent in a few months depends of course on its being most definitely remembered. The ear will not suffer the alteration of a note in a beloved melody ; and it may be safely affirmed that no one ever possessed so definite an idea of any visible object, at which he was not absolutely gazing, as thousands can summon up at any moment of their lives in the case of musical productions. The very word *Volkslied* bears witness to this definite knowledge, with the power of transmission from individual to individual and from generation to generation which it implies : and it is a striking thought that while unpretentious pictures of obscure authorship, however beautiful, might probably remain for ever in private dwellings or in village churches, a short simple and anonymous tune may become as widely known as the work of a world-famous composer.

The above are the widest and most fundamental requirements for a popular art, and the ones on which I would most insist. But, considering that numbers must take their pleasure, if at all, after a long day's work, we may further notice, in favour of Music, the state of complete physical relaxation in which it can be enjoyed, and its total independence of daylight; to say nothing of the distinctly *social* characteristics in which it is also pre-eminent, partly through the natural collecting of people both to practise and to hear it, partly by the absolute simultaneity of the impressions it produces, and the electric quality of the sympathy so evoked.

There is little fear that through a recognition of its ideal (and in great measure actual) extent the musical world will be divided against itself. The influence of an educated minority must always be sufficiently strong: would that it were always rightly used! The fact that an army of executants stands between the creative artist and his public subjects Music in one way to a special disadvantage; for among these, in addition to many of the rank and file who merely crave for the excitement of novel and amusing work, there are always some, possessed of conspicuous talent but lacking simplicity and reverence, who forget the true purpose of the art in the opportunities it gives them for personal display, and who lead away audiences capable of enjoying beautiful melody into applauding mere show. Not that the love of witnessing performance need be silly and low; qualities of vigour and decision in an executant may be interesting from a quite human point of view; but these are just the qualities which need some strength and body in the music to make themselves felt. We may hope, however, that unworthy virtuosoship will be more and more detected, and that the love of the art has its roots too deep to be permanently distorted or coerced. The people get few chances, but their instinct, healthy even where lacking refinement, has served and will serve as a sound basis for high and rapid development. Their verdicts do not extend beyond the comparatively narrow limits of their comprehension; but the comprehension is most genuine, and their positive judgments have been again and again confirmed and eventually taken up into the accepted body of opinion. Music does not stand more apart in its cosmopolitan character than in the excellence of its most distinctively popular examples. The beauty of the *Volkslieder* of the European nations has been and still is universally acknowledged by the best musicians, and many of these (as opposed to most early efforts of other arts) may be fairly called perfect. Persons who are beyond the reach of any cultivation are at all events safe from false and superficial cultivation. Whatever be the strains they enjoy, they at any rate set the example of applying real *enjoyment*, and not supposed '*accomplishment*,' as the test of what they will have: and such fine melodies as the *Marseillaise*, the *March of the Men of Harlech*, and the *Blue Danube*, which figure so prominently in the *répertoire* of the streets, might put to shame the feebly pretty tunes and feebly ugly variations which so often do duty for art in the drawing-room. Nor is it the least the case, as is sometimes asserted, that the power to appreciate fine

§ 2. The musical instinct of the people is normally sound; though it gets but little chance of true cultivation.

Importance of the *Volkslied.*

naïve tune is something which has in some way to exist among the great body of the people, and that genuine *Volkslieder* do not now appear. For instance, many persons are not aware that almost the best-known melody in Europe, and certainly one of the most beautiful, *Ach, wie ist's möglich dann—*

was written less than half a century ago by a composer of no lasting fame; and truly the happiness of having made such a tune, which can no more be kept out of the air than sunlight, must seem something better than fame, when one thinks of the number of hearts a man may so reach. Nor are tunes of this quality confined to words or popular song-books. When one marks the ease with which fine melodies are picked up in England in whatever connection, if only they be properly heard, it is easy to feel that a theme like the supremely beautiful second 'subject' in Beethoven's violin-concerto, a *Volkslied* if ever there was one, is a greater possession for mankind than all the elaborate development of that supremely beautiful work.

§ 3. Scraps of evidence of the way in which fine melody will permeate are often strangely neglected.

I suppose that everybody who is much interested in a subject, and on the look-out for scraps of evidence about it, is occasionally startled by finding that these go for the most part quite unobserved, and that what he thought commonplaces are received as paradoxes. Now at this very moment a house-painter is humming *sotto voce* Mendelssohn's *Wedding*

*March* outside my door, a baker's boy in the street is whistling *La ci darem*, and a German band a little farther on has just been playing the march from *Scipio*, to the obvious edification of surrounding nursery-maids; yet I believe that at all events the first two facts would have gone unobserved even by many of those who know the tunes. I would not say with Schumann that ' the voices of the Graces cannot be heard by reason of the multitude of fugues;' there is no incompatibility between the two things, and I have no objection to ninety-and-nine just persons singing fugues in ninety-and-nine parts (if they can get them written), provided they will allow me to believe that when a street-boy is whistling a beautiful melody in perfect tune and time, keeping step and swinging his basket in rhythm, he is not doing so in sheer vacuity and vulgarity, but with *bonâ fide* artistic enjoyment. Nor has the fact that such performances are often displeasing and worrying to others, owing to the great imperfection of the instrument, any bearing on the feeling in the performer which underlies this very feeble means of expression. It is often Music's misfortune to be overheard; but it is certainly the good fortune of the human race that they possess by nature the means, however imperfect, of reproducing musical emotions for themselves.

But, it will be objected, there are also bad and vulgar tunes which obtain the run of the streets. Doubtless: I admit of course a great deal of low taste both in and out of the streets; and I do so in complete conformity to the previous argument that pleasure must be the criterion of music; using the word *low* to imply a feeble and transient enjoyment of things which are found, as a pure matter of experience, not to appeal to those accustomed to a greater and more permanent enjoyment. But I would observe that the people have to take what they can get, and that the repertory of tunes open to the poorer classes in England is extremely limited; if they catch up clap-trap, it is greatly because they cannot pick and choose, and are at the mercy of barrel-organs: would that they got more chances, and that one had not to walk through miles and miles of London park on sunny Sunday afternoons without encountering a single band! All musicians must know the sensation of being haunted even by tunes which they absolutely dislike: and though I do not pretend that street-boys dislike the bad tunes they mechanically whistle, no one with any experience of places where the trial has been made (as in villages where the children have been taught to sing the treble of good part songs or of the choruses in the *Messiah*) can doubt that they would sing and whistle good tunes, and do, when they get the chance of knowing them, infinitely more *con amore*. If I seem to attach supreme importance to children, it is because the organism naturally tends to become set and unreceptive after a certain age: but Welsh mines and the great towns of the North could give a good account of the art whose truest home is ' in among the throngs of men.'

§ 4. It is impossible to regard the popularity of vulgar tunes as an indication in the contrary direction, till equal chances are given of picking up good ones.

So that if we cannot quite feel with Sir Thomas Browne that ' even that vulgar and tavern musick, which makes one man merry, another mad, strikes in us a deep fit of devotion, and a profound contemplation of the first composer,' it is mainly because our contemplation finds freer scope in the wide possibilities of better things.

In Music it is especially incumbent for those who have easy chances of enjoyment to think of those who have not.

In this connection it is allowable to remark that, in proportion to the lack of direct moral and intellectual stimulation in the subject-matter of an art, the duty of not allowing enjoyment of it to sink into mere personal gratification seems to need enforcement. Many of those who have easy opportunities for enjoying Art are apt to nurse themselves with the belief that they are doing something worthy and admirable in so enjoying it. But what is the legitimate recreation of busy people may be the self-indulgence of idle ones. The fashionable air which is thrown over many art-gatherings has a specially dangerous tendency; and the art where this is most prominent happens to be the very one where philanthropy has the amplest and easiest field. There is a deliberateness in the indulgence of systematic concert-going which seems to demand as a counterpoise the recognition of this fact: for while we feast in company, there are thousands with ears to hear who starve outside.

§ 5. What one may remark by attention is not a satisfactory result, but is pregnant with possibilities.

As regards the *mere fact* that a person without refined ideas or manners may possess a keen and discriminating feeling for Music, it is worth noting that a single instance is sufficient evidence. But as regards the extent to which the fact is exemplified, I am anxious not to overstate my case. What one may perceive by keeping one's ears open is to be regarded not as a satisfactory and complete result, but only as a certain indication of what might be; and deeply *un*satisfactory in so far as it falls short of that. And to any reader to whom the present views may appear exaggerated, I might point out that it is not necessary to carry their application lower than the English middle class, in order amply to bear out the positions of the last chapter as to the uniqueness of Music's influence: for the superiority in the average middle class lot to that of the poorer classes cannot be said commonly to take the line either of the capacity or the reality of keen and refined æsthetic enjoyment. But no one probably will press the attempt to distinguish the strata of musical susceptibility by the test of a shilling entrance-fee or even the possession of a cottage piano, any more than by guinea-stalls or Broadwood grands. Experience completely confirms what the argument concluded in the last chapter would have led us to expect. Good music seems to make its way like water wherever channels are open for it; and if I have dwelt chiefly on simple melodies, it is only because circumstances, not necessity, have hitherto in great measure limited the people's chances to these. We have seen that the greatest instrumental works have been fathered by Wagner with perfect justice on the dance-melody.[1] These works indeed, and their various movements, differ enormously among themselves in the amount of the distinctly popular element; the motives are clear and continuous in some, interrupted and covered in others; but it is certainly a fair tribute to their parentage to say that a person who appreciates Strauss's waltzes may as a rule be led by very easy stages to appreciate, not indeed the *Posthumous* quartetts or the last pianoforte sonatas of Beethoven, but the overtures, for example, to *Le Nozze* and *Leonora* and *Egmont* and *Prometheus* and *Euryanthe* and *Ruy Blas*, and large portions of most of the great concertos and symphonies. Sufficient proof of this may be seen at the autumn promenade-concerts at Covent Garden.[2] Nor can any one who has watched on those occasions maintain that the enjoyment is of a stupid and gaping sort: it is impossible to mistake the look of joyful welcome on many faces, when, for instance, the glorious themes of Beethoven's concertos flash forth again and again, now from the solo-instrument, now from the orchestra, and insist on being heard and recognised. It is a peculiarity of Music, due both to its addressing numbers simultaneously and to its intimate connection with the physical organism, that the effect it produces may not only be judged of by the applause, but to a great extent actually *seen* at particular instants : and if the *Rosamunde* ballet-music, which was wisely played several times last autumn, did not give incomparably more popular pleasure than the noisy 'popular' galops which usually closed the programme, I must be both deaf and blind. And it is to be particularly observed that fine melody which really speaks to the unrefined and ignorant not only produces in them as great a *mass* of enjoyment as in the cultivated amateur (for this might probably be said of the enjoyment of coarse food as compared with the amateur's enjoyment of fine claret, and to a great extent of the enjoyment of a glaring coloured print as compared with the amateur's enjoyment of a delicate engraving), but an enjoyment the *quality* of which no criterion of higher and lower pleasures can make out to be inferior.

The word *popular* a few lines above brings into notice the singular

*It rarely happens that one sees the experiment tried on a really striking scale, but the results are unmistakeable.*

---

[1] In connection with this remark, it is interesting to note the people's vindication of their own musical instinct, in respect of the fundamental and indispensable sense of rhythm, in the truly marvellous contrast between the waltzing in any common dancing-garden, or on the deck of a German steamer, and that frequently seen in more fashionable quarters. It is not surprising that the couples of the upper classes should find it impossible to dance up to the time at which their waltzes are frequently played; but why instead of checking the music, invent the fiction of 'dancing half-time,' unless through a failure to perceive that to spread three steps rhythmically over two bars of waltz-measure is a feat only comparable to the squaring of the circle ?

[2] I heard surprise expressed at our most popular English musician's having 'condescended ' to the conductorship of these concerts; *condescended* to conduct magnificent performances of the concertos, overtures, and symphonies of Beethoven, and no end of other first-class music, for the benefit of people who don't wear white gloves !

manner in which that description is perpetually applied to music. The term by rights ought as instantly to exclude, as it is actually apt to suggest, the idea of those trifling strains, the hack-work of band-masters and dance-writers, which are so common in theatres and places of public entertainment, and which may often be said not to awaken one spark of interest in any single listener. Popularity is not, as many seem to think, a speciality of strings of obvious phrases built on a simple rhythm. That music is *popular* which arrests people's attention and, when heard again, compels their recognition; not that whose highest success is momentarily to tickle their ears.[1]

But that great music should become popular in this sense, one condition, not always sufficiently realised, may in many cases be indispensable; namely, that the opportunity should be given, and taken, of hearing the same work several times. We do not walk through the National Gallery or the British Museum at five miles an hour: and if any considerable number of musical works are to become to the uncultured many what the Elgin room is to the cultured few, they must have their fair chance. I have sufficiently emphasised the fact that Music does not demand external education, and that the point where the cultivated has the advantage of the uncultivated hearer is not in being more refined or imaginative or in having wider interests, but simply in having heard more music; I will now add, in having heard a good deal of it in such a way as to become familiar with it. Regular frequenters of performances in large towns have abundant opportunities in this way: but for those whose chance of educating their ears is in any case much smaller, and who know nothing of printed scores or pianoforte arrangements, the point is doubly important, and there may be the whole difference between the second or third hearing and the first.[2] Nor is the topic less worth emphasising in the interest of many who, through no fault of their own, lose opportunities

[1] Schumann says of a gipsy-chorus in an opera which had disappointed him, 'Euphony and grace should never be found wanting, even when gipsies are the singers:' a sentence which vividly recalls the tedious and tuneless simplicity of many an operatic chorus of hunters and villagers and other such inevitable bodies of people. 'Weber has done these things better in his *Preciosa.*' Truly he has.

[2] I am of course measuring popular appreciation not by an advanced musical standard, but by the standard of the ordinary concert-going public of a higher social grade. What proportion of these, in a couple of hearings, at all grasp the construction of a long movement, in the sense that they would discover much amiss if, the 'subjects' and salient points being retained, the plan of modulation and many transitional and 'developing' passages were turned topsy-turvy? With how many of them at first does the appreciation of the wider organic coherence amount to much more than welcoming the returns of the main themes, while the rest, so far as it produces definite impressions at all, is enjoyed in a very piecemeal way? Nor, again, am I by any means asserting that music of a high class supplies an endless number of specimens which will produce astonishing popular effects; only that when such effects *are* produced in England it is normally by music belonging to that class; and that in respect of popular susceptibility the conditions are all there for multiplying the production of them a hundred-fold.

which should easily be theirs.  That music is now a perpetual feature of private evening gatherings means often no more than that it has innumerable chances of going in at one ear and out at the other; uncultivated ears—those especially of the numerous class who 'like music' but 'don't profess to appreciate anything classical'—being treated on that understanding, and naturally accepting the treatment to which they have been accustomed.  How often, in the society, for instance, of an English country-house, which is pretty sure to contain some members of this class, is the experiment tried of supplying for them the same conditions as are supplied by the barrel-organs, and giving them the same tunes, say the allegretto movement of Beethoven's sonata Op. 10, 2, on three successive evenings?  Yet that simple experiment might teach them more about classical music than attendance at a score of classical concerts, and more about their own ears than an eternity of the strains adapted to their supposed capacity.

In connection with the popular element in highly developed music, it is impossible to avoid recurring to the most prominent modern theories, and pointing out how serious is the crisis threatened in them.  Wagner, who is entirely free from musical Pharisaism, fully admits that up to this point the art has sprung from the broad foundation of the popular feeling, more especially in respect of its fundamental mainstay of rhythm.  If then it ignores its basis, a tremendous catastrophe awaits it.  And it is to that catastrophe, in the lapse of all close and coherent melodic organism, that Wagner points the way.  His views on musical structure will be more fitly noticed in connection with Opera; but the leading fallacy can be explained in a sentence, and is only a natural consequence of the curious theory as to the relation of *time* to Music, explained in the eighth chapter. After describing the fundamental impression to be received from an ideal musical work, by the metaphor of the hum of a forest on a summer night, whose multitudinous and undistinguishable voices the hearer can in no way repeat or recall, but must visit the woods again to realise, Wagner actually calls this peculiarly formless effect *melody*; in an ' uninterrupted stream' of sound 'flowing through a whole work,' and not only (as is natural in Opera) lacking the larger sort of organic coherence, but containing numberless passages and fragments which do not pretend to any sort of true melodic form, he imagines the capacity of ' infinitely richer development of melodic form than musicians have hitherto believed possible in the symphony;' and while defining melody as ' musical form,' he calls such loose conjunctions ' infinite melody,' without perceiving *infinite form* to be a contradiction in terms.   I need not repeat here in fragments the account of musical organism given in the eighth and tenth chapters: if that account be true, it is likewise true that Music attained to Beethoven's symphonies in paths where the people could follow, because it was true to the instinct which is in their very blood: through this it has been loved, dwelt on, and

§ 8. Importance of the fact that rhythmic and organic form is at the very basis of the popular feeling for Music, and equally at the basis of all that gives Music its highest and most distinctive value; recognised by Beethoven, and ignored by Wagner.

remembered.  That Wagner should perceive limitations in those symphonies, owing to their metrical form and *timidity* (poor earth-bound *Eroica*) in Beethoven's adherence to that form, may pass as a curious aberration of musical sense or as a new revelation ; but that he should glory in the notion of music which the hearer cannot at all recall, which is doomed to non-existence for him except as the vague opiate of an occasional evening, shows a curious perversity of view as to the ideal place of Music in the world.[1]

§ 9. Melody of the most direct kind, from whatever source, should be presented as much as possible on orchestras and open-air bands.

Melody of the most direct kind, however, is so obviously and necessarily the primary popular element in Music, that not only should works of striking and unmitigated tunefulness, like Sterndale Bennett's lovely *Naiads* overture, or the overtures of Auber, or the *Tannhäuser* overture and march, be well represented in every popular programme, but I cannot help wishing measures were taken in England to introduce some of the greatest vocal melodies oftener and in a more imposing manner.  Voices capable of filling vast buildings satisfactorily are very limited both in number and power of work : but why should not many glorious tunes be arranged to be played by orchestras, which waste so much time and strength on mere displays of showy sound ?  By such an adaptation the tunes may gain even in beauty as much as they lose, and may gain indefinitely in the numbers they appeal to.  I shall never forget the overpowering effect of Schubert's *Ave Maria*, played by wind-instruments and accompanied by strings, as I heard it in Dresden at one of the ordinary nightly Gewerbehaus concerts.  Do the conductors of English popular concerts know the feeling in the air when a multitude is stirred ?  If so, I should have thought that, were it only to enjoy the sense of blissful expansion in swaying the beats and pulses of that wonderful life, a sense as of controlling the powers of an invisible world, they would open more freely the treasures which lie ready to their hand.

Objections to such adaptations are quite indefensible.

Nor is it only to vocal compositions that this treatment would apply : chamber-music would afford plenty of popular beauties for the purpose. Nothing can be more blindly pedantic than to object to transpositions of this sort when judiciously made.  Unfortunately, however, such objections are often heard : thus an outcry was raised by some musical critics not long ago at the idea of arranging for a string-band a movement from Mendelssohn's octett, eminently suited for such treatment.  I have already dwelt sufficiently on the incalculable superiority in importance of musical form to musical colour : and moreover here the change is not a matter of *abstracting* colour, as in a photograph or engraving, but of giving it new body and magnificence. And it is indisputable that while beautiful melodic forms have astonishingly

[1] It is superfluous to say that Wagner's compositions present plenty of impressive music, in which, it is equally superfluous to add, the conditions of impressiveness have been duly recognised.

rapid power of arresting the popular ear, in colour it is not delicate shades and varieties but blaze and amount that the people appreciate; and that a certain force and brilliance of sound is often in the first instance necessary to make the form palpable to their ears: so that the argument from colour tends in the same direction as the argument from form. Get grand melody known, *quand même.* What sympathy is it possible to feel with amateurs who enjoy all the refinements of delicate *timbre* and exceptional individual performance at their exclusive concerts, and then object to the obvious means of presenting the substance of the beauty in the most striking and penetrating manner to the ears of less favoured hearers?

It may be observed that the truth and healthiness of the popular instinct in point of melody is the more in accordance with my general argument from its marked contrast with the feeble and debased æsthetic sense in other directions. I was struck lately with a curious instance of the blindness and vulgarity which an ordinary London audience may show when appealed to through other channels, while evincing a perfectly true and sound judgment in Music. Not long ago a piece called *The Sultan of Mocha* was played in London with great applause, the beauty and *entrain* of the music actually swamping and carrying down a plot which in point of incoherence would hardly have disgraced one of the great opera-houses. The gem of the whole was a series of short and simple ballets, a beautiful instance of the power of motion to adorn melody, and so graceful and refined in conception and detail that one felt at once how hopeless it was that it should 'take' with an Alhambra-going public. The charm of the combination, appreciable only through the interplay of delicate impressions received through two senses, was in fact quite lost, and the whole scene fell utterly flat, coming in for no fraction of the applause which was lavishly bestowed on most of the excellent melodies and execrable jokes throughout the piece. Since this was first printed I noticed the very same thing at the first performance of another opera of Mr. Cellier's, when almost the only pieces not *encored* by an enthusiastic audience were two beautifully refined little ballets. That the British public are no quicker at perceiving what is bad, a proof was afforded about the same time by the ballet of nuns in *Robert le Diable* as performed at Drury Lane. The accompanying music of this ballet is indeed so utterly weak and paltry [1] that pains on the ballet itself must perhaps be poorly

§ 10. The healthy instinct for Music contrasted with the debased taste in respect of dancing.

---

[1] I am anxious to avoid using strong expressions on mere individual bias; and therefore hope to be believed when I say that I am careful here to speak in complete submission to my own criterion, and in accordance with my experience of the effect the music described has had on others. My experience may of course be one-sided, and if I ever learn that any considerable number of people have received at all a deep and permanent impression, from, *e.g.*, this ballet-music, or even that two or three have been able to make it their spiritual food for any length of time, I will at once admit my mistake.

bestowed : nevertheless some pains were certainly taken, and the result was only not ludicrous because it was so exceedingly painful.   From the first moment when the nuns appeared with the enveloping mackintoshes which represented cerements forced out into astonishing shapes by the skirts underneath, till the final disappearance of those hideous horizontal skirts with all the waddling awkwardness which they necessarily entail on the human form, one simply felt inclined to sink into the earth ; and whatever may have been the sins of the abbess in particular, she may fairly be thought to have expiated them in condemnation to a brief space of such unmeaning contortion and grimace.   Not being able to sink into the earth, I watched the audience ; and though few applauded, it seemed to me that very few suffered.   While on this point I may remark that it is absurd to account for the shortcomings of the ballet in England by a theory of some present dearth of special genius and of particular stars. Even were particular stars necessary, which they are not, they cannot shine without a firmament.   The simple truth is that among us, who never even had a national dance, artistic dancing is an exotic dependent on passing gusts of fashion, and that the English as a people have ears but not eyes.[1]

§ 11. Mis-<br>conceptions<br>as to the true<br>and ideal<br>nature of the<br>popularity of<br>Music.

Leaving now special points of proof and suggestion as to the extent or extension of the area of Music's ever-growing influence, we may consider the subject of its popularity in a somewhat more general way.   It is a subject on which there have been many misconceptions ; and it will be by examining some of these that we shall best proceed.

Schumann's<br>remarks on<br>amateurs.

My first reference must be to the writings of Schumann.   In these there is little indeed seriously to cavil at : hatred of pedantry, contempt of mere cleverness without inspiration, overflowing geniality and kindliness, pervade them from end to end : and the one thing occasionally lacking to our complete sympathy with their spirit arises from a vein perhaps

---

[1] Another case came under my notice soon after.  Having seen in a small theatre at Milan a singularly perfect performance of a pantomimic piece, in which I do not think the most censorious critic could have found more to object to than in the spontaneous dancing of children, I was surprised next year to see the principal performer advertised to appear at Covent Garden ; and I walked down thither wondering which was the more impossible, that she should do anything inartistic and ugly, or that any solo-dancing which lacked those qualities should appear in the present day in connection with London Italian Opera.   The result was a compromise. In the *pas seul* she went through the usual miserable business, using her toes alternately to walk on the extremest tips of, and to describe horizontal semicircles in the air ; but she fell too far short of the British public's standard in shapeless bulk of muscular development to make the usual impression with these performances, and the *Morning Post* did not talk next day about a ' suavity and significance of motion charming to contemplate : ' which is a prerogative of thirteen stone and over.   Every now and then, however, in the general medley, when she was not supposed particularly to be dancing, the instinct of spontaneous motion was too strong for her, and one got a faint whiff of the Milanese delight.

unavoidable in the writings of a man whose whole career lay in the thick of musicians and musical discussion. One may feel in rising from their perusal that one has been a little too much in the atmosphere of professional orchestras and wonderful performers ; that if Music were quite such an esoteric and hothouse affair, it would hardly occupy the position that one hoped it might, and indeed that one sees it does, occupy in the world. No one appreciated the beauty and value of *Volkslieder* more than Schumann ; and it is disappointing, on the very next page to the one where he recommends attention to them as 'a treasure of lovely melodies,' to find such remarks as the following :—' " Melody " is the amateur's war-cry, and certainly music without melody is no music. Therefore you must understand what amateurs fancy the word means ; anything easily, rhyth-mically pleasing. But there are melodies of a very different stamp, and every time you open Bach, Beethoven, Mozart, &c., they will smile at you in a thousand different ways ; you will soon weary, if you know these, of the faded monotony of modern Italian opera melodies.' And again : ' In judging compositions, make a distinction between them, as to whether they belong to art, or merely serve as the entertainment of amateurs '— as if the people among whom the *Volkslied* originates and lives were not amateurs of the purest water ; and as if the names of Beethoven and Mozart and of Schumann himself were not household words, and their works household treasures, in thousands of homes whereof no single mem-ber would claim the dignity of connoisseurship. I scarcely think it a paradox to say that often it is the good music which is kept alive by amateurs, and the bad (at all events as regards *virtuoso* displays) by con-noisseurs. And the music which can only speak to Gewandhaus audiences is not the music whose existence is a great fact in the world. It is perhaps allowable rhetoric on Schumann's part to say, in his first enthusiasm about Schubert's newly-found symphony in C, that ' he who is not yet acquainted with this work knows very little about Schubert.' But it is far truer to say that he who knows and loves the peculiar quality of any one of Schubert's melodies knows a great deal about him. Elsewhere Schumann speaks with approval of the idea that progress in art ' can only be attained through the formation of an intellectual aristocracy among artists.' But Music, to be healthy, can never dispense with the broad support which comes from true though fragmentary appreciation, from natures which greet and cherish such beauties as they see, even if unable to grasp, like Schumann and his friends, the whole organism of an elaborate movement.

Not that though Schumann seems to have occasionally flouted amateurs in a somewhat indiscriminate way, his remarks are as a rule less just in their bearing on the hearers of music than on the makers and performers. The burden of his advice is always to listen and enjoy, instead of talking and carping ; and it might well be taken to heart by a certain class of concert-goers, who often seem mainly occupied in extracting the pleasure of self-importance from having a *view*—pitting compositions against each other as if they were fighting-cocks, or still more frequently ignoring the fact that the music on its own account may have some significance worth thinking about, in airing fads and fancies about particular performers. It is obviously easy to pretend to taste and insight on such points without much possibility of contradiction, and to pose when there is no danger of being knocked over : but it is impossible to help wishing sometimes to try the effect of concealing the players, and setting the critical ears which discover so much ' soul ' in one first-class performance, and none at all in another, to detect which is which.

*True appreciation of Music is often unreasonably self-distrustful ; and to flout the enormously numerous class of naïve amateurs is most unreasonable and mischievous.*    But it would be as unfair to judge the large class of amateurs by these specimens as by those whose definition of melody would be ' anything easily, rhythmically pleasing.'   My experience is that, of all sorts of amateurs, musical amateurs, in the wide sense which would include all to whom Music gives deep pleasure, stand oftenest in need of most definite encouragement and reassurance.  In a letter written three weeks before his death, Shelley remarked, ' You know my gross ideas of music, and will forgive me when I say that I listen the whole evening on our terrace to the simple melodies' (performed by Mrs. Williams) ' with excessive delight ; ' never guessing that the sentence was a contradiction in terms.   And this is the attitude one is perpetually meeting with in people whom Schumann, after his remarks on the *Volkslied*, could not but have admitted to have the root of the matter in them.   Professing to understand nothing about Music, they not only betray the sort of understanding which is worth more than all the technical knowledge in the world, but often show unwittingly a very marked amount of discrimination ; not of course in detecting everything or nearly everything which is good, but in being attracted by little or nothing which is *not* good.   It may be that musical susceptibilities of the kind Shelley describes are sometimes limited to the very shortest and simplest specimens of the art : but the combination of ' excessive delight ' in such melodies as Mrs. Williams performed, with inability to receive as much and more from such works as the *Messiah* or at least half of the movements of Beethoven's sonatas (with the one proviso that these also shall have their fair chance of sinking in), is a phenomenon which one may at any rate wait to believe in till one encounters it.

This estimate of the qualities of naïve and self-distrustful appreciation seems specially to need enforcing in the present day, just on account of the *primâ facie air* of difficulty which has increased with the modern development of the art.   One reads astonishing accounts of the way in which audiences of the last century came heard and conquered music, greeting or damning works with unanimity on the strength of a single performance : and this ready apprehension and familiar sort of treatment has a natural relation to the smaller and snugger circles (and often, it must be added, factions) in which the art was domesticated, and to stories like that of the first production of Cimarosa's *Il Matrimonio Segreto* at Vienna, when the Emperor invited all the performers to a banquet, and then sent them back to the theatre to do it again. The comparative lack nowadays of such strikingly unanimous and spontaneous response is partly owing to the very fact that the art has penetrated far more widely and deeply into the various social strata ; but partly also, it must be admitted, to the characteristics of a great deal of the music which has since been produced. A very slight and superficial parallelism may be traced between the present state of things and that which prevailed in the later middle ages ; slight and superficial, because then the divorce between the scientific and the popular elements was real, whereas now it is in great measure only apparent and partial. Still the very appearance is a fact to be most steadily kept in sight. So far as the naïve class of amateurs have become used to hearing music called very fine in which their ears do not catch and welcome the motives, so far is there a danger and difficulty which cannot be reckoned with by merely telling them, like Schumann, that they have low ideas of melody. The more it can be impressed on any such amateur in any particular case that the motives are there, if indeed they *are* there, and that—inasmuch as the keen enjoyment of *all* musical motive is one in kind, which kind he has himself realised on other occasions—there is a good chance that they will reveal themselves after a few more hearings, the better the chance that more and more great music will become popular, and that laboured and tuneless work will be detected and discredited.

The next mode of misconceiving the facts and possibilities of Music in respect of popularity is largely referable to its historical connection with Poetry ; which has had a no less disastrous influence on speculation about the subsequent position and relations of the two arts than we previously saw it to have had on views concerning the essential nature and content of the former. Comte,[1] for instance, makes a hierarchy of arts corresponding to its hierarchy of sciences, arranging them in order of decreasing generality as Poetry, Music, Painting, Sculpture, Architecture. He says that the sphere of Poetry is wider than that of the other arts, ' since it embraces every side of our existence, whether individual, domestic, or social.' And this, so far as it goes, is true ; the wider scope of Poetry as regards subject-matter admits of no doubt. But superior *generality* in this sense does not in any way involve superior *popularity* : and in trying to make out

§ 12. Comte did not perceive the peculiar causes of Music's wide popular appeal, partly owing to the old mistake of looking on its subordination to Poetry as an essential fact.

[1] Comte's views of Music are in some ways noble and interesting ; and in spite of his imagining it to be normal that Music should draw its subjects from Poetry, his appreciation of the value of Mozart's melodies seems to show that he had truly realised its independent power. But it strikes one as odder in a modern writer than in Plato to ignore the fact that the faculty of apprehending Music is a special and incommunicable, though happily a very common, gift.

that really quite distinct point, Comte sacrifices obvious facts to the simplicity and symmetry of his hierarchy.   He goes on to say that Poetry is the most *popular* of all the arts, ' both on account of its wider scope, and also because, its instruments of expression being taken from ordinary language, it is more generally intelligible than any other.'   ' Prosody,' he continues, ' the only technical element, is easily acquired by a few days' practice,'—that is, a quite uneducated Roman might have acquired by a few days' study the power of appreciating, perhaps even of reproducing, the metrical refinements of Virgil !   Nor does the argument about words express anything like the whole truth.   To say that, because words are a universal medium of expression, Poetry is universally intelligible, is something like saying that, because eyes and light are universal, the refinements of Venetian or Turneresque colouring are universally intelligible.   For, not to dwell on the fact that verbal colouring often depends on an element of subtle and complex literary association, it is the constant characteristic of intellectual poetry that appreciation of it requires a cultivated faculty for perceiving deep and often difficult relations.   Even had he said ' calculated to become the most popular after the regeneration of society,' it would have been but a guess, resting on a confusion between amount of sources of material and amount of appreciative acceptance.   In estimating the latter, we have no appeal from facts whose origin dates back to the beginning of the history of our organisms, and a change in whose nature we have no ground for prophesying.   But Music having been subordinated to Poetry in his classification, it was natural to Comte to stereotype it in this relation ; as when, in his evolution of Art out of speculative and theoretic regions, and his prophecy of its recombination with Science and its highest development in the hands of philosophers, he applies to Art in general theories which, even could we consider them sound, would apply only to Poetry, and are exceptionally inapplicable to Music.   For Poetry, alone of the arts, has Protean power, and can comprehend and follow, in their widest extent and in their minutest detail, the changing aspects and relations of life ; while Music stands of course at the very opposite extreme.   Comte has thus illustrated the danger, already adverted to, of ignoring the distinction of faculties and treating Art all in a piece.   In his own words, ' *Art* yielded to the specialising system, which, though normal for industry, is in its case abnormal ; ' and ' *Art* detached itself from the theoretic system before Science, because its progress was more rapid, and from its nature it was more independent ; ' but ' ultimately all theoretic faculties,' whether scientific or æsthetic, ' will be again combined even more closely than in primitive times.'   He supports this view by such statements as that ' the greatest masters of Music, even in modern times, have shown universality of taste,' and that ' the absence of this in the present day is but a fresh proof that æsthetic genius does not and cannot exist in times like these ' (shade of Beethoven !), ' when Art has no social purpose and rests on no philosophic principles.' I will not revert to the ' philosophic principles,' nor to the arbitrary identification of scientific and æsthetic faculties ; but the best answer to the supporting statements is flat contradiction : as it happens ' the greatest masters' of Music *have* been in a singular degree specialists, and Music *does* answer even now a most useful social purpose.

There is one other prominent writer whose views in relation to the popular character of Music cannot be passed over : for though springing from deep artistic enthusiasm, and intertwined with aims which command respectful sympathy, the views themselves are none the less derogatory to the real value of the art which they vaguely seem to glorify. In spite of the wide difference of standpoint, Wagner agrees with Comte in wholly ignoring that peculiar isolation of Music from the world of politics and speculation which we have dwelt on at length in the preceding chapters, and which will be further exemplified in the present connection. But while the French philosopher would have Music connected with all the other arts and sciences in a grand ' theoretic' scheme, the German musician would have it represent a ' national idea :' while one would fasten on it intellectual and ethical bearings which are alien to its character, the other, in pursuing a distant, and to a great extent an unreal object, is blind to that wherein its truly popular character, whether national or cosmopolitan, has consisted and will still consist.

§ 13. Wagner quite misconceives both the facts and the meaning of popularity in Music.

Wagner has given his views in a succinct and interesting form in a recent contribution to the *North American Review*. He describes how the wretched condition of German art early led him to a critical examination of German civilisation ; and how his conviction that the culture of his country was ' something unnatural, narrow, weak, incapable of producing the true realisation of any great national idea, in a word, was something altogether *un*-German,' suggested thoughts concerning the possibility of essentially changing the existing order of things. ' The German people,' he says, ' as it began to emerge from the long misery of the Thirty Years' War, saw, at the courts of its many princes, the great waste left by the death of its truly national life gradually hidden by an imitation of the sumptuous splendour of Versailles. But all that was really German seemed utterly buried beneath it, when suddenly the genius of the German race awoke anew out of its stupor, in the persons and works of great poets and musicians. Suddenly there sprang up the heroes of the great German revival. This great reawakening is the only movement that can be placed on an equality with the European conception of the Renaissance, and through it our Goethe and Schiller, Mozart and Beethoven, once more revealed the great German element in their glorious art-creations. They found no great public, no nation, to which they could speak in its own language. But in themselves the great national spirit was aroused in re-

His attempt to make out Music to be in direct and close connection with ' national ideas ' and contemporary intellectual life,

newed vigour, and only some important historical event was necessary to make it take form in *deeds*,'—a condition 'fulfilled in the great war of liberation against the world-conquering French Cæsar.' We need not take exception to anything here except as regards Music. As far as Music was concerned, 'the genius of the German race' which 'woke anew' was the well-known genius of the German race *for music*, neither more nor less. And this did not wake anew even in Mozart, much less in Beethoven; but, so far as an immense stride made by exceptional genius after a certain interval of stationariness can be spoken of as waking, it woke primarily in Bach and Handel, and was very wide awake indeed in Haydn, who all three lived absorbed in their own world of creations, Handel moreover in England, and Haydn under the wing of one of the princely families which went furthest in imitating the splendours of Versailles: but even during the Thirty Years' War it had not been by any means asleep, but had been sedulously cultivated, though as it happens no supreme name is connected with that era.[1] And it would be pure nonsense to represent national life, in the sense

which totally breaks down in the very instances he adduces.

of comprehensive patriotic and intellectual life, as 'waking anew' in such a man as Mozart; as though he had been a sort of Mazzini, instead of a simple, through-and-through, lovable, and somewhat dissipated musician, with a gift and a mission to delight the ears of men in a unique fashion for as long as we can foresee. We bless Germany for having given him to us, as we bless her for so many of his brethren: but we do not bring to or carry from *Dove Sono* any realisation of the German spirit or the German *renaissance* or national civilisation, things of which many among us have never even conceived; we simply bring the cosmopolitan power to appreciate perfect melody, and we carry away the delight which perfect melody can give. And it is precisely the same with Beethoven, though his synchronism with the climax of the great literary revival makes the confusion somewhat more natural in his case, and though in marking his general contempt for trammels and traditions we may remember with interest that he breathed the air of a revolutionary age. But he came then, or rather coming then he did just what he did, because, Haydn and Mozart having gone before, his unique and overpowering musical genius found exactly the conditions for its freest scope. Beethoven's honesty and independence, his warm heart and deeply philanthropic spirit earn him, as a man, our deep respect: but his vague democratic instincts had nothing to do with the work in which his whole life was absorbed, and were so little a proof of political sagacity that he wrote his most epoch-making work in honour of the French Cæsar aforesaid,—(it is fair to add that he tore off the title-page when Napoleon became emperor): nor had his un-

[1] Mr. Hullah has remarked how this troubled period produced, not, as might have seemed natural, a band of inventive and undisciplined geniuses, but a body of very learned and skilful organists and theorists.

defined spiritual aspirations any relation to contemporary intellectual life, or to the *Zeitgeist* which Goethe represented. The result of course is, that he is for all nations and all times which can appreciate the heights and depths of Music, and will live concurrently with all sorts of *Zeitgeist*. And the converse argument insists on suggesting itself, that, however truly Wagner may have been 'precisely the one among his countrymen who most vehemently felt the longing for a new birth of German civilisation,' and whose ' peculiarly receptive nature' was most awake to 'all the wonderful impressions his age conveyed,' his wealth of speculative and political interests has not made a Beethoven of him.

However, the patriotic spirit of a nation is doubtless fed by great work of any sort produced in it; and though the popular influence attributed by Wagner to Mozart and Beethoven would imply a depth and universality of appreciation of music which even now, after the enormous subsequent spread of musical knowledge, would be a mere dream, such a piece of enthusiasm might be passed by if it were not a link in what is meant as a continuous argument. We pass on to his description of the period of reaction and the misunderstanding of the national spirit by the restored princes. 'At such a time, just after the mightiest uprising of the national spirit for the liberation of the Fatherland, we are confronted with this picture of complete oppression of everything German, of the entire destruction of every living nucleus for the development of a domestic or political national life. The great manifestation of the national genius in the works of those mighty masters remains without a trace of influence upon the further history of the nation;' which may be marked by the way as an admission completely on my side. ' Between the people and their art, as between the people and their princes, a mutual misunderstanding, the German's misunderstanding even of himself, kept alive by fear and repression, has raised a barrier that shuts out light and air from both alike.' Very interesting again, politically: but when one thinks about Music? Did any one raise a barrier between the German and his piano? Did the police interfere with choral societies? Would Wagner seriously affirm that the sale of the works of Beethoven suffered a gradual decline, dating from the Congress of Vienna? Is it or is it not the fact, that the works of Schubert, comparatively little known in his lifetime, which closed very nearly at the same time with Beethoven's, have grown steadily in popularity ever since; national perhaps even more than Beethoven's, because many are settings of German words, but for all that cosmopolitan and eternal?

And now follows a signal instance of forcing unreal correspondences upon the phenomena of musical history. Wagner notes the decline of German literature under French influence. ' The last vestiges of Germanic character,' he says, ' were scoffed at and rooted out by the revolutionary spirit that came to us from the west.' Heine had talent, but he was not

*Wagner's connection of the political reaction with musical decline.*

of German origin, and was a spreader of the international and un-German element. Works so utterly and delightfully musical as *Masaniello* and *Guillaume Tell* are described as the glorification of the idea of revolution. But the downfall of Germanic art was completed by the advent of Meyerbeer and Mendelssohn. The description of Meyerbeer with his 'misch-masch of all styles and methods in the form of the great

His view of the popularity of Meyerbeer,

Historical Opera' is extremely true, and in Wagner's best manner. 'From Beethoven's symphonies to Meyerbeer's opera—what a fearful stride is this!' Undoubtedly: if ever any one who had deeply cared for Beethoven's symphonies came to think of Meyerbeer's operas as anything but empty and pretentious stuff with a thin sprinkling of beauties, it would be a curious phenomenon; and so far as people are led away, like babies, by glittering spectacle and glaring and attitudinising music, from what is capable of giving them far greater and more enduring delight, it is a pity. But hear what follows. 'How could the German of that day fail to take it' (*i.e.* the stride from Beethoven to Meyerbeer) 'even with enthusiasm, after his whole national character and being had been so utterly destroyed or taken away from him during those years which had passed since the war of liberation, that Beethoven's German music must seem to him something entirely foreign; something without effect upon him; the extreme extravagance of an isolated man overweighted by his genius? The German mind deserted Beethoven, whom it pronounced a mere madman, for Meyerbeer, whom it declared the greatest of modern geniuses.' As if people began to

and implication that people's ears are at the mercy of their political instincts.

be born with ears of a totally new construction, owing to a decline of 'national character' in their parents: and as if, again, the German populace had all been flocking to hear Beethoven's symphonies, and then all turned their backs and flocked to the *Huguenots* instead. That a depressed political condition should affect the musical organisation, that those who had loved Beethoven 'could not fail' to prefer Meyerbeer, as soon as political affairs got awry, is really a ludicrous notion, when one imagines the case of a single musical individual, even of one engaged in the thick of political life; to say nothing of the tens of thousands, including of course women and children, who lead a narrow civic and domestic existence without more than distant and uncomprehending glances at politics, but taking music as naturally as sunlight. No less true is it, on the other hand, that the musical signs of the times are even now not much more than signs, that very much is still wanting, and *à fortiori* was more wanting at the time Wagner is describing, to general musical culture, and that most people are like sheep, and will go to any entertainment that is in fashion, and take it as it comes. Great instrumental works have throughout worked down to the populace gradually, as they are doing now in England; and bright lights and spectacle still attract thousands and thousands even amid the strongest indications that the best music is daily gaining ground. That people 'revelled in the revolutionary music of the *Huguenots*' merely means that the *Huguenots* attracted audiences then as now ; and the only *music* in the *Huguenots* which ever entered into the popular heart is of course Luther's sadly abused and deformed, but still unspoilable chorale.

Nobody of course will dispute the advantage to Music of a free and healthy *social* life : the gathering of people together with a common aim is a necessary condition both for the actual presentation of many works, and for any wide diffusion of the knowledge of them ; though even here the natural relation of Music to desirable social habits might perhaps be more justly conceived as cause than effect. But even were we to consult common-sense by substituting 'a turn for innocent evening recreation' for Wagner's irrelevant postulates, the distinction would remain equally clear, and the confusion equally indefensible, between the general external conditions favourable to extension of the area of appreciation, and the individual's direct experience of what he knows only as addressed to his own ears.

However, while entirely repudiating Wagner's account of external causes and results, we may readily admit the coarseness and triviality of operatic art as represented by Meyerbeer. But now, says Wagner, came a finer taste and talent, and 'did its best to settle our account with the great past, a past which it found rather uncomfortable to look back upon.' Mendelssohn undertook 'to lead the educated classes of Germany as far *His account of Mendelssohn,* away from the dreaded and misunderstood extravagances of a Beethoven as from those rude theatrical orgies which his more refined taste so detested in the historical opera of his fellow-Hebrew. He was the saviour of music in the *salon*—and with him the concert-room and now and then even the church, did duty as a *salon* also. Amid all the tempests of revolutions he gave to his art a delicate, smooth, quiet, cool, and agreeably tranquil form that excited nobody and had no aim but to please the modern cultivated taste, and to give it occasionally, amid the shifting and turmoil of the times, the consolation of a little pleasing and elegant entertainment. A new idea in art was developed, the embodiment in it of a graceful, good-society element, quite foreign to the nation's character and social life.' Strange : but stranger is to come. This kind of art, it seems, ventured beyond its proper limits, and 'Robert Schumann, a tasteful composer of *and of Schumann.* little spirited and pleasant songs and pieces for the pianoforte, now began to write symphonies, oratorios, and operas.' The educated German, who no longer believed in a great living national art, saw in these works a truly reawakened 'German art-spirit,' and contrasting them with the crude realism and trivial sensuousness of Meyerbeer, 'felt himself bound to admire them enthusiastically.' 'Thus the German intellect degenerated into a condition of complete unproductiveness in art, severing the living and active bonds that bound it to a great national past, and undertaking to

create, unaided, an art intended only for amateurs and connoisseurs.'
And then we hear how I, Deborah, arose, and all the rest.

In not recog-
nising that
these com-
posers are
admired and
beloved by
people who
care quite as
much for Beet-
hoven as he
does, he is
either ignorant
or impertinent.

Now I hold it to be useless, and even foolish, to quarrel with a man
because he does not admire any particular music as much as I do : but not
to realise, as a pure matter of fact, that the profoundest admiration for the
greatest of musicians is compatible with ardent love for the two composers
who are thus set in opposition to him, to doubt or to ignore the depth of
feeling for Beethoven in thousands who can only gasp at the ascription to
Schumann of ' complete unproductiveness in art,' is either most wilful ignorance or most gross impertinence ; while to blink the fact that Mendelssohn
and Schumann, who are represented as leading the public away from
Beethoven, were the two staunchest devotees and most powerful advocates
Beethoven ever had, and did more than any other men to advance the
knowledge of his music, is something very like disingenuousness.  Of the
many hundreds of people in the world to whom the music of Beethoven
is as dear as it is to Wagner, I should doubt if half-a-dozen are so unfortunate as to be able conscientiously to endorse the above views : and the
weakness of the attempted connection between the state of the 'national
character' and the appreciation of Music stands deplorably confessed in
them.  If the popularity of Mendelssohn and Schumann is a proof of
national degradation, England at any rate must be going rapidly to the
dogs.

Wagner gives a most interesting account of the miserably hollow and
unhealthy state of the operatic world at Paris during his early stay there ;
and of the dawn of his conception, a very good one, of presenting old
legends in an operatic form which was intended to reveal the most
characteristic elements of the ' primal Germanic spirit.'  Then he describes,
again in a way which commands warm sympathy, his various efforts to
introduce reforms at Dresden, and explains the carping and wounding
criticism which he encountered on the ground that the German people
had not yet ' rediscovered its own nature.'  Then follows some rather
windy talk, with a considerable substratum of truth, about the enslaved
and conventional condition of modern society, and about Art's not being
the free and natural expression of national life.  But again we feel the
unreality as regards Music.  Instead of talking about ' some great revolution of humanity at large,' which alone ' could make the true liberty of the
individual possible,' and be ' of any saving worth to a true art,' it is
surely better to recognise that *one* true art, at any rate, has become and
is becoming more and more a tremendous social influence and a means of
wide-spread delight and sympathy, even in this contemptible modern world.

And now we come in sight of the notion which, while laudable
enough in itself, seems greatly answerable for Wagner's misconception of
the truly popular function of Music.  His aims for Music are always in

connection with the *stage*; and he tells us how the *Nibelungen* perform-ances were to exemplify what alone he ' understood by a truly *universal* dramatic art in its noblest form.' In the new dramatic institution, ' masterpieces, degraded in the everyday public service into mere styleless and tasteless performances,' and presented ' in a transient shape that was devoid of any artistic value' to ' a public made up of the most diverse elements and utterly without artistic sense,' would be given in a befitting form, and ' would awaken a conception of the true meaning of art among all who could comprehend it.' Now no one can wish to depreciate the value of occasional typical performances of the sort suggested. But to represent an art which is called ' universal' or ' national' in this peculiar sense as being *popular* would be nothing but a glaring confusion of words. How can the term *universal*, in the popular sense, be applied to an art consisting in occasional performances to which only the minutest fraction of the public can have access? The art-life of a nation depends on numberless ramifications, permeating cities and villages and homes, which, if they do not come into being through the popular instinct, will assuredly never be started from a distant fountain-head of choice per-formances, however desirable that feature may be in other ways.

In taking his view wholly from the stand-point of the *stage*, and in making occa-sional typical performances his great aim, he quite loses sight of the regions where good music is already and increasingly popular, and indeed forgets what popu-larity truly means.

The very terms of Wagner's description reveal his utter want of faith in the radical musical qualities of his nation in spite of all his devotion to the ' national idea.' To talk about occasional and exclusive performances as the means of ' awakening a conception of the true meaning of art *among all who can comprehend it* ' has a ring of Pharisaism the more distressing in that Wagner, as I have said before, is not naturally a Pharisee; so little so that a few pages earlier he has equally exaggerated on the other side, and represented the arms of those who fought the battle of Leipsic as nerved by strains which not one in a hundred of those who fought in it can have known or cared about. Meanwhile a very large number of this public ' utterly without artistic sense' and, most fortunately, ' made up of the most diverse elements' and not an artistic clique, are now finding one of their most cherished enjoyments in the wealth of beautiful music with which the skill of a single member may enrich a whole house-hold or a larger social circle; to say nothing of the innumerable choral societies and musical gatherings in which it is the exception not to find the highest class of music well represented. It is easy, of course, by totally ignoring the home and the concert-room, to avoid acknowledging how deep Music has got its roots in the popular life: but the specious-sounding dictum that ' only through the stage can national art become truly the property of the people,' will not prevent lovers of this cosmopolitan art, and ' the people' so far as they ever enter into that category, from assuming as their property all the beautiful music they can get hold of, and living on it in the most habitual and unrestrained manner. Music is this very day far more the property of the English people through the works of Handel and Beethoven alone, constantly practised and presented, running in thousands of heads, alive in thousands of hearts, than it could possibly be in the most ideal future by anything which a much improved Opera in a few great centres could do : and the stream of human happiness will go on remorselessly swelling itself from these and other sources, including even such despised tributaries as the oratorios of Mendelssohn and the chamber-music of Schumann, without much care whether it embodies a ' national idea ' or reflects the ' primal Germanic spirit.'

§ 14. The ever-widening popularity of Music may well console us, if ever its isolation from other branches of interest and culture becomes oppressive.

I hope that I have now sufficiently shown in what I hold the popularity of Music to consist : and how so far from imagining that ' to awaken a conception of the true meaning ' of the art is an operation to be gradually performed by most exceptional means on a few picked individuals, I hold that the conception—at any rate of true meaning enough to enrich and irradiate many hours of life—may be awakened in quite an easy and wholesale fashion when the means are given. That this should be so may make one sometimes inclined to call Music the highest and sometimes the lowest of the arts. There is really little meaning in calling it either : but some of the foregoing considerations may at all events be capable of affording a stimulant and solace against those times of reaction when the absence of human associations in the perception of perfect beauty puzzles and oppresses the mind. If any at such a season could find it in his heart to envy those who do not breathe the rarer air of pure artistic exaltation, and to whose spirit Music gives wings without bearing it beyond its familiar atmosphere of meditation and fancy – for these at all events keep their Pegasus where they can find him, which is a convenience for denizens of the earth—yet against the isolation of the actual inward experience he may set his knowledge of the art's wide and ever-widening appeal, and may find in its results, though not in its essence, the living interest of human sympathy.

It is very possible to generalise too widely on the importance of Art to individuals. For activity is a more essential condition of our well-being than beauty, and there are doubtless spheres where men may derive from their mere activities a constant stimulus and satisfaction, and in intellectual and spiritual conceptions may find an ideal life which leaves no sensible void. In the present constitution of society, however, the careers where a man may find himself thus situated must be acknowleged to be a small minority. The activities of most lives are in themselves dull and trivial, having little or nothing of vivid and changing interest, and no power of satisfying the imagination, leaving the mind moreover but little leisure to explore unknown worlds ; while on the spiritual side there may be more of struggle than of peace. To such lives love of beauty is like water in the desert ; and among the arts it is more especially the privilege of Music, that, penetrating where Nature's face is veiled, she can open the springs of this love to the poorest dwellers in the dingiest cities.

# CHAPTER XIX.

## THE SOUND-ELEMENT IN VERSE.

In considering a large and emotional subject, it is often useful to leave the stand-point of our own experience, to look beyond the divisions which each of us might make for himself and the various values each might himself discover in the respective features, to the divisions and values given us ready made by the sorts of hold the subject takes on different minds, the aspects in which it is reflected from different mirrors. In this way certain features are clearly distinguished which even those who are alive to all of them do not always take the trouble clearly to distinguish in their own judgments. And in the case of Poetry, the most marked fact so brought out is that many of the poetry-reading public confine their interest, or at any rate believe themselves to confine their interest, mainly to the more obvious substance of the poet's message, to what he turns out to have said at the end, to what they can remember he has said without recalling his exact words, to what they would call *par excellence* his *ideas*, with a kind of implication that, compared with that everything else is subsidiary and quasi-accidental; while to others, who are no less awake to the poet's main ideas, the interest is conveyed by what he is saying all through, by the whole tissue of his work, the most distinctively poetical qualities of which would (they feel) be absolutely unrepresented by the most literal translation or the most accurate paraphrase. This division does not of course entail a hard and fast line: no lover of Poetry belongs exclusively to the former class. But there does exist a very real distinction as regards general habit and tendency. And this corresponds to a real duality in the poet's function. He really is perpetually doing two things, which can be to some extent separately recognised, however inextricably interlaced in an actual work. On the one hand he presents things which could be presented in prose, and by dint of presenting which in impressive language a prose-writer is often said to be poetical, or even to be a poet: on the other hand he produces impressions which can only be produced in verse; he presents things of which a prose presentation is not inadequate but strictly impossible.

This distinction goes very much deeper than the obvious one so commonly made between the *matter* which a poet has to convey, and the

§ 1. The enjoyment of Poetry roughly divides itself into two kinds,

corresponding with a sort of duality in the poet's function; with the fact of his presenting ideas and producing impressions (1) which could (2) which could *not* be presented and produced by prose.

*dress* or *setting* which he finds for it.    For consider a good prose-version of a beautiful poem.    In this shape, the matter, in the above sense, is very fairly given : there are many to whom it will strongly appeal, when so presented, and who will actually get from it by far the greater part of what they could have got from the original.    The selection and treatment of topics, the perception of the deeper relations of things, the sentiments, the images, are all there ; and the result may be full and sufficient evidence of high creative genius.    But substitute the original ; and to the seeing eye very much more has been done than simply to present these things in a far more pleasing form.    The change is not just a change of dress, an improvement in the presentment of the old stuff : it is the presentment of new stuff, new food for the mind ; the new emotions evoked are realities which in the other case could never have been so much as guessed at.    No poem worth the name wholly lacks the latter kind of effectiveness ; while on the other hand lack of power to produce it may prevent persons richly endowed with all other poetic gifts from ever being poets.    It may be safely said that the power of making words, one after another, concentrate in themselves a force which seems incommensurable with their literal and logical meaning, so that language seems not so much to be investing thought as to be informing and transfiguring it, is a gift as rare as even a very large measure of those more general poetical faculties which can exist in its absence.

It is necessary to emphasise these facts from the very first, just because in Poetry, alone of the arts (as we saw in the third chapter), a content does exist independent of any sort of form addressed to the sense.    An art of language represents, not like Painting and Sculpture by imitation, but by symbols, which in our world, as it happens, are addressed primarily to the sense of hearing ; and it is on these symbols as mere sounds that the form-element of verse supervenes.    So that here discussion as to the relative value of content and form may have some meaning ; whereas a picture with its lines smudged beyond recognition, or a sonata with the notes or rhythms altered, would cease to have an intelligible content.    Thus if we compare Poetry with the other most prominent art of representation, Painting, it is obvious that the poet may act on the mind and win sympathy apart from merits and defects of form, and apart from acuteness or obtuseness of bodily sense in his audience ; whereas a painter's language *is* form, and to appreciate his drift and spirit a sympathetic sense for his language as well as a sympathetic intelligence for his ideas and feelings is requisite.    But this very fact, I say, hinders the explicit recognition that the presentation of poetic thought in poetic form is very much more than a matter of pleasing *investiture* ; that the *substance* of what is conveyed receives a new element ; in other words, that the sum of the pleasure is infinitely greater than the pleasure of the mind in the content *plus* the pleasure of the ear in a certain abstract arrangement of sounds.

---

*Marginal notes:*

This distinction goes deeper than that between the substance and the setting ;

what is sometimes represented as the dress or setting includes an element of new substance.

This point is liable to be mistaken, owing to Poetry's presenting a real content independent of form.

To the abstract arrangements of sounds, the formal element which is in-  § 2. Metre: its fundamental principle. dispensable to this wonderful result, it will be best to give some detailed attention before attempting to estimate its relations to the complete æsthetic effect. This element finds by far its most important and familiar development in *metre*. The fundamental principle of verbal metre is identical with that of the rhythmic factor of melodic forms, the recurrence of stimuli at definite intervals. A metrical scheme marks out for the line (or, if the metre is compounded of differents sorts of line, for each line) a fixed number of stresses at fixed places, and in the vast majority of metres at equi-distant places, equality being the most obvious and natural way of ensuring and establishing the sense of fixity. The line must not be too long to be easily grasped by the ear as a unit; and metres which consist in particular arrangements of such lines must, again, not be too complex for the divisions or stanzas to be recognised as larger units. In modern  The adjunct of rhyme. metres, another extremely common feature is rhyme, or similarity of clang at the end of lines. This feature, depending as it does on vowel-sounds, might seem to be properly a colour-effect; but as a matter of fact, its confinement to one position in the line, and the manner in which the ear reckons on it in co-ordinating the series of sounds into regular and coherent groups, gives it a distinct place under the head of form : indeed, varieties in the position of the rhymes are a great means of differentiating metres which in point of rhythmic structure are identical; and again, rhyme is able to bring into metre lines presenting (as often, for instance, in French verse) little or no true regularity of accent. The same remark applies in some degree to the alliterations and assonances which have in some cases acted as substitutes for metre : though in their case the ear has not the instant of its satisfaction so precisely fixed beforehand, and the satisfaction can therefore hardly be equally definite and strong.

We have seen that the primary fact in rhythm, the perpetual satisfac-  The nervous basis of rhythm : tion of expectation, is represented in the nervous organisation by the adjustment of nerve-substance in readiness for a discharge by stimulus at certain instants. In any series of stimuli which is so irregular that no set of such adjustments is established, and no certain expectations formed, there can be none of the strict satisfaction of rhythm : there may be pleasure of rises and falls, of a pleasing variety in the general stream of sounds, but not the distinctive satisfaction belonging to a series which entails such a set of adjustments, and which in the case of words is called metre. Now if we regard this principle of rhythmic stimulation in the most general way it does not matter what happens *between* the main stimuli; these spaces may be filled up with stimulation of a sort which does not interfere with the main adjustments and expectation, or it may be left destitute of any stimulation. As regards the special application of the principle to *words*, however, since language is continuous and entails in its habitual unmetrical use accented and unaccented syllables, the in-

and the peculi-
arity in the ap-
plication of the
general princi-
ple to words.

tervening spaces of time are, as a rule, naturally filled up in a metrical scheme by unaccented sound, consisting of one, two, three, or even four syllables. Exceptions of course produce feet of one syllable; as,

*Ráin,|ráin,|gó a|wáy,|*
Come a|gáin an|óther|dáy,|

or,

Ín the pen|támeter|áye||fálling in|mélody|báck.||

Such feet constantly occur at the ends of lines, where the brief interval of discontinuity serves distinctly to mark off the line. An accented sound with the unaccented sound or sounds preceding or succeeding it [1] is a

Feet: simple,

simple *foot.* As we can modify the pace with which we pronounce syllables between very wide limits, two and three unaccented syllables are often substituted for one, in lines where the metrical scheme only demands one; as, for instance, in the line

The intol|erable in|finite|desire,

where only the last two feet are normal. Feet with as many as four un-

---

[1] In musical notation the bars are arranged so that the note on which the chief accent falls is the *first* note of a bar; in the division of verse into feet, the accented syllable is often the *last* of the foot. There is no significance in this difference, which in no way affects the common feature of regular accents; and it would often be just as convenient to draw the dividing lines in verse one way as the other, and to regard any short syllable or syllables which preceded the first accent as an *anakrusis* or catch, instead of as part of a complete foot. But the difference is worth noticing, if only because failure to notice it may easily cause misunderstanding in nomenclature and description of metres, among persons whose ears have precisely the same metrical sensibilities and requirements, but of whom one is used to the look of musical notation and the other is not. The quotation on the next page affords a ready instance. There is nothing to my *eye* absolutely unnatural in marking the stanza thus:

By the|wáters of|Bábylon we sat|dówn and|wépt,
Re|mémbering|thée,
That for|áges of|ágony hast en|dúred and|slépt,
And|wóuldst not|sée—

though in reciting the passage I should make a quite noticeable pause at *wept*, and should pronounce *remembering thee* as two perfectly even iambi. Here the combinations |wépt, re| and |thée, that for| and |slépt and| represent the principle of musical bars, and if the poem were set to music (which Heaven forefend!) *wept, thee* and *slept* would fall on the first notes of their respective bars. Eyes accustomed to the look of music will have no difficulty in perceiving, in the stanza as here marked, that in the flow of sound the *re* still belongs entirely to the *mém*, and the *that for* to the *á*; it being very common in music for a long pause to occur in the middle of the bar, and for the succeeding note or notes at the end of the bar to belong, in the flow of sound, entirely to the following bar; for instance,

But in the absence of association with the look of musical bars, the above method of division might naturally suggest a complete misapprehension of the metre.

The difference, I must repeat, is a mere matter of the *eye.* Nothing can prevent *ictus* from being *ictus*: nothing can prevent our feeling an impulse to beat or stamp at the first syllables of *waters* and *Babylon* and at *down* and *wept.*

accented syllables are very rare : a splendid example of their employment is afforded by Mr. Swinburne's *Super flumina Babylonis*—

> By the wát|ers of Bá|bylon we sat dówn|and wépt,|
> Remém|bering thée,|
> That for á|ges of ág|ony hast endúred|and slépt,|
> And wóuldst|not sée,|&c.

Even here it would be possible to avoid the actual recognition of five-syllable feet, by marking thus :

> By the|wáters of|Bábylon|we sat dówn|and wépt—

but the peculiarity of the metre remains quite untouched by a change which merely consults the convenience of the eye ; and may be equally well described as the existence of four unaccented syllables between two accented ones.

It is sometimes convenient to have a name for particular collocations of sounds in which more than one accent occurs : but this is a mere matter of nomenclature, and in no way affects the principle ; such compound feet being always resolvable into simple feet containing one accent apiece. The Greek sense of *compound* foot, in application to a foot which is made **and compound.** up of two or more complete simple feet,[1] is one which we have no occasion ever to think of in English verse : but the word may serve conveniently to denote shorter collocations in which there is more than one accent.   Thus in a succession of cretics, as

> Ca ! qu'on selle,
> Écuyer,
> Mon fidèle
> Destrier,

it is more natural to regard each line as consisting of a single compound

---

[1] The reason why writers on Greek metre considered compound feet in the larger sense lies in the close connection of Greek verse, particularly lyric and choric verse, with musical performance, and the convenience of regarding as a *foot* the set of syllables which coincided with a musical *bar*. We have seen how in modern music it would be absurd to attempt to classify the actual contents of bars (looked at in the light of their complete rhythm) as feet, since the possible combinations are practically innumerable. We content ourselves with classifying the outlines or frameworks, as the $\frac{2}{4}$ framework, the $\frac{6}{8}$ framework, and so on. But with a very much simpler music, constantly associated with and in a great measure subordinate to words, and with the notes largely adapted to the natural time-relations of the syllables,

it would be natural to carry classification considerably further ; to have a name, for instance, for such a collocation as

which is to us simply one of the infinitely numerous and unnamed arrangements possible under the head of $\frac{4}{4}$ measure. This fitting of words with notes measured on a strict scale of subdivision, adapted indeed to the natural lengths of the syllables, but imposing on them an accuracy of time-proportions which is unknown to spoken prose, most imperfectly represented even in the strictest spoken verse, but entirely characteristic of melodic notes, explains how the Greek ear accurately and instinctively grasped metres which we often find too complicated to realise without laborious reference to a written scheme.

foot, accented on the first and last syllables, than to regard the metre as an alternation of trochees and feet of one syllable : and again, in

> Kéntish Sir *Býng*|stóod for his *kíng,*|
> Bídding the crópheaded|Párliament *swíng,*|

the words *Byng, king, swing,* corresponding to the dactyl *cropheaded* in the third division of the couplet, may be more naturally regarded as making up compound choriambic feet with the three preceding syllables than as monosyllabic feet on their own account. In both these cases, it will be observed, the accents fall at quite regular distances.

Metrical rhythm is imposed on, not latent in, speech. It is obvious that no single word of average length can present accents enough to give a notion of rhythm. *Incomprehensibility* makes a complete iambic line ; but only a small minority of words have even two accents. And as words normally follow one another for the sake of sense, and not for the sake of sound, it is absurd to represent metre or poetic rhythm as in some way latent, in an inchoate form, in natural human speech ; for it does not result from the *presence*, but from the *regularity*, of accents, and a *foot* has no meaning except as a unit in a *line*. ' Du bist wie eine Blume ' is verse : ' thou art like a flower ' is not inchoate verse, but prose.

The modes of marking off lines and stanzas. So much for *foot*-units. The clear division of the stream of successive feet into *line*-units may be effected in several ways, which however are by no means all mutually exclusive : (1) by an actual difference in the run of the contiguous lines, through a change in the feet which compose them ; as in the alternating hexameters and pentameters of the elegiac metre, or in the varying divisions of the alcaic stanza ; (2) by the constant occurrence, at the end of lines, of some marked feature, such as the dactyl-spondee of hexameters, or rhyme ; the latter feature, through the variety of which it is susceptible, being the great modern means of uniting small groups of lines into larger units or stanzas ; (3) by a slight break whether of sense or sound, or both, at the end of a majority of the lines, which may enable contiguous lines of most varying lengths to be perceived as separate units, (4) especially in metres where lines of an *even* number of feet alternate with lines of an *odd* number, by a definite rest of about a foot's length at the end of the latter, observed even when the sense would carry the voice on ; which not only introduces, in metres of regular construction, the principle of *regular recurrence* for the *rests* as well as for the accented sounds ; but exemplifies our further principle of *dual balance*, in giving a counterpoise to the last foot of the odd-foot lines, and thus enabling one to beat time to them just as evenly as though another foot were actually present. For instance in the stanza,

> Oft I|had heard|of Lu|cy Gray,|
> And, when|I crossed|the wild,|—|
> I chanced|to see|at break|of day|
> The sol|ita|ry child.|—|

the voice would naturally separate *wild* from *I chanced* by (approximately) a foot's length. In the same way, the lines,

Feé,|fó,|fúm,|—|
I sméll|the blóod|of an Éng|lishmán,

will naturally be pronounced with recognition of the full rest of a foot, to balance *fum*; whereas if the nonsense-syllables were Fee, fi, fo, fum, the voice would naturally go straight on to the next line. This feature of balance, aided by rhyme, appears also in cases where there is no intermixture of lines with an even number of feet, and where therefore it is impossible to represent the rest after the shorter odd-foot lines as prompted merely by an instinct of symmetrical conformance to the even-foot lines; for instance, the three-foot lines,

Tóll|for the|bráve,|—|
The bráve|that áre|no móre,|—|&c.

will take pauses about as marked as those of *Lucy Gray*; and the same principle may be perceptibly exhibited even in quite irregular measures which present no set groups or stanzas. To enter further into the varieties of line and stanza, would lead us too far; and we must now return to the more general and fundamental aspects of verse-rhythm.

Since actual stress or *ictus* is often, like the ticks of a clock, the affair of a small fraction of a second, it will be seen that there is nothing in the fundamental scheme to prevent an accented syllable from occupying the *smaller* portion of the space from *ictus* to *ictus*, and an unaccented syllable, or in exceptional cases silence, from occupying the *larger* portion. For example, in the words *perished, caverns, balanced*, each of which might form a foot, the accented first syllable takes about half as long to pronounce as the unaccented second. The whole amount of effort, however, required to pronounce a long syllable being *ipso facto* greater than that required for a short, it naturally happens that the accent falls oftener on longer than on shorter syllables: the voice having a larger task to perform, instinctively breaks upon it in a more energetic way. In syllables, moreover, containing a naturally long vowel sound, on which the voice will commonly dwell more in verse than in prose, the very act of so dwelling instinctively impresses a certain emphasis and fulness of *timbre*: thus the accent in a word like *remorse* lies rather in the emphatic dwelling on the vowel, while in a word like *revenge* it results from the forcible enunciation of the consonants. Thus there is a close, though not a constant, connection between accentuation and duration of syllables. We shall have to recur to this fact shortly.

§ 3. *Accentuation* and *duration* of syllables present a close and constant but not necessary connection.

But now comes a most important point. As regards the places where stresses of the voice actually come, verse often departs considerably from its strict metrical scheme. Some feet (if we designate by *foot* the set of syllables which, on the strict metrical scheme, would fill up an accented

§ 4. Verse often deviates from its strict scheme;

place and all the adjoining space up to another accented place) pass wholly without accent, while in others strong stress may be laid on a syllable which, according to the ideal scheme, is in an *unaccented* place ; and there will naturally be many degrees of variety short of these extreme cases. Without a certain amount of such departures, the rhythm of verse, imposed on anything so naturally unrestrained and elastic as language, would tend to a dead and sing-song monotony : for instance, it is just because English hexameters have almost invariably been written *to be scanned*, in exact conformity to the scheme of strict stresses, that the metre has obtained such an unenviable reputation.[1]   But for all that, the underlying scheme must be recognised : and the effect greatly depends on the instinctive sense of this scheme running parallel with the departures from it ; which, though more frequent than is commonly realised, leave of course sufficient landmarks—that is to say, stresses enough fall according to the strict requirements of the scheme—to preclude any doubt as to how the feet should be marked off for each line in accordance with the scheme. The loose structure of the French alexandrine may be taken as representing the opposite extreme of fault from that of the English hexameter : for the small actual difference in stress between the accented and unaccented syllables of French words, tending to preclude definite feet, tends to preclude, more especially in long lines, definite places of ideal stress.

accuracy, how-
ever, being
normally main-
tained in the
later part of
the line.

It is natural that deviations from the strict metrical scheme of accents should take place normally rather in the earlier than the later part of a line ; the accuracy of the later stresses giving the final stamp to the line as belonging to such and such a scheme. Thus in hexameters the accent on the first syllable of the last two feet is a fixed rule of the metre : and the last foot in English blank verse, though not infrequently relieved of a decided stress on its last syllable, is never reversed by receiving a stress on the first.  Greek iambic verse was less strict in this respect, probably for the following reason : that lines of six feet, that is, of mul-

---

[1] It must be added—and this important point is not enough realised—that the elasticity of language not unfrequently *favours* adherence to the strict accentual scheme. An example will make plain how the large amount of latitude permitted by speech, as regards both the time given to many syllables and the pace at which one word follows another, may allow the perfect regularity of the stresses to be preserved to the *ear*, even where apparently infringed to the *eye*. In the iambic line,

ἐκ τῶν κακῶν τῶνδ' εὐκλεᾶ θέσθαι βίον,

the two last words, if we divide off each as a foot under the scheme, may seem to de-

viate from strictness by receiving a stress on the first instead of the second syllable. But, while laying the stresses on the first syllables, it is not only possible but a natural instinct to bring them into strict accordance with the scheme, and to make the six stresses of the line fall accurately at equal distances (the accuracy becoming obvious if we beat time with the hand), by deferring the θεσ till the instant of the beat, *i.e.* by allowing slight additional time *on* or *after* the last syllable of εὐκλεᾶ—as contrasted, *e.g.*, with our treatment of the concluding three feet in the line,

ἐκ τῶν κακῶν τῶνδ' εὐκλεὴς γενήσομαι.

tiples of two feet, flow on rapidly and naturally from one to another; whereas in the five-foot lines of English blank verse, a true though faint recognition of the principle of dual balance noticed above, is apt to assert itself in a slight pause between the end of one line and the beginning of the next, the naturalness and frequency of which will be noticed if anybody tries to ignore it in reading a passage of blank verse aloud. And the foot before a slight pause is specially unable to admit liberties.

But other conditions besides position affect the limits of possible deviation. Thus English trochaic metres, where single accented alternate with single unaccented syllables, and the first accent falls on the first syllable of the line, admit of far less deviation from the strict scheme than iambic metres, where the first accent falls on the second syllable of the line. It is quite exceptional in trochaic verse for some degree of accent not to fall regularly on the odd places, according to the strict metrical scheme; while an actual reversal of a trochee into an iambus may, I think, be said to be impossible; as opposed to the distinctly pleasing effect produced by the reversal of the normal iambus into a trochee, in such a line as

*Limits of deviation exemplified in English trochaic verse;*

The lóne|cóuch of|his év|erlást|ing sléep.

It is possible in some measure to account for this peculiarity of English trochaic rhythm. The commencing accent not only establishes itself by the prominence of its position, as a very marked point on which the ear gets to reckon with confidence, the more marked probably that in English speech trochaic commencements of sentences and clauses are a small minority, but it tends to produce a certain evenly-marked rapidity in the subsequent movement, which any considerable change would tend to dislocate. Again, most English dissyllabic words are trochees, so that in trochaic metres it is exceptionally frequent for a foot to comprise a single word and not parts of two words; which naturally tends to impart a certain cut and obvious regularity to the motion. Thus in Mr. Tennyson's trochaic poem *The Captain*, out of eighty-four dissyllabic words, seventy-eight are trochees and six iambi; the first fifteen stanzas of *Locksley Hall* contain seventy-eight trochees and seven iambi. While, then, these features make trochaic metres in English seem too inelastic and monotonous for constant use, on the other hand the very fact of the above-mentioned prevalence of trochaic words, combined with the desirability, for the sake of variety and elasticity, that a single foot should *not* continually coincide with a single word, must count as a chief reason why iambic metres are *par excellence* the metres for English verse. Thus opening a blank-verse poem of Mr. Tennyson's completely at random, I find in two pages sixty-seven words distributed over the last half of one foot and the first of the next, to eleven corresponding with a single foot.

*where they are much stricter than in iambic.*

Another source of deviation from exact conformance to the ideal metrical scheme lies in the different times that syllables, and therefore feet, take to pronounce; so that even did the accents fall regularly in all the feet, they would still not be equidistant from one another. It may happen that a foot which lacks distinct accents may take longer in pronunciation than one which has a distinct accent; thus if the line,

Of man's|first dis|obéd|ience, and|the fruit,

be read naturally, the fourth foot which has no accent will occupy more time than either the third or the fifth. Far more usually, however, owing to the connection between duration and accentuation, feet which lack stress will occupy a particularly short, and feet which contain more than one stress a particularly long time. Thus in the line,

Bróught deáth|into|the wórld|and áll|our wóe,

the first foot consists of two strong and emphatic syllables, and the second foot of two extremely light and unemphatic ones; the result is that the line may be quite naturally delivered in such a manner that the first foot extends over five or six times as much time as the second. In the line,

The lóne|cóuch of|his év|erlást|ing sleép,

the second foot has a strong accent on the first, instead of, as normally in the metre, on the second syllable; and the disinclination of the voice to pronounce two heavy and emphatic syllables rapidly one after the other, causes the first three syllables of the line to extend over more time than the five succeeding ones, four of which are light in sound, and are moreover naturally given rapidly to make up for the time spent at the beginning of the line: that is, technically, a foot and a half take up more time than two feet and a half. The line,

Rocks, caves, lakes, fens, bogs, dens, and shades of death,

has eight actual stresses, all on syllables which in any case require some vocal effort, and takes at least twice as long to pronounce as an average blank-verse line. It follows, then, that no sort of strict rule of length, and no definite scheme of subdivisions, such as are entailed in the accurate dividing of musical time-values by two and three, apply to the syllables, feet, and lines of verse.[1]

---

[1] It may be convenient here to sum up the ways in which musical rhythms and developed verse-rhythms differ from one another, while agreeing in the possession of a scheme of regular accents. We have seen that in verse (1) wide latitude is allowed in the actual adjustment of accents to the scheme; (2) if we timed each foot as it passes, we should find great variety in their duration. In Music, on the other hand, constancy of accent, and so of length of bar, is a cardinal point. It is involved in the very nature of melodic form that the perception of the various relations of length which the notes present is precise, and this necessitates a standard afforded by a constant

But at this rate it would seem that *quantity* on its own account had nothing to do with metrical scheme. And in modern verse such is indeed the case ; for though quantity is a most important feature both in the production of special effects, and in assisting to give variety of movement from verse to verse, it has no essential connection with the scheme of accents. In the classical languages, however, it is otherwise : and the question of the difference is not free from difficulty, though the difficulty

§ 6. Difference between ancient and modern verse in the relation of *quantity* to the metrical scheme.

length of bar (the apparent exceptions caused by such humourings and swayings as are described in the note to chap. viii. § 3, depending for their effect on the keen instinct of the normal length which they slightly modify); while in any music containing more than one line of sounds, such precision and constancy is the most natural means for enabling the variously moving parts to present distinct and organic correspondence. We may add as a further peculiarity of verse (3) the possibility of *pauses* in such number as would dislocate the movement of melody, while made natural in verse by the natural requirements of sentences. These pauses may occur *regularly* as a true feature of the metre—thus if we expressed the metre of the above-quoted *Super flumina Babylonis* in musical notation, we should put a ⌒ mark at the end of every line—and to this, it is true, an occasional parallel might be found in melody : but a melody, though now and then it may *bear* such treatment, rarely or never *requires* it. (Such *pauses*, where in beating time one would *suspend* one's beat, must be distinguished from the complete or nearly complete *foot of silence*—demanded, *e.g.*, at the end of the shorter lines, that is in the place of the eighth and sixteenth feet, of ' common metre,' as in the above stanza from *Lucy Gray*—to which one would *give* a beat. In the latter feature no difference from music is involved, beyond the fact that, though music might introduce two similar bars of rest, it would of course not repeat the same measure for twenty consecutive periods.)

More special differences present themselves if we take our two time-units, the *foot* and the *bar*, and compare either their component elements, or the manner of their combination into longer series. A poetical foot is composed of syllables which, from the nature of language, cannot be numerous, *five* being the very outside, and of which one is not normally more than *two or three times* the length of another : whence the variety of feet in any metre is very limited,

and the flow of sound is of a simple and (between the natural pauses) of an entirely continuous kind. In verse, again, the ear is occupied with something quite apart from the sound, namely, the apprehension of the words as symbols of thought, this being its normal hourly function : it therefore takes such sops as it gets in the way of metre as an assistance and gratuity for which it is grateful, without demanding anything like strict symmetry and regularity in the lengths of the lines. These may be extremely irregular, as in many odes, and even where there is a principle of balance and symmetry, as in strophes and antistrophes, the ear has often to wait a long time for this to assert itself—so that verse may present great *irregularity* in the main metrical outline, combined with great *regularity* and simplicity in the component feet. Music is apt to reverse these characteristics. Not only may a musical note have a far longer or shorter absolute duration than the longest or shortest possible syllable, but one musical note may be *thirty-two times*, and is perpetually as many as *eight* times, the length of another in the same bar; and moreover *rests* (which must be carefully distinguished from *pauses*, and constitute, like notes, strict fractions of strict barlengths) are of constant occurrence, and are as necessary to the form as the notes themselves; so that the time-combinations of sounds and silences which may make up a bar are in number and variety quite beyond reckoning : while, on the other hand, so far as any symmetry of lengths is noticed at all, it is in that simplest and most direct dual balance of *contiguous* phrases or groups of bars, which, as we have seen, may be found pervading the most elaborate musical motions ; beyond this, the continuity of phrases and the progressive combination of smaller into larger ones preclude any suggestion of their actual lengths as forming a *scheme*, regular or irregular, such as is made possible by the distinct separateness of verse-lines.

has been made out to be greater and more fundamental than it really is. I must ask the reader to allow me to approach the subject in my own way.

Places of ideal stress in classical verse, as discovered by the English school-boy;

A school-boy who is just beginning the study of classical verse, and who scans the lines aloud in order to get the metre into his head, will invariably read each hexameter of Homer or Virgil with six regular stresses at equal distances, the first falling on the first syllable, the sixth on the last syllable but one, of the line. Similarly in scanning the iambics of Sophocles, he will give six regular stresses, of which the first will fall on the second syllable, and the sixth on the last syllable of the line. He can scan Milton in precisely the same way, giving five regular and equidistant stresses in each blank-verse line; but in so doing he will find he makes obviously unnatural departures from the normal delivery of the words. Just so in the classical languages he is certain to have sufficient conception of the way he pronounces the words when he meets them in prose, instinctively to relax and abandon the strict stresses of his scansion-lesson, when once he has got the metres into his head. And as, if gifted with an average amount of ear, he will recognise that Milton's lines, when naturally pronounced, are still lines having a distinct relation, and owing a distinct allegiance, to the strict scheme of accentuation which he brought into prominence when he scanned them, so will he be conscious of a precisely similar fact in respect of the Greek and Latin lines. The one set of sounds will still be to him a five-foot iambic metre, the other a six-foot dactylic and spondaic metre, in a real and not an arbitrary sense. And the parallelism between the two cases will be not only absolute in principle, but very close even in detail. If any one will try the experiment of reading fifty lines of Sophocles or Virgil, laying the stresses on those syllables where he would lay it if he met the word in prose, and then treat fifty lines of Milton's or Tennyson's blank-verse in the same way, he will find that the departures from what he would consider in each case the strict scheme of stresses are about equal in number; there being, in fact, no choice between a considerable amount of such departure and the sing-song effect of scanning.

which places are always occupied by long syllables.

So far, then, so good. But now comes in the further fact, which the school-boy, if left to his natural devices, would probably never have even noticed. The Greek and Latin syllables occupying the places where the accents fall in the emphatic scansion of the verses (the places of *ideal stress*, as we may call them for brevity's sake), are invariably *long*, the long syllable being occasionally resolved into *two* short ones; a *single* short syllable never occurs in those places.[1]

---

[1] Exceptions occasionally occur in Homer. Mr. Spedding, in his admirable essay on English hexameters, republished in his *Re-views and Discussions*, says that in these cases the short syllable must be abnormally lengthened. But surely the fact that in

Now we should be justified in asserting at once and *à priori*, that this coincidence cannot be accidental. An Englishman with his notions of metre formed on the verse of his own language is able, by that light and without any reference to longs and shorts as such, to pick out in classical verse places of ideal stress, which hold precisely the same relation to his natural delivery of the lines as the places of ideal stress in English verse hold to the natural delivery of English lines. A school-boy who pronounces longs and shorts no longer and shorter in Virgil than in Milton, finds in ten lines of the *Æneid* a beautiful metre; Virgil and his contemporaries found in the same lines a beautiful metre; a decisive peculiarity is in each case connected with precisely the same places in the line: to suppose that there are really *two* metres, and that the coincidence of the critical places in the two is an accident, is about as reasonable an idea as that by accident we happen to hear thunder just at the times when we see lightning. But if the coincidence is not accidental, there must be some common fact at the bottom of all the phenomena; and this fact can only be sought in the fundamental principle of rhythm and of its connection with the nervous organism. That principle, then, if precisely stated, is more general than we recognise it to be when we are thinking about stresses. It consists simply in sufficiently regular recurrence of certain stimuli for their relationship in an order to be recognised; the recognition of the *regularity* is the one prime requisite; that the stimuli in which regularity is recognised should be marked off (or at any rate should all be marked off) by actually superior force, from the stimuli which may take place between them, is *not* requisite. The fact for the occurrence of which at a particular instant the nerve-substance is adjusted, is *a* stimulus, perceived by its occurrence at that particular instant to be one of an order; not necessarily an *emphatic* stimulus.

An analogy offered by Music may be useful. In Music, though the accents are so acutely felt that the stimulus often passes all through the nervous system and prompts us to keep time by some physical movement, and though the instinctive adjustments of expectation never cease, the accented notes are not necessarily at all *louder* than the unaccented. We may go further and say that the first note of a bar, which falls in the normal place of the chief accent, may be distinctly *less* loud than other notes in the bar. In common time, for instance, if the first note is a crotchet and the second a minim, the second note will often receive the greater emphasis. In the first bar of the following melody—

*[marginal notes:]*
As the coincidence cannot possibly be accidental,

we are led to extend somewhat the statement of our fundamental principle: not emphasis, but noticed regularity, of stimuli is what is essential.

Analogy in Music.

English we perpetually accept a light syllable in a place of ideal stress is enough to suggest that these Homeric exceptions are concessions of a like kind; while, on the other hand, complete reversal of the normal pronunciation of a word is a step that even we lax moderns have never ventured on.

the notes on the first and third quaver-beats, the normally accented places, could hardly but be softer than those which precede them. But in all such cases the first place in the bar is perceived as what it is; the ear does not lose count of it; the note on it is a certain piece of *stimulus*, equidistant from the first beats of the preceding and succeeding bars, and, whether or not receiving a sound-stress, has its place in the order marked
In verse the<br>long syllables<br>mark points of<br>regular recur-<br>rence; by a downward beat (real or imagined) of the *bâton.*[1] Now in verse, a set of long syllables at equal distances is a set of regular recurrences which comes under this principle, provided only the words be pronounced with sufficient deliberation for length of syllable really to tell on the ear, a condition which in the common English pronunciation of the classical languages is far from being observed. The very attention to quantity, in hexameters at any rate, would make the commencements of the long syllables at the beginning of the feet far more truly, constantly, and noticeably equidistant than is common in the greater latitude of English verse : no case at all parallel to ' Brōught deāth | ĭntŏ | the world' which we noticed above, would be possible. The nature of language, no doubt,

[1] The same point may be illustrated by a very simple experiment, the results of which are to the full as curious as some of the more familiar delusions of the eye. Let any reader pay attention, next time his ears encounter that most irritating phenomenon, a chime of six bells playing six notes of the descending scale—

the sounds following one another with mechanical regularity and being all of equal loudness. The ear, as soon as it begins to attend, will almost inevitably divide the endless series by imposing accents at regular intervals; but the point is that it is perfectly easy to make the accentuation for oneself *in several different ways.* For instance, one can make oneself hear the series as

and the impression that the notes which one is accenting for the moment in one's own head are actually more marked than the others, that the ringer is feeling the particular rhythm which one has selected to impose, is absolutely irresistible.

entails that the truly accented syllables *are* louder than the other sounds, which the accented musical notes often are not: but for all that, the places in lines which correspond to the strong places in bars, the places which are accented in the typical metrical scheme as they are accented in normal musical rhythm, may be recognised in the absence of such extra loudness. And we have now to remember two additional facts, each of the greatest importance in stamping the sense of regular recurrences. First and chiefly, of the six long commencing syllables, *at least three* (the last two, and one or far more commonly two or three of the first four) received a *true stress* ;[1] which fact alone brings classical hexameters about as near to conformity with conditions of ideal stress as English blank-verse. Secondly, we noticed above the close connection between accentuation and duration of syllables. This would take special effect in a language and mode of delivery in which 'long' syllables were really long, really dwelt on after a fashion which we, with our different language, constant short vowels, and clipping pronunciation, find it hard to realise: and it would take effect *not only* on long syllables which were also the primarily accented syllables of their respective words, but on other long

these points, moreover, received *actual stress* about as often in classical as in modern verse;

---

[1] Mr. Spedding points out that Quintilian's rule assimilates the position of stress in Latin words very closely to the English usage, and adds that the question of the position of stress in Greek is more uncertain. But if ever a point may be decided by internal evidence, it is that the first syllable of each of the two concluding feet in hexameters must have received an actual stress as a rule of the metre, these stresses being so entirely the key-stone of the hexameter that it is impossible to conceive the existence and popularity of *two* metres, one Greek and one Latin, agreeing in all other conditions yet liable to perpetual difference in this.

The question of those marks over certain syllables which are known as the Greek 'accents' is a very perplexing one. But even if all authority were not, as it is, in favour of regarding their ancient (in opposition to their modern) employment as connected with *pitch* and not with *stress*, we have only to read twenty lines of Homer, treating them as marks of stress, to convince ourselves that the metre, which in more than half the lines will be found to go to pieces just at its critical point, would on these terms be beyond redemption by the mere regularity of the long syllables.

The argument most relied on to prove, contrary to ancient authority, that in the ancient Greek pronunciation the stresses fell on those syllables which bear the marks, is that in modern Greek they do so fall; against which, however, must be set the further fact that in modern Greek verse these syllables occupy the places of ideal stress in the metre ; that is, they hold to modern metrical schemes exactly the relation they did *not* hold to ancient ones. Confronting these two facts, we are tied up to one of two hypotheses; either the pronunciation has changed or the relation of pronunciation to metrical necessities has changed. Now having regard to the fundamental facts of human ears, nay to the single and simple nature of rhythmic stimulation through the whole range of organisms from the spider to Beethoven—if we find the words and syllables of ancient verse appearing in modern verse with complete reversal of their relation to the metrical scheme, it is surely more reasonable to argue that the method of pronouncing them has changed, than, on the mere presumption of constancy in their pronunciation, to suppose that ancient metre, in ignoring their stresses, set at nought positive and prominent facts of auditory stimulation; the positive and prominent character of which—as must surely be admitted even by those who do not perceive metre to *exist by recognising it*—would absolutely dislocate any regular arrangement of sounds which attempted to *ignore or defy it*.

while the
slower delivery
would entail
more stress
even on unac-
cented long
syllables than
we give.

syllables, which would thus obtain increased facilities for sometimes occupying the places of ideal stress. Thus we can perceive how the second
syllable of *fĕrŭnt* or δίκην would differ, as regards the amount of notice
the voice would draw to it in verse, from the long unaccented second
syllables of *pĕrĭshed* and *cávĕrns*. Even an Englishman can perceive the
line ἐγὼ δ' ἐμαυτὸν παῖδα τῆς Τύχης νέμων to be perfectly musical; but
he would hardly feel a blank-verse line ending with *Ēvāns pĕrĭshed* to be
satisfactory.

A Greek or
Roman must
have imagined
the scheme of
the hexameter
in a way iden-
tical, in its
essential point,
with the way
of the English-
man ; and
would have
beat time to
actual hexa-
meters with as
much unction.

When these latter points are considered, we may safely infer that when
a Greek or Roman imagined the metrical scheme of the hexameter in his
head, without thinking of any particular line, he imagined a scheme of
definite strong places in the bar truly and fundamentally resembling the
scheme which the English school-boy would imagine, however much
differing from the normal school-boy scheme in the refined attention to
quantity. Seeing that the *actual* main stresses did in a majority of cases
fall on these places, I should probably be correct in saying outright a
scheme of *stresses*; but I use the term *strong places* to express that particular sense of recognition which is felt, *e.g.*, in music at the first beat of
a bar, whether the note receive the emphasis of extra loudness or not.
How thoroughly the differentiating quality of the stimulus which occurs
at that place and no other is recognised (and recognised, I think it may
be accurately said, as a sense of stress *somewhere*), though it may not be
brought out to the ear by extra loudness, is shown by the physical impulse
to mark it with a beat or a tap, just as much as if it *were* brought out to
the ear by extra loudness : and as regards verse, no one who has a typical
scheme of the metre in his head will find any difficulty in beating time,
*e.g.*, to the pentameter—

Barbarous|experi|ment,||barbarous|hexame|ters,||

and giving the normal down beat to the first syllables of each foot, even
though his voice makes the second syllables both of *experiment* and *hexameters* louder than the first; a departure from the scheme as great as
would be possible in any Latin line of the same metre. Thus my point
would be perfectly well expressed by saying that a Greek or Roman would
beat time to the natural delivery of hexameters with just as much regularity and unction as an Englishman whose ideal scheme is founded simply
on stresses, and who takes little or no account of longs and shorts as such ;
the difficulty in the most extreme case being no greater than in marking
the beats to a piece of ' syncopated' music.

The great difficulty which has been found in this question of the relations of quantity to accent, a difficulty which some have been driven to
solve by imagining what would be nothing less than a fundamental
change in one of the most fundamental facts of nervous organisation, has

resulted from taking the prominence of quantity, which is so marked a feature of ancient verse, as the *most fundamental* fact about it : whereas the most fundamental fact in *all* metre must be a fixed scheme of recurrences, underlying lines which are perceived as sufficiently congruent with it for departures to be accepted by the ear with a pleased feeling that its own intuitive sense of the ideal regularity is still in a manner dominating throughout. This once granted, we may readily allow that the invariable occupation of the places of recurrence by long syllables, though not the main point, is a most important point. It must have added a delightful feature of variety and complication to that elastic working of the ear which is entailed in all enjoyment of metre ; the giving to the strong places the invariable respect of a sound of some considerable *weight* was a very delicate and peculiar means of realising the particular regularity which constituted the metre, in the midst of those various accentual departures from it which impart elasticity to verse in place of sing-song monotony. The delicacy of ear in this particular direction certainly seems to have lapsed in modern times, or at any rate finds little opportunity in the normal pronunciation of modern languages ; and even in the classical languages one of the conditions for it must have been most deliberate enunciation.[1]

*The mistake has been in taking quantity as the great fact, instead of only as the great difference, of ancient verse.*

*This being granted, it is easy to admit its immense importance, and the lapse of the delicate sense for it in modern times.*

---

[1] I heartily concur with almost the whole of Mr. Spedding's remarks on this subject. But I do not think he altogether recognises that an Englishman enjoys classical hexameters *primarily* by instinctive reference to an underlying scheme of six stresses exactly as he enjoys blank verse by instinctive reference to an underlying scheme of five stresses ; and that if he does more than this, and by really dwelling on the long syllables obtains some of the additional pleasure which Greek and Latin ears received through their refined sense of quantity, the *essence* of his rhythmic instinct is still identical with what it was when he pronounced the words in the most uncompromising English way, making *Tityre* a triplet, and so on. Mr. Spedding seems to me entirely right in considering our pleasure in the rhythm of classical verse to be a direct and instinctive one, as opposed to Mr. Munro, who considers that we attain to it by mentally superinducing our acquired knowledge of the quantities which we have lost the power of instinctively feeling ; 'that is to say,' as Mr. Spedding well objects, 'we call to mind that by the rule of the metre this syllable must, in some inexplicable way, have been felt by Virgil to be long, and that syllable to be short ; and though we cannot ourselves perceive that it is so, or understand how it could be so, we take into considera- tion the fact that it was so. And the result is " all that wondrous harmony which we feel." ' But both critics seem to me inaccurate in taking the sense of *quantity*, whether instinctive or mentally superinduced, as the fundamental point in the enjoyment, instead of the sense of *recurrence* ; and by so taking it, Mr. Spedding has been further led into what appears unwarranted scepticism as to the modern decline in appreciation of quantity. This additional refinement may, I think, be to a considerable extent acquired by a modern ear : but the resulting quality in the metre, however important, is a *secondary* one. In the fact that an Englishman, without paying any more attention to actual duration of syllables than he is accustomed to do in his own language, finds the move- ment of classical hexameters perfectly natural and beautiful, lies sufficient indica- tion that the sense of rhythm is *one*, not *two*, and that the *primary* fact in his appre- ciation is identical with the primary fact in the appreciation of the ancients ; namely, a sufficient degree of conformity to a regular ideal scheme of recurrences, which in the case of the Englishman may certainly be called stresses, and which, by whatever name we call them, did certainly in a majority of places (an average probably of four out of six) receive an actual stress.

§ 7. The relation of metre to the whole effect of Poetry.

It was impossible to avoid noticing with some care this large and vexed question of ancient and modern appreciation of metre. But a detailed discussion of particular metres and particular examples, fascinating as the subject is, lies, as I have said, quite beyond our scope ; and it is now time to pass from the consideration of metre in itself, to its place in the specific delight of Poetry.

The mere pleasure to the sense is very slight,

It is obvious, to begin with, how slight is the mere satisfaction to the sense. The 'melody of verse,' though the term is perfectly allowable, is wholly unlike melody proper. Melody proper, as we saw, is essentially a resultant of *two* factors, that of rhythm and that of pitch ; and can no more be produced by rhythm alone, apart from definite relations of pitch, than water can be produced by hydrogen without oxygen. But a rhythmic set of sounds without definite relations of pitch is just what verse presents. Thus persons may have an exceptionally delicate sense of the 'music of verse' who entirely lack 'musical ear :' for where the power to perceive the relations of notes-in-pitch is quite irrelevant, the want of it can of course be no disadvantage. The variety of vowels and consonants and of the ups and downs of the voice may greatly assist the effect on the ear ; but however superior to the dead monotony of a drummer's practice, the

and cannot be fairly tested if the words are understood.

impression is not less remote from the melody of Music. A perfectly fair measure, and indeed the only perfectly fair measure, of the amount of satisfaction that the mere sound of verse can give, is found in melodious nonsense-verses, or if the knowledge that they are nonsense be held to interfere, by melodious verses in an unknown language. It is common to consider that strikingly good verse is marked by much more *independent* beauty in the sound-element than really exists. The experiment might be tried, on a person with a good ear and ignorant of English, of introducing into a section of *In Memoriam* the following stanza, which I have seen somewhere quoted from the prose of a mathematical treatise :

> And so no force, however great,
>   Can strain a cord, however fine,
>   Into a horizontal line
> That shall be absolutely straight—

The phrase 'sound without sense' tends to conceal this.

and this stanza will be quite as impressive to him as any other. Again, the ordinary phrase 'sound without sense,' applied to musical but empty verses, is delusive if it is meant to refer the pleasure simply or even chiefly to the sound alone, as in nonsense-verses. The most musical collocations of words would not be tolerated for a couple of minutes by the emptiest-headed person, unless a considerable number of the words suggested comprehensible and pleasing images. Thus by *sound* in the above phrase we must understand musical flow *plus* pleasing fragments of image and association, and by *sense* dominating and connecting ideas.

The pleasure, then, producible by the mere sound of verse, though very appreciable, has no depth or individuality, and could only be produced in an occasional way and for a very short period at a time. And we have consequently to look far beyond the mere gratification of the ear by a more or less agreeable set of sounds,[1] for the enormous effect of metre on the presentation of thought in a language which we understand.

[1] This gratification, such as it is, is of an entirely positive kind, acting directly on the sense. It would not have occurred to me that there could be a doubt about this, had not Mr. Spencer, in his essay on the *Philosophy of Style,* taken another view. He ingeniously refers forcible style to economy of the reader's or hearer's attention, and makes out his point very successfully in many particulars; but he seems to me quite to fail in his attempt to bring the effect of rhythmical structure in verse under the same rule. He says, ' If, as we have seen, there is an expenditure of mental energy in the mere act of listening to verbal articulations, or in that silent repetition of them which goes on in reading—if the perceptive faculties must be in active exercise to identify every syllable— then any mode of so combining words as to present a regular recurrence of certain traits which the mind can anticipate, will diminish that strain upon the attention required by the total irregularity of prose. Just as the body, in receiving a series of varying concussions, must keep the muscles ready to meet the most violent of them, as not knowing when such may come; so the mind, in receiving unarranged articulations, must keep its perceptives active enough to recognise the least easily caught sounds. And as, if the concussions recur in a definite order, the body may husband its forces by adjusting the resistance needful for each concussion; so, if the syllables be rhythmically arranged, the mind may economise its energies by anticipating the attention required for each syllable.'

There is surely a confusion here between the intellect and the ear, and between two distinct meanings of perception, namely, the *recognition* of a syllable as a known word or part of a known word and the mere *hearing* of it as part of a series of accented and unaccented sounds. The 'least easily caught sounds ' are those which, from softness or indistinctness, it is *hardest to recognise* as known words or parts of known words; but these are no less easily and completely *heard* as belonging to the regular series of alternating sounds than the louder accented constituents of the series. As regards the mere act of *hearing,* the perception of the series is an affection which would be as easily produced by nonsense-syllables arranged in the same rhythm: and as for attention, not *less* but *more* of it would seem to be involved in the case of a regular accented series than in prose. For against the supposition that the ear is relieved at alternate instants from the strain of its expectant attitude, through foreknowledge of the place of the louder syllables, we must set the fact that in verse it is actively on the watch, and notices with positive satisfaction the rhythmical succession *as such*; while in an irregular series it is not the least on the watch for the purely *sound*-qualities of what is going on, but acts as the uninterested and passive conductor of symbols to the mind. The intellectual *recognition* of the sounds, on the other hand, as known words or parts of known words, is in no way facilitated by their rhythmical succession. There are as many comparatively loud and distinct syllables, and as many comparatively faint and indistinct ones, in a paragraph of prose as in an equally long paragraph of verse : and the sum of mental energy required to identify them is equal in the two cases. The fact that in the verse the *ear* is aware beforehand at what instant the louder and fainter syllables are coming cannot relieve the *intellect* of its labour of recognition ; for difficulty or ease of recognition is simply a function of the distinctness with which the syllable is heard when it comes, and of nothing else.

Mr. Spencer's analogy of muscular adjustment is misleading. For in a succession of *precisely similar* bodily impulses, we are aware of exactly what is coming, and so can prepare for it before it comes: but in the case of a mental effort we have no idea what it is to be till the matter of it is presented ; and the recognition of every syllable is a *different* act from the recognition of every other, and entails different tracts of association. The fairer analogue would be a portrait, which we certainly should not recognise any the more easily for knowing that such an effort would be demanded of us at some particular

§ 8. Metrical
features con-
nected with
special points
in the meaning
of the words.
Before seeking a general explanation, we may glance at one or two special points which, though subsidiary and of far from universal occur- rence, are of great interest and importance. To begin with, it is clear that any common quality or analogy between the *sound* of a word or group of words and its *meaning* or sentiment is completely brought out if semi-latent, or is then and there evolved, through metre and metre only ; that is, through the presence of a *norm* of sound-arrangement, modifi- cations of which will necessarily arrest attention. The stock examples—

αὖθις, ἔπειτα πέδονδε κυλίνδετο λᾶας ἀναιδής,

and

Quadrupedante putrem tonitru quatit ungula campum,

contain something like direct imitation of phenomena in which easy regu- larity of recurrence was actually a feature : but irregularity and effort find equally ready means of expression in rhythmic features, which are only brought into special notice by their contrasted and exceptional character, that is, by their occurrence as part of and in the midst of metre. The line—

Long lines of cliff breaking have left a chasm—

is a less hackneyed example than some others. Nor are such effects at all confined to pourtrayal of sensible phenomena : Pope's line—

And strains from hard-bound brains eight lines a year,

with its seven heavy accents, might attract attention even if it occurred in prose, but gains at least nine-tenths of its point from its strong con- trast with the normal movement of heroic verse. And we may refer to the same head effects where there is no directly imitative quality at all, but where a large and imposing fact or idea finds fit expression in an accumulation of weighty syllables, or in words containing an imposing array of strong and sonorous vowels. In this way the line—

Majus adorta nefas majoremque orsa furorem
Evolat—

makes a magnificent introduction to the climax of Amata's frenzy. . It is through being marshalled in the unity of a measured line that an unusual set of vowel-sounds is felt as intentional and effective : in a prose passage such an amount of assonance as this would be almost as unfortunate as a chance rhyme. So, again, the resolution of dissyllabic into trisyllabic

moment. In the case of purely physical stimulation, there is a preparation of a certain amount of nervous energy against a particular instant when the repetition of the stimulus leads to its discharge ; and if the stimulus does not come at that instant, the closing of the expected outlet for the discharge gives us annoyance. But an act of recognition is a mental process which begins naturally at any moment on the presentation of the symbol to be recognised : and what- ever its objective nervous counterpart may be, it certainly cannot be amenable to regular rhythmic discharge.

feet, which may have the more directly imitative force above noticed, as in the lines—

> The long brook falling thro' the clov'n ravine
> In cataract after cataract to the sea—

is also a frequent means of marking some point of rapidity or intensity in the sense. There could not be a more splendid instance than the italicised words in the following passage from Œnone :

> I wish that somewhere in the ruin'd folds,
> Among the fragments tumbled from the glens,
> Or the dry thickets, I could meet with her,
> *The Abominable*, that uninvited came
> Into the fair Peleïan banquet-hall, &c.

Again, metre has a most important bearing on the actual moulding of the language, originating, as it were, and informing with unexpected beauty fresh structures of word and sentence. This is exemplified in the case of *words* by the formation of striking and sonorous compounds in many languages. As regards *sentences*, the following example from Mr. Swinburne's poem *Before a Crucifix* may serve : *Metre as affecting the formation of words, and of grammatical and rhetorical figures ;*

> The suns have branded black, the rains
>   Striped grey, this piteous god of theirs ;
> The face is full of prayers and pains,
>   To which they bring their pains and prayers, &c.—

where the rhetorical figure, the repetition and inversion in the last two lines, is of course something quite distinct from the measure and rhyme, but would have been impossible without them. Or as an example of a still simpler figure, equally dependent on metre for its peculiar character, we may observe the effect producible by mere repetition of a word or group of words, not as a refrain which the ear expects, but with a very much more subtle charm. A beautiful case occurs in the *Holy Grail*— *and as permitting striking repetitions of words and phrase.*

> And he to whom she told her sins, or what
> Her all but utter whiteness held for sin,
> A man well-nigh a hundred winters old,
> Spake often with her of the Holy Grail,
> A legend handed down thro' five or six,
> And each of these a hundred winters old,
> From our Lord's time—

and again in *Guinevere*—

> For still at evenings on before his horse
> The flickering fairy-circle wheel'd and broke
> Flying, and link'd again, and wheel'd and broke
> Flying, for all the land was full of life—

in both which passages the point of the repeated words clearly depends on their occurrence in identical places of the metre.

§ 9. The more general explanation of metrical effect. The delight of tracing two separately pleasurable things fused in perfect coincidence.

These effects, however, though not uncommon, do not of course meet us at every turn. To obtain the more general explanation which we require, we must notice how often in Art the enjoyment must be traced to the perception of one thing in two relations, or, if we prefer it, to the harmonious confluence of two different lines of things. In the union of words and music, for instance, we see syllables and notes dominated by one rhythm; in the apprehension of metre, we have sounds in a frequently varied and elastic order recognised as still under the dominance of a strict scheme of stresses; in the complete effect of verse, we see the words dominated at once by the idea they express in their grammatical connection and by their metrical adjustment. It is the application of the simple metrical form, with its comparatively slight power of independent impressiveness, to material expressing a meaning totally independent of it, it is this function of two disparate elements, which is at the root of the effect. What that effect at its best can be it is as impossible for one who has not experienced it to divine, as it would be for an uninstructed person to divine the result of the combination of an acid and an alkali: or we might seek our metaphor in that unique sensation of musical concord, whose physical condition is that two different sets of stimulation shall flow on simultaneously, but without mutual interference, in the ear; the result of their joint action being something at which nobody who had only known them in separation could have given the smallest guess. In the subtler mental chemistry, to the subtler poetic perception, the combination brings a totally new intuition of language, a sense of surprising and exquisite correspondence, the union of two orders multiplying a thousandfold the vividness of the delight either alone could give, and fusing it into a kind of triumphant affection. That outflow of nervous energy which often gives to ordinary emotional expression an expansive delight unknown to our silent meditations, has its current filled, by means of rhythm, from the deeper and wider sources of our whole nervous organisation. For once physical utterance seems adequate to our emotions and cognitions: the *ictus* of the verse strikes living fire out of the neutral symbols of thought, so that hitherto undreamed-of qualities flash forth from common words. In this glow, the separate verbal units seem able to focus all the scattered suggestiveness of their associations into a single point, so as really to *mean* more than in other collocations: each word, as it has been well remarked, seems 'raised to a higher power.' And we should notice the bearing on this general explanation of the more special points of the preceding section: for any structure or use of language which seems both new and natural vivifies the sense of the twin domination to which it so willingly lends itself.

This general account of the distinctive effect of verse may seem, after all, to be rather a statement or description than an explanation. But it may not be amiss to point out that psychology presents a larger number than is usually recognised of points where the chemical analogy becomes something more than a metaphor ; where the product resulting from the combination of certain known elements is of a kind which nothing could have led us *à priori* to expect ; and where the explanation can only consist in clearly recognising the elements and the product, *plus* the fact that the result does belong to this inscrutable department of chemical *transformation*, and represents no mere *summation* of the impressive elements ; and that this region is no mere metaphorical conception, convenient in a single instance, but truly embraces a considerable number of mental phenomena, which are as real and as amenable to accurate observation as physical substances.

*This account may seem to be rather description than explanation ; but even so, it illustrates an important psychological truth.*

One more possible difficulty suggests itself.  As the pleasure in the fusion of two lines of things, which is a fundamental point in this and the following chapter, may be represented as exemplifying the principle of unity in variety, while the result of our former examination of that principle in the ninth chapter was distinctly to *discredit* it as an explanation of beauty, it may be well to point out, somewhat more explicitly than has yet been done, the difference in the two sorts of cases.  Here we are dealing with two self-complete lines of impression, united by possessing a common element—in the case of verse and song the element of *words*, the common means by which the totally different things, rhythm and music on the one hand and poetical ideas on the other, are expressed.  The unifying fact is not the mere presence of relations whereby a variety of parts are construed as a whole, but the possession by a substantive and single phenomenon of two utterly disparate and independent functions or aspects, each with its own power of appeal.  That this sort of unity in variety, where the unity is a surprising and gratuitous concordance of completely disparate things, should possess extraordinary æsthetic power, is clearly entirely compatible with our former view that the mere perception of a unity comprising a number of parts, in the absence of any further source of interest in it or them (whether the whole be intellectual, like an arithmetical progression, or material, like a prize-pig), is no sufficient guarantee of æsthetic character.

*The mode of ' unity in variety ' which the above fusion exemplifies.*

To return to our explanation of metrical effect : a further element by which it is greatly enhanced is a sense of the *uniqueness* of the particular expression.  There is a latent consciousness of the *difficulty* of conveying thought in metre, connected with the fact that only once in a million times is it so conveyed, which heightens the delight in its apparently spontaneous welling forth.  Like statues out of shapeless blocks, Poetry's most perfect utterances seem struck by magic out of the ordinary everyday mass of things said and things sayable.  The very familiarity of the verbal material makes the beauty the more startling ; for it seems

*The effect is much helped by the uniqueness of the expression.*

in a way more wonderful that such unknown possibilities should lie in words than in marble or in notes. And thus presented, what is said takes on an imperishable character. It seems said once and for ever, as though it had at last attained the expression which for all time had been awaiting it : it seems to belong to a universe instead of to an individual.

The fusion of physical and intellectual ingredients is a vital point in all distinctively poetical effects, however varying in degree of excellence.

It is of course only to exceptional works, and exceptional parts even of great works, that such a description will fully apply : but to whatever extent the description has to be diluted, the sources of the distinctively poetical effect remain the same in kind. As long as the matter of what is said retains any independent quality of interest or emotion, its gain from metrical presentation is due to the peculiar fusion of physical and intellectual ingredients, to an effect which is not the sum but the resultant of its elements, and to some accompanying sense of rarity and permanence. And any thought or fact which has any imaginative or emotional possibilities, and this too though the immediate topic be indifferent or even ugly, will if forcibly expressed in verse reap in some degree the benefits of this fusion. The effect is felt even where certain qualities in the metrical element seem somewhat incongruous with emotional work. Some of the rhymes, for instance, in Mr. Browning's *Flight of the Duchess* produce rather the impression of jokes made during the performance of a symphony : but the work is still distinctively a poem, and a very good one. But it is naturally only the best verse that reveals how deeply and subtly the elements may from the first be blended, and how little the result is described by the mere imposition of metre on poetical subject-matter ; a fact best brought home to us by the sense of entire untranslateableness in most of the poetry which seems just the best worth translating.[1]

§ 10. Differences in degree of sensitiveness to the charm of verse ;

Differences in degree of sensitiveness to the charm of this subtly woven movement of thought are, of course, enormous ; though it is probable that even persons whose misquotations of poetry betray the greatest lack of distinctive perception, and who are most contemptuous of others for what seems to them an inversion of the values of sound and sense, are still unconsciously under the spell of measured language when they hear it. It is hardly necessary to add that, though a technical acquaintance with metre may certainly facilitate the getting into sympathy with new metrical effects, the essence of the perception is entirely instinctive ; and that just as persons are often keenly appreciative of Music, while professing total ignorance of it, so persons continually profess ignorance of metre, and believe that a technical knowledge of it must reveal some quite unimagined pleasure, who show themselves instantly sensitive to a false or halting movement.

---

[1] De Nerval's translation of Heine's poems into French verse filled the author with droll despair : and he particularly stipulated for literalness and prose in the English translation. So much worse often is the spurious imitation of charm than the mere loss of it.

But while differences in the degree of the perceptive faculty are natural enough, we should hardly have been prepared for the great varieties which we find in its application. Two persons equally sensitive to the subtle charm will perceive it vividly in different places, and in places where sympathy with the special subject-matter can in no way be adduced as a reason. To such an extent is this the case that Poetry, where we should expect to find and where we do find wide agreement as to the truth and general excellence of what is set forth, is the art in the appreciation of which the indeterminate factor is often most prominent and most tantalising. The unaccountable power in special things of haunting special people is a fact which is perpetually obtruding itself above conventional agreements; and this seemingly fortuitous appeal can only be due to the subtlest variations in the interplay of intellectual and sensuous perceptions. If this were more recognised, discussion as to the relative merits of different poets and poems would assume in a much increased degree the form of a record of individual impressions as such, to the great advantage of sincere criticism. It is so natural an impulse to try to defend logically what gives one intense pleasure, that one is very apt to lay stress on its tangible external aspects as opposed to its inner essence and magic, and to claim objective validity for intangible subjective preferences. Sooner often than people are willing to allow, the point arrives at which it is best to give up the attempt at explaining in words effects which cannot even be penetrated in thought; and also to concede to others what one cannot but be goaded into claiming for oneself, the admission, namely, that a thing seen goes for more than a thing not seen, and that a pleasure which cannot be analysed can hardly be rationally called in question. Even the objective test of durability may be pressed too far, if it be made the one canon of high artistic value : for literary work may fail to satisfy it owing to verbiage lying a little off the main current of the language, and entailing new conditions and possibilities of verbal melody which are none the less genuine for their comparative transience.

It is impossible to leave this subject of the metrical element in Poetry without calling attention to the extraordinary way in which not only its special nature and value[1] but its very existence, and the peculiarity of the gift involved in its highest employment, have been ignored by writers of

*and marked variety in the places in which various people of equal sensitiveness find themselves characteristically affected by it;*

*a fact which might with advantage be more recognised in criticism.*

[1] Wordsworth, for instance, whose best versification has probably never been surpassed in natural magic, ponderously argues for the value of metre on the ground that its regularity, and our sense of having come across it on less exciting occasions, introduce what he calls 'an intertexture of ordinary feeling,' which dilutes and relieves the discomfort we might experience from the poet's more painful images : ignoring the vital point which lies in the *rarity* of metrical in comparison with unmetrical combinations— and so in an intertexture of *extra*-ordinary feeling with the presentation of thought in language. So true is it, in Mr. Ruskin's words, that 'an artist may be unconscious of the principles of his own work, and may be led by instinct to *do* all that is right, while misled by false logic to *say* all that is wrong.'

§ 11. The function and the very existence of the metrical element in verse has often been strangely ignored.

authority. Nor does this negligence of what is so characteristic of poetical beauty appear only in those general phrases and descriptions where accuracy would hardly be looked for; as when Dryden says that ' the principal end of Painting is to please, of Poetry to instruct; ' or when Reynolds remarks that ' Poetry operates by raising our curiosity, engaging the mind by degrees to take an interest in the event, keeping that event suspended, and surprising at last with an unexpected catastrophe;' which is an exact description of a sensation-novel. Such sweeping simplifications of the infinitely complex channels by which art addresses us are not likely to do much harm: but the case is more serious when the criticism which professes to be looking narrowly into the springs of artistic delight implicitly denies them all magic properties. And it is in Poetry, just because its medium is the common and universal medium of ideas, that the distinctive magic properties are most apt to be lost sight of. The name of poet is equally misused in being defrauded of what it does and credited with what it does not connote. While on the one hand the natural and pardonable habit of calling all sorts of imaginative and emotional work poetical, has further led, as we have already seen, to calling people poets who could no more have produced a stanza of poetry than flown to the moon; on the other hand, the very fact that the subject-matter of Poetry, in the universality of its range, embraces that visible world with which Painting and Sculpture also deal, together with the natural love of exercising ingenuity in marking similarities and contrasts, has often led to the most external and mechanical treatment of the special poetic art.

Lessing ignores the extent to which a poet is differentiated by the gift of *saying*;

Thus Lessing, who set himself in the *Laocoön* accurately to distinguish the nature and functions of poetic from those of graphic and plastic art, seems never to have been able to shake off the habit of judging them in reference to one another; and appears so haunted by his distinctions as to have lost all sense of Poetry's possessing any charm beyond the crude substance, which can be handled and argued about, or any special channel of emotional and artistic utterance whatever. It might sound paradoxical to say that a poet is more truly differentiated by the power of *saying*, than by any other of his qualities; though in truth a very large part of his highest function does consist in crystallising into permanent beauty what numbers have seen, thought, and felt: but that he is more differentiated by the power of saying than by the sort of things for which Lessing applauds him, is not a paradox but simple truth. After telling us that ' with the poet the execution appears to be an easier achievement than the invention,' Lessing adds that, had Virgil borrowed the idea of the entwining of Laocoön and his children by the serpents, ' then that merit which, in his work, we hold to be the greatest and most considerable, would be wanting, and the lesser merit alone remain. For to create this entwining in the imagination is a far greater achievement than the expression of it in words. On the other hand, if the sculptor had borrowed this entwining from the poet, he would still in our estimation have attained sufficient merit, although the merit of invention would have been wanting. For expression in marble is infinitely more difficult than expression in words.' So Virgil's power of verbal expression is, apparently, quite an everyday affair. The words, indeed, according to Lessing, best show their excellence, like a gentleman's dress, by escaping notice altogether. 'The poet desires to make us believe ourselves to be as conscious of his objects as if they were actually present to our senses ; and in the moment of illusion we cease to be conscious of the means, that is of the words, which he employs for this purpose.'[1] And clearly if we are to forget the words, *à fortiori* shall we neglect their rhythm. We noticed before how Lessing's vaunted discovery that words are successive and visible traits coincident,[2] led him to the wonderful conclusion that Poetry has no business with description, except of physical actions in successive parts ; but still more wonderful is the fact that his perpetual dwelling on this successiveness of words has *never once* led him to remark on their metrical adjustment as an element in poetic effect. That is to say, a book which still enjoys the highest fame as a luminous exposition of the nature and relations of Poetry contains *not one word* which is not equally applicable to prose.

*and considers the ideal state to consist in total unconsciousness of the poet's words, and à fortiori of his rhythm.*

[1] This creation of *illusion*, on which Lessing harps a good deal, is an obvious figment. The faculty of sight is here in fact as falsely glorified as that of hearing is contumeliously ignored. The power distinctly to visualise imaginary objects is one which is possessed in most various degrees, but, in the degree of perfection which could give rise to anything approaching illusion, is extremely rare. Happily it is quite unnecessary either to the production or appreciation of poetical description ; the very point of which is to seize on the *few* points which impress the imagination, and to omit the *many* which would be seen by the eye. I mentioned in a former chapter that Lessing gives as a typical, and according to him excellent, poetical description of an object, a minute and laborious catalogue of a bouquet of flowers. I hope he enjoyed the 'illusion' which the description produced : but it is worth while to quote an instance of the other kind. Take the stanza—

> Fair is her cottage in its place
> Where yon broad water sweetly slowly glides.
> It sees itself from thatch to base
> Dream in the sliding tides.

I cannot call up any vision of this scene which gives me any vivid pleasure, nor are any two visions of it that I call up alike. For visualising purposes I should be much assisted by knowing how many windows the cottage had, where the door was, how many trees there were about, and so on. Nevertheless I would assert with confidence that the stanza has produced in me, and doubtless in many others, greater rushes of delightful emotion than the sight of what is described has ever produced in any human being.

[2] There is one point in connection with this distinction which is often not sufficiently recognised ; namely, that in Poetry the parts and details of a work may be more dissociated from the main subject and dominant ideas than in Painting, where details are commonly regarded in intimate relation and subordination to the whole ; whence it follows that an inferior *poem* may contain a great deal of very superior *poetry*. Mr. Rossetti's warmest admirers would probably admit an instance of the sort in *Jenny*, where the subject and tone are disagreeable, without the excuse of high originality, and the concluding bit of moralising, which gives the idea of being meant for a justification of the poem, is a weak and irrelevant adjunct ; while of some of the beauties of detail, both in thought and expression, it would be hard to speak too highly.

On this point it is easy to foresee, and equally easy to forestall, an objection, to the effect that any imaginative work in words, whether or not possessing the form which makes it *technically* Poetry, is fairly included under that term, and that the German *Dichtung* has no technical restriction and naturally suggests the wider sense. The objection is quite irrelevant. It was fully recognised in the third chapter that the highest imaginative work might be presented apart from poetical form: and it would be just as well if we had in English a generic term for all imaginative work in words. But the dispute here is not a verbal one: I am not so foolish as to attack a German about the use of a German word: what I complain of is his professing accurately to describe and distinguish the branches of Art, while ignoring the distinctive character of a most remarkable branch, which was constantly before his eyes and from which all his examples of the more generic *Dichtung* are taken; a branch which attention to the emotions connected with it (unless this chapter has been pure nonsense) will show to have as good a claim to be considered single and unique as Painting or Music; the branch, namely, which in English we call *poetry*, in contradistinction to *prose*. The importance of this branch, and of the peculiar emotions connected with it, cannot be affected by the accident that the Germans have no specific name for it: and indeed the absence of the *name* only makes it, if anything, more incumbent on a German than on an English writer to bring out clearly the *differentia* of the *thing*.

# CHAPTER XX.

## SONG.

SUPPOSE an intelligent and sensitive child to have been born deaf, and after arriving at an age of intelligence to obtain his hearing.[1] During a week or two let him get accustomed to hear conversation around him, conducted by persons with sweet and gentle voices ; and then introduce him into the society of persons with loud and grating voices : he will without doubt be unpleasantly struck by the contrast. Now let him hear a few good vocalists sing a series of musical passages. He will find the sounds pleasanter than any he had heard in conversation, and might perhaps find excitement in trying to imitate them with his own voice : also he might reasonably ask why all the world, when they want to use their voices in speech, do not employ these pleasanter sounds, and might be told that only a minority of voices can produce them sufficiently well to be agreeable, and that even they are rapidly exhausted by so doing. The point to notice is that in the second case equally with the first the prominent phenomenon to him at the first blush would be the *quality* of the sounds. But let him now get thoroughly accustomed both to speech and singing, and two things will happen in due course. In the first place, as his knowledge of language and his delight in comprehending it increase, he will find that the singing delivery of words makes them decidedly harder to catch, and will often make unavailing efforts to follow them. In the second place, he will find that, even when he fails in this attempt, he receives from the sounds new and increasing pleasure of quite a different sort both from the intellectual pleasure of comprehension and also from his first sensuous pleasure in their sweet quality : he will find that he is gratified by certain successions, and that he gets to look out for these when the same song is repeated ; and that even when the voice sings nothing to the tune but the syllable *la* over and over again, this gratification remains unaltered. He will also find that the pleasure in rhythm which he may have received before he obtained his hearing, from seeing soldiers march past the window or from watching his sisters dance, forms a most distinct part in this new pleasure ; that he can stamp his foot to the music with even

§ 1. Imaginary case of a deaf child who obtains his hearing.

He will first be struck by the *quality* of vocal sounds ;

[1] If this supposition is too violent, we may suppose the child to be simply kept out of reach of hearing either music or speech during his early years.

greater zest than he did to the soldiers. And, if we suppose hi.n to be musically organised, another experience will follow. Some one may chirp the tune of *Rule Britannia* to him, using absolutely the minimum of vocal resonance and only just suggesting the notes, and if he is asked what it was he will answer, ' Music : ' whereas if the same question is asked after some oratorical effort delivered in the most resonant and beautiful voice, he will answer, ' It was a speech,' or ' It was a sermon,' but certainly not ' It was music.' In other words, his sense of melodic *form* is now established, and may go on developing uninterruptedly : so that looking back over his experiences he will smile at his first idea that the mere sweetness of sound which once so surprised him was what people must mean by music.[1]

but will gradually learn that it is form which constitutes Music.

§ 2. To such a person the possession by the voice of two distinct faculties would be prominently brought out.

To a person in the circumstances we have imagined, the possession by the voice of two completely distinct faculties would be brought home with exceptional vividness. The voice in fact, alone among our special organs, exercises by itself, without the use of any external material, both a function of utility and a function of art ; constituting on the one hand a medium for the symbols of speech, and on the other a musical instrument which, when in perfection, may seem preferable to all others, and even when of quite inferior quality can still present melodic forms to our ears with perfect clearness and intelligibility. Now for us, in our present stage of experience, it is easy to see that the voice may combine one of its faculties with the other after various fashions and on various grounds. It may use *notes* in delivering the words it has to *say*, as a means of making them emphatic and widely audible ; or it may use *words* in delivering the notes it has to *sing*, in order to avoid the inanity of using meaningless syllables ; for its normal business being comprehensible speech, this line of utterance is so associated with it that a protracted absence of words would be noticed as absurd. Between these two extremes there are, of course, all varieties of mean : but in the existence of the extremes we see how radically distinct (though compatible) are the aims, emphasis for words and expression for Music, to which the voice may direct its more resonant utterance. We cannot, however, suppose that in the early dawn of human history any distinct consciousness of the duality of vocal function would present itself. We need not recur here to the interesting question whether or no the voice was in a rudimentary way an organ of Music before it was an organ of Speech, that is, whether it was used to give pleasure before it was used to convey meaning. It is suffi-

---

[1] It would be interesting to discover how far a sense of melodic form could be developed in a musical child without any association at all with beauty of colour or *timbre* in the sounds. The sense of beauty or of any definite characteristic in the colour-quality of notes is abstractable with such curious completeness in the silent realisation of music in the head, that it would not at all surprise me to learn that a love of fine melody could be formed on a course of the Jew's harp. But children so instinctively sing and hum the tunes they care about that the experiment cannot be considered practicable.

cient to notice that since to articulate-speaking men Speech is a most constant and prominent fact of life, besides being both a chief result and a chief organ of development, if there be any other use of the vocal apparatus which (however remote in origin and essence) is compatible with the primary function, it is natural to look for the earliest and the closest connections between the two. Now there is no doubt that as an instrument of utility the voice early reached a comparatively high pitch of development, while as an instrument of art it could not of course forestall or outstrip the art to which it belonged; and Music till quite modern times was still, comparatively speaking, in its infancy. While, therefore, rhythmic noises and excited cries may have been a natural joy and relief to our ancestors during long prehistoric ages, still in the development of *Song* in our present conception of it, as the meeting point of Speech and Music, Speech—that is, the intentional utterance of intelligible words—may conveniently be looked on as the primary central factor; and in its gradual transformation by the other factor it will be interesting to note under what kind of influence and in what kind of way the points which differentiate Song from ordinary vocal utterances would naturally present themselves.

*The two functions were very early united in rudimentary Song.*

What, then, are these differentiating points? Two of them will be at once obvious even to a person with no musical ear: such a person hearing an ordinary song will see that the sounds differ from those of ordinary speech by being *resonant*, that is, produced by the 'singing voice,' and by presenting a certain regularity of *rhythmic accent*. The varieties of *pitch* which the tones present will not strike him as involving a difference, since the tones of speech also vary in pitch, and without a musical ear he will not detect any special reasonableness in the particular succession of intervals presented in the song. But there is a third difference which can hardly fail sooner or later to strike him, and that is that the song consists of sounds *each single and definite in pitch*; that the voice lands securely and keeps steadily on each note and does not glide and shift uncertainly up and down in undefinable stages. He might enquire why this is the case, and whether it would not be possible to keep to the natural pitch of the words as spoken, while giving them the added emphasis and sonority of the musical *timbre*. We could give to him a more satisfactory answer than was possible to the child whose sense of hearing was quite new. We could show him by experiment that the attempt to *imitate* the intonation of speech in song, to make resonant and bring out as a distinct note each embryonic and imperfect tone of our ordinary sentences, ludicrously fails. Even to discover what is the pitch of the main vowel-sounds in a sentence requires a good ear and considerable practice, and the glidings and transitions—occurring even on single syllables—are far too rapid and spasmodic for resonant utterance, which in attempting to render them falls into simple hee-hawing: moreover the sounds which are only noises,

*§ 3. Three points which differentiate Song from Speech: resonance, rhythmic accent,*

*and definiteness of each sound in pitch.*

and having no musical character have *à fortiori* no assignable pitches, form in rapid speech a preponderating majority. To return, then, to our three settled characteristics of song, regularity of *rhythm*, resonance of *timbre*, and definiteness of *pitch* for each successive sound. We have seen how close in nature is the connection between the second and third of these factors; but clearly the second and third can exist without the first, as in the rhythmless vocal deliverances of a town-crier; and the first can exist without the second and third, as when we read *John Gilpin* aloud in an easy unemotional way; and we should not consider either case to be an example of Song. It remains, then, to ascertain what fact or principle would naturally underlie the combination of the factor of rhythm with those of resonant *timbre* and definite pitch in early vocal manifestations.

To this end it will be useful to approach the subject from another side, and try to realise in what ways emotion acts on utterance. We perceive at once that violent, undignified, and unrestrained emotion results in spasmodic irregular vocalisation, and in sounds containing less than the ordinary amount of musical *timbre*, with a predominance of unmusical noises and abortive reachings at notes above or below the musical register of the voice; but that ordered and elevated emotion, on the other hand, tends naturally to sonority and regularity of utterance. And the regularity may take several forms, affecting both the *pitch* and the *time* of the sounds.

First, as regards *pitch*, if we wish to give solemn and emphatic utterance to a deeply felt sentiment, we increase the resonance of our voice and approximate to determinate musical tones; but what is more, the register of our voices in such a case naturally confines itself *within narrow limits* of pitch. For in using increased resonance we instinctively select the few notes which try and fatigue our voice least; and also since (as already pointed out) the imitation of ordinary intonation, as it might be used by a person saying the same sentence with no emotional interest in it, is impracticable, and it never occurs to us even to attempt it, there seems no object in using one note more than another, so that we instinctively gravitate towards monotone. Secondly, as regards *time*, all deliberate and dignified emotional speech aims at some sort of evenness and balance of syllable and phrase, or at any rate finds the imposition of such balance suitable to its character: and any utterance which was specially intended to attract auditors, to arrest attention and gain permanent remembrance, would naturally clothe itself in some sort of verse; that is, would adopt metrical divisions presenting something that the ear counts on, accepts gladly, and retains easily.[1]

---

[1] It seems to be a natural instinct to impose some certainty both of rhythm and pitch on words with a view to remembering them. We are told that when the Sandwich Islanders 'first began to read and spell, it was impossible for them to repeat a column of spelling or recite a lesson without chanting or singing it.' The same habit may often be noticed in children.

Here, then, in recitation of verse, we find a chance for all three factors Recitation of verse thus gives a chance for all three of the above-mentioned points. and a natural stage in the evolution of Song. The wish to be widely audible would naturally limit the reciter to the register where his voice was strongest, and also the emotion connected with verse would, as in the case of other deliberately emotional speech, tend to a limited number of sonorous tones: and under the ægis of rhythm, resonance and certainty of tone would pass out of the sphere of the town-crier's utterances and enter the region of art. For here we have a departure from ordinary intonation justified not only by emotional quality in the words but by a distinctly *musical* pleasure, the combination of definite tones with regularity of accent, that is, with a feature imposed on words by artifice. Even pure monotone would often find itself in place: for wholly blank as it is of emotional power when in an amorphous state, since the mere sensuous pleasure derived from the most beautiful voice rapidly palls on the sense in the absence of form, it may readily be vitalised and dignified by acting as a substratum to the varied motion of metre.

It may be well to remark, by the way, what was made abundantly clear The rude application of rhythm to words, in early stages, is not to be taken as implying any want of acuteness in the rhythmic sense. in the chapter on the factors of melodic form, that the sense and enjoyment of rhythm, of regular recurrence of stimuli, is something far more general than this particular application to utterance: and the rhythmic sense, even in a very early stage of human development, is far truer and keener than would be perceived if we only attended to this single application. Early verse is metrically rude, not because the sense of simple rhythm is imperfect, but because the moulding of words into metre is a matter of advanced skill, and doubly difficult with the unabundant words of a rude language; while a very slight admixture of the rhythmic element might be thankfully accepted by ears which could not but perceive that it was an unwonted gratuity in the domain of speech. Thus in the impromptu recitations, narratives, and lampoons so common among barbarians, metrical features may be present only in a very embryonic form: but this does not prove that musical elements are being gradually evolved out of speech, but that the process of application to speech of a musical element already deeply rooted in the organism was necessarily a gradual one. Dancing, clapping, stamping, use of percussive instruments, all those means of producing true regularity of stimulation which present no intrinsic difficulty, are among the most universal features of savage life, and the accuracy of their employment is a subject of perpetual comment. The full importance of this point will appear in the next chapter.

In vocal utterances, the natural way for metre to make its first entrance is simple repetition of phrase, either immediately, or at intervals in the fashion of a refrain,[1] which would clearly gain much in effect by appearing

[1] Mr. Spencer's tables of *Descriptive Socio-* *logy* supply numerous instances. The chants of the Tasmanians are described as all abounding in 'repetitions of words or lines

on a more or less even and monotonous ground.  And it is easy to see how this measured intoning, which at first presents in respect of pitch such negative characteristics, would lend itself to melodic formation. The refrains and, as metre developed, the ends of the lines, would give opportunity for recurrence of definite successions of notes, and these recurrences and cadences might grow in number.  Meanwhile the gradual development of a feeling for regular ratios between notes, in other words, the formation of a scale-system with fixity of intervals, would continue in connection with all musical manifestations, as the result of the existence, in however rudimentary a form, of purely musical (as opposed to poetical) instincts ;  instruments with a fixed succession of notes would guide and sustain the voice; and as the combination of pitch-ratios with time-ratios is the essence of all the endless combinations of melodic form, the voice in its various trials was sure to break through the bounds imposed by the normal lengths of syllables.  We have seen how absolute and accurate Music is in the employment of both its factors ; while words can yield themselves to these strict requirements without any loss of intelligi-

bility.  When, then, the power of appreciating more complicated melodic phrases had been developed, the voice would naturally not debar itself from delivering them by any sense of duty to the length of syllables natural in the normal delivery of speech.  One syllable might be held for several notes, unimportant words and syllables might be held for as long a time as important ones, words might be repeated.  Glaring reversals of natural verbal accents could be easily avoided ; but while avoiding them the melodic rhythm might lift the words wholly into its own region, justifying the transformation of their flow by the inherent agreeableness of the resulting form.

in a monotonous but not inharmonious strain.'  They have a guttural termination to all their songs, which is also a war-cry, ' Balla ugh, Balla ugh, Ugh, ugh.'  A more developed stage is represented in Sandwich Island poetry, where ' the chief art appears to consist in the compilation of short metrical sentences, agreeing in accent and cadence at the conclusion of each, or at the end of a certain number of sentences.'  It is curious to remark that the musical instinct often carries the day over the meaning of the words.  The author of the *League of the Iroquois* says, ' Their war-songs are in a dead language, or at all events the Iroquois are unable to interpret them.  They are in regular verses, or measured sentences, and were learned by them with the dance originally.' So the songs of the Dakotas are described as consisting principally in the repetition of unmeaning syllables.  The Todas, a hill tribe of India, have a gamut of five or six notes, which they ' run through in a breath, beginning with the lowest and ascending to the highest, over and over again without variation.'  Among the Mandans, ' every dance has its own peculiar song ; and that is so intricate and mysterious that not one in ten of the young men who are dancing and singing it know the meaning of the song which they are chanting over.'  We are told that among the remains of Mexican poetry ' are some verses in which, between words that are significative, interjections or syllables are interposed, devoid of any meaning, and only made use of to adjust the measure.' This is a remarkable instance of good ear ; and it is satisfactory to learn of such a people that ' on festivals they continued singing the whole day.'

In modern
Song this right
is exercised in
its fullest
extent.

Any modern song, and almost any bar in it, will show the submission of the syllables to the melodic moulding in the whole department of rhythm. Take, for example, the two following simple melodic strains:

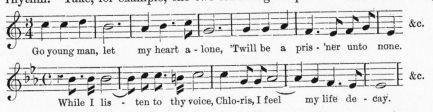

Go young man, let    my heart a - lone, 'Twill be   a   pris - 'ner unto   none.

While I lis - ten to thy voice, Chlo-ris, I feel   my life de - cay.

In the first of these couplets, two at least of the syllables which, if the lines are read, receive accents, *heart* and *be,* fall on an unaccented part of the bar, and the small and unemphatic words *my* and *'twill* on the accented beat; and of two lines of equal length one occupies four bars of music, the other only two and a third. In the second couplet, written by Henry Lawes, who was noted for his natural and easy setting of words, the musical rhythm is still more markedly independent. Yet both sound as right as possible: the new rhythm (which of course would never be thought of except in connection with the actual melody) seems as natural to the words as their own independent one. Far more violent instances are of constant occurrence: thus in a song through the greater part of which the normal verse-rhythm is retained in an exceptional degree, *O ruddier than the cherry,* there is a passage where the first syllable of the word *bluster* is held for thirty-three notes, without seeming the least absurd. We naturally find the proviso that accented syllables fall, as a rule, for the most part on accented notes; but, this one rule being observed, the melodically altered rhythm of the words is so completely justified to the ear, that it is hard to perceive, without deliberate examination, how completely in many instances the normal spoken rhythm has been departed from, and what wholly new durations and conditions are imposed on the syllables. Many poems have been set again and again to music, the melodies differing utterly in the details of their rhythm. It follows that under this handling the peculiar charm of which natural verse-rhythm is a factor is very apt to vanish; whence the wrath we have most of us experienced at musical versions of familiar and cherished lyrics: while, *en revanche,* the exquisite sense of fusion when the flow and balance of the metrical lines is preserved in the flow of a beautiful melody is quite unique in quality. It may be added, that it is through the power of Music to impose its own rhythms in perfect independence that prose as well as verse can be used for setting; as, for instance, in Handel's oratorios.[1]

[1] We noticed in the last chapter that among the Greeks the far more careful attention to quantity in the words as spoken, and the far greater simplicity of musical strains, made the close adaptation of musical bars to verse-feet possible. Probably the correspondence of word-rhythm and note-rhythm was with them about as close nor-

The voice's
assertion of
itself as an
independent
musical instru-
ment was a
very gradual
process.
Of course the change whereby the voice, while acting as the organ of developed speech, asserted itself as a musical—as distinct from a verbal—instrument, must in early days have been very gradual, depending on the slow growth of the musical art. It had progressed far enough in Plato's time to meet with his strongest reprobation; and reached its climax in some of the ecclesiastical music of the later middle ages, where all idea of intelligibility for the words was lost sight of.

§ 6. Sum-
mary of results.
So far, then, our results are as follows. We found no basis for art in mere sonority, and we found it was impossible to sing ordinary speech: but in the intoning of verse a common ground presented itself where words were intelligible and audible and where elementary musical form was possible; and when the development of melodic structure involved greater complexity of rhythm, the words could be made to follow, retaining for the most part their main accents, but otherwise very malleable. Thus in respect of pitch we seem to have passed from speech to Song by a kind of *tabula rasa* of monotone or something approximating to it, on which the various intervals of developing music gradually worked. But the following question may occur: as there is, beyond metre, a second formative factor in developed melody, namely, the definite proportions of the pitch-intervals, and as the metre has been shown to present an art-basis while the other factor was absent or wholly inchoate, was it out of the question that this other factor should also on its own account form a

Would it have
been possible to
find a satisfac-
tory formative
principle in the
pitch-relations
of notes, apart
from musical
rhythm?
similar basis? After finding reproduction of the shifting and indefinite sounds of speech impossible in the singing voice, we immediately fell back on metre for a formative principle, whereas (it might be urged) there seems to be no *à priori* impossibility of finding a satisfactory formative principle in certain ratios of intervals, while retaining the natural unmeasured flow of speech.

Now if we regard the historic development of Song, the answer is this: that the feeling for regularity of rhythmic impression is a natural fact of the organism, lying as deep in our natures as any instinct we have, and traceable to ages long previous to the dawn of distinctly intellectual processes; while systems of pitch-intervals are numerous and empirical, and have been gradually developed by conscious artistic efforts: so that emotional and poetic speech found the sense for metrical regularity and
In historical
development,
no:
recurrence ready to hand and *instinctively* utilised it; whereas the association of particular utterances with particular sets of notes would have involved the perpetual *artificial* production of new forms from the elements of some scale-system which in early times could only have an inchoate or a potential existence, that is, the making of bricks without

mally as in the cases where it is closest with us. It is therefore the more noticeable that we are expressly told that even in Greek vocal music the notes often disregarded and reversed the natural lengths and rhythm of the syllables.

straw. And apart from historic development, if we regard actual subsequent possibilities, the question whether, given a complete and convenient scale-system, the ratios of the intervals afford material out of which beautiful melodic forms can be built independently of a strict metrical element, may seem still easier to answer, and indeed to be quite out of place at this stage of our enquiry : so evident was it, in our consideration of melodic forms, that as regards sequences of unaccompanied tones the answer must be no ; that what is essentially a resultant of *two* factors cannot dispense with one of them ; that a very small number of rhythmless tones may indeed form a connected (and to quite undeveloped ears even an agreeable) group, though in the very act of imagining them it is difficult to avoid investing them with some kind of accent ; but that in a longer series the ear gets quite astray and finds no organic coherence in the mere pitch-relations of the constituent notes. Where attention is occupied with words, an occasional breaking of monotone by such groups may be a relief to the ear, as in some of the intoning and chanting one hears in foreign churches ; but we do not find in them a true basis for the development of melodic organism any more than in a succession of birds' calls, and no melodic faculty which had advanced beyond the embryonic stage could rest content with such fragments.

*and even **after** the development of a scale-system, still no,*

But there is a special reason for recurring to the point in connection with Song. For, it may be urged, does not much of what is known in modern music as *recitative* consist of such a rhythmically loose structure,[1] while nevertheless it seems to justify itself to the musical sense ? Yes ; but this is owing to a musical element the very name of which transports us at a step not only from savage strains, but from the most developed music of antiquity, to the modern era, namely, Harmony ; in our discussion of which in a former chapter it may be remembered that the point of its special relation to recitative was purposely deferred.

*until we arrive at the formative element of harmony.*

We must now refer for a moment to what we found, in that chapter,

---

[1] It should be specially realised that it is in *rhythm* (or rather in *lack* of rhythm, according to the use which restricts that word to a regularly accented series), and not (as many seem to suppose) in *pitch*, that modern recitative conforms, more or less, to the natural speech-delivery : for on this point the ear is easily deceived by the *familiar* effect which the approximation to speech-rhythm produces. It is clear, in the first place, that, while the natural speech-*rhythm* of a sentence is obvious and admits of comparatively little variety, the same words may be naturally pronounced with many different *intonations*, none of which can claim special validity. But apart from this, since the musical notes form intervals belonging to an artificial scale, and have purely musical rela- tions and necessities, no evident approximation would be possible even to an intonation of the words which, by slow and disconnected utterance, was made as free as possible from the predominant unmusical elements. And though, from the negative and conventional character which is frequent in recitative, the notes may seem to present less marked differences from the tones of solemn speech than do those of a developed tune, any one may find by trial that if he takes the words of a good recitative and speaks them with deliberate emphasis, and then compares the result with the musical notes, these go up where his went down and *vice versâ* as often as not, and that they present no sort of certain resemblance in their intervals.

to be involved in a series of chords unconnected with melody and embodying no rhythmic motive.   We saw that in such a series, each chord, being
composed of parts, has what a single note can never have, a sort of form of
its own, depending on the simultaneously felt relations of the notes which
compose it; and that if we take two in succession, we may get a decidedly
greater æsthetic effect from the changing harmony (*e.g.* in the resolution
of a discord) than is possible from the sheer emptiness of an isolated couple
of single notes.   A longer series of chords may exhibit all degrees of firm-
ness or looseness of form : it may have a definite purport and structure
which may be grasped as a unity, in which case the ear probably insists
on hearing it in some kind of accented rhythm ; or it may have no such
organism, each transition or minor group being accepted as pleasing on its
own account, not as a necessary member of a whole.   For one person who can
invent a fine melody, thousands, as we saw, can sit down and string together or 'improvise' chords and piecemeal modulations of the latter kind,
which on a fine instrument may have an agreeable effect for a short time ;
while on an orchestra they may be embroidered with all sorts of instrumental
passages.   And such series can and do stand in musical compositions as justification, support, and connection for notes and phrases which have little
or no melodic coherence of their own.   Recitative so supported serves as a
specially convenient vehicle for the emphatic and intelligible declamation
of words, since the rhythm of the words as naturally spoken can be
followed in it.   And as the old rhythmic chant, with its monotonous pitch
and its few cadences, had formed a natural feature of recitation in the old
days of bardic poetry,[1] so this totally different modern recitative, with its
varieties of pitch and its relaxed rhythm, found in the church and in the
theatre plenty of scope for its services.

§ 7. There
are all degrees
between the
barrenest reci-
tative and
melody proper.
There are of course all degrees between melody proper and such
an extreme as the kind of recitative which serves no more artistic
purpose than to make words more or less pleasingly audible through
large spaces.   Truly admirable proportions of melodic and harmonic
structure are compatible with a certain amount of metrical license :
to take the simplest possible instance, such a recitative as *Behold, a
virgin shall conceive* is really in the balance of its members a complete
organism ; and the works of Handel, Bach, and Gluck, would supply
numbers of more elaborate examples.   The safe general test is the nega-

[1] The Ambrosian chanting probably ap-
proximated to this ancient sort of recitative,
being attentive to accent and quantity during
the prevailing monotone, and reserving
melodic adornment for the ends of phrases.
The later ecclesiastical 'plain-song' seems
to have been deficient in rhythmic accent,
but here the *harmonic* element appeared,
first in the barbarous 'diaphony' and 'des-
cant,' and with gradually developing variety
and refinement.   With respect to the
rhythm, however, it must be borne in mind
that the actual mode of performance is lost
to us, owing to the extreme imperfection of
mediæval notation, exemplified, *e.g.*, in the
absence of bars and the omission of written
sharps and flats in places where they were
certainly used by the singer.

tive one : if, in a set of bars, the relative durations of the bars themselves, or the relative time-lengths of sounds and silences which they severally comprise, are susceptible of change, if no sense of dislocation results when changes are introduced, there is present no motive sufficiently organic and vertebrate to be capable of being dislocated. Abundant exercise in the application of the test will be afforded by the quotations in § 3 of the chapter on Opera.

But the actual place of recitative in modern music can only be understood by the light of a few historical facts. In the development of the art through the course of the middle ages, the governing power was Polyphony. The effect of the conjunction of two or more voices, blending and yet distinct, seemed to open up a new world ; and the ingenuity of centuries was lavished in the working out of contrapuntal tissues, inspired at first by the mere enjoyment of watching the windings and meetings and passings of the independent parts, and developed by slow degrees to accordance with a definite foundation of true harmonic progressions. Since, therefore, the attention of scientific musicians had been occupied by these matters, it was natural that, when solo-singing made its entrance into their works, it should be modest in its claims. The notes did not take possession of the words and embody them in complete melodic organisms, but followed them phrase by phrase, giving such expression as was possible in a more or less fragmentary way, and often retaining with but slight modification much of the natural spoken rhythm even of unmetrical words, while the musical intelligibility was in great measure sustained by the support of the accompanying chords. This loose form of structure reached a higher organic development and a perfection of its own in the *aria parlante* of Carissimi and the recitative of Pelham Humphreys at the end of the seventeenth century. But the fixing of the modern tonal system,[1] with the unmistakable definition of key by the dominant chord, was now practically complete ; and in the contrasts and affinities of keys and endless facilities for modulation lay the means for that immense development in the treatment of distinct rhythmic motive which makes it as cardinal a feature of elaborate compositions as of popular song : and harmony, while losing none

*Solo-singing made its entrance into Music gradually ;*

[1] It is natural that *melodic* series of notes (in contradistinction to tissues of several parts) should gain most in vividness from the definition of tonality ; since in their case the ear receives no specific gratification *at each point* from a rich changing mass of sound, but must perceive a number of successive notes as a unity; which becomes easier, the more keenly the key-relations of the component units are felt. In this connection, therefore, it is interesting to remark that the instinct for the modern tonality had existed among the people, the *trouvères*, and generally the non-scientific musicians, long before it gained acceptance in scientific works. But solo-singing made its definite entrance into serious compositions, not by adopting popular rhythmic tune, but through the attempt of the Florentine school, at the end of the sixteenth century, to create musical drama by resuscitating (as they fondly imagined) the old Greek declamation. The division between science and popular practice in the music of the middle ages is excellently treated by Mr. Hullah in his excellent sketch of modern musical history.

of its old capabilities, became also, by the same change, the minister of melody, enriching its form and explaining its modulations.

but as it has grown to perfection, the place of recitative has tended rather to decline.

And as this new wealth revealed itself, it was but natural that a separation should take place, and that recitative should sink more and more into poverty. It retained its uses indeed, the supply of melody not being endless, and some words seeming fitter for declamation than for definite song; as a relief or an introduction to tune, it may be most effective; and masters who have had fine melodic invention, and a firm instinct for balance and coherence of phrase, have been able, while relaxing strict metrical conditions, to produce results of high independent beauty, though lacking as a rule that more distinct and rarer individuality which belongs to the most clinching and organic sort of form. But it is impossible in Music to go back on our steps; and with our present experience the musical attention will rapidly weary in a prolonged recitative, from the apparent aimlessness in the succession of notes due to the deficiency of one of the two formative factors; a deficiency which can only become æsthetic through the piquancy of contrast in the re-entrance of rhythmic movement proper. Not but that persons differ much in this respect. Some are rapidly tired by the 'unchartered freedom' of loosely joined and inorganic series of phrases; while there are others to whom fine declamation and a rich harmonic accompaniment, decked and complicated with instrumental variations, will be suffi-

The place of strict rhythm in very nearly the whole of the music which is deeply cared about seems indisputable.

ciently interesting to prevent this impatience. We have already remarked how various, and how unrelated to musical development, are the degrees of susceptibility to pleasure from mere musical *tone* or colour: nor is it irrelevant to mark a similar fact as regards the mere enunciation of language; as, in the case of nations, a very little experience of the theatre will show that the French and Italians, to whom the simple act of speech, the actual movements of the tongue and lips, gives obviously a more positive delight than to us, take also a more general and positive delight in watching the speech of others. But, not to go beyond modern written compositions, it must be admitted as beyond dispute that nine hundred and ninety-nine thousandths of the music from Handel to the present hour, I will not merely say has been built on a framework of strict time-relations, but has had strict time-relations as an element in its inmost life and substance: nor can Wagner's position as the prophet of a new revelation in the light of which recitative, however amorphous, is to be esteemed regenerate and melodic, exclude much magnificent work of his own from the same category. The course of artistic development has been entirely *towards*, and not away from, the firm precision of form which is in no other way attainable. Rhythmic melody lived long ago among the people while contrapuntal artifices were dominating the churches; and, indeed, it would be absurd to treat a temporary and partial oblivion of metrical necessities, excusable in scientific music after a first plunge into the rejoicing waves of harmony, as involving an abrogation of anything so deeply implanted in our organisms as the unchangeable rhythmic sense.

Recitative in Opera has sometimes been defended as preventing a dis- agreeable and unnatural drop from music to plain speech. But this cannot excuse an invention of such inconceivable barrenness and conventionality as the *recitativo secco* of modern opera. It is a wonderful example of the power of fashion and custom, that the points at which Addison tells us ' our countrymen could not forbear laughing' are now accepted as a matter of course, and comparatively few will confess even to being bored with them. Notes so empty could indeed never give artistic point or emphasis to anything, which is perhaps fortunate, as the words are usually so silly and so unsuited to be dwelt on that the less emphasis the better : still the fact of their being sung instead of said consumes a wearisome amount of time. And it is the fashion now to disfigure even such passably amusing dialogue as that of Scribe's librettos with this dreary and alien feature. Where the musical notes have no beauty of their own, and merely serve to render tedious words and scenes which without them might pass quickly, if not agreeably, no *à priori* view that the transition from melody to recitative is more *natural* than to ordinary speech seems to have any weight. The transition from what is a pleasure to what is a nuisance is surely in every way *less* natural than the transition to what may be at worst pretty neutral.

Impossibility of defending *recitativo secco*.

The further notice of recitative, and the more detailed criticism of that peculiar species of it which has made its appearance in our own time, must be reserved for the chapter on Opera.

So much for the fundamental elements of structure, as affected by the union of musical and verbal utterances. We may now pass on to some questions of a less dry and technical kind, concerning the effect on musical art of articulate speech in its domain, and to some further modes in which the two factors of Song act on one another.

§ 8. Further questions concerning the influence of speech on the musical art.

The general historical influence may be summed up in a very few words. The human voice was naturally the first instrument, and the slay- ing of the flute-player Marsyas by Apollo, the god of the lyre, represents fairly enough the subordinate position of an instrument which from its nature was dissociated from Song. One specially important and early form in which musical elements lent themselves to the service of language was in religious celebrations : for rhythm, cadence, and tone are the natural means for enabling a number of persons to use language simultaneously, and for converting into one united utterance what would otherwise be a confusion of tongues. In its furthest ancient development, among the Greeks, Music was still in a position of tutelage to its more developed sister-arts, Poetry and Dancing ; and independent instrumental music, though asserting its rights, was quite subordinate. In the revival of Music in connection with Christian worship, the voice was of course still

The general historical influ- ence.

paramount.  For long it was the only instrument which, judged by our present standard, could be accounted satisfactory; and by means of it the art continued to develope both in theory and practice.  When the germs of modern Opera appeared in some of the miracle-plays of the middle ages, Music had made great strides, the modern scale-system was beginning to take shape, and the enormous invention of harmony and of different parts sung at the same time had given the art totally new means of effect.  But it was still predominantly vocal: nor did the great instrumental develop-ment assume importance till after the time of Handel.  Church-music and operas long held almost undivided sway, and it is only during the last hundred and fifty years that the greatest writers have thrown their utmost strength into instrumental composition.  The nature of the change in-volved in the modern development must be carefully noted; for the *historical* union of words and Music, as we saw in a previous chapter, is often treated as *essential*.  The enormous variety of modern instrumental forms, whether in chamber-music or in orchestral writing, presents countless features utterly outside the scope of voices, as well as wholly inapplicable to words.  For the nature of the voice and the nature of words (if they are to be audible and distinguishable) both demand that the structure of vocal music should be for the most part broad and simple in its lines : and even in more elaborate vocal writing each voice is bound to one more or less continuous part of limited pitch, and greatly limited also in matter of speed and difficulty.  This comparative simplicity in the two factors of Song may be associated with the further fact that in their more complex developments Poetry and Music are not only different but opposite.  Poetry suggests and compresses, and goes on perpetually saying new things; the musical organism presents, reiterates, varies, and amplifies.

§ 9. The exceptional character of the voice among instru-ments.

Speech, however, still supplies, and always will supply, the basis and starting-point for many sorts of composition.  And though Music, in all its branches, now has and claims its independent rights, the vocal and verbal elements still necessarily present features and conditions of their own.  First, then, as regards the *voice*.  Quite apart from its history, the voice is by its very nature unique among instruments.  The obvious and direct human character impressed on it by its mode of production, and by its employment of language, gives it a certain emotional quality over and above the mere musical quality of its *timbre*: and the fact that it is an absolute physical possession, as distinct from a faculty for performing on an external instrument, involves a quite special power of awakening interest; for everyone has a voice of some sort, in comparison with which the gifted and trained organ seems to accomplish miracles.  The conse-quences of this supremacy of a special instrument, dating especially from one remarkable epoch in its history, have not been an unmixed blessing to art.  In spite of the remote origin of Song, the systematic cultivation of the voice with a view to solo-singing may be said to date (in the modern era at any rate) from the foundation of the Neapolitan school of music by the great composer and teacher Alessandro Scarlatti, towards the close of the seventeenth century. At that time Italy was not only the chief but the only purveyor of cultivated voices and a good method of singing. To the intercourse which Handel enjoyed with Scarlatti and his pupils, during his three years' visit to Italy at the beginning of his career, must be attributed much of his subsequent success: to the same source also must we attribute his having written so much music for the simple purpose of vocal display. A composer of that time, to whom the beauty and capabilities of the human voice were a novel and amazing discovery, a gift of Italy to the world, was like a child with an enchanting new toy; he could not make enough of it, nor exhaust the passages adapted to show off its strength and flexibility. But though it is perhaps fortunate for Handel's reputation that his operas, in spite of the gems they contain, are never now heard as a whole, we must in judging him take account of the novelty of the field and the joy in extending it, and his achievements in the highest regions of his art may well procure for some of his less worthy voice-writing an indulgence which modern manufacturers of *bravura* passages can in no way claim.

Its more systematic cultivation has not been an unmixed benefit.

To us who have seen more of the barren glories and the paralysing influence of mere virtuosoship, passages written for the purpose of concentrating attention not on musical beauty, but on the mechanical capacities of a performer, must appear entirely contemptible, and their prevalence in modern days has simply been a blight on Song. It is saddening to see the slender wealth of naturally first-rate and carefully cultivated voice-power in existence, engaged so often in the brainless, soulless task of displaying its resources as an instrument, its colour and its compass, to the neglect of all its chances of art-presentation—sure enough of dazzling feeble hearers into the belief that tinsel is gold. To see a set of *habitués*, especially in Paris, listening to a celebrated *prima donna* in an Italian opera, is like seeing grown-up people sighing and palpitating with bliss over bonbons. The interest evoked by the melodies is so far to the good, for a love of melody of whatever kind involves a certain amount of active apprehension and a possibility of healthy growth; but this interest is faint by comparison, and the palpitations only set in with the stage of trills and cadenzas. Every formless group of sounds, every meaningless vocal trick, every little sugared turn, is followed and sucked in with a morbid kind of sensual abandonment and greeted with tumultuous bravos; this is what they call appreciating the *finesses*, which they consider a Parisian speciality. It would be absurd to vent moral indignation on what certainly cannot be plausibly connected with immoral results; but this glorification of themselves as the supreme critical tribunal, on the ground that they purr when they are tickled, is a sufficiently exasperating piece of pretension, and one unfortunately to which a certain class of *dilettanti* in every musical centre supply a parallel.

The extreme distinctness with which vocal parts stand out.
Another noticeable peculiarity of the voice is the fact of its standing, by dint of its verbal utterance, so wholly distinct from its instrumental accompaniment, that the response and interplay between the two may become quite a separate feature in vocal composition, leading to all kinds of variety of treatment. In choruses also the special differentiation of parts, which is involved in the assigning of different verbal groups or syllables of varying durations to different voices, affords peculiar opportunities for imitation and response and for effective massings and contrasts, and repetition of the same words often gives peculiar point and piquancy to the entrance of the musical subjects.

§ 10. The words : they suggest the rhythm and general character of the Music ;
Next as regards the *words* themselves. Not only may they suggest the rhythmic outline and often the general movement and character of the music, sometimes even lending themselves to spontaneous musical analogies and something like definite illustration, but in a prolonged work they give a basis and a *raison d'être* to the succession of musical paragraphs. For Music, though most precise in the form of its melodic organisms and authoritative in its manipulation of the obedient verbal syllables, is most ductile in the matter of the order, relations, and connections of these complete or quasi-complete subordinate forms in a continuous series, and will blend a stream of them with anything the unity and coherence of which is justified on its own merits to the intelligence. Thus in dramatic

and in dramatic writing they supply a unity and coherence which the stream of musical paragraphs on its own account would lack ;
writing the melodic paragraphs and passages which are self-contained enough to be susceptible of some sort of detachment in the musical memory, may often be shorter and more numerous, and may succeed each other with far less structural coherence, than would be possible where the justification was not given in the natural length, order, and character of the accompanying verbal sentences. A *scene*, as compared with an instrumental *piece*, admits of changes and counter-changes in pace and character of movement which would sound wholly irrational without such justification ; each musical sentence or section evidently having its accepted place on grounds other than its purely *structural* and musical relation to antecedent and subsequent clauses. In the binding of sections into a prolonged series, the musical sense (which is busy with the notes) comes to a kind of agreement with the understanding (which is busy with the associated words and actions) as to the amount of change and laxity that it will tolerate. It would resent, for instance, having the time altered every four

and they may even justify more definite peculiarities in the music.
bars. There are, however, certain more definite peculiarities which may occasionally present themselves in the union of words and music, the criterion of such cases being that the exact reproduction of the notes apart from the words would altogether lack point and intelligibility. These

features occur most naturally in comic writing; where oddnesses and un-expected combinations, waitings and tantalisations, dwellings on a phrase or exceptional rapidity of utterance, echo and answer between voice and accompaniment, whimsical attempts at real suggestions of external realities, seem to find a reasonable place.

Whether the union with words, in relaxing to some extent the conditions of musical structure, relaxes also the conditions of musical beauty, will be more conveniently discussed in the chapter on Opera. But we may glance here at the terms of alliance, so far as they affect the verbal element. The charm of the union will be found, then, to be indefinitely lost, if (1) the words are such as to demand a purely intellectual effort of apprehension, or (2) are strikingly weak and foolish, or (3) are in an unfamiliar language. The *first* of these three suppositions is the least practically important. The predominance of a reflective and argumentative element is too ob-viously incongruous to song to be found anywhere, except in certain parts of church compositions; and no one is likely to think of putting notes to Hamlet's soliloquy, or to a paragraph from *The Ring and the Book.* With respect to the *second* supposition, we may remark that music has rather oscillated between two extremes in its connection with words. In the later middle ages, when the best musicians wrote for Latin prose liturgies, there was no vital union of any sort: the composer used his prose pegs as he chose, and the performers took revenge on the ponderous scientific compositions they had to sing by all sorts of irreverent variations of the text. And when secular vocal music (which had of course always existed among the people) was at last received and nurtured by scientific musi-cians, the new and rapid development of its beauties seems to have had a dazzling effect; so that the words, as in the church-music, though for a different reason, received the most cavalier treatment. Anything was good enough that gave a beautiful voice the right number of syllables to sing. Addison remarked, and Beaumarchais repeated, that people sang what was too foolish to bear being said: and though exceptions were of course abundant, the last century certainly produced no body of composi-tion which, in the perfection of the alliance of music and words, can the least compare with the songs of Schubert and Schumann. Theatrical works, written as they have often been expressly for particular singers, have naturally been the chief offenders; one unfortunate result of which (as we shall see later) is that in the reaction from this degradation, the words are too often expected to supply sense and coherence not only for themselves but for the notes they go with.

The *third* of the three cases suggests several considerations as to the language of the words, and especially in respect of the unique prestige of the Italian language in connection with Opera. Considering that both

*Three charac-teristics of the verbal element by which the charm of song may suffer: the predomin-ance of a too distinctly in-tellectual ele-ment;*

*striking weak-ness;*

*and the being in an unfami-liar language.*

vocal compositions and vocal skill issued mainly from Italy at the time
when opera was spreading through Europe, we cannot indeed wonder that
Italian opera took root as such in foreign countries. The result, however,
has been to stereotype conditions most adverse to the development of art.
Though great rubbish may often be endured when delivered in English, the
hopelessly frigid and trivial dialogues and monologues so common in Italian
*libretti* would hardly pass muster in the native language of a serious nation ;
or at all events a larger number would protest against them, and we should
not see the points at which Addison's contemporaries 'could not forbear
laughing' accepted as a matter of course. It is curious how faithfully
fashion and dilettanteism has favoured this Italian domination. To take a
single instance, it was with the greatest difficulty that even Weber, when
director at Dresden, could obtain a hearing for native works or for the
native language ; and his own music was steadily ignored by the upper
classes of society until its success elsewhere made the public energetic in
their demands for it. The rage for foreign artists, and the humiliating
fact that English ones find it expedient to adopt Italian names, are indications of the same tendency. Granting all this, however, it may be objected
that the southern tongue is easy and pleasant to sing : but in the face of
the singing one has heard of English, French, and German, this will hardly
be accepted as a valid excuse for the wholesale translation into Italian which
has become a fixed custom. Every musician with a feeling for words will
write best for his own language ; and in the translator's hands any special
point and freshness which the setting has is too likely to disappear.[1]
Translations into the native language stand of course on an altogether
separate footing : but the presentation to an English audience of a French
opera in an Italian version, with the vivacious dialogue in the spoken parts
represented by the dreariest and most conventional recitative, is an
absurdity as wanton as it is inartistic.

Words need
not be of high
independent
merit to be
very suitable
for song.

We cannot at all reckon as among the conditions which make words
suitable for alliance with music, that they should be of high poetical
character. While inferior music kills good words, and while many words
of highly poetical character are quite unsuited to musical setting of any
sort, rhythmical words of comparatively ordinary character may be eminently suited to it; and in contributing to the dual effect of Song they are
often themselves so transfigured as to seem to gain entirely new point and
significance. This very fact may naturally tend to conceal the smallness
of their independent poetical merits : for even when we try to think of
them independently, the glow from another region will be apt to cling

---

[1] It would be difficult, for instance, for
English ears listening to Handel's setting of
*Alexander's Feast*, and familiar with the
line ' So Love was crowned, but Music won
the cause,' to acquiesce in ' Dir, Tonkunst,
Ehre und Dank,' as a representative of its
second clause.

about them. In throwing an indescribable romance over the most artless expressions of sentiment and over employments of poetical imagery which certainly could claim no attention on their own account, Music acts not by delusion and jugglery, but by supplying a definite beauty, which gives a substance, so to speak, in which the diffused associations suggested by the words can rest and blend.

We have considered thus far the ways in which the two factors of Song affect one another, and some of their mutual requirements. We have still to enquire what is the fundamental nature of the æsthetic effect which the union produces. The ordinary statement would of course be that the music *expresses*, or should express, the words. After the lengthy discussion in the fourteenth chapter, it is hardly necessary to point out in what a broad and general (as opposed to a detailed and exact) sense this is true; though it is naturally to melodies which have been deliberately associated with the precise meaning and sentiment of definite words that we should look for examples of the most definite and describable emotional qualities that Music can possess. With a slight amount of external assistance we can really sometimes make pretty clear distinctions. Thus, given that the theme is love, the strains in which Polyphemus addresses Galatea might make us guess, apart from title and words, the fierce rollicking nature of his passion; we shall not confound the yearning passion of Schubert's *Serenade* with the satisfied meditative rapture of *Love in her eyes*, or with the half-gay, half-tender gallantry of the guitar-song in *Don Giovanni*. But the majority even of beautiful vocal melodies will be found, by any one who tries without any external knowledge to guess the character of the words they go with, to be neutral in respect of describable emotional suggestion, except within the widest and vaguest limits, while in their own *in*describable way stirring the very depths of musical feeling. We should resent, of course, clear contradictions; we should object to glad and sportive words delivered in solemn numbers, and to excited and passionate sentiments linked to a serene or ingenuous melody. But given the most general correspondence, the music, if really worth anything, may be trusted to make it appear sufficiently definite: such is the power of beautiful melody to wed itself to that with which it is associated that the electrical union seems actually to represent an inherent oneness of purport.

It is this power in Music to *accaparer* its concomitants, and to impress the whole effect with the stamp of its own beautiful individuality, which has led to the notion that the affinity of the notes and the words is primarily and naturally a delicate instead of a general one. The instantaneous closeness of the association makes it hard to prove, by particular cases in one's own experience, that the same words would link themselves as closely with quite another tune (as might be shown in fifty other

§ 11. The music can *express* the words only in a very broad and general sense;

though a little external assistance enables the expression sometimes to seem pretty distinct,

The power of beautiful music to associate itself intimately with its concomitants creates the feeling that it is definitely and delicately expressive.

settings), and the same tune with quite other words ;[1] and when two things go exquisitely together it is hard to help conceiving them as delicately and uniquely akin.   Even a composer may very easily think and say that his music was *suggested* by the words.   He sits down with the words in his head, and his musical faculty ranges among phrases and shadows of phrases, pervaded by a certain conformity of general character, plaintive, impetuous, or whatever it be, to which the words will rhythmically go. The words, then, having been there to begin with, naturally appear to him as at the bottom of the result, and the music as in a way evolved out of them.   Had he been a versifier instead of a musician he might have equally well wrought out the words from the ' suggestion ' of the tune.[2]

The same generality of expressive character applies to single striking features in the music.

What has been said as to the expressive character of a melody or musical piece, taken as a whole, applies equally to details.   Points of change and contrast, harmonic turns, striking features of any sort, which would be really available for a very wide range of turns of sentiment and for a great variety of suggestive single words, will seem actually made for the particular verbal point which they emphasise.   Take, for instance, the point in the fourth bar on p. 324, quoted from *Die Böse Farbe* ; or the notes to *Virtue sickens* on the next page.

Mechanical imitation, admitting of various degrees.

No precise line can be drawn between this sort of expression and that more mechanical suggestion which consists in more or less direct imitation. The latter sort, while usually absurd, as we have seen, in serious music, may be in place where intentionally comic.   Thus in Pergolesi's *La Serva Padrona*, when Uberto says to the maid, ' Troppo in alto voi volate,' there is an upward flight on *volate* : and even the humour of such a concrete suggestion may be delightfully mingled with beauty, as in the debonair hopping of the accompaniment to the air *Their land brought forth frogs*.   A good instance

---

[1] The history of musical compositions abounds with instances of adaptations and changes in the connection of words and music.  An impassioned air in *Rinaldo* was adapted to a bacchanalian song beginning, ' Let the waiter bring clean glasses,' and was long popular at festive gatherings; and on several occasions Handel even laid his operas under contribution for the music of his oratorios.  Berlioz used to amuse himself by singing tunes with Italian words, and waiting till his hearers had demonstrated how successfully the character of the Italian verse had inspired the composer, before informing them that the music was from a symphony of Beethoven.  Similar tricks might really be repeated to any extent.

[2] There is no reason, in the nature of things, why the setting of words to pre-existent music should not be much more frequent than it is.  But poets, of course, write normally meaning their productions to stand independently, and introducing their own metrical effects ; while musicians do not write vocal melodies, adapted to be sung, without intending that they shall be sung, and so needing words for them from the outset.  But in writing a joint work, for the stage, for instance, a composer who had invented a good melody, of a character appropriate at a certain place in connection with certain sentiments, might fairly call on his librettist to follow him to this extent.  For one and the same meaning can be conveyed in a hundred ways in words, and set in many sorts of metrical framework, which makes it a comparatively easy task to accommodate words to music ; while a melody, once there, is a form which can only make compromises by ceasing to be itself.

of expression which is in itself less mechanically imitative than this, and enters naturally as an excellent phrase in an excellent melody, is the passage—

Yet hard to tame as rag - ing flame, And fierce as storms that bluster.

from *O ruddier than the cherry.* An equally good case, depending on harmony, is the passage from *Envy, eldest born of hell*—

Hide thee in the black - - - - est night! Vir - tue

sick - ens at thy sight! Vir - tue sick - ens at thy sight!

But the attempt to produce such effects in an isolated way, without, as here, embodying them as part of a fine form, is apt to degenerate into a barren and unimpressive sort of emphasis. A leading newspaper remarked lately, *à propos* of the *Dido and Æneas*, that it was interesting to observe Purcell's attempts ' at illustrating certain detached words by musical phrases. No sooner do such words as *storm* and *fierce* occur than a striking passage of demisemiquavers is found to give them additional import.' The import may be questioned. The same journal, in criticising another work, considered it a proof of intelligence in the treatment of the text that ' could not be sufficiently praised,' that ' whenever a sentence or a single word called for additional emphasis the composer was sure to have his *forte* in readiness.' The worth of emphasis depends of course on the worth of the music: it is easy to print the greatest rubbish in capitals.

It seems, then, that the singular charm which results from the union of words and music must have some more constant and fundamental source than such a character in the music as might lead us, if we heard it apart from the words, to surmise in a very general way the character of the words. And indeed it is obvious that something more than mere broad

§ 12. We need some more fundamental reason for the charm in the union of words and music:

resemblances in the describable character of two things is necessary to produce a sense of definite objective union: for our broad impressions of solemnity, peace, vigour, vulgarity, or whatever it may be, are common to all manner of experiences due to all sorts of phenomena, without our thereby perceiving the various sources of analogous impressions under the aspect of a single compound result. What, then, are the conditions of such union between the arts as results in compound works? That this union is desirable where attainable is clear on *à priori* grounds: for two pleasures fully realised cannot but be better than one, apart from the added pleasure in their fusion. Art, however, makes so large a demand on the attention that no two branches of it will be susceptible of simultaneous realisation unless they present some distinct element in common.[1] In the case of

---

[1] Taking the three elements of *subject-matter*, *material*, and *form*, from the tabular statement in the third chapter, we may glance at the chances they afford of organic union between the arts. First, as regards *subject-matter*, we can obviously, while looking at a picture, think of a cognate poetical passage, and enjoy each the more, feeling the kinship in penetration of the two artists: but here the union, though close, is a subjective one, a result of our own making, not constituting and presenting to us a compound object. On the stage, indeed, the poetry and the painted scene may be considered factors of a compound result: the union here, however, seems very mechanical, even if moderately permanent; we would sacrifice it in a moment for a bare barn *plus* the rare and transient personality of a great actor. Moreover, while the character of modern drama demands accessories of which no need was felt beneath the glorious sky of Athens, the artificial lighting that belongs to late hours and northern climates clearly prevents the exercise of the highest artistic qualities in the scene-painter.

Painting and Sculpture, again, can deal with the same *subject-matter*; and the *forms* of Sculpture are forms of the same objects as Painting can represent, and can be covered with colour. But here difficulties in the way of union are presented, partly by the nature of the sculptured material, partly by the fact that solidity implies perpetually shifting light and shade, and a number of different points of view, most of them close to the actual object: so that the painter's art is precluded from all its finer qualities of *chiaroscuro* and tone, from all indications of light and atmosphere, and is narrowed down to a

mechanical sort of tinting. And this tinting seems calculated to emphasise the merely imitative at the expense of the ideal qualities of sculpture, and to be inconsistent with its simple and typical character. Colour is indeed conceivable when the work is composed of its substance, as in the gold and ivory statues of Phidias, where too the independent beauty and value of the material would much enhance the sense of glory. In connection with a large scheme of colour, again, in the adornment of buildings, Sculpture was very commonly painted by the Greeks. But in detached works anything like imitative colour seems tawdry and ephemeral when laid on the surface and impertinently hiding material whose simple and imperishable aspect is precisely adapted to set forth the glories of form unobscured by secondary qualities; so that Mr. Ruskin has said, 'If we could colour the Elgin marbles with the flesh-tint of Giorgione, I had rather not have it done.' In many other branches of production which may be loosely classed with sculpture, china and terra-cotta and metal works of many sorts, an artistic use of colour, natural and artificial, is an essential element; but it would be unnatural to represent these as unions of the two main imitative arts.

It is rather in the union of Architecture with these two imitative arts that community in the element of *material* (and to some extent even of *form*) is available. First, we see that, as Painting has for its material pigments and surfaces, Architecture supplies it with the latter; and that the material of Sculpture, stone and marble, is also common to Architecture. So that these two arts of representation may become an organic part

Music and Poetry there is a community of *material,* in so far, at all events, as the words of the one and the notes of the other are given forth in a single action by the same voice ; and also in rhythm a common element of *form,* so far as the independent metrical flow of the verse makes itself felt ; which it will do provided the normal accentuation and the prominence of the rhymes be to any moderate degree preserved.   But the union of these two arts presents a quite unique vividness of effect, owing to their being presented in time and not in space, so that their appeals to the ear are, from moment to moment, fused in absolute coincidence, while at the same time their ultimate appeal is to two totally distinct faculties, the musical sense and the intelligence for verbally conveyed ideas.   The result is that here we get in its most complete form that perception of two lines of things under an aspect of unity, which we have already several times encountered in the separate domains both of Music and of verse.   Where the natural verbal flow is preserved we feel, in the set of common accents dominating both words and notes, a further perfection of fusion ; but independently of metrical conditions the words have always their own line of meaning. And the melody apart from the words, like the words apart from the melody, seems to be something which the voice, without metaphor, has to *tell* us, beautiful melody being in the most literal sense eloquent.   So that when the two phenomena are combined in Song, the duality of utterance, the expression in a single act of one set of things under the forms, simultaneously revealed, of another, in throwing, as it often does, a romance over the simplest words and subjects, gives to the indivisible effect a quality which is attainable in no other sort of artistic presentation.   How much more fundamental this quality is than the adaptation of the general character, or of certain characteristics, of the particular music to cognate qualities in the particular words, is sufficiently seen in the fact that the mere union in vocal expression of the two distinct lines of utterance begets an altogether peculiar and indisputable charm in countless cases where no such adaptation can be adduced.

One or two less vital and universal points are still worth mentioning, as entering at times into the total æsthetic effect of Song, and as made possible by the peculiar conditions of that one mode of performance.

Words can be dwelt on in Song and emphasised not only through musical resonance of voice, but by actual pronunciation and gesture, with

*and find it in the joint perception of two lines of things separately intelligible, under an aspect of unity.*

*§ 13. Less vital points.*

---

of buildings, and even their informing spirit ; Sculpture especially, through its ability to follow the lines and angles of the structure, contributing expressiveness and symbolism to every nook and corner, and ranging from more or less abstract ornament, founded generally on vegetable forms, to direct representation.

The community between Music and Poetry,

in respect both of *material* and *form,* is mentioned in the text.   A more constant and perfect community in the rhythmic element is presented by the alliance of artistic dancing with Music ; and, as they address different senses, their union may give at its best an extraordinary richness of pleasure ; but we have seen that dancing cannot be reckoned as a ' work of art.'

Opportunities
in Song for
emotional
gestures and
modes of
enunciation.
a force and passion or some kind of emotional variation which in unadorned speech would seem ludicrous, owing to the extreme divergence from the ordinary conventional standard. For accents and gestures which are as it were on the same plane as that standard would be inevitably referred to it, whereas the allied music conveys all the phenomena of utterance into another region beyond risk of comparison.

The oneness of
a voice with a
personality.
Again, the absolute oneness of a voice with a personality gives to Song, in one aspect and in rare instances, a pre-eminence among all kinds of artistic performance. In itself it seems so wholly a natural endowment that we instinctively feel in it an ideally fitting emotional outlet for any being in whose nature lies the secret of expression, and in such a one other gifts seem to associate their charm indefinably with this one. Dancing alone (if we neglect considerations of education and concomitants and the

extreme rareness of perfect solo-dancing) could be compared with Song in this respect. But apart from the great difference in the range of the music connected with the two manifestations, the singer is naturally more wholly a living part of the melody which she [1] reveals than the dancer can be of the music by which she is accompanied, or (as it should be) which she accompanies: so that the singer, in far greater degree than the dancer, is glorified by association with the supreme, independent, and permanent world of beauty with whose very essence she seems instinct. I am not comparing the whole effects of the two presentations, but a single factor only; and in the one case it seems possible for intelligence and inspiration to stand confessed in a degree to which no grace of bodily form or rhythmic movement can absolutely testify. Beautiful music is of course quite essential to the total result in dancing, but, from its externality to the dancer's actual part in the result it cannot be charged and moulded by her comprehension or emotion, and cannot in turn invest her individuality with its most ideal halo. And in feeling that her whole connection with the world of high art is perhaps confined to the mere moments of perform-ance, we may experience a half-latent but tantalising impression of transience and accident, and a doubt as to the actual relation of physical to spiritual endowment; while in imagination we picture the singer as speaking a language of which at all times, speaking and silent, she has inspired intelligence, to be showing us the forms among which she has her being, and in the love of which we joyfully recognise a common bond, so that idealisation passes readily on from the gift of the individual to the awakened and awakenable sensibilities of the race.

[1] I say *she,* not because I at all hold the view of Artemus Ward as to male performers that they 'orter lead armies on to Battel instid of shoutin in a furrin tung;' but because it must be admitted that where the most perfect success is due to the union of charm of person and personality, with an emotional activity wholly removed from the stern world of action, the implied faculties and attributes lend themselves to idealisation most naturally and spontaneously in the case of a woman.

One more remark may be made as to the combination of the gift of song with genius and other endowments. In analysing the delight we derive from the singing (with or without a fine voice in the ordinary sense) of a person whose nature is vividly interesting to us, we shall find, I think, that it is partly due to a perception of the voluntary subjection of freedom and spontaneity to law, of the singer's obedience to a definite order of presentation imagined and set forth by the genius of another. Somewhat as the essential force of words gains instead of losing by its restraint within the forms of metre, so all independent individuality seems to gain piquancy from the sense that in one direction its possessor is self-controlled into being the medium and channel of an ordered beauty existing outside the personality of this or that performer, and appealing on its inherent merits to the emotions of the listeners.

The subjection to control in the delivery of set notes enhances the charm of a singer's individuality.

Finally, it is curious to think by what a mechanical accident, as it were, the ideal power of Song over the feelings of men exists, and how easily one might conceive it eliminated from the world. For voices are not like fingers : the cases are certainly a small minority where the vocal cords are so constructed as to be able to produce musical notes of sufficient merit strongly to gratify the ear, and so to serve as adequate musical material. Had such cases been considerably rarer still, while we should have been just as we are for all practical purposes, and while speech would have been just what it is now, this one unique phenomenon of Song could never have attained high development. It is true that peculiarly gifted persons may delight us by singing even with very little ' voice,' but the place of the vocal element in Music must be admitted to be dependent on the existence of fine voices in the world. The chances are, of course, tremendous against the combination in one person of exceptional vocal cords with musical and other endowments ; and it is just the possessors of the most exceptional physical gifts who are most tempted to prostitute them. But given fairly adequate conditions, the immediate power of one being over the feelings of another seems at its maximum in a case where no external tools or appliances are involved, where nature and art appear one, where phenomena of absolute beauty can be presented as though part of the normal communication of man to man, and where in addition the use of the familiar words heightens this naturalness of address, and completes the directness and spontaneity of the effect. Many will attend when addressed in this way whose lives would otherwise lie wholly apart from the influence of beautiful and pure emotion. In the midst of this normal sad remoteness the effect of Song on the masses is like a glimpse of infinite spiritual possibilities ; and owing to the fewness of the moments where even the suggestion of a universal kinship in lofty sentiment appears possible, such occasions seem to have a very singular and impressive significance in human life.

§ 14. Fine voices are sufficiently rare to make it seem singularly fortunate that they exist at all.

The unique power of Singing over the feelings.

# CHAPTER XXI.

### THE SPEECH THEORY.

§ 1. The theory of the derivation of Music from the cadences of emotional speech.

THERE is a certain theory of the influence of speech on Music which could not be conveniently noticed till we had discussed the subject of Song. It is a theory so directly opposed to the whole exposition of this book that my answer to it has practically been already given, especially in the chapters on Association, on Melodic Form, on Expression, and on Song: but it is so important both in itself and in its corollaries, it has been so widely held in a more or less vague way, and has lately found such explicit and able advocacy, that it needs a separate survey. The theory, as put forward by Mr. Herbert Spencer in his essay on the *Origin and Function of Music,* is, briefly, that Music has its essential source in the cadences of emotional speech, and that it reacts on speech by increasing the variety, complexity, and expressiveness of those cadences.

Mr. Spencer's view that the peculiarities of emotional speech are exaggerated in song.

Mr. Spencer founds his theory on the view that the vocal peculiarities which indicate excited feeling are those which especially distinguish Song from ordinary speech, and sums them up under the heads of loudness, quality, or *timbre,* marked deviation from an average level of pitch, width of interval, and rapid rate of variation. He considers that Song arose from emphasising and intensifying these peculiarities. Deferring the question as to how far this view, if accurate, would support the theory of derivation, we may first notice how far it is from being accurate on any one of the heads. Loudness though a frequent is by no means a universal or essential element, either of Song or of emotional speech. Still less is musical resonance an essential element of the latter.

Objections to that view, as regards quality of sound;

Many of the tones of excited speech are even more removed from musical quality than those of ordinary speech, as containing a greater number of spasmodic noises and of the high harmonics which produce what we call harshness: and this must have been especially the case among our remote ancestors when the savage emotions were in the ascendant. The large part held in the emotional colouring of speech by elements which are pointedly *un*musical will appear in several ways, but this of quality is a very important one. For the emotional colouring is, of course, largely connected with the broad distinctions between the agreeable and disagreeable classes of feeling : and this distinction is mainly expressed in speech through the *quality* of the sound used, if we include under that term particular modes of attacking and bringing out the words. That increase of muscular effort on which Mr. Spencer lays stress may take effect quite as easily in increase of the harsh qualities of sound as in increase of the musically resonant qualities. Music, on the other hand, even when attempting to suggest disagreeable feelings, has never emphasised or exaggerated the harsher kinds of *timbre* or more spasmodic modes of utterance : and Wagner himself has not required that Ortrud's music shall be sung by a woman with a cracked voice, or accompanied by a cat obbligato. Even if we take the residue of tones expressing pleasing emotions and having increased resonance of an agreeable kind, and if we accept Mr. Spencer's view of such emotional speech as being prior to Music, the fact remains that agreeable sounds are only the *material* of Music ; and it is open to us to suppose that our human or semi-human ancestors, having been naturally moved to desert the region of neutral tones in order to be pleasingly emphatic, may have utilised for independent musical purposes the material of increased resonance so discovered and developed, in accordance with the well-known fact that ' organs originally adapted for one purpose have been utilised for some quite distinct purpose.' It is of course equally open to us, if we accept Mr. Darwin's hypothesis that the power of making musical sounds was acquired for sexual purposes in the pre-human stage, to suppose that the more resonant sounds, first developed in this elementary love-music, were subsequently employed where emphasis was required for purposes of emotional speech. And, looked at in the light merely of musical material, I can hardly imagine that certain vocal tones are regarded by Mr. Spencer as owing their agreeable quality simply to association with kindness and pleasing emotions. Yet he says, as though it were a *reductio ad absurdum*, that if the conclusiveness of his reasoning is not admitted, it must be supposed that vibrations causing soft sounds are intrinsically better than those causing harsh. Why of course they are intrinsically better as far as our ears are concerned, in precisely the same way as an octave is intrinsically a more agreeable chord than a sharp seventh, or a feather-bed a more agreeable couch than a heap of stones. The ear objects to the irregularities and roughnesses present in harsh sounds just as the body objects to the contact of rough irregular surfaces.

In dealing with the three remaining heads of what he considers common characteristics of emotional speech and Song, Mr. Spencer's statements seem to me even more open to exception. In the recitative which he himself considers naturally and historically a step between speech and Song, the rapid variation of pitch is impossible, and such recitative is distinguished from the tones even of common speech precisely by

and as regards rapid variation of pitch and width of interval.

being more monotonous. To suppose with Mr. Spencer that the *four-toned* recitative of early Greek poets was the slightly exaggerated emotional speech natural to them, would imply a poor idea of their emotional speech.[1] Nor does this apply only to recitative : the use of extremely few degrees of the scale is, as Helmholtz has remarked, an almost universal characteristic of all early melody. Mr. Spencer himself notices the monotony of savage dance-songs and ancient Eastern chants, and says that hence we may infer the divergence of vocal music from emotional speech to have been gradual and unobtrusive. Surely, if one thing differs from another in a special way from the very first, the theory that it diverged from it in the exactly opposite direction is not much helped by calling the divergence unobtrusive. And though it is true that developed Song and excited speech often do agree in the mere fact of deviating from an average level of pitch, the deviations, even in the most favourable instances for a comparison, are of a totally different kind ; those of speech being sudden and spasmodic, ranging rapidly up and down in a series of mere see-saws, perpetually taking very wide intervals even on a single syllable, and making nothing of a twelfth or a couple of octaves, in a way which Song, so far from exaggerating, would find it impossible and absurd even distantly to emulate. And it may be noticed, too, that even a considerable range of the voice in Song does not imply emotional conditions the least resembling those of excited speech. For speech obeys instinctively the physiological laws of emotion, which entail under excitement a larger discharge of muscular energy, and so larger vocal activity : while Song demands perpetual conscious efforts, and may bring the extremes of the vocal register quite as much into play in an adagio movement as in a presto ; so that a melody may be a considerable strain to the voice while presenting the most peaceful character.

But the objection may be brought to a more definite issue. Even in perfectly developed modern melody large intervals and extremes and rapid variations of pitch are in a very small minority as compared with their opposites. Hundreds of well-known melodies, thousands of fine and stirring melodic themes, are comprised within the limits of an octave or less; limits which, if suddenly imposed on the speaking voice, would check emotional speech nearly as much as having one's hands tied behind one's back would check emotional gestures. Again, if musical composers had begun by expressing their feelings in more extreme intervals than those of speech, and had gone on, as Mr. Spencer supposes, increasing this peculiarity, why is a semitone often the keystone of a melodic passage, and how

[1] Since more developed Greek music is often spoken of as though it were a kind of idealised declamation, it may be mentioned that Dionysius of Halicarnassus expressly points out and illustrates the absolute irrelevance of the course of the notes, in vocal melodies, to the pitch-inflections of the words as spoken.

is it that a vast number of the most emotional melodies in the world proceed almost entirely by the smallest possible degrees? In modern music, which has the assistance of harmony, the most exciting melodic passage may even consist of mere monotone. There are few things in Music more passionate than some bars in Schubert's *Addio,* where the voice repeats the same note sixteen times, and the effect is produced purely through the rhythm and harmony. On the other hand any one may convince himself that not only are the intervals used in emotional speech very large, twelve diatonic notes being quite an ordinary skip, but that he uses extremes of both high and low pitch with his speaking voice, which, if he tries to dwell on them and make them resonant, will be found to lie beyond the compass of his singing voice. In saying 'I never heard of such a thing' in a tone of strong excitement, I find that I use the high tenor B for the word *I* and the first syllable of *never,* a note far above any that I can sing, and go down for the second syllable of *never* as far as the low G or F, which is the extreme of what I can sing in that direction.

But the mere presence of these general characteristics in the succession of sounds in a melody and the succession of sounds in emotional speech, even if the parallelism were such as Mr. Spencer conceives, would be entirely insufficient to establish any sort of true kinship, whether of origin or of nature, between the cadences of speech and those of music. For instance, in delivering the word 'heigh-ho' with the expression one would naturally give as one leans back and stretches one's arms with a sense of relief and relaxation after some tedious piece of work, the voice may naturally begin at a somewhat high pitch and descend slowly and gradually over the interval of an octave, thus—

§ 2. Irrelevance of this parallelism of general characteristics, even if it were such as Mr. Spencer imagines.

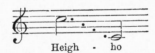

Heigh - ho

The sounds may be delivered loudly, with a good deal of singing resonance; the range of pitch is large, the combination is particularly simple and distinct, and generally the conditions for conveying a distinct emotional expression are present. Now we will take a melodic combination which keeps quite exceptionally close to the same 'cadence'—

The gradual descent from C to its octave may be made to occupy just the same time in the case of 'heigh-ho' as in the case of this final line of *Ein' feste Burg*; and this single comparison will, I think, suggest how irrelevant the general traits of loudness, resonance, &c., are to the essence of the musical effect. We may play the melodic phrase on a penny whistle or a double-bass, loud or soft, and even with very considerable variations in pace, and its musical essence and individuality is perfectly distinct and unchanged; while its expression, so far as it is describable, is of strength and confidence, and at the very extreme pole from that of 'heigh-ho.'

We may take one more instance. If some one came to me and said the weather was uncertain, when I particularly wanted to start on an excursion, I might answer, ' No, is it going to rain? dear, what a dreadful bore!' in tones which as musically represented might approximate to

No,   is   it  going  to  rain?   dear,  what  a   dread  -  ful  bore!

making a considerable descent on the syllable *dread-*. Does the emotional effect here so strikingly resemble that of the following motive—

from the march in Weber's *Concertstück*, that we should feel impelled to affiliate the latter on the former?

It is obvious, moreover, that the landmarks and directions, which the course in pitch of a single sentence may happen to trace out, may be taken possession of by the elements of melodic form with many different results. The course over the descending octave of 'heigh-ho,' for instance, is the course adopted by a large number of melodic phrases, as different from *Ein' feste Burg* as from one another. Are they all the natural progeny of 'heigh-ho'?

§ 3. Examination of the 'cadences of speech.' They are extremely uncertain and are practically innumerable.

The essence of a melodic form being independent of register and *timbre*, it is clear that in considering melodic formation and its supposed derivation from the cadences of speech, the whole point lies in the pitch-relations of the successive sounds in speech, the *tune*-element, if such there be. How completely this ground fails beneath our feet the above examples will have sufficiently shown: but it will be well to examine a little further into the so-called 'cadences of speech;' for the very phrase tends to suggest a sort of definiteness in the various series of sounds produced in speech which is quite unreal. No one who has not tried carefully and repeatedly can tell the difficulty, or rather often the impossibility, of discovering, from the infinitesimal portion of musical tone present in the ordinary intonations of speech, what actual point of pitch he uses in the successive sounds. Especially when any large interval is used, the shifting is so rapid that even this minute modicum of tone has often no certain pitch, even for a small fraction of a second; and, moreover, in repeating the same word several times over, one may vary the size of the interval within very wide limits and still convey the same ethical impression. The voice is not the least bound down to clean intervals; the common intervals of the octave and fifth may be flattened and sharpened or changed into intervals differing from them by as much as two or three tones, including all the intermediate degrees of distance, and still sound perfectly natural; [1] and twenty people might say the same few words with what would sound like similar intonation, that is, going up and down at the same places, yet differ altogether in the actual intervals. Nor is it even likely that they will at all accurately agree in the places where they go up and down. It is unfortunately impossible to convey the intonations of speech on paper; but I would undertake in a three minutes' interview to convince any one that even a quite short sentence may be naturally spoken by one person with half-a-dozen entirely distinct intonations (to say nothing of the infinite number of minor modifications which might supervene on each of these if others imitated them), while involving hardly any variation in the sort of ethical expression intended. I have seen it stated that there are opposite sorts of cadence assigned to opposed sorts of ethical intention, as that the intonation naturally ascends in supplication and descends in command. We have only to try. '*Please* give it me' is most naturally delivered with a markedly heightened pitch on the *please*, and the other three words considerably lower. The command ' Go away' may be given quite as naturally with a sudden rise on the last syllable as with a sudden drop.

*and the variations completely elude rule, even in respect of so general a feature as direction up or down.*

The few rules which can be laid down are of the most general sort, and apply merely to direction and not to interval. In one case of opposites, in the broad classes of emotions distinguished on the one hand by a character of effort and excitement and on the other by a character of relaxation and depression, there is naturally a corresponding tendency in the voice to rise or to sink. Thus a child will cry out, ' I am going to the pláy,' with a rise

*§ 4. The possible rules are extremely few and general.*

---

[1] This is very little realised, but I am entirely persuaded of its truth. In making experiments on the subject, the best way is, not first to take the sentence as spoken, and try to fix the intervals, since it is impossible to be sure of producing exactly the same intonation twice running; but to take first some fixed musical intervals, and distinctly sing them, and to work gradually down to the less distinct speech-tones. Thus, in the instance above given, 'I *né*ver heard of such a thing,' begin by taking the *I* on a high part of the speaking voice, and then *sing* the two syllables of *never*, the first on a note near the highest limit of the voice, the second an octave lower, finishing the sentence in the speaking voice at about the same low pitch as the *ver*. It will be found easy, on repeating this several times, to reduce the amount of musical *timbre* gradually, till the effect is simply of excited utterance, while the interval can still *just* be recognised as an octave. Now repeat the experiment, taking the *ne* a tone higher, and preserving the same pitch for the *ver*, and again reduce the effect to speech-intonation. The effect is still perfectly natural. All that is wanted is that the interval shall be a markedly wide one: given that, any notes will serve. The ethical effect intended increases in intensity as the interval increases, and vanishes as the interval is gradually diminished.

to the emphatic word; while ' O dear, O dear,' delivered in a tone of despondency, will sink all the way.   Even here the irrelevance of the rule as regards the actual ' cadences' can be easily shown.   For the tendency in the voice to drop after a raised emphatic syllable may make any excited sentence in which the most emphatic syllable is not the last, assume at the end exactly the same sounds in pitch as the depressed sentence.   In the sentence, ' I am going to the play to-morrow night,' the last three words may be naturally delivered in a series of sounds whose relations of pitch are indistinguishable from those of ' O dear, O dear.'   The more constant difference between excited and depressed sentences is the pitching of the one altogether in a higher and of the other altogether in a lower register; but this point is of course wholly irrelevant to melodic formation, which depends not on absolute height or depth but on *relations* of pitch.   For an emphatic syllable in the middle of an English sentence the pitch is commonly heightened, with often the hint of a very long drop just at the end of it.   For example, the words, ' I can't understand your saying so,' might be delivered with an emphatic and annoyed expression by treating *can't* or *stand* in the way described.   The sentence, ' Then you ought to have *told* me,' will grow in exasperated character the more the pitch of the *told* is heightened.   But in both these cases *stand* and *told* might be given with the same emotional significance by being emphatically pronounced on a *lower* note than the preceding syllables.   In unemphatic and unemotional speech it is only at the extreme close of sentences that we can discover any sort of definite rule.   The rule for English sentences, delivered without any special ethical emphasis, is that they descend at the close by intervals of which the average would be about a fifth, but which may be considerably more or considerably less.   The descent might be accounted for by the natural relaxation of effort when the voice feels itself just at the end of its task; but such physiological rules do not seem to have any universality of application, for in French the voice perpetually *ascends* at the close by a similar interval, in a manner which it is easier for Englishmen to appreciate than to imitate.   Compare, for instance, the normal English delivery of ' It is incredible' with the normal French delivery of ' C'est incroyable.'   On the other hand, in emotional and poetical utterance English voices perpetually reverse the characteristic, and go up instead of down at the end.   A single instance will show the contrast.   Let any one read the sentence, ' Mill's treatises are most interesting reading, especially that on Liberty:' his voice will be sure to drop on the two last syllables.   But in reading the lines—

> Now high on waves that idly burst,
>   Like Heavenly Hope she crown'd the sea,
> And now, the bloodless point reversed,
>   She bore the blade of Li'ber'ty'—

The natural rise to an emphatic syllable; which may occur as a feature in many quite different inflexions.

English sentences without special emphasis normally descend at the end;

while sentences which are emotionally delivered constantly ascend.

with any sort of emotional emphasis, it is almost impossible to avoid rising at the close.

The general rules which apply to ethical variations of intonation may be best exemplified by taking an interrogative sentence. Interrogative sentences which simply ask a question, without any expression of a bias of idea or sentiment in the speaker's mind, normally rise at the end, the accented syllable before the rise being a little depressed. A very marked rise will give the ethical colouring of surprise: on the other hand a marked drop at the end will imply that a certain definite and foreseen answer is bound to follow. For instance, if we agree that, of the following marks, ′ shall mean heightened pitch, ″ markedly heightened pitch, ‵ lowered and ‶ markedly lowered pitch, the sentence ' Did he give them liberty?' may be enunciated in at least five very distinct ways. First, ' Did he give them li‵ber′ty′?' would be the tone of quite unemotional interrogation, expressing just an ordinary desire to be informed on this particular point. ' Did he give them li‶ber″ty″?' will imply that such a proceeding was certainly not what the speaker would have expected. ' Did he give them li′ber‵ty‵?' implies that the speaker feels he may have done so, but has no strong expectation of it, and attaches some value to having the point cleared up. ' Did he give them li′ber‶ty‵?' implies very decidedly that the answer must be no; and if *did he* be heightened, and the whole range of pitch in the sentence increased, an expression of excited argument will be produced. Finally, the words may be spoken in pure monotone, which will give the impression that the question is one of a necessary series, and that the speaker has no personal interest in the answer; a historical examiner might adopt this tone to a candidate. Unemotional questions are very often asked in monotone with a pitch a little heightened above the average, and if the answer exactly follows the lines of the question, it is commonly given in monotone with a pitch a little below the average— thus, ' Ís thére ánýthíng knówn aboút ít?' ' Nò, therè's nòthìng knòwn àboùt ìt.' The effect of giving the answer here on the same note as the question would be very absurd.[1]

In the fact that such extremely loose and general rules as those I have exemplified are the only ones we can arrive at concerning the actual *pitch*

*Interrogative sentences, exemplifying varieties of inflexion according to the idea in the speaker's mind.*

---

[1] The theory mentioned in the chapter on verse, that the so-called Greek accents were in classical times indicative of pitch and not stress, will be seen now to be not without difficulties of its own, which do not seem to have been enough recognised. Fixity of relative elevation in pitch for the syllables of a word is an unknown phenomenon in modern languages, and seems incompatible with what we are accustomed to consider necessary conditions of expression. There is not a word in English, of two syllables and over, which does not alter the relations-in-pitch of its syllables, according as it occurs at the end of an affirmative or of an interrogative sentence, to say nothing of other more emotional conditions of inflection: and even monosyllables, pronounced in isolation, begin and end on distinct points of pitch which similarly vary their relations under various emotional influences.

§ 5. If we confine ourselves to cases of truly emotional expression, the 'cadences' are still more variable and indefinable, and the rules still more limited.

of the sounds employed, it is sufficiently shown what an infinite and indefinite medley are those 'cadences of speech' which we find talked of as though they were a set of universally recognised successions of tones, appropriated, one apiece, to every shade of feeling we ever experience.   It is to be noticed, moreover, that several of the examples given, where a certain cadence was natural, were not cases of *emotional* expression at all, but only of a certain opinion or expectation in the speaker's mind which was not the least connected with feeling : and if we endeavoured to extend our rules we should find that it was chiefly to cases of that class that some comparative certainty of intonation could be attached.   If we confine ourselves to truly emotional expression, the assignable rules for the pitch of the sounds will be found almost entirely to resolve themselves into the rise and fall for effort and depression, and the greater width of interval and more violent changes for greater intensity of emotion.   Nor will this latter characteristic express the *quality*, but only the *quantity*, of the emotion.   It will even do duty for exactly opposite emotions: thus precisely the same sounds in pitch may be used for the excited delivery of the words ' I *love* you ' and ' I *hate* you,' where the difference is conveyed entirely by the different *timbre* and mode of production of the sounds ; and *timbre*, I need hardly repeat, has nothing whatever to do with cadence, and offers no sort of basis for musical formation.   If we seek for some other general rule of pitch for excited utterance, beyond width of interval and suddenness of change, we shall only find it in a point which is exactly

The gliding transitions in speech, and absence of fixed steps of pitch, is the exact opposite to one of the prime conditions of melody.

*opposed* to a fundamental characteristic of Music.   All speech, emotional and unemotional, is marked by an immense amount of *gliding* transitions of pitch, and certain emotional expressions of complaint and entreaty particularly emphasise this peculiarity : while Music, as we have seen, has fixity of degree as a constant characteristic through all the numerous embryo and developed scale-systems that have been used ;[1] and when instruments, such as the singing voice or the violin, glide from fixed degree to fixed degree, the pleasure is caused by the arrival at the fixed note, after the ear has been momentarily excited by watching the course of the sound towards it : that is, by the satisfaction of an expectation which entirely depends on fixed degrees.   Thus the gliding and uncertain transitions of speech supplement its lack of rhythmical division in producing an exact opposition to the two essential factors of melodic forms.

In connection with the points urged so far, I would now ask the reader

---

[1] Many early and rude scale-systems have even avoided the smaller fixed intervals and have contained fewer steps, and some of them longer, than our developed scale of tones and semitones.  So here again, as in the former point of limitation of melody to a very few tones, we find the earlier music presenting, in respect of just those mechanical considerations which Mr. Spencer considers relevant, an even more marked difference from its putative parent, emotional speech, than the later.

to recall what has been said in previous chapters as to (1) the neutral nature of detached musical intervals and rhythmless note-fragments, and the occurrence of the same intervals and fragments in all sorts of musical forms of the most diverse characters ; (2) the close organism of musical forms, the impossibility of getting any impression of them from isolated intervals and fragments, and their distinct and indescribable musical individuality ; (3) their frequent lack of any expressive quality describable in terms drawn from the recognised category of the emotions ; and (4) the extreme width and generality of such descriptive terms even when they can be applied. Let him then compare Mr. Spencer's explanation of Music as we know it ; that the passionate and susceptible temperament of composers causes their tones and changes of voice in speech to be more marked than those of other people, and hence they are led in their music to express emotions which all feel by ' extremer intervals and more marked cadences ' than others would use ; and moreover that they are susceptible to compound emotions from things which do not affect others, which compound emotions they express in involved phrases, by combinations of the intervals and cadences in which their conversation and music is wont to express the simpler emotions. Finally, as a commentary on the comparison, I would ask him to play over the passage quoted on p. 256, or gently to whistle *Du bist die Ruh*, quoted on p. 222, and ask himself how far in either case Music owes its effect on him to ' exaggerating the loudness, the resonance, the pitch, the intervals, and the variability, which are the characteristics of passionate speech.'

§ 6. These points, and certain previous ones, confronted with Mr. Spencer's theory.

The theory may be as easily attacked on the score of its assumptions about Speech and Music separately, as of its conclusions concerning their relations. First as regards Speech, it being steadily kept in view that relations of sounds in pitch are what we are concerned with, I need hardly point out how entirely Mr. Spencer's conceptions are opposed to the view I have sketched above. In place of an infinite and indefinite medley of sound-combinations, the correspondences of which with emotion are subject to only a few extremely lax rules, and this really only in respect of such general points as width of interval and direction up or down, he seems to find a set of numerable and detachable units of tune or ' cadence,' each with its known definite expression ; a phenomenon for which I look as much in vain as I look to the clouds outside for a detailed panorama of the room I am sitting in. The most definite and assignable cadences I can find are at the end of sentences and clauses,[1] and of unemotional

The theory attacked on the side of Speech ;

---

[1] It is in the closing cadences, far more restrictedly than is generally supposed, that national differences of intonation are prominent. Languages may of course differ infinitely in *timbre* and pronunciation of vowels and consonants, and the delivery of them may differ also in *general* qualities of pitch, such as tending to monotone or travelling frequently over a large range : but actual sets of intervals having enough certainty to

rather than emotional sentences. If we go further back we are at once lost. Sentences, having to begin and go on as well as to end, do so by perpetual irregular alternations of monotone and see-sawing over intervals roughly approximating to fifths and octaves, with often much wider skips for emphatic syllables ; and precisely the same idea or emotion may, according to the particular words employed, be expressed, *quâ* pitch, in a hundred different series of tones. On this head I will add but one more argument, which further affects also the supposed connection between the ' cadences ' of speech and those of Music. We find that the *nuances* of inflection and expression in speech are appreciated and used to perfection by persons who not only cannot tell one tune from another, but cannot approximately follow a single musical interval with their voice. The absolute lack of definiteness in the intervals of speech could not receive a more clinching proof.

on the side of Music ;

Next as regards Music, Mr. Spencer position seems remote from facts equally in respect of *expressiveness* and in respect of *structure*. The ' involved phrases,' it must be observed, however much their intervals may be ' combined and complicated,' can still only mean some sort of *series* of clauses, since it is only notes *in succession* that supply any conceivable parallel to the sounds of speech. Any eight-bar melody is such an ' involved phrase,' and is bound, on Mr. Spencer's theory, to express a complex web of emotions compounded of simpler emotions, and generated in the composer (who, poor man, has just been blest by the melody's flashing across him as he lies in bed) by his contemplation of ' events, scenes, conduct, and character ; ' an idea which is quite on a par with supposing melodic construction to consist in piecing together ' intervals and cadences,' each taken from some pigeon-hole where it is kept for the special service of some simple emotion.[1]

and in respect of the supposed derivation.

Lastly, as regards the supposed derivation, it is superfluous to point out its total incompatibility with our previous account of musical motions. We may forego all reference to form [2] or to any part of our own enquiry, and

---

give sentences a sort of characteristic *tune*, occur normally at the *close*, chiefly of sentences, but to some extent of subordinate clauses.

[1] The same bugbear of perpetual definite and detailed expression leads Mr. Spencer to assign independent emotional meanings to various modes of performance, each of which may really be applied to music of the most diverse characters. For instance, he describes *staccato* as essentially appropriate to the expression of exhilaration, resolution, and confidence. I need hardly point out how a view of this sort breaks down to any one who remembers the bass accompaniment to the

wonderfully yearning and pathetic opening melody of the andante in the *Pastoral* sonata.

[2] Mr. Spencer is unable, of course, wholly to ignore the element of *form* in a melodic series of notes ; he himself describes the supposed modifications of the speaking voice under emotion as the ' raw material ' of Music, and says that the traits in question, ' *systematised*,' are the traits of Music. But, even if the traits were as accurately and constantly present in Music as he supposes, we must surely enquire how much still lies in the systematisation : the distinctive traits of a marble statue or a marble cathedral are

merely confront Mr. Spencer's theory with two simple facts of musical experience ; that the musical effect (1) may be absent in the presence of all his conditions, and (2) may be present in their absence. Thus, first confining ourselves to the cases where all the traits he considers distinctive, loudness, large range of pitch, and so on, are as far as possible present, we may still show how utterly their presence fails to account for the musical effect, by the argument which we formerly applied in the same sense to force and suggestions of physical motion ; viz. that the traits in question may all be equally there in the case of two musical pieces, one of which makes a powerful impression on us, and the other none at all. That is to say, two bits of music which equally resemble emotional speech in all the points on which Mr. Spencer founds his explanation may differ from each other by the whole amount of that emotional effect for which the explanation is wanted. And secondly, taking a melody which, so far from presenting in its succession of tones resemblances to those 'cadences' of speech on which Mr. Spencer lays stress, presents the exactly opposite qualities, if by its appeal to our melodic faculty we get from it in perfection a unique and indescribable emotional pleasure, we are certainly justified in regarding that faculty and that pleasure as in nature and origin independent of speech, however much associated with language and affected by vocal and verbal conditions in the course of their development.

How close Mr. Spencer considers the parallelism and connection to be between the actual phrases of Music and those of speech, is shown again in his further view that the *function* of the former is to facilitate the §7. Mr. Spencer's theory as to the *function* of Music.

simply traits of the raw material, *e.g.* whiteness and solidity, *systematised*, that is wrought into a *form* which appeals to the higher human faculties. And we see at once that Mr. Spencer's convenient and ambiguous 'systematisation' really stands for the whole form-element in what is *par excellence* an art of form. It is no mere matter of modern improvements, such as harmony, tonality, and modulation, which have clearly been developed in obedience to artistic sensibilities and in no way from sounds due to the physiology of speech or in imitation of instinctive vocal cadences : it applies to the very foundation of melody, to the sense of rhythm, the priority of which to any sort of emotional speech Mr. Spencer would doubtless admit ; and this independence should surely have suggested that in a more developed stage abstract forms might have an independent appeal for the ear, as well as for the eye.

The priority of rudimentary music to emotional speech, and the general irrelevance of the successions of tone in the one to those in the other, is of course quite compatible with the subsequent use, as material for musical purposes, of some few and simple phrases of speech of a comparatively definite and non-gliding character. Such instinctive modulations of speech as could be selected and adapted to Song would be mainly found in short exclamations and in closing cadences ; in elements, that is, which readily admitted of recurrence, and so of the appearance of proportion and balance ; for recurrence is obviously the stepping-stone to rhythm. The regular repetition of the same phrase or cry comes nearer music than the most excited utterances of fluent speech. A war-cry might be of such a nature, where an aid to the development of rhythmical cadence might be given by the accompanying movements, such as the step or the swinging of a club : and we noticed, in the last chapter, the natural effect on Song of the closing cadences of lines or approximately equal lengths of speech.

development of emotional and sympathetic expressiveness in the latter. He says that 'the complex musical phrases by which composers have conveyed complex emotions influence us in making the involved cadences by which we convey our subtler thoughts and feelings.' Now the incoherent 'cadences' of conversation are, as we have seen, infinite in number, and a new one is probably invented every time one of us says ten consecutive words. The coherent phrases of musicians are practically also infinite, as the combination of the pitch- and the time-factors multiplies indefinitely the possible arrangements of notes. We have seen on several grounds what a fruitless task it would be to search for definite melodic resemblances between fragments from these two infinites. We are thrown back on such occasional and general characteristics as loudness and rapidity; and I cannot think that any of us will talk louder or quicker when excited, because we find these qualities in some exciting passages of music. The argument that individuals with no sense or enjoyment of music talk as loud and excitedly as other people might perhaps be met by saying that their ancestors had enjoyed music, and transmitted the characteristic mode of utterance. But we should certainly find that a child of a savage tribe, none of whose ancestors had heard varied and rapid musical cadences, would talk just as loud and fast as English children if brought up among them. Nor do we conceive the Greeks, whose music was so much less elaborate and complex than ours, to have been on an average very inferior to ourselves in their powers of expressive utterance, and to have possessed much less developed vocal cords.

§ 8. Cruder views.

It will not be necessary, after considering Mr. Spencer's theory, to spend much time on cruder and less explicit views of the relations of speech and Music. The remark of the Abbé du Bos—one of the earliest pieces of musical criticism in modern literature—that 'just as a painter imitates the forms and colours of Nature, so the musician imitates the tones, the accents, the sighs, the inflexions of voice, in fact all the sounds by means of which Nature herself expresses her sentiments and passions,' only exposes in its baldest form a principle latent in all the modern phraseology which implies such a continuity and connection between speech and Music as would just constitute them means of graduated strength for expressing the same things. Nor would some of the more modern statements of that principle at all yield the palm in point of baldness; as, for instance, the thesis advanced not long ago by an eminent mathematician in an address to the British Association, that ' no essentially new melodic themes can be invented until a social cataclysm, or the civilisation of some at present barbaric races, shall have created fresh necessities of expression, and call into activity new forms of impassioned declamation.' *Every* original melody is of course an essentially new melodic theme in one sense: in any other sense the possibility of essentially new melodic themes has one, and only one, condition—a *new scale-system*. That such a system may be in store is quite conceivable: what is inconceivable is that it could have any reference to speech. Scales consist of fixed steps: and that they will be developed from that which is distinguished precisely by the absence of fixed steps is precisely as likely as that we shall find neatly-made fire-escapes growing in the woods.

Rousseau's views on the present question derive an interest of their own from the fact that he was in the curious position of having, as a musician, a keen appreciation of strong rhythmic tune and a keen dislike of unmetrical recitative, while at the same time far too much possessed by the idea that language must be essentially at the root of melody—which otherwise would not have been 'in conformity to Nature'—to recognise the true character of melodic form and the true place of rhythm as one of its two factors. He is thus in a perpetual state of uncertainty and compromise. He seems to connect even the rhythmic sense itself with speech: he at any rate attempts to derive musical rhythms in detail from verse-feet, and thus confuses the mere metrical outline of the bar with the infinitely various combinations of time-relations which may be included within this outline. He is always showing his sense of the indispensableness of firm rhythm by complaining of the lack of it in the contemporary French music; and yet he falls into the ordinary bungle of considering the notes-in-pitch of a melody as something which can be detached and judged apart from the rhythm. He never brings himself explicitly to recognise the power and right of Music to take possession of speech, even of prose, and to mould its flow; and denies that good melody could ever be associated with French words! It is true he knew Rameau and not Auber: but had he never heard a *Volkslied?* He says of all modern languages that as they are the productions of barbarous peoples, and therefore not naturally musical (an admission which cuts at the very root of the supposed connection), if music is to be added, great precautions must be used that the union may be sufficiently *natural* to produce illusion; not perceiving that the imposition of musical form on the words of speech must always be, from the speech point of view, *un*natural. And so little notion had he of what the voice really does in speech, that he considers the ideal recitative would deceive the ear into thinking it *was* speech—which certainly would leave nothing to desire in point of naturalness. Finally, his identification of minute slidings of the speaking voice with 'enharmonic' changes of pitch is an almost inconceivable piece of muddle: for he is speaking of such changes in connection with European music, in which they never occur as a melodic feature, and are only produced occasionally and one at a time on certain instruments, for the sake of perfect purity of intonation in harmonic progressions.

There is, however, one theory as to the connection between speech and

*Rousseau's wavering position, due to the conflict between his instincts and his theories.*

§ 9. The view that *primitive* speech contained a sort of embryonic music;

Music, which claims more particular notice. It might seem indeed only a form of that already criticised; but is far more insidious in that, while explicitly relating only to the *primitive* stage of utterance where many will carelessly grant it, it none the less enters into the whole conception of the permanent nature of the sound-art. I refer to the widely spread notion that the speech of primitive man had a special relation to Music; that his direct and normal expression of his intuitions and feelings contained the essential germs of Music, or was actually 'a sort of music.'[1]

which stands in intimate relation to the whole conception of Music most opposed to the central conception of this book.

The essential distinctness in nature of the musical element even in embryo was perhaps sufficiently insisted on in the last chapter; but the supposed musical character of early speech rests on such an easy misreading of facts, and introduces the whole false principle under so convenient a cover of remoteness, innocence, and vagueness, that it holds a very chief place among the difficulties and prejudices which the central conception of this book has to encounter: and the reference to it here affords a good opportunity for embracing those various difficulties in a connected and final summary.

Final summary of the difficulties which that central conception has to encounter.

The central conception itself, I need hardly say, is that the primary and essential function of Music is to create beautiful *objective forms*, and to *im*press us with otherwise *un*known things, instead of to induce and support particular *subjective moods* and to *ex*press for us *known* things.

General difficulties.

There is, then, (1) the initial difficulty, sufficiently exemplified in the above remark of the Abbé du Bos, and obviously due to the general association of the idea of *Art* with the definite *representation* so palpable in its poetic, plastic, and pictorial branches—the difficulty of conceiving an art as *presentative*, as primarily bound, by presenting its *own* things, whether in harmony with other things or not, to stir up its own indescribable emotions. Examining further the way in which the subject is likely to present itself to the mind, we find that (2) the habitual experience of forms which can be seen and touched is an obstacle to clearly conceiving as sensible *forms* phenomena which cannot be seen and touched; and (3) the character of the lines of sound of which we have *incessant* expe-

---

[1] It is curious to observe that Wagner, much of whose work might seem, from its efforts after detailed and impossible 'expression' and from the violent and extended intervals of its recitatives, to be an outcome of Mr. Spencer's theory, yet takes a view exactly opposite to Mr. Spencer's as to the course which the history of the musical element in human speech has taken. Holding the *earliest* efforts of speech to have come nearest to Music, he suggests that probably the first language of human beings bore a great resemblance to singing: and in speaking of Beethoven's symphonies he discovers 'the metaphysical necessity for the discovery of this completely novel means of expression in our own times, in the more and more conventional development of modern speech;' that is, speech, in spite of the enormous increase in the variety of its intonations, which he would hardly deny, has become, according to him, less and less musical.

rience, those of speech, being primarily and for the most part exclusively *expressive*, is an obstacle to recognising the character of certain *occasional* lines of sound as primarily *impressive*. These obstacles may disappear, indeed, in the very act of being explicitly noticed; but in escaping notice, they suffice to turn speculation at the very outset into the wrong channel. The mistaken view of the essence of Music seeks and finds a natural support in the mistaken view as to its essential connection with speech. While, on the one hand, the primary aspect of melodies as *forms*, as unique pieces of formed or Ideal Motion, is lost sight of—the very sound of the phrase 'abstract form' seeming, on a casual view, to have some kind of incompatibility with profound emotional appeal—on the other hand, the instinctive sense that melodies differ from visible forms in being not only forms but *utterances*, often deeply expressive utterances, and perpetually delivered by the human voice, has naturally led on to the notion that what Music represents and imitates, or exaggerates and idealises, can only be the other and commoner phenomena of expressive utterance, those, namely, produced by the voice in speech. But inasmuch as experience has habituated us to large organic structures, in which the artificial and separate character of Music is overpoweringly evident, those who desire to establish the connection naturally turn to savage nations and primitive times; neglecting the suggestive fact at their very doors, that the six or eight wordless notes which a child of four will croon over to itself with never-ceasing delight are, both in themselves and in their emotional effect, as truly and absolutely remote from speech as is the *Eroica* symphony.

And then come in the more specially misleading facts, that (4) primitive speech, in its direct and vivid contact with concrete reality and remoteness from abstract conceptions, is doubtless in a way more *poetical* than the later language where reflection has to a great extent replaced intuition; and that (5) primitive *poetry* did appear in intimate association with sonorous recitation and song;—two considerations which, taken together, seem made to create a confusion between the nature and attributes of the totally distinct elements which Song presents. Seeing that speech was often rudely poetical, and that rude poetry and music found often simultaneous utterance, how easy to slip on without analysis into the hazy notion of Herder and Comte, that the 'sort of poetry' characteristic of the primitive expression of feelings and ideas involved also a 'sort of music'; and that it is in speech (albeit essentially formless) that the essential germs of Music (albeit essentially form) are to be sought. The error is further facilitated by (6) the *rudeness* in inchoate song of the distinctively musical element, the element which is not *given in* but *imposed on* speech. The rude utterances which contain the musical element are so much *less markedly* different from the amorphous cries

*More special source of confusion, in the early relations of speech, poetry, and music.*

which do not contain them than is, *e.g.*, a modern symphony from a modern conversation—especially to *our* ears, who often find savage music and savage speech alike barbarous and ugly, and forget that we cannot judge music with the savage ear till we can remake ourselves into savages—that the separate existence and origin of the musical element may naturally fail to suggest itself, and the relative importance of the expressive and the impressive or distinctively musical aspects seem so far inverted that the very existence of the latter is ignored.

As a matter of fact, we have seen that the savage himself conveniently supplies the evidence we want in his instrumental performances, whose rhythmic and often purely percussive nature presents the distinctively musical element in undiluted purity. And the idea of rude melodic forms, developed gradually in obedience to the musical instinct (though doubtless affected by their associated words in such *general* features as length of phrase, pace of movement and so on) and instinctively imposed on words as more developed melodic forms are now more consciously imposed, may perhaps be best caught by going back to the very earliest stages, where melody was hardly represented by anything beyond its single factor of rhythm. For we have seen that it was by passing through the interlude of monotonous but rhythmical chanting, and so discarding or limiting instead of exaggerating the characteristics of emotional speech, and imposing a totally new element of form, that recitation became a basis for the development of Music. Here, then, in the action of the single factor, supervening on and not evolved from speech, may be found an illustration of the action of developing and developed melodic forms; the only difference being that the simple sense of rhythm is *so* simple that this factor might be introduced early in great completeness, even as it is presented in most complete accuracy by savage dances, clappings, &c.; while with the entrance of the pitch-factor begins the extremely slow and uncertain development of melodic form proper to what it has now become, with the perpetual chance that, through developing in association with language, it shall seem to owe to language the details of its successions-in-pitch or ' cadences.'

Final restatement of the separate source and nature of melodic form.

To pursue the subject on the positive side would, however, be merely to repeat the substance of the chapters on Association, Melody, and Song. It is enough to recall how every consideration tended to the same result; that the oak grew from the acorn; that the musical faculty and pleasure, which have to do with music and nothing else, are the representatives and linear descendants of a faculty and pleasure which were musical and nothing else; and that, however rudely and tentatively applied to speech, Music was a *separate order*, an adjustment of proportional elements of which speech knows nothing, introduced in conformance with the instincts of a pleasure to which the organism had been through long ages more and more adapted ; a pleasure greatly associated with speech, because the voice was the naturally available instrument, but which would have been in essence the same had words had no existence and *visible* signs been the ordinary medium of communication on this planet; even as it would be in essence the same to any one of us who, living in solitude, had had the music he has actually heard in his life conveyed day by day to his ears.

There is one more restricted application of the speech-theory which claims a moment's separate attention, and with which we may close the topic ; the view, namely, put forward long ago by Addison and very generally accepted without question, that *national melodies* are intimately affected by the natural intonations of speech common in a country. In the case of European nations we cannot doubt that their widely differing speech-intonations, the prevalent cadences of their sentences, are the amorphous result of all sorts of physical and linguistic differences. Melodies, on the other hand, whether characteristically national or not, are made from the intervals of *one* scale-system, the universal adoption of which in itself implies the widest agreement in the special order of sensibility addressed. We might forego all the preceding arguments, and rely simply on the contrast of these facts, to show how impossible it is that the series of notes in definite tunes should have any more connection with the definite national peculiarities of speech-cadences than with the national dress. The question of definite melodic formation must here again be carefully separated from any *general* characters.[1] Mr. Spencer is right in remarking that the Italians, who have varied and expressive speech-intonation, have also been distinguished for free and flowing melody; and that the Scotch, with a more monotonous (not necessarily, however, an inexpressive) mode of speech, have also had limited and monotonous tunes. It would be a sufficient hypothesis that the same natural causes which have led to a limited range of tones in speech have limited the voice as an instrument, that is, have limited the material for musical forms of which the voice is, for popular purposes, the prime repository. But even if the analogy be

§ 10. The idea that national airs are intimately affected by the indigenous intonations of speech.

Here again definite melodic formation must be distinguished from general characteristics such as rapidity or monotony.

---

[1] Even as regards general characters, the contrast between the speech and the music of peoples is sometimes very marked. Some races of savages are distinguished by particularly soft and musical languages, while showing no superiority in musical development. The people of New Guinea are so described ; the Samoans, with a pleasing language, have very rude percussive music, with no variety beyond two or three notes : and the same applies to other Malayo-Polynesian races, in whom the absence of more varied musical cadences should, on Mr. Spencer's theory, be the more remarkable in that they have distinct musical instinct, and are much addicted to chanting, as an accompaniment to paddling and in extempore verses and satires. The Fijians, with a remarkably rich and euphonious language and many æsthetic tastes, are pre-eminent among the peoples of the South Seas for the rudeness of their music. The Andamans, on the other hand, with a harsh and disagreeable language, are described as having a marked taste for music.

pressed to the furthest point, it is quite irrelevant to the actual structure of tunes and to their supposed derivation from speech-cadences. There is, as it happens, one noticeable peculiarity of many Scotch tunes, the avoidance of the interval of a semitone ; but for analogies to this or any other definite feature, the analogies which alone would be relevant to the theory we have been reviewing, we of course look in vain in the shifting quicksands of speech-utterances. Could any one, on the simple ground of being able to detect the nationality of a Welshman and a Scotchman by their mode of talking (to take Addison's own instance), detect which of two melodies— say *Ar hŷd y nós* and *Annie Laurie*—was the Welsh and which the Scotch one ?

§ 11. The actual relations between Speech and Music.

Having seen at such length what the relations between speech and Music are *not*, we must now conclude by briefly enquiring what they *are*, over and above those points of alliance which were sufficiently discussed in connection with the single branch of Song. I need not dwell again on the most general fact of all, our impression of music, instrumental as well as vocal, as an utterance of some true, however untranslatable, significance, and with some personality (often, I think, our own), or it may be of several personalities, projected behind it ; the sort of impression which I previously described as frequently evoking what seems more like *assent* than mere admiration ; an impulse to exclaim, at some melodic phrase, ' I should think so indeed ! ' rather than ' How beautiful ! ' This character is clearly connected with the perpetual experience of lines of sound, with varied ascents and descents and varieties of pace and emphasis, as significant in speech ; and is an instance of about as wide and pervading association as could well be. But under this most general relation of all may be ranked a number of other more special features ; which, however, are all entirely general as compared with that supposed parallelism of actual ' cadences,' of actual intervals and successions-in-pitch, which we have just been reviewing.

The general impression of music as utterance.

Many of the features of physical motion which Music may suggest may be exceptionally well presented in speech.

Thus, all those features of physical motion mentioned in the fourteenth chapter as having their counterparts in Music, which, we saw, is able to suggest definite emotions so far as the physical motions are themselves expressive of such emotions, may naturally be presented in speech. And the connection of Music with the presentation of them in speech is of course exceptionally close. For, first, in the use of language under emotion there is not only the varied play of energy parallel to that which may be manifested by muscular exercise of other sorts, but this varied play takes effect in the actual material of Sound, and so obtains the widest and easiest channel for associations with the art of sound. And, secondly, speech stands apart from other physical modes of expression in having normally a large amount of *continuity* : in the appreciation of feeling as conveyed by speech, we are accustomed to long connected lines of impression, presenting it may be many variations and contrasts of tone and character, or it may be the mere quality of even persistence; but in either case corresponding, in their character as more or less sustained chains of utterances, to the phenomena of Music, which in like manner may preserve a persistent flow, or present within a short space a marked succession of variations and contrasts.

I must repeat the previous warning, that it is not the presentation of any definable features which is at the root of musical effect: music may be slow and quick and even and interrupted and emphatic and furious and capricious and loud and soft and all the rest, and still be perfectly un-beautiful and unimpressive. But if it is musically impressive, particular features of motion will give it particular expressive characters: and then slowness becomes solemnity, and quickness becomes it may be merriness or it may be agitation, and fury becomes energy, and abruptness becomes passion, and so on. And our present point is that these characters and their intermixtures and transitions are probably more keenly felt through the experiences of speech than through any other sorts of physical motion, speech being the channel in which the varieties of psychical impulse most constantly and prominently take effect. The criterion of this influence of speech would be that, if a person of musical instinct could be imagined to live just as other men do, but to be miraculously deaf to the one pheno-menon of speech, his sense of musical expression would be found decidedly deficient.

Nor, when once the parallelism of actual intervals is given up, does it seem impossible that association may extend to less obvious features, and may exist between points in Music and speech which agree only indirectly, in the sort of relation they hold to other things in their own respective lines; for example, that a special strangeness given by some unexpected chromatic turn may involve some faint hint of the less usual accents of speech which would mark particular emotional occasions. A very frequent point, in which instinctive association with speech is undoubtedly present, is the repetition of a phrase, with or without a difference. The opening couple of bars of two of Beethoven's best known sonatas supply an instance of each kind— Repetition of phrase;

and—

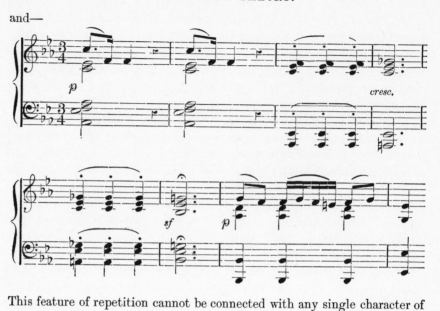

This feature of repetition cannot be connected with any single character of expression, but often resembles the reiteration of speech in conveying to the strain a special air of *intensity*, whether of some definable character— solemnity, pleading, or whatever it may be—caused by other means, or of the undefinable musical impression. In cases where this sense of intensity or persistence is not noticeably conveyed, the general feeling of music as a mode of utterance is still naturally helped by any such general points of parallelism with speech. We may find in the second of the above quotations another point of a similar kind; namely, the rising to a certain moment of climax and descent to the close, which is an extremely common feature of sentences. On the other hand, there are passages which seem to reach a climax and end on it, and which may be described as having a certain air of rhetorical emphasis; which again implies some faint reference to the phenomena of speech. In these latter instances, however, it is, I think, more doubtful how far our former criterion would apply; how far a person who had had no experience of speech, while able to hear music, would fail to receive the full emotional effect from the musical passages. There have been other applications of the idea of parallelism to which this last remark applies still more certainly; as that the effects of harmony and polyphony have some reference to the simultaneous concordant or diverging expressions of several different views by several voices. The effect of several people talking at once is, to me at any rate, so disagreeable, that I scarcely think any agreeable æsthetic effect could owe anything to association with it. Some hint of varying strains of feeling I think may be suggested by the motion of simultaneous musical parts; but it can hardly depend on even the faintest reference to their simultaneous vocal expression.

*and employ-
ment of climax.*

The list of dim affinities between Music and speech could easily be extended, but the cases I have given may serve as specimens. Far more important than the features themselves is the point that they are quite undistinctive of what is musically essential; that any one may find them as readily in music that he cares nothing for as in music that he loves; while none the less they contribute to give to music which is truly enjoyed that peculiar character of utterance, as of a revelation of unimagined things, received now, it may be, as a message from others, and now again so possessing us that we seem to find its source in the deepest springs of our own emotional nature.

Such affinities, even when they can be traced, are no guarantee of pleasurable qualities in the music.

# CHAPTER XXII.

## OPERA.

SINCE it is vocal music which finds on the stage its most prominent arena, the most fundamental points which concern Opera have already appeared in their natural place in connection with Song. It will be necessary, however, to consider the subject somewhat more in detail, and especially in connection with recent theory and practice.

First as regards *structure*. It is clear how totally alien to the varied succession of words, scenes, and events in a theatrical performance is the organism of a large symphonic movement. That sort of organism represents a growth which, having taken place from a purely musical centre through the working of purely musical instincts, naturally also represents the furthest departure of the art from alliance with extraneous adjuncts ; in other words, the furthest development of instrumental music. A similar incompatibility with the continuity of theatrical scenes must also preclude any considerable use of many features not specially associated with instrumental composition, such as fugue, ' imitation,' and the various devices which have been employed to give unity to a single complete piece of limited length. But the existence and development of these structural complexities, as we have seen all through, has in no way annulled or interfered with the instinctive and general demand of human ears for impressive motives and melodies. These are the cardinal units of Music : the effect on the musical sense of these closest and most vital organisms is the central fact of the whole art. While the most complicated musical fabric must be built clearly and intelligibly on such simpler and self-centred units of form, if it is to have any arresting and permanent power,

the simpler forms themselves, from a ' subject ' two bars long to a flowing paragraph, retain a perfectly independent power, and make exactly the same appeal as if there were no such thing as a fugue or a symphonic ' first movement ' in the world. It is clearly of these straightforward pieces of Ideal Motion that the progressive and accompanying music of theatrical scenes must in the main consist. The music of an Opera, regarded as a whole, must be a stream of more or less definite sections, worked up within certain limits, and embroidered with any amount of instrumental detail, but accompanying and adapting itself to the varied course of the extra-musical elements. And while a prolonged stream of musically inde-pendent paragraphs or lengths, whatever might be their individual charm, would lack aim and coherence apart from some external unity, it may receive in the unity of words and action a perfect justification.

But though Music does not impose on Song and Opera the reiterations and 'carryings out' and elaborations of structure which occur elsewhere, that is, does not employ *all* its resources in *one* of its branches, it is in this sense, and in this sense only, that it can be said (as it often is said) to make compromises. That it should abandon the essence of its nature, the essence which makes it delightful from moment to moment, from bar to bar, the essence of vital melodic or harmonic motive,[1] is strictly impossible without the loss of all its *raison d'être*. That laxity, therefore, in the coherence of sections, which is natural in a musical work whose unity is provided for by other than musical means, no more opens the floodgates to unmeasured declamation and recitative, whether accompanied by dry chords or by tuneless passages of florid orchestration, than the want of organic continuity in a collection of poems permits the majority of them to be out of rhythm. Such compromises of the musical to the verbal element as take effect in prolonged sections lacking the organic vitality of distinct and agreeable motive, so far from giving greater play and scope to the compound art, simply deprive the musical sounds of the power of interesting human ears. While, therefore, the plot and scenes rule the large scheme of the work, Music takes complete possession of the actual sentences as they come, and in the construction of the actual motives and sections relaxes her strict rights at most only here and there, to an extent which vivifies the sense of their main predominance.

*Music cannot abandon those most intimate organic quali-ties which enable it to be delightful from moment to moment.*

There is, however, one principle, predominant in all the larger sorts of musical organism, which is too deeply founded in the nature both of Music and of the musical sense, to be dispensed with in any prolonged musical presentation without the gravest loss ; the principle, namely, of *recurrence*. Music passes before the ear without pause : it cannot stop to be looked at : and the inevitable desire to hear impressive motives again is one which the looser succession of an opera can satisfy as well as a single compact and rounded movement. The principle, therefore, of the recurring 'subject' is a most important one. It is exemplified in a simple way by the frequent introduction into the overture of motives which are to follow in the piece, and to which the sense of recognition ensures a double and treble welcome. But a more *recherché* mode of employment (so long as it is not carried to an extent which makes it seem mechanical, like the

*§ 2. The principle of recurrence may be most effectively exemplified in Opera.*

---

[1] It was sufficiently explained in the tenth chapter, and must be specially borne in mind throughout the present one, how very much wider is the denotation of 'me-lodic motive' from what is generally under-stood by an 'air' or 'tune.'

painting of a man's name on his back) is the assigning of particular motives to particular personages or particular recurrent ideas in the piece, so as to make the recurrence a distinctly dramatic effect; a feature of which Wagner was the first to perceive the great possibilities. The extraordinary ease and rapidity with which any striking music becomes identified with that in association with which it is presented may give such motives the power of seeming not so much to symbolise as actually to express what is assigned to them; but the primary source of their value is, of course, the delight of the ear in hearing again and again what has once struck it.

The *Leitmotiv.*

§ 3. Wagner's confusion on the subject of organic structure.

There should not be any difficulty in perceiving the complete compatibility of the two facts, (1) that the structural conditions of an opera, where the stream of music is supported and justified by a progressive series of scenes and words, are totally different from the structural conditions of a large musical organism, such as a symphonic movement, which must be rounded off into a self-complete unity by purely musical means: and (2) that the musical series must not be a series of orderless sounds or fragments of phrases, but must consist of sections [1] or groups of bars linked together by the firm bond of melodic coherence, seeing that Music would cease to be Music if it resigned its intimate organic qualities. It would be useless to insist further on these facts, after the detailed discussion of musical form in the eighth and tenth chapters, were it not for the great confusion in which Wagner has involved the really simple point. For he talks of developing the ' symphonic form ' in union with the drama; and expressly anticipates from the mere evolution of a series of musical phrases out of the successive sentences of a poem—the poem itself being necessarily constructed without the slightest reference to the purely musical conditions of large musical organism exemplified in the symphony—a richness of *purely musical* development which will infinitely exceed that hitherto attained by the symphony; as though richness of development could be a possible result of perpetual differentiating, without any necessity of integration. Of course if Wagner or any one else succeeded in investing the successive periods of a poem with a succession of musical sections all of which were beautiful (and some of which, as in operatic concerted pieces, might naturally attain within themselves to considerable complexity of organism), that would be a most satisfactory result: but the *invention* of any number of beautiful *forms* would have absolutely no relation to *development* of *form*, in that wider general sense which implies the binding together of a prolonged series of formed parts under aspects of structural

---

[1] I must again warn readers who do not recall the account of melodic organism in the tenth chapter, against understanding by this word musical lengths of a distinctly detachable kind, that is, with the unmistakable beginning and end which we identify with a single complete melodic form.

unity. That development is best exemplified in our old comparison of the large instrumental movement with its germ in the dance-tune: there we have a true logical and historical development of form, resulting in a large and complex series—in place of a small and simple series—of related clauses, both the simple and the complex series being accepted by the musical intelligence as in a true sense a single and self-complete whole. Yet it is actually a further advance in this direction, a truly musical development of form to a point beyond that obtained in the symphony, that Wagner asserts to be attainable through the medium of a verbal basis, with which music is obliged to link itself sentence by sentence and paragraph by paragraph, and which necessarily and confessedly takes no account whatever of the laws and conditions of prolonged musical unity; as though by arranging a number of animals (I fear that in view of modern recitative we must make a good many of them invertebrates) tail to head, we should evolve a single markedly superior vertebrate organism.

The fact is that the word *form* has been a complete stumbling-block to this writer. He nowhere distinguishes its several senses, or the several grades of closeness of organic coherence which it includes : and the special application of it to the perceptions of the human senses, the notion of a form as a set of impressions which the eye or ear, with their well-known and limited range of action, can grasp and integrate, seems never to have dawned on him in the course of his theorising. Thus while he seeks to dignify the musical element of Opera by vague talk about ' infinite melody,' the ' large melody which comprises the whole dramatic-musical piece,' and while, as we saw, he actually gives the name of melody (and assigns therefore the character of form) to the undivided and multitudinous murmur of a forest, he perpetually overlooks the humble fact that while melody does not the least want to be infinite, it does very much want to have one bar intelligibly and organically connected with the next, and even with the next but one, and as a rule even the one beyond that ; and that the ear's impression of what it is receiving from moment to moment is not the least affected by the knowledge that these present strains belong to a ' melody ' so large that it will be going on three hours hence. It may sound attractive to make the poet remark to the musician, ' Throw yourself fearlessly into the sea of music : spread your melody boldly, so that it may flow through the whole work like an uninterrupted stream ; with it reveal all that I pass over in silence, because you alone can reveal it.' But unfortunately notes, like syllables, when spread too boldly may result in nonsense. And we have thoroughly seen what indispensable conditions for musical coherence are (1) firmly measured rhythm [1] and (2) a certain

*His failure to distinguish the various senses of the word form;*

*and his notion of ' spreading melody boldly.'*

---

[1] It is difficult to avoid frequent repetition of this point, and impossible to add at every repetition the slight amount of qualification that it demands; the statement of which will be found at p. 155, *note*, pp. 261–2, and p. 461. I would specially refer to the *test* of organic motive mentioned in the latter place.

definiteness and steadiness of key. Seeing how systematically these conditions have been ignored (in spite of brilliant exceptions) in the recitative-portions of Wagner's operas, it is surely odd to find him complaining in an injured tone of the view, 'instilled into people's minds,' that his theory 'comprised just that element which had always seemed to them eccentric and displeasing' in his compositions. Consider the following specimens picked at random from the second act of *Lohengrin* :

furcht - bar töd - lich Gift, das uns-re Schmach und ih - re

Freu - - den en - - de! Du fürch - - ter - li - ches

Weib! was bannt mich noch in dei-ne Nä-he? Wa-rum lass' ich dich nicht al -

- lein, und flie-he fort, da - - hin, da - -

- hin,— wo mein Ge - wis - sen Ru-he wie-der fänd'!

and again—

In these passages, which are fair specimens of their kind, there is clearly no musical substance or vitality whatever. They wholly fail to satisfy any condition which discriminates a really organic succession of notes from a mere set of orderless and arbitrary phrases, tacked on, fragment after fragment, to the pronunciation of certain words; whether it be our technical test, of collapse of form by change of time-relations, which will at once convict them of having no form to collapse; or the more popular criterion, that each note and bar, at any rate after several hearings, shall be recognised and welcomed as right and unalterable in its place. An ordinary amateur might hear strains of this sort in

Unmelodic and inorganic character of the passages quoted from *Lohengrin.*

connection with the same words and situations a dozen times, and be none the wiser if the greater part of them had been altered on each occasion; and even an experienced musician, after careful attention, might be sorry to have to bet on anything half a bar ahead. Chords and orchestral passages may mechanically bind together such unrelated note-fragments into a nerveless string, but never into the loosest sort of organic union; and the stamp of their restless aimless impotence is the fact that *more than half* their chord-support consists of mere diminished sevenths, that keyless chord which is the eternal bane of so-called 'dramatic' music. As a contrast to the above I should be glad to quote the section in the scene where Lohengrin first appears, ending with 'Elsa, ich liebe dich,' where the vocal part, while still retaining quite the nature of free recitative as opposed to set *aria*, is supported by a truly fine rhythmic motive of quite sufficiently sustained coherence. But, unfortunately, in the portion of the work delivered by solo voices there are a dozen pages of the former sort for one of the latter: elsewhere, as in *Tristan*, the proportion is even larger.[1] If this is little recognised, it is because Wagner, with all his indisputable superiority of musical genius, has really reaped to the full the benefit of

*That so much will pass muster which is totally uninteresting and unpleasing is owing to the chaotic state of the public mind in respect of Opera.*

the chaotic state of the public mind on the subject of Opera. The great majority of opera-goers go expecting to have a certain number of scenes and situations set off by fine voices and brilliantly lighted spectacle, while the whole is filled up with musical sound in the same sort of conventional way that the back of the stage is filled up with scenery; but without a notion of having more than a fraction of the time occupied with vivid enjoyment of the music, with definite melodic motive at which it will repay them to prick up their ears. And this being their standard of the evening's amusement, they are grateful for scenes and situations which at any rate possess a certain romance, and for getting their accustomed quota of musical enjoyment of a really superior quality; and can hardly understand the irritation felt by those who have a higher idea of operatic possibilities, when a vein so splendid proves to be also so unabundant, and when a man capable of writing the better parts of *Lohengrin* and *Tannhäuser* is found capable also of wearying and distressing hopeful and attentive ears for whole quarters of an hour at a time.

Holding fast, then, to the principles of melodic motive set forth in previous chapters, we cannot look for the development of form in general

---

[1] It is impossible to help recalling Rousseau's criticism of Lulli's recitatives: ' Comme la mesure ne s'y fait sentir ni dans le chant, ni dans la basse, ni dans l'accompagnement, rien n'est si traînant, si lâche, si languissant que ces beaux monologues que tout le monde admire en bâillant.' ' Sans les bras et le jeu de l'actrice je suis persuadé que personne n'en pourrait souffrir le récitatif, et qu'une pareille musique a grand besoin du secours des yeux pour être supportable aux oreilles.' Unfortunately Wagner's recitatives are often delivered by kings and heralds and people whose *bras* and *jeu* are not particularly interesting.

from defiance of the primary conditions of form in particular. Nor is it possible to allow, even to those special structural changes which Wagner has really in great measure introduced, any such vital importance as is often attributed to them. They consist chiefly in dispensing with the more obvious points of division which mark off a scene into definite musical pieces—solos, duets, trios, finales, and so on. This characteristic is clearly not to be judged of in the abstract, but in reference to the particular works in which it is presented. So far as the avoidance of marked divisions may lead a writer into forgetting that the musician's business is, *quand même*, to produce satisfactory bits of music, whether they end with the dominant and tonic chords or not, and into imagining that a paragraph is relieved of the duty of containing pregnant and coherent sentences by the substitution of commas for full stops and the avoidance of capital letters, it has its dangers. We can hardly be properly grateful even for getting rid of the padding of *recitativo secco*, as long as the substitute is the sort of recitative of which I have just quoted examples. On the other hand, so far as the continuity is a continuity of firm periods, each of which, long or short, has true organic qualities, it will of course be delightful, if only because it involves a large supply of the very thing we want. So far as such music is given us, we certainly shall not hanker after set *morceaux* ; and shall admit the flow of music through places where the voice-parts are not, as well as where they are, predominantly melodic, to be both musically and dramatically beneficial. For the orchestra supplies a means of retaining musical coherence without any interruption to the dramatic flow of remarks : and vocal passages more or less sporadic in themselves, and entirely removed from any conventional form of piece where the dramatic character of the performers is liable to suffer, may be sustained and united by clear and continuous orchestral motive with a specially delightful effect, for which operatic scenes give unique opportunities.

§ 4. Wagner's obliteration of strongly marked divisions in the musical sections, though it has proved to have serious drawbacks, is on the whole commendable ;

Given, then, a sufficient amount of good organic music, of whatever sort—and this, not the continuity or discontinuity of the sections, is the vital and unchangeable point—we may admit the continuous mode of structure to be an advantageous one, and shall not complain even if the linking of sections involves a considerable interspersion of fragments and passages of more transitional aim and character. Orchestral continuity at any rate shuts off the chance of puerile and unmusical passages of vocal display, and of interrupting applause. But we cannot allow much reality to the prime reason usually assigned for the avoidance of set pieces ; that it is *unnatural* to impose distinct musical divisions on the normal flow of dramatic action, and that to do so is to demand of Poetry unwarrantable concessions. An opera is not a drawing-room comedy ; it is a representation which has to be accepted entirely on its own ideal level ; and to object on the ground of unnaturalness to the observance of natural musical conditions, which in no way interfere with

though the reason usually assigned for it has not much reality.

our perception of the relations of the characters or the significance of the scene, is like objecting to conversations in a tragedy for being conducted in blank verse. With equal reason Rousseau complained of vocal duets as unnatural, on the ground that two people do not talk at once; he therefore required that duets should be strictly dialogues, or that if the parts were occasionally combined they should move in thirds and sixths! The appeal to Nature, which in Rousseau's day led to so many odd conclusions, has of course only to be pressed to put an end to Opera altogether. It is possible, no doubt, for set pieces to occur in places so dramatically incongruous as to offend common sense. But the interest in the progress of the drama will certainly not be damped by an occasional full close and a frank admission to the ear that one musical paragraph is over and another is going to begin; and a scene where the words are at once of such fiery interest, and so closely involved in rapid logical sequence as to present no natural divisions, is not adapted for musical investiture at all.

*The avoidance of repetition of words and phrases is a very unessential point.*

Similar reasons preclude us from attaching any particular importance to a point in the verbal structure, on which Wagner lays particular stress in reference to the libretto of *Tristan*; namely, the studied avoidance of repetition of words or phrases. The conditions of musical structure often make verbal recurrences a specially agreeable feature, as is proved in vocal music of every class; and the sentiments which are most naturally associated with song lend themselves readily to such a mode of expression. To make a virtue, then, of foregoing this feature, and of setting so many thousand words, straight on end, to so many thousand notes, suggests again an arbitrary and mechanical theory of amalgamation. Not that there would be anything to object to in such a setting if it were beautiful throughout; but Music, in transfusing situations and sentiments with her own emotional power, may certainly resent restrictions as to the mode in which she is to *débiter* words and sentences, and may claim to bring them, with full liberty, and on her own responsibility, into the mould of her own forms.

*§ 5. Expression. All those modes of expressing sentiments which have already been discussed find their largest scope in Opera.*

So much for *structure*: next as regards *expression*. On this head there is nothing to add in principle to what has been said in preceding chapters. All that power of correspondence with definable moods and sentiments which Music possesses is naturally called on to the utmost in operatic composition. But the distinct scenes and personages of Opera naturally add, by association, many apparent shades of expression to the music, which can hardly be said to be objectively there, inasmuch as a blind person ignorant of the language would hear and enjoy the music without perceiving them, but which none the less become an inseparable part of the effect. Thus *Non più andrai* has obviously a gay, gallant, military sort of movement; but it has been also called *mock-heroic*; and well as the word applies, I hardly think that particular shade of expression would be perceived apart from the particular address of Figaro to Cherubino. Whether or not this special instance commends itself, it is clear, from the extreme breadth and generality of the extra-musical emotions which Music can in itself suggest, that any delicacy and distinctiveness of expression which seems to make particular pieces *belong*, to special characters and situations must be chiefly the result of association. That whole large class of operatic heroines in whose personation prima donnas are always said by the newspapers 'to realise the dreamy idealism of the character,' and who are for the most part amiable young ladies alternating between the joys and pangs of love, might sing each other's melodies, sprightly, melancholy, or passionate, in the most impartial manner. Zerlina certainly has a *naïveté* and charm of her own; but I doubt if it would have been perceived that she ought to have been a *rustic* if she had happened to be a lady, difficult as it may be now to imagine a change in her condition; and the reason she is so distinct an individual is really that she has tunes of such peculiarly good quality to sing, not that either libretto or music mark her out in any way as a vivid human character. And as regards more special points of expression, the passionate vein of some agitated passage might often do duty equally for joy or anger; the thrilling phrase with some wild and emphatic note might clinch the idea of death either for self or for rival, of agonised renunciation or of wild resolve. Such examples hardly need to be multiplied.

But besides the more simple and direct correspondence of the musical with the external idea or character, there is another possible sort of correspondence (the principle of which was noticed in Chap. XV. § 5), that, namely, of a relation between successive parts of the music to a relation between successive parts of the verbal or scenic presentation: and this, comprising as it does extensive possibilities in the way of parallel ebb and flow, crisis and contrast, much increases the range of musical expressiveness. It is naturally in Opera that such features are predominant. To take one instance, in *La Serva Padrona* the maid alternates lento and allegro passages, in a song where she addresses pathetic remarks to her master and intersperses *sotto voce* asides in comment on the effect. Often, as here, the transitions are such as might occur in independent instrumental music. Often, however, the concomitants justify an amount of modification, interruption, and comminution in the music which would otherwise be unnatural; compromises, if we like to call them so, but not entailing any serious or continuous sacrifice of coherent musical phrases; the actual points of interruption being marked by their brevity and their exceptional character as contrasted with the normal flow. In respect of these features, again, it is to be noticed that the effect is really, for the most part, a general one, and would equally well suit a considerable variety of incidents or of successions of verbal sentiment, however much it becomes in each case identified with the

*The correspondence of contrasts and transitions in the music to analogous features in the scene;*

the expression here being really of a very general kind, though made to appear precise by the definiteness of the action and words.
special situation at which it occurs. When the heroine leaves off with a start on a high note accompanied by a striking change of harmony, the plot is obviously thickening, but the mere sounds do not reveal how. The sudden interruption of some soft and tender passage with a crash, a change of *tempo*, and some amount of orchestral tumult, would lend itself to a variety of easily imagined surprises : or the supervention of a hush and a subdued movement in simple colouring on an agitated and ornate duet or trio represents in itself a deep but quite vague emotional change, which might fitly embrace several different sorts of detail. And in every such case the effect naturally *seems* accurately descriptive of what is on hand.

The power of association to give rise to indescribable correspond- ences.
But association will do more even than this ; as we saw in the chapter on Song, it will give rise to an exquisite and quite indescribable feeling of affinity between a line of musical and a line of extra-musical impressions, even in cases where the music, taken on its own ground, is not either directly or indirectly suggestive of any definable emotions or circumstances. Every reader will recall instances where he has known and loved such music before connecting it with its words or anything else, and will re- member how, when he has heard it in its place, the concomitants, though in no way essential to begin with, have gradually become part and parcel of the charm. This power of Music, provided it be in itself attractive, to mingle its independent stream freely with all sorts of words and scenes, and in many cases to make, so to speak, its own affinities as it goes along, is a fact of enormous importance to Opera ; the sphere of which would be disastrously circumscribed if Music were confined to being always very definably of this or that emotional character, and were debarred from all alliances outside the range of true poetical inspiration.

Occasional ex- pression by marked me- chanical fea- tures.
We may rank under a separate head of expression, mentioned in the chapter on Song but chiefly exemplified in Opera, cases where the feeling of analogy with the accompanying verbal idea is created not by any emo- tional colouring belonging to the series of notes as music, but by some marked mechanical feature in them ; the occurrence of which may be said to represent a true, though rare, exception to the law of formed and agree- able musical phrases, since the intellectual sense of analogy may here have æsthetic value in the absence of any true satisfaction to the purely musical sense. The exception really proves the rule ; for it is just through the rarity of such features that they can be effective. An instance may be found in the expression of stern fixity given to the decree of the oracle of Apollo, in Gluck's *Alceste*, by the iteration of a single note. This feature is so simple and positive, and so strongly contrasted with what is usual in music, that it makes its own point and justifies the brief absence of true musical formation.

Another special sort of case, which may be conveniently though not very logically included under the topic of expression, is where the charm of the

union between music and other things results not so much from its express- The combina-<br>tion of beauty<br>with absurdity.
ing as from its pointedly *not* expressing them. The combination of beauty
with some measure of absurdity, a phenomenon quite unique in its æsthetic
effect, is also one to which Song, especially in theatrical performance, gives
extraordinary scope ; and the reason why good burlesque and good comic
opera are so rare lies in the absence of the delicate aptitude for a kind of
inward irony to which this twin result appeals. This serio-comic vein was
perhaps specially favoured by the robust *naïveté* of an earlier stage of the
art, and fails somewhat in an age when the muse varies between knitting
her brows and splitting her sides, too intentionally serious to be touching,
or too intentionally comic to be amusing : but even in the modern deluge
of forced and of vulgar work, cases might be cited, coming under the rough
category of comic writing, where Music's readiness to lend a tender grace
to homely and even to whimsical things has been strikingly displayed, and
where the boundary line between jest and pathos, I might almost say between laughter and tears, seems to be of the most shadowy kind. Even
in pure mock-heroic the incongruity sometimes seems only to add a delicate
edge to the natural flavour of the music ; and no one surely would exchange
the half ecclesiastical aroma of the drunken porter's ' Deo Gratias ' in *Le
Domino Noir,* or the trio in Zerlina's chamber in *Fra Diavolo,* for any
amount of professedly *bouffe* writing.

Finally, we may rank under the head of expression those blendings of Dramatic effect<br>in concerted<br>pieces.
song whose effect depends on something more than plurality of voices,
namely, on plurality of personalities. I do not mean by this, what is too
obvious to need enforcing, that the interaction of the dramatic personages
and the interplay of remarks afford the most favourable opportunity for all
the literally expressive and dramatic features that Music may present : [1] but
rather that, even in the absence of such most distinctive characters, the
mere fact of being delivered by different people standing to each other in
certain dramatic relations, and the emphasis thus given to the sense of
individuality amid harmony, may immensely enhance the charm of operatic
concerted music and invest it with a peculiar romance or humour. The
individuality of the parts receives often additional prominence from the
mode of delivery, *e.g.* from each singer's marking his or her more emphatic
notes by making one step forward and spreading out his or her arms ; this
attitude of giving something to the audience, which would be absurd and
exaggerated in a concert-room, seeming appropriate enough in the costume
of the stage. Very slight dramatic incidents may contribute largely to

---

[1] An excellent example (which I have encountered only as this chapter is going through the press) may be found in the garden-quartett of *Mefistofele* ; where the mocking tone of the sham-lover is conveyed by merely giving him semi-quavers against the crotchets of the others, and the hesitancy and agitation of Margherita are perfectly expressed by the simple device of syncopating her notes.

the result.  Thus in *Rigoletto*, the opera where sense and decency have perhaps been most conspicuously outraged, and where the general dramatic interest is of the lowest and most trifling kind, the celebrated quartett owes much of its charm to the simple point that two of the singers are not supposed to know that the others are near them, which gives piquancy to the contrast in the strains they sing.  An effect resting on a similar basis was a very pretty feature in a little piece of Mr. Sullivan's, called *The Zoo*; where an andante duet between two lovers was accompanied by an allegro statement from the second lady of the number of buns and lollipops she had been consuming.  The special order of effect is quite as well exemplified in such a case as this as in many much more ambitious attempts; and if it is not in any strict sense dramatic, it is at all events intimately connected with the delivery of music by dramatic personages whose history and relations are to some extent present to the mind.

The combination of parts may also, of course, often give peculiar point to some direct piece of dramatic intention, by the mere fact of enabling several people to talk at once.  Arne, in his *Judgment of Paris*, introduced one of the first examples of such a concerted piece in a trio for three soprano voices, where each reiterates the words 'Turn to *me*, for *I* am she.'

§ 6. Necessity of independently agreeable quality in the great bulk of the music of an opera.

I have already incidentally adverted to the necessity of independent impressiveness in the great bulk of the music of an opera; of such agreeableness of quality as would convey real pleasure, however far short of the complete pleasure, to a person who did not catch the words or see the scene.  This topic needs the more careful consideration in that the view itself is easily liable to misrepresentation, while the contradictions of it may assume various very plausible forms.

False and superficial objections to this view; as that it demands a sacrifice of dramatic expression;

It is easy, for instance, to stumble over the word *independent*, as though it involved oblivion of the expression and dramatic suitability which are naturally looked for in operatic music.  Whether music which is not on its own merits *im*pressive can be *ex*pressive at all, unless in a perfectly barren sense, is a question which, though practically answered in the fourteenth chapter, assumes primary importance in connection with Opera, and must be further considered in a few moments.  Meanwhile I need hardly dwell on the normal compatibility of the impressive and expressive characters, having already occupied so much space with discussion of the manner and degree in which Music may overlap the definable sphere of ordinary human sentiments; and having just explained that, so long as no sacrifice is made of direct musical beauty, association is always ready to extend the scope of this power by the gradual creation of genuinely-felt though inexplicable analogies.

that it implies that an opera gains nothing from scenic presentation;

Again, the demand for inherent musical beauty is sometimes taken as implying that a good opera might be satisfactorily transferred to a concert-room: as though vindication of the qualities necessary to render effective a single element in a compound result were to assert that the single element is worth as much as the whole result. I have, moreover, dwelt especially on the facts (1) that the delight bred from the union of the distinct lines of impression is something quite beyond the mere sum of the two, and (2) that the successive musical sections depend entirely on the scene and action for explanation and justification of their succession.

It may sound plausible, again, to represent insistence on the rights of Music as a vulgar preference for having one's ears tickled to the lofty delight of witnessing 'dramatic interpretation:' as though what is meant by the rights of Music were ministration to the fame and fortune of soprano acrobats. This fiction of a dilemma, in which the choice is between surrendering the claims of one's ears for firm and coherent motive and betraying an itch for the tricks and roulades one most abhors, is less excusable now than in Gluck's time. 'I wished,' Gluck said, 'to confine Music to its true province, that of strengthening Poetry by the expression of the sentiments,' &c.; and he compared the function of Music towards Poetry to the aid ' which liveliness of colouring and the happy combination of light and shade afford to a correct and well-designed picture.' ' I have therefore carefully avoided interrupting a singer in the warmth of a dialogue in order to wait for a tedious ritornel, or stopping him in the middle of a speech either for the purpose of displaying the flexibility of his voice on some favourable vowel, or that the orchestra might give him time to take breath before a long-sustained note.' Perfectly right, of course : Gluck's practical reforms were altogether to be applauded. The only mistake is in not seeing that the points described are duties owed primarily *to the music*, rather than by the music to the poetry. In being delivered from long passages of vocal gymnastics Music is being not ' confined ' but set free, is not putting off her rights of beauty but shaking off the trivialities which more than anything else defraud her of those rights. Not that Gluck was blind, even in theory, to the independent conditions of vital musical organism ; as he showed by dwelling on the fatal effects which the slightest alterations may produce. ' Make the least change,' he said, ' in *Che farò senza Eurydice*, and it will become an air for a puppet-show.' Quite so : that is the sort of melody which truly ' strengthens the expression of sentiments ; ' and it may be hinted that if Gluck had written rather more of such unchangeable music, and rather less of the declamatory recitative (good though much of it be of its kind) ' which everyone admires and yawns at ' and few indeed recall or live on, his operas would hardly have lost their vitality. What a satire, indeed, are the surviving beauties of the *Orphée* on the theory of humble musical subordination ! Who would ever have read or heard of the libretto or its sentiments, but for the ' seconding ' music ? How many of the thousands who have loved *Che farò* have regarded the music as an adjunct to something more import-

that it implies a low desire to have one's ears tickled ;

this last objection being less defensible now than in the days of Gluck.

Music is strong to aid and second Poetry through retaining, not through surrendering, strength and beauty of its own.

ant than itself, or would have recalled a couple of lines of the words on their own account ? It is not by *adding* 'liveliness of colouring or 'happy combination of light and shade,' but by *possessing* perfectly beautiful and definite melodic form, that such music acts as it does : it would be powerless to second words and sentiments but for its own inherent strength. Nor does such language imply either complaint of an inadequate libretto, or oblivion that true operatic effect is entirely a joint one. The libretto is perfectly adequate—as even libretti with less interesting scenes, with balder words, and generally still more unfit for independence, may be fairly adequate—just because the 'seconding' power of Music will lift them into her own region and make them one with herself, in an effect which alone she would be powerless to attain.

§ 7. The doctrine that Music is to bow down before the eternal rights of Poetry.

This last point brings us face to face with the most comprehensive and *ad captandum* form of the fallacy under the protection of which Music is to be excused, when it likes, from gratifying the musical sense ; the doctrine that henceforth every composer with high aspirations is ' to consider it his task to express a preconceived poetical idea by means of sound,' and is 'to bow down before the eternal rights of Poetry.' Not of course that any one will object to a composer's considering this his task, as long as he produces enjoyable music ; and that enjoyable music can be produced by persons who do consider this their task has been sufficiently proved ; only they cannot be allowed to excuse themselves for producing *un*enjoyable music on the plea of bowing down before any eternal rights whatever.

The invocation of the Choral Symphony.

The general use made of the name of Beethoven in connection with the above fallacy, has been already noticed : but the special instance most insisted on has a special relation to our present topic, having been used to show how Beethoven, tottering on the final Pisgah-peak of the Symphony, pointed on to the Wagnerian Opera. It is a real curiosity in the way of finding a text for a theory. Beethoven is represented as having felt ' the demand of a previous poetic inspiration,' and being the spiritual father of those who bow down, on the ground that in one movement of one symphony (which by bad luck was the last he completed) he introduced a chorus, and made them sing some stirring words to an utterly musical and rhythmic tune of the most catching and popular character. In the same sense Shakespeare proclaimed the insufficiency of men and women for dramatic purposes by introducing beings of another order into the *Tempest* ; and in the same sense Beethoven himself proved the inadequacy of his musical resources and the necessity of henceforth bowing down before the eternal rights of birds, by a well-known passage in the *Pastoral* symphony.

§ 8. The limits of the dispute : it does not concern differences in *musical* appreciation.

But while we cannot allow Beethoven as the figure-head of a view which he never once expressed and which his whole practice belies, the view may still claim to be examined on its own merits in connection with the field of art to which it has been specially applied. It is necessary first of all to

make the limits of the disputed question perfectly clear. I am in no way
arguing with those who perceive musical beauty in some places where I do
not, or who perceive in other places a higher degree of it than I do. On
the contrary, I try elsewhere to show how baseless and unmeaning such
argument is apt to be; and how so far as A receives any musical enjoyment
which is compatible [1] with the complete enjoyment of all that B enjoys, B
is simply so much the worse off for being deaf to it. But the parts which
are able on their independent merits to attract and interest the ear are, of
course, not representative of a theory of complete dependence and subordination. In respect of them Wagner is simply a successful composer,
not a ' daring innovator.' They are fundamentally on the same line as all
other music that attracts and interests the ear; and so far as such music
is given us, we will not quarrel with the giver as to whether the exquisite
harmony of two things can be held to imply the evolution of one out of
the other. The parts I am concerned with are successions of notes which
do *not* attract or interest the ear. The view of dependence which I dispute is that Music acts on the drama not, or not only, by shedding the
light of its own beauty in broad masses and in vivid points; but by
bringing out in close detail a ' melody contained in the poem; ' which
' melody ' may and often does take the shape of successions of notes that
convey no pleasure to the musical sense, but are none the less felt, in some
mysterious way, to ' express ' the words they go with. And my point is
that the alliance of these notes with words is not dramatic interpretation
or expression, but at best arbitrary symbolism and at worst mere mechanical
emphasis, which even as emphasis defeats its own object; and that the
notes, having *ex hypothesi* no independent value, are simply an element
of weariness in a drama.

Here then is a plain issue. If, when I complain of a large number of
pages in Wagner's operas as unbeautiful, his adherents told me that they
found them the reverse, it might still, I think, be proved to them that
successions of notes which will not stick in the head, which might go
another way on another night without detection, which, in other words, are

---

[1] This is a very necessary condition, and
applies to any sort of comparison of musical
tastes. There are many pieces of Wagner's
music which one hears quoted and played on
pianos as special gems, and in which one
may perceive really remarkable excellence,
while still receiving from them a certain impression of cloyingness, mannerism, want of
complete robustness, and occasionally vulgarity. The orchestral opening to the fourth
scene of the second act of *Lohengrin* is so
beautiful as in some measure to atone for
the dreary waste preceding it, which is
tolerably high praise; but when one hears
this, and the introduction to the third act of
the same opera, and other impressive and
characteristic passages, talked of as though
they were on an unsurpassed level of excellence, one may be pardoned for doubting
whether those who so talk have really felt
*quite* all there is to feel in certain very familiar works, say the first movements of the
*Pathétique* and *Pastoral* sonatas. Will that
introduction to the third act of *Lohengrin*
find itself *quite* comfortable among the motives of the seventh symphony, in ears to
which the motives of the seventh symphony
are supreme? If so, so much the better.

wholly inorganic, must give a less sum of pleasure than successions of notes which *will* stick in the head, which when they recur *insist* on being welcomed, every note in its place, with joyful recognition, which, in other words, are wholly organic. And it might further be proved that *tremolando* passages of diminished sevenths are at any rate not original; and that firm rhythm and well-defined tonality are such rooted and essential elements of the great music which the whole musical world has admired and continues to admire, that it is, to say the least, odd if they can be discarded at a moment's notice. But at the same time if my friends continued to say they enjoyed these same pages, that would be a fact I could never get behind. But what they do tell me is that the pages I object to are *dramatic*; that if I want beauty I must go elsewhere, or at least to some other part of the same opera (where I gladly admit the possibility of finding it), but that successions of musical sound can possess dramatic value which have no *locus standi* as music; in other words, that combinations of notes can find some short cut to being effective and expressive without passing through the stage of interesting or satisfying the musical sense.

The defence set up for an immense amount of recent music is not that some find it musically agreeable, but that it is dramatic.

It should surely be obvious that since notes can get no musical quality or coherence out of words, they can only add anything to the effect of words by bringing a quality and coherence of their own, *i.e.* by giving the distinctive impression of agreeable melodic and harmonic form. Consider the converse case, and suppose the material, that is, the separate words, to be taken out of a poem of Tennyson's, to be arranged in inconsecutive fragments, and then set to music. Would it be thought a valid answer, to a person who complained of their inanity, that it was unfair to judge of their merits apart from the notes? Yet what more sense is there in calling formless and unrelated successions of musical sound *music*, and then saying, as is perpetually said, that it is *unfair* to judge them *as* music, or to consider them as entities at all apart from the words? It need hardly be repeated that judging them as music does not mean obstinately treating them as if we were in a concert-room; that the demands of the ear do not shut out the sense of dramatic suitability, and the delight in the fusion of the musical with the extra-musical elements.

§ 9. The absurdity of saying that successions of notes are not to be judged with reference to their effect on the musical sense.

We have seen how, in spite of the very broad and general nature of the emotional conditions which Music will normally express, the mere adjunct of definite words and scene will make the particular alliance with music seem equally definite; so that plaintive or passionate strains, which on their own account could only be described by such general adjectives, will truly wed themselves to a particular dramatic situation as though they were the inevitable outcome of it. But to be soul-stirring, such association demands independent coherence and vitality in the two things: it makes concrete the connection between them only when they are alive and akin, to begin with, by the abstract resemblance of each having something to tell,

§ 10. Association can only set up magical correspondences between music and other things on condition of the music's possessing independent charm.

and it would do little to galvanise such 'dead formalism' as Music has recently been described to be when left to its own resources. No amount of hearings of *Tannhäuser* would make me feel this kind of association between the words and situation of the tournament of song and the music sung by the competitors (with the exception of Tannhäuser's own song), simply because I see no independent beauty in the music. If I knew every bar by heart, I should simply know, as a matter of fact, that each note comes where it does with such and such a word, but the association being purely mechanical would give me no additional pleasure. It will be remembered that it is in the subtle and harmonious blending of things *severally impressive in their kind,* that we found our general principle and condition of magical correspondences in Art. The union of verbal phrases with note-phrases which, to a person who did not catch the words and did not look at the stage, would have no charm (and few will deny this to be the case with such passages as I have quoted above), is not spiritual fusion but mechanical welding; however much the writer, who confessedly sits down to evolve music out of long strings of extra-musical conceptions, may deceive himself as to the expressive power of his symbols.

People are somewhat apt to lose sight of this fact from thinking only of short single fragments When a man shouts—

Or - trud

accompanied by the inevitable harmony, a diminished seventh, it may seem to 'express' the fact that he has something disagreeable on his mind; what is lugubrious or violent has of course an exceptionally good chance of being 'expressed' by what is ugly, shiftless, or abrupt as music. In the same way spasmodic orchestral scurryings are a favourite means of musically 'pourtraying' agitation and distress, and vague *tremolando* chords of suggesting mystery. But any value which can be attached to such effects depends on their rarity, as in the somewhat analogous case of metrical irregularities in Poetry. When formless passage succeeds formless passage, when the music is sustainedly incoherent, the symbols of the intended qualities lose every vestige of interest. We see at once how mechanically set and obvious the means for 'expression of sentiments' in such circumstances must be. The notes will go slow when the sentiment is grave, will quicken up when the sentiment is gay; there will be some marked minor intervals when the sentiment is sad, and some chromatic ones when the sentiment is agitated; when there is a 'transition in the sentiment' there will be some modulating chords, helped out by some orchestral noise if the transition of sentiment means a little excitement; the æsthetic result being about equivalent to what would be produced by printing words of joy red, words

The mechanical character of 'expression by formless and unrelated fragments.

of grief black, words of jealousy green, words of thought brown, and so on. When there is no particular sentiment, as in the lengthy remarks of the male personages, before the appearance of the hero, in the first act of *Lohengrin*, there is no reason why the notes should do anything in particular; so it seems a pity that there, at any rate, they should not have taken the opportunity of being agreeable. This of course is not a description of what recitative need be, but of what it perpetually is. There are all degrees between coherence and absolute incoherence, between the most beautiful melodic recitatives of Handel and Gluck and those quoted at the beginning of this chapter. But a composer who has not grasped the idea that there is no road to true musical expression save through the exercise of true musical genius in the invention of true musical form, who thinks that successions of notes can retain the character of expressive utterance while abandoning the conditions which give them a hold on the ear, must of course be in special danger in any field where the conditions may be to some extent relaxed. In prolonged recitative, even where rhythm and key are not wholly flouted, there must always be a tendency to lose clear, strong, and individual movement: where the object is just to emphasise certain words, it must often be a matter of indifference whether we have *tweedledum* or *tweedledee*, in the same sense that it is a matter of indifference whether we have a word italicised or underlined. And it is to the keeping of the ear on the stretch by a system of note-underlining, that Music is reduced by the loss of its inherent rights and the abandonment of organic periods.

I need hardly pause to answer the ordinary superficial objection that the productions of the other arts may impress the imagination even in the absence of the qualities included broadly under the term beauty. We have seen [1] how essentially Music lacks the conditions which apply, in this respect, to the arts of representation—as, in Painting, the skill of accurate delineation, and the distinct and far-reaching suggestions of the subject-matter and treatment; and in Poetry, the sense of subtle relations, and the infinitely delicate and complex associations of language; which admits of the rarest and most forcible use on almost any theme, and within the briefest space. A passage of *sound* can suggest no delicacy of detailed resemblance, can open up no distinct vistas of external or speculative interest: the rare and forcible use of *notes* has no meaning apart from satisfaction of the ear's claim for what is enjoyable, individual, and rememberable: the sole employment offered to the mind under what is musically ugly or unpleasing, as against the manifold activity evoked in other cases, is the bald reflection that 'the situation demands' what is ugly or unpleasing; a refuge in which even the least exacting imagination must surely soon find itself rather cramped. In tracing the causes of the

*Marginal notes:*

Inevitable tendency in prolonged recitative to lose individual movement, and to degenerate into barren emphasis which soon ceases even to be felt as emphatic.

Futility of the objection that in other arts imaginative interest is not confined to the region of the beautiful.

---

[1] See especially the first part of chap. xvii.

unique dependence of Music on its own immediate resources, we have seen how entirely the test-question must always be, Is such and such a sound-motion a source of assured delight to the sound-sense? Do the melodic and harmonic combinations commend themselves to their sole arbiter?' And this position is confirmed by our more recent observation of the utterly mechanical nature of any 'dramatic suitability' which tries to elude the test; of the ease of imparting to inorganic successions of notes external aspects of 'expression;' and pretending that characters with which Music—so long as she is true to herself—can indeed invest her very loveliest forms, will flourish equally in defiance of the ear's conditions and in the absence of any forms to invest.

I have said that it is the frequent and continuous, not the brief and occasional, abandonment of organic structure which is objectionable. More or less fragmentary pieces, either of orchestral 'passage-writing,' or it may be of colour-effect from some solo-instrument such as a horn, or of unmetrical declamation, may come in with propriety and effect, but only on condition of their being sparingly and frankly used. But since the making of fragments is cheap and easy, while fine melodic motive will not come even to genius except in special moments and often as the result of long search, the temptation is always to string fragments together, and impose on the public the notion that the disconnected and spasmodic character of the series is part of the 'dramatic' business. Whenever a fine soprano voice takes some unexpected notes in a high register, accompanied by some marked bodily movement, one is sure to hear that word 'dramatic:' many indeed seem to appropriate it to the extreme or chromatic intervals which have much the same relation to truly dramatic musical effects as the jerky antics of a marionette to truly dramatic gesture. In a certain way the most dramatic parts of a play, where the turns of events and remarks are apt to be sudden and swift, and where set and sustained pieces of music are out of place, expose the composer to particular difficulties in the invention and concatenation of phrases; and with an idea that the inability to develop long melodic motives excuses him from being melodic or supplying any basis of rhythmic continuity, he is very apt to shut off music, and to turn on noisy orchestral passages interspersed with short 'declamatory' tags. A notable example of this may be found in *Guillaume Tell*, an opera in the first half of which the composer has altogether surpassed himself, and which goes literally to pieces in the apple-scene, at the very crisis of the plot.

In face of a theory which specially insists on detailed illustration of the verbal text, it is half amusing to note how completely those particular musical points which *can* truly go beyond the normal general agreement, and *can* make a detail of the music seem one with a detail of verbal expression, are precluded by Wagner's habit of 'throwing himself

*The brief and occasional abandonment of organic structure is allowable and effective:*

*but composers are tempted into whole long scenes of fragments by the very ease of stringing them together; and especially at important crises.*

§ 11. The very points where detailed expression is possible, especially by striking harmonic features, depend entirely on the true organic form which Wagner's recitative discards.

fearlessly into the sea of music' and despising the firm support of measure and key. These detailed points are naturally for the most part connected with *harmony*. We saw in the chapter on that subject how individual and arresting the effect of a single chord might be; and in association with words and scenes, such features may become dramatic in an extraordinary degree: as Wagner himself says, 'one single harmonic turn is capable of the most touching changes of expression.' We saw the effect of a single chord in a perfectly naïve melody of Auber's, and in an equally simple one of Schubert's; we might add another harmonic feature from the table-music towards the end of *Don Giovanni*, which, while acting as the simple accompaniment of the simplest of melodies, seems to suggest with superb irony the whole impending doom. But such luck comes only to one who deserves it; we saw how harmony waits on melody, and how thrilling harmonic points cannot be shed *ad libitum*, but depend entirely on occupying a particular position in a particular organic form. They can no more be got otherwise than a painter can get the effect of his high lights in an orderless conglomeration of blotches and streaks. No focussing of beauty or expression is possible at any point of such series of patches as I quoted from *Lohengrin*. All that harmony can do in cases like that is mechanically to support the patches and peg them together; it can never vitalise them. Precisely similar remarks apply to less concentrated musical features; as, for instance, to the above-mentioned use of syncopation in the garden-quartett of *Mefistofele*; as good an instance as could be wished of the dependence of thrilling dramatic expression on independent and duly conditioned musical substance—on definite beauties which genius brings forth, not by throwing itself vaguely into the sea of music, but by hunting patiently for pearls.

§ 12. The perpetual expression-in-detail which is musically impossible is dramatically unnecessary.

It is clear that any musical features, whether of striking contrast, or of special harmonic vividness, or of any other sort, which give the chance for the most vivid sense of union with their dramatic concomitants, must on musical grounds be occasional only: we cannot have marked contrasts and vivid harmonic features every four or six bars. But on verbal and dramatic grounds also this most detailed sort of expression is only occasionally wanted. It is as absurd to suppose that there is a definite dramatic turn of feeling or a 'motive of dramatic action' to be musically 'expressed' every ten seconds, as to expect the heroine to be momentarily alternating between smiles and scowls. And when this is recognised, and the more general sort of correspondence between the musical and the dramatic passages is realised as the normal condition of union, the demand that the music, if continuous, shall be in itself agreeable, receives additional force: on no other terms can words gain in anything except tedium from a forced alliance with notes and intervals with which they have no more connection than with geometrical curves.

At any rate those who are not wearied may be lauded for their patience, but hardly for their artistic perception. It may, no doubt, be the case that some persons are so constituted as to prefer a long speech or dialogue delivered in fragmentary phrases of musical sound, to the same words delivered in the speaking voice, or to silence. But inasmuch as a million ways exist of being fragmentary and inorganic to one of being the reverse, it is at any rate impossible to claim much merit for such settings. Again, the background of fine and varied musical colour which a large orchestra, play what they will, can hardly help producing, may have the same kind of general stimulating and supporting influence that it sometimes has on purely subjective trains of thought and emotion, vaguely enhancing the pleasure of watching the dramatic situations, and blending with the colour-effects (usually, it must be admitted, of a very crude sort) presented to the eye. This indefinite effect was sufficiently noticed in the chapters on Colour and on the two ways of hearing Music, nor do I wish to undervalue it. But its value is comparatively small and short-lived, and, as we saw, is smallest in the case of those who seek for something more. The glory of sound-colour and mass is in seconding not supplanting form : and when Music fails or ceases to convey individual melodic and harmonic impressions, the finest voices and the most richly coloured orchestral passages will not be able for many minutes to keep up the fiction that the ear which is groping and leaking is really grasping and assimilating.

§ 13. Some may prefer even incoherent and joyless musical phrases to common speech or to silence;

and others may be impressed by the mere mass and colour of sound;

but such pleasure must be very short-lived.

Not of course, as I must once more repeat, that truly strong and organic music is bound to reveal its qualities in a moment. At first much of a symphony of Beethoven or a fugal chorus of Bach may make on many as undefined an impression as that produced by the most *nohow* parts of operas : but the final verdict on all of these must rest not on any such result, but on the conscious and definite perception of their beauties by those who obtain more complete knowledge of them. Wagner, however, expressly presents his work 'not to the connoisseur but to the public,' and conceives that the 'infinitely rich and ramified details of the large melody which comprises the whole dramatic-musical piece' are 'to reveal themselves to the most naïve layman as soon as he may be sufficiently collected to receive the impression.' And this in the same breath that he adduces as a characteristic, and indeed a merit, of the great 'forest-melody' by which he illustrates his ideal of operatic music, that the hearer cannot the least possess or recall it, or obtain any notion or reminiscence of it in his own home, but 'must return to the woods,' *i.e.* to his stall at the opera, 'on a summer-night. Would it not be folly if he were to catch a sweet wood-bird, so as to train it at home to whistle a fragment of that great forest-melody ? ' Whistling may not be the best medium; but so far as he possesses at home any means, whether in himself or in some domestic

§ 14. Wagner's profession of presenting his work to the 'naïve layman.'

'wood-bird,' of reproducing at will such beauties as voice or pianoforte can reproduce, and thus facilitating and stamping his acquaintance with them, he is not so much foolish as fortunate. The compliment paid here to the naïve layman is in fact about as left-handed as that paid to melody by calling it infinite. What naïve laymen are interested in, first and foremost, is not the maze but the clue; not 'infinitely ramified details' which they cannot get hold of, but clear and continuous motive which they can.

§ 15. Unreality in the identification of musician and poet.

Finally there is a strong unreality about Wagner's theory from a practical point of view. If the words of a play which lasts for four hours are to be 'expressed' by notes, clause after clause, in the detailed way which Wagner assumes possible, and more especially if the notes are not to be bound to independent musical beauty, the words ought at any rate to be most remarkably well worth expressing. What, then, is to happen next? Is not the rarity of the special poetic gift and function somewhat ignored in the broad compliment to the abstraction, Poetry? We have only to look round to see that poets are not musicians, nor musicians poets, even in the most indirect and potential sense; the characteristics which they necessarily possess in common may be reduced to a more or less emotional temperament and a correct ear for time, both shared by them with thousands of non-inventive persons. Yet we must admit, supposing the close and special alliance of detail after detail in the two utterances to be possible, that the poet who plans his poem so that it 'can penetrate to the finest fibres of the musical tissue,' and who 'has perfectly mastered the inexhaustible power of expression of the symphonic melody, so as to be induced to meet its finest and most delicate nuances,' will have at any rate a tolerable aptitude for Music; and a cognate completeness and delicacy of perception of the other art would be required from the musician. Poet and musician seem really driven to be one: for the picture of the musician humbly sitting, waiting to be fertilised, and then inventing the music implicit in some one else's poem, is grotesque and self-contradictory. But even Wagner would allow that, just as a total absence of ear for tune would prevent the greatest of poets from appreciating a melody, so some quite independent musical aptitude is necessary to the ideal compound artist, to enable him to evolve and write down in correct score the melody implicit in his poem. Now assuming that the next hundred years, like the last, will produce a limited number of people endowed with the necessary independent musical aptitudes, what ground have we for expecting the possession by any one of these of such dramatic genius and such power of verbal expression as truly to entitle him to the name of a poet? The chances against the union of the two gifts are a million to one. While Wagner cannot dispense in 'musicians of the future' with the special musical aptitudes possessed by those of the past, he in fact demands in addition a totally new set of aptitudes.

Such a change, it need hardly be said, is without any sort of precedent or analogy. The argument on this more external ground entirely corresponds with our former objections. It is just this attractive-sounding theory of amalgamation of 'finest fibres' and 'infinitely ramified details' which, we saw, cut at the root of musical coherence, and so of musical beauty and effect. In such a theory a musician truly embraces a cloud, and his artistic offspring may too probably, like Ixion's brood, turn out a double failure, neither music nor poetry. Meanwhile the particular poetry before which the sister-art is to 'bow down' does not seem likely to attain extremely lofty flights. Fortunately there is no need that it should : it is in fact only a simple and elementary sort of poetry which is really suitable for musical setting, and the simplest dramatic thread and most ordinary words will serve as a basis for a beautiful opera. Only in face of the librettos at present existing in the world Music may perhaps fairly claim to stand upright a little longer.

*Fortunately, Music is content with simple situations and a kind of poetry which it certainly does not require genius to produce.*

# CHAPTER XXIII.

## MUSICAL CRITICISM.

§ 1. The small place which Music holds in literature.

In the *Confessions of an Opium-Eater* De Quincey has remarked with surprise how few are the worthy and illuminating utterances which can be adduced on the subject of Music, considering the conspicuous place the art has held both in the ancient and in the modern world. His observation refers rather to general literature, but it is easy to extend its application; and to show moreover that so far as the preceding views and arguments are just, the fact is far more true than surprising, and illustrates, and is illustrated by, other experience.

The highest function of the art-critic:

Criticism is a word which covers a great deal of ground. It does duty equally for the most profound and illuminating instruction and for the most transient record of hasty opinions. But in its highest aspect, at any rate, the function of the art-critic is that of an interpreter. By his greater sympathy with his subject, and knowledge of its special scope and function in relation to the whole imaginative activity, he may really fulfil the enviable part of making others see and appreciate marvels otherwise quite beyond their ken; and it is hard to over-estimate the influence of this kind which one man may have, where the subject is adapted to such treatment. Those who depreciate the seeing with the eyes of others, which is to many in the first instance the only means of seeing worthily at all, simply ignore what to those who experience it is a definite and indisputable possession: and it is unfortunate that in subjects where intuition seems predominant, as especially in Art, the very person most fitted to act as a guide may be apt to distrust the value of guidance. Having by nature the instinct and power of direct vision, and having all his life found this element predominating in all his judgments, he can with difficulty believe in sight at second hand, unless perchance he has himself experienced a similar benefit in being told what to look at and what to look for in some other region of Art where he is less of a master.

which has no place in Music.

In one of the arts, however, those who have so far agreed with me will agree that criticism of the entirely enlightening kind never did and never can exist. The true *interpreter* of Music must always be the performer, not the critic; and the latter, from a feeling that he must explain something, is in constant danger of mistaking his vocation. Many seem to find this a difficult notion to catch. The soothing and stimulating effects of Music, regarded merely as beautiful sound, are so marked and universal, and pass often by such imperceptible degrees into the perception of objective musical ideas, that persons of general culture, the limits of whose musical instinct or proficiency chance to confine their experience rather to the former end of the series, are apt to suppose that the keener and more comprehending musical pleasure must be just a more intense and sustained one of the same kind as their own, and that where they imagine occasional streams and groves or catch intermittently the thread of musical assertion and response, Beethoven would trace landscapes and watch dramas; thus mistaking secondary, momentary, and accidental suggestions of music for its true essence and the primary source of its creator's impulse. Moreover a cultivated person may be not unnaturally loth to admit the existence of quite unknown regions; and finding perhaps that, in the absence of any strong or subtle sense of form and colour, his general knowledge, intelligence, and sympathy have carried him with admiring interest through scores of picture-galleries, he may feel that it must be very much against Music if here his general powers will not come in. The indefinite emotional stirrings of beautiful sound are excellently described by De Quincey; but he makes the common mistake of intellectual writers in taking these indefinite effects (whose power and value I have fully recognised) for the substance of what is there; in supposing that the inward and indescribable character of musical impressions means that they are necessarily vague and subjective. The greater indeed the hearer's power of reflection and imagination, the more likely (in the absence of definite musical instinct) that he will make music the background to his own thoughts and aspirations, or take the critic's ideas on trust. Nevertheless true art is objective; and the definiteness in form which first-rate music presents to the hearing ear is compatible with a sense of mystery and infinity which no vagueness can emulate, and which will gain nothing from a score of possible (and very often entirely different) subjective interpretations. In a similar way many who derive a large amount of true perceptive pleasure from some compositions and some parts of compositions, but find others above their heads, suppose that a more gifted or more cultivated faculty would reveal some symbolic purpose and meaning, that it would show them *different* things, instead of the *same* things *better* and more of them. Instead of sticking to the music and asking, 'What does it say?' to which a few more hearings might give them the answer, they look outside and ask, 'What does it mean?' and feel sure the composer could have told them.

We can easily see how the elimination of the interpreter's duties narrows the musical critic's sphere. Poets, painters, and sculptors deal

*The common idea that Music has an assignable meaning and can be interpreted by experts.*

§ 2. Limitation of the musical critic's sphere.

with a world of facts which are independently appreciable. The art of many of the greatest of them has been steeped in a particular vein of ideas and sentiments : and apart from this, their work is grounded everywhere on truth and Nature and on a feeling for the connections of the visible and spiritual world, and they themselves have the most definite relation to their environment and their fellows. It is true that the greatest masters have often worked with little self-consciousness or self-analysis, and no sense of a special aim or mission, but have simply followed out an irresistible inward impulse, not guessing to what an extent their natural vision was revelation for the world. But a critic who enters into the ideas of the men and of their time, and who knows what Nature is like, has at any rate solid ground for explaining effectively their standpoint, and the kind and measure of their success; and we can many of us fully sympathise with Dorothea's sudden awakening to the significance of saints with architectural models in their hands and hatchets in their heads. In visible art containing no religious or symbolical motive, the critic still commands in the selection and treatment of the subject-matter topics on which he will at any rate be intelligible to a large body of the public, and which may afford him the very best text for interesting lessons on ancient and modern life. All such topics disappear when we enter the world of sound. We have seen how it is owing to her nature, and not through having appeared on the earth in her full stature and beauty at a time of teeming industrial life and of conflicting and vanishing creeds, that Music, while exercising a most powerful cosmopolitan influence, reigns independently of any great phases or currents of human existence and thought. No such book as *Modern Painters* could possibly be written in connection with this art; for all criticism which depends on a consideration of external facts and relations is excluded in a region where there are no such facts and relations to consider.[1]

---

[1] Critics who, like C. H. Bitter, perceive in the great *B Minor* Mass 'a musical commentary in Bach's own didactic argumentative manner on the principal doctrines of Christianity,' have, no doubt, a limitless range for their interest; and it is a pity this writer could not foresee how much, *e.g.*, the doctrine of the Procession of the Holy Ghost would gain in intelligibility to quite a number of London amateurs during the spring of 1876, through the medium of Bach's learned and lucid exposition. The scarcely less bold assertion by Mr. Haweis of the principle that it is allowable for music to be dull, and to 'express uninteresting successions of emotion,' is an instance of the straits to which an able writer is reduced by that disastrous and unmeaning premiss that 'Music covers the whole of life,' and that 'every moment of our lives,' and therefore the dull ones, 'is a fit subject for music.'

I have been sometimes asked by professedly unmusical persons why there cannot be some treatment of Music analogous to that criticism of Poetry which deals with the form, the metrical and verbally musical dress of the thought. The answer of course is that the poetical criticism always includes reference to the subject-matter, and to the mode in which it is presented and transfigured; the very duality of subject-matter and form, the fact of definite investiture, supplies the interesting topic: while in Music the subject-matter throughout is not *invested* in form, but *is* form.

The same isolation which prevents an explanation, and so a criticism (in the highest sense), of melodies or musical works as a whole, affects also their details. A word or phrase in a poem, a figure or part of a figure in a picture, may be picked out and dwelt on in relation to the whole work, and may be made a nucleus for all manner of interesting considerations. In Music, though the relation of a chord or phrase to its surroundings may be *technically* criticised, no words can penetrate or enhance its effect. In details, as in leading conceptions, force or appropriateness or namby-pambiness, or whatever it may be, can be to a great extent *proved* in the arts of representation, only *felt* in Music.

When once the uniqueness and isolation of musical experiences is recognised, it becomes obvious moreover that *description* has not a much wider field than *interpretation*. Set attempts in that direction continually take the form of a mere piling up of big words. Whether a person knows the special composition or is only about to make its acquaintance, he can hardly gain much by being told, for instance, of Schumann's quintett, that 'ecstatic inspiration, lofty expression, fine mastery of passion, noble feeling, wealth of imagination, fresh and healthy images, and a happy issue, are here united in a rare degree.' This specimen fairly represents an enormously large number of the sentences written about musical works. It is inevitable that vapouring phrases should specially abound in respect of those unique and exciting utterances which themselves admit of no confirmation or confutation by being confronted with external reality: and multitudes who feel truly and acutely are unfortunately, in respect of verbal expression of their feelings, very much at the mercy of the jargon they find in vogue around them.

*Description has hardly a wider field than interpretation.*

There is doubtless a natural reason why those technically acquainted with the art of Music should be popularly supposed to be in possession of secrets which are hidden from others, or rather why the nature of the secrets should be misunderstood. There is a curious contrast between the width of the instinctive appreciation of this art, and the esoteric and apparently mysterious nature of its technicalities. An immense number of persons who are habitually enjoying music have not the slightest idea what a *key* or a *modulation* means; while of those who have musical knowledge in the sense that they can perform and read music with facility, not one in fifty has any technical acquaintance with the simplest elements of harmony and structure: and it is natural that such persons should often vaguely imagine that only professed students can know exactly what the creators are at, or be justified in speaking with decision about their creations. It would be absurd to underrate the value of such technical acquirements, even as regards appreciation: they often immensely facilitate the process of making acquaintance with new works and give certainty and tenacity to the memory; to say nothing of the insight

*§ 3. Reason why the secrets of which musical experts are thought to be in possession are misunderstood.*

they give into the *craft*, the pleasure of perceiving wherein lie the special points of skilful and original workmanship. But it is very important that those who lack them should realise that they make no vital revelations; that perception and enjoyment may be absolutely perfect without them. That music which a person's natural capacity and experience in the way of hearing and attending enable him to appreciate, he will appreciate; and though the power of technical analysis might give him considerable extraneous interest, it would not alter the essence of the impression, or make it at all more delightful to him.[1] The great advantages which result from practical or theoretical study, in the way of rapid and lasting acquaintance with musical works, should make those who possess them anxious to recognise all that is implied in these facts; the chief point being that it is not so much milk instead of strong meat that the untechnical lover of music requires, as judicious and condensed administration of the stronger diet; and especially, what has been already so much insisted on, repetition of the same work till its motives are in a true sense familiar. Berlioz complains that about Music people expatiate in perfect ignorance who would never so commit themselves on other arts: I am far more often annoyed by the remark from those who appreciate much, and might easily appreciate more, in the truest way, that they 'understand nothing about it;' which is like professing to 'understand nothing about' human beauty on the ground of not having minutely studied human anatomy.

While on the subject of the relations of technical acquirements to popular appreciation, it is just worth noting that there is music which may be interesting to the performers without being so to the auditors:

---

[1] Equally erroneous with the supposition that technical acquaintance with the laws of harmony will give the ear some new kind of appreciation of beauty, is the idea that discoveries about the physical laws of sound and the physiology of the ear have in some way explained *Music*: whereas all they have done is to explain the *material* of Music. The theory of sound is an exceptionally well-understood and self-complete branch of physical science, just as Music is an exceptionally popular and self-complete art: but the two are absolutely distinct. Science explains the gradual adoption of a certain system of notes, giving admirable scope for the variety of proportional forms of which Music consists, and assigns reasons why some of these notes, sounded simultaneously, are concordant and others discordant: but in this direction it does not get beyond the bare and wholly unemotional elements, the bricks and mortar out of which melodic and harmonic forms are built. The actual definite effect on us of this or that musical motive as it is evolved before our ears—technically a series of time- and pitch-relations, æsthetically a free form charged with divine vitality—is no more explained by physiological facts than the effect of a drawing of Leonardo is explained by the natural actions of the eye in following straight lines and curves. For realisation, however, of the general characteristics of musical impressions, some sort of conception of their relation to the organism and of the most elementary facts of the nervous system does certainly seem requisite: not because such a conception at all explains the inner mysteries, but because without it people are likely to blunder, or to accept blunders, on the very threshold of the subject. I need only refer to the remarks about the 'tyranny of rhythm,' quoted in the eighth chapter.

and though a large number of those who naturally lead public opinion on the subject are alternately the one and the other, and run the risk of being bored as well as boring, it may be not amiss that they should occasionally brace and perhaps correct their taste and judgment by an elimination (performed partly by self-analysis and partly by watching other people's experience) of the element of merely technical interest.

I hope that in the course of this enquiry I have shown some reason to believe that, if the functions of musical criticism are limited, so also is its necessity, and that the grounds which preclude verbal interpretations and set verbal descriptions lie at the root of the art's wide comprehensibility and diffusion. The very fact that not one in a hundred of those who care for Music take the smallest interest in any external treatment of it is as good an indication as could be had of its exceptionally swift and easy channels to the comprehension and the heart. At the same time there is plenty for words to do. The natural conditions of musical life render the history of the art and its votaries rich in those chance incidents and remarks which may often throw a light and reveal a truth better than more deliberate criticism, and in which many a sedative might be found for those who are perpetually haunted by the spectre of some inner meaning: and the difference Music offers from the arts of the study and the studio in enlisting for its presentation large bodies of artists, among whom a special *esprit de corps* and a peculiar life and language might be expected to develop, is specially prolific in anecdotic interest. But work of a more serious kind is not wanting. We have had in England excellent recent examples of studies of particular composers, none the less interesting for the fact that the theme, when judiciously treated, is not an endless one; and, more important still, we have accounts and general analyses of particular works of a really educating sort. These accounts, to be useful, are necessarily somewhat technical; but the custom of giving quotations, and guiding the listener's attention to the noticeable points, conveys the elements of technical knowledge to all who can in some degree follow music with their eye, an acquirement as common and easy among amateurs as the actual realisation of it through the eye apart from performance is rare even among connoisseurs. And with this backbone of solid stuff, a running commentary of verbal description is often vivid and felicitous.

§ 4. The necessity, no less than the functions, of musical criticism is limited:

but criticism of the right sort has an abundant field.

Criticism of the right sort, however, speaks for itself and is received with avidity. More useful matter for my present purpose will present itself in connection with criticism which appears mistaken or misleading, and which includes several varieties not as yet mentioned. In the first place, then, newspaper-critics of so-called 'light music' perpetually, as I think, miss the important points in a way which makes their praise and blame equally undiscriminating and worthless. This sometimes seems to

§ 5. Instances of misleading criticism: in respect of 'light music,' through misapprehension of the popular capacity, imply a failure to recognise the value of melodic pleasure, and perhaps a certain individual lack of melodic instinct; but it is chiefly to be regretted in that it apparently assumes as an axiom the inability of the people to appreciate good music.  It would perhaps be useless for newspapers to be always criticising the ordinary run of plays and entertainments by a standard of very high æsthetic excellence, and here they may reasonably consider it as much as can be fairly demanded if an audience gets a tolerable amount of interest and amusement of a not unhealthy kind ; but I hope I have not totally failed in showing that with Music it is otherwise, and that good melody is a treasure of which the people have the key. Why, then, should a critic say less than the plain truth ?  The compositions of Offenbach will afford an example.  One knows the general tone in which they are criticised, and all the stock phrases which as a rule reach their utmost limit of severity in the expression 'pretty jingle.'  This may be damning with faint praise ; but why should music be praised at all which fails to satisfy any conceivable canon of goodness ?  According to our previous argument, the word *bad* may be fairly used (absolutely or relatively) of music—(1) which gives no pleasure, (2) which gives extremely slight and transitory pleasure, (3) which gives pleasure superior in these respects, but shown by experience to be incompatible with more deep and lasting pleasure given by other music.  I am keeping strictly to experience when I say that by far the greater part of Offenbach's music, like so much of the 'popular' music of the present day, comes under the second head. He has written many works containing not one single melody which gets hold of the popular ear, still less of the popular heart.  That people go to hear these works is owing to the great reputation which he has made by other melodies which *have* got hold of the popular ear, and to the fact that the *mise-en-scène* and the miserable jokes and horse-play of the ordinary opera-bouffe are in accordance with the popular taste : but any musician may say with certainty of tunes of such very simple form that, if he cannot recall them himself, and does not hear snatches of them either among the audience issuing from the theatre or afterwards, they have made no strong or permanent impression, and as mere rhythmical jingle they do not deserve even so mild an adjective as pretty.  With regard to the less numerous class of Offenbach's melodies which *have* spread and lived among the people, it must be experience again which settles whether or not they belong to the third of the above classes.  There are persons who seem to have the power of getting pleasure from a very wide range of melody ; and as far as I can judge, it would be in no way true to say (as some will say) that the width is in the inverse ratio of the depth. Moreover, there are degrees between strong love and indifference, and acquaintance with a higher style of music may reduce without annulling earlier partialities.  From my own experience and such other as I have

as exemplified
in the case of
Offenbach ;

had access to, I should say that a small minority of Offenbach's melodies possess an enduring charm of fine (occasionally even very fine) quality; but these, though among the number which the people find out, and the critics might find out by watching the people, are usually swept along with all the rest into the category of ' pretty jingle.'

A more important point is the influence of fashion on Music, as affecting the tone of musical criticism, and converting to an unworthy alliance what should be a strong resisting force. It is specially common, in respect of this inward and indescribable art, to find persons possessing a capacity for valuable enjoyment, whose instincts are yet not sufficiently keen and certain, or whose self-distrust is too great, to allow them to *préciser* their own requirements. Such persons are of course at the mercy of any conventionalities around them; and failing to interrogate their own impressions directly, and to find out what is really enjoyable to themselves from the only possible authority, go on living a barren existence, assisting unquestioningly at what is in vogue, and getting from the sense of a duty performed a satisfaction which partially compensates them for a great deal of tedium. Given, then, the peculiarities which mark out Music as the special art of evening assemblies, and we get the exact conditions for the deadening interaction of fashionable sheepishness and blind and narrow criticism. It is naturally in large and wealthy centres that misleading influences of this conventional kind find fullest scope: and in London they tend to stereotype a certain set of performances which greatly conceal the true position of the art in the nation. Just because the press has an air of representing the prevalent taste, it acts mischievously when on extraneous grounds it assumes in the public an interest which has little true vitality, or confuses what is vital with what is conventional. London newspapers go everywhere: and the prominence they give almost daily during the season to fashionable entertainments would countenance the notion that Covent Garden is a real head-quarters of English musical life—a title which might with far more justice be claimed for many a provincial practice-room.

It needed no special insight of Wagner's to detect the general weakness of modern Opera; nor can he feel much flattered at the now stereotyped laudations of his own works from critics who continue to puff, as the most approved upper-class digestive, the strains he most despises and the *tours de force* of high soprano voices. One particular point, the imposition of a single foreign language on all works which enter the great English opera-houses, has been already noticed; but it would be lucky if the indictment could stop there. It is curious how the whole level of things tends to alter as soon as one enters Covent Garden. The enormous size of the theatre, to begin with, casts a blight over everything that is not spectacle; and the extraordinary dreariness of

*and in respect of Italian Opera, through the paralysing influence of fashion.*

seeing a few beings straying about in the distance on that Sahara of a stage, or seated on an oasis of a sofa, and talking about the dullest intrigues in *recitativo secco*, perhaps accounts for its appearing high humour when Figaro hops on one leg, or makes a dab of soap over the face of the man he is shaving. It is small wonder if artists fail in making emotional or amusing what is so essentially dull and puerile : the wonder lies in an audience which can be satisfied by cake with so very few plums in it, and which, so far from crying out (as Wagner says) for perpetual melody, will sit through a whole scene of this kind for the sake of a single one. No audience untrammelled by fashion and precedent, in a performance of its own choosing, would stand even for five minutes being thus bored by what appeals neither to their ears nor to their understanding ; and as to my certain knowledge there are many whose occasional visits to the Opera result in a feeling of bewilderment as to whether they or the rest of the world are mad, I think it is important that the fact of there being audiences who do stand it should not be misunderstood. The misfortune is, not that people's ears should be wearied (as any one who watches carefully may see that English ears *are* wearied) by nine-tenths of such operas as *Aïda*, or *La Favorita*, or *Le Prophète*, but that their newspapers should make them believe what wearies them to be fine stuff, worthy of its *mise-en-scène* ; so that either they persuade themselves they are enjoying the music, when all that really impresses them is the voices and the spectacle, or else, still more disastrously, they get to dissociate the idea of *fine* music from that of music *to be loved*.

The case of Opera presents peculiar facilities for bolstering up, for long periods at a time, works wholly destitute of popular power. An opera is such an expensive affair that the very fact of its being *there* imposes it to some extent on the public, which has no chance of making a wide independent choice ; and as the assistance of brilliant scenes, a fine band, and favourite singers can be ensured, and appearances can thus be kept up, people are very ready to eke out their own inadequate enjoyment with a belief in what they consider skilled opinion. The brighter features of the case in some ways make the drearier ones the more irritating. The repertory contains some operas of dramatic interest, a few with a sustained flow and many more with an intersprinkling of musical beauty, of various degrees of excellence. Even where neither element is independently interesting, the combination may produce here and there exciting scenes, and afford occasional points to gifted artists. Such instances are the text which critics should seize on, in order to point out the contrast, and to urge that there is no inherent necessity for three hours of tedium as the price of twenty minutes of enjoyment. It is their business to separate the wheat from the chaff; not to represent a sickly fashionable vogue, which makes no distinction between the two, as healthy and genuine popularity. This language can

Hollowness of the interest in which newspapers would find the culmination of English musical life.

hardly be accused of exaggeration. It is professedly in the singers, not
the music, that the staple attraction both of Italian operas and of guinea
concerts consists; and different parts and songs are the permanent trapezes
on which they are to exhibit their skill. The consequence is that, if the
whole musical pleasure of the London Italian season could be summed up,
the average result per hour and per person would be a humiliating one
for the most elaborate and expensive entertainments of the largest city in
Europe. However agreeable to *dilettanti* after dinner, the pleasure of
being tickled ceases absolutely with the tickling; and even putting the
*roulade* business aside, when music depends for its whole effect on the
moment of performance and on being presented by most exceptional
instruments, simple addition shows how small is its total æsthetic value.
Luckily, though fine voices are rare and expensive andbelong to the
moneyed classes, fine tunes are common and cheap and belong, or may
belong, to the people. Many critics might get a condensed and much-
needed lesson in the physiognomy of genuine musical enjoyment by
sitting in the empty stalls and watching the pit and gallery at the next
performance of the *Beggars' Opera*; a work, by the way, for preferring
which to the Italian fashions of its own day, the British public were
politely compared by an eminent contemporary critic to the cat that was
changed into a fine lady, but could never resist the temptation of pursuing a mouse.

It is difficult to say exactly what amount of influence on the right side
criticism might have in these matters, though easy to see how its
flattering and conventional tone acts like a dead weight on the wrong.
Just because of the enormous size of the present 'musical public' and
its consequent want of homogeneousness, just because 'musical taste' has
come to have all sorts of different meanings, and is diffused in a fragmentary way, in all degrees of genuineness and spuriousness, through a
concert-room or a theatre, is it important to recognise the danger of
general assumptions, and of establishing on fortuitous and extraneous
grounds a prestige which is not checked off by the criterion of vital enjoyment. Such assumptions take various forms. The commonest, perhaps,
is the ignoring of the entire individuality of all the most valuable musical
impressions, and the perpetual reference to 'styles' and 'schools,' as if
the features implied in a special style or school were a guarantee of pleasure-
giving qualities. Music is valuable when *this* motive, and *this*, and *this*,
give to numbers of those who hear them that peculiar delight which is at
once perfectly distinct and perfectly indescribable; not because it is
written in the 'flowing Italian style,' or belongs to the 'lively French
school.' The flowing Italian style comprises the sickliest sentimentalities
of Bellini and Donizetti, and the noblest scenes in *Guillaume Tell*; the
lively French school confounds the tinsel of Adam with the gold of Auber.

§ 6. Danger
of general as-
sumptions;
illustrated by
the common
talk about
'schools' and
'styles' and
'prevailing
taste.'

And it is hard to guess why the almost unbelievable inanities of the *Bohemian Girl* are so frequently resuscitated, unless it be in order to assert the existence of an ' English school.' Melody is far too much a hit-or-miss affair with individuals for sweeping formulæ to be anything but misleading; and the very assumption that there is naturally a prevailing ' taste,' which must be satisfied by certain external characteristics of the music, tends to foster the external point of view, and a disposition which is not taste but fashion. When we read that Pergolesi's *Olimpiade* and Beethoven's *Fidelio* failed on their production from ' not hitting the prevailing taste,' that even the entirely naïve and popular music of the *Beggars' Opera* did not prevent the success from being for some time dubious at the first performance, and remember the unbounded popularity which in the case of the two latter works followed in the briefest space of time, we see that the unreal notion of something in a ' style,' apart from the special content, may be as dangerous to good new as it is artificially protective of bad old work.

§ 7. The fruitlessness of argument and impossibility of proof in matters of musical feeling.

We have seen the danger which the musical critic runs in trying to *describe* and *interpret*: closely connected with this are the troubles which beset him when he attempts to *argue*. Having in the first instance commonly set up a subjective criterion of good and bad, he is apt to take refuge, when pressed for reasons, in tautological expressions. He will say that the good music (*i.e.* what pleases him) expresses great ideas, and the bad uninteresting or trivial ones; that the good is characterised by deep thought and the bad by absence of thought, and so on; but if the ideas and thoughts are musical ones, this, though very likely true, is obviously only a restatement of his opinion. Mr. Ruskin finds no difficulty in showing the vulgarity and brutality of the introduction of ruffians stripping to bathe in a picture of the Baptism of Christ; any one who differed from him would have to try to show by facts that such accessories are common or appropriate on solemn occasions. But in Music, under the most favourable conditions for a similar criticism, that is, where the alliance with something external, such as words, seems to give a kind of fulcrum for argument, no such demonstration can be given, simply because no appeal from the individual consciousness to facts is possible. I may *feel* with no less force the vulgarity of the *Cujus Animam* in Rossini's *Stabat Mater*, but I can give no *criticism* of it worthy of the name. Again, I may be shocked by the musical irreverence of the way in which Meyerbeer winds up the overture to the *Huguenots* with the theme of Luther's glorious chorale, and here I may plausibly adduce a *primâ facie* unfitness in the conversion of a familiar psalm-tune into a jig; but had Meyerbeer made the tune himself and then treated it in the same way I should have disliked his treatment equally, and have had nothing to appeal to. One sometimes hears vague references to the ' consensus of the musical world;'

but this will not afford much assistance, partly because in many cases all that can fairly be meant is the musical world of a special country or period, partly because this world is not coincident with the world of connoisseurs, and partly because even among them the consensus is often imaginary.

Not that I would advocate, and least of all in conversation, a pedantic reserve. The experience of one person may be of great service to another, partly in showing points to notice, partly by sheer infection. We cannot be always taking a census of the greatest happiness of the greatest number, or keeping in mind an *arrière-pensée* about such a criterion. But arguments on art have special risks. It is hard indeed to make the intuition of others an article of as vivid faith as our own; and in Music there is a special difficulty in realising that a keen pleasure is derived from strains which one can perfectly follow, but only with the result of finding them trivial or tiresome; or that strains which powerfully move oneself fall dead on another person's ears. Thus, though sympathy in perception of beauty is one of the most exquisite of pleasures, which it is a pain to miss, yet where agreement turns out to be hopeless, so impregnable seems the standpoint of one's individual sensations that there may be a dismal and cross-grained satisfaction in the mere attitude of resistance, of which I perhaps tasted a grain in writing just now the sentence about the *Cujus Animam*. And in more deliberate criticism, while any careful record of experience is valuable, good sense and good temper may easily fail on ground where the want of tangible relationship to other things prevents the possibility of obtaining new points of view and new lights, and so new means of estimation and comparison, and where consequently to explain and convince is hopeless. On such ground it is little wonder if the *odium musicum* sometimes approximates in character to the *odium theologicum*.

Differences of musical taste are as striking as they are ultimate. There are some of an entirely generic sort, such as that which we have encountered more than once in this enquiry, of pedantic science *versus* popular instinct. This was curiously exemplified during the great days of Italian music in the last century, by a very prevalent superstition that the subordination of contrapuntal devices to melody marked a decline in the art. Pergolesi was blamed by high authorities for not having written his *Stabat Mater* in the style of the sixteenth century : and the celebrated Mattei called the taste of the people ' frivolous and depraved,' because they preferred the songs of the gondolieri to 'a learned and ingenious kind of music, full of harmony and contrivance.' But musical pedants still have the ears of men, and are rarely consistent. The very Jomelli to whom Metastasio wrote, grieving that in the mazes of scientific elaboration he had lost the power of touching the heart, pronounced the emphatic ' This is invention ' of Piccini's *La buona Figliuola*, which had amazing popularity among all classes.

§ 8. The ultimate and inexplicable nature of the differences;

illustrated in
Mazzini's and
Schumann's
estimate of the
*Huguenots*;
As a special and very interesting sample of complete difference of view about the same composition, we may select the following quotations from the writings of two most earnest devotees of Music. Mazzini says that the *Huguenots* ' stands alone, a beacon to indicate to future composers the course through which Music may be directed towards a high social aim.' ' The sense of a guiding Providence pervades the whole work. The very presence of Marcel on the stage arouses in the heart of the spectator the sense of a providential influence at work to bring about the triumph of good,' &c. ' Of German descent, though born in Italian Istria, one might almost fancy this combination of the two elements in his own person significant, symbolic, and prophetic. The figure of Giacomo Meyerbeer appears before us as the first link between the two worlds, the complete union of which will constitute the highest music of the future.' Compare with this Schumann's criticism of the same composer and the same work; which made him ' weary and inattentive from anger,' and which he follows from ' the ridiculously trivial sanctity ' of the overture on through the whole course of intrigue and carnage, indignant that one of the bloodiest of religious dramas should be ' degraded to the level of an annual fair-farce, in order to raise money and noise with it.' ' To startle or to tickle is Meyerbeer's maxim, and he succeeds in it with the rabble. And as for the introduced chorale, which sets Frenchmen beside themselves, I declare that if a pupil brought such a lesson in counterpoint to me I should certainly beg him to do better in future. How overladen yet empty, how intentional yet superficial! What blacksmith's work, that the mob may not fail to observe it, is this eternal chanting of Marcel's *A Firm Fortress!* Then a great deal is said about the dedication of the swords in the fourth act. I acknowledge that it has much dramatic movement, some intelligent striking turns, and that the chorus especially is of great outward effect; situation, scenery, instrumentation work together, and as the horrible is Meyerbeer's element, he has written this with warmth. But if we look at the melody from a musical point of view, what is it but a vamped-up *Marseillaise?* Is there real art in producing effect with such means at such a passage? I do not blame the use of every means in the right place; but we must not exclaim " Glorious! " when a dozen of drums, trumpets, and ophicleides are heard at a little distance in unison with a hundred singing men. One Meyerbeerian refinement I must mention here. He knows the public too well not to know that an excess of noise stupefies at last. How cleverly he goes to work then! After such explosions as that mentioned above, he gives us whole arias with the accompaniment of a single instrument, as if he meant to say, " Behold what I can do with but small means! Look, Germans, look! " '

and in Maz-
zini's view of
German music.
Mazzini's descriptions of German music have a still more remarkable sound. ' German music consumes itself uselessly in mysticism.' The

melody in German music 'is short, timidly and slightly designed.' 'German music is eminently elegiac; it is the music of remembrance, of desire, of melancholy hopes, of sorrows which no human lip can console— a music as if angels lost to heaven were hovering around.' And this is of what we are accustomed to consider by far the boldest and most ample melodies, and by far the most robust and all-embracing music in the world. What is the good of arguing? It had not *spoken* to Mazzini.[1] His words are rather descriptive of what we have called the indefinite than of the definite musical pleasure: music which merely ' embraces you with a chain of gradations linked by a master's hand, and surrounds you and cradles you upon a wave of chords,' is not music which to you, then and there, is presenting strong and individual melodic motive. Nor is the converse fact wanting. Many tunes which are the daily bread of the Italians, and wholesome where indigenous, are to many of us as disagreeable and cloying as overripe pears: but so far as any one has received large masses of delightful emotion from such tunes, that is a fact which it is impossible to get behind or call in question. The most one can say, and perhaps to some extent prove, is that larger masses of more delightful and more varied emotion are produced by other music which, as a fact, and not on any *à priori* grounds, will not, or will very rarely, go in the same head with vivid delight in the modern Italian.

These remarks apply with especial force to conversation. Few subjects in the present day are more widely discussed than Music: no subject admits less of profitable discussion, as opposed to a mere airing of opinions. The fact that a musical work cannot well be talked about during its performance, and is not as a rule reproducible or quotable at pleasure, the separation of the times when people talk and theorise from the times when they actually realise music, makes an additional difficulty, over and above the peculiar character of the impressions and the want of a generally understood vocabulary. It follows that in general society musical talk almost always sinks into that most barren and wearisome region, the discussion of the merits or demerits of different executants and *virtuosi*. But even where it is easy to recall the exact points on which stress is to be laid, and where each person has command of the technical materials necessary for discussion and is anxious to appreciate the other's ideas, it is a common experience that differences of opinion on this subject are mutually irritating rather than mutually instructive. It is curiously little recognised that when it comes to a simple question of liking, disliking, or regarding with indifference a succession of notes of which those who

*Special application to conversation.*

---

[1] I have heard from a friend intimately acquainted with Italy that he has found Italians devoted to Verdi's melodies, who, without prejudice and after honest endeavour, could not manage to perceive even in choice specimens of Mozart any charming or arresting quality.

differ would seem each to have an equally definite and complete knowledge, discussion has no standpoint, and the simpler the strain, the stranger, the less analysable, and the more irritating the difference. But if direct justification of particular musical proclivities is in the main impossible, some comfort may be found in the compatibility of wide differences in the estimation of some compositions with a common admiration of a vast number of others.

Many will be the readier to admit the expedience of toleration in Music, from a recollection of the different ways in which they themselves have been impressed by different compositions at different times. It is not only that taste gradually develops, and so music once dear becomes commonplace and music once uninteresting becomes dear : we have seen that a trained faculty and taste are liable to similar phases in respect of almost all compositions short of the strongest and purest. Moreover, both the rapidity and the order of musical development differ greatly in different cases, so that the power of appreciating the same composition will form and culminate at very various times in different lives. But it is, after all, on a clear perception of the grounds why differences are beyond analysis and argument, that a plea for mutual tolerance can be most successfully founded.

§ 9. Such uncertainty as the test of pleasure presents need neither confuse our views nor paralyse our efforts.

This impossibility of marking off *good* and *bad* by objective tests and rigid lines in this particular sphere of art is manifestly nothing more than a corollary from the argument which was applied in the sixteenth, seventeenth, and eighteenth chapters. If pleasure is the criterion of music's essential worth, we cannot refuse to consider both surface and depth in our measurement : it seems as impossible to deny the epithet *good* to the music which can give some degree of durable enjoyment to large numbers of human beings, as to that which can give a greater degree of more durable enjoyment to a smaller number.[1] Bad music is bad in the comparative sense that it can give, at best, a small sum of pleasure, and either has not sufficient individual impressiveness for any one to feel a longing for its exact recurrence, or is rapidly tired of when it recurs ;

[1] It would be idle to attempt to compare or equate surface and depth, even if all good music got an equal chance of being known. But it is worth while to point out, by an example, one special way in which the superiority of one piece of good music to another is often satisfactorily indicated. Suppose it to be true (which I am far indeed from asserting) that the sum of pleasure derived in a year from the strikingly beautiful and popular overture to *Tannhäuser* is greater than that derived from the first movement of the *Eroica* Symphony. The broad ground to take would be, of course, that in proportion as musical experience spreads, will the superiority of the latter be more widely felt : but my present point is that those who enjoy the overture most are just those who enjoy the symphony more. The perception of a ' thin vein of genuine trash ' is no more a proof of inferior enjoyment in Music, than the perception of a similar characteristic in Goethe's works renders the able critic who has supplied me with the phrase a less appreciative admirer of their merits than other people.

which means that it lacks any element of durability. The criterion is so safely applied in an immense number of cases that we need hardly distress ourselves at the existence of a debateable region where its application is uncertain and difficult. The very difficulty of taking the census reveals most satisfactorily the enormous width of the ground the census has to cover. And certainly no doubts need paralyse our efforts to extend among the people those opportunities of hearing and enjoying, every extension of which will further prove the fundamental similarity of thousands and thousands of human ears, and will more and more remove from our test the charge, on the one hand, of admitting as good what connoisseurs would condemn, and, on the other, of seeming to confine the verdict to connoisseurs.

# APPENDICES.

———◦◦◦———

## APPENDIX A.

### ON PLEASURE AND PAIN IN RELATION TO THE EVOLUTION OF THE SENSES.

IN the first chapter, I adverted to the idea that the development of pleasure and pain admits of the same kind of explanation, on the theory of natural selection, as do the numerous advantageous physical conditions to the survival of which that theory supplies a clue. Suppose, for example (to take a perfectly crude and simple instance), that lying in the sun tends to develop an eye in some creature; the idea would be that it would constitute an advantage to the creature to *like* lying in the sun, since if he likes it he will do it again, and in time will get the rudiment of an eye, which may be further developed by the same habit in his descendants. But to begin with, no one accustomed to distinguish between *physical* and *psychical* phenomena can fail to see that it is only to the former that natural selection, which is a principle of physical life, can truly apply. Every stage of the deductive zoology can be imagined without any supervention of psychical phenomena at all. It is impossible to treat physical and psychical events as parts of a single chain, and to credit a feeling, *as such* and irrespective of its physical basis, with causal efficacy in a physical order; and if a psychical phenomenon cannot form a link in a physical nexus, so neither can its presence or absence be a condition of advantage or disadvantage as regards physical existence.

We do, however, as a matter of fact, live in a world of psychical phenomena, in a world of sentient creatures. And if we find that in them the *physical* impulse or motion towards doing anything is connected with a certain *psychical* phenomenon, known also as impulse, no confusion need result from speaking of the impulse as a condition of the action, even if the word *impulse* be understood in a psychical sense; since, the connection being invariable, the appropriate physical changes will be necessarily involved. But is the case the same with *pleasure?* If the connection between pleasure and psychical impulse were of an equally *invariable* sort, if pleasure and pain were essentially involved as objects in those impulses of selection and rejection with which they are so commonly associated, it would doubtless be intelligible though inaccurate, to substitute the object, pleasure, as the necessary condition of the action. But this connection is so little invariable that careful self-examination will fail to make it good even in the most general and fundamental instances. Thus even in the case of hunger which has not reached the stage of violence, we can often dissociate the object of the impulse, eating, both from the attainment of pleasure and the avoidance of pain.[1] And this being so, we can clearly dissociate the psychical life from pleasure and pain, without landing ourselves in any theory of automatism; for *impulses* might remain, and take their place, when they occurred, among the other neutral phenomena of feeling, of which a great part of all psychical life consists.

And it is possible to carry our view of the externality of pleasure to the conditions of advantage a step further, if, in addition to this position that impulse can exist independently of pleasure, we may also hold that pleasure can exist independently of impulse. This will perhaps be less readily granted: for pleasure seems only definable as a mode of consciousness which we seek to retain or to reproduce—a definition which clearly involves impulse. It appears to me, however, that the *essence* of pleasure is *un*definable; and that the above definition, though applying very well to our own ordinary experience, overshoots that essence. Even in our own experience, many pleasures are so passive in character that the impulse to retain them is of a wholly potential kind; a baby may resist being taken out of a warm bath, but can the essence of his pleasure in it from moment to moment be really held to involve an impulse towards retention? And as we descend the scale of creation to simpler and simpler organisms, the necessity of the ingredient of impulse seems to get more and more shadowy, and the essence of pleasure seems more and more able to resolve itself into an experience without any reference beyond the immediate instant.

We may readily grant, however, that in *established* cases of kinds of action which have tended to preservation, and which have, in virtue of that fact, been preserved and now exist, the union between pleasure (or avoidance of pain) and psychical impulse is fairly close and constant; that the impulse towards the pleasure and the impulse towards the action are often felt as identical, and have a similar appearance of directive force towards advantageous results. But when we are considering the effects of natural selection, we must suppose *new* cases; for natural selection supervenes on events which, so far as it is concerned, are strictly accidental. Now the process by which the psychical order of phenomena rose into distinctness was of course an infinitely *gradual* one; we cannot conceive the more fundamental impulses and pleasures as new things, turning up suddenly like chance variations of structure. The physical connection between organisms and their environment has grown in complication as the organisms have become more and more differentiated in structure, and the objective phenomena of selection and rejection of certain objects and actions have, on the *physical* side, made up part of this gradually complicated connection; while in the concurrent and correlated increase of general psychical vitality, the *psychical* impulses, the *feeling* of selection and rejection have had their natural part; as also have the phenomena of pleasurable sensation attaching to certain kinds of normal function. It is clearly, then, outside such stereotyped aspects of life as this that we must look if we are to establish any correct sort of essential connection between natural selection and pleasure. But when we come to *new* cases, we find no essential bond between our three factors of impulse, pleasure, and advantage implying opportunity for development by natural selection; and they may fall apart in various ways. Thus natural selection may refuse its ratification to actions where impulse and pleasure remain in accord; a creature or a race might have deleterious impulses, and in

[1] I am indebted for this view to my friend Mr. Henry Sidgwick, whose chapter on 'Pleasure and Desire,' in the *Methods of* *Ethics*, contains a most forcible statement of it.

that case its life might be a short, but there is no *à priori* reason why it should not be a merry one. Again, though pleasure, and not pain, is the concomitant of established impulses, *till* an impulse has been established through proving advantageous to existence, there is no evidence that it will be pleasurable in its results rather than painful ; and though in the latter case further experience might show that it was also disadvantageous, and that, either through its cessation in the individual or through the extinctive powers of natural selection, no habit was established, yet the existence of the pain, prior to the weeding out of its conditions, would remain an ultimate and irreversible fact. The case of pain introduces special difficulties as to the historical relations of the phenomena into which it enters to natural selection. For there is clearly a great difference between pleasure and pain, as regards their relation to advantage and so to natural selection, in the following respect. Where advantage can be connected with *pleasure*, it results from doing and repeating the pleasure-causing action; and the preservation of the creature or its race, so far as it has been thus conduced to, appears to constitute a stamp of approval *both* of the action and of the pleasure, it not seeming necessary (except for purposes of strict accuracy already discussed) to make a separation between the two : but where advantage can be connected with *pain*, it results from *not* doing, from avoiding repetition of the pain-causing action ; and the preservation of the creature, so far as it has been thus conduced to, appears to constitute a stamp of approval for the sensibility to pain, but of *dis*-approval for the action. We might, it is true, without absolute contradiction, attribute to natural selection the double function of *weeding out* deleterious actions by extinction of the creatures who continued to do them, and of *fostering* pain after trial of deleterious actions, through the survival of creatures to whom advantage accrued from early learning by pain to avoid such actions.[1] But then, when once we begin to consider pain as an advantage which has been fostered, and try to adjust the ratio of painfulness and advantageousness, we cannot altogether ignore the ordinary common-sense view that insensibility to injury is, as a rule, a proof of robustness ; or, more precisely, that insensibility to pain from deleterious events or courses is an indication of advantageous physical conditions.

It seems, then, that there is only one way in which pleasure and pain can be truly connected with natural selection ; namely, in respect of their *present distribution*. If pleasure is a function of certain modes of physical change, it will not naturally continue to co-exist with modes of physical change which tend to *destroy* existence; that is to say, when we find pleasure *now* in connection with impulses, it is naturally in connection with the only impulses which are there *now* for it to be connected with, those, namely, which, by tending to preservation, have themselves survived. Again, if pain is a function of certain modes of physical change which tend to destroy existence, whether by positive injury or by prevention of the preservative conditions and actions, a contradiction would be involved in its co-existence with conditions or actions which, by having persisted, prove themselves to belong to the non-destructive class.

Perhaps the commonest form in which pleasure and pain are vaguely credited with objective powers, is not so much in the connection of natural selection with

---

[1] I have here adopted for convenience the inaccurate phraseology of ordinary usage : strictly, for *learning by pain* we should substitute the physical correlative, viz. certain nervous affections or processes following on a physical impulse and tending to prevent the repetition of that impulse.

particular pleasures and pains as in a more general sort of argument, of this kind: that as it may be assumed that creatures in whom the agreeable did not predominate over the disagreeable sensations would perish off the face of the earth through a palpable want of the necessary adaptation to environment, therefore pleasurable sensation in general must be an advantageous thing. But here of course is involved the same fallacy as before: the psychical phenomenon of pleasure is not regarded in its true relation to objective facts, as a *sign* of serviceable and selected activities, but is treated as on the same plane with some kind of physical adaptation. And we argue as before that agreeable sensation, being connected with nervous processes, which in turn are connected with particular activities, cannot of course exist unless the activities are there; and the only activities which can be there are necessarily just those which are in proper relation to the environment, so have survived, whether by natural selection or otherwise, and so have a tendency to survival : but the essential physical processes are those which are represented in feeling as the impulse, for example, to eat, not those which are represented in feeling as enjoyment of eating.

So far we have been entirely concerned with pleasures and pains in connection with which an active impulse is found ; and in the gratification of the impulse, provided it be of the advantageous kind, pleasure, though not an essential constituent, has been a very constant concomitant, developing at the same time and seeming to work altogether in the same direction as the impulse, and in fact so fused with it in feeling that the dual nature of the psychical phenomenon has to a great extent passed unnoticed. It is clear that the only pleasures and pains with which the deductive zoology can have anything to do are those where such an impulse exists, where a choice, a preference or rejection, is implied. For no advantage in the struggle for existence could possibly accrue to any creature in connection with sensibilities which did not take effect in some kind of action : natural selection preserves existence, not enjoyment; activities, not passive sensibilities. The choice may be either to do something immediately conducive to the existence of the individual, as eating, or conducive to the propagation of the race ; or to do something which modifies structure advantageously, as in our imaginary case of the creature who got the rudiment of an eye by habitually lying in the sun. The latter case, it will be at once noticed, differs from the ordinary actions which conduce to individual advantage, in the wide disconnection of the advantageous result, the possession of a serviceable eye, from the pleasurable conditions of its attainment : the creature's impulse, as represented in consciousness, is not towards light nor towards getting an eye, but primarily towards warmth, or something equally undifferentiated. When he begins to perceive the first glimmerings of light, this is a sign that the advantage has begun ; for with the appreciation of the difference between light and darkness, when, for example, some approaching object temporarily obscures the light, the perception of objects has been started ; and this advantage may appear in a rudimentary form at an early stage of development : but it is quite discontinuous with the pleasure-tending impulse. If now we proceed to consider the action of the higher senses after the formation of their organs, we shall find this want of connection between what tends to pleasure and what tends to advantage become so marked as to set these senses in a position of real contrast with the lower.

To take vision first. Employment of its eyes by a creature which has got them, and the results of that employment, seem indeed to present a certain analogy to the processes and results in cases where, as in our crude instance of the differentiation of an eye, structure has been advantageously modified by persistence in some pleasurable action. Thus a creature who has impulses to move his eyes will gain the unsought advantage of further development of their structure, leading to increased scope, quickness, and precision. Here, then, the relation of impulse and movement to subsequent advantage seems clear; but what has become of pleasure? The enjoyment of mere *light*, when it is differentiated from warmth, must be extremely slight; in our own highly organised stage it can hardly be said to exist, apart from enjoyment of definite objects and of colour; and even if we choose to consider that light, like warmth, may have been perceived with direct satisfaction at an early stage of evolution (as when our old friend was lying in the sun and getting the rudiment of an eye), we can hardly suppose enjoyment of it to have formed an element in any creature's consciousness when using its sight in the search for prey or the avoidance of enemies. And in any case it is the history of our own pleasures which we are seeking to trace; and for us it is undoubtedly enjoyment of *colour* which constitutes the true pleasure of visual sense-impression. And distinction of colour is wholly a matter of the elements of the retina; it has no connection with *movements* of the eye, such as would be specially advantageous to a creature for purposes of getting sustenance or avoiding dangers. Colour is marked and enjoyed rather in *absence* of movement, by steady passivity. There results a difficulty in connecting this pleasure either with impulse or advantage : the impulse favourable to it would be a pure negation, the impulse to do nothing, which certainly would never get stamped as favourable to existence ; and though the power to *discriminate* colours, when got, is an advantage, it is just *not* the discriminative act (till high mental elements, such as the sense of gradation and contrast, have been developed), but the purely passive reception, to which pleasure attaches. Or if it be said that the mere *recognition* of a colour would be an advantage, as aiding towards recognition of an object, still that fact does not suggest to us any active impulse by following which sensibility to particular colours might be attained.

A further difficulty in connecting enjoyment of colour with advantageous impulses will appear, if we consider what is the place of colour in the environment, as compared, for instance, with that of food. The physical cause of colour is ethereal waves of various lengths; and such waves are a perpetual daily element of the terrestrial environment, the particular wave-length of this or that series of waves, as it is reflected from any terrestrial object, depending entirely on certain conditions in the object, and not in the slightest degree on the existence or the whereabouts of eyes. The special consequences as regards living creatures are evident. While the external conditions for satisfying hunger are small and occasional fragments of the environment, which have to be distinctly searched for and selected, the external conditions for perceiving colour are there, all round, all day long, and not only do not need to be searched for and selected but cannot, except by an impulse of avoidance resulting in positive movements, be rejected. The irrelevance of enjoyment to the attainment of definite objects, the absolute divorce between pleasure and selective and preservative action, is here of the most marked description. In such a case advantage would lie, not in particular impulses, but in variations of structure, either accidental or developed by the exercise of function, and unconnected with impulse towards pleasure or any other object ; and pleasure could only supervene as the unsought and inexplicable subjective counterpart of the nervous processes involved in the gradual differentiation of the organ and its functions.

The case of the ear is very similar. The waves of aerial vibration which are perceived as sound, travel, like the light-waves, in all directions, and during the period of their occurrence pervade the whole environment. Their causes, like those of colour, must have been quite independent and accidental as regards rudi mentary organisms : the physical conditions must have been practically all external, since only the most infinitesimal fraction of the sounds which may have gradually impressed primitive creatures could have been made by themselves. And it is difficult to conceive how any impulse tending to pleasure could have led any creature to put itself in the way of hearing sounds. Such an impulse is, indeed, even harder to imagine in the case of sound than of colour. For in the first place the physical conditions of sound are not, like those of light, continuously for hours together all about in the environment; sounds are for the most part occasional and intermittent things, impossible for unintelligent creatures to put themselves specially in the way of : and in the second place, apart from imagination and association, the louder sounds of nature differ from bright colours in not seeming particularly pleasurable things; and the more striking and impressive they are the less agreeable do they appear, both as causing a physical shock or start and in primitive life probably suggesting danger. Perception and discrimination of sounds would doubtless be an advantage when attained ; but the attainment, as in the case of the eye, would be come about through variations and differentiation of structure entailing new and unsought sensibilities.

To sum up the case, then, as regards colour and sound. The relation of the senses concerned to advantage in the struggle for existence differs, first, from that of the senses which pertain to eating and reproduction, in being entirely indirect : the advantage of seeing and hearing things does not consist in seeing and hearing, but in subsequent proceedings; not in perceiving approaching prey, but in catching it ; not in becoming aware of dangerous proximities, but in getting away from them. The case of the higher senses differs, secondly, from that of any more general mode of affection (as of warmth) which may have been present during the slow processes of differentiation of structure, inasmuch as the physical facts of colour and sound seem to preclude the hypothesis of a habit gradually formed in conformity to some constantly recurring embryonic impulse, and leading to perpetual subjection of the organism to appropriate conditions. And as a result, the primitive use and development of these particular senses seem to stand markedly out of relation to pleasure. This may, perhaps, be best appreciated by noticing how impossible it is to apply in their case phrases which, though inaccurate, are with the necessary proviso intelligible, in application to the other senses ; as that it would be an advantage to a creature to feel pleasure in a thing, inasmuch as pleasure would lead to repetition. Repetition of what? of some action : but (1) no action will provide the sensorium of any creature with a colour or a sound, unless the physical conditions are there; (2) when the physical conditions are there, the perception of the phenomena does not require any action ; (3) the movements of seizing and avoiding and the like, in which the perception must result if it is to be even indirectly preservative, are exactly contrary to the conditions of passivity favourable to the appreciation of the phenomena; the enjoyment of which would, therefore, seem to be not only something over and above perception and discrimination, but to a great extent incompatible with the only circumstances where perception and discrimination would be serviceable. So that, on the whole, the development of pleasurable capacity in connection with the development of the sense seems in these cases entirely disparate from, and unrelated to, either impulse and action, or advantage in the struggle for existence.

---

## APPENDIX B.

### ON RHYTHM IN RELATION TO THE NOTION OF SUCCESSION IN TIME.

THE question as to the formation of the notion of Time and the relation of succession is too remote from our main subject to warrant any lengthy discussion here. There is, however, one theory of great ingenuity which, as it connects this formation directly with the sense of hearing and with rhythmic movements, seems to come fairly within our scope; and the more so since a notice of it may indirectly serve to make the distinctive character of the *pitch-dimension* of Chapters VII. and VIII. more easily intelligible. The theory, as stated by Dr. Hughlings Jackson, rests on the view that the two divisions of the auditory nerve are afferent, the one to centres in the medulla oblongata for movements of the heart, and the other to centres for locomotion in the cerebellum. The nerve has therefore much muscularity in dependence on it, namely, the movements of the head and neck, and thus indirectly locomotor movements, and the all-important movements of the heart-beat. This association of *movement* with the auditory sense is supposed to account for our sense of the time-relation of successive impressions, just as the *movements of the eye* are beyond all doubt at the root of our notion of the extension, and the outsideness to one another, of things in space. With regard to *Space*, Dr. Jackson says with perfect truth, ' We could have no notion of extension by mere impressions on the retina; there must be movements of the eyeballs. To suppose that we know the shape of an object by the merely sensory process of an object, as it were, imprinting itself on the retina, is to suppose that the position of the several retinal elements in relation to one another is known already. These can only be learned by movements. Similarly,' he argues with equal truth, ' to say that, since the ear receives sounds in succession, this kind of reception gives one an idea of their time-relation, assumes that particular intervals,' *i.e.* time-intervals, ' are already known : ' and these Dr. Jackson holds can also be learned by movements, those namely of the heart.

Now, tempting as must appear any explanation of the notion of succession in Time analogous to that of extension in Space, this view ' that our ideas of time have final, although unconscious, reference to the rhythm of the heart,' seems open to the gravest objections. There is doubtless a parallelism of a *negative* kind, a parallelism of *error* in the assumptions, which Dr. Jackson confutes, that extension in the one case and succession in the other are ideas essentially present in the simple sense-impressions with which we learn to connect those notions. But when we attempt *positive* explanation, and compare the movements involved in the two cases, the analogy breaks down.

Extension is connected wholly with things in space, that is, things outside one another and with their several parts outside one another; this outsideness is learnt by the special movements of the eye which bring the most sensitive part of the retina to bear cn each object or part of an object in turn, and the relative positions of the points seen correspond to the various parts of the retina, with each of which a special movement is associated. Movements associated with sensations of touch might suffice in the same way to give some imperfect sense of extension ; and locomotor movements have certainly played an important part in the formation of our complete conception of Space, which seems to contain, beyond extension, the notion of being able to move through it. But the multitude and delicacy of the eye's experiences are such that, even quite unassisted, it would be competent to the formation of a perfect notion of extension ; and we may say, with small error, that that notion is only a generalised abstraction from experiences of ocular movements. Now, the point to notice is this : that these particular movements, and therefore the generalised conception of them, are *wholly devoted to and concerned with one class of impressions*, those, namely, which light brings to the retina : the impressions of light on the retina and these special muscular movements of the eye are in our experience indissolubly associated, and their range is absolutely coextensive and conterminous. That relation between retinal impressions which we call extension is generalised from a set of movements which unceasingly attend those retinal impressions, and have no other object or function.

Now, what is the bearing of this on succession in Time ? The analogue in Space of things in Time is a series of points in a line. For simplicity we may take two points : we have seen, then, that constant experience of the movement of the eye from one point to the other would suffice to give us the notion of the outsideness of one to the other ; in fact, that the gradually generalised idea of such experience *is* that notion. But then, as we have seen, it is the special movement devoted to certain special sensory impressions, and to nothing else, which would give the relation ; that particular movement and no other ; it is not merely *synchronous* movement ; for instance, if we exercised some of our muscles while our retina remained immovably fixed in the direction of the points, such movements would of course be wholly irrelevant to the space-relation of the points. Yet it is to this latter sort of movements, and not to the special ocular sort, that the movements by which Dr. Jackson attempts to explain the notion of succession are analogous. If we take two sense-impressions perceived as successive, we look in vain for any special movement associated with them, which can possibly put them outside one another in a time-relation. We may receive two auditory impressions, and a certain number of heart-beats may take place during the interval between them : but there is absolutely nothing to refer the change of state, involved in this movement of the heart, to the two auditory impressions, in the way that the change of state involved in the movement of the eye from one point to another was necessarily referred to the two visual impressions. It is a *synchronous*, but *irrelevant*, change of state. Assuming the relation of succession in the heart-beats to be already known, we might conceivably use them as a measure : but then we have to come down to the heart-beats themselves, and ask how the notion of succession is to be got into *them*. We are talking about the formation of a general idea : now, a general idea must be formed from particular elements which reach consciousness ; and this is not ordinarily the case with the heart-beats at any rate of those beings who are capable of forming general ideas. But even supposing them to reach consciousness, as in certain bodily states they do, they are felt merely as a set of precisely similar events. We have no consciousness of a change of physical state connecting one with another ; there is no movement which, by its intimate association with a pair of such sense-impressions, while still remaining—as movement—distinct from them, can set one outside the other for us.

Nor is this all. Dr. Jackson seems to assume a special connection between the ear and Time as a known fact, apart from theory. 'That the ear has to do with Time as the eye has to do with Space is,' he says, 'a truism.' With all deference to so distinguished an authority, I cannot admit that it is even true. The sense of vision has almost a monopoly of the idea of *extension* : whereas in the idea of *succession* it is hard to see that one sense can claim any special superiority over another, or that sense-perceptions of any kind have more part than the purely intellectual faculties. The notion of succession pervades the whole of our experience through and through ; and the means by which it is acquired are probably purely mental acts, attention to and comparison of impressions or ideas in respect of such qualities as distinctness, greater or less isolation from irrelevant or subordinate concomitants, and so on. The notion of Time is thus much more ultimate and difficult to account for than that of Space; and it is everywhere assumed in our explanation of Space by movements.

If we want an analogy to visual extension in the region of sound, it is certainly to *Pitch* and not to Time that we must go. The resemblance is very well put by Helmholtz. 'It is an essential character of Space that at every position within it like bodies can be placed, and like motions can occur. Everything that is possible to happen in one part of Space is equally possible in every other part of Space, and is perceived by us in precisely the same way. This is the case also with the musical scale. Every melodic phrase, every chord, which can be executed at any pitch, can be also executed at any other pitch in such a way that we immediately perceive the characteristic mark of their similarity. On the other hand, also, different voices, executing the same or different melodic phrases, can move at the same time within the compass of the scale, like two bodies in Space, and, provided they are consonant in the accented parts of bars, without creating any musical disturbances.'

---

## APPENDIX C.

### ON DISCORD.

MR. GRANT ALLEN, in his recent book on *Physiological Æsthetics*, adopted the words 'maximum of stimulation with minimum of fatigue' as the general formula for the conditions of peripheral stimulation most favourable to pleasure in the case of the higher sense-organs. I wish to point out some considerations which seem to detract from the value and generality of this formula. One obvious objection may be seen at once to be the use of the subjective word 'fatigue' for the expression of objective phenomena in physiology : and it is ultimately owing, as I believe, to this dangerous and misleading use that the other weak points in the formula, if such indeed they prove to be, easily escape detection.

To illustrate my first objection, we may take a case or two where the sort of ratio expressed in the formula seems familiar to us. We say, for instance, that a skilful violinist extracts from his strings the maximum of transverse with the minimum of longitudinal vibration ; or that mountain-air enables us to walk a maximum number of miles with a minimum of fatigue. In either case the two terms of the ratio are clearly distinct things, which may be conceived as increasing together or decreasing together, or one of which may increase as the other decreases. Now let us look at the word ' fatigue ' as used in the formula. It relates simply to physiological facts, to the molecular disturbances of stimulated organs in which wear is outrunning repair, and which are thus being brought further and further from the state they were in to start with, without a chance of recurring to that state during the continuance of the stimulation ; [1] a condition whose relation to the condition of stimulation *without* ' fatigue ' finds a rough parallel in the difference of behaviour of two bodies respectively moved from a position of un-stable and of stable equilibrium. But, holding fast to this objective view of the terms employed, we see of course that the need of repair is simply dependent on the amount of disturbance or wear ; that the unfatiguing and the fatiguing stimulation are not two distinct things which can be separately appraised, but are *continuous*, one being an excess of the other beyond the line where perpetual repair is possible. So that our formula seems reduced to ' a maximum of getting up to the line with a minimum of going over it.'

Cases where the formula is really applicable are those where *several* sets of nerve-fibres are concerned. For instance, we can speak of a surface covered with strips of the primary colours as inducing the maximum of stimulation with the minimum of fatigue ; since here, while the eye ranges about, each colour affords a rest to the nervous elements stimulated by the other two ; whereas the same surface covered by one of the colours, and stimulating a single set of elements, would cause a maximum of fatigue. Again, by improving the quality of a musical note, that is, by calling into play more nervous elements in response to the additional harmonic vibrations, we increase the general stimulation without making it anywhere excessive. But the case of single and simple phenomena, or single and simple parts of compound phenomena, is of course an entirely different thing ; and here the only way in which we can get any scientific conception including the idea of ' maximum of stimulation ' seems to be by taking into consideration a new term—the *time*, namely, during which the stimulation lasts, and by substituting for ' minimum of fatigue ' the maximum of time during which the sensation is pleasant. Take the case of a fine musical note : if this be of only moderate strength, it can be listened to for a good many seconds with satisfaction : if, on the other hand, it be extremely loud, it may be pleasant for a moment, pleasanter perhaps to many people and in some states of the organism than the gentler note, but rapidly becomes almost unendurable. We may assume, then, that for any given state of a particular organ a particular period of stimulation has corresponding to it a maximum intensity of stimulation, which constitutes the condition most favourable to pleasure for that period. But the two factors obviously vary inversely ; [2] if we increase the loudness of the note we diminish

---

[1] *Stimulation* is used throughout in a physiological sense, to express the movements which constitute the response of the peripheral nervous elements to physical stimuli.

[2] They probably vary inversely in a very

the time during which it is agreeable : and on the subjective side we have very uncertain and limited power of comparing things so heterogeneous as greater intensity and greater prolongation of pleasure ; so that, if we ourselves cannot decide in what case pleasure is really most favoured, the physiological conditions most favourable to it become a somewhat indefinite object of search. Our two *maxima*, however, must clearly lie well within the points where, on the one hand, the amount of stimulation would reduce the time of possible pleasurable endurance of it to zero, and where, on the other, the length of time during which it was endurable would imply an almost inappreciable amount of it.

To return to our formula. The use of the word ' fatigue ' seemed to lead to difficulties ; but if we relegate it to its rightful place on the subjective side, there are doubtless feelings connected with the higher sense-organs to which it seems quite fairly applicable ; and it is incontestable that the physiological counterpart of these feelings is an excess of stimulation in the organs concerned. But my main objection is of a much more serious kind ; since, if substantiated, it connects the lax use of the word, not with a weakness or want of clearness in definition, but with a certain amount of failure in the apprehension and discrimination of facts. These facts are most prominent in the domain of Sound : and the special point to be here discussed is as follows :—We find the word ' fatigue ' used to express the objective counterpart not only of what is *felt as fatigue, e.g.* the too prolonged continuance of a loud note, but of what is *felt as discord,* an ultimate and wholly different sensation. The two objective phenomena agree probably in the general character of wear and tear as the two subjective sensations agree in the general character of unpleasantness : but, the natural supposition being that under this most general head the two former differ from each other no less than the two latter, is it not rash to identify them under a common name, when we should never dream of so confusing their psychical counterparts ? Discord is not felt the least as fatigue : if, then, we give the name ' fatigue ' to the physiological counterpart of discord, are we not likely to overlook the extreme speciality which that particular form of wear and tear (if so it be) must possess, and to rest content with a most imperfect explanation ?

It is hardly necessary to remind my readers that the sensation of musical tone is produced by continuous regular nervous stimulation, and that the sensation of discord is due to rapid ' beats,' that is, to a series of augmentations and diminutions of stimulation interposed in the regular series, and caused physically by the interferences of sound-waves of nearly equal lengths. The separate beats are as little present to consciousness in the pure sensation of discord as the separate vibrations in the pure sensation of tone : the sensation seems quite unique and beyond analysis. The manner of connecting the unpleasantness of the sensation with the theory of stimulation and fatigue is clearly shown in Chapter VIII. of Helmholtz's *Ton-Empfindungen,* which forms a convenient text for the objections I would venture to raise. He points out that a nerve is

complex way. For the subjective phenomena, and doubtless therefore the objective, are *gradated* as the limiting instant is approached when pleasantness vanishes : and the steps of gradation, and the proportion of the whole time which elapses before the decline sets in, probably differ according to the degree of stimulation ; that is to say, with change of stimulation, the part of the time during which the sensation is most pleasant may vary differently from the whole time during which its pleasantness remains above zero. The matter lies quite beyond the reach of experiment, as the subjective facts can never be rendered sufficiently distinct and isolated for accurate examination.

deadened by strong stimulation, and rendered less sensitive to fresh irritants : a
rest, however, enables it to recover its sensibility, and the time of rest necessary
in the case of the more delicate sensory organs is extremely short.   Now the
intermittence which beats cause in the stimulation gives the nerves an opportunity
for recovery and repair during each minute period of interruption, and they thus
present themselves to each fresh attack of the stimulus in a state of renewed
nutrition and irritability.   They are therefore subjected to a series of more violent
shocks than in cases of unintermittent stimulation, and this violence, as Helmholtz holds, sufficiently explains the unpleasant sensation.   He illustrates this
position by the case of the eye, pointing out that by looking for even a moment
at the sun the sensibility of the retina is so blunted that we see a dark spot when
we turn our eyes to the sky ; that on coming out of darkness into full daylight
we first feel blinded, but the sensibility of our eyes is soon so far blunted that
this degree of brightness is found very pleasant ; and that so, ' by the continuous
uniform action of the irritation of light, this irritation itself blunts the sensibility
of the nerve, and thus effectually protects this organ against too long and too
violent excitement.'   Intermittent flashes of light, on the other hand, permit
fresh renewals of irritability, and so act with more intensity, and ' everyone knows
how unpleasant and annoying is any flickering light, even if it is relatively very
weak.'

With respect to stimulation so violent as that caused by looking at the sun,
the statement that the blunting of the nerve-sensibility acts as a natural pre-
ventive of ' too violent excitement' is surely too general.   For, though the power
of producing the subjective impression of *light* is at once considerably blunted, it
would be rash to assume that the peripheral nerve-elements concerned in that
impression play no part in the sensation of increasing *discomfort*, which would
result if a person's eyes were forcibly kept open and exposed for some time to
the direct action of the sun.   But anyhow here the stage of possible comfort is
instantly passed : that stage in the eye's power of adaptation lies within a certain
limit of stimulation.   Thus, when the retina encounters ordinary daylight after
total darkness, nervous wear outruns repair (that is, on the subjective side, discomfort is felt), until the stored-up superfluity of irritability has run down, so to
speak, after which wear and repair go on equally.   The stages of the shifting
ratio between wear and repair might be roughly illustrated by a steel spring,
which will yield and then remain steady under certain weights, but which, if the
pressure be excessive, will rapidly pass all the positions of steadiness and snap ;
the range of normal and reparable wear, the counterpart of agreeable sensation,
corresponding to the steady positions of the spring.   Under direct exposure to
the sun, the snapping comes, that is, the molecular disturbance far outruns all
chance of recovery, in an almost inappreciable time.   But this would happen
whether the sensibility of the retina had been previously blunted or not : let us,
then, neglect such violent cases, which tend to confuse the subject, and confine
ourselves to the limits within which regular stimulation is the counterpart of
endurable and agreeable sensation, as only here can the problem of intermittence
and its effects be introduced.

Now, in trying to connect the unpleasant sensation corresponding to intermittence with *intensity* of stimulation, understood in the ordinary and natural
sense, we at once come across a difficulty which is not removed by the undoubted
fact that the intermittence enables the nerves in some measure to renew their

irritability, and which may be illustrated by the following case :—Suppose that a person with good eyesight reads a book for half an hour by a strong and agreeable light, or looks for the same time at a bright landscape, or merely sits talking in a sunshiny room. The sensibility of his eyes is not to his knowledge affected by the process; for aught he is aware of, the page or the landscape or the room looks as bright at the end of the time as at the beginning, and the blunting of irritability must at any rate have been very small. Now suppose him to read a book or sit in a room illuminated by a much lower but still sufficient light, and let the light flicker. The discomfort will be very decided : but it seems impossible to make out that the normal kind of stimulation of the end-organs connected with sight is more *intense* here than in the former case. The stimulation has no doubt been more intense than if the light, instead of flickering, had remained steady at its highest strength : but the light in the first case we considered was very much stronger than this; and in order to make out the intensity of stimulation or molecular disturbance in that first case to be *less* than in the second, we should have to suppose a self-protection amounting to a great and continuous blunting of the power of response to stimulus; and, as this would be represented in consciousness by the reduction of the page or room to darkness long before the expiration of the half-hour, the supposition is contradicted by facts. The subjective feeling of brightness was far greater at every instant of time in the first case than in the instants of greatest brightness, when the nerve-irritability was most thoroughly renewed, in the second : and the subjective feeling of brightness is the concomitant of a high amount of stimulation. It seems illogical, then, to imagine greater *violence* of stimulation in the second case. The question as regards the eye is complicated by the fact, to which Helmholtz does not call attention, that much of the discomfort caused by flickering is due to the perpetual *muscular* readjustments necessitated by the variations in the strength of the light. But if we agree to neglect this element, the proposed explanation could only pass muster in a case where the light, supposing it to be steady, was as strong as the eye could comfortably stand, in which case making it flicker and so permitting renewals of nervous irritability would send the sensation over the line of discomfort : if we look at a less extreme case, we seem driven to connect the unpleasantness not with *excessive* response of the nerves to stimulus, but with a special feature of *discontinuous* response, whether referable to perpetual stoppings or perpetual startings or both. We need phrases like ' violence of stimulation ' or ' excessive response' (which are both better than ' fatigue ') to express the excessive molecular disturbances which would be caused by increasing the steady light on the page or in the room till it was disagreeably dazzling : we want another expression for the exceptional order of disturbance introduced by the repeated intermittences. It is not of course meant that the latter may not be in some way included under the general rule of wear and repair : but it is in itself a quite different species of wear from that involved in excess of the regular and normal stimulation. A man's frame will need repair after rolling a truck along rails for three hours, and also after setting it going, letting it stop and setting it going again, and continuing this jerky labour for an equal time : but the movements in space and the work done will be very different in the two cases.

When we pass to the ear the problem becomes much simpler and more distinct, for several reasons. First, we get rid of the irrelevant element of *muscular* fatigue, caused by adjustments of the pupil to varying degrees of light. Secondly, the visual intermittences are felt *as such*, and the confused feeling of discomfort may seem fairly describable by the word 'fatigue'—especially under cover of the associated muscular feelings, whereby the difference from the normal fatigue caused by excess of light is necessarily much disguised; whereas in discord the intermittences are not perceived as such, but give rise to a new sensation to which no one would dream of applying the name 'fatigue.' Again, confusion is avoided in the case of the ear by the organ's very limited power of self-adaptation. For the ear seems little liable to anything analogous to being first dazzled (like the eye in emerging into daylight from the dark) and then getting its sensibility blunted to the comfortable pitch which represents equilibrium between wear and repair. Deafness of course ensues from prolonged exposure to excessive sound, but this is owing to real structural injury: and in the case of musical tone,[1] at any rate, I do not think it is ever the experience of a healthy ear to find a single sound intolerably loud for a few seconds, and then to get reconciled to it; whenever it is disagreeably loud to begin with, it gets worse.

Let us now take two means of stimulation for the ear analogous to our former two cases of the strong steady light and the weaker flickering light: they will evidently be a loud single tone or concord and a soft discord, say a very loud octave and a very soft discord of a semitone, played on a finely-toned organ. The former is of course felt as pleasant, the latter as unpleasant: and in consistency it is sought to connect the former sensation with a lesser and moderate amount, the latter with a greater and violent amount of stimulation. But the actual physical stimulus is obviously very far greater in the case of the loud concord than of the soft discord: the whole burden of the explanation must therefore be thrown on the other factor of stimulation, namely, the degree of irritability or molecular instability in the organs concerned. First, then, with respect to the loud concord, in order to make out the stimulation in the case of this, the *greater*, stimulus to be *less* than that caused by the soft discord, we should have to suppose the sensibility or power of response to be very greatly and rapidly deadened: but we have sufficient proof that the nerve-elements are performing their functions in a highly vivacious and persistent way, in the fact of our continuing to hear and appreciate the sound for many seconds just as perfectly as we did at first. Secondly, with respect to the discord, we can take this as soft as we please; so that the relation of the perpetually repaired organs to the intermittent stimuli is not analogous to that of an eye brought from darkness into daylight, but brought from darkness into obscure twilight; and in such a case 'intensity of stimulation' ought not in reason to outrun the conditions of agreeable sensation. For, looking at our two factors of stimulation, we see that it is only the *amount of stimulus* which can be indefinitely varied, and there is an obvious limit to the extent to which we can draw on the other factor, that of *irritability dependent on nutrition*. The perfection of nutrition and repair cannot be more than perfect; it cannot be carried, cannot therefore carry irritability, beyond a certain natural point; so that, however unstable be the condition of maximum irritability, we ought by diminishing the strength of the physical stimulus to be able to avoid causing wear to outrun repair. While granting, of

---

[1] With respect to extremes of non-musical sound, opinions may vary. The getting accustomed to such an extreme, in the sense of gradually becoming able to distract attention from it, hardly implies that the acoustic sensibility has been deadened. Here again it is almost impossible to isolate the phenomena sufficiently for experiment.

course, that the greater the irritability the less the stimulus which will suffice to cause the amount of stimulation corresponding to *unpleasantness*, we still know that the amount of stimulation which normally corresponds to *pleasantness* is a very considerable one : and we cannot postulate the perpetual renewal of such a miraculous amount of irritability as would be required to bring stimulation up to and far beyond this point even under the action of a very weak stimulus. The intermittent stimulus produces, according to Helmholtz, ' a much more intense and unpleasant excitement of the organs than would be occasioned by a continuous uniform tone.' More unpleasant certainly : but the assumption is that it is more unpleasant simply *by dint of* being more intense, however soft the sound, in face of the fact that more intense excitement still, caused by a much greater stimulus acting regularly on organs which are proved by the concomitant sensation to remain perfectly responsive and undeadened, is felt as pleasant. And over and above all this, if it *were* more intense in the manner imagined, it ought to be felt as *loudness* : ' loudness,' as Mr. Grant Allen himself remarks in one place, ' is the subjective concomitant of intensity in stimulation.' And the sensation of loudness has absolutely no relation to that of discord, which retains its unique character even when barely audible.

In this connection I may quote an illustration given by Helmholtz, which seems to me delusive. He says, ' If a tuning-fork is struck and held at such a distance from the ear that its sound cannot be heard, it becomes immediately audible if the handle of the fork be revolved by the fingers. The revolution brings it alternately into positions where it can and cannot transmit sound to the ear, and this alternation of strength is immediately perceptible by the ear. . . . Just as this alternation of strength will serve to strengthen the impression of the very weakest musical tones upon the ear, we must conclude that it must also serve to make the impression of stronger tones much more penetrating and violent than they would be if their loudness were continuous.' No doubt a change or movement serves often to direct attention to feelings which when uniform were too slight to be noticed : a change even to a *lesser* degree of stimulation might have this effect, if the attention had got deadened by the monotony of a prolonged impression. But the change here described by Helmholtz would be consciously perceived as a *change of loudness*. In just the same way, with a very much greater strength of tone, if the alternations were slow enough to be perceived as separate, they would be recognised as alternations of loud and soft sound, the loudness, unless very extreme, being in no way unpleasant. Now by artificial means we can introduce into a single continuous tone, that is, into a simple series of regular stimulations, an intermittence similar to that produced by natural interference in the compound series whose counterpart in consciousness is the sensation of two discordant tones. Let us then, by way of getting a new point of view, suppose the alternations to get faster and faster till they merge in consciousness into one continuous sensation. What quality or qualities should we expect this sensation to have? We know that there has been no change in the nature and amount of the respective physical stimuli as they gradually got crowded nearer together : *à priori* therefore we find no reason to suspect much change in the nature and amount of the physiological response to each of these stimuli : and hence we should expect that the psychical representative of this response would continue to be the sensation of loudness up to the end of the process. And such we find by experiment to be the case : the quality of loudness remains when the sensation has become single and unintermittent. But experiment reveals another quality which we could not have predicted : the sensation is not one of loudness only, but is distinctly unpleasant and jarring. Again, if we made the experiment with a soft sound, the rapid alternations of strength, when merged in one sensation, could only bring its loudness up to the low level of what were its louder parts when it was felt as intermittent ; but the same jarring quality would be experienced as in the other case. And just so discords, when soft, give a sensation which is not ' penetrating and violent,' but disagreeable in a special and unique way.

The following consideration may set the difficulty in a still clearer light :—A continuous low note, having, say, 120 vibrations to the second, is pleasant : a higher note of equal apparent strength with several thousand vibrations to the second, having its regular series of vibrations interrupted 120 times every second, is unpleasant ; so is a discord of two high notes with the same number of beats or interruptions. But here the periods given to the nerves for renewal of irritability are *equal in number* in the two cases of the unpleasant and the pleasant sensation. What right, then, have we to account for the contrast by speaking of the stimuli as ' wastefully attacking the fibres and end-organs concerned ' (to quote Mr. Grant Allen) in the one case, and as blunting and so protecting them in the other ?

I will adduce only one more argument. If the same kind of stimulation, when excessive, caused the unpleasant sensations both of over-loudness and of discord, those who are able to experience one ought, under the appropriate conditions, to agree in experiencing the other. But it is not uncommon to find that of two persons who are equally susceptible of annoyance from over-loudness, one is keenly sensitive to discord and the other totally unconscious of it.

To sum up. The disputed view, when clearly drawn out, implies variety in *degree*, but not in *kind*, of the stimulation proper to the several end-organs. This stimulation is felt as pleasant up to the point at which nervous wear begins decidedly to outrun repair ; when it is felt as unpleasant this point has been passed. The point itself is supposed to be the resultant of two factors : one is the amount of the physical stimulus, which must be called excessive, in relation to a particular state of the organs, whenever the action cannot last for an appreciable time without seriously disturbing the balance between wear and repair : the other is the degree of nutrition and consequent molecular instability in the organs concerned, which must be called excessive, in relation to a particular amount of stimulus, if discomfort is experienced under the action of an amount of stimulus which at other times may be found quite pleasant. We took cases where one sensation was pleasant and another unpleasant, in spite of much greater violence of stimulus in the former case : and to account for this according to the theory, recourse was inevitably had to the second factor—the irritability of the nerves, supposed to be deadened in the former case, perpetually revivified in the latter. We objected to each feature of the explanation : to the *deadening* in the case of the continuous tone or concord as being contradicted by the continued vitality of the subjective feeling ; to the *revivification* in the case of the discord (1) as needing often to be miraculous in degree in order to account for the facts, (2) as bound, so far as it did occur, to produce the normal concomitant of intensity of stimulation —loudness, and not something quite different. Next, we found a case where a pleasant and an unpleasant sensation were produced under conditions which, as regards opportunity for renewal of irritability, were identical. Finally, we noticed that, whereas two sensations depending on precisely the same physiological facts ought to be equally awakenable under the appropriate stimuli, cases were common where one was so awakenable and the other not.

We seem thus driven to assume the existence of some other *kind* of nervous disturbance, connected specially with interruptions supervening on a mode of motion which has been sufficiently established to become, so to speak, familiar. We find an illustration, perhaps even a true analogy, in the effect of interruption of any regular rhythm which is being watched by the eye or ear (*e.g.* in observing the pendulum or ticking of a clock), or produced by our own voluntary muscular actions. In this comparison whole sense-organs, and actions slow enough to be consciously and completely followed, take the place of the infinitely minute nervous elements and infinitely rapid movements we have been considering. And here we assuredly should never think of accounting for the unpleasant sensation by 'intensity of stimulation,' the feeling of being baulked and disappointed being totally different from that of over-strain or fatigue; not more different, however, than is the feeling of discord from the oppression of excessive sound. If the new and special phenomenon, in either the illustrating or the illustrated case, is to be brought on the objective side under the general rule of wear and repair, it must probably be by supposing energy to be stored up ready for discharge, which, when the regular and established stimulus does not come, is discharged unnaturally, so to speak, and against resistance: as Mr. Grant Allen well expresses it with regard to rhythm, 'if the opportunity for the discharge is wanting, the gathered energy has to dissipate itself by other channels, which involves a certain amount of conflict and waste.' If the suggested analogy be applicable, we may imagine the new phenomenon of discord to appear in consciousness as soon as the frequency of the baulkings, or whatever we are to call them, has become sufficient to bring this sort of conflict up to a certain pitch of intensity.

I may just remark, in passing, that this case of discord serves well to illustrate in how extremely small a degree considerations of peripheral nerve-stimulation can really penetrate into the secrets of artistic beauty. A discord is always a discord wherever it occurs, and has the same wearing effect on the peripheral organs: but the action of the higher co-ordinating centres so overrides the natural character of the sensation as to convert it into an all-important feature of modern music, the simplest bit of which is often crammed with discord. We may see here the most extreme case of the difference, pointed out at the beginning of the first chapter, between a wearing affection of one of the differentiated sense-organs and literal pain: for a sensation of the literally painful kind could never have its quality reversed by a relation to another sensation which is to follow it. The very exceptional and distinct manner in which a particular sound-impression, unpleasant in isolation, is made pleasant by a definite relation to another sound-impression, may be taken, moreover, as illustrating the wider fact—the simple and direct way in which, in this domain of Sound, Form, *i.e.* the perception of relations in the elements of sensuous material, assumes pleasurable qualities. It helps us to understand that this perception of relations, however much transcending mere sensuous impression and in that way intellectual, is far too entirely and directly grounded in very unique affections of sense to be connectible with any of the more general sorts of intellectual activity: which, again, accounts for its exceptionally early and distinct occurrence in the experience both of the individual and the race.

A few words may be added on the subject of *colour-discord*. To put a simple case : why is immediate juxtaposition of orange and vermilion on one surface disagreeable ? Mr. Grant Allen tries to bring such facts under his general formula on the ground that the same class of optic fibres is stimulated by each of the two colours, and that over-stimulation therefore ensues. But if the orange part were vermilion, like the other, stimulation of the same class of optic fibres would be carried still further and a still greater degree of over-stimulation would result, whence we should logically expect an intensification of the same subjective feeling. This objection is, in fact, the one which Mr. Sully made in his review of Mr. Allen's book in *Mind*, and his *reductio ad absurdum* was perfectly sound, that 'it would follow that the same colour spread over a large surface would produce the pain of chromatic dissonance in its maximum degree.' To this Mr. Allen replied that though all dissonance is fatigue, all fatigue is not dissonance. No : but even if we could conceive for the moment that the lesser stimulation, being still excessive, was cognised as a special form of discomfort—*colour-discord* —while the more excessive stimulation was cognised as the normal discomfort known as *fatigue*, what are we to say if we find a case where the feeling of the lesser stimulation answers to the above description, but the feeling of the greater is not fatigue but *pleasure ?* If 'fatigue' is one in kind (as the old formula and the arguments in support of it throughout imply), how will Mr. Allen explain the fact that we are annoyed by a mixed mass of pink and scarlet geraniums, but are pleased by an equal mass of the flowers when they are all scarlet, seeing that the conditions are more favourable to 'fatigue' in the latter case ? He adds, ' What would Mr. Sully say to a person who argued that on Helmholtz's principles one and the same note continued for a long time would produce in the maximum degree the pain of musical dissonance ?' But this remark, proposed as an absurdity, really suggests the very difficulty which I have found in accepting Helmholtz's principles of musical dissonance as complete : and indeed the remark has its exact parallel and converse in the argument which forms the gist of this Appendix. I have argued that, on the theory that stimulation is one in kind and only varied in degree and is completely expressible in terms of intensity, it is impossible to explain how it happens that its subjective concomitant in certain cases is an impression not of loudness but of discord : conversely, had I taken discord as the chief and central phenomenon, the fact with which I should have confronted the theory would have been that the feeling of the stimulation due to a loud continuous note is unaccountably not discord but loudness. The above remark proposed by Mr. Allen may in fact be used as a *reductio ad absurdum* of the view he adopts on musical discord, exactly parallel to Mr. Sully's *reductio ad absurdum* of his view on colour-discord. Mr. Sully, after his criticism on this point, adds, ' We do not say that these disagreeable combinations may not be brought under such a principle of painful stimulation as that laid down by Mr. Allen, but if so, it must be effected in quite another way.' This appears to me to be a suggestion parallel in kind to that advanced above as to the supervention, in cases of intermittent nervous stimulation, of some special kind of dissipation and disturbance : but if such facts really exist in the case of discordant colours, they are probably of a much more obscure kind, since they can hardly depend on anything so simple as interruptions of an established rhythm.

Two further points may be mentioned in opposition to the view that 'fatigue' or excess of normal stimulation is a sufficient explanation of colour-discord. First, to return to our example of vermilion and orange, the special unpleasantness ceases when the one is made to shade off into the other : and yet here again the same optic fibres are used to a greater extent, as the eye passes and repasses along the surface, than when it was more restrictedly occupied with the dividing line where the two colours lay side by side without gradation. Secondly, the briefest time will suffice for the unpleasant sensation to be felt. This is an objection which we are precluded from urging in the case of note-discord, because there the 'fatigue' was connected with intermittences of which a large number occur in a second : but colours, however discordant, cause no such intermittences, and the 'fatigue,' if such it be, ought in reason to grow by gradual and sensible degrees, just as it would in the case of a single bright colour when looked at continuously.

All things considered, one is led to guess that the extent to which explanations resting on peripheral nervous conditions apply to sensations of colour-discord and concord must be very limited. They may cover, for instance, such broad effects as the obviously resting action of complementary colours, which affect different sets of fibres : but one seems more and more driven to refer the more delicate shades of feeling to associational and intellectual elements. This would seem to be the case even with single colours which are not bright, stimulating, or fatiguing, and can be looked at for a long time without serious discomfort, but which are simply ugly. Again, it is impossible to abstract the colour from the object; and even beautiful colours displease us in inappropriate and unusual positions. Such associations, however, as we can consciously discover will often be found provokingly insufficient if pressed as explanations. For instance, the pleasantness of the gradation from bright red to orange, as compared with their immediate juxtaposition, might perhaps suggest a connection with the frequency of such gradation in nature, as, for example, in sunsets. But then we also continually find in nature a total absence of gradation in nearly related tints whose juxtaposition is nevertheless felt to be delightful ; as in looking at a light blue sky through blue-green leaves. And indeed a *slightness* of divergence in colours often seems the essential feature of their *harmony*; whence a new difficulty in accepting as final and complete the view that 'those combinations produce discord which successively stimulate the same class of structures.' And these experiences of colour-effects often occur in isolated acts of observation without any relation to surrounding conditions; so that they cannot possibly be explained on the same grounds as the presence in music of sound-discords, which are enjoyed as parts of a complex and *organic* whole. Such considerations are almost enough to make one despair of anything like an exact and complete *rationale* of colour-discords and affinities : it would at any rate lie far beyond the scope of any conceivable formula.